THE REVELS PLAYS

Former editors
Clifford Leech, F. David Hoeniger
and E. A. J. Honigmann

General editors
David Bevington, Richard Dutton,
J. R. Mulryne and Eugene M. Waith

EVERY MAN OUT
OF HIS HUMOUR

MANCHESTER
UNIVERSITY PRESS

THE REVELS PLAYS

THE REVELS PLAYS

EVERY MAN OUT OF HIS HUMOUR

BEN JONSON

edited by Helen Ostovich

MANCHESTER
UNIVERSITY PRESS

Manchester and New York

*distributed exclusively in the USA
by* Palgrave

Introduction, critical apparatus, etc.
© Helen Ostovich 2001

The right of Helen Ostovich to be identified as the editor of this
work has been asserted by her in accordance with the Copyright,
Designs and Patents Act 1988.

Published by Manchester University Press
Oxford Road, Manchester M13 9NR, UK
and Room 400, 175 Fifth Avenue, New York, NY 10010, USA
http://www.manchesteruniversitypress.co.uk

Distributed exclusively in the USA by
Palgrave, 175 Fifth Avenue, New York,
NY 10010, USA

Distributed exclusively in Canada by
UBC Press, University of British Columbia, 2029 West Mall,
Vancouver, BC, Canada V6T 1Z2

British Library Cataloguing-in-Publication Data
A catalogue record for this book is available from the
British Library

Library of Congress Cataloging-in-Publication Data applied for

ISBN 0 7190 1558 8 *hardback*

First published 2001

10 09 08 07 06 05 04 03 02 01   10 9 8 7 6 5 4 3 2 1

Typeset in Plantin
by Best-set Typesetter Ltd., Hong Kong
Printed in Great Britain
by Bookcraft (Bath) Ltd, Midsomer Norton

TO MY DAUGHTERS
JENNIFER AND ELLIS

Contents

Illustrations

General Editors' Preface

Clifford Leech conceived of the Revels Plays as a series in the mid-1950s, modelling the project on the New Arden Shakespeare. The aim, as he wrote in 1958, was 'to apply to Shakespeare's predecessors, contemporaries and successors the methods that are now used in Shakespeare's editing'. The plays chosen where to include well-known works from the early Tudor period to about 1700, as well as others less familiar but of literary and theatrical merit: 'the plays included', Leech wrote, 'should be such as to deserve and indeed demand performance'. We owe it to Clifford Leech that the idea became reality. He set the high standards of the series, ensuring that editors of individual volumes produced work of lasting merit, equally useful for teachers and students, theatre directors and actors. Clifford Leech remained General Editor until 1971, and was succeeded by F. David Hoeniger, who retired in 1985.

The Revels Plays are now under the direction of four General Editors, David Bevington, Richard Dutton, J. R. Mulryne and Eugene M. Waith. Published originally by Methuen, the series is now published by Manchester University Press, embodying essentially the same format, scholarly and high editorial standards of the series as first conceived. The series concentrates on plays from the period 1558–1642, and includes a small number of non-dramatic works of interest to students of drama. Some slight changes have been made: for example, in editions from 1978, notes to the introduction are placed together at the end, not at the foot of the page. Collation and commentary notes continue, however, to appear on the relevant pages.

The text of each Revels play, in accordance with established practice in the series, is edited afresh from the original text of best authority (in a few instances, texts), but spelling and punctuation are modernised and speech headings are silently made consistent. Elisions in the original are also silently regularised, except where metre would be affected by the change; since 1968 the '-ed' form is used for non-syllabic terminations in past tenses and past participles ('-'d' earlier) and '-èd' for syllabic ('-ed' earlier). The editor emends, as distinct from modernises, the original only in instances where error is patent, or at least very probable, and correction persuasive. Act divisions are given only if they appear in the original or if the structure of the play clearly points to them. Those act and scene divisions not in the original are provided in small type. Square brackets are also used for any other additions to or changes in the stage directions of the original.

Revels Plays do not provide a variorum collation, but only those variants which require the critical attention of serious textual students. All departures of substance from 'copy-text' are listed, including any relineation and those changes in punctuation which involve to any degree a decision between alternative interpretations; but not such accidentals as turned letter, nor necessary additions to stage directions whose editorial nature is already made clear by the use of brackets. Press corrections in the 'copy-text' are likewise collated. Of later emendations of the text, only those are given which as alternative readings still deserve attention.

One of the hallmarks of the Revels Plays is the thoroughness of their annotations. Besides explaining the meaning of difficult words and passages, the editor provides comments on customs or usage, text or stage-business—indeed, on anything judged pertinent and helpful. Each volume contains an Index to the Commentary, in which particular attention is drawn to meanings for words not listed in *OED*, and (starting in 1996) an indexing of proper names and topics in the introduction and Commentary.

The introduction to a Revels play assesses the authority of the 'copy-text' on which it is based, and discusses the editorial methods employed in dealing with it; the editor also considers the play's date and (where relevant) sources, together with its place in the work of the author and in the theatre of its time. Stage history is offered, and in the case of a play by an author not previously represented in the series a brief biography is given.

It is our hope that plays edited in this fashion will promote further scholarly and theatrical investigation of one of the richest periods in theatrical history.

DAVID BEVINGTON
RICHARD DUTTON
J. R. MULRYNE
EUGENE M. WAITH

Preface

When I first started working on *Every Man Out of His Humour* as my doctoral project, I had no idea that almost fifteen years later I would still be obsessively annotating, reconstructing, and laughing at this play. I am grateful for the encouragement I received at the University of Toronto, both from my supervisors, Brian Parker and Alexander Leggatt, whose advice and close readings of my drafts were invaluable, and from others who read, listened, or offered opinions and support; notably, F. David Hoeniger, S. P. Zitner, William Blissett, John Astington, and H. J. Mason (who explained the etymology of the Greek parenthetical remark in the 'Apology'). I am also obliged to the School of Graduate Studies for the travel grant allowing me to examine otherwise inaccessible materials at the Victoria and Albert Museum in London; and to the Social Sciences and Humanities Research Council of Canada for the financial support without which the dissertation could not have been undertaken or completed. The National Library of New Zealand interrupted microfilming priorities to supply me with a copy of the first quarto; D. F. McKenzie, then at the Victoria University of Wellington, kindly facilitated my request.

For this updated and revised edition, I owe more than I can express to David Bevington for his enthusiasm, his meticulous attention to detail, his forbearance, and his generosity in encouraging me in this project. His guidance as General Editor and his friendship have been inspirational. I am also grateful to Martin Butler for his advice on my argument concerning place in the Paul's Walk scene for the version called ' "To behold the scene full": Seeing and Judging in *Every Man Out of His Humour*', in *Re-presenting Ben Jonson: Text, History, Performance*, edited by Martin Butler (London, 1999). I also acknowledge the permission granted by the editors of *English Literary Renaissance* to re-use portions of my essay ' "So sudden and strange a cure": A Rudimentary Masque in *Every Man Out of His Humour*', which first appeared in volume 22.3 (autumn 1992). Finally, I am happy to acknowledge the assistance of the Arts Research Board of McMaster University which funded my checking of texts and contexts in the British Library.

HELEN OSTOVICH
McMaster University

Abbreviations

REFERENCE WORKS

Aubrey   John Aubrey, *Brief Lives*, ed. Richard Barber (Woodbridge, 1982).

Baskervill, *Jig*   Charles Read Baskervill, *The Elizabethan Jig and Related Song Drama* (Chicago, 1929; rpt New York, 1965).

Baker   Christopher Paul Baker, *Ben Jonson and the Inns of Court: The Literary Milieu of 'Every Man Out of His Humour'* (Diss. Chapel Hill, 1974).

Bates   E. S. Bates, *Touring in 1600: A Study in the Development of Travel as a Means of Education* (London, 1911).

Brissenden   Alan Brissenden, *Shakespeare and the Dance* (Atlantic Highlands, NJ, 1981).

Browne   Sir Thomas Browne, *Pseudodoxia Epidemica*, ed. Robin Robbins (Oxford, 1981).

Bryson   Frederick R. Bryson, *The Sixteenth-century Italian Duel* (Chicago, 1938).

Byrne   Muriel St Clare Byrne, *The Elizabethan Home* (London, 1930).

Chalfant   Fran S. Chalfant, *Ben Jonson's London: A Jacobean Placename Dictionary* (Athens, GA, 1978).

Chambers   Edmund K. Chambers, *The Elizabethan Stage*, 4 vols (Oxford, 1923).

de Bruyn   Lucy de Bruyn, *Mob-rule and Riots: The Present Mirrored in the Past* (London and New York, 1981).

Dent   R. W. Dent, *Proverbial Language in English Drama, Exclusive of Shakespeare, 1495–1616: An Index* (Berkeley, 1984).

De Vocht   Henri de Vocht, *Comments on the Text of Ben Jonson's 'Every Man Out of His Humour': A Research about the Comparative Value of the 'Quarto' and the 'Folio'*, in *Materials for the Study of Old English Drama* 14 (1937).

DNB   *The Dictionary of National Biography.*

Erasmus   Erasmus, *Colloquies*, trans. Craig R. Thompson (Chicago and London, 1965).

Finkelpearl, *Histrio-Mastix*   Philip J. Finkelpearl, 'John Marston's *Histrio-Mastix* as an Inns of Court Play: A Hypothesis', *HLQ* 29 (1966): 223–34.

Finkelpearl, *Temple*   Philip J. Finkelpearl, *John Marston of the Middle Temple: An Elizabethan Dramatist in His Social Setting* (Cambridge, MA, 1969).

Florio   John Florio, *A World of Words* (London, 1598).

Gesta Grayorum   Gesta Grayorum, ed. W. W. Gray, Malme Society Reprints 41 (Oxford, 1914).

Grose   [Francis Grose], *Dictionary of the Vulgar Tongue: A Dictionary of Buckish Slang, University Wit, and Pickpocket Eloquence*, rev. and enl. 1811 (Northfield, IL, 1971).

Gurr   Andrew Gurr, *The Shakespearean Stage, 1574–1642*, 2nd ed. (Cambridge, 1980).

Henke   James T. Henke, *Courtesans and Cuckholds: A Glossary of Renaissance Dramatic Bawdy (Exclusive of Shakespeare)* (New York and London, 1979).

Howard   Clare Howard, *English Travellers of the Renaissance* (London, 1914).

Hoy   Cyrus Hoy, *Introductions, Notes, and Commentaries to the Texts in 'The Dramatic Works of Thomas Dekker'*, Edited by Fredson Bowers, 4 vols (Cambridge, 1979–80).

Johansson, *Law*   Bertil Johansson, *Law and Lawyers in Elizabethan England as Evidenced in the Plays of Ben Jonson and Thomas Middleton* (Stockholm, 1967).

Johansson, *Religion*   Bertil Johansson, *Religion and Superstition in the plays of Ben Jonson and Thomas Middleton* (Upsala, 1950).

Judges   A. V. Judges, *The Elizabethan Underworld* (London, 1930).

Linthicum   M. Channing Linthicum, *Costume in the Drama of Shakespeare and his Contemporaries* (Oxford, 1936).

Manningham   John Manningham, *The Diary of John Manningham* (Hanover, NH, 1976).

Nason   Arthur Huntington Nason, *Heralds and Heraldry In Ben Jonson's Plays, Masques, and Entertainments* (New York, 1907).

OCD   *The Oxford Classical Dictionary*, 2nd ed. (Oxford, 1970).

OED   *Oxford English Dictionary.*

Onions   C. T. Onions, *A Shakespeare Glossary* (Oxford, 1911).

Partridge, *Accidence*   A. C. Partridge, *The Accidence of Ben Jonson's Plays, Masques, and Entertainments* (Cambridge, 1953).

Partridge, *Syntax*   A. C. Partridge, *Studies in the Syntax of Ben Jonson's Plays* (Cambridge, 1953).

Partridge, *Bawdy*   Eric Partridge, *Shakespeare's Bawdy* (London, 1947).

Partridge, *Slang*   Eric Partridge, *A Dictionary of Slang and Unconventional English* (London, 1961).

Prothero   G. W. Prothero, ed., *Select Statutes and other Constitutional Documents Illustrative of the Reigns of Elizabeth and James I* (Oxford, 1963).

Randolph   Mary Claire Randolph, 'The Medical Concept in English Renaissance Satiric Theory: Its Possible Relationships and Implications', *SP* 38 (1941): 125–57.

Rastell   John Rastell, *Difficult and Obscure Words and Terms of the Laws of this Realm*, 1579 (New York, 1969).

Rubinstein   Frankie Rubinstein, *A Dictionary of Shakespeare's Sexual Puns and their Significance*, 2nd ed. (Basingstoke, 1984, 1989).

Schmidt   Alexander Schmidt, *Shakespeare-Lexicon*, 2 vols (Berlin, 1923).

Skeat   Walter W. Skeat, *A Glossary of Tudor and Stuart Words, Especially from the Dramatists* (Oxford, 1914).

Small   Roscoe Addison Small, *The Stage-Quarrel between Ben Jonson and the So-called Poetasters* (Breslau, 1899).

STC   A. W. Pollard and G. R. Redgrave, *Short Title Catalogue of Books Printed in England, Scotland and Ireland . . . 1475–1640*, 2 vols (London, 1976, 1986).

Steggle   Matthew Steggle, *The Wars of the Theatres: The Poetics of Personation in the Age of Jonson*, English Literary Studies (University of Victoria, 1998).

Stone   Lawrence Stone, *The Crisis of the Aristocracy 1558–1641* (Oxford, 1965).

Stow   John Stow, *The Survey of London*, 2 vols, ed. Charles Kingsford (Oxford, 1908).
Sugden   Edward H. Sugden, *Topographical Dictionary to the Works of Shakespeare and his Fellow Dramatists* (Manchester, 1925).
Tilley   Morris Palmer Tilley, *A Dictionary of the Proverbs in England in the Sixteenth and Seventeenth Centuries* (Ann Arbor, 1950).
Wheeler   Charles Francis Wheeler, *Classical Mythology in the Plays, Masques, and Poems of Ben Jonson* (Princeton, 1938).
Williams   Gordon Williams, *A Dictionary of Sexual Language and Imagery in Shakespearean and Stuart Literature*, 3 vols (London, 1994).

PERIODICALS

BJJ   *Ben Jonson Journal.*
ELH   *English Literary History.*
ELR   *English Literary Renaissance.*
ELN   *English Language Notes.*
ES   *English Studies.*
G&R   *Greece and Rome.*
HLQ   *Huntington Library Quarterly.*
MaRDiE   *Medieval and Renaissance Drama in England.*
MLQ   *Modern Language Quarterly.*
MP   *Modern Philology.*
N&Q   *Notes and Queries.*
PLL   *Papers on Language and Literature.*
RD   *Renaissance Drama.*
RES   *Review of English Studies.*
SB   *Studies in Bibliography.*
SEL   *Studies in English Literature.*
ShS   *Shakespeare Survey.*
SQ   *Shakespeare Quarterly.*
SP   *Studies in Philology.*
ThN   *Theatre Notebook.*
YES   *Yearbook of English Studies.*

JONSON TEXTS

Alc.   *The Alchemist.*
BF   *Bartholomew Fair.*
Cat.   *Catiline*
CisA   *The Case Is Altered.*
Conv.   *Conversations with Drummond.*
CR   *Cynthia's Revels.*
DisA   *The Devil Is an Ass.*
Disc.   *Discoveries.*
E. Blackfriars   *Entertainment at Blackfriars.*
EH   *Eastward Ho!*
EMI (Q)   *Every Man In His Humour*, quarto edition.
EMI (F)   *Every Man In His Humour*, folio edition.
EMO   *Every Man Out of His Humour.*

Ep. Epigrams.
F1 Jonson's *Works* (1616).
F2 Jonson's *Works* (1640).
Gifford   William Gifford, ed., *The Works of Ben Jonson*, 9 vols (London, 1816).
GM The Gypsies Metamorphosed.
H&S   C. H. Herford, P. and E. Simpson, eds, *Ben Jonson*, 11 vols (Oxford, 1925–52).
Hym. Hymenaei.
ML Magnetic Lady.
MQ Masque of Queens.
NI The New Inn.
NT Neptune's Triumph.
Poet. The Poetaster.
PR Pleasure Reconciled to Virtue.
Q1 Holmes's quarto (Adam Islip, 1600).
Q2 Holmes's quarto (Peter Short, 1600).
Q3 Ling's quarto (1600).
Schelling   Felix E. Schelling, introd., *Ben Jonson. The Complete Plays*, 2 vols (London, 1910).
Sej. Sejanus.
StN The Staple of News.
SW Epicoene, or The Silent Woman.
Und. Underwoods.
Volp. Volpone.
Whalley   Peter Whalley, ed., *The Works of Ben Jonson*, 7 vols (London, 1756).

OTHER ABBREVIATIONS

Chars.   Characters.
F   Folio.
Ind.   Induction.
n   note (follows line number).
Q   Quarto.

All Jonson references are to the Herford and Simpson edition, unless a Revels text is specified. The line-numbering of Shakespeare's plays is that of the single Arden 2 editions. All Dekker references are to the editions of Fredson Bowers, *The Dramatic Works of Thomas Dekker*, 4 vols (Cambridge, 1953–61) and A. B. Grosart, *The Non-dramatic Works of Thomas Dekker*, 5 vols (London, 1884–6). Marston references are to the edition of A. H. Bullen, *John Marston, The Works*, 3 vols (London, 1887), unless otherwise indicated. Nashe is quoted from R. B. McKerrow, *The Works of Thomas Nashe*, 5 vols (Oxford, 1958). Chapman, unless otherwise indicated, is taken from *The Plays of George Chapman: The Comedies*, edited by Allan Holaday (Urbana, 1970). Beaumont's *The Knight of the Burning Pestle* is quoted from the Revels edition, as is *EMI* (*Q*).
    Most old-spelling sources have been silently modernized.

Introduction

The First Quarto (Q1)

William Holme, Jonson's first publisher, entered *EMO* in the Stationers' Register on 8 April 1600. The entry reads:

> 8 Aprilis
>
> William holme. Entred for his copie vnder the handes of master Harsnet. and master wyndet warden. A Comicall Satyre of euery man out of his humour. vj d.[1]

Holme's edition of *EMO* (*STC* 14767) was printed by Adam Islip. Islip is not identified by name on the title-page, but the same title-page ornament appears in *Marie Magdalen's Lamentations for the Losse of her Master Jesus*, 'Printed by Adam Islip for E. White 1601' (*STC* 17569); and the ornaments on A3 and B1 recur in Islip's books printed between 1596 and 1602[2]. W. W. Greg has pointed out that, although Islip did not often appear as a dramatic printer, he had produced an edition of Peele's *David and Bathsabe* the year before, in 1599.[3]

The format of *Q1* can only loosely be described as quarto, since only signatures P, Q, and R (also H in the British Library copy) are true quarto-size, 'the rest being of that puzzling size (it might be called "bastard quarto") which is commonly folded in fours, and agrees in size and shape with a normal quarto, but according to wire and water marks should be an octavo'.[4] Two compositors set the text, evidently based on fair copy prepared for the printer by Jonson himself.[5] The title-page asserts that *Q1* represents the text 'AS IT WAS FIRST COMPOSED / by the Author B. I. / *Containing more than hath been Publickely Spo-/ken or Acted*'. Jonson does not indicate how much of the play was cut for performance, or how much he added after the performance, but he does defend his original conception of the final scene, which he was forced to rewrite after the play opened. Both the revision and the original ending appear in the quartos. Stage directions are prolific, with entrances and exits usually marked at the appropriate point of occurrence during the scene. The few initial directions for scenes mention entries, extras, and stage-properties. The printer may be responsible for the two errors in speech-prefixes: at 2.2.137, the speech-heading was omitted, thereby attributing Deliro's speech to Macilente; at 5.3.432, Fungoso's speech was incorrectly assigned to the Drawer. An error in scene-numbering (2.2 is labelled SCENA TERTIA) may also be the printer's.

For this edition, I examined all five extant copies of *Q1*: the Huntington Library copy and the Wellington, New Zealand, copy (Alexander Turnbull Library, National Library of New Zealand) are in almost perfect condition, although the title-page of the latter has suffered some damage on the exposed edges (see p. 97); the Boston Public Library copy (G.3973.8) has cropped running-titles; the British Library copy (C.34.i.29) has a repaired title-leaf, A4, B4, and H3 are mutilated, with a portion of the text lost, and A1 (the blank leaf before the title) and R3–4 (containing the apology for the original catastrophe) are missing; the University of London copy (Durning-Lawrence Library 31893) lacks A2–3 (title-page, names of the actors, character-sketches from Asper to Saviolina, inclusive), Q3 is damaged with parts of some lines obliterated, and R4 has been literally cut, the half-page containing Macilente's final speech having been removed. *Q1* collates A–R4 in a well-spaced format, using the same running-titles recto and verso.

The punctuation—probably Jonson's own, as A. C. Partridge suggests[6]—is spare and straightforward. I found no variants in accidentals, apart from anomalies caused by uneven inking, misaligning, or dirt-marks which might be misconstrued as accidentals emendation. On B1 recto (Ind.7), for example, 'vnder' looks something like 'vn'der' in the Boston quarto, but the mark is simply a smudge; similarly, in the Huntington quarto, '*manfrede*' on O1 recto (4.5.111) seems to be followed by a very faint and minute apostrophe—Herford and Simpson recorded it as such in their collation—but no mark at all appears in the other four copies. A similar explanation may account for what appears to be '*no:*' in the Boston quarto's R3 recto, instead of the '*not*' that appears elsewhere (see the collation for Apology 17).

I found only three substantive printing variants in *Q1*, described in the collation notes for 'ingenious' (Chars.2), 'dew' (Ind.93), and 'unicorn's' (5.3.173). As for substantive errors in *Q1*, I could find only one. At 4.5.111, the compositor rendered a word, indecipherable ever since, as '*manfrede*' (altered in the folio to 'vndertake'); I have revised it to 'mansuete' (see commentary note). At 4.3.23, the word 'not' may have been omitted by the compositor, thus rendering Puntarvolo's statement puzzling to the modern ear: 'That I may choose to give my Dog or Cat Fish, for feare of Bones' (L4r). Clearly a negative is implied, if not stated. Why would Puntarvolo wish to sign a bond that encourages him to expose his dog or cat to needless risk of death by choking—or even indigestion—when he could reduce that risk, and so safeguard his chances of gaining twenty-five thousand pounds? Nevertheless, I have not revised this line.

Press-correction for *Q1*, it seems, was thorough. The extant copies have very few substantive errors, and a minimum of accidentals errors, or even merely typographical errors for that matter, although turned letters (t (F1v) and (u 14r)), substituted letters (c for e (Q2r)) and letters rising in the forme (11r in the British Library copy; C2r in all but the Huntington copy) do occur. By and large, the text is remarkably clean and careful, probably testifying the authorial involvement in reading proofs.

The Second Quarto (Q2)

Holme appears to have rushed the second quarto (*STC* 14768) into print, after selling out the first within about eight months, a wild success by play-publication standards. Although the printing of plays was generally a risky business, a second edition—a rare event in the working lifetime of any publisher—promised to double profits from the original publication.[7] Holme evidently determined to work quickly and to save costs where possible. *Q2* is essentially a good copy of *Q1*, with variations in spelling and punctuation attributable in part to the decision to save a sheet of paper on the reprint. *Q2*'s printer was nominally Peter Short—his device and initials appear on the title-page—but the copy-text of *Q1* was divided for distribution to two printing-houses, A–I2 going to Peter Short, and I3–R4 to Adam Islip.[8] Short reset his half as A–H4, and Islip reset the remaining half as I–Q4, each man saving two leaves or four pages.

Greg has meticulously described the process whereby the seventeen sheets of *Q1* were reset for the sixteen sheets of *Q2*.[9] Briefly, Short moved the title-page forward to A1r , and the 'Names of the Actors' to A1v, saving two pages; compressed the Characters into three pages; and, in order to save his fourth page, adopted a thirty-seven-line page instead of the thirty-six of *Q1*. By the end of E, he could drop his extra line and follow the original page for page. Islip had only three pages to save (R4v of *Q1* was blank), and did so by rescuing space around headings and directions, and occasionally tucking in lines that had previously been turned over. These methods allowed him to agree with his copy-text by the end of Q2r and then reproduce the original thereafter. As Greg remarks, 'The reprint is astonishingly exact'. The chief difference is that Peter Short normalized, according to Elizabethan custom, instances in which *Q1* had used 'u', 'v', 'i', and 'j' in the modern convention; Islip, not surprisingly, retained the anomalies.

This edition collates the two extant copies of *Q2*: the one in the Dyce Collection, Victoria and Albert Museum (D 26 Box 23 6), is a good copy; and the other, the Bodleian copy, is defective at the top outer corners of A–C3, and badly stained on Q4.

The Third Quarto (Q3)

The third quarto (*STC* 14769), also issued in 1600, has been regarded with suspicion for three reasons: there is no record of a transfer of rights to Nicholas Ling;[10] the brevity of the imprint and the failure of Ling's device to appear in other books of that date suggest fraud or piracy;[11] and critics have simply been unwilling to credit the play as a best-seller, thus preferring to believe that the 1600 imprint is a forgery.[12] The absence of a recorded transaction, however, is not evidence of 'skulduggery', since entrance in the Stationers' Register was voluntary.[13] Without objection from Jonson or Holme, Nicholas Ling apparently acquired the right to issue the third quarto in 1600, and subsequently, upon his retirement, assigned his rights to John Smethwick, although the title does not appear in the list of books officially transferred on 19 November 1607. Aside from speculations based on absence and denial, which Peter Blayney calls 'inane conspiracy theories' as credible as folklore or myth,[14] no typographical evidence contradicts or throws doubt on the 1600 title-page date. No one, on the other hand, doubts that *Q3* is a careless, and probably hurried, version of *Q2*. Four different printing-houses worked on parts of *Q3*: William White produced A–C4; Valentine Simmes may have been responsible for D–H4; probably Simon Stafford, or possibly Edward Allde, set I–M4; a fourth house, not yet identified, put out N–Q4.

Various inaccuracies plague the text: two pages of sheet N are tranposed; errors of *Q2* are repeated (for example, 'PASTIDIUS' instead of 'FASTIDIUS' at Chars.33); new errors result from words misread ('rarefi'd' at 2.1.361 became 'ratifide' in *Q3*), altered (*Q1*'s

'Shot-sharkes' at 5.3.1 became 'Shotmarkes' in *Q2*, and 'Shot-makers' in *Q3*), inserted ('might see' in *Q2* at 2.1.258 became 'might but see' in *Q3*; 'that you' at 5.1.65 became 'that that you' in *Q3*), or omitted ('horse' at Chars.40).[15] Among its few attempts at substantive emendation, *Q3* makes a notable correction of the repeated 'one and twentieth' (see 1.3.52 and collation note) by omitting the second occurrence. Other creditable changes appear in the spelling of 'peremptory' at 5.3.275 and in the Greek transliteration in Apology 2.

For this edition, I examined four copies of *Q3*: the Huntington, the Folger, the Dyce (D 25 H.75), and the British Library (C.57.C.22) copies. *Q3* has no authority, but is helpful in illustrating printing-house practices and in raising questions about the transmission of the text, particularly in those instances where *Q3* and *F1* agree. The usual finding is that *Q3* agrees with *Q2*; where *Q3* differs from *Q2*, it usually differs from *Q1* and *F1* as well. Most of the agreements between *Q3* and *F1* are in accidentals, but some of the alterations constitute semi-substantive changes from *Q1*. The stronger pointing (replacing a comma or dash with a full stop) sometimes eliminates the notion of interrupted speech; the emendation of the subject–verb agreement error at 3.1.168 ('yond' gallants obserues us') may not render accurately the 'fustian' fashionable drawl that Clove affects. Most of the changes represent (*a*) attempts to improve the pointing by inserting commas to mark off interjections and direct address; and (*b*) attempts to clarify the sense by inserting full or partial stops. Such changes probably represent various printing-house styles, not Jonson's own corrections. But there is a positive consideration that emerges from the agreements between *Q3* and *F1*. The findings suggest that editors should closely examine evidence of practice common to two or more printing houses before attributing accidentals emendation to the author.

The First Folio (*F1*)

No explicit record exists of the transfer of *EMO* to another printing house until 28 April 1638. William Stansby printed it in the 1616 folio (*STC* 14752) with a special title-page appearing in many of the copies acknowledging John Smethwick's rights: 'Printed by William Stansby / for *Iohn Smithwicke*'. The acknowledgement, however, appears only in one original state (in a change introduced after printing had begun) and in the corrected states, but not in the reset and large-paper states.[16] Some accommodation was presumably reached, since Richard Bishop, prior to his printing of the second folio in 1640, acquired both John Smethwick's rights to *EMO*, and Stansby's rights to 'Master BENIAMIN JOHNSONS *workes*. his part':

28 Aprilis 1638

Master Bishop.   Assigned ouer vnto him by vertue of a note under the hand and seale of master Smethw\<i\>cke and subscribed by Master Bourne warden all the Right and interest in a play called Euery man out of his humour by Ben: Johnson. vj d.[17]

4 Martij 1638 [1639]

Master Bishop.   Assigned over vnto him by vertue of a deed of bargaine and sale vnder the hand and seale of William Stansby lately deceased and alsoe by vertue of a note vnder the hande and seale of Elizabeth Stansby the widdow of the said William these Copies and partes of Copies following which were the Copies of the said william. *saluo Jure cuiuscunque* xxviij s. vj d.[18]

The folio version, based on *Q1*, appears on pages 73–175 (signatures G1–P4) of the 1616 folio (*STC* 14751/14752). Although alterations in the text are not so major as to produce a distinctly different play (as in *Every Man In His Humour*), the folio offers a considerably revised ending, as well as persistent changes in spelling, punctuation,[19] wording, scene-division, and stage-directions. The extent to which these alterations represent Jonson's rethinking has been debated at length. Henri de Vocht, in his thorough documentation of *F1*'s revision of *Q*, states categorically that Jonson had no hand in the textual alterations;[20] Herford and Simpson argue just as forcefully that the folio represents Jonson's final concept of the play.[21] In a more even-handed bibliographic view, Johan Gerritsen claims that, because the first quire to go to press was G, the initial quire of *EMO*, the play is 'by far the most heavily corrected' in *F1*, simply because printer and author had to work out a *modus operandi* for shifting the format from quarto to folio, one that would permit a pleasing uniformity in the printing of the plays throughout the folio volume.[22] But Kevin Donovan adds the caveat that most variants in spelling and punctuation, like changes in capitalization and font, are not authoritative results of press correction, but rather are 'clearly compositorial'.[23] Fredson Bowers argues at greater length, even while conceding that Jonson may be 'a partial exception', that 'a reprint even if revised in some respects by the author is ordinarily not taken to be so authoritative in its accidentals as in its substantives . . . It follows that even in a revised edition the authority of an accidentals variant that the editor may prefer is moot, for usually each successive reprint merely modernized (according to the standards of its day) the copy from which it was set.'[24]

Some of the substantive changes from Q to $F1$ reflect conformity to the statute of 3 Jac. I, c. 21 (January 1606) which levied a fine of £10 for blasphemy; and further substantive changes of the same kind in $F2$ are responses to the more rigorous anti-profanity statutes of 19 February 1623 and 26 July 1635.[25] These changes do not necessarily imply Jonson's hand in $F1$, of course, any more than they can imply it for $F2$ (1640), since Jonson died three years before $F2$ was published. Other substantive changes are harder to explain, even as a product of the sixteen-year gap between Q and $F1$. What Peter Ure said of the text of *Bussy D'Ambois* is also true of *EMO*: 'about half the reviser's busy activity seems to have been totally wasted . . . and has neither weakened nor strengthened his original; he fidgets with the text'.[26] The 'fidgets' in *EMO* include shifting the article from Q's 'a' to F's 'the' (3.1.205); adding modifiers, as when Q's 'gentlemen' becomes F's 'good gentlemen' (3.1.338); eliminating modifiers, as when Q's 'good sort' becomes F's 'sort' (3.1.379); and altering contexts—Q's 'chronicle' and 'virtuous man' become F's more specific '*Acts, and Monuments*' and '*Martyr*' (3.2.126–7), or Q's faintly biblical 'scriptures' becomes F's less specific 'manuscripts' (3.1.450), or Q's 'in faith' becomes F's 'I feare' (3.3.32). Arguably, some of the changes signal Jonson's sensitivity to shifts in colloquial usage—Q's 'perriwigs' becomes F's 'perrukes' (5.3.227)—or a dropping away from precious academic language to ordinary English, as in Q's 'the *Theorie*' becoming F's 'thy instructions' (4.3.3). Sometimes F's changes seem merely to waffle: in revising Q's 'Crush out the humour of such spongie soules' (Ind.144), 'Crush' becomes 'Squeeze' in F's corrected state, and 'soules' becomes 'natures' in the reset state. Where 'Squeeze' has the merit of expanding the alliteration of the line, 'natures' merely muddies the rhythmic emphasis of the angry Asper, who tends to prefer monosyllabics to begin and end his downright verses.[27] On occasion, genuine grammatical correction seems to be the issue: Q's 'proper' becomes F's 'properer' (4.3.160); or Q's 'an ingenious' becomes F's 'as ingenious a' (4.3.339).

The one consistent feature of this debate over Jonson's hand in the emendations of *F1* is that the emendations represent highly wrought second thoughts on how to turn a play (regarded in the early modern period as light reading) into a 'work', in the conventional sense of 'serious text for an educated reader'. The paradox of 'play' as 'work' lies behind this anonymous gibe attacking Jonson's intellectual presumption for establishing the precedent of publishing *ephemera* in folio:

> To Mr. Ben Jonson demanding the reason
>   why he called his plays works.
>
> Pray tell me, *Ben*, where doth the mystery lurk?
> What others call a play you call a work.[28]

Partly to forestall such criticism, the folio may have permitted conventions of scholarly publication to over-burden a text that had already proved itself in practice to be eminently readable.

For this edition I collated three copies of the 1616 folio: two large-paper copies, one from the Folger and the other from the British Library (*STC* 14751) and one regular-size copy, also from the British Library (*STC* 14752). In addition, I examined one copy of the 1640 folio (*STC* 14753) from the British Library, but *F2* has no authority.

This edition

The present edition is based on *Q1*. This choice has already been substantially argued in my discussions of the coinciding accidentals emendation in *Q3* and *F1*, and of the altered accidentals, scene-division, stage-directions, and wording in *F1*. The original text of 1600 is both vivid and valid. More to the point, it is this text which first made Jonson's literary reputation and influenced playwrights throughout the seventeeth century. The decisions of those previous editors who rejected the profanities and stylistic eccentricities of *Q1* I view as 'the niceness of a few (who are nothing but form)' (Ind.264–5), nor can I agree with Gifford that 'To shock or nauseate the reader, by bringing back what the author, upon better consideration, flung out of his text, though unfortunately not without example, is yet a species of gratuitous mischief, for which simple stupidity scarcely forms an adequate excuse' (vol. 2, 39n). Even if *Q1* does not represent Jonson's final intention (assuming that Jonson made many, if not all, of the changes in the final version of 1616), it vehemently represents Jonson's intention in 1600. As such, *Q1* has importance both for its historic value as the record of a playwright just arriving at the peak of his powers, and for its intrinsic value as a theatrically innovative and influential experiment, supported by non-theatrical and extra-dramatic frames of character-sketches, critical comment, and apology. I do not dispute the value of the folio text in itself, but I can neither accept it as superseding the quarto text nor see the point of a conflated or eclectic text—a version of the play that was not composed by the playwright nor staged by any contemporary company. Where both texts have authority, the choice of copy-text must derive from other considerations, as John Jowett has eloquently argued in his study of the early quartos: 'In the Folio, though it is essentially a modified reprint, the most distinctive features of the Quarto are weakened, abandoned, or dispersed. The Quarto is in various senses more textually significant; it is also more culturally significant, more Jonsonian'.[29] In the few cases where *F1*'s revision has clarified *Q1*'s work, I have incorporated the changes: these include the correction of 'good' to 'God', thus retaining the joke at 3.1.55; the modification of the confusing syntax at 4.3.309–10; and the elimination of the speech-heading errors at 5.3.60 and 5.3.432. Similarly, at Ind.49.1, 3.1.122, 3.1.135, and 3.3.67.1, I have retained *F1*'s supplements to *Q*'s stage-directions by adding perhaps redundant explanations, nevertheless useful as visual aids for a reader. But where the editing of *F1* seems to have altered the purpose or character of the original, or to have worked from different principles, I have merely noted the changes.[30] Following the same logic, I have concluded the play with the original catastrophe in order to convey Jonson's conception as it was initially written and performed in 1599.

All variants which have a substantive or semi-substantive value are recorded in the collation notes. I have followed *Q1*'s scene-divisions, except for 5.4, which I have marked off as a separate scene for the catastrophe, partly to simplify the reader's comparisons to the revised catastrophes located in Appendix A, and partly because some link between 5.3 and the original catastrophe may be missing. Entries, exits, and other stage-directions are largely as they appear in *Q1*. In order to keep the Grex's comments distinct from the dialogue in the play proper, I have marked off the Grex sections with horizontal lines; in *Q*, the shifts to the Grex are indicated by brackets in the margin. Verse lines, including shared lines, appear as iambic pentameter where scanning permits. Otherwise, I have retained short or extrametrical lines on the assumption that they reflect Jonson's intention, but have collated *F1*'s attempts to regularize them. Stage-directions added in this edition and not in *Q* or *F* are in square brackets and are not collated.

While translating Jonson's pointing into modern punctuation, I have silently shortened sentence lengths, taking my cues from Jonson's colons. Jonson's use of the question mark was, on the other hand, more modern than most of his contemporaries': *Q* uses the exclamation mark instead of consistently allowing the question mark to serve both interrogative and exclamatory functions, as was then the custom. Consequently, where a question is rhetorically possible, I have retained the question mark. Otherwise, I have reverted silently to the exclamation mark. As for the vexed problem of parentheses, the rhetorical implications of this punctuation is clear in 3.3 (K4v), in which parenthetical puffs of tobacco smoke, represented textually as (*Tab.*) . . . (*Tab.*), segment Brisk's sentence and draw attention to his self-important output, ludicrously parodying the significant shifts in tonality usually associated with bracketed remarks. Macilente's dig, 'I ne're knew *Tabacco* taken as a *parenthesis* before', suggests that, for Jonson, punctuation should convey to the reader what the actor's voice, expression, and gesture relay in the theatre, reflecting the similar concern of Renaissance rhetoricians vis-à-vis their audience. With this in mind, I have tried to resolve conflicts between grammatical and rhetorical punctuation by silently excising parentheses which serve merely syntactical functions, and by retaining those that surround remarks which the speaker intends should be heard by at least some of his listeners, but which he may at times be directing to the audience, rather than to all the listeners on stage. These remarks usually involve a change of tone, often to sarcasm or scepticism, but not excluding a variety of emotional or intellectual states (anger, indifference, surprise, amusement, or self-justification). Where parentheses mark interrupted thoughts, I have used dashes. Because this text abounds in interrupted speeches, I have used correspondingly what might otherwise be considered a disproportionate number of dashes, as at 3.1.367–89.

Jonson's parentheses, perhaps more than any other punctuation marks, indicate the great theatrical liveliness of the text. In them, the reader, forced to distinguish shifts in tone and address, recognizes the dynamics of Jonson's 'language, such as men do use' (*EMI* (F), Prologue, 21), with its jerky rhythms and cross-currents of thought, 'pouncing convulsively from one idea to another' as it follows and tries to contain 'the involutions of the thinking mind'.[31] His extraordinary sensitivity to the spoken word is best expressed by Jonson himself: 'Language most shows a man: speak that I may see thee.'[32]

2. GENRE

'of a particular kind by itself'

Comical satire

Jonson celebrated his originality in *EMO* by inventing a new generic label for it: comical satire, defined by Cordatus as 'strange and of a particular kind by itself, somewhat like *Vetus Comedia*' (Ind.227–8). In coining 'comical satire', Jonson seems to emphasize 'satire' as the *kind* and 'comical' as the *particular* mode, a *strange* defamiliarization of terms that nevertheless sets up satire as the genre's primary element, deploying laughter as a weapon against a panorama of butts—topically aimed at particular persons as well as types—with daring disregard for conventional expectations of plot.[33] The 'comical' modifier allows Jonson to juggle and reverse New Comedy conventions of the blocking figure (Sordido, Deliro), the young man in love—here only with clothes or himself (Fungoso, Brisk), the *miles gloriosus* (Shift), and the parasite (Carlo), and completely sabotage the romantic 'cross-wooing' (3.1.520) of popular Elizabethan comedy by pillorying courtship and marriage at every turn. Social critique, 'somewhat like' the Aristophanic pattern of *Vetus Comedia*, not the resolution of a single dramatic narrative, is the play's point.

This radical revision of satire for the early modern stage erupted out of the vogue for satirical writing in the 1590s, inspired by classical precedents that swung between two extremes: Juvenal's crude vituperation and Horace's more tolerant and playful irony.[34] The Elizabethan preference for vitriolic direct abuse, understood as effective denunciation of sin in the puritan invective of Gosson (*The School of Abuse*, 1579) and Stubbes (*The Anatomy of Abuses*, 1583), suggests that the squeakiest wheel broadcasts the most efficacious morality. When satirical zeal in verse escalated towards the end of the decade into the scabrous particularity of Hall's *Virgidemiarum* in 1597, Marston's *Scourge of Villainy* and Guilpin's *Skialetheia* in 1598, and Middleton's *Micro-Cynicon* in 1599, the result was twofold. The Archbishop of Canterbury and the Bishop of London banned verse satire on 1 June 1599. Within a few months of the book-burnings, Jonson produced his first 'comical satire', in which the motifs of verse satire (the figure of the satirist, the parade of fools and knaves, the intemperate railing) structure the drama.[35] Even repeating the term 'satire', no matter how modified, so soon after the ban suggests that Jonson meant some idea of succession to be inferred.

The proper form and tone of satire were clearly hot intellectual issues among Jonson's fellow writers.[36] Typically, Jonson opposed the dominant trend by choosing to incorporate the Horatian mode. The choice is obvious in *The Poetaster*, where Horace plays a major role, and in *Cynthia's Revels*, in the figure of Crites; but even in *EMO* the play moves from Juvenalian fulmination to Horatian tongue-in-cheek amusement, ending on Asper's mildly self-deprecating quip that the audience's appreciation will 'make lean Macilente as fat as Sir John Falstaff'. The critical view that Jonson equates Old Comedy (*Vetus Comedia*) only with abusive Roman satire does not coincide with Jonson's practice in the first comical satire. The Juvenalian outbursts of both Asper and Macilente provide only one kind of perspective on society, and are themselves put into other ironic perspectives, either explicitly by the Grex or implicitly by the self-revealing observations of various characters in the play proper. To complicate further the controversy over the dominant satirical style, Jonson creates distinctly Menippean features in the country-house visit of 2.1 and the Paul's Walk excursion of 3.1 in which groups of voluble eccentrics damn themselves out of their own mouths with ludicrous arguments and attitudes. The constant adjustment in perspective necessitated by these shifts in style points to Jonson's adaptation of the Horatian point of view with its self-scrutiny and moderation, best expressed in raillery, not in railing.[37]

The significant element in this adjustment of perspective is Jonson's attribution of 'comical' to 'satire'. Jonson has his critical spokesman ask and answer the question '*Quid sit comedia?*' (3.1.523–32) at first with an appeal to the classical dictum that the stage should mirror life, but then adding crucial provisos on attitude. Cordatus defines the comical as not only 'ridiculous'—provoking laughter at follies—but also 'pleasant'—good-humoured, merry, and just plain funny. This description seems close to Horace's view of the comical in satire, in that he too preferred to make his point by jesting (*ridiculum*), not by vituperation. But the meaning of *ridiculum* shifts in translation. Sidney's description of comedy as 'ridiculous and scornful'[38] gives a more pointedly derisive and mocking slant to the 'ridiculous'—common in English usage—than does Jonson's direct source, Minturno's '*certe iucundam, atque ridiculam*', where the joking tone, as in Horace, is uppermost.[39] In other words, the English edginess of 'provoking laughter *at*' has to be distinguished from the more benign and general Latin sense of simply 'provoking laughter', especially given Jonson's predilection for using words in the sense of their Latin roots. Jonson's other term, 'pleasant', qualifies his meaning more narrowly: although 'pleasant' included a contemporary sense of 'ridiculous' as laughing at absurd behaviour (*OED* 4), the ridicule was more jocular than abrasive. The combination of 'pleasant' and 'ridiculous' suggests a comical tone that is tolerant, wry, and informal—a far cry from Juvenal's *saeva indignatio*.

The moderating influence of attaching 'pleasant' to 'ridiculous', both 'accommodated to the correction of manners', suggests the equally moderating influence of attaching 'comical' to 'satire'. By so doing, Jonson shifts away from the cutting didacticism of satire to the cathartic effects of mirth. As Asper puts it, 'We hope to make the circles of your eyes / Flow with distillèd laughter' (Ind.214–15). The result is a salutary and satisfying complementarity in which laughter takes the sting out of censure.

The humours play

Although 'humours play' has been taken as the equivalent of satirical comedy, strictly it applies to the method of character analysis and portrayal, and not to dramatic construction.[40] In *EMO*, the action depends primarily on humours, because it is the humours themselves, in all their various pathologies, trivial or profound, that provoke it. Without them the action could not occur.

The humours tradition derives from medieval physiology, itself derived from classical practice. It postulated four liquids or humours preserving the body (blood, phlegm, black bile, yellow bile). Any imbalance in the system, whether discernible in disease or in personality, was attributed to the dominance of one physiological humour. Throughout the sixteenth century, the term had acquired transferred meanings related to disposition and by the 1590s frequently appeared in studies of manners to suggest whim, affectation, dominant mood, or ruling folly.[41] By the time of Chapman's *An Humorous Day's Mirth* (1597), the immediate precursor of

Jonson's humours plays, the metaphorical sense of 'humour' defined by Asper in the Induction, 86–112, had really already been established.

Although fellow writers clearly influenced Jonson's strategy of exposing folly embodied in humours, and Jonson certainly did not discount the 'disposition of those times wherein they wrote' (Ind.260–1), he also absorbed the analogous principle of *hybris* in Aristophanes' comedies.[42] In ancient Greek, *hybris* denoted the aggressive spirit of display in certain animals, like the strutting and crowing of cocks. In humans, it appears as immoderate self-absorption: an excessive spirit of aggression fostering excessive indulgence which then fosters the excessive aggressiveness, *ad infinitum*. It may express itself as excessive eating, drinking, or sexual activity, like Carlo Buffone's, or it may apply to any venture which expends surplus energy wastefully or ludicrously, as in Puntarvolo's 'strange performances' or Brisk's smoking, viola-da-gamba-playing, and boasts of athletic prowess. It also includes more obvious aggression in physical abuse (the murder of the dog in 5.1, the attack on Carlo in 5.3), even suicide (3.2), and verbal taunts, jeering, and derisive laughter (*passim*). Aristophanic *hybris*, simply put, generates egocentric energy. Like Jonson's 'humour', *hybris* is ultimately a pejorative term indicating a morally unjustifiable, voluntary abuse of power.[43] It was also legally wrong. In Athenian law, it denoted acts of aggression, usually assault and battery or damage to public property (like the charge of 'riot' in 5.3), but not excluding anything from ridicule to rape. Such behaviour was considered an offence against the state, not merely against an individual, just as Asper insists that the abuses effected by unrestrained humours create 'the time's deformity' (Ind.118), and diminish the quality of life in the Fortunate Isle of England. Significantly, in Athens the act had to proceed from a certain attitude of mind, culpably 'self-indulgent egoism',[44] and this is precisely the attitude that Jonson captures in his humours.

To note the similarity in attitude is not, of course, to imply exact correlations with Aristophanes. But Jonson was reformulating and reaccentuating the conventional genres of his day, and Aristophanes was incorporated into this feat of 'generic engineering'.[45] Aristophanes tends to build his plays around one great eccentric. Philokleon, in *Wasps*, possibly the original 'humorist', is the jury-addict whose son attempts to put him out of his humour of judging by staging the mock trial of a dog who stole a cheese. Misled by a trick,

Philokleon acquits the guilty dog and thus is shocked out of his humour. What characterizes Aristophanes' humours characters is their imposition of a 'fantasy of total selfishness' on a community that will not listen to reason—that is, to reason as the humours characters perceive it.[46] Once Philokleon is convinced that serving the law is corrupt, he becomes totally anarchic, revelling in drunken self-indulgence by beating off neighbours, fighting with his son, and wrestling with a naked flute-girl. With the same single-mindedness, Dikeiopolis in *Acharnians* revenges himself on the warmongers of Athens who refuse to endorse his peace movement; he concludes a private peace with the enemy, and celebrates by mocking and excluding the other citizens. Asper's humour of moral indigna- tion and Macilente's humour of envy are equally self-absorbed: when reason fails to reform behaviour in London, the play- wright Asper constructs a fantasy in which Macilente exploits and explodes other humours and is rewarded by a final private vision of well-being. For in Jonson's comical satire, humours characteri- zation is not restricted to one or two 'humorists'. Instead, Jonson fills the stage with humours, each one colourfully distinguished from the others in manifestations ranging from Macilente's compulsive envy to Puntarvolo's eccentric chivalry or Fungoso's fashion fetish. The accumulated humours, variously thwarted, com- plicated, or fulfilled during the play, give the 'attentive auditor' a whole spectrum of social behaviours to respond to by laughing, by thinking, and, most importantly, by recognizing in them his or her own follies.

Farce

Although Jonson frequently criticizes farce in all its forms—jigs, ballads, motions, Tudor moralities, interludes, and all '*theatrical* wit, right stage-jesting, and relishing a playhouse, invented for scorn, and laughter'[47]—what he is criticizing is the meretricious provocation of empty laughter. In practice, Jonson uses farce to structure his plays and to render analytical complexities in accessibly physical form. He also destabilizes audience expectations by parodying form itself, and by reducing to the level of farce other generic modes, especially those he feels have been trivialized already: the prodigal son story (Fungoso); the morality play (Sordido); the Arthurian legend (Pun- tarvolo); the Petrarchan love-story (Deliro); the cony-catching tale (Shift). This subsuming and farcifying of other genres is part of what

Robert Watson sees as Jonson's subversive attack on the conventionality of his dramatic rivals and their audiences by ambushing 'not only a variety of hackneyed traditions, but also the intellectual complacency that sustained those traditions'.[48]

In doing this, Jonson relies on many of the standard formulas of the sixteenth-century farce or stage jig. Its dominant elements are crude colloquial dialogue, frequent mocking asides, and rapid physical action. Its characterization depends on stock types like the shrewish sensual woman, the duped husband, the swaggering gallant, the intriguer, and the clown. In the ballad-jig, generally the woman has to choose between two wooers: the prodigal gallant, whom she finally rejects, and the tradesman, whom she abuses as a clown.[49] Fallace's reduction of Deliro's courtship to a game of peek-a-boo (4.1) follows the same pattern. Other ballads depict a rustic clown, like Sogliardo in 1.2, boasting of his wealth. Moralities offer fools who sing nonsense songs and dance, like Carlo in 5.3.127–9, unaware of the retribution their own actions may provoke. The monologue of the Vice in morality plays is related to the clown's set-piece in later comedy, like Carlo's frequent lectures on gentlemanly behaviour, his discourse on pork (5.3.136–66), and his extra-dramatic address in the Induction. The virtuoso clown performance is the two-voice dialogue or song, like Launcelot Gobbo's in *The Merchant of Venice* 2.1, or Feste's impersonation of the parson in *Twelfth Night* 4.2.[50] Carlo's two-cup routine in 5.3 is of the same order. Low comedy frequently draws on tavern foolery with drunks, drawers, and quarrels over tavern reckonings,[51] such as also appear in the Mitre scene of *EMO*. The puppet play or 'motion', of which the two-cup routine is a variation, uses the same motifs, especially the flyting match erupting into physical attack, a staple farce-routine dating back at least to the marital squabbles and spouse-beatings of the Noah play in the mystery cycles and still standard in Punch-and-Judy shows. Shift avoids a beating in 5.2 by abject capitulation; Carlo's recognition of the danger signs (5.3) comes too late. Conventions of the jig include insulting asides, burlesques of current issues, and especially the device of presenting personal or social satire in the form of news or gossip retailed by the fool, this last to such an extent that the presence of the word 'news' in titles, songs, and dialogues usually indicates a burlesque or satirical treatment.[52] Sogliardo's '*que novelles?*' (5.2.68–9) plays on this expectation.

According to Bergson, farce mechanizes the human in its focus on the simplicity underlying complexities of behaviour. Our laughter is a desensitizer, a response to the threat of being reduced to mere cogs of instinct: we are at the mercy of our bellies and groins, and we make light of it. The construction of farce depends on arithmetical and symmetrical patterns derived from principles of repetition: the duplication of events, characters, ideas, words; their inversion in reversals and oppositions; and the coincidental intersection of two or more independent series of events, which seem as a result to have a cause and effect relation.[53] Characters may imagine they are duping those around them, but they are chiefly fooling themselves. They may even be capable of recognizing and commenting on the follies of others without recognizing that all the characters, themselves included, are counterparts of one another. For such comedy to work, the characters must be mechanical and two-dimensional, not only repetitive in themselves but also capable of being repeated by others: this is the connection between the would-be fashionable gallants, Brisk and his mirror-image Fungoso, eventually inverted and parodied by Macilente at one extreme (3.3) and Sogliardo at the other (5.2). The key structural feature of farce is this persistent cumulative arrangement of pairs, trios, quartets, like the marvellously proliferating rustics of 3.2 or officers of 5.3. The artificiality of these arrangements, parallel in progression despite antithesis in substance, distances the characters from the laughing audience. Farce characters must be incapable of genuine socialization (Clove and Orange represent extreme cases, the one speaking in trendy buzz-words, the other replying with meaningless catch-phrases) and consequently the audience sees only a ludicrous pattern, not people.[54] Techniques of stylized movement (the strolling sequence of 3.1), equally stylized tableau (the placement of observers and actors in 2.1), and acrobatic mime (accompanying Brisk's story of the duel, 4.3) contribute to the distancing. In fact, once emotional self-awareness develops in caricatures, and the audience responds to it, the nature of the comedy changes to something more complex and poignant: Jonson relies on this shift in sensitivity to work the scene of Macilente's vision of the queen (5.4), even though he inverts and lightens the effect in the return to the frame: 'How now, sirs? How like you it? Has 't not been tedious?'

The recognizable formulas of farce work hand in hand with stock characters. Through repetition, inversion, and amplification, farcical actions and types are capable of almost infinite variety, readily fitting themselves to Jonson's satiric panorama of incontinent 'humorists'.

3. THE ARISTOPHANIC MODE

'somewhat like *Vetus Comedia*'

As one of his contemporaries remarked in 1602, Jonson 'has become nowadays something humorous and too-too satirical up and down, like his great-grandfather Aristophanes'.[55] The assimilative nature of Jonson's classicism often makes it difficult to determine the sources of his borrowings.[56] Throughout his career, Jonson certainly made clear his debt to the past, but asserted the autonomy and integrity of the artist, ancient or modern, 'every man in the dignity of his spirit and judgement' free to supply something 'to illustrate and heighten . . . invention' (*EMO* Ind.253–63): 'For to all the observations of the *Ancients*, we have our own experience: which, if we will use, and apply, we have better means to pronounce. It is true they opened the gates, and made the way, that went before us; but as guides, not commanders' (*Disc.* 132–7). Cordatus's brief history of comedy turns on Aristophanes both as the apex of Old Comedy ('in him this kind of poem appeared absolute and fully perfected', Ind.254–5), and as the underlying inspiration for the genre's continuing development. Jonson argues that successive playwrights, trying to make an individual contribution to a genre already 'perfected' by Aristophanes, felt free to alter or augment the form, limited only by 'the elegancy and disposition of those times wherein they wrote' (Ind.260–1), and that this licence is equally the prerogative of modern writers.

Jonson's attraction to Old rather than New Comedy has to do in part with his habitual testing of accepted authority, and in part with certain predispositions he shares with Aristophanes. Old Comedy is urban, unromantic, flamboyantly scoffing, and reductively earthy. Like Jonson, Aristophanes was admired for his technical originality, and was considered more intellectual, sceptical, and irreverent than his contemporaries.[57] Ironically, again like Jonson, his reputation as a fearless moralist was enhanced by the larger-than-life physicality of his stage conceptions.[58] Because his characters ballooned into caricatures, audiences and critics assumed that this exaggeration had a didactic purpose that transcended its value as entertainment. Aristophanes' focus was social and broadly political, concentrating on abuses by self-centred power-seekers and on the consequences of such behaviour for the city. His plays were vehicles not only for social but also for literary theory.[59] In all these areas, Aristophanes, like Jonson, explored the connections between crude, mundane reality and higher human aspiration or potential; in Jonsonian terms, he was trying to reconcile the belly and the groin with the spirit or understanding.

What Jonson perceived as essential to his own and to Aristophanic comedy was the reliance on farce to express serious themes, and the shifting of perspective as characters alternated between their assigned roles in the dramatic illusion and their function as representatives of the audience, observing and commenting on stage action.[60] The object was to involve spectators in new ways of seeing by keeping them continually aware of the fact of performance. The comprehensive perspective that evolved, Jonson hoped, might give them a more clear-sighted understanding of human nature.

The chorus

The Aristophanic chorus has formal functions that facilitate the audience's reception of the play. During the *agon*, the chorus observes the conflict and pronounces the verdict without intervening, although the chorus may be partisan or even divided against itself. It also performs intermediary functions between the actors and the spectators: it consciously fills in gaps to cover off-stage business, frees the drama from the limitations of stage time and space, and introduces new characters or incidents. In general, the choric role is to dispute in the first half of the play, and gradually to be reconciled and united by the end of the second half.[61]

The Grex fills these functions in *EMO*: Cordatus and Mitis are explicitly present as 'censors' (Ind.152). They wrangle over such issues as decorum in characterization (1.3, 4.4) and in stage action (3.2, 5.1), scene-division (1.3, 2.1, 4.5, and 5.3), and personal satire (2.2, 3.1, 4.4, and 5.3). They comment on setting and on entrances, frequently when the characters are still liminally off-stage; sometimes they are made aware that their conversations are interrupting or delaying the production, notably in the Prologue's refusal to play his part (Ind.285–307), but also in Mitis's 'O, peace! You break the scene!' (1.1.36) and Cordatus's suggestion that they stop arguing and 'give way to the actors' (3.1.531–2).

The Aristophanic chorus's most characteristic feature is the *parabasis*, an abuse-match conducted while the action is in hiatus and the actors have left the stage, and directed at the audience by the chorus, who now behave as if they were visitors to the city during the festival for which the play is being performed.[62] The chorus leader generally criticizes Athenians, and offers advice, particularly extolling the poet, at the expense of his rivals, as a moralist or innovator. In *Clouds*, the chorus leader appears as 'Aristophanes' himself, cheekily defending his new play:

> You know me: I'm a man of ideas.
> Not a long-haired freak. I don't serve
> The same plots up in play after play:
> Mine are clever and sparkling and new.[63]

The rest of the chorus then continues the diatribe as it applies to the shortcomings of at least some of the spectators: in *Wasps*, the chorus accuses the audience of 'slow-witted dullness':

> when your Saviour sowed new Ideas by the sackful,
> your heads were so hard that you ruined his crop.
>   Nothing came up.[64]

This invective alternates with invocations to the gods or other placating songs. The whole exercise ostensibly promotes *homonoia*, the community of mind that strengthens the city against its external enemies by purging it of vice, but the *parabasis* may in fact be delivered ironically, as to incorrigibles.[65] From this point of view, the *parabasis* includes the audience in the play both as objects of satiric attack and as sharers of an in-joke on society at large. At the same time, by cutting across theatrical illusion, it operates like a Brechtian alienation effect, ridiculing the conventions of the theatre, even the most essential convention of actors giving a performance and spectators watching it.

Although the *parabasis* usually appears in the middle of an Aristophanes play, Jonson adapts it to fit the Elizabethan convention of the induction, and by so doing creates a whole new approach to induction-writing.[66] Asper addresses most of his remarks directly to spectators in the Globe, defending his own work as moral and denigrating the productions of other poets as time-serving and hypocritical. He intermittently praises the audience to win sympathy, but interrupts this traditional rhetorical ploy by collapsing into hysterical abuse of specific targets among the spectators. In a variation on the typical style of Aristophanic anapests, in which the chorus leader delivers as many of his lines as possible in one breath, raising his voice to a scream to drown out opposing views,[67] Asper works himself up into such a frenzy of invective against 'the time's deformity' (118) that he shouts down the responses of Cordatus and Mitis, overwhelming them with mimicry and sarcasm, and finally leaves the stage with a defiant taunt. The Grex then continues the discussion of poet and play until interrupted first by the Prologue, then by Carlo, and finally by Macilente beginning the play proper. Some of the later Grex commentaries, notably at the end of 2.1 and 3.1, seem to resume the *parabasis* by asserting the right to challenge authority, even if only by grumbling and carping. This strategy of hostile interruption, in Aristophanes as in Jonson, complicates the social critique with clever reversals and antitheses between city and country, new ways and old, physical buffoonery and mental gymnastics, naivety and sophistic trickery, all of which mark Old Comedy structures.[68]

The one element of the Aristophanic chorus that Jonson does not capture in the Grex is the sheer numbers. He compensates for this lack by redistributing the choric role erratically throughout the play proper among various observers and commentators who mirror the Grex by framing the actions of other characters, as in plays-within-the-play. The strategy is a kind of doubling. Carlo and Macilente, either jointly or separately, appear most often in the commentator role, but many of the others have at least one turn at it. In its simplest form, as in 1.2, Macilente observes Sogliardo from a hidden position while Carlo, though accompanying Sogliardo as his friend, indicates by asides that he too is observing Sogliardo satirically. Covert observation expands in degree and kind during the course of the play. We observe Sogliardo observing Puntarvolo in 2.1, and himself being observed by Puntarvolo and Carlo in 3.1. By 4.3.90–6, Sogliardo is ridiculed by Carlo and 'some dozen or twenty gallants' in an off-stage perspective through a keyhole, and by 5.2 several witnesses on-stage see him inflate himself in the charade with Saviolina and just as publicly deflate at the end of the scene, when his hero Shift is exposed as a fraud. A similar compilation of scenes could be devised for most of the other characters. The variation and integration within this choric technique give the impression of on-going satiric exposure provoking a range of responses that depend on wildly differing levels of intelligence and sensitivity. And the satiric responsiveness evoked by this conscious theatricality of the chorus convention implicates the theatre audience as well, seated or standing in rows, watching these inner-play watchers over the shoulders of the vigilant Grex.

The rhetoric of comic exposure

Although Aristophanes claims to be rescuing the state from moral torpor, his tone is usually ironic and jesting; the social reforms he stages are acted out by grotesque caricatures who are themselves targets of comic exposure.[69] The pattern of Jonson's play follows a similar sequence of shocking characters out of their humours by systematically degrading and humiliating them before witnesses who make the exposure possible and effective. Crude language is an indispensable feature of this process: it replaces physical aggression in acting out hostilities and thus bypasses the inhibitions society usually imposes on aggressiveness. Passing verbal attack off as a joke disarms critical thought and modifies the appearance of aggressiveness, making it easier and less potentially dangerous to laugh at someone else's expense.[70] Freud points out that sharing a joke becomes a means of creating rapport within a group: 'Every witticism . . . demands its own public, and to laugh over the same witticisms is a proof of absolute psychic agreement.'[71] This rapport is vital to understanding Aristophanes and Jonson because both playwrights deny that they use obscenity and crude physical comedy in general, except to make higher satiric and moral points accessible to the audience: 'not too refined and dainty for *you*, of course, but rather more intelligent than smutty farce'.[72] Their purpose differs substantially from that alleged of their contemporaries, whose only aim was to provoke laughter of any kind. Jonson claims that he is 'much distasted with the immodest and obscene writing of many, in their plays' (*CR* Ind.174ff.), and that he loathes 'the use of such foul and unwashed bawdry as is now made the food of the scene'— 'nothing but ribaldry, profanation, blasphemy, all licence of offence to God and man is practised' (*Volp.* Epistle, 46–7, 36–7). 'If you find their plays funny,' Aristophanes remarks of his rivals, 'then don't laugh at mine.'[73]

Yet comic invective is ubiquitous in Jonson, as in Aristophanes. At the simple level of name-calling, the naming of the *dramatis personae* turns characters into caricatures by magnifying the physical or psychological dimension of their 'humours' to the point of absurdity: Macilente is 'Skinny', Deliro is 'Crazy', Sogliardo is 'Hog'. The naming sketches inhuman, fantastic, or undeveloped figures, designed to preach a thesis along grotesque lines, a comic technique earlier mastered by Aristophanes.[74] Another aspect of invective is the grotesque Circean transformation of characters into inanimate or subhuman form, fixing them in absurd postures, like Aristophanes' choruses of birds and wasps, or the giant dung-beetle that transports the hero to Olympus in *Peace*. Jonson's grotesque is similarly reductive: Carlo pictures Sogliardo as 'holding his snout up like a sow under an apple tree' (4.3.93), Macilente as a 'lean mongrel . . . chap-fallen with barking' (1.2.214–15), and Puntarvolo as 'the sign of the George' (2.1.146), stiff 'as if he went in a frame, or had a suit of wainscot on' (274–5). Aristophanes frequently creates grotesque effects through parody. The philosophical bombast with which Socrates, suspended in a basket above the stage to facilitate higher thought, attempts to impress Strepsiades in *Clouds* is similar to the pseudo-intellectual name-dropping of the Clove and Orange sequence in 3.1.[75] The messenger's mock-Euripidean description of Lamachos's exploits on the battlefield in *Acharnians*, delivered with asides puncturing the heroics, resembles Brisk's story of his duel and torn clothing in 4.3.[76] The ultimate invective in Aristophanes is personal satire; but in this area Jonson had to be far more circumspect, usually diluting attacks on specific targets by burying their traits in otherwise unrecognizable personalities.[77]

Obscenity is both the most common and the most potent weapon for attacking and exposing pretentiousness. Explicit bawdy as an aggressive tactic appears less frequently in Jonson than in Aristophanes, who crams his plays with direct references to bowels, genitals, and intercourse.[78] In *EMO*, explicit bawdy tends to be interrupted, as in 2.1.23–6, where Brisk's pompous question, 'Whither should I ride but to the court?' is put down by Carlo's vulgar suggestion, 'your hot-house, or your—', cued by the sexual implication of 'ride'. Clearly he means to say 'whorehouse', a term synonymous with hot-house in any case, but Brisk changes the subject before the anticipated word is uttered. Explicit bawdy also appears as strategy of group aggression, in which spectators on- or off-stage enjoy complicity with one set of performers against another. In 5.2, Sogliardo addresses Saviolina as though she were a common whore ('*Bona roba*', 68) and makes crude sexual overtures to her ('Hot and moist? Beautiful and lusty?', 64–5), believing all the while that he is behaving like a perfect courtly gentleman. The fact that Saviolina accepts this vulgarity as the witty play-acting of the true gentleman she thinks she discerns under Sogliardo's gross exterior adds to the in-group's enjoyment.

By and large, in *EMO* at least, Jonson prefers double entendre to explicit bawdy. Often the jokes involve dramatic irony; that is, the audience hears bawdy which the speaker does not intend, but which pertains to the speaker's characterization. Sogliardo's involuntary obscenities in 5.2 qualify under this heading. Sometimes most or all of the performers are aware of the obscenity and the performance

operates hypocritically on two levels at once, as performers disguise
or distort their recognition of bawdy meanings: the Arthurian
charade between Puntarvolo and his wife (2.1.305–65) portrays high
romance as well as erotic fantasy, but the eavesdroppers mostly hear
it merely as vulgar titillation. The crudeness of spectators on or off
the stage is made clear in Carlo's frequent capping of non-sexual
subjects with sexual jokes, as in his sexualizing of the sundial conceit
(214–15, 269–70).[79] On the other hand, Shift's posted notice apparently offering himself as a gentleman-usher (3.1.91–7) also reads as
an advertisement for prostitution, and this latter obscene meaning
is certainly intended by the writer, a pimp under one of his aliases.

In Jonson as in Aristophanes, while gross sexual jesting keeps
company with wit and literary parody, the effect is not pornographic.
The sexuality integrates with the densely physical language dealing
with moral correction ('I'll strip the ragged follies of the time /
Naked as at their birth—', Ind.15–16), envy ('O, I could eat my
entrails / And sink my soul into the earth with sorrow!', 1.2.39–40),
and social climbing (a well-dressed fool can take virtue 'by the
shoulders or the throat / And kick him down the stairs', 3.3.19–20),
as well as all the various forms of invective. The bawdy provides an
earthy contrast to artificial stances, cuts through and exposes
humbug, adds spice to satire, and enlivens and intensifies parody.
Besides acting as a vivid means of communication with the audience, it articulates the notion that human nature demands a healthy
balance between the physical and the rational, and that artificial
systems of thought or action corrupt this naturally ethical balance.[80]
The concrete, often outrageous language becomes a kind of self-
assertion of the common citizen against the superior powers of
gods and society: ordinary human vulgarity, violence, and indepen-
dence, expressed in insulting and exulting over others, are the only
weapons, exaggerated because of the need to counter the magnified
tyranny of the opposition.[81]

Structure

Aristophanes freely experiments with the traditional dramatic structure of comedy.[82] The plot is invented and original, and even when
the setting is realistic, the distorted reality of the situation comments
satirically on Athenian institutions and attitudes, while the action
expands into the realm of the fantastic to allow the hero to accomplish the impossible.[83] In speaking of the structure of Aristophanic

action, one has to revise one's notion of 'plot'. Otherwise, the conclusion that there *is* no plot is inescapable. His comedies are not
plots of intrigue or incident, and are not concerned with unravel-
ling complex situations. Instead, they isolate moments of hyperbolic
and fantastic comic vision, exposing characters and the consequences of their behaviour to the laughter of the audience. Formal
integration is less important than dazzling the audience with the
rhythms, balances, and incongruities of the comic pacing. To some
extent, the structure has the fluidity of a modern revue with its
cumulative effects created by the variety of perspectives—comic bits,
mood pieces, monologues, duologues, ensemble scenes—on one
general subject or theme that unifies the whole.[84]

At the centre of an Aristophanic comedy is a philosophical
problem which, despite the fantasy that develops from it, grows out
of witty perceptions of contemporary issues. The dramatic materials derive from the collision between traditional beliefs and the
new intellectual developments in scientific speculation and in
systems of rhetoric or religion.[85] Athenian and Elizabethan tastes,
including the passion for litigation, were remarkably alike; and educated readers in the sixteenth century were drawn to Aristophanes
because his drama seemed to arraign and prosecute the social, economic, political, and religious vices of their own times.[86] Aristophanic structure presents the play as a legalistic statement of cases
with defences, proofs, evidence, witnesses, and judgement. From the
point of view of 'action', usually the first scene of the play establishes the idea that no action is possible in a corrupt and self-seeking
world where morality is a mask for injustice and greed; the only
course is to transcend the real world by establishing a private world
in which all wishes are satisfied, all enemies powerless, and all convention overturned by the hero's boundless self-assertion.[87] Since
nothing is really happening except in fantasy, the play does not
develop in a well-made plot-line of rising and falling action. The
question is, as Katherine Lever put it, 'whether Aristophanes
intended one scene to *develop into* another', and 'whether *development* is the only relationship between scenes'.[88] It is more fruitful to
see the scenes as offering lateral views that form a rhythmical pattern
of balances and contrasts. Once the action of the play has been arti-
culated by a single large controlling concept—like the desire to
shame people out of their humours—it is fuelled and propelled by
a series of smaller concepts—the idiosyncratic humours themselves—which laterally augment and reinforce the situation at the

heart of the plot by defining it with particular details and specific comment.[89] This presentation of lateral views works out the implications of the theme through counterpoint, like a fugue in music. The cumulative effect of echoes, inversions, and layered variations builds the main weight of the dramatic structure, which assumes in its audience a philosophical and aesthetic delight in complexity.[90]

The Aristophanic plot inclines, then, toward the intellectual rather than emotional engagement of the audience. It has no suspense rooted in intrigue, no romance, no lovers reunited by fortune. The hero is usually a grouch who expresses his dissatisfaction with the world in images of physical pain or disease (as do Asper and Macilente) in order to demonstrate from the very beginning that 'reality' as he construes it is wrong, and that his inversion of it by the end constitutes the only curative and right action. Very loosely, the comic movement of the play is from oppression to freedom: the hero begins in dismay at the perversion of order in society, the dismay leads him to carry out bizarre actions which shift the plot into fantasy, and his action ends in some glorious fulfilment.[91] In the process, the hero has to turn the tables on his enemies, who are at first stronger than he, but then are worsted and expelled.[92] These antagonist figures are all impostors who intrude on the hero in one way or another, 'impudent and absurd pretenders' and 'swaggering liars', each boasting of special merits, 'the whole gallery of quacks and humbugs standing for various professional classes in socety'.[93] In Jonsonian comedy, the impostors assail the hero with their superficial variety, but they have only one generic character, 'swaggering imposture', and one generic role in the action: to interrupt or upstage the hero with obnoxious self-vaunting, and to be beaten, mocked, or otherwise mishandled and driven away.[94] The reduplication of the impostor is integral to the action both as a tactic of farce and as a strategy of theme, exploring the kinds of humours defacing society. Not merely episodic, the best impostor scenes, such as 2.1, 3.1, and 5.2–3, generate momentum and demonstrate unity of action by choreographing impostors in groups, smaller groups within the larger, each dancer dancing his own dance within the larger dance.

The expulsion of the impostors completes the *agon* and complements the transformation of the hero. The expulsion is usually symbolic, a survival of the death-and-resurrection motif in seasonal ritual, in which negatives are destroyed by an act of simulated violence in order to facilitate the influx of a positive good for the city at large.[95] So in *EMO* Carlo has his lips sealed; Shift is brought to

his knees and expelled with curses; Sordido hangs himself and is
then recalled to life for moral conversion; Fungoso hides under a
table, rises for his humiliation, and is redeemed; Brisk is derided and
left in the underworld of the Counter awaiting trial; and Macilente,
initially prostrated by bitter envy, rises socially and sartorially by
mid-play, and is ultimately resurrected spiritually by his vision of the
Queen. These comic transformations are to be understood as efficacious at stopping social error: 'Unlikely conversions, miraculous
transformations, and providential assistance are inseparable from
comedy. Further, whatever emerges is supposed to be there for
good: if the curmudgeon becomes lovable, we understand that he
will not immediately relapse again into his ritual habit.'[96] But
such an ending does not make promises of happiness for all those
whose humours have been blasted. If Sordido and Macilente find
redemption, assuredly Carlo, Puntarvolo, Brisk, Deliro, and Fallace
do not.

The *exodos*, or finale, celebrates the new order in a symbolic marriage to indicate the rejuvenation or restoration of an ideal, and,
through this temporary union, reintegrates the hero with the rest of
humanity. The mute bride of the final scene is allegorical; she exists
solely for the purpose of rewarding the hero, treating him with 'royal,
and even divine, honours'. The moment is pure ritual: 'There is
nothing whatsoever in the previous incidents of an Aristophanic plot
to prepare the spectator for any such conclusion'.[97] This figure closes
almost all of Aristophanes' plays: Opora (or Fruits-of-Summer) in
Peace, Reconciliation in *Lysistrata*, the Peace Treaties in *Knights*, and
especially (in the Jonsonian context) Basileia, Queen of Heaven, in
Birds. Basileia represents in tangible personal form the idea that her
groom Peisetairos acquires power and self-definition within his universe. Not just a fertility symbol, she is:

A sort of Beauty Queen,
the sign of Empire and the symbol of divine supremacy.
It's she who keeps the keys to Zeus' thunderbolts
and all his other treasures—Divine Wisdom,
Good Government, Common Sense.[98]

The symbolic bride is the final perspective from which we view
the hero's action: she sanctions his deeds, but the sanction and its
seriousness beneath the jesting are unexpected. Before her appearance, the angle of perspective on the action has been determined by
one of the stock comic types: the *eiron* or roguish ironist-hero; his

companion, the *bomolochos* or buffoon; and his antagonist, the *alazon* or impostor.[99] In Aristophanes' comedy, when the last impostor is expelled, that third position offering a perspective on the action is filled by the mute figure of the bride with her tacit approval of the hero's deed. The buffoon, an essentially festive character, remains to help celebrate. But in *EMO* the buffoon Carlo is expelled as well as the impostors, and his absence from the final scene gives unusual weight to the appearance of the queen. Her power to purify and assimilate Macilente extinguishes the other remaining point of view, that of the ironist. Her serene assumption of social and moral corrigibility becomes the only perspective.

4. THE INNS OF COURT MILIEU

'according to the elegancy and disposition of those
times wherein they wrote'

Dekker's satirical pot-shot at Jonson in *Satiromastix*, forcing 'Horace'/Jonson to 'swear not to bombast out a new play with the old linings of jests stolen from the Temple's Revels' (5.2.295–6), makes two points pertinent to *EMO*: first, that Jonson consciously borrowed from the Inns of Court revels, especially from those of the Inner or Middle Temple; and second, that Jonson was well enough acquainted with the lawyers and law students to be a sharer in their entertainments and in the kind of wit that shaped them. A survey of Inns of Court traditions can help to explain such key Jonsonian features as the complex, boldly critical tone of 'comical satire', the bantering relationship that *EMO* establishes with its audience, and the special significance of the Queen's sudden appearance in the catastrophe.

The origin of Jonson's friendships among the young intellectuals at the Inns is not known, but their effects were profound and lasting. According to Aubrey, John Hoskyns of the Middle Temple was Jonson's intellectual 'father': 'Sir Benet [Hoskyns' son] . . . told me that one time desiring Mr. Jonson to adopt him for his son, "No," said he, "I dare not; it is honour enough for me to be your brother: I was your father's son, and it was he that polished me." '[100] Richard Martin, the Christmas prince of the 1597/8 Middle Temple revels, extricated Jonson from threats of prosecution over the 'Apologetical Dialogue' appended to *The Poetaster* in 1601; Jonson dedicated the play to him in the 1616 Folio. Jonson's admiration and exasperated affection for John Donne (Lincoln's Inn) are persistent features of his conversations with Drummond in 1618. Some of his friendships at the Inns may have come about through former schoolmates at Westminster School, from which Jonson graduated in 1590, or through his former schoolmaster, William Camden, 'the most learned, and my honoured friend', to whom he dedicated the folio revision of *Every Man In His Humour*. Unable to afford a university education, Jonson was apprenticed to a bricklayer, and, apparently to escape this line of work, joined the army in 1591 to serve in the Low Countries. On his return, he cultivated his intellectual interests and, like the Inns of Court gentlemen, probably spent his afternoons at one of the many local playhouses. By the end of 1594, Jonson, now married, must have decided to make a name and a modest living for himself as a playwright, following the path taken by university wits like Nashe, and to begin by learning stagecraft as an actor, as Shakespeare had done. Jonson's talents as a player were apparently minimal, according to Dekker and Aubrey.[101] Jonson himself seems to have had an equally low opinion of his early plays; at any rate, none survives to indicate why Francis Meres named him along with Shakespeare as 'among our best for tragedy' in *Palladis Tamia* (1598).

The turning point in his career was the performance of *The Isle of Dogs* some time before 28 July 1597. His role as actor and part-author brought him a contract with Henslowe, two months imprisonment and interrogation in the Marshalsea prison by order of the Privy Council, and an enhanced reputation as a satirist among the Inns of Court students, many of whom were satirists themselves. Nashe, the play's originator, fled London, admitting afterward to having composed the induction and first act. The content of the play can only be guessed at: the Isle of Dogs, the peninsula across the river from Greenwich, may have been treated as a liberty for snarling satirists attacking some political figure. The high level of veiled political analogy in Day's later *Isle of Gulls* (1606) may be some indication of how the Nashe–Jonson satire worked. In any case, the frequency of dog-jokes in *EMO* suggests an oblique tie-in with *The Isle of Dogs*, and implies that the Inns of Court gentlemen found the play's satirical daring to their taste. Afterwards, Jonson's career was on the upswing: the success of *The Case Is Altered*, performed by the fashionable Chapel Children, was followed by various collaborations in works now lost, and by the popular *Every Man In His Humour* (1598), 'sundry times publicly acted', according to its Q title-page in 1601. Jonson's continuing popularity at the Inns of Court is suggested in John Marston's revision of *Histriomastix* for the 1598/9 revels at the Middle Temple, subsequently performed at Blackfriars in November 1599: it presents an admiring portrait of Jonson as Chrisogonus, the nonpareil philosopher-cynic-stoic.[102] Very likely, admirers at the Inns were responsible for advising Jonson before his trial for the murder of the actor Gabriel Spencer in a duel on 22 September 1598: Jonson escaped hanging by pleading 'benefit of clergy', an archaic law originally designed to protect priests, not classicists.

The world of the law and the world of the theatre were not as dissimilar as they might at first appear. Both nurtured talented men whose skilled rhetoric and self-presentation fitted them for positions of influence, whether political, financial, or literary. The Inns of Court were not simply amalgamated law schools. Each inn was also a professional association for class-conscious graduates and practising lawyers, and, just as importantly, a private club. In Jonson's day, legal education was almost mandatory for the younger sons of the nobility and gentry: the object was not only to learn the law in order to protect and enhance the family estate but also to pick up the courtly airs and graces of nearby Westminster, in hopes of finding powerful patronage for a career in government or the royal household.[103] The Inns were more frequented by the gentry than both universities together; in fact, since the universities were geared to clerical education, the more secular students, after a year or two at Oxford or Cambridge, chose to broaden their education with cultural activities in London at one of the Inns of Court. Here, education meant more than a foothold in the legal and social establishment. Especially between 1590 and 1610, the Inns fostered a catalytic atmosphere for literary reaction, arising from their tradition of free and candid speech, their growing disenchantment with Elizabethan power structures, and their arrogant, histrionic 'sense of belonging to an elite of wits in a world of gulls'.[104]

The satirical point of view blossomed in an educational environment that valued critical acumen. Much legal training was rhetorical, in *bolts* (lectures by a senior member of the Inn) and *moots* (debates in which bold conduct often won legal points, despite contrary precedents). It is to this environment of 'Humanity and Liberty'—learning and licence—that Jonson admiringly refers in the 1616 Dedication to *EMO*. Even the Inn revels were 'playful models of statecraft', 'an educational parody of the actual government at

Whitehall'; serious didactic purposes often underlay the antics.[105] The revels mock-kingdom was both a means of preparing the young lawyers for government service by rehearsing their diplomatic skills and a means of conveying astute political messages to the Queen under the pretence of Christmas games. These entertainments, attended by the court and eminent members of government, were influential outside the Inns precisely because of this blend of epideictic flattery and witty criticism.

The lawyers' mode of expression had considerable appeal for Jonson, whose standards for judgement were intellectual and social, rather than sentimental or religious; he attacked follies that were 'intellectually undesirable'—based on ignorance or stupidity—rather than those that were 'morally heinous'.[106] In fact, Jonson's comical satires equate intellectuality with moral superiority, a view contrary to the clever Vices and rationalist villains of theatrical tradition, in which intellectuals had been portrayed as demonic.[107] In part at least, this attitude may be attributed to the matriculation revolution of 1570–1608, which resulted in oversupplying society with professional graduates and scholars who became the 'alienated intellectuals' of late Elizabethan and early Stuart England.[108] It may also account for Jonson's popularity with students not only at the Inns but also at the universities. By 1602, Jonson was virtually a cult figure at Cambridge, where the literary avant-garde had all read his plays in quarto, whether or not they had actually seen performances in London.[109]

EMO was not only Jonson's biggest hit as a printed text but also the most popular play-text published by anyone in the period. Its influence as a model is obvious in the Cambridge playwrights' *Return from Parnassus, Part II* (1601/2), a comical satire about the failure of the scholar (like Macilente) to find a place in society; it borrows Jonson's humours characterization, realistic London setting, and selection of satirical targets, and relies on a similarly intense level of audience provocation.[110] Its structure, like Jonson's, resembles some of the features of the Inns of Court revels in its heavy use of parody, mock trials of pretentious fools, and lateral co-ordination of scenes in a loose processional movement.

The general format of the Inns of Court revels depended on the creation of a saturnalian fantasy-world: a mock-state with its own prince and court, proclamations, edicts, and progresses. Just before Christmas, each Inn selected a prince to lead its revels and to rule until Candlemas or Shrovetide. During the revels, students were in charge, supplanting the usual Inn rule, which was by benchers (during the term) and barristers (during vacation). Typical revels ceremonies included elaborate emblazoning of the prince's titles, job descriptions of court officers and knights, declaration of laws, arraignments of 'criminals', presentation of plays, and ceremonious visits to the country, city, and court. Finally the prince 'died' and the revels ended.[111] The shape of events within this loose structure was threefold: first, a ponderous movement towards disruption of order; then, the bringing of culprits to trial; and, finally, the restoration of authority through various face-saving expedients. Thus, 'The Night of Errors' in the *Gesta Grayorum*, during which visitors from the Inner Temple were subjected to 'disordered Tumult' and insults, was a prologue to an elaborate statement of renewed friendship between the two Inns.[112] The 1597/8 Middle Temple invitation to Lincoln's Inn also erupted into disorder, 'practic'd factiously' by the Clerk of the Prince's Council against the Prince's state, and the situation was similarly resolved two days later after a series of arraignments. On both occasions, the incidents were partly spontaneous high-spirited trouble-making and partly planned stratagems for staging a wide variety of rhetorical games: trials, letters mending diplomatic ties between Inns, banquet speeches, and masques. The whole scheme of riot, redress, and formal renewal of order was fully in the spirit of the revels, 'all part of the rag'.[113]

This description suggests several particular ways in which *EMO* models itself on the form and content of the revels, although this is not to discount any more general source of fantasized folly to which Erasmus and More were indebted. Asper's choice of setting, the Fortunate Island, resembles the topsy-turvy revels land of fools, which is explicitly associated in the induction with the actual audience, and which is finally resolved into an idealized vision of England. Asper's zeal for social reform transmutes itself into Macilente's disruptive malicious energy, fomenting the disorder in the play by means of which society is purged and renewed. The first half of the play is concerned with the gradual assembly of self-displaying characters engaging in various rhetorical games as members of competitive, ever-expanding, and shifting groups whose allegiances are constantly tested and redefined. Fungoso, Brisk, and Saviolina recall particularly common revels targets. But the most important points of contact between the Inns of Court revels and *EMO* are Jonson's recreation of the 'ragging' revels tone and his controversial use of the image of the Queen to end the play.

The tone of the revels may be defined as ironic interplay between real life and play-acting; the irony included the relationships between actors as members of the Inn, actors as characters within a sustained fiction, actors as audience for one another, even actors as actors, as well as the relationship between actors and the actual audience. The comedy of festive role-playing depended on the true condition and the mock condition of the lawyer-prince being recognized together: 'the role was transparent, but maintained in utmost ceremony', with conscious theatricality and witty self-mockery preventing a decline into mere fantasy.[114] By drawing on this multiple tone for *EMO*, Jonson hoped to establish the same relationship with his audience: that is, a rapport growing out of in-group jokes and playfully aggressive put-downs which provide an implicit extradramatic commentary on events, characters, and observers both fictive and real.[115]

This bantering revels style, refined to an art in the previous decade by sophisticated clowns such as Richard Tarlton,[116] was enjoyed and exploited by Queen Elizabeth and those of her court not too cowed to participate. Elizabeth declared at the end of the *Gesta Grayorum* that she 'wished that their sports had continued longer, for the pleasure she took therein' and made the final recorded quip of the revels herself by mocking some courtiers for dancing after the brilliantly choreographed 'mask of Proteus' had ended: 'What! Shall we have bread and cheese after a banquet?' She also habitually engaged in witty skirmishes with players, as she did at Kenilworth in 1575 when she quibbled with the 'Lady of the Lake' and concluded, 'Well, we will *common* more with you hereafter.'[117] To 'common' meant to share good fellowship with others, to participate in conversation, to take a part in common with them in a way that minimized status (*OED* 1–3). 'Commoning' forged group intimacy and shared amusement by provoking and indulging the aggressiveness of a particularly assertive audience;[118] and it is this 'commoning' relationship that Jonson recreates in *EMO* by means of the frame, the internal Grex commentaries, and the related in-group sniggerings and carpings of different combinations of observers imbedded in the play proper. To take these choric voices as purely Juvenalian railing, arrogant moralizing, or bitter elitist sneering is seriously to misinterpret the play's prevailing tone.[119]

The Inns saw their revels as 'witty inventions . . . mocking . . . at our own follies', and 'using pleasures, as sauces for meats of better nourishment'.[120] Sexual levity, predictably in any college

production, was the sauce that most frequently flavoured their satirical attacks. Among those listed as homagers and tributaries of the
Prince of Purpoole is a brothel-keeper:

> *Lucy Negro* [probably a real Lucy Black], Abbess *de Clerkenwell*, holdeth
> the Nunnery of *Clerkenwell* with the lands and privileges thereunto belong-
> ing, of the Prince of *Purpoole* by night-service in *cauda*, and to find a choir
> of nuns, with burning lamps, to chant *Placebo* to the gentlemen of the
> Prince's Privy-Chamber, on the day of his Excellency's coronation.[121]

The other favorite topics, many continuing from late medieval satire,
were fashions in clothes and taverns, and fads of various kinds:
heraldry and emblem-making; 'best-sellers' like the *Arcadia* and
Euphues; affectations such as carrying a toothpick or smoking; and
travel—although recurring references to 'Turks' probably meant
gangs of apprentices, with whom Inns gentlemen often fought.[122]
Revels witticisms were frequently quibbles on the legal forms and
jargon in which the young members were being instructed, as in, for
example, the prince's 'gracious, general and free pardon' with its list
of exceptions that finally excluded everyone.[123] These legal parodies
usually had bawdy implications. Many of those excluded from the
general pardon stood accused of sexual misdemeanours or dysfunction, such as persons who have 'occasion . . . or possible means
to entertain, serve, recreate, delight, or discourse' with a 'gentlewoman', 'publicly, privately, or familiarly', but 'shall faint, fail, or be
deemed to faint or fail in courage . . . or in act'. Sometimes speeches
were tightly packed with legal vocabulary and syntax just for the
pleasure of hearing the rhetoric back up on itself, as in Puntarvolo's
contract in 4.3. The hallmarks of such parody are excessive length,
the over-use of prepositional phrases, densely involved subordinate
clauses, the reduplication of synonyms or alternatives, and such
recurrent legal terms as *case, cause, frustrate, grief, disease, apparels,
exception*, and the many others noted in the commentary on this
play.[124]
    Elizabethan legal procedure, pedantic and unduly respectful of
forms, threatened to reduce the whole system to an elaborate intellectual game,[125] and the revellers exaggerated this idiosyncrasy of
the law with their emphasis on specifically verbal jokes. In the
Middle Temple's revels of 1597/8, for example, 'Bestia' (Charles
Best) was indicted for shifting his speech to 'wrest, turn, pervert,
misconster, and catachristically abuse the honest, civil, chaste, pure,
and incorrupt meanings' of such words as 'standing, members,

dealing, truncheon, quiver, evidences, weapons'. Bestia's reply to the charge of 'perverting honest speeches into unhonest meaning' was that 'the words they were his, but the sense was in the audience, and every one of them brought hither a mind of his own'.[126]

Tickling the minds of the audience with sexual innuendo, in-jokes and absurd concatenations is typical of revels prose. Those speeches that are not explicitly or covertly ribald rely on calculated impudence. John Hoskyns's 'Fustian Speech' was not only a reply to Charles Best's 'Tufftaffeta Speech', in which tobacco was hailed as politically powerful, but also an oblique chaffing of Sir Walter Ralegh, the Prince d'Amour's chief guest for the evening and reputedly the discoverer of tobacco:

> I see no reason why men should so addict themselves to take *tobacco* in Ramus' Method; for let us examine the complots of politicians from the beginning of the world to this day: What was the cause of the Repentine mutiny in Scipio's camp? It is most evident it was not *tobacco*. What was the cause of the Aventine revolt, and seditious deprecation for a Tribune? It is apparent it was not *tobacco*. What moved me to address this expostulation to your iniquity? It is plain it is not *tobacco*. So that to conclude, *tobacco* is not guilty of so many faults as it is charged withal; it disuniteth not the reconciled, nor reconcileth the disunited; it builds no new cities, nor mends no old breeches; yet the one, the other, and both are not immortal without reparations.[127]

Clove's fustian talk (3.1.175ff.) is a tribute to Hoskyns's manipulation of rhetorical sound over substance of argument. Brisk's attempt to present himself as a powerful lover by smoking his pipe with authority translates the fustian argument into a visual mode. Brisk is apparently an inept smoker (3.3.38–9, 71), and in any case Saviolina is repelled by the fumes (118–19, 130–1, 133–6). The only other smokers in the play, Shift and Sogliardo, are exposed in a mocking perspective through a keyhole: 'and there we might see Sogliardo sit in a chair, holding his snout up like a sow under an apple tree, while th'other opened his nostrils with a poking-stick to give the smoke a more free delivery' (4.3.92–5). Similarly impudent, Sir Francis Beaumont's 'Grammar Lecture', probably delivered at the Inner Temple in 1601, gives a flippantly satirical description of law students, whom he categorizes under three headings: the 'puny' or young student, a 'soft imitating piece fit for the impression of either plodder or reveller',[128] like the spongy Fungoso; the reveller, a sophisticated dilettante with habits remarkably similar to Fastidius Brisk's; and the plodder, the student who actually intends to practise law, as Fungoso pretends in conversation with his uncle or father. Beaumont describes the 'etymology' of getting money from one's parents or from one's merchant, as Fungoso and Brisk habitually attempt to do, and the 'very vile syntaxis' of spending the money on books (which, as in Fungoso's successful stratagem, should merely be the excuse for the loan) instead of 'good clothes, through which he is fit for revelling and courtship'.[129] This tension between professional and elitist goals at the Inns of Court produced among the more sensitive, such as John Donne, an equivocality that expressed itself in the figure of ironic deprecation, rhetorically aligning the speaker with elitist pleasure over mercenary industry, even while acknowledging the contradiction implicit in the pose, since even idealists have to earn a living: the opening lines of 'Satire 2', in which Donne represents himself as one free of the competition for status and power—'I do hate / Perfectly all this town'—might have been spoken by the frustrated Asper/Macilente.[130]

The Inns of Court entertainers often risked including sociopolitical content which might have offended if uttered directly, but was made acceptable by indirect allusion and analogy. Plays touching on religion and government, topics forbidden in public performance by the Proclamation of 16 July 1559, were allowed at the Inns. Through carefully constructed symbols and icons, they dramatized dangerous material for a closed audience 'in such a way that their loyalty to the monarch seemed never to be in question'.[131] The revellers were permitted considerable licence in expressing astringent criticisms by developing a peculiarly English twist to classical myths within which to couch their views.[132] This creation of a fiction through which to voice criticisms or obtain preferment was part of the 'histrionic self-presentation'[133] common at the Inns and at court. Lawyers like Plowden and Bacon had been responsible for shaping the Queen's image by secularizing the cult of the Virgin Mary into the cult of Elizabeth, virgin queen of two bodies, the body natural and the immortal body politic.[134] This symbolism merged with other classical and romantic myths in which the Queen appeared to subsume, as in Lyly's *Endymion*, the roles of goddess (Diana, Pallas, Cynthia, Astraea) and unattainable monarch-mistress (Gloriana), with a result that has been called 'Petrarchan politics'.[135] The Queen's exercise of power was bound up in her use of courtly love romance fictions, and those who wanted political favour had to play the game. Homage to Elizabeth, 'the incomparable Empress of the

Fortunate Island', as she is styled in 'The Masque of Amity' at Gray's Inn (1594/5),[136] suggests that she is the perfect queen of an ideal state, where confusion and discord have no place.

Initially, the main purpose behind this courtly pretence, especially as the Inner Temple saw it in 1561, was to assure the succession through a royal marriage to Lord Robert Dudley, a member of that Inn. Dudley, as prince of the Inner Temple revels, presented a wooing allegory in the masque of *Desire and Beauty* in which Pallas herself urges Elizabeth to marry.[137] The Queen's presence, both symbolically in the play and actually in the audience, made for a double show. The same advice appeared even more dramatically in the Gray's Inn entertainments at Whitehall, 5 March 1564/5, which the Queen interrupted to remark to the Spanish ambassador, 'This is all against me'. Yet, despite the fact that, when the same subject was raised in Parliament, she called it 'treason', she heard the lawyers out.[138] The 1575 entertainments at Kenilworth, however, marked a change in the view of Elizabeth's power. She was no longer featured as potential bride and mother, but dominated the scene as a 'regenerating and liberating force' in a more spiritual, mystical, even transforming sense: 'Elizabeth brings in her person power to charm and to free—gods bring her gifts, wild men are tamed, the fearful set free.'[139] Similarly, the civic pageants in the Low Countries during Leicester's progress in 1586 present Elizabeth as a figure of victory, liberty, and justice in the face of tyranny; a view continued in Peele's *Descensus Astraeae* in the Lord Mayor's Show of 1591; and in the Middle Temple revels of 1597/8, where she is praised as 'the only divine pattern of all creatures'.[140]

The effect of this later view of the Queen can be clearly seen in Jonson's original ending to *EMO*, which could be pertinent only to an audience educated in such iconography. When the actor portraying the Queen, no doubt in splendid costume, appears on the stage and Macilente collapses in '*very wonder*' (5.4.0.2), the *tableau vivant* captures the whole era's tradition of masque, show, and civic pageant in one brief electric moment. The visual impact is all. Then Macilente, '*rising and recovering heart*' (0.3–4), confirms the significance of the royal image in his poetry and in his decorous kneeling after line 21, as befits the wild man tamed. Ideally the miracle on stage should reflect a similar catharsis in the audience. Elizabeth, as queen, embodies 'religious and mystical powers sufficient to release men from their bondage; indeed, she seems to be the Truth that sets men free'.[141]

Like the Inns of Court masques—and like Jonson's masques to come—the 'pageant' ending of *EMO* operates epideictically as both flattery and counsel, as idealization and as instruction for 'attentive auditors'. The Queen becomes an emblem of the perfectability, or at least corrigibility, of human nature. But the very artificiality of the scene is also a reminder that natural men and women are mocked by their own humours and passions, creatures of flux. Their hope of transformation into better beings lies in the transcending power of art. This 'pageant' ending is the significant ending Jonson intended *EMO* to have, the ending he defended in print, and the one he insisted on publishing in the quarto and substantially reproducing in the folio. Why? Perhaps because it offers hope as an antidote to satiric aversion. The original catastrophe moves the diverse human spectacle of folly into a sustaining harmony equivalent to an act of grace. It is not surprising that Jonson should have been dissatisfied with the alternative endings forced upon him. He did not want an empty Macilente, a mere shell drained of malice. He wanted a positive emanation of social good, one that, filtered through the frame of actor-playwright and Grex, could accompany the audience out of the theatre.[142]

5. THE THEATRE AND THE PLAY

'to behold the scene full'

EMO's brief stage history has weighed heavily in the modern perception of the play as unperformable. Length alone would, of course, indicate that the published version is unsuitable for production; the quarto's title-page admits freely that the play was printed 'AS IT WAS FIRST COMPOSED / by the Author B. I. / *Containing more than hath been Publickly Spo-/ken or Acted*'. The advertisement appended to 'The Characters' indicates that the performed version was controversial ('many censures fluttered about it'), but controversy in itself is not an indictment. It may be rather an enticement to repeated performance and publication. It certainly indicates lively reaction, a desirable response in the playhouse. Inevitably, when artists attempt to sweep out the old and install the new, they raise a lot of dust. Dramatists who want to revolutionize or redefine an audience's relationship to the stage have little hope of doing so if they cannot express ideas through their chosen medium: the physical space of the theatre itself. What follows is a discussion of Jonson's exploitation of that space.

Stage history and stage potential

According to the 1616 folio title-page, *EMO* was 'Acted in the year 1599 / By the then Lord / CHAMBERLAIN / his Servants'. The theatre was the newly constructed Globe, which had opened in August or September 1599. The exact date of the first performance is unknown, but it may have been between 15 November and 20 December; and the existence of the revised ending suggests that the performance was repeated. This approximation is based on the date of the Paul's Boys' revival of *Histriomastix*, 13 November (Clove mentions the title at 3.1.139), and the subsequent court performance of *EMO* during the Christmas season, between 26 December 1599 and Twelfth Night 1600.[143] The play was later revived at James's court on 8 January 1605. The only recorded performance after this date was at the Theatre Royal in July 1675.[144] However, Restoration comments suggest that it was 'very satisfactory to the town' when it was 'acted but now and then',[145] and that it was 'accounted an excellent old comedy'.[146]

Later critical response to the play has not been kind, perhaps because of the changing tastes of the eighteenth century, which, by keeping *EMO* off the stage, made it a pariah, victim of its own history of non-performance. In 1753, Bishop Hurd spurned the play as 'abstract' and 'unnatural', despite his admission that 'this comedy has always had its admirers'.[147] In 1764, one of them, David Erskine Baker, praised the characters as 'perfect originals', not unlike 'several well known existents in real life', and suggested that, with cutting, 'this play might be rendered extremely fit for the present stage'.[148] In 1784, Thomas Davies agreed, calling critical opposition 'ill-founded', and also mentions that Foote imitated *EMO* 'in some his farces [*sic*], in which some of his actors have spoken to others on the stage from the gallery and the boxes, to the no small entertainment of the spectators'.[149] In the absence of modern stage performance, these insights have remained hypothetical.

Perhaps as a result, critics since the mid eighteenth century have made a point of discrediting *EMO* as drama, praising it as daringly innovative while damning it as unstageworthy. Clearly few, if any, of these critics have actually had their opinions validated by a production. Nevertheless, the tendency among twentieth-century critics has been to toe the standard line drawn by Herford and Simpson (1.21): Jonson's first comical satire is 'abortive as a drama, but of the most brilliant literary texture', a 'magnificent perversion' of the successful comic method used in *Every Man In*. Helena Watts Baum agrees: Jonson 'threw away . . . [his] skill in handling comic material' in the play. More recent critics adopt a similar half-admiring, half-dismissive stance: Knoll calls it 'an intellectual's play'; Barish sees it as a 'heroic failure, a brilliant and original failure'; for Parfitt, it is an experimental 'demonstration rather than exploration'; and, for Barton, 'a conspicuously brilliant as well as an infuriating work', 'defiantly idiosyncratic'.[150]

The major defender of *EMO*'s worth as a stage play, W. David Kay, describes the play as the watershed in Jonson's work, marking his break with contemporary fashions in drama and the start of his specifically literary career.[151] The salient points of Kay's argument are worth repeating. Kay disputes assumptions that *Every Man In His Humour* was better received by the public than *EMO*. He points out that Robert Allot, editor of *England's Parnassus* (1600), cited seven quotations from *EMO*, and only two from *EMI* (*Q*); that *EMO* was the first of Jonson's plays to be published in quarto, and also the first to be revived at James's court (*EMI* was revived a month later, on 2 February 1605). There is no evidence that *EMO* was a popular failure. The only negative criticism is of the original ending, which was apparently received well at court in 1599, if not at the Globe. If the play had not been considered effective as theatre, repeated performance and court revival would have been unlikely. Finally, the unusual demand for the printed version in 1600, when three editions appeared successively over a period of eight to twelve months, suggests the popular desire to relive the theatre experience. This excitement over *EMO* may have led to the printing of *EMI* (*Q*) and *Cynthia's Revels* in 1601, and perhaps to the later revision of *EMI* (*F*) as well.

As Kay's argument suggests, Jonson's success was both dramatic and literary. In fact, it may well be a false distinction to separate the two kinds of success, since the original audiences did not do so. Jonson's tragedies, for example, did not begin a trend for accuracy in the treatment of Roman history; they were spurned both as drama and as literature. Jonson gained his reputation as the leading 'humorist' of the time as a direct result of his transformation of the light comedy of humours into an effective vehicle for dramatic satire. At the same time, it established him as a major influence, artistic and intellectual, on the direction that comedy—city comedy in particular—was to take during the next decade, and indeed throughout the seventeenth century.[152]

If the eighteenth and nineteenth centuries ignored Jonson's

innovations, the twentieth may finally have educated audiences to appreciate them. An audience exposed to Bertolt Brecht's theatre is to some extent already acclimatized to Jonsonian practice. Brecht's illusion-breaking techniques and 'alienation effects' bear a close resemblance to Jonson's theatrical self-consciousness and his parody of stage convention. Both playwrights reject 'well-made' plots and empathetic identification with characters. Both mingle the highbrow with the lowbrow to startle the audience into a critical frame of mind. Both emphasize the social realities that override conventional morality and demonstrate its naivety. But live theatre has been superseded by television, a more accessible and more pervasive influence on the modern audience. The satirical revue, rising out of the internationally acclaimed Cambridge production *Beyond the Fringe* (1960), ultimately reached its largest audience in television's *Monty Python's Flying Circus*. The *Python* method is essentially parodic, revelling in absurd transformations of television conventions like the game-show or the interview, and connecting scenes with a free flow of association, assisted by choric interruptions. Its comedy combines the intensely verbal with the ludicrously physical in bizarre and savage attacks on pretentiousness. Extensive sarcasm, implied brutality, fulminating rages, gratuitous obscenity: these tactics are *Python* hallmarks, and not all that far from Asper/Macilente's aggressive monomania, Puntarvolo's 'silly walk' and equally silly medievalism, and Carlo's gush of poisonous similes. The other potent influence on recent audiences is the cinema. To cite only one representative favourite, Juzo Itami's *Tampopo* (New Yorker Films Release, 1987) is a social satire in a gentler, but recognizably Jonsonian, vein. Opening with an induction that mirrors the movie audience, the film works out its central theme through several tangentially connected vignettes, all of which parody film conventions and, by so doing, accumulate satirical meanings. Almost any Woody Allen movie plays with these same motifs, including direct audience address and critical re-evaluation of artistic concerns and generic expectations. These twentieth-century trends in theatre, television, and cinema suggest that modern productions and modern audiences are recapturing the attitude of mind that relished the iconoclastic dramaturgy of *EMO* in 1599.

The Globe and Jonson's dramaturgy

The new Globe Theatre itself may have been the inspiration for Jonson's conception of staging in *EMO*. Certainly its size alone—

Richard Hosley estimates that the stage measured 41 feet 6 inches by 27 feet 8 inches[153]—would have been a challenge to a playwright like Jonson who loved rather 'to behold the scene full and relieved with variety of speakers to the end than to see a vast empty stage and the actors come in one by one as if they were dropped down with a feather into the eye of the audience' (2.1.582–6). Jonson's preference for long crowded scenes arises directly from his innovative theatrical principle of developing place as synonymous with meaning. When several simultaneous activities occur in the same scene, the audience watches and evaluates them *because they are all on stage together*. This makes for dramatic complexity. And when these activities take place in a real locale, the concreteness of the scene, even on a bare stage, enriches the viewers' experience by confirming their prior knowledge of social conditions assumed to be features of place at that particular site. In effect, the audience engages in the stage image and accepts the stage's ambivalence, seeing the familiar rendered unfamiliar by a process of repression and selection that allows spectators both to recognize and to be surprised by the representation of a familiar space transformed for use on stage.[154] Reliance on place, Jonson discovered with this play, was crucial to his comic depiction of English behaviour. In *EMO*, that place is the Globe, which becomes the constant reminder of everyday performance in London life. Jonson makes use of every known feature of the Globe, with the possible exception of the trap.[155] His virtuosity appears in the play's self-conscious theatricality and in its open focus on staging and scene management from roof to platform of 'this fair-filled Globe' (*Q*'s revised catastrophe, 36). Needless to say, self-referentiality was not new in English theatre, but its 'scope and drift' (Chars.106–7), its complete absorption of what in another play would have been plot, were startlingly new.[156]

Perhaps the best place to begin in Jonson's *tour de force* is with the staging of the Grex, a cleverly localized variation on contemporary choric precedents as in Kyd's *The Spanish Tragedy*, Peele's *The Old Wives' Tale*, and Greene's *James IV*. Cordatus and Mitis remain on stage throughout the play as representatives of the audience, probably sitting forward and to one side of the platform, although Davies's comment on Foote's staging suggests that the Grex might sit above, either actually among the paying spectators or on the upper stage. Either location has its advantages. By remaining on the platform and even obstructing sight lines, the Grex becomes a constant reminder of the spectators' roles in the theatre as both irritating distractions and gratifying 'understanders'. If Cordatus and Mitis are seated above, the distance from the platform may make them less obtrusive, and consequently less significant for the audience, who could ignore them during much of the action. On the other hand, the gallery-level location and the fact that the audience could view their faces instead of their backs might increase the sense of the Grex as a mirror of proper audience response.

Whatever the location, the Grex provides a vital perspective on the theatricality of the whole play. It cannot be right to assume that Jonson designed the Grex only for the published version of *EMO*. In fact, the play concentrates as much on watching audiences as it does on watching players. The Grex's commentary is not particularly intrusive. Those comments that begin or end scenes cover natural breaks in the action, and perform other dramaturgical functions pertaining to setting and characterization; and those that interrupt scenes rarely exceed five lines. Jonson virtually insists that the spectators be conscious of attending a theatre performance. Watching the mechanics of performance and sorting out the difficulties of scene changes minimize any tendency of the audience to be drawn into the illusion of the play. Running gags like the quick changes of costume between Brisk and Fungoso repeat the puncturing of stage illusion. This open theatricality gives an edge to spectating, because the audience's awareness of the stage management, guided by the Grex's conversation, is neither subliminal, peripheral, nor retrospective, as it is with plays in which stage illusion is the object. Here the acting space is at the same time both the real world and the imaginary place.

This double vision of the stage as both real and illusory lets Jonson have his cake and eat it too, especially in the liberties he takes with conventional comic 'laws' like those of time and place. Judging from Fungoso's letter to his father (3.2.29), the play is set at Shrovetide, the three-day saturnalian carnival of self-indulgences, or 'humours', which 'every man' must give up, or be 'out' of, for Lent. Traditionally this is the time for parades of apes and fools, of men readying themselves for penance and absolution, symbolically accompanied by beasts that embody their excesses:[157] hence the focus of the play's imagery on swine and dogs. In visual terms, it is the time when the fat figure of Carnival battles the lean figure of Jack-a-Lent, and hence the continual on-stage presence of either Carlo or Macilente, or both, as unofficial lords of misrule.[158] In contrast to the expansiveness of symbolic 'play time', 'Grex time' is strictly the three hours' performance from the second sounding before the induction to the epilogue some 4400 lines later.[159]

The same doubleness applies to place. 'Grex place' is always the Globe Theatre. In what may be a parody of the chorus in *Henry V*, Jonson has the Grex 'cram /Within this wooden O' (*H5* Prol. 12–13) so many changes in setting that Cordatus is eventually forced to warn: 'Lose not yourself now' (5.3.345). The deliberate double vision of time and place, unlike Shakespeare's, is not intended primarily to charm the spectators into supplying with their imaginations what the staging lacks, but rather to eliminate their sympathetic involvement in the situation by emphasizing its artificiality. 'Play place' is alarmingly elastic, stretching from country to city to court, from farms and manors to city house and garden, church, tavern, prison, and palace. Normally Jonson condemns such 'admirable dexterity' in setting (Ind.278). But here, along with the swirl of characters in crowded scenes, the excesses in changed location simply add to the satiric spirit of the whole.

For the most part, scene-division in Jonson's original conception of the play seems to be governed by setting, with each new scene bridging gaps in time and changes of place, but 5.3 defies that principle, whirling us from the Mitre to Deliro's house, back to the tavern, then the Counter, and, in the quarto, even to the court, before returning us to the frame location—the theatre—which, of course, we have never left. This last scene is really just a vertiginously accelerated version of the already rapid (or, more accurately, increasingly rapid) continuous staging of the earlier scenes, in which the Grex comments on actors entering almost before the players of the previous scene have exited. Continuous staging was common in Elizabethan stage practice, but Jonson makes us directly conscious of it as a strategy of flamboyant and excessive theatricality. This is immediately apparent in Act 1. The brevity of scene 1 is more a joke for the reader than the spectator: when Mitis, irritated by Cordatus's pedantry, snaps, 'O, peace! You break the scene', sure enough, the scene is broken, and scene 2 begins. At this point, Macilente lies down on the platform and remains in that position until half-way through the next scene (1.3.87). In terms of continuous time and place, Act 1 is clearly one long scene. In terms of dramatic occasion and satiric focus, it is not. Scene 1 acts as a bridge between the 'reality' of the frame and the fun-house mirror of the play proper; it encourages the audience to recognize echoes of Asper's rage against the world and his violent images of destruction in Macilente's opening remarks. Scene 2 offers a variety of perspectives on social inequities and human shortcomings in the Grex's commentary on the new characters, in Macilente's envious grumblings, in Carlo's covert mockery of Sogliardo and later fear of Macilente, and in Sogliardo's preening stupidity. By contrast, scene 3 avoids interaction, simply juxtaposing Sordido's greed with Macilente's contempt both for the grain-hoarder and for himself.

Neoclassical convention dictates that exits and entrances determine scene-division. This is manifestly not the intention in *EMO*, although the folio scene-division mistakenly reverts to that practice. The choppiness of the short scenes imposed on the folio text is an artefact of editing. It denies the play's long swelling movements, a rhythm that would be obvious to an audience right from the beginning. Exits and entrances are merely part of the flow. The induction alone is full of to-ing and fro-ing. In Act 1 no one enters or leaves scene 1; Sogliardo and Carlo enter and exit during the progress of scene 2; Sordido enters at the end of scene 2, and Macilente exits in the middle of scene 3. Elsewhere, even the Grex is 'loath to interrupt the scene' because it depends on the playwright's almost seamless accumulation of activity in which 'all his actors so strongly pursue and continue their humours' (4.5.165–6). The length, because it allows the playwright to keep 'the scene full and relieved with variety of speakers' (2.1.582–3), complements the growth and interplay of humours characters:

> Why, therein his art appears most full of lustre and approacheth nearest the life, especially when, in the flame and height of their humours, they are laid flat. It fills the eye better, and with more contentment. How tedious a sight were it to behold a proud, exalted tree lopped and cut down by degrees, when it might be felled in a moment! And to set the axe to it before it came to that pride and fullness were as not to have it grow.
>
> (4.5.167–74)

In general, Jonson's concept of what constitutes a scene is determined by two factors, both of them related to performance. One is Jonson's orchestration of 'crescendo effects':[160] his characteristic method of visualizing a play in terms of the climactic placement of crowd scenes. He sets up several trickles of egocentric activity, keeping them separate at first, then running them together, swelling them with cross-currents until they flood before subsiding again. Consequently, the movement of each act is either towards or away from a long scene which illustrates this merging of several streams of humours. To attempt to convey such diffuse social relationships by altering the shape of his argument and presenting it in orderly single scenes, as Mitis requests (2.1.577–9), would defeat Jonson's purpose in creating a surface impression of kaleidoscopic chaos in the first place.[161] Jonson constructs the flagrant theatricality of the whole as a deliberate tactic to keep his audience aware that the chaos is a metaphor for the characters' personal confusion, not a sign of the playwright's faulty artistry. The busy-ness of the scene is a trans-fer to the theatre of the push and shove for place which Jonson sees as the defining conditions of Elizabethan life: a satiric '*imitatio vitae, speculum consuetudinis, imago veritatis*' (3.1.526–7), a hurly-burly of blindly conflicting energies. This leads to the second factor governing Jonson's scene-division. The scenes have to be of a certain magnitude—in length as in number of incidents—not only to satisfy Jonson's artistic craving for crowded scenes and his appreciation of their truth as pictures of society's hustle, but also—unlike those authors who carelessly 'outrun the apprehension of their auditory' (Ind.280–1)—to facilitate the audience's grasp of diverse stage actions. The Grex serves this second function by separating the actions into shorter or longer units based on the ebb and flow of characters on the stage, and the satiric occasion for which they are assembled.

Jonson's stage technique of 'fill[ing] the eye' depends on his use of several simultaneous stage locations. Simply having the Grex con-tinually on the stage accomplishes a double focus for the spectators, always forcing them to keep watch on two places at once. But Jonson is rarely satisfied with only two points of view. He finds new ways of using the whole milieu—roof, gallery, platform, and pit—to sur-prise the audience with altered perspectives on conventional stage illusion.

The second sounding of trumpets which begins the induction was a warning familiar to Elizabethan playgoers. But Jonson makes the convention unfamiliar by drawing attention to the musicians who, according to Asper (at 151, 156, and 211), are waiting too long before giving the third sounding that should start the performance. The suggestions of actual backstage tension, Asper's nervous energy, and the improvised feel of the conversation with Cordatus and Mitis complicate the audience's response to stage illusion apparently before the play has even begun.

A similar complication arises in the references to the 'heavens' and the stage posts. Asper sarcastically maintains that he knows 'the time's condition' too well to be taken in by illusion:

> You might as well have told me yond is heaven,
> This earth, these men, and all had moved alike.   (Ind.125–6)

'Yond' is the underside of the roof, called the 'heavens', which was painted with sun, moon, and stars, and probably the signs of the zodiac.[162] 'This' is the platform, and 'these' the stage posts. Pointing to them ironically, Asper distinguishes between the artificial world of the Globe and the real globe moving on its axis. This frank acknowledgement of the actual affects the audience's later perception of Sordido scanning the heavens for evidence of rain at 2.1.518–19, and probably shaking his fist at them during his tirade against 'these star-monger knaves' and 'sky-staring coxcombs' (3.2.13–18). In the same way, the audience accepts Carlo's comparison of the 'well-timbered' Prologue to one of the stage pillars supporting the roof when he suggests: 'he would ha' made a good column, an he had been thought on when the house was a-building' (Ind.321–3). Looking at the stage post itself, instead of seeing a stage illusion, makes suspending disbelief more difficult when Fungoso and his tailor make notes on Brisk's suit from behind a pillar (3.1.278–308). It is not that the audience resists the illusion of being in Paul's Walk, but that it is always consciously combining recognition of the illusory place with the real theatre space, and each change adds density and complexity to the stage picture.

But explicit awareness of playing space does not always originate in the extra-dramatic frame. Sogliardo, the thick-witted *nouveau riche* of the play proper, suggests 'under this terrace' (2.1.182) as a hidden vantage point from which he, Brisk, Cinedo, and Carlo may observe Puntarvolo's domestic dramatics. The terrace, or balcony, may have projected outward from the first gallery level of the tiring-house façade. Beneath this projection would have been sufficient space for actors to conceal themselves.[163] Deliro might conceal himself there as well at 4.1.50. The terrace itself probably contained at least two wide openings.[164] One may have been reserved for the Grex. Another was certainly used for Puntarvolo's dialogue with the Waiting-Gentlewoman (2.1.195.1–268.1, 301.3–340) and his Lady 'above' (195) at a window. Projecting downwards from the overhang of the terrace were hooks from which an arras might be hung (see

5.1.38); Sordido may have used one of these hooks to rig the ropes for his attempted suicide (3.2).

Beneath the terrace were the two stage doors generally used for exits and entrances, and sometimes for specific locations. Cordatus designates one as being the west door of St Paul's, the usual location for posting advertisements (3.1.3–4). Both doors are used in the domestic squabble at 4.1.114–24. The mere opening of doors attracts attention to scene-changes: 'O, here they come from *sealed and delivered*' (4.4.84); 'Here come the gallants' (4.5.181–2). When one door is localized, as in 2.1, where the terrace and the door beneath it are clearly Puntarvolo's house, then the other door may be obscured, perhaps by a property-tree, to suggest a different space through which Cinedo may exit (13) and re-enter (120.1); so too Puntarvolo with the Huntsman and the dog (188.4–5), and Sordido and Fungoso (280.1), who remain where they cannot be seen by the women at the window (301.1–2). At its fullest, the scene has to accommodate twelve actors in various locations: the two women above; Puntarvolo and the dog below the window, but to the side and forward on the platform; Carlo, Brisk, Cinedo, and Sogliardo huddled under the terrace; Sordido and Fungoso on the other side of the stage; and the Grex at one side but well forward. This is probably more confusing to read than to see. In fact, since most members of the audience saw the action from an elevated position in the galleries, their vantage point facilitated appreciation of spatial relationships between players, or among groups of players.[165]

If Jonson is zealous in exploiting the physical resources of the theatre, he is equally adroit in exploiting its human resources. Despite the large number of roles, Jonson allows almost every bit-part the kindness of a characterizing line to speak. In addition, the play is constructed for efficient doubling. Although Henslowe's records suggest that eighteen men and six to twelve boys commonly made up an acting company, *EMO* can be staged with thirteen men and three boys. (See Appendix C.) Aside from Jonson's specific references to and uses of physical locations at the Globe, and his exploitation of human resources, Jonson plays many games with stage business and effects, complicating the presentation of illusion as reality. The Grex is to be perceived as 'real' and its conversation as extempore, although the audience knows that Cordatus and Mitis are actors pretending to be spectators. Asper is part of that putative reality as the playwright, and part of the illusion of the play proper in his role as Macilente; but he is also recognized as an actor playing the playwright, and doubling as Macilente. This doubleness is complicated in Carlo, who plays the same role under the same name both in the play proper and in the induction, where he claims to know the author personally, but he does not make clear whether the author he means is Jonson or Asper.

This interplay between reality and illusion is a factor in almost every scene, but with varying degrees of ironic consciousness. The Prologue who refuses to say his part in face of Cordatus's sarcasm (Ind.285–307) is less surprising than Clove and Orange, who are introduced as extras to swell the scene in Paul's walk 'by chance' (3.1.40). Other extras in the play, however, have specific functions, even if the quantity in which they appear borders on the surreal. For example, the several rustics of 3.2, although comically excessive in number, assist in the stage business of Sordido's hanging and provide the motivation for Sordido's conversion. The several officers who appear with the Constable in 5.3 serve similar functions by clearing the stage after the attack on Carlo, and arresting Fastidius in preparation for the final dishumourings at the Counter.

Quality, not quantity, causes the play to shift to a completely different blend of illusion and reality, with no apparent hint of irony, in the masque-like vision of the Queen in 5.4. Suddenly the entire preceding five acts take on the character of grotesque antimasque, and the true perspective on society crystallizes in the purifying wonder of the vision that restores Macilente to hope and moral wholeness. The antimasque world, as Stephen Orgel points out, is a world of particularity and mutability; the masque world is one of abstractions and eternal truths. Of the moral life at the centre of a masque, Orgel states: 'All the masque can do . . . is to offer a moment in which a vision of an ideal becomes a poetic and dramatic experience—becomes, in other words, a reality.'[166] This reality is not antithetical to satire; in fact, the desire for perfection is satire's other face, the bright ideal inseparable from the shadow of mockery. The sudden flight into masque is a logical extension of the experiments with theatricality that have marked the play from that moment in the Induction when Asper alters the conventional distance between stage and spectator by suddenly noticing the audience: 'I not observed this throngèd round till now' (Ind.49). The uncertainty, in Jonson's day as in our own, of how to understand this masque-like vision is also part of the complex tone established by the Induction. The spectator is expected to balance Asper's *furor poeticus* and the Grex's seriousness with Carlo's irreverent geniality, which seems to 'place' the preceding speakers as unduly high-minded.[167] This is in part an Aristophanic puncturing of dramatic mood: 'The framework of speciously serious argument is the mere vehicle for an attack whose technique and rationale have to be understood in terms of the genre's licence for scurrile entertainment.'[168] But it is to geniality that the play finally returns in the last conversation with the Grex.

Different yet again is the effect created by Puntarvolo's dog. As an animal on stage, the dog has no notion of the difference between illusion and reality. Anything it does on stage will be perceived by the audience as hilariously puncturing dramatic illusion, especially when the other actors mention it, as in Carlo's comments on the dog's melancholy appearance (2.1.234) and its attentiveness to its stiff master, looking 'as if he went in a frame, or had a suit of wainscot on, and the dog watching him lest he should leap out on 't' (274–6). Concern for the dog's well-being becomes a constant motif, once the travel scheme is set forth. Carlo facetiously worries about the effects of going barefoot on 'a dog that never travelled before' (544); Fastidius Brisk inquires politely after the dog's health (3.1.252), as does Saviolina later (5.2.6–7); Puntarvolo sees threats to the dog everywhere—in his fear that it might be lost (3.1.58–9, 4.5.130, 5.1.18–30), in Shift's boast that he can teach the dog to take the whiff (3.1.482–3), and even in the possibility that it might 'turn Turk' (4.3.16). Death by ingestion is mentioned on three occasions (2.1.545–50, 3.1.62–3, and 4.3.23–6) but the audience does not accept the dog as a likely victim even after Macilente poisons it in 5.1. The shock value of this scene, especially if the dog is skilled at playing dead, once more upsets the balance between theatrical illusion and reality, because the audience has accepted the dog as real, not as acting, and because in fact it has had no necessary stage business to perform up to this moment. Its natural behaviour has been all that the staging required.

The balance is further upset by metaphorical associations with the dog. Puntarvolo's greyhound is an expensive breed, displaying its master's status as a wealthy gentleman, but most proverbial associations with 'dog', listed in Tilley, indicate contempt for the animal as greedy, idle, sycophantic, cowardly, and foolish. Colloquial usage of 'dog' and variants as a coarse expletive was associated with sexual perversion and whoredom of both sexes, especially male homosexual prostitutes;[169] hence the offence taken by the Groom (5.1) and Shift (5.2) when charged with keeping or stealing a dog. The image of the snarling dog was associated with the satirical playwright, a 'one-headed Cerberus' with '*caninum appetitum*' (Ind.336, 332), with the 'bandog' (2.1.382) gibes of Carlo, described as 'an open-throated, black-mouthed cur / That bites at all' (1.2.234–5), and with the envious Macilente, 'A lean mongrel . . . chap-fallen with barking at other men's good fortunes' (214–16). Chance itself is a fawning dog (2.2.9–10). Deliro is a 'good bloodhound' (4.3.121), tracking down debtors; Fungoso wastes resources to 'dog the fashion' (4.5.126); and Saviolina calls her taunters 'goodly beagles' (5.2.122). The actual presence of a dog on the stage who becomes a focus for various double entendres and running gags keeps returning the metaphorical to the bottom-line physical. The reductivity of actual performance is never clearer than in Carlo's zany suggestions of the uses to which the dead dog may be put (5.3.219–35), and in the graphic retaliation by which Carlo himself is muzzled.

This return to the concrete is evidence of Jonson's sense of theatre. Paradoxically, by concentrating so completely on the physical resources and limitations of the stage, Jonson transforms theatre facts into metaphors, which he uses to propound a thesis on how to see and judge. Constantly standing theatrical convention on its head, juggling levels of meaning, and playing a shell game with time and space, he encourages the audience to think about the implications of what they are seeing. Like the book in *Tristram Shandy*, the theatre in *EMO*—stage, audience, performance—becomes the unifying image within which social relationships and apparently digressive actions achieve coherence.

Seeing and judging: spectators and perspective

In the theatre, the Grex has a delightful duality. As extra-dramatic characters in the frame, the Grex figures insinuate the play into the audience's world, and share the audience's point of view by sitting and watching; at the same time, they are actors, and belong to the world of the play. Jonson complicates this duality when he confronts the audience with images of itself not only in the frame but also in the play proper. In part, Jonson sees the theatre as a therapeutic hall of mirrors, purging playwright, actors, characters, and audience alike; by the end of Act 5, everyone, whether in or out of the play, has been satirically 'Anatomized in every nerve and sinew' (Ind.119) and put 'out of his humour'. In the course of attacking bad or 'sick' taste in his characters and his spectators, Jonson also pursues a philosophical goal, attempting to clarify the relationship between aesthetic taste and moral judgement. To accomplish these diverse goals, he invents a complex framework of chorus-figures who set up multiple perspectives on one another, and whose interactions demonstrate the satiric, aesthetic, and moral points of the play.

Jonson's crowded stage gives a sense of almost cinematic montage, surveying a whole world of self-absorbed individuals who correspond to one another only in their singleminded pursuit of private obsessions. Although the numbers on stage increase and diminish, the focus of the play never changes: Jonson attacks what he sees as the social corruptions of his times. But he lives in an era in which 'The days are dangerous, full of exception, / And men are grown impatient of reproof' (Ind.122–3). In order to pre-empt possible criticism, Jonson splinters his attack by adopting several ironic masks, none of which wholly represents Jonson himself. Instead, he divides the social criticisms among many mouthpieces who serve limited satiric functions, and who are not only the attackers but also the attacked. To co-ordinate these functions, Jonson constructs nesting frames of chorus/commentators, including a 'reality frame' which engages the audience directly in a constant process of observation and evaluation.

The 'reality frame' encompassing the play is the audience's awareness of Jonson as the playwright and of themselves as the ultimate critics. Jonson appears only briefly as a parody of himself in Carlo Buffone's ironic toast to the audience at the end of the induction. Carlo, himself the quintessential parasite, represents Jonson as a voracious dinner guest who 'comes abroad now and then, once in a fortnight, and makes a good meal among players' (330–2), although at home he subsists on 'beans and buttermilk'. Carlo also claims that Jonson is a mean drunk with an inflated self-image, 'as though he would work wonders when he comes home' (338–9), a man who would swallow five cups of wine in rapid succession and then 'look villainously when he has done, like a one-headed Cerberus (he do'not hear me, I hope)' (335–7). Arrogance and violence are also part of Asper's personality, but these are satirical distortions of himself that Jonson gives to Asper, rather than an equation of Jonson and Asper. Ironic facets of Jonson appear in all the characters, or at least in those capable of critical observation.

The audience, the 'Gentlewomen (I am sworn to put them in first) and gentlemen' (326–7) of Carlo's replacement-prologue, is a constant feature of the outer frame of the play. Asper makes an attempt

to control his rage at vice when he realizes that he is talking to Cordatus and Mitis in the presence of 'this throngèd round' (49). He
flatters his 'Gracious and kind spectators' (50) as 'judicious friends'
(54) whose intelligence and attentiveness he will reward with the
unflinching accuracy of his depictions of 'the time's deformity'
(118). But this flattery is only for those auditors who 'join their profit
with their pleasure, / And come to feed their understanding parts'
(200–1) in the theatre. Asper vituperates—at length and in the style
of assaultive detail now associated with John Cleese—those with
'neither art nor brain' (177), who come to the theatre not to see, but
to be seen. These ignorant gallants he will 'purge' of follies and affectations through the 'pills' (174) which his play will make them
swallow. The play's final references to the real audience are not just
conventional flattery. They confirm that the purge has been effective. Cordatus, now out of his humour of 'censuring', defers to the
opinion of the spectators: 'Besides, here are those round about you
of more ability in censure than we, whose judgements can give it a
more satisfying allowance. We'll refer you to them' (5.4.47–50). Even
Asper, still in his costume as Macilente, is 'out of humour for
company': 'I stand wholly to your kind approbation, and, indeed,
am nothing so peremptory as I was in the beginning' (57–8). The
'reality frame' spectators are important because they (or we) are
constant features of the play, involved *in* it, yet not really *of* it, always
aware of watching the play over the shoulders of Cordatus and Mitis,
and subsequently of any of the other characters who assume the
temporary role of spectator. In addition, the divergence between the
actual spectators of Jonson's day and the scripted stage-sitters
emphasizes another satiric dimension. The Globe did not permit
stage-sitting in 1599. The Globe audience, therefore, would recognize, *via* Cordatus and Mitis, a satiric allusion to the private
theatres.

   This heightened awareness of satiric dimension and multiple
perspectives focuses the audience on the difficulties of judging, a
process that the play means to elucidate. It is also the essential
difference between the conventional framing device used by other
playwrights as a way into and out of the illusion of the inner play,
and Jonson's nest of five frames, which he uses to indicate the
relativity of human perspective and intelligence. Each of the successive frames reflects the diminished capacity of the characters
included within it.

   The first scripted frame of the play consists of Asper, Cordatus,

and Mitis. Asper is the author of the play about to be presented.
Like Jonson, he uses the play as a forum for pointed social criticism.
His is the voice of the angry idealist: '*furor poeticus*' itself, full of 'constant courage and contempt of fear' (Ind.146, 120), and uncom-
promising in his hatred of aesthetic, ethical, and verbal abuses. His
violent reaction to Mitis's colloquial use of the word 'humour' so
unhinges Asper that he cannot even continue his own diatribe
without prompting:

> *Mitis.*   Ay, I pray you proceed.
> *Asper.* Ha? What? What is 't?
> *Cordatus.*   For the abuse of humour.
> *Asper.* O, I crave pardon. I had lost my thoughts.   (83–5)

Cordatus is finally driven to apologize to the audience for the mad
playwright.

Cordatus and Mitis have a moderating influence both on Asper
and on the play. Their interests are primarily aesthetic. Mitis usually
voices a critical concern: 'Does he observe all the laws of comedy
in it?' (231); 'Methinks . . . he dwelt somewhat too long on this
scene: it hung i' the hand' (2.1.573–4). Cordatus usually defends the
play against Mitis's objections. As the Grex, they provide a direct
focus on Jonson's dramaturgical problems, and simultaneously
provide an insight into the patterns of critical argument that recur
in the inner frames of the play. Mitis, 'a person of no action, and
therefore . . . no character' (Chars.110–11), argues from a dogmati-
cally conventional point of view: he prompts or sets up certain
issues, derides (albeit gently), declines to debate, and is finally
silenced. Cordatus, 'the author's friend' (Chars.106), is aggressive
in vindicating Asper's artistic principles: his role is to expound.
Together they represent an inclusive and conscious frame for
Jonson's satirical purpose.

Carlo Buffone and Macilente operate as the second-frame inner
chorus of the play proper. They are satirical versions of the first-
frame commentators. Carlo is the negative railer and detractor, the
thoughtless buffoon; he enjoys exposing fools for his own idle
amusement, not out of any moral conviction. Macilente, on the
other hand, does want to effect intelligent conversion where he can
(as in his attempts to free Deliro from romantic illusions). But, when
he fails, he settles for exposure and suppression of folly as at least
an ethical and social improvement, one that satisfies his gnawing
envy of the good fortune he desires for himself, but sees wasted on

the ignorant. These second-frame commentators promote excess rather than the moderation urged by the Grex. As critics, they find their targets in the ethical vacuity of the world around them. Their tactics are debunking and deflating. They are not, however, merely critics. They also devise action and incite others to perform it. As playwrights, they are twisted variants of Asper's and Jonson's impulse to speak out. Carlo is a master at setting up the less aware characters of the inner frames to act out his scenarios; Macilente finishes the script by supplying the stinging catastrophe: 'He carries oil and fire in his pen, will scald where it drops' (1.2.216–17). Together, they combine direct action, unavailable to the Grex, with some critical detachment, bounded by their limited consciousness of social and aesthetic abuses.

The characters of the third frame, Puntarvolo and Deliro, are even more limited in their consciousness of social and aesthetic concerns; however, they are also men who seem to have existence beyond the humours ascribed to them. They have the doubleness of function and the access to shifts in point of view that characterize the first- and second-frame chorus-figures. For one thing, they are able to criticize less aware characters with a certain wit and detachment. Puntarvolo notes Brisk's courtly effeminacy (2.1.382–3) and later castigates Carlo for his hypocritical friendship with Sogliardo (4.3.100–4). Deliro defends Macilente's character and shows contempt for Brisk's in a few succinct statements which raise Deliro in the audience's estimation (2.2.279–302). Furthermore, Puntarvolo and Deliro extend the satiric distortions of the playwright-figure. They script scenarios which they then act out with their wives (Puntarvolo's have enjoyed a long run; Deliro's always bomb). They become trapped in the skits set up by Carlo and Macilente. Finally, they exact a kind of vengeance by turning on one tormenter with the help of another, conveniently evading the question of personal responsibility. So Puntarvolo, mocked by Carlo in a series of tasteless jokes about the dead dog, turns on Carlo and, aided and abetted by Macilente, seals his lips with wax. It is Macilente who is not only the undiscovered murderer of the dog but also the inciter of the verbal attack on Puntarvolo and the physical attack on Carlo. Similarly, Deliro, victim of Macilente's plan to shock him out of his mad attachment to his wife, has Brisk arrested for debt, only to discover Fallace in the arms of the jailed courtier. Egged on by Macilente, who forced this unwanted awareness on him, Deliro can only pursue his prosecution of Brisk with more vigour.

What Macilente fails to achieve in Puntarvolo and Deliro—clear consciousness of folly—Sordido achieves for himself in his frustrated suicide attempt (3.2). When he loses faith in his almanac readings, Sordido, like the old morality-play figure of Despair, hangs himself: an impressive spectacle, literally undercut by the five or six comic rustics who rescue him. The rustics' dismayed reaction to their good deed brings about Sordido's conversion, 'by wonder changed' (119). Deliro and Puntarvolo are also shocked out of humour, but they do not achieve Sordido's level of charity and renewed sense of humanity. In fact, Mitis objects strenuously to the scene's improbability and lack of decorum in the context of comedy. Cordatus can defend it only with an obscure classical precedent, to which Mitis rejoins wryly: 'Your memory is happier than mine' (158). But Jonson liked the scene well enough to repeat it in another physical and spiritual resurrection, when Macilente collapses in *very wonder* before *rising and recovering heart* (5.4.0.2–4), a changed man. The chief difference between the two scenes is that, whereas Macilente's experience is solitary and serious, Sordido's is overrun by waves of bumbling rustics doing farcical double-takes. From the moment Sordido swings by his halter, rustics tumble on to the stage, *one after another* (3.2.65.1). First they express horrified compassion for the hanged man, except for the irritable Second Rustic, who seems to be a habitual complainer. Next they congratulate the First Rustic for his quick action, all apparently patting him on the back, except again for the Second Rustic, who chastises Sordido. Then, with shocked recognition, they join the Second Rustic in berating the First Rustic for saving the life of a 'viper'. Finally, after Sordido's conversion, they all marvel at the miracle. These automatic waves of repeated *volte-faces* distance us from the serious implications of Sordido's act, but the rustics' transparent sincerity draws a more complex response. Their speed in saving a life and their genuine pleasure at the goodness of another—whether the First Rustic's or Sordido's— are considerations that one would admire in the most polished gentlemen. The mirror which they hold up to Sordido effectively purges him because they clearly are incapable of deceit. Through them he sees his own anamorphosis, 'monstrous in true human eyes' (105) and also sees the way to a better perspective on himself, '"graced with love"' (121). Despite their yokelisms of manner and speech, the rustics humanize the satiric impulse, making its effects momentarily civilized and benign.

The fourth-frame characters in the play's nest of receding

chorus/commentators are flat creations, distinguished solely by the singleness of their humorous obsessions. The only doubleness in these characters arises from their arrangement in mirrored pairs of mentor and novice: Shift and Sogliardo, the would-be gentlemen; Fastidius Brisk and Fungoso, the would-be fashion-plates; Saviolina and Fallace, the would-be witty court-mistresses. None of these characters shows any awareness of others. They are incapable of conversation. They talk only about their affectations, no matter what other topic is proposed. They also have no scripting abilities that might allow them to save face once they are humiliated in public. Mere puppets, they are part of the London 'motions' to which the characters often refer as popular entertainment. They are dishumoured to the extent that their superficial affectations are halted, but they have no existence beyond the humours they have lost. These fourth-frame characters are wholly limited and completely unconscious of the social, ethical, or aesthetic concerns that modify the outer frames of the play.

And what is at the centre of all these frames? The tiny emblematic portrait of Clove and Orange, effete and effeminate 'strangers to the whole scope of our play—only come to walk a turn or two i' this scene of Paul's by chance' (3.1.38–40). Jonson offers this apparently irrelevant twosome as an apt satiric thrust at a society based on bad taste and empty affectation. Rank poseurs, on the prowl for sex and drink, they flash their version of intellectual repartee without any sense of 'the barrenness of their lives and rhetoric'.[170] They are signs of the times.

If the whole point of Jonson's social criticism were simply an abrasive scourging of the flat and defenceless characters of the inmost framed groups, then the satirist would be shown as superior to what he satirizes, and the audience would be invited to share that single stance. But this is not the point of view Jonson invites. To some extent, in fact, he vitiates the aggressiveness of his satire by demonstrating that it is not all one way, and that satire has a way of rebounding on its initiators. This is, in part, a self-defensive ploy. Jonson anticipates and frustrates his own critics by attacking himself first; that is, he does not allow his satirists (functions of his own satiric impulse) to criticize with impunity. By diffusing the satiric functions through several graduated frames of increasingly more limited and distorted perspectives, and by making each chorus-figure double, in that he is both satirically attacking and satirically attacked, Jonson forces the audience to participate more fully in a wide range of ethical and aesthetic choices. Simply put, the off-stage spectators realize, by looking over the shoulders of several other spectators on the stage, that a single viewpoint does not permit them to see the different angles that will give their judgement a three-dimensionality they can rely on as objective.[171] The recognition of multiple perspectives is what frees observers from subjective narrow-mindedness, which Jonson satirizes as 'humours' or, at their most superficial and 'sick in taste' (Ind.130), mere affectations 'of such spongy souls / As lick up every idle vanity' (144–5). Spectators whet their tastes and hone their judgements by acquiring the habit of looking at the same thing from a variety of perspectives. This does not mean that spectators adopt the judgements of others. It means that they take an imaginative leap into another's position and see how a phenomenon looks to them from his point of view.[172]

This concept of imaginative leaps into a plurality of perspectives is the key to understanding the lateral unfolding of the several humorous activities through which the play develops tension. The elaborate framing structure is a technique that, virtually by defini-tion, eliminates conventional plot. Instead, it substitutes vignette or 'cameo' performances as more functional in co-ordinating multiple perspectives on the satiric butt of the moment. The vignettes illus-trate a range of follies in an ethical vacuum, observed by people who, some more and some less, remember what values used to be. The assembling and regrouping of critical observers co-ordinate the parts into a sophisticated revue with a variety of comic turns: one-liners, comic dialogues of cross-purposes, monologues, slapstick, in-jokes, an animal act, and frenetic ensemble scenes. What links these various routines together within the satiric framework is the two running gags which begin in 2.1: the dog jokes, and Fungoso's attempts to copy Brisk's wardrobe. Both of these gags carry con-siderable dramatic and thematic baggage, and by Act 5 are instru-mental in the dishumourings. The dog jokes reach their apogee in Macilente's murder of the dog, which precipitates the dishumour-ing of Shift, Sogliardo, Carlo, and Puntarvolo. The clothing gag involves behind-the-scene quick-changes as each costume moves from Brisk to Fungoso, and double-takes when Brisk appears in yet another outfit. It ends in the dishumouring of Fallace, Deliro, Fungoso, and Brisk—and ultimately of Macilente, Asper, the Grex, and the off-stage audience as well. The ordering of the whole has a rapid, choreographed flow that illustrates the satire's general applic-ability by exaggerating the profusion and pervasiveness of the behaviour of the criticized and the critics. In this array of human folly, Jonson musters a mad variety of perspectives that may render the viewers sane.

Illustrating place and meaning: Paul's Walk

Why did Jonson select Paul's Walk as the play's central site? If we accept Stephen Mullaney's definition of the city as a 'projection of cultural values and beliefs: as a casting of ideals and ideologies into concrete form, an inscription of cultural practices and concerns in the very landscape of community', then Jonson has cast the city of London into the satirical nutshell of St Paul's.[173] Whatever the status of the cathedral as a spiritual or religious centre in Jonson's day, the popular perception of St Paul's as a *mikrokosmos* was already recorded in Robert Greene's *Cony-catching* pamphlets and other similar tales (see 3.1.2–3n). In these stories, city rogues and thieves prey upon the courtiers, professionals, tradesmen, students, and tourists who loiter in the aisles to see the fashions, conduct business, gossip, and smoke. Jonson discards any two-class view which too neatly suggests that criminals and riffraff are not like us: the Paul's Walk scene demonstrates that hungry predators and parasites lurk in all classes and occupations. The largest building in London, and more like a shopping mall than a cathedral, St Paul's embodied the sprawling urban marketplace, and encouraged the buying and selling of goods and persons within a monumental setting which virtually ritualized, even blessed, the negotiation of social and economic power.[174] Jonson takes the implications of the St Paul's promenade only a few steps further when he interprets this negotiation as an obsessively competitive dance.

That St Paul's is intended to be a central paradigm for the interpretation of place and behaviour in London is clear from its central location in the play's structure. It not only occupies most of Act 3 but also marks the turning points of the various strands of action. Before the Paul's Walk scene, the characters each introduce their humours; during the scene, they parade their humours in particularly intense displays; after the scene, they suffer reversals until, by the end of the play, everyone is out of his humour. St Paul's is the perfect showcase for those humours, pumped up and performed for the audiences who throng there as participants and observers. Throughout the scene, we watch characters titillate themselves with exercises in one-upmanship and flattering imitation, in bids to acquire position, prestige, or privilege. Like the actual places visited and frequented by citizens of London, as described in Stow's *Survey*, St Paul's serves as a rhetorical *locus communis*, a site of 'potential meaning, open and available to various figures and uses, even capable . . . of antithetical or ambivalent significance'.[175] Jonson, like Stow, invokes the traditional cultural values of an urban site, and then records the encroachment on those values by the overflowing unruly city swelling its limits, forcing channels for the upwardly mobile and their hangers-on, and inundating its original structures.

The Paul's Walk scene begins with Cordatus explaining to Mitis that the place and the meaning it represents are inseparable. Catching sight of Shift, who is stealthily hanging up advertisements on one of the stage doors, Cordatus instructs the spectator to imagine the place as authentic ('presuppose the stage the middle aisle in Paul's') and the character as an edifyingly typical 'illustration', spontaneously performing actions that anyone would expect to see in Paul's Walk near the west door, where the unemployed posted bills offering their services for hire. Every subsequent character who appears on stage is on the make in one way or another, looking for money to borrow, wager, or spend. Most of them, like Shift, are obsessed with selling themselves to the highest bidder, but have no sense of their own folly, and no instinct about being judged by on-stage or off-stage audiences. 'This is rare', Shift remarks in relief, looking around, seeing empty space, and assuming he has gotten away with something; 'I have set up my bills without discovery' (3.1.21–2). Although the doubleness of the moment is funny— Cordatus and Mitis have just been talking about him, and thousands in the Globe have watched him—his comment also establishes his behaviour as immediate, natural, real. He seems to be a genuine and typical frequenter of Paul's Walk, not now performing for an audience, as he is later in the scene.

The same is true of Clove and Orange, who enter separately and greet each other with apparent surprise at mid-stage. Their accidental meeting introduces another ingredient that establishes the place as authentic, *like* a theatre without *being* a theatre. Have they wandered into the Globe actually imagining themselves to be in St Paul's? Can they not distinguish between the two role-playing sites? The degree to which they are to be understood as extemporized or fortuitous figures is never defined: on the one hand, they seem to have stumbled into the scene, 'mere strangers to the whole scope of our play', but on the other hand they are recognized as characters

by Shift and as types by Cordatus. The implications muddle our separation of illusion and reality. Apparently irrelevant scene-fillers,
Clove and Orange are meaningful in that their self-serving postures
and chatter perfectly reflect the St Paul's milieu. As William
Haughton's clown, Frisco, describes it in *Englishmen for My Money*,
Paul's Walk is a kind of 'open house' filled with a 'great store of
company that do nothing but go up and down, and go up and down,
and make a grumbling together' (2.1.882–90).[176] Haughton's brief
scene (merely fifty lines) lacks Jonson's choreography, but highlights
the key factors of identifiable types, movement, and babble.[177] Clove
and Orange signal the same elements as they begin the assembly for
the promenade in Paul's Walk by greeting each other as partners,
obeying the stage-direction, '*They walk together*' (3.1.42). Eventually,
everyone will walk.

Although the Grex offers no further verbal views until the end of
the scene, its presence on the Globe stage and its non-verbal or para-
verbal responses to dialogue and action frame the Paul's Walk
sequence and provide the off-stage audience with a necessary perspective on place and meaning. The Grex's constant participation
in the spatial experience of the play is an essentially Aristophanic
borrowing: Cordatus and Mitis mediate between the performance
by the actors and its reception by the audience, thus supporting the
unity of imagined space in which the action plays out. Cordatus has
seen rehearsals of this play before, and enjoys guiding the responses
of Mitis (and through him, us) for whom the play is a new experience. They both share a certain pleasure in watching the apparently
random activity of various groups of performers suddenly co-
ordinate itself into an aesthetic pattern of meticulously kept rhythms
resonating between and among pairs of men. And even when they
disagree or are wrong, their pleasure at puzzling out meaning com-
municates itself to us, the off-stage audience. Jonson makes no
attempt to represent the strolling in Paul's Walk as an unmediated
experience, even though he manipulates some of the action into
seeming spontaneous or accidental. With the Grex as model and
guide, defining the scene's elements, Jonson specifies location,
formal arrangement of characters, and movement, thus fixing the
performance image precisely as a compositional entity. In addition,
he fills the scene with references to sizes, shapes, colours, and physical eccentricities, supported by verbs (*see, seem, look, observe*), nouns
(*eye, judgement, illustration*), and demonstratives (*here, there*) which
mirror the audience's act of watching and emphasize the idea of a

theatre as a *theatron* or 'seeing place'.[178] The audience's desire to judge derives from this physical focus on spectating and the awareness, by way of the Grex, that viewers interpret what they view differently. When Jonson allows us to eavesdrop selectively on various conversations in Paul's Walk, he is substituting one kind of choric commentary on events for another, and steering the audience into a response to what they overhear from that more complicated remove.

Once the Grex retreats into critical silence, the dance of observers and participants in Paul's Walk begins in earnest. The burden of explicit commentary comes from within the dancing groups who gradually crowd the stage with their physical and verbal eccentricities. The scoffer, Carlo Buffone, takes part in Puntarvolo's self-consciously stage-managed entrance and display. With his retinue—Carlo and two servants, one leading his dog, the other holding his cat in a bag—Puntarvolo moves with his characteristic stiffness. His first stage-business in Paul's Walk fussily calls attention to himself. He removes his cloak, hands it to the servant holding the cat, and orders the servant leading the dog to 'follow me closer' (3.1.57–8), eliciting the farce that ends with Puntarvolo's later reproof, 'Sirrah, keep close; yet not so close, thy breath will thaw my ruff' (273–4). With his entourage, the knight makes a stately progress around the stage until he reaches the door, where he pauses to read the posted bills. This group is more complex than Clove and Orange, not simply because the numbers have doubled—or tripled, if you count the animals. The significant addition is the complication in verbal and non-verbal communication, which forces us to keep reassessing the situation: Carlo speaks sycophantically to the knight, but mutters rebellious asides to the servant with the dog; whatever the servant's reaction (the text does not specify), the audience watches him for responses. As a further complication, Puntarvolo and Carlo are planning a joke at the expense of a third man, Sogliardo, who has not yet appeared. Their complicity emerges as they chortle over the advertisements. And the audience cannot ignore the dog, which, while not consciously acting, is nevertheless performing. The sick cat is probably not a live actor: all we see is a bag which the servant may manipulate like a hand-puppet.

As a counterpoint to the large group, Macilente, Deliro, and Fastidius Brisk enter and begin to stroll in what Brisk calls 'the *Mediterraneum*', a fashionable name for Paul's middle aisle. An elaborately dressed courtier, Brisk tries to draw all eyes and admiration to himself, as he demonstrates how his hair, in the stiffly upswept 'predominant' style, recovers its height after he removes his hat, simply 'with once or twice stroking up your forehead thus' (100–1). Too self-obsessed to register disapproval in others, he does not interpret Deliro's silence or Macilente's sarcasm as contempt. A similar blindness to his audience occurs when the crude *nouveau-riche* Sogliardo enters, in a costume too elegant for his manners, and fails to read the mockery in Carlo's and Puntarvolo's suggestion that he choose himself a gentleman-usher from the advertisements. The combination of body configuration, movement, gesture of hand, torso, and foot, facial expression, costume, location on the stage, all work together to generate that necessary precedent to judgement, the receiving of several conflicting perspectives at once, an effect more like life in a real place than like artistic unity of action and expression.

The stage is now crowded with ten actors and two animals in the Paul's Walk site, and two privileged members of the audience marking the site of the Globe. Their carefully blocked entrances and the display of their humours have been illustrating the difference between the experience of obsessive participants and the more objective observations of onlookers, whether those onlookers are understood as part of the Paul's Walk milieu or of the Globe frame. Nevertheless, Jonson makes it clear that the apparently discrete experiences of unaware participants and aware observers are on a continuum that places all of us as performers and audiences in all kinds of social or aesthetic dramas.[179] Clove and Orange represent the furthest extreme of this complex duality. Hoping to impress the other strollers, Clove and Orange pause in mid-stroll, executing what seems to be a nested performance within a performance within a performance. Clove's rather dim idea emphasizes St Paul's Cathedral as the foremost site of competitive theatricality and one-upmanship in London, not only materially, in terms of clothing, retinue, and other signs of social status, but also intellectually:

> *Clove.* Monsieur Orange, yond gallants observes us. Prithee let's talk fustian a little and gull 'em, make 'em believe we are great scholars.
> *Orange.* O Lord, sir!
> *Clove.* Nay, prithee, let's, by Jesu. You have an excellent habit in discourse.
> *Orange.* It pleases you to say so, sir.
> *Clove.* By this church you ha', la. Nay, come, begin. (168–75)

Their act fools nobody. The text places Carlo's group, including servants and dog, at the stage door, their backs turned to read the bills, while Macilente's group ambles and chats together across the stage.

Macilente's one line during the 'great scholars' act suggests an interrupted conversation: he pivots for an appraising glance in passing, and remarks, 'O, here be a couple of fine tame parrots' (181–2). The two chief satirical spokesmen and their associates thus form an uneven frame of indifferent non-observers around the eccentric figures of Clove and Orange whose performance ends bathetically as they realize that no one, not even the dog, is paying any attention to them: 'Let us return to our former discourse,' says Clove, 'for they mark us not' (200–1). This is one of the comic highlights of the scene, and one that can be comically exaggerated if the on-stage audience, the still-silent Cordatus and Mitis, ignore them as well. That a complex satiric framework of critical commentators and observers should disregard the two characters whose sole purpose for being in the play is to be recognized as symbols of the place—this is an extraordinary testament to the ironies of obsessive self-display.

Arid circularity is the most important physical and verbal feature of this scene, a feature of which the constant pacing in Paul's Walk reminds us. The circularity suggests the impossibility of permanent gain, because walking in a round implies the opposite of progress. It also visualizes Jonson's contempt for this kind of social circle by rendering it as a rotating exhibition within a closed world whose lack of discernment perpetuates empty values in the repetition of a mindless pattern. The next movement of the scene, a masterpiece of ensemble choreography, gradually reduces that pattern to the mechanics of clockwork dolls. The whole crowd begins to stroll and to eye one another. The social climber Fastidius Brisk wants to join Puntarvolo, an established courtier, but is frustrated by his companions' decision to snub the other party:

> *Fastidius.* Mass, yonder's the knight Puntarvolo.
> *Deliro.* And my cousin Sogliardo, methinks.
> *Macilente.* Ay, and his familiar that haunts him, the devil with a shining face.
> *Deliro.* Let 'em alone. Observe 'em not.   (202–6)

As they deliberately turn away in one direction, '*Sogliardo, Puntarvolo,* [*and*] *Carlo walk*' in the other. At some point during the two groups' circling of the stage, Fastidius manages to detach himself from Deliro and Macilente, and fasten on to Puntarvolo. Jonson's elaborate marginal stage-direction suggests the extent to which he visualized the choreography of this whole scene: '*Here they shift. Fastidius mixes with Puntarvolo; Carlo and Sogliardo; Deliro and Macilente;*

Clove and Orange: four couple' (246.1–4). The change-over probably involves a gradual shift of companions over twenty-four lines, beginning with an earlier stage-direction, after Puntarvolo initially interrupts his conversation to greet the eager-to-fawn Brisk, 'Save you, good Monsieur Fastidius', with the marginal stage-direction, *'They salute as they meet in the walk'* (231–2, 232.1). Step by step, Fastidius Brisk sidles into position near the knight, managing to separate him from Carlo and Sogliardo, who move as a couple some distance away from Brisk and Puntarvolo. The jockeying for place in this sequence (247–57) gives spatial support to the complex verbal interactions of unctuous sycophants, dupes, and hustlers: Fastidius's sycophantic greeting of Puntarvolo and his 'fair dog' is matched by Puntarvolo's equally sycophantic interest in meeting 'a merchant of any worth' like Deliro to back his travel scheme, and by Deliro's in improving his own financial and social status through a nodding acquaintance with a wealthy knight while ignoring a boorish kinsman and a crude parasite.

Once the characters begin to rotate in four couples, the blocking of the movement shows us human desires in a concrete pattern. The artifice of couples in a stylized processional dance, like a pavan,[180] comments satirically upon the egotistic toadies who throng the middle aisle of St Paul's looking for patrons and admirers to support their habit of self-love. The dance pattern constructs a psychological mirror for fawning hypocrites, each couple imitating and outdoing the others in maintaining distances, managing approaches, responding to tensions. In terms of the perspective created for the audience, the blocking of the dance allows some of the actors to relate to the spectators directly, inviting their collaboration in the intimacy or distance suggested by the simultaneous staging of several performances at once.[181] Apparently Deliro and Macilente, and Clove and Orange, are strolling downstage as the other two couples stroll upstage, or perhaps they rotate in a circle, two couples moving clockwise and the other two counterclockwise, since the sequence is punctuated by greetings between pairs. As they reach the front of the stage, each of the couples has a 'bit' to perform. The slow retreating and advancing movements between couples allow Macilente opportunities to make caustic asides. Carlo delivers his set speech to Sogliardo on gentlemanly deportment. Presumably Sogliardo tries to adapt his facial expressions and posture to Carlo's instructions, perhaps trying them out on Clove and Orange, who should be passing by during this speech. The strollers come full circle after Carlo's sudden exit. His unconventional 'congee', the leave-taking at the end of a dance, concludes the pavan as the dancing couples once more break into casual groups: '*Exit* CARLO *Sogliardo mixes with Puntarvolo and Fastidius*' (272–272.1).

The strolling movement does not stop, but the formal precision of the rotating couples ceases, perhaps to make room for the next dancer, Fungoso, whose single-minded object is to obtain an exact copy of Brisk's suit. Fungoso performs a figurative galliard,[182] a fast-paced and focussed virtuoso display of leaps and pauses. Transmitting details of Brisk's satin suit ('Do you mark how it hangs at the knee there?'; 'For God's sake, do, note all. Do you see the collar, sir?'), Fungoso capers around the preening courtier while his tailor jots notes. The breathless urgency of Fungoso's exclamations and the economy of the tailor's replies suggest the whirlwind quality of this comic performance, an effect accentuated by its tunnel-vision and its frantic entrance and exit. Fungoso and the tailor see and respond to nothing but the suit. Fungoso does not hear his uncle Sogliardo's greeting. The only long speech in the whole sequence of thirty-four lines is Fastidius's, but neither Fungoso nor the tailor listens. The reductiveness creates a superbly comic effect: Brisk, like the others on parade, is nothing but a stuffed suit. And it sums up the social whirl in Paul's Walk where the dance consists of fancy footwork to obtain funds or set fashions: Brisk, Puntarvolo, Fungoso, and later Shift all openly seek a sponsor to 'impart' money; Carlo is Puntarvolo's parasite, and Macilente has become Deliro's; Sogliardo, Macilente, and Fungoso all want to wear clothes as beautiful as Brisk's. As observers of the scene, the two servants with the dog and cat, the two critics Cordatus and Mitis, and quite possibly a clutch of extras, keep 'the scene full' in true Jonsonian style, providing yet another on-stage audience for the dancers' vanity.

Carlo's return marks the beginning of the last movement of the scene, during which all the characters gradually exit. Carlo heralds the entrance of Shift and at the same time indicates that the choreographed strolling continues:

> Here he comes. Nay, walk, walk, be not seen to note him, and we shall
> have excellent sport.
>
>   *Enter* SHIFT; *walks by and uses action to his rapier.*   (318–20.1)

The next several speeches provide ironic stage-directions as the observers, pretending not to observe, describe Shift's sighs and flourishes with his weapon. At the same time, such remarks as this one from Puntarvolo, ''Slid, he vented a sigh e'en now, I thought he would have blown up the church' (321–2), continue to cement the association between affectation and place. The object of Shift's strange sword-dance in Paul's Walk is to attract a civic-minded admirer 'to impart some ten groats or half a crown' to an ex-soldier (386). Macilente and Deliro exit in disgust. Shift's efforts end when Fastidius, who has refused to lend him money, suddenly realizes that he has allowed Deliro to leave without 'imparting' the three or four hundred pounds that Fastidius wants to borrow. He exits running. Clove's and Orange's farewells precede Shift's new attempt to elicit funds by offering to teach Sogliardo how to smoke. Shift's final boast that he could 'make this dog take as many whiffs as I list, and he shall retain or effume them at my pleasure' (482–3) immediately offends Puntarvolo by its undervaluing of a dog that could be worth twenty-five thousand pounds in travel wagers. The knight calls his servants and exits in a huff: 'Pardon me, my dog shall not eat in his company for a million' (487–8). After Sogliardo and Shift dance a little bergomask of pleased rapport, they exit with Carlo. Paul's Walk is empty: the promenade is over for the day.

The Grex has the last word on the unconventionality of the whole scene. Mitis objects to the play's failure to live up to his expectations of romantic comedy. He is uneasy over what he has recognized as a satirical scene 'thus near and familiarly allied to the time' (521). Cordatus silences this objection by asking if the audience can come up with a better definition of comedy than the playwright's temporary borrowing from Cicero '(till he have strength to propose to himself a better)':

> *imitatio vitae, speculum consuetudinis, imago veritatis*: a thing throughout pleasant and ridiculous, and accommodated to the correction of manners. If the maker have failed in any particle of this, they may worthily tax him, but if not, why, be you (that are for them) silent, as I will be for him; and give way to the actors. (526–32)

This reply conveniently twists the Ciceronian tag to emphasize Jonson's theory of how comedy can modify satire to produce a salutary effect. Ironically, however, Cordatus does not try to account for the Busby Berkeley routine that marks the centre of the scene and the point of its satire—what Mitis felt to be too 'familiarly allied to the time'.

First and foremost, the whole scene calls upon the London audience's insider knowledge of the place and its customs. Because they know Paul's Walk, and expect to see the attitudes and situations that typify it, spectators might experience several conflicting impressions. Since they are watching events in a place familiar to them, they might feel excited by the representation of that place within a new space, the stage, and proud to feel somehow associated with it. They might feel more critically aware, simply because they are in a position to comment on the accuracy of the representation. They might bond with other spectators who also feel a personal involvement in the show, as a result of their first-hand experience with the St Paul's setting. They might feel superior to audiences who do not share that intimacy and who may feel excluded from the scene because they do not 'get it'. Habitués of St Paul's might identify with the elite groups on the stage, or they might find the staged caricatures threatening or invasive, because their familiarity with St Paul's convinces them that the play exposes their own affectations too directly or personally. And yet the raising of the artistic pitch of Paul's Walk by virtually turning random and narcissistic individual movements and desires into a celebratory ballet, no matter how ironic, might be a cathartic experience. The transfiguration into dance is a fantasy enhancement that beautifies as it essentializes. It co-ordinates time, motion, and rhythm into a meaningful pattern even while it ridicules. It reminds us of the shared joys of urban life, and modifies our atavistic territorial need to mark boundaries, display superior resources, and herd together for defence.

Agreement among the viewers is not the issue here. The multifarious pondering of place, event, and character is precisely what Jonson wants to evoke through his complex system of observers and participants. The long full scene of Paul's Walk, with its detailed stage-directions, demonstrates Jonson's original staging concept by helping readers visualize the theatrical space and comprehend the momentum generated by the overlapping plural actions. By splitting the stage into several simultaneous acting areas, he can define divergences of perception or sensibility spatially. At the same time, by alternating the focus from group to group and by changing the pace of stage movements and delivery, he can create a multiple complex tension on the stage that denies the audience comfortable or simple responses.[183] Through participating in these diverse points of view, the audience may acquire discernment, sense what is appropriate, and arrive at judgements that have the ethical and aesthetic 'feel' of objectivity. That is as close as anyone can get to right answers.

6. JONSONIAN AGGRESSION AND SOCIAL PERFORMANCE

'Who is so patient of this impious world
That he can check his spirit, or rein his tongue?'

'Now, sir, if you had stayed a little longer, I meant to have spoke your prologue for you, i' faith' (Ind.285–7). Cordatus's sarcastic reprimand of the Prologue for the play's late start, delivered from the privileged standpoint of the playwright's friend and nominated critic, rebounds in a way as disconcertingly for the audience as for Cordatus himself. Accepting the sarcasm as a serious offer of 'kindness' (296), and legalistically holding him to it, the Prologue manages to disrupt not only the performance of the play but also Cordatus's presentation of himself as a man of 'discreet and under-standing judgement' (Chars.107). By the Prologue's parting vow, Cordatus is baffled with rage and embarrassment—'''Sdeath, what a humorous fellow is this?' (Ind.309)—and neither Mitis's wry under-statement nor Carlo's amused gibe at his 'fustian protestations' (313) calms him down. He interrupts Carlo to curse the Prologue again ('Hang him, dull block!', 320) and vents his irritation after Carlo's exit with unexpected disparagement of Carlo himself. Cordatus's loss of composure jeopardizes the audience's reliance on him as an infallible spokesman for the playwright; from this moment on, Cor-datus is a man as capable of error as any in the audience. At the same time, this brief episode alerts the audience to the subtleties of social performance seen from Jonson's point of view. Jonson's characterization indicates an interest not so much in the inner lives of individuals as in the public interaction of persons in social groups. His characters, unlike Shakespeare's, for example, rarely soliloquize. He gives no privileged views of unguarded, internalized landscapes. Even Macilente's long monologues, as in 1.1, are merely a testing of various public self-presentations, a search for an appropriate personal style or tone to suit his current circumstances. The motives and responses of character rubbing against character, not intrigues or cross-wooings for their own sake, are what determine the action of particular scenes; and what the audience sees on stage is generally what can be seen in life itself: the outside of things, the shows which people put on and by which others try to understand them.

Much of this deduction from observed interaction derives from the 'rules' people perceive as governing social behaviour, rules to which each person at first conforms, but then bends to fit his own individuality. In a sense, Jonson applies to human relationships the same criterion he applies to literary matters: conventional rules are not laws, and people are not bound to follow them. Although people may try to shape themselves according to an accepted type, or preconceived image in isolation, their attributes actually emerge in social relationships, and change according to the situations and persons with whom they are associating. Most individuals can draw on a plurality of social selves or personas as they go through a process of assessing a situation, choosing an appropriate persona, and then modifying its presentation as the social interaction develops. Because this expressive process is contingent on personal response to a specific social scene, no one account of the social meanings given to one's own actions or those of others can be accepted as objective or neutral in resolving ambiguities.[184] An incident or scene becomes more understandable when observers can round out its context with as many points of view as possible: even in Cordatus's brief wrangle with the Prologue, Jonson projects four—five, if we count the possible mute reactions of Carlo's Boy—which the spectators may consider in interpreting the episode. The minute and dislocating details of stage moments such as these, and the frequency with which such revealing interactions occur in Jonson's work, compel the audience to adopt an analytical attitude towards human nature, an attitude quite unlike that usually evoked in the dramas of Jonson's contemporaries.

This analytical attitude is, in general, a feature of satire; it is also a feature of dramaturgy. From the sociological point of view, a theatrical performance, inasmuch as it reflects the dynamic social process by which individuals shape their identities, has theoretical implications for understanding social behaviour, especially the relationship between roles and personalities.[185] If the theatrical performance is satirical, the implications and the consciousness of implications increase. Satire is concerned primarily with role-playing and particularly with attack and aggression in social activity. Satirists assume that society shares certain intellectual and moral standards which validate the ridicule of aberrant social performances.[186] Whether or not satirists are playwrights, they conceive of their art in terms of drama and their characters in terms of performance, mimicking their victim's voice, or caricaturing his or her image, making distinctions between the impression the performer wishes to make, or thinks he or she is making, and the impression received by various critical observers. Because they are concerned with social process, satirists place their victim within groups of co-performers and audiences, some of whom may imitate, expose, or rival the performance being staged. Jonson may have been the first 'social psychologist' to make extensive use of the overtly dramaturgical standpoint both as an 'analytical tool' and as a 'determinant of action', in order to elucidate the complexity of human behaviour;[187] simply put, he explains what people do by looking at how they present themselves as actors in specific social scenes. Jonsonian actors perform to establish a personal identity, and they are defensive about their performances because they fear exposure as mere actors. The reactions of the group before whom they perform will, by accepting or rejecting the performance, affect their perceptions and future presentations of self.

The dominant feature of life in social groups is the concern for dignity, and the dynamics of groups vary in the extent to which they support that preoccupation. Generally a group will cover up the lapses of its members in order to avoid diminished prestige or, worse, contempt.[188] So Cordatus and Mitis cover up Asper's hysterical loss of focus when the word 'humour' first becomes an issue (Ind.83–5), and defend his idiosyncrasies when he leaves the stage; and so Mitis defers to Cordatus's judgement at the end of the induction, or at least does not contradict him, in order to salve his self-esteem after the demoralizing encounters with the Prologue and Carlo. To preserve self-esteem, individual performers often foster the impression that they had ideal motives for acquiring the role which they are performing, that they have ideal qualifications for the role, and that it is not necessary for them to swallow indignities, insults, or 'party' lines in order to sustain the role.[189] This is the impression Asper insists on in his role as fearless playwright; what upsets Cordatus is the disruption by the Prologue and Carlo of a similar impression of himself as fearless critic. Conversely, the obstruction of that impression of fearlessness is the cause of Macilente's bitter resentment against society; he sees himself reduced to playing a part beneath his dignity, feigning deference and gratitude to those who are undeservedly fortunate: ' "I thank you, sir." [*Aside*] I know my cue, I think' (2.2.22). Macilente distances himself from his role by showing that he is aware that he is putting on a performance, and by giving little signs that subtly mock that performance: his asides, his reference to cues, and his exaggerated emphasis all demonstrate in a privately face-saving way his control over those actions that constitute the public performance.[190] At the same time, by seeing himself as an actor, and by being aware of the variety of audiences before whom he is playing, he draws attention to the roles being played by the other characters, and his perception of their less-aware role-playing allows him to deride them, thus defending his own superior worth in his own eyes.

The theatre audience too is aware of the levels of role-play-within-the-play and is likewise distanced from the action in order to judge from a superior position. But the role-player prefers to restrict views. Because an individual likes to foster the impression that the routine he is currently performing is his most genuine or indeed his only routine, he has to segregate his audiences. By doing so, he ensures that the audience before whom he performs another part in a different setting will not pierce his disguise.[191] The Clove and Orange, for example, who greet Shift as idle men-about-town are directing themselves to a different audience from the one they try to impress with their 'great scholars' act. Shift tries to keep his identities as Signor Whiff and Master Apple John separate from the noble-soldier-reduced-to-beggar routine that he enacts for Brisk, and separate again from the *ersatz* highwayman he concocts for Sogliardo's consumption. As these examples suggest, people spend a considerable amount of time experimenting with the expression of multiple and often incompatible versions of themselves, no one of which singly encapsulates the whole self, and all of which may help protect the self from complete exposure.[192]

Such multiple performances are difficult to sustain within marriage: both of the marriages in *EMO* founder on the problematics of role-playing. Jonson creates a deliberate disjunction between the apparent compliance suggested by the wives' relative silence and their rejection or at least disapproval of their husbands, revealed in the stage-directions. The result suggests that one source of marital dysfunction (a dysfunction at the heart of all Jonson's comedies) is the implicit defamation of wives who, despite the public honour conferred by marriage, are assumed to perform only a sexual role in the union, a role that, for the women diminished by it, feels dishonourable. Both Lady Puntarvolo and Fallace are staged to provoke prurience in their male audience, on and off stage, although the women's refusal to comply with male sexual fantasies proclaims that their seductive images are at odds with their action. Their conventional postures elicit the same initial response from the viewer as do depictions of courtesans in early modern pornography: framed by open windows or open doors, the women signal sexual availability. More specifically, they illustrate two versions of female sexuality in marriage. In one, Jonson creates a compliant wife, Lady Puntarvolo, who ends up rejecting the pornographic role imposed on her by her husband. In the other, he creates Fallace, the wilful wife who seizes the pornographic advantage, turns her gaze lustfully beyond her husband, and asserts her own erotic pleasure.

Lady Puntarvolo seems to be the conventionally chaste obedient wife, but, when her husband's foreplay inadvertently exposes her to the mockery of eavesdroppers, she takes a firm independent stand. She has been expected to perform a provocative but private charade at her window to please her husband's eccentric sexual palette. In this domestic game, Sir Puntarvolo plays a knight-errant looking for lodging at a hospitable castle. His wife's waiting-gentlewoman first appears at the window to describe the magnanimity of her absent lord (an act designed by Puntarvolo to flatter himself); then the wife appears at the window, and the game of courtly seduction begins. The tone of these exchanges is difficult to assess: on the women's part, the tone possibly projects contempt, to judge from the waiting-gentlewoman's opportunities for sarcasm, or perhaps simply embarrassment, or even indifference brought on by too many repetitions of a stale encounter. On the other hand, Puntarvolo's generally quixotic behaviour suggests a high level of courtly earnestness. But the eavesdroppers certainly find the charade both stilted and ludicrous, as suggested by Carlo's disgust:

> What? A tedious chapter of courtship, after Sir Lancelot and Queen Guinevere? Away! I mar'l in what dull cold nook he found this lady out, that (being a woman) she was blessed with no more copy of wit but to serve his humour thus. 'Sblood, I think he feeds her with porridge, I! She could ne'er have such a thick brain else. (2.1.345–50)

Sir Puntarvolo's awareness that neighbours are watching his performance makes him swim even more enthusiastically with 'the current of his humour' (302–3), as one observer notes with shock. His language leans heavily on dubious metaphors of entry: he seeks 'a smooth and secure passage' for his travels and begs the lady to permit him 'to enter your fair castle and refresh me' (325–31). Her reply also plays with common metaphors of ingress and sexuality: although she does not usually 'admit any entrance to strangers', yet she is so impressed by the knight's 'innated virtues and fair parts' that she resolves 'to entertain you to the best of my power' (333–7). But once the women become aware of the ring of oglers, the domestic role-playing ceases permanently. Lady Puntarvolo says only one

line more, after opening her door and discovering all the visitors—
a discovery that may comically include the whole theatre audience:
'God's me, here's company! Turn in again' (365). The level of language drops with a thud as she registers the public humiliation for
what should have remained a harmless if irritating game. After all,
Lady Puntarvolo has leaned out of her window to conduct an adulterous liaison with her own husband, an adultery for which he has
written the script, even if she perhaps does not desire it for herself.
After the leering community relieves her of this role-playing burden,
she restores her self-esteem by closing her windows and doors
against further psychic intrusion. Her shame at having been displayed pornographically for voyeurs makes her reject sexual fantasy
altogether. Anything we hear of her later in the play suggests that
she has chosen to live in unstimulating retirement: no kinky sex, no
travelling to exotic places, and no further appearances on stage.

With Lady Puntarvolo, then, Jonson chooses to close the door on
sexuality, and deny the equation of woman or wife with the body.
But with Fallace, Jonson found other means to disrupt the pornographic staging of women: by reversing the usual direction of the
gaze. He represents this middle-class *nouveau-riche* wife in a particularly unsettling way as she swoons with erotic longings for the
handsome courtier Fastidius Brisk. The pronunciation of Fallace's
name may be designed to support her sexuality, whether italianately
tri-syllabic (Fal-la-che) or anglophonic: Fall-ace emphasizes the
'fall' of the fallen woman, with a play on 'false', 'fallacy' (in the sense
of trickery or deception), and perhaps 'phallus', as a kind of complement to her sexual fantasies. She daydreams about how Brisk's
'graces disperse contentment through all my senses', and envies
women who have received his kisses, praises his face, his body,
especially his 'tongue able to ravish any woman i' the earth!'
(2.2.333–47). As she leaves the stage, she sighs out a licentious
prospect: 'Well, I will not altogether despair. I have heard of a
citizen's wife has been beloved of a courtier, and why not I? Heigh
ho! Well, I will into my private chamber, lock the door to me, and
think over all his good parts, one after another' (2.2.353–7). Here
are the metaphors of ingression and sexual assets, repeated from
Lady Puntarvolo's domestic dialogue. But Fallace's double entendres tease the audience into responding as voyeurs to her autoerotic
suggestions of what will happen behind her locked door. In an early
modern version of *What the Butler Saw*, the audience projects the
keyhole through which it may spy luscious female sexuality, self-

absorbed in a fantasy of erotic fulfilment. Whereas Jonson's pornographic depiction of Fallace seems to represent her as a sexual
object, the uneasiness that this scene arouses comes from the fact
that Jonson actually constructs Fallace as a self-sufficent sexual
subject, orgasmically stimulated not by Brisk but by her fantasy of
him, and thus not really needing him at all for the gratifications of
her private chamber. She is, in other words, appropriating pornography for her own pleasure, not for the pleasure of the male voyeur.
In fact, in Fallace's final scene with Brisk, alone together at last, she
is irritated by his attempt to kiss her in inappropriate circumstances.

Fallace's preference for the Brisk of her imagination conflicts with
Deliro's expectation of her role as his wife. Fallace, like Lady Puntarvolo, is expected to play the part of the courtly beloved within a
set especially designed for her performance: Deliro encloses her
in a perfumed garden and serenades her with bands of musicians
while he peeks at her from behind bushes. Unlike Lady Puntarvolo,
Fallace refuses to comply with the scenario. Her flight from her
husband's fantasies at first expresses itself in disdainful rejection. Of
his garden strewn with flower petals and sprayed with additional
scent, she remarks: 'Here's a sweet stink indeed! / What, shall I ever
be thus crossed and plagued? / And sick of husband?' (96–8). She
rejects his conventional lover's gift of gloves, and then complains
when the servant takes them away. Whatever Deliro does, she puts
him in the wrong, metaphorically slamming doors in his face, and
yet he cannot resist her. Even Macilente is so stunned by her beauty
that he envies and resents Deliro both for possessing such a wife
and for not knowing how to keep her. Indeed, Macilente not only
wants to adore her—he wants to *be* her: 'What moved the heavens,
that they could not make / Me such a woman?'—or, better yet, why
could he not be transformed into 'some fair water-nymph' (158–63)
who might magnetically lure the world to destruction, like a siren
or a fishy Helen of Troy? The death-blow to the Deliro marriage
comes when Deliro decides in Act 4 to have Brisk arrested for debt.
Fallace becomes violently enraged, shrieks, 'I'll not bide here for all
the gold and silver in heaven', and slams the stage door as she exits.
Deliro chases her through the door, but, as he disappears, Fallace
re-enters '*running*' by another door, '*claps it to*', and holds it closed,
perhaps with Fungoso's help, while her husband, trying to placate
her, apparently struggles to get in (4.1.115–26). The farcical pursuit
through slamming doors ends with her success in holding the door
against him. For Fallace, as for Lady Puntarvolo earlier, keeping the

door closed becomes a sign of sexual autonomy and, to Jonson's satirical eye, a judgement against sexually obsessed husbands. Although the play ends with the exposure of Fallace as the false wife, bearing out Macilente's opinion, 'Would any woman but one that were wild in her affections have broke out into that immodest and violent passion against her husband?' (4.2.3–6), clearly Deliro's own immoderate behaviour has been responsible for the shambles their marriage becomes.

What this focus on staging at windows and doors illustrates is the lack of appropriate or sensitive responses to women's choices in marriage. Jonson shows us only a simple binary here between the wife who says no after complying dutifully for years with the demands of a peculiar and increasingly less cautious husband, and the wife who says no because she cannot comply dutifully with the demands of a husband she cannot desire. Certainly the dislocating emphasis on saying no counters the sexualized view of women prompted by the iconography of windows and doors in which they are staged, an iconography that screams yes! In both cases, the husband bears the brunt of the blame for the derailed marriage, because the husband is perceived as having failed his masculine duty to be adult and civilized in his actions—that is, cultivated, gentlemanly, wittily humane, spiritually (not just materially) generous. But if a man fails in courtship, within or without marriage, he has other options: Puntarvolo, Deliro, and Brisk all find themselves compensating for failures with women by means of various face-saving techniques that temporarily restore some sense of self, at least within male groups.

Personal identity is something which is undertaken as a project on a trial-and-error basis. If the project is not sufficient to establish the performer in one role, then he seeks out alternative settings in which he may perform a role.[193] This concern with roles and audiences suggests that individuals are 'as much manipulators of social relations as manipulated by them'.[194] The balance between the two, Jonson suggests, depends on one's responsiveness to social interaction. Brisk actually seems to prevent reciprocally sustained involvement in conversation because he is distracted by the impression or production of his own affectations.[195] His rhetoric, routine in the fashionable group to which he aspires, is frequently an additional bar to communication because his inflated latinate vocabulary and loose syntax distort or exaggerate his descriptions of life at court, so transforming reality that normal discourse is flummoxed.[196] 'I cannot frame me to your harsh vulgar phrase', he declares to Carlo after failing to make himself clear; ''Tis against my *genius*' (2.1.98–9).

In order to interpret Brisk, his hearers have to 'cross-negotiate accounts' by accumulating other reports.[197] Certainly, the impression that Brisk tries to create of his popularity and influence at court (see 2.1.457–508, 2.2.238–73, 3.1.91–120, 4.3.379–438, 4.5.16–32) is greatly undermined by Macilente's report to Deliro that Brisk is not a leading actor at court but rather 'like a zany to a tumbler, / That tries tricks after him to make men laugh' (4.1.86–7), and his somewhat different account to Carlo and Puntarvolo, placing Brisk as one 'frothy fool' among many (4.3.193–206). These reports follow the scene in which the audience obtains a first-hand view of Brisk virtually tripping over his various personas, enacted or invoked—the sophisticated pipe-smoker, the musician, the dancer, the gymnast, the wit—in his efforts to impress. As a result, the audience sees him trapped satirically among Saviolina's outright rebuffs and rudenesses, Macilente's ambiguously face-saving remarks and hostile muttered asides, and Cinedo's busy smoke-screening assistance. Ironically, Brisk even provides his own charivari, the discordant noise-making that usually accompanies public ridicule, by playing his own 'rough music' on the viola da gamba.[198] He finally acknowledges his disgrace by begging Macilente: 'Report it not for a million' (3.3.149). Yet, once his audience changes, Brisk is able to recover his poise and renew his affectations. His account of his duel with Luculento (4.3.379ff.) glows with bravado. An actual duel in which the combatants rip each other's clothes, trip over their own spurs, and flee the field is scarcely likely to arouse admiration. But Brisk's rhetoric of violence, by placing the emphasis on his manly assertiveness and sophisticated appearance, serves, as the action itself could not, to enhance his sense of personal prestige and worth.[199] ''Fore God,' Puntarvolo remarks, apparently without irony, 'it was a designment begun with much resolution, maintained with as much prowess, and ended with more humanity' (440–2).

To some extent, obvious in Brisk's experience and perhaps less so in Macilente's envious desire to have (or become) Fallace, men compensate for rejection from women by substituting or preferring male flirtations.[200] Cinedo offers Brisk far more gratifying access to erotic encounters than either Fallace or Saviolina, and the duel with Luculento, which ended when the two men 'embraced and marched hand in hand up into the presence' (4.3.436–7), echoes the game in a more courtly mode. Sogliardo discovers, whispering with Cinedo (2.1.156.1), that he need not deny his attraction to young men, and subsequently hires Shift for sexual as well as fashionable pursuits (as suggested by Shift's posted advertisements). Puntarvolo forgets his failure with his wife when he parades through town with his entourage of eagerly dutiful servants, animals, and parasites. The man-and-dog bond, parodied and equivocally sexualized in other male pairings (Brisk–Fungoso, Macilente–Carlo, Deliro–Macilente, Puntarvolo–Carlo, and so on), becomes the standard for social relationship. The master–servant or master–dog connection marks the debasement of classical male friendship because it does not support or repeat the Orestes–Pylades or Damon–Pythias ideal of physical and spiritual intimacy. Disproportion or grotesque reduction in rank, commodification of the body in Paul's market, and superficiality of courtly affectation replace that intimacy with sexual service. The vulgarization of male bonding is implicit in Carlo's protests that he admires Macilente 'above the love of women' (4.3.230), and his persistent expression of a desire to eat his flesh, bite his ear, or melt in contact with him remind us that male fellowship, even when not primarily sexual, has an erotic charge that stimulates hostile wit and aggressive behaviour.

The unstable relationship between aggressive rhetoric and violent action, particularly where face-saving is at stake, is difficult to gauge, especially when the attack is a concerted team effort. A team is 'a kind of secret society', generated by a basic human need for companions with whom to enter into 'collusive intimacies and backstage relaxation', although the intimacy tends to be formal, lacking personal warmth.[201] Persons in groups tend to be subversive; that is, the process of identifying one's self in public in the context of one group involves challenging and even dissolving the identities of other persons and groups.[202] The feeling of almost militant solidarity generated by membership in a group is both a powerful invitation to hostilities against outsiders and an effective defence from retaliatory attack. Although Macilente, for example, begins as a powerless railer on the sidelines of society, he eventually acquires the requisites for membership in a group: appropriate gear (3.3), associates who both fear and admire him (4.3.229–31, 333–4), and occasions for displaying his skills in action (4.5, 5.3). The trick played on Saviolina is an excellent example of how the group dynamic operates for the mutual satisfaction of its members, establishing an identity they all want to share.

Macilente introduces the trick in a way that prompts Fastidius and Puntarvolo to act voluntarily in accordance with his plan. He guarantees Fastidius's co-operation by suggesting to him the possibility of exposing Saviolina as 'too self-conceited', rather than incontrovertibly witty. Puntarvolo joins the team apparently for the sport of it, and perhaps also as a return on Fastidius's participation in the knight's travel wager. Macilente co-opts Carlo for his natural scoffing talent, even though Carlo's usefulness is limited to backstage arrangements: ensuring Sogliardo's presence, and arranging the victory celebration at the Mitre. Finally, the team absorbs Fungoso merely to cheer him up.

Macilente's dominance of the group is essentially directive, rather than dramatic.[203] He allocates the parts and co-ordinates the timing; Sogliardo is the unwitting dramatic focus of the performance, eager to be presented at court and never quite catching on to the fact that he is being duped by the rest of the group. The performance of the practical joke involves both the group members and their target in a temporary play-world with saturnalian laws and carnivalesque customs of its own.[204] The prospect of laughter has a bonding effect; it sharpens the group's aggressive behaviour and produces fellow-feeling among the participants. At the same time, it draws lines separating the insiders, who enjoy the dramatic ironies of the set-up, from the outsiders.[205] Sogliardo is not a fully fledged member of the group; he is co-operating in the group performance, but is not a party to the 'inside secrets' of the exclusive inner circle, and his enjoyment comes from the giddy excitement of performing well before a fine court lady, proving himself a courtier among courtiers. The group's target, Saviolina, on the other hand, aware that a joke is being performed, but unaware of its secret strategy, smirks at her visitors in the belief that she cannot be outwitted.

The idea of playing out a riddle to which each side thinks it has the answer motivates the dramatic performance of both the insiders and the outsiders. Because each side expects to turn the tables on the others, each enjoys the preparation for the satiric moment, outdoing one another in courtly compliments that become progressively more mocking. The mockery is largely mimicry, based on Puntarvolo's and Fastidius's initial assertion about the gentleman who 'doth so peerlessly imitate' a clown that 'it is not possible for the sharpest-sighted wit in the world to discern any sparks of the gentleman in him when he does it' (5.2.38–9, 41–4). Saviolina registers her contempt for their estimation of her wit by repeating their words with mocking emphasis: 'sparks' (47, 49), 'clown' (58, 62), and several variations on 'see' and 'sight'. Because she does recognize Sogliardo's ludicrously inept performance as a performance, she assumes that his travesties of courtly compliment are proofs of his 'real' identity as a gentleman-mimic, and not proofs of his essential boorishness. Her increased mimicry of the group, sign of her increased self-confidence, aligns her with the rare and witty stranger whom she has, by her superior intelligence, 'deciphered' (71, 80–1): 'Not decipher him, quoth you?' she sneers (92). Mimicry becomes the chief weapon of the group mockers as well: 'Why, has she deciphered him, gentlemen?' Macilente asks (95). Fastidius delivers the final ironic echo: 'She deciphered him at first' (119). The same pattern of double-edged mimicry emerges with other terms denoting clarity of sight and wit: 'discern' (72, 116); 'perceive . . . as clear as noonday' (76–7, 118–19); 'judgement' (75, 85, 101). The mimicry is accompanied by constant testing for firmness of position, each member of the group leading Saviolina into ever stronger assertions of her superiority: Puntarvolo asks, 'In earnest, lady?' (73); Fastidius finds it 'strange . . . her ladyship should see so far into him' (89–90); Fungoso declares it a 'wonder' (94); and Macilente begs, in face of Saviolina's laughter, 'Nay, lady, do not scorn us' (102). In fact, Saviolina is so convinced that she has outwitted the group that she cannot take in the truth, until she looks at Sogliardo's calloused palm and hears his ingenuous explanation: 'Tut, that was with holding the plough' (115). The group-members' elation at their victory prompts them to prolong their exhilaration by pursuing Saviolina for further jeering; Fastidius's remark, 'Nay, let's follow it while 'tis hot' (127), is a typical response to successful group aggression.[206]

Hostile wit, according to Freud, requires at least three persons: one to make the joke, one to be the butt of the joke, and one to laugh.[207] A group is a breeding ground for hostile wit, and where no out-group target exists, as in the scene with Saviolina, it stimulates intra-group aggression.[208] The effects of abusive in-group joking are usually controlled by the participants' loyalty to the group, their prudence in selecting jokes, and the accepted level of 'teasing' to test a group-member's ability to take a joke, that is, to sustain a friendly manner while not feeling it.[209] All three of these checks against dissonance break down when Macilente incites Carlo to heckle Puntarvolo about the dead dog, pushing verbal hostility into active side-taking and physical attack.

Macilente has never, as the theatre audience is well aware, been loyal to a group. He has always taken a discrepant role, pretending to support members of various groups while openly or secretly selling them out to one audience or another. In the Deliro family triangle, for example, he openly tries to disabuse Deliro regarding his wife's perfections (4.3.149–77), but fails; he is more successful in exposing humours secretly, while posing as a friend: arranging for Brisk's arrest for debt, Fallace's attempt to rescue him, and Deliro's discovery of the guilty pair. Carlo too thinks little of loyalty; good timing, a dissembling tongue, and a guileless face—an actor's tools—can protect him from suspicion: 'What Lynceus can see my heart?' (4.3.108–9). Unfortunately, Carlo forgets to weigh these factors when he accepts Macilente as his partner. Well primed with drink, he assumes he is safe from reprisals simply because he has a partner whose co-operation and support he thinks he can count on in a secret alliance against the other members of their team. Carlo and Macilente consolidate their new alliance in derogatory behind-the-scenes laughter at the absent Puntarvolo and Sogliardo (5.3.104–14), and, as a result of this apparently spontaneous demonstration of unanimity, Carlo agrees to harass the knight, with Macilente's backing (118–25).

Carlo's pact with his secret sidekick heightens the already intoxicating effects of 'old sack' and the vicarious enjoyment of high-jinks and reversals at court. The result is a bubbling overflow of anarchic exhilaration that translates into wild rhetorical energy, generating hyperbole, surrealist fantasy, and sublime nonsense. He suggests remedy after remedy to revive or replace the dead dog by quackery—'if he be not outright dead, there is a friend of mine, a quacksalver, shall put life in him again'; taxidermy—'flay me your dog presently (but, in any case, keep the head) and stuff his skin well with straw'; simulation—'or, if you like not that, sir, get me somewhat a less dog and clap into the skin'; or black magic—'you may have (as you come through Germany) a familiar, for little or nothing, shall turn itself into the shape of your dog . . . for certain hours' (5.3.190–235 *passim*). This burst of satiric invention is 'both virulent and affectionate':[210] Carlo depends on the ambivalence of his joking relationship with Puntarvolo (whom he addresses familiarly as 'Sir Puntar') to protect him from the consequences of his verbal hostility in a situation that calls for restraint or at least avoidance of conflict. Macilente stimulates aggression on both sides of the contest by alternating between *sotto voce* reinstigation of Carlo's attacks—

'Nay, to him again' (175); 'Nay, Buffone, the knight, the knight!' (209–10)—and exacerbation of Puntarvolo's sense of injury—'God's precious, knight, will you suffer this?' (195–6); 'Sir Puntarvolo, 'sdeath, can you be so patient?' (231).

Ridicule, especially with the acquiescence of the group, neutralizes the power of the victim, who ceases to have the status of a person in the ridiculer's consciousness.[211] Puntarvolo's *amour-propre* will not tolerate such dehumanization. His violent retaliation is a tit-for-tat, a way of denying Carlo's status as an appropriate representative of the group, and therefore denying the worth of his offensive remarks as an interpretation of reality. The resort to violence is a cultural expectation, especially in one whose favorite self-presentation is as a knight-errant. The proper response to provocation in round-table etiquette is to lash out, so that bystanders will respect and approve the immediate assertion of dignity; the failure to act in line with this code may lead to social emasculation or even exclusion from the group.[212] Carlo suffers both sanctions. His cowardice in face of physical attack loses him whatever advantage his verbal prowess had gained him earlier; when even Macilente joins the knight's side, Carlo's hope of rescue vanishes, and with the sealing of his lips his only potent weapon—his tongue—is rendered *hors de combat*.

Macilente's betrayal of Carlo, like his other betrayals including his murder of the dog, places Macilente in a dubious position. He is a renegade, disregarding the social bonds which restrain or modify most socially aberrant behaviour. On the other hand, he defends himself by taking a moral stand against socially accepted corruption in a world in which the vilest person, provided he has money enough, 'shall not only pass, but pass regarded' (3.3.11–14), and where the idea of rewarding merit is considered puritanically fussy and 'a disease in nature' (4.3.199–201). Such attitudes suggest that 'it is better to be true to the ideals of the role than to the performers who falsely present themselves in it'.[213] His justification for this belief appears in his reward: 'a spirit as sweet and clear / As the most rarefied and subtle air' (5.4.18–19), purged of all moral taint by the Queen's transforming power. In the second half of this final scene, the audience is reminded that Asper, another self-proclaimed renegade, wrote and played the part of Macilente, and that Macilente's actions thus have authorial approbation. Asper announced from the beginning his contempt for social bonds that facilitate or wink at corruption:

> My soul
Was never ground into such oily colours
To flatter vice and daub iniquity

. . .

I fear no mood stamped in a private brow,
When I am pleased t'unmask a public vice.   (Ind.11–13, 19–20)

Just as Macilente detects hypocritical or intellectually flimsy social performances for the purpose of exploding such humours in the play proper, so Asper identifies corrupt self-presenters both in society at large—the strumpet, the ruffian, the broker, usurer or lawyer, the courtier—and in the theatre audience itself. There he spies among the rest 'a sort of fools, so sick in taste / That they condemn all physic of the mind' (130–1), whom he gives 'pills to purge, / And make 'em fit for fair societies' (174–5).

But Jonson does not necessarily advocate the methods of an Asper or a Macilente to achieve a better society. This would be to minimize the varieties of life that emerge in rascals like Carlo or Shift, or in courtiers like the stiff-limbed Puntarvolo or the transparent poseur, Fastidius Brisk. Rather, the whole spectrum of roles, actors, and audiences can enrich the understanding of social performance by showing that a single model of behaviour is inadequate in a social process that demands a complex shifting from one role to another. As one social psychologist remarked, concerning a single participant's view of an episode: 'One didn't discover the *causes* of that action, nor did one discover the *truth*: one obtained a perspective.'[214] By imposing too many sharp distinctions, or by trying too hard to see clear and consistent patterns of behaviour, an audience may 'lose sight of the sense of confusion and ambiguity that had its important role to play in shaping the Renaissance sense of self'.[215]

This awareness of a perplexing, even indiscriminate multiplicity of conflicting selves is what shapes the Jonsonian perspective. It is inherent in inconsistent self-presentation and in the groups whose aggressiveness tries to impose unilateral views. It is what finally decides Cordatus and Mitis to 'ha' done censuring now' (5.4.43). Jonson's mild refusal to add a final judgement to what has been a highly judgemental play suggests a sane exit from the satirical world where toleration was not a virtue. With all humours now written and played out, Jonson does not mean to offer his spectators a narrow 'humorous' judgement as a final point of view, but to let them alone to 'feed their understanding parts' (Ind.201).

NOTES

1 Edward Arber, *A Transcript of the Register of the Company of Stationers of London, 1554–1640*, 5 vols (London, 1875–94), 3.159.

2 J. A. Lavin, 'Printers for Seven Jonson Quartos', *Library* 25 (1970): 331.

3 W. W. Greg, 'Notes on Old Books', *Library* 3 (June 1922): 57.

4 W. W. Greg, 'The First Edition of Ben Jonson's "Every Man Out of His Humour"', *Library* 1 (1920): 155.

5 It had been thought that only one compositor set *Q1*, but Kevin J. Donovan distinguishes two on the basis of the spelling variants; see 'Jonson's Texts in the First Folio', in Jennifer Brady and W. H. Herendeen, eds, *Ben Jonson's 1616 Folio* (Newark, 1991), p. 36, 21n.

6 A. C. Partridge, *Orthography in Shakespeare and Elizabethan Drama: A Study of Colloquial Contractions, Elision, Prosody and Punctuation* (London, 1964), p. 130.

7 Peter W. M. Blayney, 'The Publication of Playbooks', in John D. Cox and David Scott Kastan, eds, *A New History of Early English Drama* (New York, 1997), pp. 396, 412–13.

8 I am indebted to Peter Blayney, who, when he was working on Elizabethan printing houses at the Folger Shakespeare Library in Washington DC, kindly relayed information to me about the printers of *Q2* and *Q3*.

9 My comments on printers in this paragraph are derived from Greg, 'The First Edition', pp. 156–8.

10 Evelyn May Albright, *Dramatic Publication in England 1580–1640: A Study of Conditions Affecting the Content and Form of Drama* (New York, 1927), p. 332. Albright suggests that Ling published *Q3* 'probably without permission'.

11 Greg, 'The First Edition', says that the date is 'open to doubt' (p. 159) and that the imprint is 'a little suspicious' (p. 160). *H&S* (3.411) feel 'a little uneasy' about the date as well.

12 W. David Kay, 'The Shaping of Ben Jonson's Career: A Re-examination of Facts and Problems', *MP* 67 (1970): 228–30.

13 Blayney, pp. 403–4.

14 Blayney, pp. 403, 383–4.

15 Albright, pp. 332–42, offers further rationalizations and explications of *Q3*'s errors.

16 For the details on these states of the folio see James A. Riddell, 'The Printing of the Plays in the Jonson Folio of 1616', *SB* 49 (1996): 149–68, esp. 153–4; and 'Addendum: The Printing of the Plays in the Jonson Folio of 1616', *SB* 50 (1997): 408–9.

17 Arber, 4.417.

18 Arber, 4.432–4.

19 Features of the elaborate system of punctuation include the ubiquitous use of the comma to separate syntactical units, not only before or after vocatives and interjections, but also paradoxically and pedantically between the two parts of any compound structure already linked by 'and'; the increase in the use of dashes and exclamation marks; and the substitution of colons for semicolons.

20 See de Vocht, whose contempt for the folio is apparent on every page.

21 'The Folio of 1616', in *H&S*, 9.13–73, and their specific refutation of de Vocht's arguments, 'An Attack upon the Folio', pp. 74–84.

22 Johann Gerritsen, 'Stansby and Jonson Produce a Folio', *ES* 40 (1959): 53.

23 Donovan, p. 25. On the unnecessary aspect of such changes, Partridge, *Orthography*, remarks: 'Many changes were of the fussy, pedantic order, not vital; for Jonson already knew how to punctuate when he published his first Quarto, *Every Man Out of His Humour*, in 1600' (p. 137).

24 Fredson Bowers, 'Notes on Editorial Apparatus', in Mary-Jo Arn and Hanneke Wirtjes, with Hans Jansen, eds, *Historical and Editorial Studies in Medieval and Early Modern English* (Groningen, 1985), p. 151.

25 Albright, p. 190.

26 Cited in Nicholas Brooke, ed., *Bussy D'Ambois*, Revels (Manchester, 1964), p. lxvi.

27 Riddell (1996) reaches the same conclusion on p. 151.

28 *H&S*, 9.13.

29 John Jowett, 'Jonson's Authorization of Type in *Sejanus* and Other Early Quartos', *SB* 44 (1991): 64.

30 For a fuller argument on the validity of texts other than the final version see James McLavery, 'The Concept of Authorial Intention on Textual Criticism', *Library* 6 (June 1984), esp. pp. 130–3.

31 Jonas A. Barish, *Ben Jonson and the Language of Prose Comedy* (New York, 1970), pp. 47, 62.

32 *Discoveries*, in George Parfitt, ed., *Ben Jonson: The Complete Poems* (London, 1975, 1988), p. 435.

33 See M. H. Abrams, *A Glossary of Literary Terms*, 4th ed. (New York, 1981), pp. 167–8, on the distinctions between comedy and satire; and Steggle, pp. 10–11, 24–6, who argues that Jonson's term includes the literary and the topical. On the specific Old Comedy similarity see Jeffrey Henderson, 'The *Dēmos* and the Comic Competition', in Erich Segal, ed., *Oxford Readings in Aristophanes* (Oxford, 1996), citing *Frogs* on the function of the comic poet: 'to say much that is humorous and much that is serious, and to win the prize by playfulness and mockery, worthily of the festival' (p. 65). Henderson argues that old comic poets pictured themselves as competing for the favour of the *dēmos* with humorous spectacles of a special kind, for which they had public permission and approbation, and which influenced public thinking about matters of major importance.

34 Among the many commentaries on the genre during the early modern period, the most comprehensive is still Alvin Kernan, *The Cankered Muse: Satire of the English Renaissance* (Hamden, CT, 1976), pp. 64–80.

35 This generic shift has been exhaustively argued, notably by C. R. Baskervill, *English Elements in Jonson's Early Comedies* (Chicago, 1929; rpt New York, 1965), ch. 3; O. J. Campbell, *Comicall Satyre and Shakespeare's Troilus and Cressida* (San Marino, CA, 1938) ch. 1 and 2; Kernan, ch. 3. See also Raman Selden, *English Verse Satire, 1590–1765* (London, 1978), ch. 2.

36 See James S. Baumlin, 'Generic Context of Elizabethan Satire: Rhetoric, Poetic Theory, and Imitation', in Barbara Kiefer Lewalski,

ed., *Renaissance Genres: Essays on Theory, History, and Interpretation* (Cambridge, MA, 1986), pp. 448–56.

37 Selden, pp. 13–28, 44. Cf. the Horatian epigraphs on *Q1*'s title-page and final page, and other references in the annotation. Henderson also notes the combination of playfulness and comic ridicule in Old Comedy, citing *Lysias* 24.18: 'My accuser is not being serious but playful, his purpose not persuasion but ridicule, as if making some fine joke', and pointing out that the distinction between abuse and jesting called for 'nice judgment': 'One man's joke is another man's slander' (p. 90). Puntarvolo's attack on Carlo in 5.3 illustrates what happens when the jester goes too far, and the butt is over-sensitive.

38 Sidney, *An Apology for Poetry* (Cambridge, 1951), p. 30.

39 Henry L. Snuggs, 'The Source of Jonson's Definition of Comedy', *MLN* 65 (1950): 543–4; and Baumlin, pp. 451–2.

40 Campbell, p. 2.

41 See Baskervill's analysis of its shades of meaning in Fenton's *Tragicall Discourses* (1567) as 'clearly anticipatory' of Jonson's usage, pp. 46–54. For other meanings in the 1590s see pp. 59–72.

42 The following in based primarily on Douglas M. MacDowell, '*Hybris* in Athens', *G&R* 23 (1976): 14–31. See also, in the same volume, N. R. E. Fisher, '*Hybris* and Dishonour', 175ff.

43 MacDowell, p. 21.

44 MacDowell, p. 27.

45 Robert N. Watson, '*The Alchemist* and Jonson's Conversion of Comedy', in Lewalski, p. 337.

46 See K. J. Dover, *Aristophanic Comedy* (London, 1972), p. 88.

47 *Discoveries*, in Parfitt, p. 454.

48 Watson, p. 334.

49 C. R. Baskervill, *The Elizabethan Jig and Related Sang Drama* (Chicago, 1929; rpt New York 1965), pp. 191–2. Baskervill's descriptions of early jigs provide an invaluable source for understanding the structures of early comedy.

50 Baskervill, *Jig*, p. 87.

51 Baskervill, *Jig*, pp. 47, 301.

52 Baskervill, *Jig*, pp. 60–76.

53 Henri Bergson, *Le Rire: Essai sur la signification du comique* (Geneva, 1945), pp. 63–7; Jessica Milner Davis, *Farce* (London, 1978), p. 62.

54 Bergson, pp. 94–5.

55 Jesse Franklin Bradley and Joseph Quincy Adams, *The Jonson Allusion Book* (New Haven, 1922), p. 33. For other recognitions of Jonson's debt to Aristophanes, see *H&S*, 11.319–20, 337.

56 Coburn Gum, *The Aristophanic Comedies of Ben Jonson: A Comparative Study of Jonson and Aristophanes* (The Hague and Paris, 1969), p. 132. However, the shape and flavour of Aristophanic situations have a way of recurring in Jonson. Strepsiades, the farmer in *Clouds*, like Sordido, is anxious to escape his financial difficulties, and therefore sends his status-seeking fashionable son Pheidippides (Fungoso) to Socrates' school (Inns of Court) to learn 'wrong argument' (i.e., legal/verbal tricks). After the second parabasis, Strepsiades appears with a calendar, checking off days (like Sordido with his prognostication) until he has to face his creditors and be summoned to court as a crook (cf. Sordido

and his 'precept', 1.3.88ff.) At one point, as a trick to outwit the law, Strepsiades considers hanging himself; by the end of the play, he is 'converted' to love for the gods and rejects selfishness and dishonesty, again like Sordido in 3.2. In *Wasps*, Philokleon, like Sogliardo, is schooled for the salon, but manages to reduce its elegant intellectual refinement to his own vulgar level through bathos and crudity; as at Saviolina's reception, 5.2, the party blows up in the giver's face. The chief difference is in agency; Philokleon deliberately sabotages the occasion, but Sogliardo is merely the dupe of Macilente and the others.

57 Dover, p. 214.
58 Dover, p. 227.
59 Katherine Lever, *The Art of Greek Comedy* (London, 1956), p. 154, points out that *Frogs, Wasps, Clouds*, and *Thesmophoriazusae* articulate views on dramatic poetry based on wide appreciation of Greek literature.
60 See Kenneth McLeish, *The Theatre of Aristophanes* (Bath, 1980), pp. 79–92, for a discussion of the puncturing and restoring of stage illusion.
61 Francis Macdonald Cornford, *The Origin of Attic Comedy* (1934; rpt Gloucester, MA, 1968), pp. 79–81; and Lever, p. 127.
62 Dover, p. 49; and see Cornford, pp. 92–5.
63 Trans. Kenneth McLeish (Cambridge, 1979), p. 26.
64 Trans. Douglass Parker (Ann Arbor, 1961), p. 82.
65 Dover, pp. 51–2.
66 See Stephen C. Young, *The Frame Structure in Tudor and Stuart Drama* (Salzburg, 1974), pp. 125–47; and Thelma Greenfield, *The Induction in Elizabethan Drama* (Eugene, 1969), pp. 67–96.
67 Cornford, p. 92.
68 See Charles Segal, 'Aristophanes' Cloud-chorus', in Erich Segal, ed, *Oxford Readings in Aristophanes*, pp. 165–76; and in the same volume, Oliver Taplin, 'Fifth-century Tragedy and Comedy', pp. 14 and 26, in which Taplin argues that interruption is also a feature of audience rapport (laughter, catcalls, comments) and becomes part of the performance in that the actors have to accommodate audience response.
69 Jeffrey Henderson, *The Maculate Muse: Obscene Language in Attic Comedy* (New Haven, 1975), p. 12. Nevertheless, as Henderson points out in 'Comic Hero Versus Political Elite', in Alan H. Sommerstein, Stephen Halliwell, Jeffrey Henderson, and Bernhard Zimmermann, eds, *Tragedy, Comedy and the Polis* (Bari, 1990), p. 307, the victim of comic abuse is usually rich, powerful, or well-born, not one of the ordinary citizens—unless the citizen gets above himself by wangling an undeserved place among the elite.
70 Henderson, *The Maculate Muse*, pp. 29.
71 *Wit and its Relation to the Unconscious*, trans. A. A. Brill (London, n.d.), p. 233.
72 *Wasps*, p. 26.
73 *Clouds*, pp. 13–14.
74 David Grene, 'The Comic Technique of Aristophanes', *Hermathena* 50 (1937): 89–90.
75 Gum, pp. 146–7. See also *Disc.* 3292–3300.
76 Barish describes other rhetorical parodies in Sordido (3.2), Fallace (4.1), and Brisk (4.5), pp. 108–12.
77 Exceptions may include the parody of Charles Chester in Carlo

Buffone; Steggle, pp. 27–8, argues persuasively for that satirical target. See also Steggle, 'Charles Chester and Ben Jonson', *SEL* 39:2 (spring 1999): 313–26. Clove uses some Marstonian vocabulary, but does not otherwise resemble Marston. The likelihood is that some of the caricatured features in various characters were recognized as personally satiric by at least some of the audience, especially members from the Inns of Court. For further discussion of personal satire see Gum, ch. 6; *H&S* 1.381–4; and Small.

78 Lois Spatz, *Aristophanes* (Boston, 1978), p. 17.

79 Dover, p. 38, remarks on the frequency of this habit in Aristophanes.

80 McLeish, p. 93; and James D. Redwine, 'Beyond Psychology: The Moral Basis of Jonson's Theory of Humours Characterization', *ELH* 28 (1961): 326.

81 Dover, p. 41; and Fisher, esp. p. 180. Henderson, 'The *Dēmos* and the Comic Competition', in Segal, *Oxford Readings in Aristophanes*, adds that in Aristophanes' theatre 'The *dēmos* is here sponsor, spectator, and judge of agonistic performances' (p. 70) and that comic ridicule acts in interest of the *dēmos* as a 'social mechanism' in which 'ridicule is a kind of kangaroo court' (p. 88), exposing errors known to exist in politics or private life, even though legal evidence cannot confirm them.

82 Sir Arthur Pickard-Cambridge, *Dithyramb, Tragedy and Comedy*, rev. T. B. L. Webster (Oxford, 1962), p. 195, describes the traditional sequence of prologue, *parados*, *agon*, *parabasis*, iambic scenes, and *exodos*. Jonson's games with the conventions of comic structure in *EMO* have recently been summed up by Janet Clare, 'Jonson's "Comical Satires" and the Art of Courtly Compliment', in Julie Sanders, with Kate Chedgzoy and Susan Wiseman, eds, *Refashioning Ben Jonson: Gender, Politics and the Jonsonian Canon* (London, 1998), pp. 32–3.

83 Spatz, p. 23.

84 McLeish, p. 158, and Leo Aylen, *The Greek Theatre* (London and Toronto, 1986), pp. 151–4.

85 Dover, pp. 109–10.

86 P. Walcott, 'Aristophanes and Other Audiences', *G&R* 18 (1971): 48; and Katherine Lever, 'Greek Comedy on the Sixteenth-century Stage', *Classical Journal* 42 (1946): 173.

87 Henderson, *The Maculate Muse*, p. 57.

88 *The Art of Greek Comedy*, p. 121. Italics mine.

89 McLeish, p. 159.

90 Aylen, pp. 141–3, concludes on the basis of the fugue analogy: 'We cannot apply rules derived from the comedy of plot [to fifth-century plays]. All we can do is to try and sense each play's own rhythm as a totality.' John M. Potter, 'Old Comedy in *Bartholomew Fair*', *Criticism* 10 (1968): 294, suggests a similar, though rather more geometrical, view of Aristophanic structure: 'A single episode is related not to the other episodes but to a central theme or conflict which is expressed in the agon and the resolution of the play. Thus the structure is not A leads to B leads to C leads to Y, but A, B, and C lead to Y.'

91 Spatz, p. 60; McLeish, pp. 17, 50, 64–9.

92 Cornford, p. 26.

93 Cornford, p. 122. Henderson, 'Comic Hero Versus Political Elite', adds that 'The comic hero's heroism is the achievement of something that ordinary people would have liked to achieve but could not', and that the hero's act is thus *political*: by somehow bypassing an otherwise intractable problem, he assists or improves the state (p. 310). This 'wish-come-true' has its echo in *EMO*'s quasi-political final affirmation in which the queen integrates Macilente seamlessly into the ideal society she represents.

94 Cornford, p. 129.

95 Cornford, pp. 11–13. But this does not necessarily imply the conventional 'happy ending' of comedy: Charles Segal, 'Aristophanes' Cloud-chorus', points out that the abrupt surprise ending of *Clouds* seems to be a reversal of the earlier scenes, but actually maintains the unhappy reversals caused by faulty education (pp. 176–8)—a destructive state of events also evident in *EMO*; and Thomas K. Hubbard, 'Appendix 2: Ben Jonson and the *Clouds* Parabasis', in *The Mask of Comedy: Aristophanes and the Intertextual Parabasis* (Ithaca and London, 1991) pp. 231–42, esp. 239–40, surveys unhappy endings in Jonson's other comedies.

96 Northrop Frye, *Anatomy of Criticism* (Princeton, 1957), p. 170.

97 Cornford, pp. 56, 62. M. S. Silk, 'Aristophanic Paratragedy', in Sommerstein *et al.*, *Tragedy, Comedy, and the Polis*, has defined this kind of typically Aristophanic moment as 'paratragic': without being parodic or even tragic, the moment collides with and dislocates the ordinary comic/satiric context that precedes it, subverting it by offering a positive and recognizably serious alternative point of view (pp. 481, 496). The technique explains why Jonson preferred his original ending, and why he defended its recognizable qualities in his 'Apology'.

98 For the full description of Basileia see the William Arrowsmith translation (Ann Arbor, 1961), p. 95.

99 Frye, p. 172. In practice, of course, these roles are not so clearly differentiated: the protagonist may play the buffoon either partly, like Dionysus in *Frogs*, or almost entirely, like the Sausage-seller in *Knights*, Strepsiades in *Clouds*, and Philokleon in *Wasps*, with a diluted ironist role relegated to the companion or son.

100 Aubrey, pp. 170, 179.

101 *H&S*, 1.182.

102 Finkelpearl, *Histrio-Mastix*, 228, 232. Finkelpearl points out the unlikelihood that a novice's play honouring a playwright of a rival company would have been performed first at Paul's. But see James P. Bednarz, 'Marston's Subversion of Shakespeare and Jonson: *Histriomastix* and the War of the Theaters', *MaRDiE* 6 (1993): 103–28, which postulates a 'close symbiotic relationship' of critical exchange between *Histriomastix* and *EMO*.

103 Stone, pp. 690–2. Margaret Knapp and Michal Kobialka, 'Shakespeare and the Prince of Purpoole: The 1594 Production of The Comedy of Errors at Gray's Inn Hall', *Theatre History Studies* 4 (1984): 70, note: 'The curriculum at the Inns was flexible, largely voluntary, and covered a wide variety of subjects in the arts and humanities as well as law. The

ultimate purpose of the Inns was to develop future statesmen, justices, and scholars, and therefore the students' time was taken up not only with the study of legal subjects, but also with the development of such courtiers' skills as dancing, fencing, writing poetry, and acting in plays and masques.'

104 Finkelpearl, *Temple*, p. 73. But see William J. Bouwsma, 'Lawyers and Early Modern Culture', *American Historical Review* 78 (1973): 303–27: the arrogance was based on very real cultural power, in which the lawyer was the 'secularizer' and 'agent of change' (p. 322) who used the common law as the foundation for order and meaning, peace and prosperity, for all subjects in all classes of the realm.
105 Baker, pp. 79–80; and Marie Axton, 'The Tudor Mask and Elizabeth Court Drama', in Marie Axton and Raymond Williams, eds, *English Drama: Forms and Development* (Cambridge, 1977), p. 32.
106 Helena Watts Baum, *The Satiric and the Didactic in Ben Jonson's Comedy* (Chapel Hill, 1947), p. 33.
107 Paula Glatzer, *The Complaint of the Poet: The Parnassus Plays, A Critical Study of the Trilogy performed at St. John's College, Cambridge, 1598/9–1601/2* (Salzburg, 1977), p. 185.
108 Louis A. Knafla, 'The Matriculation Revolution and Education at the Inns of Court in Renaissance England', in Arthur J. Slavin, ed., *Tudor Men and Institutions: Studies in English Law and Government* (Baton Rouge, 1972), p. 126.
109 Glatzer, p. 199.
110 See Glatzer, pp. 173–84.
111 For an extended description see Finkelpearl, *Temple*, pp. 32–44.
112 *Gesta Grayorum*, ed. W. W. Greg, Malone Society Reprints 41 (Oxford, 1914), p. 22.
113 D. S. Bland, ' "The Night of Errors" at Gray's Inn', *N&Q* 111 (1966): 127–8.
114 M. C. Bradbrook, *The Rise of the Common Player: A Study of Actor and Society in Shakespeare's England* (London, 1962), p. 261.
115 R. B. Parker, 'The Problem of Tone in Jonson's "Comicall Satyrs" ', *Humanities Association Review* 28 (1977): 43, 57–8; and Bradbrook, p. 136.
116 See Bradbrook, ch. 7.
117 Bradbrook, p. 248. Italics mine.
118 R. B. Parker, p. 59.
119 Finkelpearl, in 'The Use of the Middle Temple's Christmas Revels in Marston's *The Fawne*', *SP* 64 (1967): 209, concludes that the revels connection with Marston's work helps define the tone of his play, not as 'dark bitter comedy suffused with sex loathing and disillusion' (a charge often levelled at Jonson as well), but in the 'spirit of revels with their playful irreverence and "solemn foolery" '.
120 *Gesta Grayorum*, pp. 2, 24, 41.
121 *Gesta Grayorum*, p. 12. The puns are typical of Inns of Court jokes: night-service reverses the honourable sense of knight-service, and in *cauda* refers to a legal entail, as well as a piece of sexual tail.
122 Baker, p. 121.
123 *Gesta Grayorum*, pp. 14–18.

124 R. J. Schoeck, 'Inns of Court Nomenclature', *N&Q* (1953): 2–4, and 'Rhetoric and Law in Sixteenth-century England', *SP* 1 (1953): 110–27; Baker, p. 110.

125 Johansson, *Law*, p. 31.

126 Quoted at length in Baker, pp. 133–5.

127 John Hoskyns, ' "Fustian Speech" from *Le Prince d'Amour*', in H. H. Hudson, ed., *Directions for Speech and Style* (Princeton, 1935), appendix B, pp. 111–12.

128 Mark Eccles, 'Francis Beaumont's *Grammar Lecture*', *RES* 16 (1940): 406.

129 Eccles, pp. 408–9.

130 See Ronald J. Corthell, ' "Coscus onely breeds my just offence": A Note on Donne's "Satire II" and the Inns of Court', *John Donne Journal* 6:1 (1987): 25–31.

131 Marie Axton, *The Queen's Two Bodies: Drama and the Elizabethan Succession* (London, 1977), p. 12.

132 Axton, *The Queen's Two Bodies*, p. 61.

133 Stephen Greenblatt, *Renaissance Self-fashioning From More to Shakespeare* (Chicago, 1980), p. 162.

134 Axton, *The Queen's Two Bodies*, pp. 12ff.

135 Greenblatt, p. 166. See also Jean Wilson, *Entertainments for Elizabeth I* (Woodbridge, 1980), pp. 10–15.

136 *Gesta Grayorum*, p. 31.

137 Axton, *The Queen's Two Bodies*, pp. 40–3.

138 Axton, *The Queen's Two Bodies*, pp. 49–50.

139 David M. Bergeron, *English Civic Pageantry 1558–1642* (London, 1971), p. 35.

140 Finkelpearl, *Temple*, p. 59.

141 Bergeron, p. 63.

142 For a more extended discussion of the catastrophe's iconographics see Helen Ostovich, ' "So Sudden and Strange a Cure": A Rudimentary Masque in *Every Man Out of His Humour*', *ELR* 22:3 (1992): 315–32.

143 *H&S*, 9.186. Small's suggestion of February/March for the first public performance does not fit with the dates for court performance. The dates at court are those on which John Heminges was paid for appearances by the Lord Chamberlain's Men, *Declared Accounts*, 543, n. 57. Bednarz, pp. 112–21, argues for an earlier date of late October or early November: according to him, *EMO* was performed first; then Marston based *Histriomastix* on Jonson's invention of the comical satire, especially devising Chrisoganus as an imitative Asper/Jonson and concluding the play with an appearance by the Queen; and Jonson responded to this virtual plagiarism by mocking Marston as 'Clove', a character added to the print version of *EMO* in early 1600. Steggle disagrees in *The Wars of the Theatres*, p. 27. The chief difficulty in making any assertion is the lack of evidence. It is equally possible that Marston saw or heard about *EMO* while Jonson was still writing or while the cast was rehearsing, and tried to 'scoop' Jonson by putting on *Histriomastix* first. I suspect Clove was always part of Jonson's design, and not just a barbed afterthought directed at Marston, from whom Jonson had himself borrowed 'Briscus', englished as 'Brisk'.

144 Robert Gale Noyes, *Ben Jonson on the English Stage: 1660–1776* (Cambridge, MA, 1935), p. 296. The prologue and epilogue written for this performance appear in Appendix D.

145 Noyes, p. 296, citing Downes, *Roscius Anglicanus* (1708), pp. 8–9.

146 Gerard Langbaine, *English Dramatic Poets* (Oxford, 1691), pp. 290–1; and Noyes, p. 297.

147 Richard Hurd, 'Dissertation on the Provinces of the Drama', in *Works (1811)* (Hildesheim, 1969), 2.53.

148 *Bibliographia Dramatica*, rev. and enl. Isaac Reed (to 1782) and Stephen Jones (to 1811) (London, 1812), 2.205.

149 Thomas Davies, *Dramatic Miscellanies* (Dublin, 1784), 2.74; 2.59.

150 Baum, p. 147; Robert P. Knoll, *Ben Jonson's Plays* (Lincoln, 1964), p. 47; Barish, p. 104; George Parfitt, *Ben Jonson: Public Poet and Private Man* (New York, 1976), p. 45; and Anne Barton, *Ben Jonson, Dramatist* (Cambridge, 1984), p. 63; and 'Shakespeare and Jonson', in Kenneth Muir, Jay L. Halio, and D. J. Palmer, eds., *Shakespeare, Man of the Theatre* (Newark, 1983), p. 160. One of the few praisers of the play is Alexander Leggatt, *Ben Jonson: His Vision and his Art* (London, 1981), pp. 190–8.

151 Kay, especially pp. 228–31.

152 On Jonson's immediate influence see Brian Gibbons, *Jacobean City Comedy: A Study of Satiric Plays by Jonson, Marston, and Middleton* (London, 1968), especially ch. 4 on the Comical Satires. For his later influence see among others: R. J. Kaufman, *Richard Brome, Caroline Playwright* (New York, 1961), ch. 3; Albert S. Borgman, *Thomas Shadwell: His Life and Comedies* (New York, 1928); and Pralay Kumar Deb, *Jonson and Congreve: A Study of their Comedies* (Calcutta, 1976).

153 Richard Hosley, 'The Shape and Size of the Second Globe', in C. Walter Hodges, S. Schoenbaum, and Leonard Leone, eds, *The Third Globe* (Detroit, 1981), p. 101. Hosley's measurements apply to the first Globe as well as to the second.

154 D. Cole, *The Theatrical Event: The Mythos, a Vocabulary, a Perspective* (Middletown, 1975), ch. 3, esp. pp. 63–6.

155 As J. W. Saunders remarks in 'Staging at the Globe, 1599–1613', *SQ* 11 (1960): 402, Jonson 'plays with the new theatre like a child with a new toy', filling *EMO* with 'delighted references to the different parts of the "throngèd round"'.

156 After the failure of Beaumont's *The Knight of the Burning Pestle* (1607), self-referentiality on that scale was not attempted again until Buckingham's *The Rehearsal* (1671–5) (significantly, also the time of *EMO*'s revival), and Sheridan's *The Critic* (1779).

157 Rudolph Chris Hassell, *Renaissance Drama and the English Church Year* (Lincoln, 1979), pp. 13, 45, 118.

158 See Neil Rhodes, *The Elizabethan Grotesque* (London, 1980), pp. 138ff., for an extended discussion of this motif.

159 David Klein, 'Time Allotted for an Elizabethan Performance', *SQ* 18 (1967): 434–8.

160 Leo Salingar, 'Comic Form in Ben Jonson: Volpone and the Philosopher's Stone', in Axton and Williams, *English Drama*, p. 52.

161 Freda L. Townsend, *Apologie for Bartholomew Fayre* (1947; rpt New York, 1966), p. 76.

162 Gurr, p. 121.

163 Gurr concludes that there is no discovery-space *per se*, pp. 124–5, 132.

164 Saunders, p. 413, conjectures that two bay windows were located over the stage doors on either side of the platform, with no central balcony. Gurr, p. 134, prefers the idea of a continuous gallery above the platform with window-like openings that might be designated variously as windows, walls, balcony, or terrace, depending on the text. The consensus is with Gurr.

165 Bernard Beckerman, 'The Use and Management of the Elizabethan Stage', in Hodges *et al.*, *The Third Globe*, p. 162.

166 Stephen Orgel, *The Jonsonian Masque* (Cambridge, MA, 1965), pp. 73, 185.

167 Gibbons, pp. 73–4.

168 Stephen Halliwell, 'Aristophanic Satire', *YES* 14 (1984): 18.

169 J. W. Binns, 'Women and Transvestites on the Elizabethan Stage: An Oxford Controversy', *Sixteenth Century Journal* 5 (1974): 101–2.

170 John J. Enck, *Jonson and the Comic Truth* (Madison, 1957), p. 58.

171 Michael Denneny, 'The Privilege of Ourselves: Hannah Arendt on Judgment', in Melvyn A. Hill, ed., *Hannah Arendt: The Recovery of the Public World* (New York, 1979), p. 250. Denneny does not discuss Jonson, but in his discussion of Arendt talks about values embedded in personal and group choices which have a bearing on Jonson's theories of judgement and the development of discrimination through responsible participation in social decisions.

172 Denneny, p. 264. Stanford B. Garner, Jr, *The Absent Voice: Narrative Comprehension in the Theater* (Urbana, 1989), ch. 5, makes a similar argument from the theatrical point of view when he describes *Volpone*, in words that apply equally to *EMO*, as a 'drama of overwhelm', which assaults and accosts its audience with 'the anarchy of possibility': 'Its multiplicity of incident, dramaturgically freed of anticipations and liaisons, gives the play's development in performance a complication always burdened with the imminent and the unknown, and consequently effects an enormous strain on the audience's efforts to organize incident into narrative', a process which constantly forces spectators to lose track of and then recover the play's meaning (pp. 100, 120–1).

173 Steven Mullaney, *The Place of the Stage: License, Play, and Power in Renaissance England* (Chicago, 1988), p. 10.

174 See H&S, 9.444–5, for contemporary details about St Paul's and its denizens. Dekker, *The Gull's Horn-book* (1609), ch. 4, 'How a gallant should behave himself in Paul's Walks', follows Jonson closely.

175 Mullaney, pp. 16–18.

176 Albert Croll Baugh, ed., *William Haughton's 'Englishmen for my Money; or A Woman Will Have her Will'* (Philadelphia, 1917).

177 For a discussion of the babble/Babel trope in Haughton and other dramatists of the period see A. J. Hoenselaars, 'Reconstructing Babel in English Renaissance Drama: William Haughton's *Englishmen for my Money* and John Marston's *Antonio and Mellida*', *Neophilologus* 76 (1992): 464–79. The implications certainly fit Clove and Orange's 'great

scholars' charade, with its incomprehensible references to ancient and modern studies.

178 Stanford B. Garner, Jr, *Bodied Spaces: Phenomenology and Performance in Contemporary Drama* (Ithaca and London, 1994), pp. 53–4, writing of similar practices in Beckett's late plays.

179 Richard Schechner, 'Magnitudes of Performance', in R. Schechner and W. Appel, eds., *By Means of Performance: Intercultural Studies of Theatre and Ritual* (Cambridge, 1990), pp. 27–8. Schechner's anthropological examination of ritual performances in the Third World (chanting, dancing, re-enactments) in particular sanctified places during specific holiday periods has had some influence on my understanding of Jonson's choreography in St Paul's during Shrovetide, but only through my extrapolation, not through Schechner's direct discussion of early modern theatrical practices.

180 'Usually a grave, stately dance in duple time; danced as a processional opening to balls and on other solemn occasions. It appears to have developed from the basse dance, and many variations were current, some of them relatively quick.' See Brissenden, p. 116. Brissenden describes its use as part of ritualized performances at the Inns of Court (pp. 6–7), and in another staged group dance in *Much Ado About Nothing* (pp. 49–52).

181 J. L. Styan, 'Stage Space and the Shakespeare Experience', in Marvin and Ruth Thompson, eds, *Shakespeare and the Sense of Performance: Essays in the Tradition of Performance Criticism in Honor of Bernard Beckerman* (Newark, 1989), pp. 197–8.

182 'A lively dance in triple time with leaping steps and intricate variations; often danced after a pavan. Also called the cinquepace or sinkapace from the French cinq pas (five steps), referring to the five steps which are danced to six beats, the fifth being without a step. The most popular quick court dance for couples in the sixteenth century, it also gave special opportunity for virtuoso solo displays by men dancers.' See Brissenden, pp. 113–14; for its application in *Twelfth Night* see pp. 57–9.

183 P. R. Williams, 'Ben Jonson's Satiric Choreography', *RD* 9 (1978): 138, 145.

184 Rom Harre and P. F. Secord, *The Explanation of Social Behaviour* (Oxford, 1972), pp. 146–51.

185 Richard C. Trexler, 'Introduction', in Richard C. Trexler, ed., *Persons in Groups: Social Behaviour as Identity Formation in Medieval and Renaissance Europe* (Binghamton, 1985), p. 16.

186 Douglas Gray, 'Rough Music: Some Early Invectives and Flytings', *YES* 14 (1984): 24.

187 Harre and Secord, pp. 206–10, attribute the historical origins of this analytical concept to Erasmus, *The Praise of Folly*, and its practical application to Jonson, specifically *The New Inn* (1629). However, social playacting is as much the mode of *EMO*, and is a decisive factor in all of Jonson's plays; cf. *Disc.* 1108–9: 'For though the most be players, some must be *spectators*.'

188 Peter Marsh, 'Identity: An Ethogenic Perspective', in Trexler, *Persons in Groups*, p. 20.

189 Erving Goffman, *The Presentation of Self in Everyday Life* (New York, 1959), p. 46.
190 Harre and Secord, pp. 207–8, on 'role-distance'; Goffman, p. 187, on 'derisive collusion' with one's audience.
191 Goffman, p. 48.
192 Goffman, p. 207.
193 Marsh, p. 29. See also my article on self-labelling subcultural groups, '"Jeered by Confederacy": Group Aggression in Jonson's Comedies', *MaRDiE* 3 (1986), especially 115–16.
194 Ronald F. E. Weissman, 'Reconstructing Renaissance Sociology: The "Chicago School" and the Study of Renaissance Society', in Trexler, *Persons in Groups*, p. 42.
195 Goffman, *Interaction Ritual: Essays on Face-to-face Behaviour* (New York, 1967), pp. 21, 121–2.
196 Marsh, 'Rhetorics of Violence' in Peter Marsh and Anne Campbell, eds, *Aggression and Violence* (Oxford, 1982), p. 108.
197 Marsh, 'Rhetorics of Violence', p. 109.
198 Gray, p. 25.
199 Marsh, 'Rhetorics of Violence', p. 116.
200 See Mario di Gangi's brief discussion of *EMO*'s master–servant relationships in *The Homoerotics of Early Modern Drama* (Cambridge, 1997), pp. 67–72, to which my discussion in this paragraph is partly indebted.
201 Goffman, *Presentation of Self*, pp. 104, 206, 83.
202 Trexler, p. 15.
203 Goffman, *Presentation of Self*, pp. 97–102.
204 Johan Huizinga, *Homo Ludens* (1950; rpt Boston, 1972), p. 12.
205 Konrad Lorenz, *On Aggression*, trans. Marjorie Latzke (1967; rpt London, 1969), p. 253.
206 Cf. Kastril's pursuit of Surly at the end of *Alc.* 4.7; and the Ladies Collegiate's repeated atttacks on Morose in *SW.* See Ostovich, '"Jeered by Confederacy"', pp. 120, 124.
207 Freud, p. 144.
208 Lionel Tiger, *Men in Groups* (London, 1969), p. 131.
209 Goffman, *Presentation of Self*, pp. 212–28.
210 Gray, p. 30.
211 Robert C. Elliott, *The Power of Satire* (Princeton, 1960), p. 85; see also pp. 53–4.
212 Leonard Berkowitz, 'Violence and Rule-following Behaviour', in Marsh and Campbell, p. 92.
213 Goffman, *Presentation of Self*, p. 165.
214 Marsh, 'Rhetorics of Violence', p. 102.
215 Weissman, p. 44.

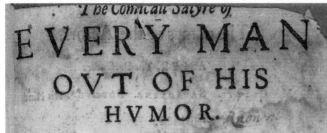

The Comicall Satyre of

EVERY MAN
OVT OF HIS
HVMOR.

AS IT WAS FIRST COMPOSED
by the Author B. I.

Containing more than hath been Publickely Spo-
ken or Acted.

VVith the seuerall Character of euery Person.

Non aliena meo pressi pede | * *si propius stes .*
Te capient magis | * *& decies repetita placebunt .*

LONDON,

Printed for *William Holme,* and are to be sold at his Shop
at Serjeants Inne gate in Fleetstreet.
1600.

Epigraph] The Latin motto, lines 10–11 on the previous page, appears on all the title-pages, *Q* and *F*, but is identified as being by Horace only in the large-paper *F1* and in *F2*. The lines are a slightly altered composite taken from *Epistles* and *Ars Poetica* (*H&S*, 9.396). Cf. the final advertisement following 5.4, which concludes the reading of the play with the same comic-arrogant tone. The borrowings in their original contexts are italicized here: (*a*) from *Epistles* 1.19.21–2: 'Libera per vacuum posui vestigia princeps / *Non aliena meo pressi pede*' ('I was the first explorer who, unguided, made tracks in unknown territory; / *I did not follow in the footsteps of others*'); (*b*) from *Ars Poetica* 361–5: 'Ut pictura, poesis; erit quae, *si propius stes*, / *Te capiat magis*, et quaedam, si longius abstes. / Haec amat obscuram, volet haec sub luce videri, / Judicis argutum quae non formidat acumen: / Haec placuit semel; haec *decies repetita placebit*' ('A poem is like a painting: *if you examine it up close*, / *one will strike you more*; and another, if you stand further back. / One likes to hide in a shadow; another intends to be seen under a light, / unafraid of the critic's piercing scrutiny: / one has pleased a single time; the other *will continue to please after ten repeated viewings*').

The Names of the Actors

[*The Frame*]

ASPER, the Presenter [author of and chief actor in the performance].

GREX [Asper's guests]:

  CORDATUS [ASPER's friend and spokesman].

  MITIS [another friend].

[Prologue, an actor in the Induction].   5

[*The Performance*]

MACILENTE [an envious scholar, played by ASPER].

CARLO BUFFONE [a parasite].

  [A Boy, serving CARLO BUFFONE.]

PUNTARVOLO [a knight].

  His Lady.   10

  [Her] Waiting Gent[lewoman].

  Huntsman.

  Servingmen, two.

  Dog and Cat.

FASTID[IUS] BRISK [a courtier].   15

  SAVIOLINA [a court lady, BRISK's mistress].

The Names] *Q and F present the names of Performance characters in columns according to relationships. In Q, reading downwards, the first column lists six names (upper case)—Macilente, Puntarvolo, Carlo Buffone, Fastidius Brisk, Deliro, and Fallace—and the second lists dependants (lower case, with proper names in italics) related to the first column, connected by large brackets; similarly, the third column lists six names (upper case)—Sordido, Fungoso, Sogliardo, Shift, Clove, and Orange—and the fourth lists bracketed dependants (lower case) of the third column and extras. The exceptions are noted below. The Frame names (Asper at the top and the Grex at the bottom) appear literally as a frame around the names of the characters in Asper's play. In F, the third column has seven names, beginning with Saviolina, and makes no attempt to align the upper-case names in columns one and three; columns one and two are separated from columns three and four by a solid line dividing the list in half.* 1. ASPER] *Q, F (centred separately on the first line).* 2. GREX] *Q, F (centred separately on a line following the columns of names).* 3–4.] *Q, F (centred on the last line).* 9. PUNTARVOLO] *Q;* PVNTERVOLO *F.* 16. SAVIOLINA] *grouped with* BRISK, *this ed.; in Q, begins the second column, apparently to maintain the balance of six names in each of columns one and three; in F, begins the third column.*

99

CINEDO, his Page.
DELIRO [a merchant].
  FALLACE [DELIRO's wife].
  FIDO, their servant.   20
  Musicians.
SORDIDO [a wealthy farmer, DELIRO's father-in-law and father
    of FALLACE and FUNGOSO].
  His Hind.
  Rustici [country bumpkins].
FUNGOSO [a law student, SORDIDO's son and FALLACE's
    brother].   25
  Tailor.
  Haberdasher.
  Shoemaker.
SOGLIARDO [a would-be gentleman, SORDIDO's brother].
  SHIFT [a pimp].   30
CLOVE and ORANGE [coxcombs].
[A Notary.]
[Two] Drawers [at the Mitre Tavern, one named GEORGE].
Constable and Officers.
A Groom.   35
[An Actor portraying the Queen.]

---

17. CINEDO] *Q, F (italic, lower case).*   20. FIDO] *Q, F (italic, lower case).*
23. Hind] *Q;* Hine *Fa;* Hinde *Fb.*   24. *Rustici*] *F; in the last column
grouped with the extras in Q.   After l. 36.] F2 adds:*
    The principal comedians were
    Ric[hard] Burbage.   Joh[n] Hemings.
    Aug[ustus] Philips.   Hen[ry] Condel.
    Will Slye.   Tho[mas] Pope.

[Characters]

ASPER his Character

He is of an ingenious and free spirit, eager and constant in
reproof, without fear controlling the world's abuses; one
whom no servile hope of gain or frosty apprehension of danger
can make to be a parasite either to time, place, or opinion.   5

[CHARACTERS]] *Mostly italic in Q1 and F, except for subtitles giving the names.*
Q1 and F1 head the page with a device.   2. ingenious] *Q1b, F; ingenuous*
Q1a.

Characters] Jonson's satirical sketches prepare the reader for his characters' 'humours', or social and moral flaws in the play. He imitates the style
of Nashe's *Pierce Penniless* (1592) and Lodge's *Wit's Misery* (1596), with their
scoffing racy realism, rather than the measured tone of Theophrastus
(*c.* 371–*c.* 286 BC), Aristotle's most famous pupil, whose works offered models
for the study of Stocism and Neoplatonism in the late sixteenth century.
Jonson was certainly aware of Casaubon's Latin translation of Theophrastus's *Characters*, published in 1592 and reissued, enlarged, in 1599; nevertheless, his own 'Characters', both here and in *CR*, read more like epigrams
on particular persons than studies of universal types. The first deliberate imitation of the Theophrastian *Characters* was Joseph Hall's *Characters of Virtues
and Vices* (1608), followed by the more famous *Characters* of Sir Thomas
Overbury, whose first published collection was appended to the 1614 second
impression of his poem, *The Wife*. See Benjamin Boyce, *The Theophrastan
Character in England to 1642* (Cambridge, MA, 1947).
    1. *ASPER*] a stern faultfinder: 'Aspero, *sharp, sour, rough, craggy, eager,
severe, surly, unpleasant, churlish, rude, austere, hard, grievous, fierce, stubborn,
rigorous, rugged, stinging, biting*' (Florio). Another source for the name lies in
the scholia of Terence, among whose various dissenting voices debating
points of grammar and meaning is Aemelius Asper, a second-century writer
of commentaries subsumed into what are now known as the Donatan
scholia. Jonson's Asper, like Donatus's, comments on the action as 'a stage
equivalent of a marginal gloss' (Steggle, p. 24). See also Steggle, 'Jonson's
Every Man Out and Commentators on Terence', *N&Q* 44 (242):4 (Dec.
1997): 525–6.
    2. *ingenious*] having high intellectual and creative capacity (*OED* 1, 3).
Often, as in *Q1a*, confused with 'ingenuous': having a noble disposition,
honest and frank.
    3. *controlling*] rebuking.
    5. *parasite*] sycophant. See *scurrilous*, 23n below.

MACILENTE

A man well parted, a sufficient scholar, and travelled; who
(wanting that place in the world's account which he thinks his
merit capable of) falls into such an envious apoplexy, with
which his judgement is so dazzled and distasted that he grows   10
violently impatient of any opposite happiness in another.

PUNTARVOLO

A vainglorious knight, over-Englishing his travels, and wholly
consecrated to singularity; the very Jacob's staff of compliment; a sir that hath lived to see the revolution of time in   15
most of his apparel. Of presence good enough, but so palpa-
bly affected to his own praise that (for want of flatterers) he

6. *MACILENTE*] '*lean, meagre, gaunt, barren, thin*' (Florio). These charac-
terisitics are associated with the figure of the malcontent, the ascetic scholarly railer against vice.

7. *well parted*] 'endowed with good natural abilities' (Gifford).

sufficient] (*a*) qualified, capable (*OED* 3); (*b*) used of legal testimony and
documents that are complete, sound, and effective for the designated
purpose (*OED* 2a).

8. *wanting*] lacking.

10. *dazzled*] confounded.

distasted] disgusted.

12. *PUNTARVOLO*] '*a nice, coy, affected, scrupulous, self-conceited fellow*'
(Florio). The name might also be translated as 'gamester' for its association
with gambling games of the period. *Punto* is the ace of trumps, a top card
in *primero*, an early form of *ombre*, the gambling card-game played in Pope's
The Rape of the Lock. In *Bassett*, a card-game that originated in fifteenth-
century Italy and became wildly popular in seventeenth-century England
and France, a punter is a gambler who stakes against the bank: if he is lucky,
he can win a fortune, but he is more likely to lose because of the bank's sta-
tistical advantage. See *Games and Gamesters of the Restoration* (London,
1930), pp. 271–7, 281, and William Andrew Chatto, *The Origin and History
of Playing Cards* (London, 1848), p. 147.

13. *over-Englishing his travels*] over-elaborating the contractual conditions
of his travel wager by attempting to list all contingencies in plain English, as
described at 4.3.1–57.

14. *singularity*] an affectation of eccentricity, 'specially . . . to provoke
beholders' and acquire 'a mark' of notoriety (*Disc.* 701–4).

Jacob's staff] obsolete instrument for taking altitudes (*OED* 2); metaphorically, measuring Puntarvolo's emulation of the high-flown language and
dated manners of chivalry, as at 2.1.196ff.

15–16. *a sir . . . apparel*] a man so old that his clothes have gone completely out of fashion.

16. *presence*] bearing, dignified appearance.

commends himself to the floutage of his own family. He deals
upon returns and strange performances, resolving—in despite
of public derision—to stick to his own particular fashion, 20
phrase, and gesture.

CARLO BUFFONE

A public, scurrilous, and profane jester that, more swift than
Circe, with absurd similes will transform any person into

---

18. *floutage*] mockery.

19. *returns*] returning from hazardous journeys; originally a fashionable
form of gambling at court. The traveller would bet a sum of money that he
would return from his trip in a specific condition or by a certain date; others
would bet that death or accident would prevent the successful completion
of the venture; and the odds might range from two-for-one to five-for-one
(as in the proposal at 2.1.525ff.). Such speculation became common after
1595, when bankrupts and adventurers undertook ridiculous expeditions for
high stakes. See Will Kemp's account of how he danced the morris from
London to Norwich on a wager, in *Kemp's Nine Days' Wonder* (1600); and
Howard, p. 95.

strange performances] bizarre feats undertaken for wagers. The term 'performance' has a quasi-legal sense of executing or discharging a promise
(*OED* 1), like the contract drawn up in 4.3. Cf. *Gesta Grayorum*, p. 39: 'Item,
no Knight of this Order shall put out any money upon strange returns or
performances to be made by his own person; as, to hop up the stairs to the
top of St Paul's, without intermission; or any other such like agilities or
endurances, except it may appear that the same performances or practices
do enable him to some service or employment; as if he do undertake to go
a journey backward, the same shall be thought to enable him to be an Ambassador into Turkey.'

22. *CARLO BUFFONE*] A 'carl' is a common or base fellow, a churl (*OED*
2); probably a reference to Charles Chester, on whom Carlo is loosely based;
see 5.3.200n and Matthew Steggle, 'Charles Chester and Ben Jonson', *SEL*
39.2 (1999): 313–26. 'Buffone' is Italian for 'clown', but also derives from
'bufe', thieves' cant for 'dog'. Carlo is associated with canine terms applied
both to him by others (cf. 'feast-hound or banquet-beagle', 25), and by him
to others (cf. 1.2.214). See introd., pp. 50–1, for discussion of the dog jokes
permeating the play.

23. *scurrilous*] The Roman parasite, or *scurra*, sought out invitations to
dinners of the wealthy (hence, 'feast-hound or banquet-beagle'), and repaid
his hosts by entertaining the party with indiscriminate verbal attacks and
tasteless witticisms, malicious and spiteful in delivery; see Mary A. Grant,
*The Ancient Rhetorical Theories of the Laughable, University of Wisconsin Studies
in Language and Literature* 21 (1924): 95.

24. *Circe*] the sorceress in the *Odyssey* who transformed men into swine.

absurd similes] a feature of the grotesque style, as in Rabelais or Nashe.
Neil Rhodes describes this 'gymnastic verbal performance' as depending on
unlikely analogies, especially to physical incongruities. See *The Elizabethan
Grotesque* (London, 1980), pp. 22–4.

deformity. A good feast-hound or banquet-beagle that will   25
scent you out a supper some three mile off and swear to his
patrons (*God damn me*) he came in oars when he was but
wafted over in a sculler. A slave that hath an extraordinary gift
in pleasing his palate, and will swill up more sack at a sitting
than would make all the guard a posset. His religion is railing,   30
and his discourse, ribaldry. They stand highest in his respect
whom he studies most to reproach.

FASTIDIUS BRISK

A neat, spruce, affecting courtier, one that wears clothes well
and in fashion; practiseth by his glass how to salute; speaks   35
good remnants (notwithstanding the bass-viol and tobacco);
swears tersely and with variety; cares not what lady's favour
he belies, or great man's familiarity: a good property to
perfume the boot of a coach. He will borrow another man's

27. (*God damn me*)] *Q;* (Dam him) *F.*

26–8. *swear . . . sculler*] swear to his hosts, with an oath, that he came to
the party in a large and expensive boat with pairs of oars powered by
oarsmen, when in fact he took cheaper and socially less impressive transport
in a light craft rowed by one man with a light oar, or scull, fixed to the stern
(Grose). Dekker cautions a would-be gallant to 'hate a sculler (remember
that) worse than to be acquainted with one o'th' scullery. No, your oars are
your only sea-crabs' (*Gull's Horn-book* 2.252).

30. *than . . . posset*] than would serve to provide the troops with a drink
of hot milk curdled with ale or wine.

33. *FASTIDIUS BRISK*] In Florio, 'Fastidio' and 'Fastidioso' mean
'*tedious, loathsome*', '*accloying*', and importunate. Onions defines 'Brisk' as
'smartly dressed'. Both Guilpin and Marston apply the term to affected
dandies (Small, p. 185). *H&S* cite two references to Fastidius Brisk in
Burton's *The Anatomy of Melancholy*, suggesting that the name had become
synonymous with the type of the fashionable gallant.

34. *neat*] finical, foppish (Schmidt).
affecting] full of affectation (Schmidt).

35. *practiseth . . . salute*] rehearses elaborate greetings before his mirror.

36. *remnants*] scraps or fragments; used contemptuously of conversation
padded with borrowings, or 'retailing others' wits' in Marston's phrase
(*Scourge of Villainy* IV, 61); e.g., Brisk quotes from Daniel's popular sonnet
sequence to Delia (Small, p. 185).

(*notwithstanding . . . tobacco*)] still continuing his attempts at fashionable
music-making and smoking; see 3.3 for the puncturing effect these have on
Brisk's conversational style, when he fails to impress his mistress.

38–9. *good property . . . coach*] The highly perfumed Brisk would improve
the scent of the air in the recess where attendants sat inside the coach. The
implication is that servants usually smell of sweat or bad breath.

horse to praise, and backs him as his own. Or, for a need, on   40
foot can post himself into credit with his merchant only with
the jingle of his spur and the jerk of his wand.

DELIRO

A good doting citizen, who, it is thought, might be of the
Common Council for his wealth. A fellow sincerely besotted   45
on his own wife, and so rapt with a conceit of her perfections
that he simply holds himself unworthy of her. And in that
hood-winked humour lives more like a suitor than a husband,
standing in as true dread of her displeasure as when he first
made love to her. He doth sacrifice twopence in juniper to her   50

---

40. *praise*] appraise.

backs . . . own] rides the borrowed horse as if he owned it. *Backs* may also
suggest that he uses the horse as a security for loans.

for a need] needing cash.

41. *post*] ride in haste. Although Fastidius's spurs and riding switch
suggest he owns a horse, he travels 'on foot'; cf. the article of behaviour in
the Middle Temple Revels, 1597/8: 'That no Knight go booted and spurred
with a switch or rod, to make men wrongfully suspect that he keeps a great
horse when he hath none' (Baker, p. 154). Carlo's request to view Fastidius's
horse at 2.1.42 is ignored, presumably because the horse does not exist, or
because it is not the fashionable mount he claimed.

42. *jingle of his spur*] Impractical spurs were the symbol of the frivolous
court-gallant, a type Jonson presents as an easy victim of sharpers in *Alc.*:
'bury me a lodestone / To draw in gallants, that wear spurs' (1.3.69–70).

jerk of his wand] flourish of his riding switch. Such a whip was a symbol
of social status, the perquisite of authority at a time when the flogging of
inferiors was endemic (Stone, p. 35).

43. *DELIRO*] '*a fool, a sot, a gull, a dotrell, a swerver from reason, bestraught-
ed of his wit. Also peevish and fond*' (Florio). The name also suggests a pun
on 'lira', Italian money, appropriate for the character of a usurer.

44–5. *of . . . wealth*] rich enough to be on the municipal governing body.

48. *hood-winked humour*] blindfolded, as in the game of Blindman's Buff.
Adults played the game for titillation, as in John Day, *Humour Out of Breath*
4.3, in *The Works of John Day*, ed. A. H. Bullen (London, 1963), p. 463:
'*Florimell*. But how if you take me? as I know that will be your aim? / *Hort-
ensio*. If I take you prisoner, madam, you must either be hood-winked yourself, or give your conqueror a kiss for your ransom.'

50. *made love to her*] wooed her.

juniper] a coniferous evergreen whose seeds and wood were burnt as air
purifiers (*OED* 1); Jonson's metaphor suggests religious incense-burning.
H&S cite Burton's claim that the sweet scent of juniper smoke relieves
melancholy.

every morning before she rises, and wakes her with villainous-
out-of-tune music which she out of her contempt (though not
out of her judgement) is sure to dislike.

FALLACE

Deliro's wife and idol, a proud mincing peat, and as perverse   55
as he is officious; she dotes as perfectly upon the courtier as
her husband doth on her, and only wants the face to be
dishonest.

SAVIOLINA

A court lady whose weightiest praise is a light wit, admired by   60
herself and one more, her servant Brisk.

SORDIDO

A wretched hobnailed chough, whose recreation is reading of
almanacs, and felicity, foul weather. One that never prayed but
for a lean dearth, and ever wept in a fat harvest.   65

51–2. *villainous-out-of-tune music*] Marston's *The Malcontent* begins with
'*The vilest out-of-tune music being heard*', 1.1.0.1. Dekker announces in the
first sentence of *Gull's Horn-book* (2.201): 'I sing . . . to be laughed at',
describing his 'tunes' as 'scurvy noise'. In all three, the sound announces
satirical intention.

54. *FALLACE*] 'Falace, *false, deceivable, deceitful, fraudulent, guileful*'
(Florio). 'Fallacia' suggests illusion, or delusion.

55. *peat*] a petted darling (Onions).

57. *face*] effrontery.

58. *dishonest*] adulterous.

59. *SAVIOLINA*] '*pretty* [somewhat] *wise, wary, or witty. Also nice, coy,
puling, self-conceited, humorous*' (Florio). The name also plays on Vincentio
Saviolo, author of a book on duelling techniques (1558), translated and published in London, 1595. Saviolina is reputedly an acute fencer in matches of
wit.

61. *servant*] admirer.

62. *SORDIDO*] '*a niggard, a palterer, a dodger, a penny-father* [hoarder of
small   change], *a   miser,   a   pinch-penny,   a   covetous   wretch
. . . corrupt, unclean, . . . unhonest*' (Florio).

63. *hobnailed chough*] tedious rustic miser, who would wear hobnailed
boots and chatter like a *chough*, or jackdaw, a bird of the crow family which
repeats whatever it hears, and tends to filch and hoard small objects.

64. *almanacs*] popular calendars that predict weather and crop yields; in
1.3, Sordido relies on his almanac to plan his grain-hoarding.

felicity, foul weather] whose happiness depends on foul weather. Crop
failure enables him to reap huge profits by selling the grain he has hoarded
in anticipation of poor harvests.

65. *lean dearth*] i.e., crop failure.

FUNGOSO

The son of Sordido, and a student: one that has revelled
in his time, and follows the fashion afar off like a spy.
He makes it the whole bent of his endeavours to wring sufficient means from his wretched father to put him in the   70
courtier's cut, at which he earnestly aims, but so unluckily that
he still lights short a suit.

SOGLIARDO

An essential clown, brother to Sordido, yet so enamoured of
the name of a gentleman that he will have it though he buys   75
it. He comes up every term to learn to take tobacco and see
new motions. He is in his kingdom when he can get himself
into company where he may be well laughed at.

---

66. *FUNGOSO*] '*spungy, airy, light, as a mushroom*' (Florio). The implication is that Fungoso (*a*) soaks up the humours of others like a sponge, and
(*b*) is an upstart; cf. 'mushroom gentlemen', 1.2.164.

67. *revelled*] taken part in the revels at the Inns of Court. The revels
included banquets, dances, plays, and witty exercises, and ran approximately
from Christmas to Candlemas, sometimes persisting until Lent (Finkelpearl,
Temple, pp. 34–6).

69–72. *bent, aims, lights*] terms taken from archery: the bow is bent, the
archer takes aim, shoots, and the arrow 'lights' or lands on the target. If it
'lights short', he has fallen short of the target. The archery metaphor also
puns on Fungoso's *bent*, or inclination, for high fashion rather than legal
study; and sets up the law-court joke of his being *short a suit*: he cannot argue
for enough money from his family (*suit* as petition) to keep up with his sartorial aim (the perfect *suit* of clothes).

71. *courtier's cut*] fashion worn by courtiers.

73. *SOGLIARDO*] '*slovenly, sluttish, or hoggish. Also a lubbard, a loggerhead,
a gull, a fool, a flatterer, a cogger*' (Florio).

74. *essential clown*] essentially a boor or rustic.

75–6. *though he buys it*] even if he has to pay for it.

76. *term*] a London law-term, when visitors flocked to town: Hilary
Term, 11–31 January; Easter Term (the 'movable' term because it follows the
church calendar), approximately 15 April to 8 May; Trinity Term, 22 May to
12 June; and Michaelmas Term, 2–25 November (Johansson, *Law*, pp.
15–16).

learn . . . tobacco] Pipe-smoking was a fashionable affectation for would-
be gallants.

77. *motions*] (*a*) puppet-shows; (*b*) applications made to a court or judge
during a court action, to obtain some ruling necessary to the progress of that
action (*OED* 13, 8b). Throughout the play, legal puns often act as extra-
textual in-jokes for the Inns of Court students in the audience.

SHIFT

A threadbare shark. One that never was soldier, yet lives upon   80
lendings. His profession is skeldring and odling, his bank
Paul's, and his warehouse Pict Hatch. Takes up single testons
upon oaths till doomsday. Falls under executions of three
shillings, and enters into five-groat bonds. He waylays the

---

79. *SHIFT*] rogue; cf. 'The Fraternity of Vagabonds ... with a description of the crafty company of Cozeners and Shifters Whereunto also is
adjoined the Twenty-five orders of Knaves, otherwise called a Quartern of
Knaves', by John Awdeley, 1561 (Judges, p. 51). E. A. J. Honigmann argues
that Shift satirically personates John Weever, a hanger-on in Jonson's circle;
see *John Weever: A Biography of a Literary Associate of Shakespeare and Jonson*
(Manchester, 1987).

80. *shark*] sponger and petty swindler (*OED* sb.2).

80–1. *soldier . . . lendings*] Awdeley classifies this confidence trick as the
work of either a 'ruffler' or a 'courtesy-man'. 'A Ruffler goeth with a weapon
to seek service, saying he hath been a servitor in the wars, and beggeth for
his relief', but his trade is robbery, open or disguised. The courtesy-man
ingratiates himself with well-dressed young men or honest citizens, seems
ashamed of his poverty, and begs 'liberality', pleading his war-experience and
his honesty (Judges, pp. 53, 56–7). A proclamation of 1598 'for suppressing
of the multitudes of Vagabonds' specifically addressed the problem of 'able
men, neither impotent nor lame, exacting money continually upon pretence
of service in the wars without relief; whereas many of them never did serve'
(*Proclamations* 2.356, in the BL).

81. *skeldring*] fraudulent begging, especially by rogues posing as wounded
or demobilized soldiers (Gifford, Schmidt).

odling] cheating (*H&S*).

81–2. *his bank Paul's*] his criminal bailiwick is St Paul's Cathedral, a
popular meeting-place for citizens seeking business and leisure, and hence
for confidence tricksters and pickpockets, as in 3.1. Greene's *Cony-catching*
pamphlets describe Paul's as a lair of gentleman-pickpockets (Judges, pp.
1679, 196–9).

82. *warehouse*] safe place where he stores stolen goods.

Pict Hatch] 'a rendezvous of thieves and prostitutes located behind a
turning called Rotten Row [a red light district] on the east side of Goswell
Road'; the name derives from the half-door surmounted by spikes which was
often used in brothels (Chalfant).

Takes up] He borrows.

testons] sixpences.

83. *upon . . . doomsday*] ambiguous: (*a*) Shift swears on the final judgement of his soul to repay the debt; (*b*) he is always swearing to repay, but
never means to do so.

executions] writs of execution, whereby the officer of the court is empowered to seize the goods or person of a debtor in default of payment (*OED* 7).

84. *shillings*] A shilling was worth twelve pence, or one-twentieth of a
pound.

groat] four pence. Shift is a very petty criminal.

reports of services, and cons them without book, damning   85
himself he came new from them, when all the while he was
taking the diet in a bawdy house, or lay pawned in his chamber
for rent and victuals. He is of that admirable and happy
memory that he will salute one for an old acquaintance that
he never saw in his life before. He usurps upon cheats, quar-   90
rels, and robberies which he never did, only to get him a name.
His chief exercises are taking the whiff, squiring a cocatrice,
and making privy searches for imparters.

CLOVE and ORANGE

An inseparable case of coxcombs, city-born; the *Gemini* or   95
twins of foppery: that, like a pair of wooden foils, are fit for
nothing but to be practised upon. Being well flattered, they'll
lend money, and repent when they ha' done. Their glory is to

---

85. *services*] bold and daring military actions (Gifford).

cons . . . book] memorizes them, so that he will seem to be a soldier fresh from the field.

85–6. *damning himself he*] swearing blasphemously that he.

87. *taking the diet*] undergoing a cure for venereal disease.

lay . . . chamber] was forced to stay in his room because he had pawned his clothing.

89. *salute one*] greet a person. Shift pretends to recognize strangers as old friends, as part of his con game.

90. *usurps upon*] wrongfully appropriates, lays false claim to.

92. *exercises*] activities.

taking the whiff] smoking.

squiring a cocatrice] escorting, protecting, and exploiting a whore; pimping.

93. *making privy searches*] looking around covertly.

imparters] a delicate euphemism for persons who will lend or give him money.

94. *CLOVE, ORANGE*] imported aromatic delicacies. Both substances were used in pomanders—scent containers, often shaped like oranges—to perfume the air and inhibit infection from foul odours. The names suggest the men's affectation, effeminacy, and irrelevance to native English manhood. In particular, *Orange* implied 'lover' or 'paramour'; the fruit was associated with the golden apples of the ancients, and hence love or lust. Nashe joked about an alternative mistress, 'leman, or orange' in *Lenten Stuff* 3.197.

95. *case*] pair.

96. *foils*] rapiers.

97. *practised upon*] (*a*) used, like wooden swords, for training bouts; (*b*) fooled, tricked.

feast players, and make suppers; and in company of better
rank (to avoid the suspect of insufficiency) will enforce their   100
ignorance most desperately to set upon the understanding of
anything. Orange is the more humorous of the two; whose
small portion of juice being squeezed out, Clove serves to stick
him with commendations.

CORDATUS   105

The author's friend; a man inly acquainted with the scope and
drift of his plot; of a discreet and understanding judgement;
and has the place of a moderator.

MITIS

Is a person of no action, and therefore we have reason to   110
afford him no character.

99. feast] *Q;* invite *F.*   102–3. whose small portion of juice being
squeezed out] *parenthetical in Q, F. Q and Fa wrongly insert an extra parenthesis—*(being—*cancelled in Fb.   After* 111.] *Device acts as filler in Q, F.*

---

99. *players*] actors.

100. *suspect of insufficiency*] suspicion of intellectual incompetence.

100–1. *enforce their ignorance*] either (*a*) strain their inadequate mental
powers; or (*b*) assert their own stupidity in the attempt to sound learned.

101. *set upon* (*a*) begin working at, attack (*OED* 127, 132c); (*b*) advance
a theory about (*OED* 148d); (*c*) sink or founder in (*OED* 10).

102. *humorous*] preposterous, given to silly self-indulgences or humours.

103–4. *Clove . . . him*] *H&S* cite the housekeeper's practice of suspending
an orange or lemon stuck with cloves over the wine in a cask, in order to
prevent fustiness. When Orange attempts to clear the air with feeble banter,
Clove sticks by him with praise.

105. *CORDATUS*] prudent, wise (Latin). As his testy temper in the induction indicates, he has trouble living up to his name. Like Asper (see note 1
above), Cordatus is another 'assertion of literary affinity' in having the name
of a prominent commentator in the Donatan scholia on Terence (Steggle,
p. 24).

106. *inly*] intimately, deeply.

106–7. *scope and drift*] Nashe used a similar expression in his marginal
gloss on *The Isle of Dogs* in *Lenten Stuff* (1599), 3.153–4: 'I having begun but
the induction and first act of it, the other four acts without my consent, or
the least guess of my drift, or scope, by the players were supplied, which bred
both their trouble and mine too.' Nashe fled into the countryside when
Jonson was arrested for writing those 'other four acts'.

108. *moderator*] arbitrator or judge, deciding issues in, as well as presid-
ing over, the play.

109. *MITIS*] mild; gentle and kind (Latin). But his comments to Cordatus are often wryly ironic.

[ADVERTISEMENT]

It was not near his thoughts that hath published this either to
traduce the author, or to make vulgar and cheap any the peculiar and sufficient deserts of the actors; but rather (whereas   115
many censures fluttered about it) to give all leave and leisure
to judge with distinction.

113–17.] *Roman in Q; not in F.*

112–17.] De Vocht (p. 92) misinterprets this advertisement as meaning
that the play received 'a cold welcome' on stage, because of its too erudite
tone and its thinly veiled criticisms. Jonson himself refers only to objections
raised by the original conclusion of the play. See 'Apology' (Appendix A:I).
   114–15. *any . . . deserts*] any of the distinguished and substantial merits.

Debt → Many playwrights were im-
prisoned for debt — no
guaranteed continuous income.
↳ Counters ie Wood St./Poultry
Canter / Kings Bench →
central part of London life →
central part of the city ... not
places of punishment but
holding pens / spectacle for
tourists or to induce shame.

St Pauls walk — characters humours
are introduced + then emphasised
if St Pauls walk scene →
meeting place for rogues, scholars
to argue, fight, drink + trade —
juxtaposition between location +
social classes

Induction

At the second sounding, [enter] GREX:
ASPER, CORDATUS, [*and*] MITIS.

Cordatus. Nay, my dear Asper—

Mitis.   Stay your mind—

Asper.   Away!

   Who is so patient of this impious world
   That he can check his spirit, or rein his tongue?
   Or who hath such a dead unfeeling sense
   That heaven's horrid thunders cannot wake?   5
   To see the earth, cracked with the weight of sin,

0.1–2.] *This ed.*; Euery man out of his Humor. / *Inductio, sono secundo.* /
GREX. / *Cordatus, Asper, Mitis. Q;* EVERY MAN OVT / OF HIS HVMOVR. / *After
the second Sounding.* / GREX. / CORDATUS, ASPER, MITIS. *F*   1. Asper] *Q,
F. All proper names in Q are italic, and are abbreviated for speech-headings; F uses
roman capitals, also abbreviated for speech-headings.*

0.1. At the second sounding] This musical warning, probably by a trumpeter on the roof above the stage (Gurr, pp. 121, 123), also precedes the induction in *CR* and the speech of Envy in *Poet.* The third sounding announces the prologue (*H&S*). The first sounding apparently warned spectators to take their places.

   GREX] invited guests, or company; perhaps clique (Latin). The term suggests audience rather than chorus, but the kind of audience Jonson expects them to be is made clear in the course of the Induction. Asper acts as a member of the Grex in commenting on the writing and viewing of plays before joining in the performance as an actor.

   0.2.] Although modern editors tend to list characters in the order in which they speak, *Q*'s list suggests the order of appearance. Asper seems to stride on stage pursued by his companions, rejecting their pleas for restraint physically as well as verbally.

   1. *Stay your mind*] Give yourself time to consider; restrain yourself.

   2. *patient*] forbearing, capable of enduring; cf. Macilente's opening speech, 1.1. Both characters inveigh against the stoic habit of mind. *H&S* cite Juvenal, 1.30–1, as the source. Asper's complaint is echoed by Ingenioso '*with Juvenal in his hand*', 2 Return from Parnassus 1.1.90–1: '*Difficile est, Satyram non scribere, namquis iniquae / Tam patiens vrbis, tam ferrens vt teneat se?*' ('It is difficult not to write satire; for who is so forbearing and so tolerant of this unjust city that he can restrain himself?').

   3. *check . . . rein*] terms of horsemanship, meaning 'control'.

Hell gaping under us, and o'er our heads
Black rav'nous ruin with her sail-stretched wings,
Ready to sink us down and cover us:
Who can behold such prodigies as these   10
And have his lips sealed up? Not I. My soul
Was never ground into such oily colours
To flatter vice and daub iniquity,
But with an armèd and resolvèd hand
I'll strip the ragged follies of the time   15
Naked as at their birth—
Cordatus.   Be not too bold—
Asper. You trouble me!—and with a whip of steel
Print wounding lashes in their iron ribs.
I fear no mood stamped in a private brow,
When I am pleased t'unmask a public vice.   20
I fear no strumpet's drugs, nor ruffian's stab,
Should I detect their hateful luxuries;

---

9. us:] *Q, Fa (vs.); vs! Fb.*   11. soul] *Q, Fb;* language *Fa.*   16. birth
—] *Q, F (* birth:*).* Be] *Q;* (Be *F.* bold—] *This ed.;* bold, *Q;* bold. *F.*
17. me!—] *This ed.;* me, *Q;* me) *F.*

---

8. *with . . . wings*] like a bird of prey, ready to swoop on its quarry.
10–11.] Most satirists defend their art as a personally necessary and
socially profitable vent for anger or melancholy; e.g. Lucilius comments that
the satiric spirit demanded some outlet: '*evadat saltem aliquid aliqua*' (Frag.
632); Juvenal explains: '*indignatio facit versum*' (1.79); Puttenham defends
satiric epigrams as purging: 'men would and must needs utter their spleens
in all ordinary matters also or else it seemed their bowels would burst'; both
Nashe (*Strange News* 2.239) and Jonson (*Poet.* 5.1) equate vomiting with
releasing the 'invective vein'. 'The satirist's justification of his genre as a virtuous and admirable means to a catharsis of his own feelings was thus an
integral part of the defense of his work which every satirist, alert to his own
interests, was bound to make sooner or later' (Randolph, pp. 154–6). Whereas
Carlo has his lips sealed up in 5.3, Macilente goes on to complete a cathartic experience and rejoin the Grex as an altered Asper.
12–13.] painting metaphor, illustrating Asper's refusal to be sycophantic:
he cannot draw a pretty picture of an evil society.
15–16. *strip . . . Naked*] Cf. Marston, *Scourge of Villainy* 9.129–30: 'I'll strip
you nak'd, and whip you with my rhymes, / Causing your shame to live to
after times'.
17. *You trouble me!*] directed at Cordatus for interrupting.
19–20.] Cf. Marston, *Scourge of Villainy* 10.5–6: 'I dread no bending of an
angry brow, / Or rage of fools that I shall purchase now'.
21. *drugs*] poisons.
22. *luxuries*] lusts.

No broker's, usurer's, or lawyer's grip,
Were I disposed to say they're all corrupt.
I fear no courtier's frown, should I applaud   25
The easy flexure of his supple hams.
Tut, these are so innate and popular
That drunken Custom would not shame to laugh
In scorn at him that should but dare to tax 'em.
And yet, not one of these but knows his works,   30
Knows what *damnation* is, the *devil*, and *hell*,
Yet hourly they persist, grow rank in sin,
Puffing their souls away in perj'rous air
To cherish their extortion, pride, or lusts.
Mitis. Forbear, good Asper. Be not like your name. 35
Asper. O, but to such, whose faces are all zeal,
And with the words of Hercules invade
Such crimes as these; that will not smell of sin
But seem as they were made of sanctity—
Religion in their garments, and their hair   40
Cut shorter than their eyebrows—when the conscience
Is vaster than the ocean, and devours

---

29. 'em] *Q, F ('*hem*). All instances of this word, too frequent to list, have been modernized in the same way.*   39. sanctity—] *This ed.;* Sanctitie; *Q;* Sanctity! *F.*   41. eyebrows—] *This ed.;* eie-browes; *Q;* eye-browes! *F.*

---

23. *grip*] extortionate hold.
26.] his frequent bowing, the sign of a toady.
27. *popular*] common and vulgar.
28-9.] that habitually debauched behaviour is so brazen that it invites open laughter at satirists who attack vice.
32. *rank*] grossly luxuriant, corrupt, foul-smelling, coarsely licentious.
33. *perj'rous*] lying.
35. *name*] a stern faultfinder; cf. Chars.1n.
36. *zeal*] used particularly of Puritan religious enthusiasm.
37. *with . . . Hercules*] ranting insanely like Hercules in his madness. Jonson, like his source, Juvenal (2.19–20), registers contempt for what he considers a travesty of Hercules's moral and rhetorical strength. He may also be thinking of the Globe Theatre's sign, Hercules bearing the globe on his shoulders; the words of Hercules would then refer to actors' lines, an appropriate analogy for hypocrites (Greek *hupokrites*, actor).
38. *that . . . sin*] who piously and hypocritically profess purity.
40-1. *hair . . . eye brows*] referring to the Puritan hairstyle, but the phrase is Juvenal's (2.14–15), describing the affectations of homosexuals posing as Stoics. For both writers the target is hypocrisy.

More wretches than the Counters!

Mitis.   Gentle Asper,
Contain your spirit in more stricter bounds,
And be not thus transported with the violence   45
Of your strong thoughts.

Cordatus.   Unless your breath had power
To melt the world and mould it new again,
It is in vain to spend it in these moods.

Asper. I not observed this throngèd round till now.
                              Here he makes address to the people.
Gracious and kind spectators, you are welcome.   50
Apollo and the Muses feast your eyes
With graceful objects; and may our Minerva
Answer your hopes unto their largest strain.
Yet here mistake me not, judicious friends:
I do not this to beg your patience,   55
Or servilely to fawn on your applause,

49.1] *Fa, appearing at 48.1; cancelled in Fb; not in Q.*

---

43. *Counters*] or Compters, the two city prisons regulated by the sheriffs
of London, primarily for debtors, but accommodating felons as well if the
Newgate and Ludgate prisons were full. Asper castigates the Puritans for
condemning, with their repressive notions of 'conscience', more Londoners
than could be crammed into the city's jails.

49. *I not observed*] The non-periphrastic construction of a negative statement was common in the sixteenth century, but more usually the negative
followed the verb (Partridge, *Syntax*, p. 9).

round] audience area of the Globe Theatre.

51. *Apollo and the Muses*] Apollo, the Greek sun god, was also god of
enlightenment, associated particularly with music and poetry; hence the nine
Muses, representing various studies in the arts.

52. *Minerva*] Roman goddess of wisdom, corresponding to the Greek
goddess Pallas Athene, known for her sound judgement in the arts of both
war and peace. Her association with Apollo and the Muses is indirect in classical literature, but Jonson is drawing on the Inns of Court tradition of
Minerva as a symbol of the Queen's body politic, and the lawyers as servants
of Minerva, hence, public servants who had special licence both to advise
the Queen and to entertain her in the revels with dancing and plays. Thomas
Blenerhasset's *Revelation of the True Minerva* (1582), which may be an
embroidered account of an Inner Temple revels, presents her as a figure of
immortality and heavenly wisdom, symbolizing the Queen as head of both
church and state, and associating her with the Muses, the Graces, and the
Nine Worthies. See Marie Axton, *The Queen's Two Bodies: Drama and the
Elizabethan Succession* (London, 1977), pp. 39–51, 67–9.

53. *unto . . . strain*] to the utmost.

Like some dry brain despairing in his merit.
Let me be censured by th'austerest brow
Where I want art or judgement. Tax me freely.
Let envious critics with their broadest eyes   60
Look through and through me. I pursue no favour.
Only vouchsafe me your attentions,
And I will give you music worth your ears.
O, how I hate the monstrousness of time,
Where every servile imitating spirit   65
(Plagued with an itching leprosy of wit)
In a mere halting fury strives to fling
His ulc'rous body in the Thespian spring
And straight leaps forth a poet, but as lame
As Vulcan or the founder of Cripplegate!   70

60. critics] *Q (Critickes);* censors *F.*

58–63.] Asper challenges all critics to attempt to discredit his work. Being 'censured' did not imply only adverse criticism; cf. Marston's praise of 'True-judging eyes, quick-sighted censurers' in '*In Lectores prorsus indignos*', 87, *Scourge of Villainy.*

59. *art or judgement*] not equations but alternatives, though closely linked: the writer shows art in his conception and expression, judgement in his handling of his material.

Tax] censure, assess, charge.

60. *envious*] carping.

broadest eyes] most sweeping and comprehensive gaze.

65. *imitating*] plagiarising.

66–9. *Plagued, itching leprosy, ulc'rous, lame*] Formal verse satires, epigrams, comical satires, and satiric comedies depict human vices and follies through metaphors of venereal diseases (characterized by itching), plague, leprosy, and varieties of festering growths and deformities—all were physical commonplaces, transposed for satirical purposes (Randolph, pp. 136–7).

67. *halting*] lame, defective; cf. Marston, *Scourge of Villainy* 5.18: 'Rude limping lines fits this lewd halting age.'

68. *Thespian spring*] the Muses' fountain of poetic inspiration, as in *Disc.* 2488–91. Jonson mixes this classical reference with the tradition of biblical rivers like the Jordan in which diseased pilgrims immersed themselves for cure.

69. *straight*] straightaway, instantly.

70. *Vulcan*] Hephaestus, Greek god of the forge, crippled when Zeus hurled him out of Olympus.

founder of Cripplegate] According to popular legend, Cripplegate, one of the seven gates in the London Wall, was constructed by a lame beggar, rich from alms-gathering. The church of St Giles-Cripplegate, named for the patron saint of cripples, stood just north of the Cripplegate postern; *H&S* cite the myth of St Giles's refusal to be cured of lameness himself, 'so that

Mitis. In faith, this humour will come ill to some.
　　You will be thought to be too peremptory.
Asper. 'This humour'? Good. And why 'this humour', Mitis?
　　Nay, do not turn, but answer.
Mitis.　　　　　　　　　　Answer? What?
Asper. I will not stir your patience. Pardon me.　　　　75
　　I urged it for some reasons, and the rather
　　To give these ignorant well-spoken days
　　Some taste of their abuse of this word *humour.*
Cordatus. O, do not let your purpose fall, good Asper.
　　It cannot but arrive most acceptable,　　　　　　　80
　　Chiefly to such as have the happiness
　　Daily to see how the poor innocent word
　　Is racked and tortured.
Mitis.　　　　　　　Ay, I pray you proceed.
Asper. Ha? What? What is 't?
Cordatus.　　　　　　　For the abuse of humour.
Asper. O, I crave pardon. I had lost my thoughts.　　　85
　　Why, *humour* (as 'tis, *ens*) we thus define it
　　To be a quality of air or water,

---

he might mortify the flesh more effectively'. The church was actually founded
by Alfun in the eleventh century; see Philip Norman, 'London City Churches
that Escaped the Great Fire', *London Topographical Record* 5 (1908): 99–109.
Stow (p. 32) claims a tradition, unsubstantiated, of miraculous cures for the
many cripples in the area. Hoy (1.57) notes a similar image of the lame imi-
tator of other men's ideas in Dekker's *The Seven Deadly Sins* (1606).

　71. *come ill*] seem offensive.

　72. *peremptory*] (*a*) dogmatic or obstinate (*OED* 3, 4); (*b*) arbitrarily dismissive of another opinion; based on the legal term applied to one-sided but
binding objections or writs (*OED* 1).

　73. *'This humour'*] pointed mimicry of Mitis's casual use of the word at
71. In response, Mitis turns away, perhaps in embarrassment, or even irritation, until Asper apologizes at 75.

　77. *well-spoken*] derisively, of the 'refined' speech fashionable among the
ill-educated but upwardly mobile social set.

　81. *happiness*] strength of mind.

　84. *Ha? . . . What is 't?*] Absorbed in contemplation of verbal abuses,
Asper has apparently not heard the last five lines.

　86–112.] Here Jonson distinguishes between a physiological disruption in
the four humours (see 97) that may distort personality, and the superficial
love of 'singularity', affectation in dress or manner.

　86. *ens*] a school term, signifying a substance or existence (Whalley), and
used to herald an answer or definition.

And in itself holds these two properties:
Moisture and fluxure. As for demonstration,
Pour water on this floor, 'twill wet and run;   90
Likewise, the air, forced through a horn or trumpet,
Flows instantly away, and leaves behind
A kind of dew; and hence we do conclude
That whatsoe'er hath fluxure and humidity,
As wanting power to contain itself,   95
Is *humour*. So, in every human body,
The choler, melancholy, phlegm, and blood,
By reason that they flow continually
In some one part and are not continent,
Receive the name of humours. Now thus far   100
It may by metaphor apply itself
Unto the general disposition;
As when some one peculiar quality
Doth so possess a man that it doth draw
All his affects, his spirits, and his powers   105
In their confluxions all to run one way:
This may be truly said to be a *humour*.
But that a rook, in wearing a pied feather,
The cable hatband, or the three-piled ruff,

---

93. dew] *Qb, F;* due *Qa.*

---

89. *fluxure*] fluidity.

93. *dew*] condensation.

99. *not continent*] incontinent; not readily restrained, flowing.

105. *affects*] feelings.

106. *confluxions*] actions of flowing together; a Latin neologism invented by Jonson.

108. *rook*] lout; literally, a raucous-voiced bird of the crow family, which nests in dense colonies.

pied feather] parti-coloured plume, perhaps dyed to match a costume. Feathers 'peaking on top of their heads', as Stubbes put it, were fashionable on the headgear of both sexes, particularly at court (Linthicum, p. 221, citing *Anatomy of Abuses* (ed. Furnivall), p. 50).

109. *cable hatband*] a twisted cord of gold, silver, or silk worn around the hat (*H&S*).

three-piled ruff] fashionable multi-layered ruff which, instead of extending at right angles to the neck, hung down from the top of a high stock fastened up to the chin (Linthicum, p. 160).

A yard of shoe-tie, or the Switzer's knot   110
    On his French garters, should affect a humour,
    O, 'tis more than most ridiculous!
Cordatus. He speaks pure truth. Now if an idiot
    Have but an apish or fantastic strain,
    It is his humour.
Asper.   Well, I will scourge those apes,   115
    And to these courteous eyes [*Indicating audience*]
        oppose a mirror
    As large as is the stage whereon we act,
    Where they shall see the time's deformity
    Anatomized in every nerve and sinew,
    With constant courage and contempt of fear.   120
Mitis. Asper—I urge it as your friend—take heed:
    The days are dangerous, full of exception,
    And men are grown impatient of reproof.

---

113. truth. Now] *This ed.;* truth: now *Q;* truth now *F.*

---

110. *A yard of shoe-tie*] A fashionable shoe lace required a yard to a yard
and a half of ribbon (Linthicum, p. 243). A lady's shoe-tie was worn by her
lover as a conspicuous sign of favour; Brisk wears Saviolina's as an earring
(2.1.482–3).

Switzer's knot] a style worn by Swiss soldiers: the garter was tied below
the knee in a thickly knotted bow of two or three loops, the ends hanging
down the calf; illustrated in James Robinson Planche, *A Cyclopaedia of
Costume* (London, 1879), 2.200.

111. *French garters*] probably of silk or taffeta, rather than English worsted
or crewel. Men's garters were like small sashes, costing a pound or more,
depending on the decoration: gems, spangles, embroidered flowers, gold
fringe, or lace (Linthicum, p. 263).

115–19. *scourge, mirror, Anatomized*] Images of the body, especially
medical imagery, characterize Renaissance satire as 'a scourge, a whip, a
surgeon's scalpel, a cauterizing iron, a strong cathartic all in one; its mission
is to flay, to cut, to burn, to blister, and to purge; its object is now a culprit,
a victim, a criminal, and now an ailing, submissive patient, a sick person
bursting with contagion; and the satirist himself is a whipper, a scourger, a
barber-surgeon, an executioner, a "doctour of physick"' (Randolph, p. 125).
H&S cite Marston's *Scourge of Villainy* (1598); Baldwin's *Mirror for Magis-
trates* (1559); Stubbes's *Anatomy of Abuses* (1583); and Nashe's *Anatomy of
Absurdity* (1589).

116. *oppose*] set opposite to their gaze, where they may see themselves.

122. *exception*] (*a*) objection, faultfinding (*OED* 6); (*b*) in law, objection
that limits or bars an opponent's court action because of countervailing
rights or insufficient evidence (*OED* 4).

Asper. Ha, ha!

You might as well have told me yond [*Pointing to roof*
    over stage] is heaven,   125
This [*To platform*] earth, these [*To stage posts*] men, and
    all had moved alike.
Do not I know the time's condition?
Yes, Mitis, and their souls, and who they be
That either will or can except against me?
None but a sort of fools, so sick in taste   130
That they contemn all physic of the mind,
And like galled camels kick at every touch.
Good men and virtuous spirits that loathe their vices
Will cherish my free labours, love my lines,
And with the fervour of their shining grace   135
Make my brain fruitful to bring forth more objects
Worthy their serious and intentive eyes.
But why enforce I this? As fainting? No.
If any here chance to behold himself,
Let him not dare to challenge me of wrong,   140
For, if he shame to have his follies known,
First he should shame to act 'em. My strict hand
Was made to seize on vice, and with a grip
Crush out the humour of such spongy souls
As lick up every idle vanity.   145

124. Ha, ha!] *Q; an extrametrical foot at end of the previous line in F.*
138. this?] *F; this, Q.*   144. Crush] *Q; Squeeze F.* souls] *Q, Fa; natures*
Fb.

---

129. *except against*] make an objection against.
130. *sort of fools*] group or gathering of fools; cf. *Stultorum plena sunt omnia*
('All places are full of fools'), used as an epigraph both by Marston, *Scourge*
of Villainy 9, and by Dekker, *Gull's Horn-book.*
131. *contemn*] scorn, disdain.
physic] medicine.
132. *galled*] made sore by chafing.
137. *intentive*] paying assiduous attention.
138. *enforce*] argue forcibly, with a secondary sense of compelling the
observance of a law (*OED* 14).
fainting] (*a*) in law, 'Faint pleading is a covenous, false, and collusory
manner of pleading to the deceit of a third party' (*OED, Faint* 1b); (*b*) sham-
ming or feinting, as in fencing and boxing, threatening a thrust or blow in
order to divert attention from the real point of attack.
140. *challenge*] (*a*) accuse (*OED* 1); (*b*) in law, to object or take exception
to (*OED* 3).

Cordatus. Why, this is right *furor poeticus!*
  [*To audience*] Kind gentlemen, we hope your patience
  Will yet conceive the best, or entertain
  This supposition: that a madman speaks.
Asper. [*To actors off-stage*] What? Are you ready there?—Mitis,
    sit down,   150
  And my Cordatus.—[*Calling to trumpeters*] Sound, ho,
    and begin!—
  I leave you two as censors to sit here,
  Observe what I present, and liberally
  Speak your opinions upon every scene,
  As it shall pass the view of these spectators.   155
  [*Calling*] Nay now, you're tedious, sirs. For shame,
    begin!—
  And, Mitis, note me if in all this front
  You can espy a gallant of this mark,
  Who (to be thought one of the judicious)
  Sits with his arms thus wreathed, his hat pulled here,   160
  Cries mew, and nods, then shakes his empty head,
  Will show more several motions in his face

---

151. Sound, ho] *Q* (Sound hoe); Sound hough *F.* 161. mew] *Q, F* (meaw).

---

146. furor poeticus] inspired frenzy attributed to poets; cf. the poet's name in *2 Return from Parnassus.*

151. *Sound, ho!*] probably a request for the third sounding, nevertheless delayed until 283; cf. 211: 'I'll haste them sound.' *F*'s reading of 'hough'—usually pronounced 'hock'—means 'clear the throat of phlegm'; a possible gibe at the actors. *Q*'s spelling simply suggests an interjection to attract attention.

152. *censors*] judges.

157. *note me*] note, or note for my sake. The 'me' is ethical dative, indicating a person to whom the verb bears indirect application.

front] collectively, the faces of the audience (*OED* 2, 3).

160. *arms thus wreathed*] Asper folds his arms, demonstrating the posture of melancholy; see T. W. Craik, 'Reconstruction of Stage Action', *Elizabethan Theatre* 5 (1975): 87.

his hat . . . here] hat-brim pulled over the eyes, another conventional pose of melancholy, as in *LLL* 3.1.14–15: 'with your hat penthouse-like o'er the shop of your eyes'.

161. *Cries mew*] makes a derisive catcall or bird-like jeer (*OED, Mew* int. and sb.3).

162. *several*] various.

162–3. *motions . . . Nineveh*] puppet-shows; frequently burlesques of

Than the new London, Rome, or Nineveh,
And now and then breaks a dry biscuit jest,
Which, that it may more easily be chewed,   165
He steeps in his own laughter.
Cordatus.   Why? Will that
Make it be sooner swallowed?
Asper.   O, assure you!
Or, if it did not, yet as Horace sings:
Jejunus rare stomachus vulgaria temnit;
'Mean cates are welcome still to hungry guests'.   170
Cordatus. 'Tis true, but why should we observe 'em, Asper?
Asper. O, I would know 'em, for in such assemblies
They're more infectious than the pestilence,
And therefore I would give them pills to purge,
And make 'em fit for fair societies.   175
How monstrous and detested is 't to see
A fellow that has neither art nor brain
Sit like an Aristarchus, or stark ass,
Taking men's lines with a tobacco face,

---

plays, like the puppet-play in *BF* 5.4. *H&S* identify 'Nineveh' as a produc-
tion of the Jonah and the whale scene from Lodge and Greene's *A Looking
Glass for London and England* (1598); and 'Rome' as a travestied version of
Julius Caesar, mentioned in other plays of the period.

164. *dry biscuit jest*] stale joke; refers to the alehouse practice of floating
dry bread or toast in mugs of ale as a bar-snack (cf. 5.3.26–7). Shakespeare
uses a similar metaphor in *AYL* 2.7.39–40 when Jaques describes Touch-
stone's brain as being 'as dry as the remainder biscuit / After a voyage'.

166. *steeps*] soaks; see previous note.

169–70.] from Horace, *Satires* 2.2.38 (*H&S*). Jonson's translation is free;
more literally, 'A hungry stomach rarely despises meals'.

170. *Mean cates*] humble fare.

still] always.

174. *pills to purge*] emetics or laxatives, picking up on the medical imagery
found earlier at 115–19 (see note).

177. *art*] the playwright's skills, e.g., in language.

178. *Aristarchus*] Aristarchus of Samothrace, *c.* 217–145 BC, the Greek
scholar who wrote commentaries on several playwrights. Asper clearly considers him a model of the bad critic, as indicated by his deliberate mispro-
nunciation of the name as *or stark ass*.

179–80. *Taking . . . In snuff*] taking offence at or exception to lines
spoken in the play. Snuff originally meant the unpleasant smell from the

In snuff, still spitting, using his wried looks, 180
In nature of a vice, to wrest and turn
The good aspect of those that shall sit near him
From what they do behold! O, 'tis most vile!
Mitis. Nay, Asper—
Asper. Peace, Mitis. I do know your thought:
You'll say, 'Your audience will except at this!' 185
Pish! You are too timorous and full of doubt.
Then he, a patient, shall reject all physic
'Cause the physician tells him, 'You are sick';
Or, if I say that he is vicious,
You will not hear of virtue. Come, you're fond. 190
Shall I be so extravagant to think
That happy judgements and composèd spirits
Will challenge me for taxing such as these?
I am ashamed.
Cordatus. Nay, but good pardon us.
We must not bear this peremptory sail, 195
But use our best endeavours how to please.
Asper. Why, therein I commend your careful thoughts,
And I will mix with you in industry
To please—but whom? Attentive auditors,

185. 'Your audience . . . this!'] *Q (your . . . this?);* your guests here will except at this: *F.*

---

smoking snuff of a candle, but here refers to the acrid smell of tobacco, and hence a sniff of disgust. The 'tobacco face' and 'spitting' are contortions associated with pipe-smoking.

180. *wried*] twisted, contorted.

185. *except at*] take exception to, object to; cf. 129, *except against.*

186. *Pish!*] explosive sound of contempt.

187–90.] 'If a listener rejects my good advice, he is like a patient refusing to accept a medical diagnosis of his own illness; or if I attack his vices, you'll defend him by saying that I mustn't preach about "virtue".'

190. *fond*] crazy, foolish.

194. *I am ashamed*] I am ashamed of (or for) you.

good] (*a*) intensifies the apology; (*b*) possibly a vocative, meaning 'good sir' (cf. *Tp.* 1.1.3: 'Nay, good, be patient'); (*c*) corruption of 'God'. Cordatus has little reason for apologizing except as an intercession for Mitis, under attack for seeming to disagree with Asper. If 'God pardon us' is the correct reading, it represents a mild imprecation to lower the pitch of the conversation.

195. *bear . . . sail*] sail on peremptorily, disregarding the audience's sensibilities.

Such as will join their profit with their pleasure,   200
And come to feed their understanding parts.
For these, I'll prodigally spend myself,
And speak away my spirit into air;
For these I'll melt my brain into invention,
Coin new conceits, and hang my richest words   205
As polished jewels in their bounteous ears.
But stay, I lose myself and wrong their patience.
If I dwell here, they'll not begin, I see.
Friends, sit you still and entertain this troop [*Gesturing to audience*]
With some familiar and by-conference.   210
I'll haste them sound. [*To audience*] Now, gentlemen, I go
To turn an actor and a humorist,
Where (ere I do resume my present person)
We hope to make the circles of your eyes
Flow with distillèd laughter. If we fail,   215
We must impute it to this only chance:
'Art hath an enemy called Ignorance'.   *Exit.*

207. lose] *Q, F (* loose*).*

---

200. *profit . . . pleasure*] Jonson frequently repeated this maxim, derived from the *Ars Poetica* and perpetuated by Sidney and other Renaissance critics (see *H&S*).

203.] and use up my creative energy delivering speeches.

204. *melt . . . invention*] distil my imagination into new dramatic form.

205. *conceits*] dramatic concepts, fancies.

207. *their patience*] the audience's patience.

208. *they'll not begin*] The actors won't enter while the author is still on stage. Besides, Asper must change costume to play Macilente, the part that opens 1.1.

210. *by-conference*] chitchat; idle talk.

211. *I'll haste them sound*] I'll have the musicians play the third sounding. With this tactic, Asper will force the Prologue to begin, giving himself some time to dress as Macilente. Nevertheless, the third sounding is delayed until 283.

212. *humorist*] (*a*) person subject to 'humours' or fancies (*OED* 1); (*b*) facetious or humorous talker, actor, or writer (*OED* 2, citing this passage as its earliest instance).

216. *only*] sole, single.

217.] In Nashe, *The Anatomy of Absurdity*: 'Science hath no enemy but the ignorant'. McKerrow (4.31) traces the proverb to the *Adagia* of Gilbertus Cognatus: '*Ignorantia scientiae inimica*' ('Ignorance and knowledge are enemies'). Quotation marks do not necessarily indicate actual quotation from another work, but may simply lend conspicuity and authority to *sententiae*, either invented by Jonson or in the public domain.

Cordatus. How do you like his spirit, Mitis?

Mitis. I should like it much better if he were less confident.

Cordatus. Why, do you suspect his merit? 220

Mitis. No, but I fear this will procure him much envy.

Cordatus. O, that sets the stronger seal on his desert. If he had no enemies, I should esteem his fortunes most wretched at this instant.

Mitis. You have seen his play, Cordatus? Pray you, how is 't? 225

Cordatus. Faith, sir, I must refrain to judge. Only this I can say of it: 'tis strange and of a particular kind by itself, somewhat like *Vetus Comedia*: a work that hath bounteously pleased me. How it will answer the general expectation, I know not. 230

Mitis. Does he observe all the laws of comedy in it?

Cordatus. What laws mean you?

Mitis. Why, the equal division of it into acts and scenes, according to the Terentian manner; his true number of actors; the furnishing of the scene with *grex* or chorus; 235 and that the whole argument fall within compass of a day's efficiency.

---

237. efficiency] *Q;* business *F*

221. *envy*] hostile ill-will, malice.

222. *that . . . desert*] i.e., the jealousy of Asper's detractors merely confirms his merit. Asper is fortunate in having such foolish enemies.

228. Vetus Comedia] Old Comedy, the Greek comedy that culminated in the plays of Aristophanes, in which the chorus alternately punctured and upheld dramatic illusion; plots were fantastic, loosely constructed, and unrestricted by time or place; and the wit was personally satiric, generally irreverent, and sexually crude. For further discussion, see introd., pp. 18–28.

231. *laws of comedy*] Here follows a survey of the development of the comic form in which Jonson sees the playwright's guiding principle as intelligent innovation, based on a synthesis of his predecessors' achievements and an understanding of the spirit of his own times.

234. *according . . . manner*] in the manner of Terence (195–159 BC), the Roman playwright whose practice in writing comedy derived largely from the New Comedy of Menander (see 256n below). Terence, however, divided his plays into five acts; he also invented a new style of prologue that dealt with literary criticism, and avoided monologues by adding listeners on stage to provoke dialogue (as Mitis and Cordatus do when they speak to Asper). Generally Terence's style (like Jonson's) resembles everyday conversation and thus seems to promote stage realism (*OCD*).

236. *argument*] plot.

237. *efficiency*] operative agency (*OED* 1).

Cordatus. O no, these are too nice observations.

Mitis. They are such as must be received, by your favour, or
it cannot be authentic.   240

Cordatus. Troth, I can discern no such necessity.

Mitis. No?

Cordatus. No, I assure you, signor. If those laws you speak of
had been delivered us *ab initio* and in their present virtue
and perfection, there had been some reason of obeying   245
their powers. But 'tis extant that that which we call
comedia was at first nothing but a simple and continued
satire, sung by one only person, till Susario invented a
second; after him Epicharmus a third; Phormus and
Chiomides devised to have four actors, with a prologue   250
and chorus, to which Cratinus long after added a fifth

---

248. satire] *Q;* Song *F.*

---

238. *nice*] (*a*) foolish (*OED* 1); (*b*) strict or fastidious in literary taste
(*OED* 7c).

239. *received*] adopted.

by your favour] excuse me, with your permission; forgive me for differing
with you.

244. *ab initio*] from the beginning.

virtue] (*a*) superiority or excellence; (*b*) vigour.

246. *extant*] manifest; usually part of a phrase in early usage: 'extant to
the sight, to be seen' (*OED* 2).

248. *satire*] a sprawling, inclusive term, but mainly meant '(1) a poem, (2)
approaching and practically synonymous with invective, (3) whose mission
is didactic—the reprehension of vice and folly' (Randolph, p. 126).

248ff.] *H&S* point out that Jonson's history of the number of actors in
Greek comedy is a Renaissance invention; 'Aristotle expressly says in the
Poetics (5.3) that nothing is known on the subject'. Most of the poets he cites
are lost to posterity, except as names in commentaries.

Susario] Susarion of Megara is supposed to have originated comedy in
Attica, between 581 and 560 BC. However, he probably was not from Megara,
the only known quotation from his work is probably not authentic, and the
name itself is probably fictitious (*OCD*).

249. *Epicharmus*] Sicilian writer, active between 500 and 470 BC. He
wrote Doric comedy that was as colourful and sophisticated as Attic comedy,
with which it has been only hypothetically connected (*OCD*).

Phormus] Syracusan writer of comedy and contemporary of Epicharmus;
supposed to have invented long cloaks for actors and a new form of *skene*
(*OCD*).

250. *Chiomides*] one of the earliest writers of Attic Old Comedy (*OCD*).

251. *Cratinus*] 519–422 BC. With Aristophanes and Eupolis, he forms a
trio of Old Comedy's greatest poets. Richly inventive, allusive, and exuberant, his plays moved Old Comedy in the direction of personal satire (he

and sixth; Eupolis, more; Aristophanes, more than they:
every man in the dignity of his spirit and judgement supplied something. And, though that in him this kind of
poem appeared absolute and fully perfected, yet how is   255
the face of it changed since in Menander, Philemon,
Caecilius, Plautus, and the rest, who have utterly

---

254. something] *Q;* some thing *F.*

---

attacked Pericles in two productions), his chorus established direct contact
with the audience, and he often parodied himself as a notorious drunkard
(so too Jonson's self-deflating burlesque in Ind.329–42). His work survives
in numerous fragments, and is commented on in contemporary and later
Hellenistic writings (*OCD*). In *Knights*, Aristophanes describes his rival (with
ironic sympathy) as an ageing has-been, now the butt for invective he had
used against others (Thomas K. Hubbard, *The Mask of Comedy* (Ithaca,
1991), pp. 74–5).
  252. *Eupolis*] 446–412 BC. His comedy, bitter and indecent, tended to
target intellectuals and flatterers in a milieu of social decline. No complete
play survives, but, as with Cratinus, many fragments and commentaries indicate his place in the history of comedy (*OCD*). Aristophanes parodied
Eupolis's abusive style in the second parabasis of *Knights* (see Hubbard, pp.
83–7). Francis Meres suggested that he was Nashe's model for frank personal satire: 'As Eupolis of Athens used great liberty in taxing the vices of
men, so doth Thomas Nashe: witness the brood of the Harveys!' (Chambers,
1.324–5, cited in Steggle, p. 25).
  Aristophanes] See introd., pp. 18–28.
  255. *absolute*] perfect, complete.
  256. *Menander*] 342–292 BC, the major playwright of New Comedy, in
which settings were contemporary, plots domestic, and devices conventional
(foundlings, kidnapped daughters, scheming slaves). His plays were adapted
by Roman poets who admired his life-like characters, colloquial speech, rapid
dialogue, and gently ironic tone (*OCD*). Surviving in several fragments,
Roman reconstructions, and one intact play, *Dyskolos* (*The Misanthrope*), his
work strongly influenced seventeenth-century playwrights in England and
France. He is now considered the father of the comedy of manners and thus,
indirectly, of modern romantic comedy and the sit-com.
  Philemon] *c.* 360–263 BC, a rival of Menander. He was criticized for ver-
bosity, but credited with wit, lucid plotting, and verisimilitude in characterization, language, and situation (*OCD*). Fragments of his work survive.
  257. *Caecilius*] d. 168 BC, a Roman comic poet influenced by Menander,
and highly regarded for his plots and emotional power (*OCD*).
  Plautus] 254–184 BC. Like his contemporary Terence, Plautus, the more
prolific playwright, adapted Menander for the Roman stage, but was less
interested in artistic unity. He often invented his own material, expanding
the roles of parasites and pimps, and parodying Roman customs within the
Greek scene. With his irreverent wit and hyperbolic imagination, he was considered the Roman Aristophanes.

excluded the chorus, altered the property of the persons,
their names, and natures, and augmented it with all
liberty, according to the elegancy and disposition of those   260
times wherein they wrote! I see not then but we should
enjoy the same *licentia* or free power to illustrate and
heighten our invention as they did, and not be tied to
those strict and regular forms which the niceness of a few
(who are nothing but form) would thrust upon us.   265

Mitis. Well, we will not dispute of this now. But what's his
scene?

Cordatus. Marry, *Insula Fortunata*, sir.

Mitis. O, the Fortunate Island? Mass, he has bound himself
to a strict law there.   270

Cordatus. Why so?

Mitis. He cannot lightly alter the scene without crossing the
seas.

Cordatus. He needs not, having a whole island to run through,
I think.   275

Mitis. No? How comes it then that in some one play we see

---

258. *property of the persons*] propriety, or decorum, in constructing
characters.

261–2. *I . . . enjoy*] I don't see why we should not enjoy.

262. licentia] See above 231n on the laws of comedy, and *Disc.* 129–42.

264. *niceness*] foolishness; strictness of literary rule-following, as at 238n.

264–5. *a few . . . form*)] *H&S* suggest that this comment is a glance at
Kyd and Daniel, both established men of letters who had written rigidly
Senecan dramas.

268. *Marry*] common oath that largely lost its religious origin, swearing
by the Virgin Mary.

Insula Fortunata] (*a*) Like Elysium, a term used by Spenser and others
as a compliment to Elizabeth, the name refers to the mythical Greek land
for the spirits of heroes, a blissful alternative to the torments and gloom of
Hades; also called the Islands of the Blessed. (*b*) Literate Elizabethans would
have recognized it as the land of fools, birthplace of Folly in Erasmus's *The
Praise of Folly*: 'I was brought forth even amidst the Islands which . . . are
called fortunate' (trans. Sir Thomas Chaloner, 1549, b2v–b3). See Arthur F.
Main, ' "Fortunata" in Jonson's *Every Man Out of His Humour*', *N&Q* 199
(1954): 197–8.

269. *Mass*] by the mass, a conventional oath swearing by the eucharist
(*OED* 6).

276. *some one play*] Probably, as *H&S* suggest, Shakespeare's *H5* or
Dekker's *Old Fortunatus*, both on stage in 1599; but also a reminder of
Sidney's *Defence of Poesy* ('you shall have *Asia* of the one side, and *Affrick* of
the other, and so many other under-kingdoms, that the player, when he

so many seas, countries, and kingdoms passed over with
such admirable dexterity?

Cordatus. O, that but shows how well the authors can travel
in their vocation and outrun the apprehension of their   280
auditory. But leaving this, I would they would begin once.
This protraction is able to sour the best-settled patience
in the theatre.   *Sound the third time.*

Mitis. They have answered your wish, sir: they sound.

Enter Prologue.

Cordatus. O, here comes the Prologue.—Now, sir, if you had
stayed a little longer, I meant to have spoke your prologue   285
for you, i' faith.

Prologue. Marry, with all my heart, sir, you shall do it yet, and
I thank you.   [*Going*]

Cordatus. Nay, nay, stay, stay!—Hear you?

Prologue. You could not have studied to ha' done me a greater   290
benefit at the instant, for I protest to you I am unperfect,
and, had I spoke it, I must of necessity have been out.

Cordatus. Why, but do you speak this seriously?

Prologue. Seriously! Ay, God's my help, do I! And esteem
myself indebted to your kindness for it.   295

Cordatus. For what?

Prologue. Why, for undertaking the prologue for me.

---

279. travel] *Q, F* (trauaile). 283. *Sound the third time*] after 284 in Q;
The third sounding. F, appearing after l. 287. 284.1.] *Q;* PROLOGVE. *F,* after
l. 287.1. 295. God's] *Q;* wit's *F*

---

cometh in, must ever begin with telling where he is, or else the tale will not
be conceived'). Cf. Jonson's echo of it in the Prologue of *EMI* (*F*) (Gurr,
pp. 164–5).

279. *travel*] Modern spelling of the *Q* and *F* 'trauaile' loses the pun on
'travail', drudge or labour.

288–9.] The abortive prologue was evidently a popular gag; in *1 Return
from Parnassus*, the Prologue utters one word of address, 'Gentle—' before
being silenced by the Stage Keeper, who refuses to permit the speaking of
drivelling compliments.

292, 293. *unperfect, out*] not word-perfect in the part, and hence, 'out', or
reduced to silence. Cf. Shakespeare, Sonnet 23: 'As an unperfect actor on
the stage, / Who with his fear is put besides his part'; or Dekker, *News from
Hell* (1606): 'in a dumb show (with pitiful action, like a player, when he's out
of his part) made signs' (2.144).

Cordatus. How? Did I undertake it for you?

Prologue. Did you! I appeal to all these gentlemen whether   300
    you did or no? Come, it pleases you to cast a strange look
    on 't now, but 'twill not serve.

Cordatus. 'Fore God, but it must serve, and therefore speak
    your prologue.

Prologue. An I do, let me die poisoned with some venomous   305
    hiss, and never live to look as high as the twopenny room
    again.   *Exit.*

Mitis. He has put you to it, sir.

Cordatus. 'Sdeath, what a humorous fellow is this? [*To audi-*
    ence] Gentlemen, good faith, I can speak no prologue,   310
    howsoever his weak wit has had the fortune to make this
    strong use of me here before you. But I protest—

> *Enter* CARLO BUFFONE *with a* Boy [*and wine*].

Carlo. Come, come, leave these fustian protestations. Away,
    come, I cannot abide these grey-headed ceremonies. Boy,
    fetch me a glass quickly, I may bid these gentlemen   315
    welcome, give 'em a health here.

>   *Exit* Boy.

303. God] *Q;* me *F.*   312.1.] *Q;* CARLO BUFFONE. *F, and in margin: He*
enters with a boy, and wine.   316.1.] *In Q, appears at the end of l. 319; not in F.*

300. *all these gentlemen*] the audience.

302. *serve*] serve as an excuse.

305. *An*] if.

305–6. *die . . . hiss*] theatre metaphor, comparing the hissing audience to
a serpent.

306. *twopenny room*] 'To enter the yard cost a penny; to enter the galleries
cost another; and to sit in comfort in the higher galleries cost another.' The
exclusive lords' rooms, closest to the stage, cost sixpence (Gurr, p. 121). The
twopenny room seems to have been a popular haunt of pickpockets and prostitutes; *H&S* cite several contemporary references.

309. *'Sdeath*] by God's death, a common oath.

312. *strong*] severe, burdensome, flagrant; with wordplay on the antithesis of *strong* and *weak* (311).

313. *fustian*] inflated, turgid, or inappropriately lofty language; bombastic
ranting. Literally, coarse cloth.

protestations] excuses. Carlo deliberately uses an inflated term.

314. *grey-headed ceremonies*] hoary, outmoded conventions.

315–16. *quickly . . . here*] 'quickly, so that I may welcome these gentlemen
and drink to their health'. Grammatically, an elliptical construction with two
parallel predicates, virtually identical in meaning (the second explains the
first) and sharing the same modal verb, 'may'.

I mar'l whose wit 'twas to put a prologue in yond
sackbut's mouth. They might well think he'd be out of
tune, and yet you'd play upon him too.

Cordatus. Hang him, dull block!   320

Carlo. O, good words, good words! A well-timbered fellow, he
would ha' made a good column, an he had been thought
on when the house was a-building.

Enter Boy *with a glass.*

O, art thou come? Well said. Give me, boy, fill . . . so.
Here's a cup of wine sparkles like a diamond. [*To audi-*   325
ence] Gentlewomen (I am sworn to put them in first) and
gentlemen, a round, in place of a bad prologue. I drink
this good draught to your health here, Canary, the very

323.1.] *Printed over at the right margin of Q; not in F.*

318. *sackbut*] a bass trumpet with a slide like a trombone's for alternating the pitch (*OED* 1a). The instrument, perhaps like the actor playing the
Prologue, has a nasal whining sound. *Sackbut* may also suggest a butt or cask
of sack, implying that the actor is drunk.

319. *play upon him*] pun: (*a*) manipulate, as an instrument; (*b*) tease or
trick with wordplay; (*c*) mock. Cf. *Ham.* 3.2.355–62: 'You would play upon
me, you would seem to know my stops . . . 'Sblood, do you think I am easier
to be played on than a pipe?'

320. *block*] (*a*) wooden head on which hats or wigs were shaped; figuratively, a stupid person (*OED* 4); (*b*) an obstruction (*OED* 11); (*c*) a piece of
wood that acts as a support in carpentry (*OED* 6). Cordatus intends the first
two meanings; Carlo plays on the third.

321. *well-timbered*] (*a*) well-built; (*b*) 'well-hung' (Henke); (*c*) blockheaded.

323. *when . . . a-building*] The Globe Theatre had just been built in 1599.

324. *Well said*] well 'sayed, or assayed; well done.

326. *put them in*] Although Carlo claims that he is addressing the ladies
first out of politeness, his object is the sly innuendo of sexual ingression
(Henke); cf. *1 Honest Whore* 5.2.304–6.

328. *Canary*] (*a*) a light sweet wine from the Canary Islands (Onions);
(*b*) punningly, a drink appropriate for a man who sees the world in canine
terms: see Chars.17n. According to Pliny the Elder, the Canary Islands, or
Canaria (Isles of Dogs), were so named after the large dogs which roamed
there; cf. Charles Earle Funk, *Thereby Hangs a Tale* (New York, 1950). In the
anonymous *The Conquest of the Grand Canaries* (1599), pp. 23–4, the derivation 'is by interpretation, dogskind, for they [the islanders] ran as swift as
dogs, and were as bloodthirsty . . . (like unto mad curs, agreeing with their
name *Canaria*)'.

elixir and spirit of wine. (*He drinks.*) This is that our poet
calls Castalian liquor, when he comes abroad now and   330
then, once in a fortnight, and makes a good meal among
players, where he has *caninum appetitum*. Marry, at home
he keeps a good philosophical diet, beans and buttermilk.
An honest, pure rogue, he will take you off three, four,
five of these, one after another, and look villainously when   335
he has done, like a one-headed Cerberus (he do' not hear
me, I hope), and then, when his belly is well ballast' and
his brain rigged a little, he sails away withal, as though he
would work wonders when he comes home. He has made
a play here, and he calls it *Every Man Out of His Humour*.   340
'Sblood, an he get me out of the humour he has put me
in, I'll ne'er trust none of his tribe again, while I live.
Gentles, all I can say for him is, you are welcome. I could
wish my bottle here amongst you, but there's an old rule:
'No pledging your own health'. Marry, if any here be   345
thirsty for it, their best way that I know is sit still, seal up
their lips, and drink so much of the play in at their ears.
                                       Exit [*with* Boy].

Mitis. What may this fellow be, Cordatus?
Cordatus. Faith, if the time will suffer his description, I'll give

---

329. (*He drinks.*)] Printed over at the right margin of Q; not in F.
337. ballast'] Q, F (ballac'd).   342. ne'er trust] Q; trust F   After 347.]
On separate line F adds GREX.

---

329. *elixir*] alchemical term for a potion that renews or prolongs life.
330. *Castalian*] (*a*) from Castalia, the Muses' sacred spring on Mount
Parnassus; (*b*) pun on Spanish wine from Castile.
332. caninum appetitum] a dog-like (i.e., greedy) appetite.
334. *take you off*] drink off. The *you* is an impersonal dative with no specific reference.
336. *one-headed Cerberus*] Cerberus, the three-headed dog who guarded
the gates of Hades, could be bribed with sops, bread soaked in wine.
do'not] colloquial usage for 'doth not'. The modern contraction 'don't' did
not appear in literature until after 1660, apparently first in the dialogue of
Dryden's plays. See Partridge, *Syntax*, pp. 8–9, and *Accidence*, p. 258.
337. *ballast'*] ballaced or ballassed, the sixteenth- and seventeenth-
century form for 'ballasted'; freighted or loaded, like a ship rendered steady
under sail by a sufficient weight in the hold (*OED* 1).
338–9. *as though . . . home*] as if he were a ship on a return voyage laden
with miraculous goods that would bring him public acclaim at home. The
simile suggests an absurd demeanour of heavily weighted cockiness.
341. *'Sblood*] by God's blood, a common oath.

it you. He is one, the author calls him Carlo Buffone, an   350
impudent common jester, a violent railer, and an incomprehensible epicure: one whose company is desired of all
men, but beloved of none. He will sooner lose his soul
than a jest, and profane even the most holy things to
excite laughter. No honourable or reverend personage   355
whatsoever can come within the reach of his eye but is
turned into all manner of variety by his adulterate similes.

Mitis. You paint forth a monster.

Cordatus. He will prefer all countries before his native, and
thinks he can never sufficiently, or with admiration   360
enough, deliver his affectionate conceit of foreign atheis-
tical policies. But stay, observe these. He'll appear himself
anon.

Enter MACILENTE, *alone.*

Mitis. O, this is your envious man, Macilente, I think.

Cordatus. The same, sir.   365

363.] *Q; not in F.   alone*] *This ed.; solus Q.*

---

350. *He . . . calls him*] he is one whom the author calls. A colloquialism
which inserts the personal pronoun 'him' as a substitute for the relative
pronoun 'whom', omitted earlier after 'one' (Partridge, *Syntax*, p. 70).

351–2. *incomprehensible*] immense, uncontainable (*OED* 1).

357. *adulterate similes*] specious comparisons.

361. *affectionate conceit*] affected or elaborate metaphorical discourse.

363.1.] This SD is part of Jonson's deliberate campaign to demonstrate his
virtuosity as a playwright by standing theatrical convention on its head. He
ends the induction with an entrance, not an exit.

alone] The original Latin *solus* may also mean 'only' or 'lonely'.

Act I

Macilente. Viri est, fortunae caecitatem facile ferre:
　　'Tis true, but stoic. Where in the vast world
　　Doth that man breathe that can so much command
　　His blood and his affection? Well, I see
　　I strive in vain to cure my wounded soul,　　　　　　5
　　For every cordial that my thoughts apply
　　Turns to a cor'sive and doth eat it farther.
　　There is no taste in this philosophy.
　　'Tis like a potion that a man should drink,
　　But turns his stomach with the sight of it.　　　　　10
　　I am no such pilled cynic to believe

1.1.0. ACT I SCENE I] ACTVS PRIMVS. SCENA PRIMA. *Q*; *Act I. Scene I.* /
MACILENTE *F.*　　11. pilled] *Q, F (*pild*)*.

1.1.] The scenes in this act take place in the country on Sogliardo's estate.
　1.] 'It is man's lot to endure the blindness of fortune submissively'; conventional sentiment, source unknown.
　2. *stoic*] characteristic of the school of Greek philosophy founded by Zeno, *c.* 300 BC, known for its austere ethical doctrines; in Jonson's day, specifically noted for its repression of emotion, indifference to pleasure or pain, and patient endurance. Macilente rejects this philosophy by 10, although he does retain the stoic view that, except for the ideal sage (perhaps the role Macilente sees himself fulfilling), all men are fools. Cf. Asper's opening speech in the Induction, and Marston, *Scourge of Villainy* 2.5–6: 'Preach not the Stoic's patience to me; / I hate no man, but men's impiety'.
　3. *so much*] thus entirely.
　4. *blood*] passions.
　affection] emotional state.
　7. *cor'sive*] corrosive.
　8. *taste*] relish or zest; pleasant savour.
　11. *pilled*] (*a*) threadbare, beggarly (*OED* 3, citing this usage); (*b*) covered with fur (*OED, Piled* ppl. a.*3*, 1), alluding to the dog-like behaviour associated etymologically with 'cynic'. According to the *OED, pild* (*Q* and *F*) might mean 'pilled', 'piled', or 'peeled', depending not on the pronunciation but on the context.
　cynic] member of a sect of philosphers in ancient Greece founded by a pupil of Socrates, and marked by an ostentatious contempt for ease, wealth, and pleasure. The name derives from the Greek word for 'dog', associated

That beggary is the only happiness;
Or (with a number of these patient fools)
To sing 'My Mind to Me a Kingdom Is'
When the lank hungry belly barks for food.   15
I look into the world, and there I meet
With objects that do strike my bloodshot eyes
Into my brain; where, when I view myself—
Having before observed this man is great,
Mighty, and feared; that, loved and highly favoured;   20
A third, thought wise and learned; a fourth, rich
And therefore honoured; a fifth, rarely featured;
A sixth, admired for his nuptial fortunes—
When I see these (I say) and view myself,
I wish my optic instruments were cracked,   25

---

25. my optic instruments] *Q* (my *Optique* instruments); the organs of my sight *F*

---

with the sect's public attacks on vice; cf. Diogenes's harangue in Lyly's *Campaspe* (Revels), 4.1.28–9: 'Ye call me dog: so I am, for I long to gnaw the bones in your skins!'; or Henry Peacham's *The Garden of Eloquence* (1593), in which the shameless railer is represented as a barking dog.

14. *'My . . . Is'*] Sir Edward Dyer's hymn, in Byrd's *Psalms, Sonnets, Songs of Sadness and Piety, Made into Music of Five Parts* (1588), no. 14. Jonson relates the austerity of the cynics to that of the Puritans, neither of whom, in his view, took recidivist human nature into account. C. F. Angell, in 'A Note on Jonson's Use of Sir Edward Dyer's "My mynde to me a kingdome is"', *PLL* 10 (1974): 417–21, points out that Jonson rejects the conventional belief that intellectuality prevents worldly corruption and sin. In *CisA*, Onion quotes Dyer's line (1.2.39–42) but proves by Act 5 that the mind left to its own devices degenerates into appetite and wilfulness; similarly, in *Disc.* 1469–71: 'when men's minds come to sojourn with their affections . . . their diseases eat into their strength'.

15. *hungry belly barks*] an almost Brechtian put-down of cynics (for railing) and stoics (for complacent hymn-singing). The remark is class-conscious: the cynics addressed the general populace, while the stoics cultivated the upper classes. Satirists also pictured themselves as barking dogs, 'showing their fangs, snapping, and sinking their pointed teeth deep in some sinner's vitals' (Randolph, p. 153). The phrase itself occurs both in Horace, *Sat.* 2.2.18, and in Erasmus, 'Penny-pinching', p. 493.

16–32.] The reverse of Shakespeare's Sonnet 29, 'When in disgrace with fortune and men's eyes'; for Macilente, nothing compensates his envy at the successes of others.

22. *rarely featured*] uncommonly handsome.

And that the engine of my grief could cast
Mine eyeballs like two globes of wildfire forth
To melt this unproportioned frame of nature.
O, they are thoughts that have transfixed my heart
And often, i' the strength of apprehension,   30
Made my cold passion stand upon my face
Like drops of sweat on a stiff cake of ice!

GREX

Cordatus. This alludes well to that of the poet:
    Invidus suspirat, gemit, incutitque dentes,
    Sudat frigidus, intuens quod odit.
Mitis. O, peace! You break the scene.   35

Enter SOGLIARDO *with* CARLO BUFFONE

ACT I   SCENE 2

Macilente. Soft, who be these?
    I'll lay me down a while till they be past. [*He lies down.*]

32. sweat] *Q;* dew *F.*   36.1.] *Q; not in F.*   1.2.0. ACT I SCENE 2] SCENA
SEC. *Q; ACT I. SCENE II. /* SOGLIARDO, CARLO BUFFONE, MACILENTE. *F.*
In *F,* the scene begins after l. 5.

26–7. *engine . . . forth*] Metaphors of war-machines recur regularly
throughout the play. Randolph (p. 135n) refers to such standard satirical
weaponry as sallies and charges against vice; cannon volleys and musket discharges of words; exploding powder-mines of jests; campaigns, battering-
rams, and bullets of hyperbole.

26. *grief*] (*a*) anger (*OED* 4); (*b*) wounded self-esteem (*OED* 2, 7); (*c*) in
law, a wrong or injury documented in a formal complaint or demand for
redress (*OED* 2b).

27. *wildfire*] a composition of highly inflammable substances, readily
ignited and very difficult to extinguish, used in warfare (*OED* 3).

28. *unproportioned*] unjustly apportioned.

34–5.] 'Jealous, he sighs, groans, and grinds his teeth; / His sweat runs
cold, gazing on what he hates.' *H&S* cite Caelius Firmianus Symposius,
whose epigram, '*De livore*', read '*fremit*', not '*gemit*'; but they locate Jonson's
source for the misquotation, attributed to Virgil, in Mignault's commentary
on Alciati's *Emblemata* (Antwerp, 1574), 71.211.

36. *break*] interrupt.

1.] This opening half-line may have been completed by mute stage-
business of trying to hide before the decision uttered in the next line; or it
may be the second metrical half of the last line of 1.1.

2. *I'll . . . down*] an anti-heroic comic reversal of expectation in staging:

GREX

Cordatus. Signor, note this gallant, I pray you.
Mitis. What is he?
Cordatus. A tame rook. You'll take him presently. List.   5

Sogliardo. Nay, look you, Carlo, this is my humour now: I have
     land and money, my friends left me well, and I will be a
     gentleman whatsoever it cost me.
Carlo. A most gentleman-like resolution.
Sogliardo. Tut, an I take an humour of a thing once, I am like   10
     your tailor's needle: I go through. But for my name,
     signor, how think you? Will it not serve for a gentleman's
     name when the 'signor' is put to it? Ha?
Carlo. Let me hear. How is 't?

9.] *Q; not in Fa, although the catchword* CAR. *appears at bottom of p. 90. Fb adds a line to the bottom of p. 90, and changes the catchword.*

Maciente remains in this position even after meeting Sogliardo (see 172–3) and apparently continues supine until he exits at 1.3.87. Shakespeare may have begun the twist of having a central character act in a prone position by showing Falstaff in his first appearance on stage caught 'sleeping upon benches after noon' in *1H4* 1.2. In *Antonio and Mellida*, Marston frequently depicts Antonio as falling to the ground; in 4.1 he utters many of his lines from that prostrate position.

3. *this gallant*] Sogliardo.

5. *rook*] i.e., lout, as at Ind.108; cf. 'chough' (Chars.63), 'gull' (1.2.37), 'painted jay' and 'popinjays' (2.2.209, 212) and *passim*. For satirical terms of abuse based on birds, insects, or animals with qualities unattractive to man, see Randolph, p. 135.

take him] see through him.

7. *friends*] relatives.

well] well-to-do, wealthy.

7–8. *I will . . . cost*] Wealth was displacing birth as the key social signifier: 'who can live idly and without manual labour and will bear the port charge and countenance of a gentleman, he shall be called master' (Prothero, p. 177).

10. *an I*] if I.

11. *your . . . through*] Sogliardo wants to portray himself as manly and decisive, but tailors, often butts of jokes, were considered effeminate and ineffectual; the needle has phallic implications.

12ff.] *H&S* cite Gifford in noting that Carlo's lessons in gentlemanly behaviour (41–152) derive from Erasmus's 'The Ignoble Knight', pp. 428ff. Dekker, in *The Gull's Horn-book*, expands Jonson's points.

Sogliardo. *Signor Insulso Sogliardo.* Methinks it sounds well.   15
Carlo. O, excellent! Tut, an all fitted to your name, you might
very well stand for a gentleman. I know many Sogliardos
gentlemen.
Sogliardo. Why, and for my wealth I might be a justice of
peace.   20
Carlo. Ay, and a constable for your wit.
Sogliardo. All this is my lordship you see here, and those farms
you came by.
Carlo. Good steps to gentility too, marry. But, Sogliardo, if
you affect to be a gentleman indeed, you must observe   25
all the rare qualities, humours, and complements of a
gentleman.
Sogliardo. I know it, signor, and, if you please to instruct, I
am not too good to learn, I'll assure you.
Carlo. Enough, sir. [*Aside*] I'll make admirable use i' the pro-   30
jection of my medicine upon this lump of copper here.

---

15. Insulso] (Latin) without salt; hence, insipid, tasteless, witless.

16. *an . . . name*] if you were dressed to suit your name.

19–20. *justice of peace*] an unpaid position as local administrator and
judge. Sogliardo's mention of 'wealth' in the same breath may be a satiric
reminder that justices frequently embezzled public money collected as taxes
and fines; cf. Egerton's statement in the Parliament of 1597–8: 'Justices of
Peace were like dogs in the Capitol, that, being set to bark at rebels, set themselves to annoy the good subjects . . . Their greediness was the grievance of
the people' (de Bruyn, pp. 36–7).

21. *constable for your wit*] proverbial for foolishness (Dent C616).

22. *lordship*] title and property (traditionally including village, church,
and fields) of a lord of the manor, not a member of the peerage. A lord of
the manor may purchase, inherit, bequeath, or sell his title, but has little
social standing, despite Sogliardo's boasts: he may not call himself lord
(Sogliardo selects an Italian title instead) or be granted a coat of arms
(although he purchases one in Act 3). The title today does not necessarily
include real property rights, though it may retain ancient rights to collect
tolls within the manor; hence Sogliardo's concern with Macilente's trespass.
See 'Manorial and Other Feudal Titles: An Introduction', *The British Heraldic
Archive*, http://www..kwtelecom.com/heraldry/manor/html, where modern
sales of lordships are recorded.

25. *affect*] pretend, aspire.

26. *rare*] colloquially, splendid, excellent (*OED* 6b).

complements] accomplishments (*OED* 7); attributes that make up the
whole, make a person complete or perfect (*OED* 3, 6).

30–1. *projection . . . copper*] in alchemy, the casting of powdered philosopher's stone (called 'medicine' because it cures all disease) upon a base metal
to effect a transmutation into gold. Carlo sees Sogliardo as a base source for
gold.

[*To Sogliardo*] I'll bethink me for you, sir.
Sogliardo. Signor, I will both pay you and pray you, and thank
    you and think on you.

GREX

Cordatus. Is not this purely good?   35

Macilente. [*Aside*] 'Sblood! Why should such a prick-eared
    hind as this
    Be rich? Ha? A fool? Such a transparent gull
    That may be seen through? Wherefore should he have
    land,
    Houses, and lordships? O, I could eat my entrails
    And sink my soul into the earth with sorrow!   40
Carlo. First, to be an accomplished gentleman, that is, a
    gentleman of the time, you must give o'er housekeeping
    in the country and live altogether in the city amongst gal-
    lants, where, at your first appearance, 'twere good you
    turned four or five hundred acres of your best land into   45
    two or three trunks of apparel. You may do it without

---

35. *purely good*] perfection itself. Cordatus takes a connoisseur's pleasure
in enjoying the 'humour' of the characters on-stage.

36. *prick-eared*] (*a*) usually applied to the erect ears of dogs (*OED* 1), but
by extension may include other animals (a hind was a female deer); (*b*) said
of the apparently prominent ears of a man whose hair is cut short and close
(*OED* 2).

hind] (*a*) rustic, boor; originally, a farm labourer; (*b*) deer (see previous
note).

42–3. *give . . . country*] In London, the only substantial city in England,
entertainment became big business in the 1590s (Camden published a guide-
book in 1600): aside from playhouses, there were lions at the Tower, bear-
baiting at Paris Garden, brothels, various freaks in prisons and madhouses,
and the prospect of violence in streets and taverns (Stone, pp. 386–90).
During 1596 and frequently thereafter, in attempts to solve the problems
caused by absentee landlords, insufficient farm-produce, and unemploy-
ment, the government issued proclamations instructing gentlemen to return
to their country estates, but to little effect. See L. C. Knights, *Drama and
Society in the Age of Jonson* (London, 1937), pp. 108–17; and acts on maintaining tillage and husbandry, in Prothero, pp. 93–6.

Dept as social process – Johnson views city as a site for consumerist seduction → counter used for people who use

debt
climb
social
ladder
↓
social
capital =
good will
sympathy
+ connections
created by interaction between
social networks

going to a conjurer. And be sure you mix yourself still
with such as flourish in the spring of the fashion and are
least popular. Study their carriage and behaviour in all.
Learn to play at primero and passage, and (ever when   50
you lose) ha' two or three peculiar oaths to swear by that
no man else swears. But, above all, protest in your play
and affirm 'Upon your credit, as you are a true gentleman', at every cast. You may do it with a safe conscience,
I warrant you.   55

Sogliardo. O, admirable rare! He cannot choose but be a
    gentleman that has these excellent gifts. More, more, I
    beseech you!

Carlo. You must endeavour to feed cleanly at your ordinary,
    sit melancholy, and pick your teeth when you cannot   60
    speak. And when you come to plays, be humorous, look

---

47. *conjurer*] magician or witch, able to change objects or persons into
other shapes or things by means of supernatural aid.

still] on every occasion, invariably.

49. *least popular*] least vulgar, most removed from the common people
(Whalley).

carriage] social conduct, deportment.

50. *primero*] a card-game in which the winner holds either the 'prime' (the
highest point-count) or a flush (cards of one suit). See *The Letters and Epigrams of Sir John Harington*, ed. Norman Egbert McClure (Philadelphia,
1930), pp. 418–19.

passage] 'a game at dice to be played but by two, and it is performed with
three dice. The caster throws continually till he hath thrown doublets under
ten, and then he is out and loseth, or doublets above ten, and then he passeth
and wins' (Charles Cotton, *The Compleat Gamester*, in *Games and Gamesters
of the Restoration* (London, 1930), p. 81).

51. *peculiar oaths*] Jonson satirized the fashion for eccentric cursing in
EMI (*Q*) 3.2.134–59, where Stephano rehearses at the stage-post, imitating
Bobadill's style of swearing.

53. *credit*] honour, reputation.

54. *cast*] throw of the dice.

56. *admirable*] wonderfully (colloquial).

59. *ordinary*] tavern or eating-house serving public meals at a fixed
price.

60. *pick your teeth*] a fashionable affectation; cf. 4.1.39 and note. Dekker,
Gull's Horn-book, 2.232, advises the would-be gallant to be seen after dinner
'to correct your teeth with some quill or silver instrument, and to cleanse
your gums with a wrought handkercher: It skills [matters] not whether you
dined or no'.

with a good starched face, and ruffle your brow like a new
boot; laugh at nothing but your own jests, or else as the
noblemen laugh—that's a special grace you must observe.
Sogliardo. I warrant you, sir.   65
Carlo. Ay, and sit o'the stage and flout, provided you have a
good suit.
Sogliardo. O, I'll have a suit only for that, sir.
Carlo. You must talk much of your kindred and allies.
Sogliardo. Lies! No, signor, I shall not need to do so. I have   70
kindred i' the city to talk of. I have a niece is a merchant's
wife, and a nephew, my brother Sordido's son, of the Inns
of Court.
Carlo. O, but you must pretend alliance with courtiers and
great persons. And ever when you are to dine or sup in   75
any strange presence, hire a fellow with a great chain
(though it be copper, it's no matter) to bring you letters,
feigned from such a nobleman or such a knight, or such
a lady, to their 'worshipful, right rare, and noble qualified
friend or kinsman, *Signor Insulso Sogliardo*': give yourself   80

---

62. *starched face*] stiff either with haughtiness, or with cosmetics, like the
courtier in *CR* 3.4.26–8 'that weighs / His breath between his teeth, and dares
not smile / Beyond a point, for fear t'unstarch his look'.

62–3. *like . . . boot*] Wide-topped boots were the fashion; the tops were
carefully folded below the knees, or 'ruffled', to expose the embroidery or
lace on the boot-hose (Linthicum, p. 262).

66. *sit o' the stage*] a policy at some theatres. The Globe did not usually
accommodate stage-sitters, but Cordatus and Mitis, guests of the playwright,
behave in a more genteel fashion than is described here. Cf. Dekker, *Gull's
Horn-book*, ch. 6, 'How a Gallant should Behave Himself in a Play-house';
and Sir Francis Beaumont, *The Knight of the Burning Pestle*, in which two citizens join the stage-sitters (who may have been actual spectators, not mute
actors).

flout] scoff.

70. *Lies!*] The absurdly incomplete echo of 'allies' points up Sogliardo's
self-importance and stupidity. He thinks he is being invited to invent prestigious family connections, but believes his kindred is already powerful
enough: his niece Fallace is married to the wealthy merchant, Deliro, and
his nephew Fungoso is a law-student.

71. *niece is*] niece who is. Omission of the relative pronoun is a stylistic
mannerism peculiar to Shakespeare and Jonson, often after notional verbs
(Partridge, *Syntax*, p. 69).

72–3. *Inns of Court*] law school and professional offices which constituted
the third university of England, after Oxford and Cambridge.

76. *great chain*] the steward's badge of office.

style enough. And there (while you intend circumstances
of news, or enquiry of their health, or so) one of your
familiars (whom you must carry about you still) breaks
it up as 'twere in a jest and reads it publicly at the table;
at which you must seem to take as unpardonable offence   85
as if he had torn your mistress' colours, or breathed upon
her picture, and pursue it with that hot grace as if you
would enforce a challenge upon it presently.

Sogliardo. Stay! I do not like that humour of challenge. It may
be accepted. But I'll tell you what's my humour now. I   90
will do this: I will take occasion of sending one of your suits
to the tailor's to have the pocket repaired, or so, and there
such a letter as you talk of (broke open and all) shall be
left. O, the tailor will presently give out what I am upon
the reading of it, worth twenty of your gallants.   95

Carlo. But then you must put on an extreme face of discon-
tentment at your man's negligence.

Sogliardo. O, so I will, and beat him too. I'll have a man for
the purpose.

Macilente. [*Aside*] You may. You have land and crowns. O   100
partial fate!

---

86. mistress'] *Q, F* (mistresse).   88. enforce] *Q;* advance *F.*

---

81. *intend*] Latinism: direct words or attention to (*OED* 5); set out to
relate (*OED* 6b).

83. *familiars*] intimate companions, entourage.

83–4. *breaks it up*] 'opens, by breaking the seal' (*H&S*).

86. *your mistress' colours*] A gentleman wore the colours of the lady
he admired, and by means of colour symbolism could carry on a silent
conversation or flirtation with her; e.g. blue for constancy, green for hope,
pale yellow for jealousy, bright yellow for joy (Linthicum, pp. 25–6). Cf.
CR 5.2.28–35.

breathed upon] sullied or spoke dispraisingly of (Gifford); perhaps, panted
lustfully.

92. *to the tailor's*] Sogliardo exposes himself as a coward by deciding to
have his letter read, not by a courtier whose behaviour might result in a duel,
but by a tailor, a lower-class and generally ridiculed figure, who could quickly
spread the gossip with impunity.

97. *man's*] manservant's. Also 98. The servant is to be blamed and beaten
for leaving the letter in the suit pocket.

100. *crowns*] gold coins.

101. *partial*] unfair.

Carlo. Mass, well remembered: you must keep your men
  gallant at the first—fine pied liveries laid with good gold
  lace. There's no loss in it. They may rip 't off and pawn
  it when they lack victuals.   105

Sogliardo. By 'r lady, that is chargeable, signor. 'Twill bring a
  man in debt.

Carlo. Debt? Why, that's the more for your credit, sir. It's an
  excellent policy to owe much in these days, if you note
  it.   110

Sogliardo. As how, good signor? I would fain be a politician.

Carlo. O, look where you are indebted any great sum: your
  creditor observes you with no less regard than if he were
  bound to you for some huge benefit, and will quake to
  give you the least cause of offence, lest he lose his money.   115
  I assure you, in these times, no man has his servant more
  obsequious and pliant than gentlemen their creditors, to
  whom, if at any time you pay but a moiety or a fourth
  part, it comes more acceptedly than if you gave 'em a
  New Year's gift.   120

Sogliardo. I perceive you, sir. I will take up and bring myself
  in credit, sure.

Carlo. Marry, this: always beware you commerce not with
  bankrupts, or poor needy Ludgathians. They are impudent creatures, turbulent spirits. They care not what   125

---

103. *pied liveries*] parti-coloured uniforms.
  laid] embroidered. 'Laid-work' or 'couching' was embroidery with gold
thread, in this case attaching lace trim laid flat on the surface of the cloth
(*OED*, *Couching* 2).
  106. *By 'r lady*] by our lady, an oath referring originally to the Virgin Mary.
  chargeable] financially burdensome.
  108. *credit*] reputation as a gentleman; but with an ironic pun, since lavish
spending will ruin a man's credit financially, if he cannot pay for the goods
he has been entrusted with.
  109. *policy*] stratagem.
  109–10. *if you note it*] if you pay attention to how the game goes.
  111. *politician*] shrewd player of the game.
  113. *observes*] attends.
  121–2. *bring . . . credit*] runs up debts, go on credit.
  123. *commerce*] do business with, deal commercially.
  124. *Ludgathians*] bankrupts committed to the debtors' prison at Ludgate
(*H&S*).

violent tragedies they stir, nor how they play fast and
loose with a poor gentleman's fortunes to get their own.
Marry, these rich fellows that ha' the world, or the better
part of it, sleeping in their counting-houses, they are ten
times more placable, they. Either fear, hope, or modesty   130
restrains them from offering any outrages. But this is
nothing to your followers. You shall not run a penny more
in arrearage for them, an you list, yourself.

Sogliardo. No? How should I keep 'em then?

Carlo. Keep 'em? 'Sblood, let them keep themselves! They are   135
no sheep, are they? What? You shall come in houses where
plate, apparel, jewels, and divers other pretty com-
modities lie negligently scattered, and I would ha' those
Mercuries follow me, I trow, should remember they had
not their fingers for nothing.   140

Sogliardo. That's not so good, methinks.

Carlo. Why, after you have kept 'em a fortnight or so and
showed 'em enough to the world, you may turn 'em away
and keep no more but a boy. It's enough.

Sogliardo. Nay, my humour is not for boys. I'll keep men, an   145

126–7. *fast and loose*] literally, a confidence trick, like a shell-game,
depending on sleight-of-hand: observers gamble on whether or not an intricately looped belt is fixed to the table.

129–30. *they . . . they*] Pleonastic pronominal subject repeated at the end
for emphasis; in Jonson, the repetition is usually an indication that the
speaker's emotion has been aroused (Partridge, *Syntax*, pp. 29–30).

130. *placable*] peaceable, unwilling to offend.

133. *an you list*] if you please. Carlo's advice is that Sogliardo himself need
not run up debts on account of his servants.

138–40. *I would . . . nothing*] i.e., I would have those servants who serve
me bear in mind that their fingers can be used for pilfering from rich household where their master visits.

139. *Mercuries*] Mercury was the god of thieves; for the view of Mercury
as a menial as well, see Cupid's taunting of his 'light feather-heel'd coz',
CR I.I.

144. *boy*] A boy generally was cheaper to maintain and gave better value
than a manservant; cf. 'The Citizen at Home', in *Dialogues from Hollyband*
(1573), reprinted in Byrne, p. 33: '*Gossip.* You have there a pretty boy, and
quick of wit. / *Father.* I promise you that I will draw out more service of that
boy, than of three servants which will do nothing else than to make great
cheer, and play at dice and cards.'

145. *My humour . . . boys*] Sogliardo's domestic bias hints, perhaps
unconsciously, at a sexual preference.

I keep any. And I'll give coats, that's my humour. But I
lack a cullisen.
Carlo. Why, now you ride to the city, you may buy one. I'll
bring you where you shall ha' your choice for money.
Sogliardo. Can you, sir?   150
Carlo. O, ay! You shall have one take measure of you and make
you a coat of arms to fit you, of what fashion you will.
Sogliardo. By word of mouth, I thank you, signor. I'll be once
a little prodigal in a humour, in faith, and have a most
prodigious coat.   155
Macilente. [*Aloud*] Torment and death! Break head and brain
at once
To be delivered of your fighting issue!
Who can endure to see blind Fortune dote thus?
To be enamoured on this dusty turf?
This clod? A whoreson puckfist? O God, God, God, God!
(*etc.*)   160

---

146. *coats*] liveries (Nason, p. 90). Also, to *give coats* is to display a coat
of arms. See next note.

147. *cullisen*] heraldic term for the badge designed to accord with the
family coat of arms and worn on the sleeve, breast, or back of the livery;
the badge was sometimes identical with the crest or some charge in the
escutcheon (heraldic shield) and sometimes a variation (Nason, p. 58).

149. *choice for money*] 'Nobility got by purchase is commonly an object of
ridicule' (Erasmus, p. 426). The money would be paid to the kings of arms,
the three chief officers of the College of Heralds, who had authority to grant
arms and crests to deserving applicants, but they frequently abused this privilege (Nason, pp. 66–7, 90). An Inner Temple manuscript satirizes this abuse:
'And if need be, a King of Heralds shall give him for money arms newly
made and invented with a crest and all: the title whereof shall pretend to
have been found by the said Herald in the perusing and viewing of old registers' (Stone, p. 49). Heraldic confirmation, the more elaborate the better,
became a major weapon in the battle for status, as the newly rich and
respectable attempted to camouflage dubious origins.

151. *one*] one who devises coats of arms, but the metaphor, 'take measure
. . . fashion', suggests a tailor.

156–7.] 'Oh, agony! May my head split open—anything to escape the conflicting thoughts pouring out of my brain!' Macilente is torn between envy
of Sogliardo's wealth and contempt for his ignorant misspending of it.

159. *dusty turf*] mere clod (see next line).

160. *puckfist*] puffball fungus, hence, an empty boaster; an abusive term
consistent with the satiric practice of giving men names of plants with
unpleasant characteristics (Randolph, p. 135); cf. 'Fungoso', or 'bullrushes'
and 'mushroom', 163. Dekker and Webster, in *Westward Ho!* (1604), refer to
a 'Captaine Puckfoist', 4.1.63. *H&S* cite other references in Jonson.

I could run wild with grief now to behold
The rankness of her bounties, that doth breed
Such bullrushes—these mushroom gentlemen
That shoot up in a night to place and worship!

[*Sogliardo, hearing Macilente, moves towards him.*]

Carlo. Let him alone. Some stray, some stray.   165
Sogliardo. Nay, I will examine him before I go, sure.
Carlo. The lord of the soil has all wefts and strays here, has
he not?
Sogliardo. [*Still approaching Macilente*] Yes, sir.
Carlo. [*Aside*] Faith, then I pity the poor fellow. He's fallen   170
into a fool's hands.
Sogliardo. [*To Macilente*] Sirrah, who gave you commission to
lie in my lordship?
Macilente. Your lordship?
Sogliardo. How? My lordship? Do you know me, sir?   175
Macilente. I do know you, sir.
Carlo. [*Aside*] 'Sheart, he answers him like an echo.
Sogliardo. Why, who am I, sir?
Macilente. One of those that fortune favours.

163–4. *mushroom . . . night*] a frequent description of upstarts, in JONSON
and elsewhere. See *H&S*.

165. *stray*] Carlo implies that Macilente is a stray dog. In law, a domestic animal found wandering ownerless within a lordship was impounded by
the lord, and (if not redeemed within a year and a day after the lord posted
its description in two market towns) was forfeited to the lord's use; cf. *Estray*,
in Rastell. For another figurative use of the term see *2H6* 4.10.24–5: 'Here's
the lord of the soil come to seize me for a stray, for entering his fee-simple
without leave'.

167. *wefts*] waifs, frequently found in combination with 'strays', from
the legal phrase, 'waifs and strays': property of some kind, usually stolen
goods abandoned by a thief during hue and cry, which, if unclaimed by the
owner during the pursuit or a subsequent trial, falls to the lord of the manor
(*Waifes*, in Rastell). Figuratively, homeless persons or animals (*OED*,
Waif 2).

172. *commission*] warrant, or legally delegated authority.

173. *lie*] reside, with wordplay on 'lie recumbent', since Macilente has
been doing so.

174, 175. *lordship?*] Macilente's echo is malicious; Sogliardo's is naively
self-important.

177. *'Sheart*] by God's heart, a common oath.

Carlo. [*Aside*] The periphrasis of a fool. I'll observe this better.   180
Sogliardo. That fortune favours? How mean you that, friend?
Macilente. I mean simply—that you are one that lives not by
    your wits.
Sogliardo. By my wits? No, sir, I scorn to live by my wits, I. I
    have better means, I tell thee, than to take such base   185
    courses as to live by my wits. 'Sblood, dost thou think I
    live by my wits?
Macilente. [*To Carlo*] Methinks, jester, you should not relish
    this well.
Carlo. [*Aside*] Ha? Does he know me?   190
Macilente. [*To Carlo*] Though yours be the worst use a man
    can put his wit to of thousands, to prostitute it at every
    tavern and ordinary, yet methinks you should have turned
    your broad side at this, and have been ready with an
    apology able to sink this hulk of ignorance into the   195
    bottom and depth of his contempt.

---

182. mean simply—that] *This ed.;* mean simply; That *Q;* mean simply. That
F.

---

180. *periphrasis of a fool*] Carlo wryly observes that Macilente's seeming
praise of Sogliardo as one whom fortune favours is in fact a roundabout
(periphrastic) way of describing a fool, as in the Latin proverb, *Fortuna favet
fatuis* ('Fortune favours fools'). Jonson also quoted this proverb in the
opening line of the prologue to *Alc.* (*H&S*).

184. *I scorn . . . wits*] Macilente has suggested that: (*a*) Sogliardo does not
have to earn his living in various employments in order to survive; (*b*) his
wits in any case are not sufficient to support him. Sogliardo ironically emphasizes his own stupidity by expressing scorn at the very idea of being able to
earn his living, and by failing to comprehend the insult in the second.

191-6.] Macilente reproves Carlo for encouraging and then laughing at
the witless Sogliardo, who is beneath even a common jester's notice.

192-3. *at every tavern*] 'Hence the point of Dekker's fling at Jonson in
Satiromastix: "In briefliness, when you sup in taverns, amongst your betters,
you shall swear not to dip your manners in too much sauce, nor at table to
fling epigrams, emblems, or play-speeches about you (like hail-stones) to
keep you out of the terrible danger of the shot, upon pain to sit at the upper
end of the table, a'th left hand of Carlo Buffon"' (*H&S*); also discussed in
Small, p. 36.

194-6. *broad side . . . depth*] a metaphor of naval engagement. Carlo, as
the agile vessel with weapons, should have exploded the hulk or large transport ship of Sogliardo's clumsy pretentions with one broadside blast; that is,
a simultaneous discharge from all the artillery on one side of the ship.

195. *apology*] defence.

Carlo. [*Aside*] 'Sblood, 'tis Macilente! [*To Macilente*]—Signor,
you are well encountered. How is 't? [*Aside to Macilente*]
O, we must not regard what he says, man. A trout. A
shallow fool. He has no more brain than a butterfly. A   200
mere stuffed suit. He looks like a musty bottle, new wickered: his head's the cork—light, light. [*Aloud*] I am glad
to see you so well returned, signor.

Macilente. You are? Gramercy, good Janus.

Sogliardo. [*Aside to Carlo*] Is he one of your acquaintance? I   205
love him the better for that.

Carlo. [*Aside to Sogliardo*] God's precious, come away, man.
What do you mean? An you knew him as I do, you'd shun
him as you'd do the plague!

Sogliardo. [*Aside to Carlo*] Why, sir?   210

Carlo. [*Aside to Sogliardo*] O, he's a black fellow. Take heed on
him.

Sogliardo. [*Aside to Carlo*] Is he a scholar or a soldier?

Carlo. [*Aside to Sogliardo*] Both, both. A lean mongrel, he
looks as if he were chap-fallen with barking at other men's   215

---

199. *trout*] proverbially caught by tickling (Dent, T537).

200. *shallow*] (*a*) a reference to the depth of water in which a trout might
swim; hence (*b*) trite, superficial.

201-2. *like . . . wickered*] Sogliardo looks like a bottle of wine, set into
a wicker basket, as was the practice with Chianti, for example; but here
the bottle/Sogliardo is stale, and the wicker/clothing new, indicating
that Sogliardo's outwardly spruce appearance is at odds with his actual
boorishness.

201. *musty*] spoiled or soured; trite.

202. *his head's . . . light*] continuing the wine-bottle analogy: Sogliardo's
head is like the cork, lightweight or trivial.

204. *Gramercy*] many thanks (French, *grand merci*).

Janus] The Roman god welcoming the new year had two faces, one turned
to the past, and one to the future; later, an image of hypocrisy or double-
dealing. See Tilley, J21 and Dent, F20. The name may refer as well to a facial
expression, as at 5.1.56ff: in *CR* 5.4.233, the Janus look is an 'oblique leer';
in Dekker and Webster's *Westward Ho!* 5.1.261, 'a squint' (Hoy, 2.233-4).
Macilente is calling Carlo a devious hypocrite for flattering Sogliardo to his
face, but sneering at him behind his back.

207. *God's precious*] an oath: by God's (Christ's) precious body.

211. *black*] evil, fierce, formidable.

215. *chap-fallen*] literally, with the lower jaw hanging down in extreme
exhaustion; slack-jawed, and hence hollow-cheeked; cf. the description of
Horace/Jonson in *Satiromastix* 5.2.262, as 'so lean a hollow-cheeked scrag'.
Figuratively, dejected or dispirited.

good fortunes. 'Ware how you offend him. He carries oil
and fire in his pen, will scald where it drops. His spirit's
like powder, quick, violent: he'll blow a man up with a
jest. I fear him worse than a rotten wall does the cannon,
shake an hour after at the report. Away, come not near   220
him.

Sogliardo. [*Aside to Carlo*] For God's sake, let's be gone. An
he be a scholar, you know I cannot abide him. I had as
lief see a cockatrice, specially as cockatrices go now.

Carlo. [*To Macilente*] What, you'll stay, signor? This gentle-   225
man, Sogliardo, and I are to visit the knight Puntarvolo,
and from thence to the city. We shall meet there.

Exeunt CARLO *and* SOGLIARDO.

Macilente. Ay, when I cannot shun you, we will meet.

'Tis strange. Of all the creatures I have seen,
I envy not this Buffon, for indeed   230
Neither his fortunes nor his parts deserve it.
But I do hate him as I hate the devil,

---

224. lief] *Q*, *F* (*leeue*).   227.1.] *Q*; *not in F.*

216–17. *oil . . . scald*] Horace/Jonson in *Satiromastix* 5.2.320–1, has to
swear 'not to make scald and wry-mouth jests'. 'The satirist's pen . . . oftentimes spurts or drips oil and fire from its nib on the evil place and scalds
and blisters but at the same time cauterizes' (Randolph, p. 145).

217. *pen, will*] pen that will.

218. *powder*] gunpowder.

220. *report*] sound of the cannon blast.

224. *lief*] gladly, willingly.

cockatrice] a basilisk, the legendary reptile that kills with its glance (Dent
c496.2); cf. E. Topsell, *History of Serpents* (1608), cited in Browne, 2.811: 'the
beams of the cockatrice's eyes, do corrupt the visible spirit of a man, which
visible spirit corrupted, all the other spirits coming from the brain and life
of the heart, are thereby corrupted, and so the man dieth'. Hence, a prostitute; either because of the fascinating gaze with its promise of sexual 'death'
= orgasm, or because the prostitute can corrupt and kill with venereal disease
(Henke). Williams explains the etymology on analogy with *meretrix* (whore
in Latin, but the basis of jokes on 'merry tricks'), citing the warning in
Wilkins, *Miseries of an Enforced Marriage* (1605–6), not to waste money on
'your punks, and your cock-tricks'.

230. *envy*] feel jealousy at his superior advantages.

Buffon] punning on Carlo's name and the common noun/adjective referring to vulgar jest. The stress on the first syllable is likely to have reminded
the audience of 'bufe' or 'buffa', the cant-word for dog; cf. 234, 'open-
throated, black-mouthed cur'; also, the scornful reference to 'buffon, barking
wits' in *Poet.* 5.3.371–2.

Or that brass-visaged monster, Barbarism.
O, 'tis an open-throated, black-mouthed cur
That bites at all, but eats on those that feed him;   235
A slave that to your face will, serpent-like,
Creep on the ground, as he would eat the dust,
And to your back will turn the tail and sting
More deadly than a scorpion. Stay. Who's this?
Now, for my soul, another minion   240
Of the old lady Chance's: I'll observe him.

                                            [*Remains lying down.*]

        Enter SORDIDO *with a prognostication*[, *reading*].

                        ACT I   SCENE 3

Sordido. O rare! Good, good, good, good, good! I thank my
        Christ, I thank my Christ for it!
Macilente. [*Aside*] Said I not true? Doth not his passion speak

241.2.] *Q; not in* F.

1.3. ACT I SCENE 3] SCENA TER. *Q*; *Act I. Scene III. / SORDIDO,
MACILENTE, HINE. *F*   2. Christ . . . Christ] *Q*; Starres . . . Starres *F*

   233.] Barbarism has a brass face as a sign of its brazen (outrageous, insolent) qualities.
   236. *slave*] villain, rogue.
   237. *as*] as if.
   240. *minion*] darling.
   241.2. prognostication] The annual weather forecast was a separate work
from the almanac, but since 1540 the two had been bound in the same
volume: almanac and calendars first, then a separate title-page and the prognostications, as in Thomas Buckminster, *An Almanac and Prognostication for
the Year 1598*, introd. Eustace F. Bosanquet (London, 1935), pp. 7–8. Besides
monthly weather predictions, the format included gardening notes, dates of
terms and holidays, favorable days for weddings, times of eclipses, seasonal
phenomena, hours of moonlight, and astrological tips for better health. The
prognostication was satirized in the Middle Temple Revels, 1597/8, beginning with a zodiacal description of the female body, and ending with sexually charged predictions about the weather and diseases affecting courtiers
(cited in Baker, pp. 128–9).
   1.3.] *H&S* note parallels (especially 126–39) to the case of Archer, an
Essex farmer who was convicted in the Star Chamber 'For enhancing the
price of corn'. See, also, Overbury's 'Engrosser of Corn', in *The Overburian
Characters*, ed. W. J. Paylor (Oxford, 1936), pp. 65–6: 'When his barns and

Out of my divination? O my senses,
Why lose you not your powers and become   5
Dead, dull, and blunted with this spectacle?
I know him. 'Tis Sordido, the farmer,
A boor, and brother to that swine was here.

Sordido. Excellent, excellent, excellent! As I would wish, as I
would wish!   10

Macilente. [*Aside*] See how the strumpet Fortune tickles him,
And makes him swoon with laughter—O, O, O!

Sordido. Ha, ha, ha! I will not sow my grounds this year. Let
me see. What harvest shall we have? June? July?

Macilente. [*Aside*] What is 't? A prognostication raps him so?   15

Sordido. 'The twentieth, twenty-first, twenty-second days,
rain and wind'—O, good, good. 'The twenty-third and
twenty-fourth, rain and some wind'—good. 'The twenty-

---

6. Dead . . . blunted] *Q*; Dull'd, if not deadded *F.*   14. June? July?] *Q*
(*Iune, Iulie?); June, July, August? F.*   15. What is 't? A] *This ed.*; What is
't a *Q*; What is 't, a *F*; What, is 't a *Schelling.*   16. twentieth . . . twenty-
second] xx. xxi. xxij. *Q, F (and thus with other numbers in this passage to l. 20;
subsequent numbers are spelled out in full).*

---

garners are full (if it be a time of dearth) he will buy half a bushel i'th' market
to serve his household . . . The poor he accounts the justice's intelligencers,
and cannot abide them.' So also in *A Knack to Know a Knave* (1594), ll.
1263–72 in the Malone Society Reprint (Oxford, 1964) on indicting miserly
landowners at the Assizes: 'he keeps corn in his barn, and suffers his brethren
and neighbours to lie and want, and thereby makes the market so dear, that
the poor can buy no corn'. The initial visual image of Sordido with book in
hand is an emblem of the grasping farmer representing Mammon, or greed;
Marston's character, 'Mamon', in *Jack Drum's Entertainment* (1600), F3, is
greeted as though he were the emblem: 'Welcome, *Erra Pater*, you that make
prognostications for ever. Where's your almanac?'

4. *divination*] guess that Sordido is lucky at 1.2.240–1 ('another minion /
Of the old lady Chance's'), now confirmed by Sordido's opening lines.

6. *Dead*] deadened; the modern term replaced 'dead' and 'deadded' (*F*)
after 1650 (Partridge, *Accidence*, p. 194).

8. *swine was*] swine who was. The swine features prominently on
Sogliardo's coat of arms. See Appendix B.

15. *raps*] affects with rapture, transports (*OED* vb.3, 2b).

16. ff.] The style of the prognostication exactly reflects Buckminster's:
part of July's forecast reads, 'The xxjiii. day seasonable wether. The xxv. and
xxvj. dayes, some thunder and shewers are suspected. The xxvji. and xxvjii.
dayes variably enclined. The xxjx. and xxx. dayes very hotte' (c4).

fifth, rain'—good still. 'Twenty-sixth, twenty-seventh,
twenty-eighth, wind and some rain'—would it had been   20
rain and some wind. Well, 'tis good (when it can be no
better). 'Twenty-ninth, inclining to rain': inclining to
rain?—that's not so good now. 'Thirtieth and thirty-first,
wind and no rain.' No rain? 'Slid, stay! This is worse and
worse. What says he of St Swithin's? Turn back, look: 'St   25
Swithin's . . .'—No rain?

Macilente. [*Aside*] O, here's a precious filthy damnèd rogue
    That fats himself with expectation
    Of rotten weather and unseasoned hours!
    And he is rich for it, an elder brother: 30
    His barns are full, his ricks and mows well trod,
    His garners crack with store. O, 'tis well—ha, ha, ha!
    A plague consume thee and thy house!

Sordido. O, here! 'St Swithin's, the fifteenth day, variable
    weather; for the most part, rain'—good—'for the most   35
    part, rain.' Why, it should rain forty days after now, more
    or less. It was a rule held afore I was able to hold a plough,
    and yet here are two days no rain. Ha! It makes me muse.
    We'll see how the next month begins, if that be better.
    'August: August first, second, third, and fourth days, rainy   40
    and blustering'—this is well now! 'Fifth, sixth, seventh,
    eighth, and ninth, rain with some thunder'—ay, marry,
    this is excellent! The other was false printed, sure. 'The
    tenth and eleventh, great store of rain'—O, good, good,

---

38. Ha!] *This ed.;* ha? *Q, F*   40. August: August first] *Q; September,* first
F

23–4. '*Thirtieth . . . rain*'] Sordido, upon reading this, turns back to St
Swithin's Day (15 July) because of the proverb, 'If it rain on St Swithin's Day
/ It will continue for forty days', alluded to later as a 'rule' (37). He then
checks the weather from 15 July to 23 August. *F*'s alteration of these dates
to August and September confuses the reference to the St Swithin's (also
spelled St Swithun's) proverb (de Vocht, pp. 88–9).

24. '*Slid*] abbreviated oath: by God's eyelid.

28–9.] similar to the 'farmer, that hang'd himself on th'expectation of
plenty' (*Mac.* 2.3.4–5); see 143 below, and 3.2. The scarcity and expense of
grain became a very serious problem in 1594–7, when harvests were poor
because of excessive rain (de Bruyn, p. 56).

31. *ricks . . . trod*] stacks of grain packed down firmly in storage so that no
space is wasted.

32. *garners*] storehouses for corn; granaries.

good, good, good! 'The twelfth, thirteenth, and four-   45
teenth days, rain'—good still. 'Fifteenth and sixteenth,
rain'—good still. 'Seventeenth and eighteenth, rain'—
good still. 'Nineteenth and twentieth'—good still, good
still, good still, good still, good still! 'One-and-twentieth,
some rain.' Some rain? Well, we must be patient and   50
attend the heavens' pleasure. Would it were more, though.
'The one-and-twentieth—two-and-twentieth, three-and-
twentieth, great tempest of rain, thunder and lightning.'
O good again, past expectation good!
I thank my blessèd angel! Never, never   55
Laid I penny better out than this,
To purchase this dear book: not dear for price,
And yet of me as dearly prized as life,
Since in it is contained the very life,
Blood, strength, and sinews of my happiness.   60
Blessed be the hour wherein I bought this book,
His studies happy that composed the book,
And the man fortunate that sold the book:
Sleep with this charm, and be as true to me
As I am joyed and confident in thee.   65

Enter a Hind *to* SORDIDO *with a paper.*

Macilente. [*Aside*] Ha, ha, ha! I' not this good? Is 't not
    pleasing, this? Ha, ha! Gods! ha!

52. The one-and-twentieth—] *This ed.; Q and F have a comma, which seems
to deny the prediction that Sordido has already read for that date. To resolve the
problem, Q3 simply omits the date, and continues with* the two and twentieth.
65.1.] *Q; in margin of F: The Hine enters with a paper.*   67. ha, ha! Gods!
ha!] ha, ha? / Gods ha? *Q, turned over on to the end of l. 66; a separate
line in F:* Ha, ha, ha! God pardon me! ha, ha! *In Q the laughter is clearly
extrametrical.*

56. *penny*] the usual price for an almanac; *H&S* cite several contemporary references.
57. *dear*] Sordido plays on two meanings in a common pun: (*a*) precious,
loved; (*b*) costly.
59. *life*] essence; playing on *life* meaning 'existence' in 58.
62. *studies happy*] labours beneficial or prosperous.
64. *charm*] blessing just chanted in 61–3, which apparently has talismanic
power.
65.1 *Hind*] Servant, especially a farm servant or agricultural labourer
(*OED* sb. 2, 2).
66.] The laughter in this line is extrametrical, as is the choked-off
blasphemy. The metrical line reads: 'I' not this good? Is 't not pleasing, this?'

Is 't possible that such a spacious villain
Should live and not be plagued? Or lies he hid
Within the wrinkled bosom of the world,
Where heaven cannot see him? 'Sblood, methinks   70
'Tis rare and admirable that he should breathe and walk,
Feed with digestion, sleep, enjoy his health,
And—like a boist'rous whale swallowing the poor—
Still swim in wealth and pleasure. Is 't not strange?
Unless his house and skin were thunder-proof,   75
I wonder at it. Methinks now the hectic,
Gout, leprosy, or some such loathed disease
Might light upon him, or that fire from heaven
Might fall upon his barns, or mice and rats
Eat up his grain, or else that it might rot   80
Within the hoary ricks, e'en as it stands.
Methinks this might be well, and after all
The devil might come and fetch him. Ay, 'tis true.
Meantime, he surfeits in prosperity,
And thou, in envy of him, gnaw'st thyself.   85
Peace, fool. Get hence, and tell thy vexèd spirit,
'Wealth in this age will scarcely look on merit'.   *Exit.*

---

71. admirable] *Q;* strange *F*   72. digestion] *Q, F* (disgestion).   87. SD
Exit.] *Q; not in F*

---

67. *spacious*] large-scale (*OED* 4b, citing this passage as its earliest
instance).

75. *thunder-proof*] impervious to thunder-bolts hurled by an angry god.

76. *hectic*] fever accompanying wasting diseases, especially tuberculosis,
and characterized by flushed cheeks and hot dry skin.

78. *fire from heaven*] *H&S* cite popular literature about the judgement
of God on farmers. The image of the leviathan, 73, or the legend of
Bishop Hatto of Bingen who, along with his hoarded grain, was eaten
by a plague of rats, as at 79–80—a tale retold by Thomas Coryat in *Coryat's
Crudities* (Glasgow, 1905), 2.295—also belongs to the popular moral
tradition.

82. *Methinks . . . well*] This seems to me a suitable punishment.

83. *The devil . . . him*] A favourite set-piece in morality plays, it appeared
in *The Castle of Perseverance* (*c.* 1440), *Mankind* (1465), Wager's *The Longer
Thou Livest* (1559), Fulwel's *Like Will to Like* (1568), Greene's *Friar Bacon
and Friar Bungay* (1589), and Marlowe's *Doctor Faustus* (1589). Jonson uses
it himself in *DisA.*

85–6. *And thou . . . fool*] addressing himself.

87.] presented as an aphorism, though not a common proverb.

Sordido. Who brought this same, sirrah?

Hind. Marry, sir, one of the justice's men. He says 'tis a
  precept, and all their hands be at it.   90

Sordido. Ay, and the prints of them stick in my flesh
  Deeper than i' their letters. They have sent me
  Pills wrapped in paper here that, should I take 'em,
  Would poison all the sweetness of my book
  And turn my honey into hemlock juice.   95
  But I am wiser than to serve their precepts,
  Or follow their prescriptions. Here's a device
  To charge me bring my grain unto the markets.
  Ay, much!—When I have neither barn, nor garner,
  Nor earth to hide it in, I'll bring it, but till then   100
  Each corn I send shall be as big as Paul's.
  O, but (say some) the poor are like to starve.
  Why, let 'em starve. What's that to me? Are bees

---

100. but till] *Q;* till *F*

88. *this same*] the paper; Sordido's emphatic colloquial expression suggests a rustic dialect and conveys a degree of annoyance or contempt (Partridge, *Syntax*, pp. 56–7). *Sirrah* also expresses condescension towards a
social inferior.

90. *precept*] court order, here requiring Sordido to produce his grain for
sale at market. A proclamation was issued on 31 July 1596 against covetous
farmers and engrossers; local sheriffs had to submit monthly surveillance
reports on its enforcement by justices of the peace (de Bruyn, pp. 56–7).
Another proclamation, issued 23 August 1598, was directed against any
hoarding or wasting of corn, 'especially such as so contemptuously and
unchristianly either have fed dogs, or made starch' for their own vanity or
profit, instead of sustaining the poor in a time of dearth; see *Proclamations*
2.355, in the BL.

all . . . it] all the authorities have signed the court order.

91. *sticks . . . flesh*] like a brand.

93–7. *Pills . . . prescriptions*] pharmaceutical puns based on precept/pre-
scription, both written orders from an authority, playing on the legal sense
of asserting a right or claim (*OED, prescribe,* 6).

93. *in paper*] 'Pills were usually wrapped in gold or silver leaf' (*H&S*).

96. *serve*] observe, obey.

99. *much!*] indicates contemptuous recognition of an ironic fact or situation; a sarcastic interjection.

101. *Paul's*] St Paul's Cathedral, then the largest building in London,
larger than the present structure; cf. Dekker, *The Dead Term* 4.47. Sordido
means that he'll bring his corn to market only if he can't hide it, and each
grain would have to be monstrously huge to thwart his intention.

102. *like*] likely.

Bound to keep life in drones and idle moths? No.
Why such are these that term themselves the poor,   105
Only because they would be pitied,
But are indeed a sort of lazy beggars,
Licentious rogues, and sturdy vagabonds,
Bred (by the sloth of a fat plenteous year)
Like snakes in heat of summer out of dung,   110
And this is all that these cheap times are good for;
Whereas a wholesome and penurious dearth
Purges the soil of such vile excrements,
And kills the vipers up.
Hind.   O but master,
Take heed they hear you not.
Sordido.   Why so?
Hind. They will exclaim against you.   115
Sordido.   Ay, their exclaims
Move me as much as thy breath moves a mountain.
Poor worms, they hiss at me, whilst I at home
Can be contented to applaud myself,
To sit and clap my hands, and laugh and leap,   120
Knocking my head against my roof with joy
To see how plump my bags are, and my barns.
Sirrah, go, hie you home, and bid your fellows
Get all their flails ready again' I come.
Hind. I will, sir.   *Exit* Hind.   125
Sordido. I'll instantly set all my hinds to threshing

---

124. again'] *F*; againe *Q*.   125.] *Extrametrical line.*   Exit Hind.] *Q; not in F.*

---

104. *Bound . . . moths*] bound to keep drones and idle moths alive by labouring in their stead.

107. *sort*] band or group, as at Ind.130.

108. *sturdy*] (*a*) defiant, disobedient (*OED* 5); (*b*) able-bodied, robust (*OED* 7).

110.] referring to the common belief that snakes, along with eels, salamanders, and certain crustaceans and insects, were bred by spontaneous generation; cf. Browne, 3.28, and Pliny, *Natural History* 10.86–7.

116. *exclaim against*] accuse loudly, blame.

118ff.] From Horace, *Sat.* 1.1.64–7: 'He is like the rich miser in Athens who, they say, used thus to scorn the people's talk: "The people hiss me, but at home I clap my hands for myself, once I gaze on the moneys in my chest"'.

124. *again' I come*] against or in anticipation of my coming.

Of a whole rick of corn, which I will hide
Under the ground, and with the straw thereof
I'll stuff the outsides of my other mows.
That done, I'll have 'em empty all my garners   130
And i' the friendly earth bury my store,
That, when the searchers come, they may suppose
All's spent, and that my fortunes were belied.
And, to lend more opinion to my want
And stop that many-mouthèd vulgar dog   135
(Which else would still be baying at my door),
Each market day I will be seen to buy
Part of the purest wheat, as for my household,
Where, when it comes, it shall increase my heaps.
'Twill yield me treble gain at this dear time,   140
Promised in this dear book. I have cast all.
Till then, I will not sell an ear. I'll hang first.
O, I shall make my prizes as I list!
My house and I can feed on pease and barley.
What though a world of wretches starve the while?   145
'He that will thrive must think no courses vile.'   *Exit.*

GREX

Cordatus. Now, signor, how approve you this? Have the
    humorists expressed themselves truly, or no?
Mitis. Yes, if it be well prosecuted. 'Tis hit hereto happy
    enough, but methinks Macilente went hence too soon.   150

146. SD] *Q; not in F.*

---

129. *mows*] stacks of cut grain or hay in a barn.
132. *searchers*] government inspectors authorized to prevent farmers from
cornering markets of essential products for purposes of exploitation and
profiteering. Specific provisions for searchers to discover where corn was
wasted appeared in the 23 August 1598 proclamation (*Proclamations* 2.355,
in the BL).
133. *belied*] misreported, lied about.
135. *many-mouthèd vulgar dog*] a variation on the Hydra, common as a
figure of the mob, here representing the many mouths of the poor and
envious, baying and yelping for food.
136. *still*] continually.
141. *cast*] forecast.
146.] represented as proverbial, but having no known source.
149. *prosecuted*] continued, followed up.
hit] on target.

He might have been made to stay and speak somewhat
in reproof of Sordido's wretchedness, now at the last.

Cordatus. O no, that had been extremely improper. Besides,
he had continued the scene too long with him as 'twas,
being in no more action.   155

Mitis. You may enforce the length as a necessary reason, but,
for propriety, the scene would very well have borne it, in
my judgement.

Cordatus. O, worst of both! Why, you mistake his humour
utterly then.   160

Mitis. How? Do I mistake it? Is 't not envy?

Cordatus. Yes, but you must understand, signor, he envies him
not as he is a villain, a wolf i' the commonwealth, but as
he is rich and fortunate. For the true condition of envy
is *Dolor alienae felicitatis*, to have our eyes continually fixed   165
upon another man's prosperity—that is, his chief happiness—and to grieve at that. Whereas, if we make his monstrous and abhorred actions our object, the grief we take
then comes nearer the nature of hate than envy, as being
bred out of a kind of contempt and loathing in ourselves.   170

Mitis. So you'll infer it had been hate, not envy in him, to
reprehend the humour of Sordido?

Cordatus. Right. For what a man truly envies in another, he
could always love and cherish in himself, but no man
truly reprehends in another what he loves in himself.   175
Therefore, reprehension is out of his hate. And this distinction hath he himself made in a speech there (if you
marked it) where he says, 'I envy not this Buffon, but I
hate him'.

Mitis. Stay, sir: 'I envy not this Buffon, but I hate him'. Why,   180
might he not as well have hated Sordido as him?

Cordatus. No, sir. There was subject for his envy in Sordido:
his wealth. So was there not in the other: he stood pos-

---

180. Why,] *This ed.; why Q, F.*

156. *enforce*] put forward as an argument.

157. *propriety*] stage decorum, or appropriateness of action, time, place,
character, or language. Cf. 'improper', 153.

165. Dolor alienae felicitatis] grief or resentment at another's good
fortune.

176. *reprehension*] the act of rebuking, or finding fault.

sessed of no one eminent gift, but a most odious and
fiend-like disposition that would turn charity itself into   185
hate, much more envy, for the present.

        Enter CARLO BUFFONE, SOGLIARDO,
        FASTIDIUS BRISK, [*and*] CINEDO.

186.1–2.] *Q; not in F.*

  186. *much . . . present*] rather than mere envy, in this case.

Act 2

ACT 2 SCENE I

Mitis. You have satisfied me, sir. O, here comes the fool and
the jester again, methinks.

Cordatus. 'Twere pity they should be parted, sir.

Mitis. What bright-shining gallant's that with them? The
knight they went to?   5

Cordatus. No, sir. This is one Monsieur Fastidius Brisk,
otherwise called the fresh Frenchified courtier.

Mitis. A humorist too?

Cordatus. As humorous as quicksilver. Do but observe him.
The scene is in the country still, remember.   10

Fastidius. Cinedo, watch when the knight comes, and give us
word.

2.1.0.1. ACT 2 SCENE I] ACTUS SECUNDUS, SCENA PRIMA *Q*; *Act II. Scene
I.* / FAST. BRISKE, CINEDO, CARLO BVFFONE, SOGLIARDO. *F, appearing
after l. 10.*

2.1.] The scene, still in the countryside, now shifts to Puntarvolo's house, as
Carlo warned at 1.2.225–7. Jonson emphasizes this change at 2.1.4–5 and 10.

1–3. *fool . . . parted*] Usually 'fool' and 'jester' are synonyms referring to
one person, but here they are 'parted': Sogliardo is the fool, and Carlo the jester.

5. *knight*] Puntarvolo.
went to] paid a visit to.

7. *Frenchified*] implication of effeminacy and affectation; see *Ep.* 88,
'On English Monsieur': 'Would you believe, when you this Monsieur see,
/ . . . That he, untravelled, should be French so much / As Frenchmen in
his company should seem Dutch?' The French accomplishments were social,
not intellectual. The Elizabethans saw Paris-educated young men as ignorant
and affected; Sir Robert Dallington, *View of France* (1598), described the
French as effusive, inconstant, and undiscriminating (Howard, pp. 105–9).

8. *humorist*] person given to 'humours', fantastic and whimsical.

9. *humorous as quicksilver*] volatile and capricious. *Quicksilver* is mercury,
liquid and mobile at ordinary temperatures.

11. *Cinedo*] homosexual (Latin). Marston, *Scourge of Villany* 3.49, speaks
of 'fair Cinaedian boys' in the context of pederasts and 'male stews'.
Although the text is not overtly sexual, whenever a character is named the

Cinedo. I will, sir.   *Exit.*

Fastidius. How lik'st thou my boy, Carlo?

Carlo. O, well, well. He looks like a colonel of the pygmies'   15
horse, or one of these motions in a great antique clock.
He would show well upon a haberdasher's stall at a
corner shop rarely.

Fastidius. 'Sheart, what a damned witty rogue's this? How he
confounds with his similes!   20

Carlo. Better with similes than smiles. And whither were you
riding now, signor?

Fastidius. Who, I? What a silly jest's that? Whither should I
ride but to the court?

13. SD *Exit.*] *Q; not in F.*   16. antique] *Q1, Q2, F;* anticke *Q3.*

---

equivalent of 'Bum-boy', the subtext has to accommodate double entendres
or salacious action, as at 154–6.

   15. *pygmies*] *The Voyages and Travel of Sir John Mandeville, Knight* (*c.* 1583),
ch. 64, treats 'of the Land of Pygmy, the people whereof are but three span
long'. Pygmies also figure in Pliny's *Natural History* 7.2, and Homer's *Iliad*
3.6. Laureo reads 'a tale of Pignies' in Latin in Dekker's *Patient Grissel* 5.1.4
(Hoy, I.174). Pygmies, probably played by boys, appeared in *The Masque of
Proteus* which ended the *Gesta Grayorum*, 1594/5.

   16. *horse*] cavalry.

   motions] clockwork figures.

   antique] 'Antic' is a parallel form of 'antique'; both words, though distinct
in sense, were spelled 'anticke' as in *Q3*. If 'antique' (*OED* 3) is intended
here, then the meaning is 'old-fashioned'. If 'antic' (*OED* 3), then it refers
to bizarre detail in art and architecture, like a grotesquely grinning face.
Carlo's ludicrous similes comparing Cinedo to a pygmy, a clockwork puppet,
and a tradesman's mannequin suggest that 'antic' is punningly intended,
along with leering or simpering stage business for the boy.

   17. *haberdasher's stall*] selling either hats, notions and fashion accessories,
or a variety of small wares (*H&S*). Cf. Marston, *Scourge of Villainy* 7.180–1,
attacking effeminacy: 'Out on these puppets, painted images, Haberdashers'
shops'.

   19–20.] Fastidius refers to Carlo, but is not speaking aside; he means
Carlo to hear him.

   21. *Better . . . smiles*] Better to tease with fanciful word play than to
deceive with flattering smiles. Carlo plays on two meanings of 'confound':
(*a*) confuse, embarrass; (*b*) destroy, ruin.

   21–2. *whither . . . now*] The full answer to this question is delayed until
133–42. Brisk wants to observe Puntarvolo's eccentricities at first hand.
Carlo asks the question in the spirit of a malign second banana, hoping to
elicit some humorous statement he can then mock.

   23–4. *ride . . . court*] Fastidius Brisk's temporizing answer is the one to be
expected from a courtier, for whom there would be no point in going anywhere else.

Carlo. O, pardon me, sir, twenty places more: your hot-house,   25
or your—

Fastidius. By the virtue of my soul, this knight dwells in
Elysium here.

Carlo. He's gone now. I thought he would fly out presently.
These be our nimble-spirited *catsos* that ha' their evasions   30
at pleasure, will run over a bog like your wild Irish; no
sooner started but they'll leap from one thing to another
like a squirrel, heigh!—dance, and do tricks i' their discourse, from fire to water, from water to air, from air to
earth, as if their tongues did but e'en lick the four ele-   35
ments over, and away.

Fastidius. Sirrah Carlo, thou never saw'st my grey hobby yet,
didst thou?

26. your—] *Q;* your whorehouse—*F*

25. *hot-house*] bath-house and massage parlour; synonymous with whorehouse (see *Ep.* 7), also suggested by the implied rhyme of 'your' and 'whore'.
Carlo is taking *ride* to mean 'copulate': in Middleton, *A Mad World, My
Masters* 5.2.90, when the constable reports seeing suspicious fellows 'riding
a-horseback', Sir Bounteous replies, 'A pox of all asses still, they could not
ride afoot unless 'twere in a bawdy-house' (Williams).
27. *this knight*] Puntarvolo.
28. *Elysium*] the Fortunate Isles; cf. Ind.268n. The sound and original
spelling *Elizium* compliment Elizabeth.
29–36.] Not an aside: Carlo's comments are ostensibly for Sogliardo's
edification, but the 'Irish' reference prompts Fastidius to initiate the hobby-
horse discussion that follows (see 37n). Whereas Carlo taunts Fastidius for
skittish changes of subject and superficial dabbling in various courtly
humours, Fastidius hears his criticisms as compliments.
29. *He's gone now*] Fastidius, rapt in admiration of Puntarvolo's estate, is
ignoring Carlo and Sogliardo. Carlo proceeds to use Fastidius as a case in
point, illustrating courtly affectation, which *H&S* identify specifically as Fastidius's irritating habit of leaving his sentences unfinished (Macilente also
criticizes Fastidius for this trick at 3.3.43–4 and 83–5). Carlo is unlikely to
be referring to Puntarvolo's absence from home, given the rest of his speech.
30. catsos] from Italian, *cazzo*, 'a man's privy member' (Florio); a frequent
term of abuse. Cf. Castilio's page, Catzo, in Marston's *Antonio and Mellida.*
evasions] Latinism: sallyings forth (*OED* 4).
31. *will run . . . Irish*] i.e., with swiftness and agility. Essex found during
his Irish campaign that he could not defeat Tyrone in 1599 because the Irish
foot soldiers were too adept at guerrilla warfare, striking the enemy and then
escaping through swampy land, where pursuit by the English, using conventional battle tactics in an unfamiliar landscape, was impossible.
37. *Sirrah*] common form of address to an inferior.
hobby] a small horse, originally bred in Ireland for ambling or pacing

Carlo. No. Ha' you such a one?

Fastidius. The best in Europe, my good villain, thou'lt say,   40
when thou see'st him.

Carlo. But when shall I see him?

Fastidius. There was a nobleman i' the court offered me one
hundred pound for him, by this light. A fine little fiery
slave, he runs like a—O! excellent, excellent!—with the   45
very sound of the spur.

Carlo. How? The sound of the spur?

Fastidius. O, it's the only humour now extant, sir: a good
jingle, a good jingle!

Carlo. [*To Sogliardo*] 'Sblood, you shall see him turn morris   50
dancer! He has got him bells, a good suit, and a hobby-
horse.

---

49. jingle] *Q, F* (gingle).

(*OED* I). Dekker points out in *Gull's Horn-book* (2.229–30) that the fashionable mount for a 'true humorous gallant' is 'an Irish hobby', elsewhere referred
to as a 'galloway-nag'. See 50–1n and 51–2n below.

40. *villain*] class-conscious term of familiarity, like 'Sirrah' (37), stressing
Fastidius's social superiority, but also suggesting a perhaps flirtatious appreciation of Carlo's malicious wit; cf 'sweet mischief' at 119.

44. *by this light*] an oath: by the light of this day.

49. *jingle*] noise made by large loose rowels on the spur; a court fashion
not intended for riding (the rowels were blunt) and even awkward on
foot: see 4.3.424–31. Gifford cites the activity of beadles and choir boys
in collecting 'spur-money' from those who jingled during divine service
in St Paul's and other cathedrals. A church ruling of 1598 warned choris-
ters to follow their prayer books more closely, 'rather than spend their
time in talk and hunting after *spur-money*, whereon they set their
whole minds, and do often abuse divers if they do not bestow somewhat on
them'.

50. *him*] Fastidius.

50–1. *morris dancer*] The morris is a strictly patterned and controlled
country dance, performed at May-games by six dancers in elaborate dress
with bells attached to their lower legs; hence, the jingling sound. The dancers
were accompanied by fantastic characters (including the hobby-horse) performing grotesque and often sexually explicit movements to counterpoint
the formal dancers; cf. Brissenden, p. 19. Manningham (p. 89) attests to the
currency of Carlo's joke: 'October 1602. One Mr. Ousley of the Middle
Temple, a young gallant, but of a short cut, overtaking a tall stately stalking
cavalier in the streets, made no more ado but slipped into an ironmonger's
shop, threw off his cloak and rapier, fitted himself with bells, and presently
came skipping, whistling, and dancing the morris about that long swaggerer,
who staringly demanding what he meant, "I cry you mercy," said the
gent[leman], "I took you for a maypole."'

Sogliardo. [*To Carlo*] Signor, now you talk of a hobby-horse,
I know where one is, will not be given for a brace of
angels.   55
Fastidius. How is that, sir?
Sogliardo. Marry, sir, I am telling this gentleman of a hobby-
horse. It was my father's indeed, and (though I say it—
Carlo. —that should not say it). On, on!
Sogliardo. —he did dance in it with as good humour and as   60
good regard as any man of his degree whatsoever, being
no gentleman. I have danced in it myself too.
Carlo. Not since the humour of gentility was upon you? Did
you?
Sogliardo. Yes, once. Marry, that was but to show what a   65
gentleman might do in a humour.
Carlo. O, very good!

GREX

Mitis. Why, this fellow's discourse were nothing, but for the
word 'humour'.
Cordatus. O, bear with him. An he should lack matter and   70
words too, 'twere pitiful.

51–2, 53. *hobby-horse*] (*a*) a fantastic character in the morris dance. A
wicker or light wooden horse is fastened around the waist of the dancer, concealing his legs with a long foot-cloth. The dancer then imitates a horse by
frisking and plunging (*Nares*, *OED* 2); (*b*) because of the sexual implications of
the dancer's movements, the term came to refer to any lustful person, especially a promiscuous woman (*OED* 3b).
    54. *is, will*] is that will.
    54–5. *brace of angels*] pair of gold coins worth 10*s* each.
    58–9. *(though . . . it)*] proverbial (Dent, s114).
    61. *regard*] public approval.
    68–9. *nothing . . . 'humour'*] Cf. Ind.73ff. Tucca in *Poet.* 3.4.188–91 also
comments on the ubiquity of the word in the theatre: 'I would fain come
with my cockatrice one day, and see a play; if I knew when there were a good
bawdy one: but they say, you ha' nothing but *humours, revels,* and *satires,* that
gird, and fart at the time, you slave.'

Sogliardo. Nay, look you, sir, there's ne'er a gentleman i' the
    country has the like humours for the hobby-horse as I
    have. I have the method for the threading of the needle,
    the—   75
Carlo. How, the method?
Sogliardo. Ay—the legerity for that, and the wehee and the
    daggers in the nose, and the travels of the egg from finger
    to finger: all the humours incident to the quality. The
    horse hangs at home in my parlour. I'll keep it for a   80
    monument as long as I live, sure.
Carlo. Do so. And when you die, 'twill be an excellent trophy
    to hang over your tomb.

---

77. wehee] *Q, F (*wigh-hie*)*.

---

74. *threading . . . needle*] a step in the morris, probably involving a single
file of dancers passing through the arched arms of two others, common in
country dances.
    77. *legerity*] dexterity.
    wehee] whinny of the hobby-horse in a burlesque of horse-like activity; the
term is onomatopoetic.
    78. *daggers . . . nose*] another feat of dexterity, perhaps, as *H&S* suggest,
a survival of a sword dance.
    travels . . . egg] possibly a trick of legerdemain involving the rolling and
balancing of an egg on the fingertips. It may also refer to the St George
mumming play known as the Pace-Egg play, still performed on Easter
Sunday or Monday in rural areas of Westmoreland, Derbyshire, and
Lancashire: hard-boiled eggs are dyed, carried in a basket by the mummers,
used in tricks and games of various sorts, and then distributed to the
audience and eaten. The performances end with singing and may include
morris-dancing, or at least a hobby-horse figure. For articles on this
tradition, see *The English Mumming Play: An introductory bibliography*,
ed. Eddie Cass, Michael J. Preston, and Paul Smith (London, 2000),
pp. 20-1.
    79. *all . . . quality*] all the tricks suited to the skill of the performer.
    81. *monument*] commemoration of morris dances gone by. The preten-
tious term suggests to Carlo the ridiculous idea of a tomb decoration, which
Sogliardo takes seriously.
    82. *trophy*] originally a token of victory in war, usually arms taken from
the enemy and prominently displayed; figuratively, any evidence of valour,
power, or skill, in this case bathetic: the hobby-horse is a crude clown's role,
requiring more energy than skill.

Sogliardo. Mass, and I'll have a tomb, now I think on 't. 'Tis
    but so much charges.   85
Carlo. Best build it in your lifetime, then. Your heirs may hap
    to forget it else.
Sogliardo. Nay, I mean so. I'll not trust to them.
Carlo. No, for heirs and executors are grown damnably care-
    less, specially since the ghosts of testators left walking.   90
    [*Aside to Fastidius*] How like you him, signor?
Fastidius. [*Aside to Carlo*] 'Fore heavens, his humour arrides
    me exceedingly.
Carlo. [*Aside to Fastidius*] 'Arrides' you?
Fastidius. [*Aside to Carlo*] Ay, pleases me. A pox on 't! I am so   95
    haunted at the court and at my lodging with your refined
    choice spirits that it makes me clean of another garb,
    another strain, I know not how—I cannot frame me to
    your harsh vulgar phrase. 'Tis against my *genius*.
Sogliardo. [*Interrupting*] Signor Carlo.   [*He talks to him aside.*]   100

---

98. strain] *Q;* sheafe *F.*

    84–5. *tomb . . . charges*] Funeral arrangements for the rich were 'grandiose
in scale and portentous in style'; great figured tombs, conspicuously coloured
and gilded, and ostentatiously located, cost around £1000 in 1600 (Stone,
pp. 572–81).
    86–90. *Best . . . left walking*] To avoid the ruinous cost of outrageous
tombs, heirs would manipulate the wills through legal hair-splitting, regard-
less of the wishes and instructions of the dead. The ghosts stopped walking,
or haunting the heirs, presumably because the survivors were not disturbed
by guilty conscience.
    91. *How . . . signor?*] Carlo is offering Sogliardo to Fastidius as an
amusing specimen or curiosity in the display of humours.
    92. *arrides*] amuses, makes laugh; a fashionable Latinism. *H&S* cite *CR*
3.5.82 and 4.3.257, where an affected courtier also uses the term. Cf. Manningham, p. 90: 'One told a jest and added that all good wits applauded it;
a way to bring one to a dilemma, either of arrogance in arriding, as though
he had a good wit too, or of ignorance, as though he could not conceive of
it as well as others'.
    95. *A pox*] a curse; literally, the boils of plague or syphilis.
    97. *garb*] manner or style (*OED* 3).
    98. *strain*] style or turn of expression; *OED* 12c cites Milton using 'garb'
and 'strain' in describing extravagant language.
    99. genius] Another Latinism: (*a*) natural inclination or taste; (*b*) spirit,
essential self; (*c*) a man's guardian 'angel', prompting him to good deeds and
protecting him from evil; both *Hym.* 538 and *ML* 3.4 are cited in Wheeler,
p. 103.
    100.] Sogliardo, perhaps unnerved at being talked about and resentful at

GREX

Cordatus. This is right to that of Horace: *Dum vitant stulti vitia in contraria currunt*. So this gallant, labouring to avoid popularity, falls into a habit of affectation ten thousand times more hateful than the former.

Carlo. [*Aside, to Sogliardo*] Who, he? A gull! A fool! No salt in   105
him i' the earth, man. He looks like a fresh salmon kept
in a tub: he'll be spent shortly. His brain's lighter than his
feather already, and his tongue more subject to lie than
that's to wag. He sleeps with a musk-cat every night, and
walks all day hanged in pomander chains for penance. He   110

---

104. more hateful] *Q*; hatefuller *F*

being cut out of the conversation, evidently complains about Fastidius, to judge from Carlo's propitiating reply at 105–14.

101–2. Dum . . . corrunt] 'In avoiding vices, fools run into their opposites' (Horace, *Sat.* 1.2.24). The modern proverbial equivalent might be 'Out of the frying pan, into the fire'.

103. *popularity*] popular, meaning vulgar, taste, like Sogliardo's.

105. *salt*] wit.

106. *i' the earth*] in the world; that is, anywhere, whatsoever.

107. *spent*] exhausted by spawning (*OED* 5b); all his energy expended.

108. *subject to lie*] inclined to feather-brained exaggeration or distortion.

108–9. *than . . . wag*] than the feather is to flutter. Cf. the description of 'Don Fashion' in Guilpin, *Skialetheia*, 'Satire 5', ed. D. Allen Carroll (Chapel Hill, 1974), pp. 129–31: 'Oh brave! What, with a feather in his hat? / He is a dancer you may see by that; / Light heels, light head, light feather well agree.'

109. *musk-cat*] (*a*) a container full of musk, to scent him for the next day; (*b*) literally, a civet-cat or other animal prized as a source of musk for perfume; (*c*) a harlot (Williams).

110. *hanged in . . . chains*] wearing pendant perfume containers, but referring to the practice of exposing the dead bodies of certain executed criminals to the public view. G. B. Harrison, *A Last Elizabethan Journal* (London, 1933), p. 64, notes for 11 January 1600: 'A Fencer Hanged. Henry Adlington, a fencer, was hanged without the bars of Aldgate for killing a man there, and after hanged in chains on the Mile's End'. *Pomander chains* are scent cases hanging at the neck, wrist, or girdle, often made of filigreed gold or silver, or shaped into oranges (each segment holding a different scent) or snails; see Case 15, Jewellery Room, Victoria and Albert Museum. Gifford cites a recipe for pomander paste: 'but six grains of musk, ground with rose water, and tempered with a little civet' (Marston, *The Malcontent* 5.1.17–18).

has his skin tanned in civet to make his complexion
strong and the sweetness of his youth lasting in the sense
of his sweet lady. A good empty puff. He loves you well,
signor.

Sogliardo. [*Aside to Carlo*] There shall be no love lost, sir, I'll   115
assure you.

Fastidius. [*Interrupting*] Nay, Carlo, I am not happy i' thy love,
I see. Prithee, suffer me to enjoy thy company a little,
sweet mischief. By this air, I shall envy this gentleman's
place in thy affections, if you be thus private, i' faith.   120

Enter CINEDO.

How now? Is the knight arrived?

Cinedo. No, sir, but 'tis guessed he will arrive presently, by his
forerunners.

Fastidius. His hounds! By Minerva, an excellent figure! A
good boy!   125

Carlo. You should give him a French crown for it. The boy

120.1.] *This ed.; placed after l. 121 in* Q; CINEDO. F, *placed after l. 121.*

---

111. *tanned*] preserved, like fine leather.

111–12. *make . . . strong*] (*a*) maintain the youthful texture of his skin; (*b*) nourish and protect his constitution. Strong perfumes were thought to be a preservative against diseases that might impair beauty and prowess.

112–13. *lasting . . . lady*] having an enduring and arousing appeal to his mistress.

113. *puff*] libertine, often with homosexual emphasis. Cf. Marston, *Antonio and Mellida* 3.2.30, 108, 112, where an effeminate 'treble minikin' is called 'musk-cod' and 'puff-paste'.

117. *happy . . . love*] favoured by your attention.

118. *suffer*] allow.

119. *sweet mischief*] patronizing term of endearment, addressed to Carlo; see 'villain', 40, and 'Sirrah Damnation', 132–3.

this gentleman's] Sogliardo's. This comment, as at 19–20, is not necessarily spoken aside; Fastidius's complaint at being ignored is more playfully malicious than Sogliardo's self-conscious whispers at 100ff.

123. *forerunners*] (*a*) harbingers sent before to prepare the way and herald a great man's approach; (*b*) four-runners, punning on hounds running on their four legs before the hunter, a joke caught by Fastidius in the next line.

124. *figure*] figure of speech, pun.

126. *French crown*] (*a*) écu, a French coin, cast with the king's head on the obverse, and, on the reverse, a cross of four fleurs-de-lys around an H, for Henri IV (*H&S*); (*b*) the baldness produced by syphilis, known as the 'French pox' (Partridge, *Slang*).

would find two better figures i' that, and a good figure of
your bounty beside.

Fastidius. Tut, the boy wants no crowns.

Carlo. No crown. Speak i' the singular number, and we'll   130
believe you.

Fastidius. Nay, thou art so capriciously conceited now. Sirrah
Damnation, I have heard this knight Puntarvolo reported
to be a gentleman of exceeding good humour. Thou
know'st him. Prithee, how is his disposition? I ne'er was   135
so favoured of my stars as to see him yet. [*To Cinedo*] Boy,
do you look to the hobby?

Cinedo. Ay, sir. The groom has set him up.

Fastidius. 'Tis well.   [*Sogliardo walks aside with Cinedo.*]
[*To Carlo*] I rid out of my way of intent to visit him and   140
take knowledge of his—nay, good Wickedness, his
humour, his humour!

Carlo. Why, he loves dogs, and hawks, and his wife well. He
has a good riding face, and he can sit a great horse. He
will taint a staff well at tilt. When he is mounted, he looks   145
like the sign of the George, that's all I know—save that

---

127. *figures*] punning on figures of speech and the representations cast on
the coin.

figure] impression, manifestation; sum of money.

129. *wants no crowns*] needs no tips.

130. *No crown*] no bald spot caused by syphilis. Carlo's implication is
that Fastidius, as a promiscuous courtier, might infect his catamite,
Cinedo.

132. *conceited*] (*a*) full of rhetorical conceits or metaphors; (*b*) clever; (*c*)
full of yourself.

138. *set him up*] put the horse in Puntarvolo's stable.

140. *rid . . . of intent*] rode out of my way on purpose.

141. *nay, good Wickedness*] cf. 'Sirrah Damnation', 132–3 above. This
protest suggests that Carlo has taken some salacious meaning from Brisk's
previous words, or that Brisk has paused to suggest such meaning; perhaps
'take knowledge of his—' suggests carnal knowledge of Puntarvolo or his
wife.

144–8.] Like the heroes of legend, Puntarvolo has all the old-fashioned
knightly skills: he can ride a *great horse*, or war-horse; *taint a staff well at tilt*,
break a lance skilfully in tilting (*OED, Taint* v, 5b); and *brandish* and *break
his sword*, wield a heavy military sword, rather than the rapier commonly in
use among courtiers. Carlo compares him to *the sign of the George* in being
as unbending as an inn-sign and looking like a sign's painted depiction of St
George, the quintessential English knight of chivalry.

instead of a dragon, he will brandish against a tree, and
break his sword as confidently upon the knotty bark as
the other did upon the scales of the beast.

Fastidius. O, but this is nothing to that's delivered of him!   150
They say he has dialogues and discourses between his
horse, himself, and his dog; and that he will court his own
lady as she were a stranger never encountered before.

Carlo. Ay, that he will, and make fresh love to her every
morning. This gentleman [*Indicating Sogliardo*] has been   155
a spectator of it.—Signor Insulso!

       [*Sogliardo*] *leaps from whispering with the Boy.*

Sogliardo. I am resolute to keep a page.—Say you, sir?

Carlo. You have seen Signor Puntarvolo accost his lady?

Sogliardo. O, ay, sir.

Fastidius. And how is the manner of it, prithee, good signor?   160

Sogliardo. Faith, sir, in very good sort. He has his humours
for it, sir: as first (suppose he were now to come from
riding, or hunting, or so) he has his trumpet to sound,
and then the waiting gentlewoman, she looks out, and
then he speaks, and then she speaks. Very pretty, i' faith,   165
gentlemen.

Fastidius. Why, but do you remember no particulars, signor?

Sogliardo. O, yes, sir. First, the gentlewoman, she looks out at
the window.

Carlo. After the trumpet has summoned a parle? Not before?   170

Sogliardo. No, sir, not before. And then says he—ha, ha, ha,
ha! (*etc.*)

Carlo. What says he? Be not rapt so!

Sogliardo. Says he—ha, ha, ha, ha! (*etc.*)

Fastidius. Nay, speak, speak!   175

Sogliardo. Ha, ha, ha! Says he, 'God save you'—ha, ha! (*etc.*)

Carlo. Was this the ridiculous motive to all this passion?

Sogliardo. Nay, that that comes after is—ha, ha, ha, ha! (*etc.*)

156.1.] *In margin of F; not in Q.*   *Sogliardo*] *This ed.; He F; not in Q.*
159. ay] *Q, F (*I*).*

---

150. *to that's . . . him*] compared to what is said about him.
154. *make fresh love*] court her as if for the first time.
158. *accost*] address, woo, usually in an aggressive sense (*OED* 6, 7).
161. *good sort*] fine manner, high style.
170. *parle*] parley, negotiation before active strife begins (term from seige warfare).

Carlo. Doubtless he apprehends more than he utters, this
    fellow, or else—   *A cry of hounds within*   180
Sogliardo. List, list! They are coming from hunting. Stand by,
    close under this terrace, and you shall see it done better
    than I can show it.
Carlo. So it had need. 'Twill scarce poise the observation else.
Sogliardo. Faith, I remember all, but the manner of it is quite   185
    out of my head.
Fastidius. O, withdraw, withdraw! It cannot be but a most
    pleasing object.

[Carlo, Sogliardo, and Fastidius, with Cinedo,
conceal themselves so that they may observe and comment
aside among themselves on Puntarvolo's behaviour.]

Enter PUNTARVOLO, *[and]* a Huntsman
with a Greyhound.

180.1. SD] *Over to the right, at the margin, in Q at ll. 181–3, indented to accom-*
modate SD; in left margin of F, with no indentation.   188.4–5.] *Q; Act II. Scene*
II. / PVNTARVOLO, HUNTSMAN, GENTLE- / WOMAN. *In margin: To the rest.*
F.

---

182. *under this terrace*] beneath the gallery, which probably projected no
more than two or three feet from the tiring-house façade. The upper area
may have been partitioned to accommodate the lords' rooms and/or a sup-
plementary playing space. Under this gallery was another space, perhaps an
alcove, optionally enclosed with hangings, which could be used for essentially static tableaux, such as the eavesdroppers perform in this scene; see
Gurr, pp. 121, 134–8.

184. *poise the observation*] repay or be worth watching. The metaphor is
of scales: watching Puntarvolo would have to weigh more as information on
balance than Sogliardo has been able to communicate.

188.5. *Greyhound*] an expensive animal, bred for speed, and frequently
associated with gentlemen, often appearing on escutcheons representing
some noble virtue; see Manningham, p. 32. The ubiquity of Puntarvolo's
dog suggests its emblematic function as a badge of knightly status and
honour; proverbially, 'He cannot be a gentleman that loveth not a dog'
(Vincent Stuckey Lean, *Lean's Collectanea* (Bristol, 1902), p. 438). On
the other hand, it may invite recognition of the caustic colloquialism,
'You are a fine man, an you had a fine dog', as in Beaumont's *The Knight*
of the Burning Pestle 3.535–6. In sexual terms, *dog* was associated with a
homosexual or heterosexual lecher, especially in amorous pursuit, as Puntarvolo is in this scene; it also appears as a euphemism for genitals
(Williams). Hence the affront taken by the groom asked to 'hold my dog',
5.1.17 and ff.

Puntarvolo. Forester, give wind to thy horn.—Enough! By
this, the sound hath touched the ears of the enclosed.   190
Depart, leave the dog, and take with thee what thou hast
deserved: the horn, and thanks.

[*Exit* Huntsman.]

Carlo. Ay, marry, there's some taste in this.
Fastidius. Is 't not good?
Sogliardo. Ah, peace! Now above, now above!   195

The Waiting Gentlewoman *appears at the window.*

Puntarvolo. Stay! Mine eye hath (on the instant) through the
bounty of the window received the form of a nymph. I
will step forward three paces, of the which I will barely
retire one, and (after some little flexure of the knee) with
an erected grace salute her: one, two, and three.—Sweet   200
lady, God save you.
Gentlewoman. No,   forsooth,   I   am   but   the   waiting
gentlewoman.
Carlo. He knew that before.
Puntarvolo. Pardon me. *Humanum est errare.*   205

195.1. Waiting Gentlewoman] *Q; gentlewoman F.*

189–92.] The lines and SD suggest potential for comic stage-business. The
Huntsman may play too long, too unskilfully, or too enthusiastically on the
horn, whereupon Puntarvolo may seize it at 'Enough', and return it to him
at his dismissal. The horn also suggests the common insult of the cuckold's
horns: this insult may be all the huntsman deserves, rather than the anticipated tip.

190. *the enclosed*] an affected way of saying 'the persons inside this house'.

195.1. window] i.e., gallery above the stage.

199. *flexure . . . knee*] bowing.

200. *erected grace*] graceful gesture of greeting after straightening up, following the bow (but debatably with unintended erotic play on the idea of
erection).

202. *forsooth*] truly, indeed.

205. Humanum est errare] proverbial: 'To err is human', as in 'To
err is human, (to repent is divine,) to persevere is diabolical' (Dent,
E179).

Carlo. He learned that of a Puritan.

Puntarvolo. To the perfection of compliment (which is the dial
of the thought, and guided by the sun of your beauties)
are required these three projects: the *gnomon*, the *puntilios*, and the *superficies*. The *superficies* is that we call 'place';   210
the *puntilios*, 'circumstance'; and the *gnomon*, 'ceremony';
in either of which, for a stranger to err, 'tis easy and facile,
and such am I.

Carlo. True, not knowing her horizon, he must needs err—
which I fear he knows too well.   215

Puntarvolo. What call you the lord of the castle, sweet face?

Gentlewoman. The lord of the castle is a knight, sir: Signor
Puntarvolo.

Puntarvolo. Puntarvolo? Oh.

Carlo. Now must he ruminate.   220

Fastidius. Does the wench know him all this while, then?

---

206. Puritan] *Q;* his chaplain *F*   209. projects] *Q;* specials *F*

---

206. *Puritan*] facetious jibe, probably at Puritan preachers, whose emphasis on original sin and the anti-humanist ethic made them frequent butts of
Inns of Court witticisms; e.g., 'A puritan is such a one as loves God with all
his soul, but hates his neighbour with all his heart' (Manningham, p. 219).

207. *dial*] sundial, here a metaphor for measuring the merit of a compliment given to a beautiful woman (the 'sun' whose presence inspires the
flattering thought).

209. *projects*] a draughtsman's scale drawings; here, naming various technical features of the sundial. The design includes the *gnomon*, a rod which
casts a shadow to indicate the correct hour on the sundial; the *puntilios*, the
various points on the circumference of the sundial which are touched by
the shadow-line at certain hours; and the *superficies*, the sundial's face, with
the sector and the rays for measuring the hours (de Vocht, p. 83).

210–13. *The* superficies . . . *I*] In Puntarvolo's conceit, the parts of the
sundial represent the site (*superficies*) and occasion (*puntilios*) inspiring his
thought, and the decorum or appropriateness (*gnomon*) of his remarks,
in any of which it was easy for him, as a supposed stranger, to make a
mistake. (The mistake was identifying the Waiting Gentlewoman as the lady
of the household.)

212. *facile*] Latinate doubling of the English 'easy', not necessarily arch
or affected (*OED* 1, 2b), similar to the modern 'nice and easy'.

214. *not . . . err*] Carlo quibbles on (*a*) the geographical region within
which Puntarvolo 'errs' or wanders (*OED* 1b); (*b*) her range of knowledge
and experience (*OED* 2b); (*c*) the horizontal position taken by a woman
before a man 'errs' or sins sexually.

Carlo. O, do you know me, man? Why, therein lies the syrup
of the jest: it's a project, a designment of his own, a thing
studied and rehearsed as ordinarily at his coming from
hawking or hunting as a jig after a play.   225
Sogliardo. Ay, e'en like your jig, sir.
Puntarvolo. 'Tis a most sumptuous and stately edifice. What
years is the knight, fair damsel?
Gentlewoman. Faith, much about your years, sir.
Puntarvolo. What complexion or what stature bears he?   230
Gentlewoman. Of your stature, and very near upon your
complexion.
Puntarvolo. Mine is melancholy—
Carlo. So is the dog's, just.
Puntarvolo. —and doth argue constancy, chiefly in love. What   235
are his endowments? Is he courteous?
Gentlewoman. O, the most courteous knight upon God's
earth, sir.
Puntarvolo. Is he magnanimous?
Gentlewoman. As the skin between your brows, sir.   240
Puntarvolo. Is he bountiful?
Carlo. 'Sblood, he takes an inventory of his own good parts.

227. What] *Q;* of what *F.*   237–8. upon God's earth] *Q;* in Christian land
F.   242. 'Sblood] *Q;* 'Slud *F.*

222. *syrup*] sweetness, like the icing on the cake.
225. *jig . . . play*] a bawdy farce, written in rhyme, which was sung and
danced as a theatrical afterpiece (Hoy, 4.27).
226.] Sogliardo is agreeing with Carlo and addressing Fastidius; the colloquial use of *your* is impersonal, suggesting common knowledge, not
possessive.
234.] proverbial: 'as melancholy as a dog' (Dent, D438).
235. *argue*] betoken.
236. *courteous*] courtly and chivalrous.
239. *magnanimous*] Magnanimity, a prime virtue in medieval ethics,
denoted outstanding greatness of soul, moral authority, and nobility of
judgement based on wisdom and prudence. Cf. John Skelton, *Magnificence*
(1516?) for a detailed exposition of kingly generosity of spirit and action.
240. *As . . . brows*] proverbial (Dent, S506); used to corroborate and
emphasize (*H&S*).
241. *bountiful*] Charity, or generosity to followers, was another ideal of
noble behaviour, related to magnanimity; see 'To Penshurst', *The Forest*
(1616).
242. *he*] Puntarvolo.

Gentlewoman. Bountiful? Ay, sir, I would you should know it.
   The poor are served at his gate early and late, sir.
Puntarvolo. Is he learned?   245
Gentlewoman. O, ay, sir. He can speak the French and Italian.
Puntarvolo. Then he is travelled?
Gentlewoman. Ay, forsooth, he hath been beyond-sea once or
   twice.
Carlo. As far as Paris, to fetch over a fashion and come back   250
   again.
Puntarvolo. Is he religious?
Gentlewoman. Religious? I know not what you call religious,
   but he goes to church, I am sure.
Fastidius. 'Slid, methinks these answers should offend him.   255
Carlo. Tut, no. He knows they are excellent and to her capac-
   ity that speaks 'em.
Puntarvolo. Would I might see his face!
Carlo. She should let down a glass from the window at that
   word, and request him to look in 't.   260
Puntarvolo. Doubtless, the gentleman is most exact and
   absolutely qualified! Doth the castle contain him?
Gentlewoman. No, sir, he is from home, but his lady is within.
Puntarvolo. His lady? What, is she fair? Splendidious? And
   amiable?   265
Gentlewoman. O Jesu, sir!

---

246. ay] *Q*, *F* (*I*).   247. travelled] *Q*, *F* (trauail'd).   266. O Jesu] *Q*;
O, Lord *F*

255. *'Slid*] an abbreviated oath: by God's eyelid.
255–7.] Brisk wonders if the statements that Puntarvolo has travelled
only twice and goes to church only occasionally might be offensive. Carlo
recognizes that the Gentlewoman's answers are part of the prearranged
scenario, calculated to make the 'wandering stranger' more attractive,
but geared to her limited invention. Certainly she may simply be performing her part unwillingly, perhaps sarcastically, not entering into the spirit of
romance suggested by Puntarvolo's leading questions about himself. If
so, Puntarvolo would have to either ignore her attitude or forgo the daily
fantasy.
264. *splendidious*] brilliant, magnificent, as at 239n. An inflated term,
seemingly a Jonsonian coinage. *OED* incorrectly gives a citation from *Volp.*
2.2 (1605) as its earliest use.
265. *amiable*] worthy to be loved.

Puntarvolo. Prithee, dear nymph, entreat her beauties to shine
on this side of the building.

> *Exit* Gentlewoman *from the window.*

Carlo. That he may erect a new dial of compliment with his
gnomons and his *puntilios.*   270

Fastidius. Nay, thou art such another cynic now, a man had
need walk uprightly before thee.

Carlo. Heart, can any man walk more upright than he does?
Look, look: as if he went in a frame, or had a suit of wainscot on, and the dog watching him lest he should leap   275
out on 't.

Fastidius. O villain!

Carlo. Well, an e'er I meet him in the city, I'll ha' him jointed.
I'll pawn him in Eastcheap among butchers else.

Fastidius. Peace! Who be these, Carlo?   280

> *Enter* SORDIDO *with his son,* FUNGOSO.

> [*Carlo, Fastidius, and Sogliardo remain hidden.*]

Sordido. [*To Fungoso*] Yonder's your godfather. Do your duty
to him, son.

Sogliardo. [*To Fastidius*] This, sir? A poor elder brother of

---

268.1.] *Q; in margin of F at ll. 271–2: Gent. leaues / the window.*   279. butch-
ers] *Q;* the butchers *F.*   280.1.] *Q; Act II. Scene III./* SORDIDO,
FVNGOSO, LADY. *In margin: To the rest. F.*

269.] bawdy quibble about erection based on the sundial analogy of 207ff.

271. *such another*] such a notable (colloquial).

273–6.] The stage-business of Puntarvolo's characteristic 'upright' posture and movement, as though stretched on a rack or stiffened in a picture-frame, is an on-going visual comment on his unbending rectitude and knightly honour. The dog's alert attendance is also part of the running joke.

274–5. *wainscot*] wooden panelling used to line the walls of a room.

276. *on 't*] of it.

278. *jointed*] pun: (*a*) mended by a cabinet-maker; (*b*) disjointed or cut into roasting-sized pieces by a butcher.

279. *Eastcheap*] the eastward continuation of Cheapside, dominated by 'a flesh market of butchers there dwelling on both sides of the street' (Stow, p. 194).

281. *your godfather*] Puntarvolo.

283. *This*] Sordido.

mine, sir, a yeoman, may dispend some seven or eight
hundred a year. That's his son, my nephew, there.   285
Puntarvolo. You are not ill-come, neighbour Sordido, though
I have not yet said welcome. What, my godson is grown
a great proficient by this!
Sordido. I hope he will grow great one day, sir.
Fastidius. What does he study? The law?   290
Sogliardo. Ay, sir. He is a gentleman, though his father be but
a yeoman.
Carlo. What call you your nephew, signor?
Sogliardo. Marry, his name is Fungoso.
Carlo. Fungoso? O, he looked somewhat like a sponge in that   295
pinked doublet, methought. Well, make much of him. I
see he was never born to ride upon a mule.

Enter Gentlewoman *above.*

Gentlewoman. My lady will come presently, sir.

---

296. doublet] *Q*; yellow doublet *F.*   297.1.] *Q*, at end of l. 299; Returnd
aboue. F, in margin.

---

284. *yeoman*] a step down in class from a 'gentleman', a yeoman might
possess considerable land; cf. 291–2n. below.
may dispend] who has an income of, or may spend.
288. *proficient*] advanced student.
by this] by now, by this time (Partridge, *Syntax*, p. 53).
291–2. *gentleman . . . yeoman*] Despite persistent attempts to forbid the
status-seeking lower classes a law-school education, as in King James's order
in 1604 that 'none be henceforth admitted into the society of any House of
Court that is not a gentleman by descent' (Stone, p. 33), a substantial per-
centage of entrants nevertheless continued to be yeomen: see Louis Knafla,
'The Matriculation Revolution and Education at the Inns of Court in
Renaissance England', in *Tudor Men and Institutions*, ed. Arthur J. Slavin
(Baton Rouge, 1972), pp. 232–64.
295. *sponge*] See Chars.66n.
296. *pinked doublet*] jacket with detachable sleeves, decorated with patterns of small holes or slits exposing linings or shirts of contrasting colours
(Linthicum, pp. 153–4). Benchers at the Inns of Court tried to forbid the
wearing of frivolous clothing by law students and members of the bar. Manningham (p. 81) records an incident in October 1602 in which Justice Wray
ordered a fantastically dressed barrister either to remove himself from the
court or to suffer disbarment.
297. *mule*] the traditional transport to court for judges and sergeants-at-
law. Carlo's point is that Fungoso looks too frivolous to succeed in the con-
servative law profession.

Sogliardo. O, now, now!

Puntarvolo. Stand by. Retire yourselves a space. Nay, pray   300
you, forget not the use of your hat. The air is piercing.

                    Sordido and Fungoso withdraw
                    at the other part of the stage.

        Meantime, the Lady *is come to the window.*

Fastidious. What? Will not their presence prevail against the
current of his humour?

Carlo. O, no. It's a mere flood, a torrent, carries all afore it.

Puntarvolo. [*Declaims*] *What more than heavenly pulchritude is*
        this?   305
    What magazine or treasury of bliss?
    Dazzle, you organs to my optic sense,
    To view a creature of such eminence!
    O, I am planet-struck, and in yond sphere
    A brighter star than Venus doth appear.   310

Fastidius. How? In verse?

Carlo. An ecstasy, an ecstasy, man!

Lady. Is your desire to speak with me, sir knight?

Carlo. He will tell you that anon. Neither his brain nor his
body are yet moulded for an answer.   315

301.1–3.] *Q; Sordido & Fun-/goso with-draw / to the other part / of the stage,
while / the lady is come / to the window. F, in margin.*

---

301. *forget . . . hat*] A key symbol of early modern society, the hat was
'forever being doffed and donned to emphasize the complex hierarchy of
ranks and authorities' (Stone, pp. 34–5). In giving Sordido permission to put
his hat on, Puntarvolo shows magnanimity, a quality on which he prides
himself. Compare Hamlet's similar request to the obsequious Osric, *Ham.*
5.2.92–105.

302. *their presence*] the presence of Sordido and Fungoso.

304. *mere*] utter, nothing less than complete (*OED* 4).

carries] which carries.

306. *magazine*] storehouse.

309. *planet-struck*] struck with awe, ecstatic (see 312) as one confronting
his destiny, whether pleasurable (as here) or malign (as at 5.3.522) (Dent,
P389). Astrologically, the planets were thought to control fate.

314–15.] Carlo explains the stage-business of Puntarvolo's pause and stiff
body-language before he can deliver his ludicrously Latinate circumlocution
and the bow that accompanies it.

Puntarvolo. Most debonair and luculent lady, I decline me as
low as the basis of your altitude.

Cordatus. He makes congees to his wife in geometrical
proportions.
Mitis. Is 't possible there should be any such humorist?   320
Cordatus. Very easily possible, sir. You see there is.

Puntarvolo. I have scarce collected my spirits, but lately scattered in the admiration of your form, to which (if the
bounties of your mind be any way responsible) I doubt
not but my desires shall find a smooth and secure   325
passage. I am a poor knight-errant, lady, that, hunting in
the adjacent forest, was by adventure, in the pursuit of a
hart, brought to this place; which hart, dear madam,
escaped by enchantment. The evening approaching,
myself and servant wearied, my suit is to enter your fair   330
castle and refresh me.

316–17. as low] *Q;* low *F.*

316. *debonair*] gentle, gracious; *de bonne aire*, of good disposition.
luculent] brilliant; *OED*'s first instance of this sense, though it is not a new
coinage.
316–17. *I . . . altitude*] I prostrate myself before your feet. Puntarvolo uses
the language of geometry, in which the *basis*, or base, is the line or surface
of a plane or solid figure on which it stands (*OED* 9) and the *altitude* is the
height of a triangle or other figure measured by a perpendicular from the
vertex to the base (*OED* 2).
318. *congees*] ceremonious bows.
318–19. *in geometrical proportions*] (*a*) in angular bows; (*b*) with a geometrical conceit punning on *basis* and *altitude* (see 316–17n).
322–3. *scattered*] dazzled and confused.
324. *responsible*] correspondent, responsive (*OED* 1).
325–6. *desires . . . passage*] pun suggesting that Puntarvolo's chivalric
fantasy is a sexual stimulant. Masquerade is frequently a sexual game in
Jonson, as in *Ep.* 25, 'On Sir Voluptuous Beast'; the attempted seduction of
Celia in *Volp.* 3.7.220–34; and the Stuffs' marital games in *NI* 4.3.64ff.
328. *hart*] female deer. The heart/hart pun on the lover's pursuit was a
romantic cliché.

Lady. Sir knight, albeit it be not usual with me (chiefly in the
absence of a husband) to admit any entrance to strangers,
yet in the true regard of those innated virtues and fair
parts which so strive to express themselves in you, I am   335
resolved to entertain you to the best of my unworthy
power, which I acknowledge to be nothing, valued with
what so worthy a person may deserve. Please you but stay
while I descend.

Puntarvolo. Most admired lady, you astonish me.   340

> *She departs [with her* Gentlewoman], *and*
> *Puntarvolo falls in with Sordido and his son.*

Carlo. What? With speaking a speech of your own penning?

Fastidius. Nay, look! Prithee, peace!

Carlo. Pox on 't! I am impatient of such foppery.

Fastidius. O, let's hear the rest.

Carlo. What? A tedious chapter of courtship after Sir Lancelot   345
and Queen Guinevere? Away! I mar'l in what dull cold
nook he found this lady out, that (being a woman) she

340.1–2.] *Appears in Q after l. 339 (Shee departs: and Puntarvolo falls in with*
Sordido, / and his sonne.); Shee departs:/ Puntaruolo falls / in with Sordido, / and
his sonne. F, in margin.

---

  333. *entrance*] quibble on sexual ingression (Henke), picking up on a
similar hint about entering at 330.
  334. *innated*] innate; frequent about 1550–1650 (*OED*).
  334–5. *fair parts*] quibble on sexual organs (Henke).
  336. *entertain*] quibble on 'occupy or please sexually' (Henke).
  340. *astonish*] stun, overwhelm by the presentation of something
unlooked for. The implication is that the knight understands that the lady
reciprocates his feeling for her.
  340.1. *departs*] exits from the gallery, in order to descend backstage, and
re-enter on the main stage at 364.1.
  340.2. *falls in with*] joins on-stage. Puntarvolo enjoys having Sordido and
Fungoso watch his odd mating ritual, and chats with them while the lady
exits above and comes down behind the façade of the tiring house to enter
on the main stage at 364.1. The interval also allows Carlo and his companions
to comment on what they have seen.
  345–6. *Sir Lancelot . . . Guinevere*] generic terms for adulterers, ironic in
this pretence of cuckoldry between Puntarvolo and his wife. See Marston,
The Malcontent 1.3.53, and Dekker, *Satiromastix* 3.1.163; *H&S* point out
Jonson's hostile references to 'Arthurs', 'Tristrams', and 'Lancelots' in the
'Execration upon Vulcan' (*Und.* 43).

was blessed with no more copy of wit but to serve his
humour thus. 'Sblood, I think he feeds her with porridge,
I! She could ne'er have such a thick brain else.   350
Sogliardo. Why, is porridge so hurtful, signior?
Carlo. O, nothing under heaven more prejudicial to those
ascending subtle powers, or doth sooner abate that which
we call *acumen ingenii*, than your gross fare. Why, I'll make
you an instance: your city wives. But observe 'em. You ha'   355
not more perfect true fools i' the world bred than they
are generally, and yet you see (by the fineness and
delicacy of their diet—diving into the fat capons,
drinking your rich wines, feeding on larks, sparrows,
potato pies, and such good unctuous meats) how their   360
wits are refined and rarefied, and sometimes a very quintessence of conceit flows from 'em, able to drown a weak
apprehension.
Fastidius. Peace! Here comes the lady.

        Enter the Lady *with her* Gentlewoman.

Lady. God's me, here's company! Turn in again.   365
                    And, seeing them, turns in again.
Fastidius. 'Slight, our presence has cut off the convoy of the
jest.

---

349. 'Sblood] *Q;* 'Slud *F.*   364.1, 365.1 SD] *This ed. follows Q, but splits
the SD to include the lady's last line (Enter Ladie with her Gent., and seeing them,
turnes in againe.); Lady, with her / gent. descended,/ seeing them, / turnes in
againe. F, in margin.*

---

348. *copy*] abundance (*OED* 1); cf. the scholarly virtue of *copia*, fluency
on a given subject.
349. *porridge*] Carlo's assumption is that a diet of thick porridge produces
equally thick or dull wits. See his later comments on the virtues of pork as
'your only feed', 5.3.136–66; he seems to be an exponent of the 'you are what
you eat' theory.
354. acumen ingenii] acuteness of mental power.
355. *But*] Only, simply.
359–60. *larks . . . potato pies*] considered aphrodisiacs; see *1 Honest Whore*
2.1.36 and 4.1.95–6.
363. *apprehension*] intellect, understanding.
365. *God's me*] God save me.
Turn in] turn back, exit into the house.
366. *convoy*] artful management, art or trick (*OED* sb.1, 2).

Carlo. All the better. I am glad on 't, for the issue was
very perspicuous. Come, let's discover, and salute the
knight.   *Carlo and the other two step forth to Puntarvolo.*   370
Puntarvolo. Stay! Who be these that address themselves
towards us? What, Carlo? Now, by the sincerity of
my soul, welcome, welcome, gentlemen. And how
dost thou, thou grand scourge, or second Untruss of the
time?   375
Carlo. Faith, spending my metal in this reeling world, here
and there, as the sway of my affection carried me, and
perhaps stumble upon a yeoman fewterer, as I do now,
or one of fortune's mules laden with treasure, and an
empty cloak-bag following him, gaping when a bag will   380
untie.

---

370. SD] *Q; Carlo, and the o-/ther two, step / forth. F, in margin at ll. 366–70.*
374. grand scourge] *Q, F (Grand Scourge).*   374–5. second Untruss of
the time] *Q, F (Second Vntrusse of the time).*

---

368. *issue*] outcome.
369. *perspicuous*] easily understood, transparent.
discover] reveal our presence.
salute] greet.
374. *grand . . . Untruss*] Scourging is associated with the satirist, as in
Marston, *Scourge of Villainy.* To untruss is to unfasten garments, especially
as preparation for a lashing, as in Nashe, *Pierce Penniless* 1.159, referring to
Munday (?), 'The Exploits of Untruss' (McKerrow, 4.90); similarly, the subtitle for *Satiromastix: Or the Untrussing of the Humorous Poet.* By innuendo,
Carlo, the 'impudent common jester' of Ind.351, is carrying on the task of
Marston and Munday (*H&S*).
376. *metal*] coin, money; punning on 'mettle', natural vigour. 'Spending
my mettle' has the further connotation of 'expending my semen'.
377. *affection*] feelings.
378. *yeoman fewterer*] (*a*) dog-keeper; one that leads a greyhound for the
chase (Whalley): a sly dig at Puntarvolo, who has been holding his own dog
since the dismissal of the Huntsman; (*b*) perhaps a punning reference to
Puntarvolo's knight-errantry, with an undercurrent of sexual gibing at
knightly phallic symbols: a 'fewterer' is a knight who puts away his lance or
spear into the support attached to his saddle, as in Spenser, *FQ* 4.6.10. In
this reading, Carlo mocks Puntarvolo's deliberate archaisms as well as his
chivalric charade.
379–81.] The metaphor defines the relationship between Sogliardo, the
treasure-laden mule, and Carlo, the follower eager to profit from him.

Puntarvolo. Peace, you bandog, peace! What brisk
   Nymphadoro is that in the white virgin boot there?
Carlo. Marry, sir, one that I must entreat you take a very particular knowledge of and with more than ordinary   385
   respect: Monsieur Fastidius.
Puntarvolo. [*To Fastidius*] Sir, I could wish that, for the time
   of your vouchsafed abiding here and more real entertainment, this my house stood on the Muses' hill, and
   these my orchards were those of the Hesperides.   390
Fastidius. I possess as much in your wish, sir, as if I were made
   lord of the Indies, and, I pray you, believe it.
Carlo. I have a better opinion of his faith than to think it will
   be so corrupted.
Sogliardo. [*To Sordido*] Come, brother, I'll bring you   395
   acquainted with gentlemen and good fellows, such as
   shall do you more grace than—
Sordido. Brother, I hunger not for such acquaintance. Do you
   take heed, lest—   *Carlo is coming toward them.*
Sogliardo. Husht! [*To Carlo*] My brother, sir, for want of edu-   400

---

382. Peace, you bandog] *This ed.;* Peace you Bandogge *Q;* Peace, you, Bandogge *F*   399. SD] *In Q appears at end of l. 400; F has* SD *in margin at ll.*
400–1.

---

382. *bandog*] (*a*) originally, a dog chained up on account of its ferocity;
(*b*) fierce mastiff, used in bear-baiting; (*c*) figuratively, one who reviles or
lampoons indiscriminately.
   383. *Nymphadoro*] 'Nimfadoro, . . . an effeminate wanton, milk-sop, perfumed ladies-courting courtier' (Florio). Marston uses the name for a
courtier in *Parasitaster, or The Fawn* (1606).
   white virgin boot] Puntarvolo seems contemptuous of this effeminate
footwear, but young Fungoso is especially impressed by both boots and spurs
at 414–18.
   387–8. *vouchsafed abiding*] deigning to grace with your presence (a fashionable phrasing).
   388. *real*] (*a*) ample, bountiful; (*b*) royal (*H&S*).
   389. *Muses' hill*] Mount Parnassus.
   390. *Hesperides*] mythical sisters in whose garden, at the western limits of
the world, grew golden apples.
   393–4.] Carlo's equivocal put-down suggests that Puntarvolo will not be
taken in by Fastidius's hyperbole, a pale imitation of Puntarvolo's courtly
rhetoric.
   400. *Husht!*] Hush!

cation, sir, somewhat nodding to the boor, the clown. But
I request you in private, sir.
Fungoso. [*Aside, staring at Fastidius*] By Jesu, it's a very fine
suit of clothes.

GREX

Cordatus. Do you observe that, signor? There's another   405
humour has new cracked the shell.
Mitis. What? He is enamoured of the fashion, is he?
Cordatus. O, you forestall the jest.

Fungoso. [*Aside*] I mar'l what it might stand him in!
Sogliardo. [*To Fungoso, as Carlo joins Sordido*] Nephew?   410
Fungoso. [*Aside*] 'Fore God, it's an excellent suit, and as neatly
becomes him. [*To Sogliardo*] What said you, uncle?
Sogliardo. When saw you my niece?

403. Jesu] *Q;* heauen *F.*   411. God] *Q;* mee *F.*

401. *nodding to*] inclining toward; probably with a play on 'noddy', or
fool.

402. *in private*] The expression suggests two scenarios: (*a*) Before
Sogliardo greets his nephew, he attempts to do his brother 'grace' by engaging him in conversation with Carlo. However, Sordido is unwilling and
suspicious (398–9), concerned about the weather (518–19), and perhaps
eager to exit (532–3), as may be indicated in mime. Carlo returns to gibe
at Puntarvolo and Fastidius by 457, but he may have rejoined them at
any time between 410 and 450. (*b*) Sogliardo draws Carlo aside briefly to
apologize for his brother's rudeness; Sordido may have refused even to
greet Carlo, behaviour befitting a 'boor' and 'clown'.

403–4. *very . . . clothes*] Fungoso's humour (obsession with fashionable
clothes) ignores sumptuary legislation intended to suppress social mobility
by preserving class distinctions in dress. Elizabeth issued ten proclamations
during her reign enforcing the 1533 Sumptuary Act, a revision of the
1463 statute, but Parliament finally repealed it in 1603 (Stone, pp. 28–9).
Article 24 of the 29 articles of behaviour in the Middle Temple Revels,
1597/8, warns students against 'transgressing the Statute of Apparel' (Baker,
p. 132).

406. *cracked the shell*] burst into being, like a newborn chick.
409. *stand him in*] cost him.
413. *niece*] Fallace, Fungoso's married sister, living in London.

Fungoso. Marry, yesternight I supped there. [*Aside*] That kind
    of boot does very rare too.   415
Sogliardo. And what news hear you?
Fungoso. [*Aside*] The gilt spur and all. Would I were hanged,
    but 'tis exceeding good! [*To Sogliardo*] Say you?
Sogliardo. Your mind is carried away with somewhat else. I
    ask what news you hear?   420
Fungoso. Troth, we hear none. [*Aside*] In good faith, I was
    never so pleased with a fashion, days of my life! O, an I
    might have but my wish, I'd ask no more of God now but
    such a suit, such a hat, such a band, such a doublet, such
    a hose, such a boot, and such a—   425
Sogliardo. They say there's a new motion of *The City of
    Nineveh*, with Jonas and the whale, to be seen at Fleet
    Bridge. You can tell, cousin?
Fungoso. [*Aside*] Here's such a world of question with him
    now! [*To Sogliardo*] Yes, I think there be such a thing.   430
    I saw the picture. [*Aside*] Would he would once be

---

418. you?] *Q; you, vncle? F*

415. *boot*] By 1585, gallants wore boots exclusively; previously such
footwear was fashionable only for riding. The vogue was for soft Spanish
leather with wide tops, draped into 'ruffles' and turned down to display the
hose (Linthicum, p. 246).
    rare] excellently, as applied to comparatively trivial objects (Partridge,
Slang).
    417. *Would . . . hanged*] mild oath, meaning 'I'd stake my life on the truth
of this'.
    422. *days of my life*] in all the days of my life.
    424. *band*] flat linen collar, just beginning to be worn with the ruff. Orna-
mental bands, especially Italian cutwork or purl-trimmed, with a tiered ruff,
cost £6 or £7 a set (Linthicum, pp. 155–6).
    425. *hose*] included upperstocks, or breeches, and netherstocks, or stock-
ings (Linthicum, p. 210).
    426–7. *motion . . . The City of Nineveh*] puppet-show. See Ind.162–3n.
    427. *Jonas*] Jonah.
    427–8. *Fleet Bridge*] one of the four bridges across the Fleet Ditch, asso-
ciated with crude city tastes in entertainment; its puppet-shows are also mentioned in *Volp.* 5.4.77 (Chalfant).
    428. *cousin*] kinsman; in this case, nephew.
    429. *Here's . . . him*] He's making such a fuss with all his questions.
    431. *picture*] advertisement.

satisfied! Let me see: the doublet, say fifty shillings
the doublet; and between three or four pound the
hose; then boots, the hat, and band—Some ten or eleven
pound would do it all, and suit me for the heavens!   435
Sogliardo. I'll see all those devices, an I come to London once.
Fungoso. [*Aside*] God's lid, an I could compass it, 'twere rare!
[*To Sogliardo*] Hark you, uncle.
Sogliardo. What says my nephew?   440
Fungoso. Faith, uncle, I'd ha' desired you to have made a
motion for me to my father in a thing that—Walk aside
and I'll tell you, sir—No more but this: there's a parcel
of law books (some twenty pound's worth) that lie in a
place for little more than half the money they cost, and I   445

---

434. the hat] *Q;* hat *F*   444. pound's] *Q, F* (pounds*)*.

432–5.] moderate prices. Despite variables of design and fabric, Fungoso
could purchase a modest doublet for 50*s*, or £2 10*s*, French hose for £3 or
less, boots for another 10*s*, and £4 for a felt hat and simple band (Linthicum,
pp. 199, 204–10, 246), for a total of £10.

435–6. *for the heavens*] i.e., perfectly. The phrase may simply be another
mild oath ('by heaven'), or suggest a theatre-conscious seating arrangement:
Fungoso will be so well-dressed that he could join the high-fashion crowd
'over the stage i' the lords' room', mentioned at 476. The heavens was the
underside of the penthouse roof over the stage; the lords' room was in the
gallery under the roofed area.

438. *compass*] achieve, attain.

442. *motion*] legal application made in the course of a lawsuit; see
Chars.77n.

444. *law books*] abstracts of court records dating from the Middle Ages.
Actual textbooks became available from 1600 (e.g.,William Fulbeck,*A Direc-
tion or Preparative to the Study of the Law*, 1600), but Fungoso would have
had access only to the reprints of Plowden *et al.* discussed at 447-8n below.
I have listed only editions and prices available before 1600; I am grateful to
R. J. Fehrenbach, General Editor, *Private Libraries in Renaissance England*,
College of William and Mary, Williamsburg, Virginia, for checking invento-
ries in his database for me. Other legal publications in use were Littleton,
Tenures (1557), costing 4*d* to 6*d* in 1597;William Rastell, *A Collection of Entries*
(1566), probably his edition of Littleton, 12*d* in 1593; and John Rastell, *An
Exposition of Certain Difficult and Obscure Words,* 6*d* in 1597.

twenty pound's] *Q*'s 'pounds' could be modernized as pound's or pounds';
'pound' was used collectively to denote more than one, as in 'three or four
pound', 433, 'some twelve pound or twenty mark', 446, and elsewhere.
According to inventories of 1597–9, Fungoso could purchase all the books
he mentions for £2 6*s*, far below the estimate he gives here.

444–5. *lie in a place*] are for sale in a bookshop.

think, for some twelve pound or twenty mark, I could go
near to redeem 'em. There's Plowden, Dyer, Brooke, and
Fitzherbert—divers such as I must have ere long—and
you know I were as good save five or six pound as not,
uncle. I pray you, move it for me.   450
Sogliardo. That I will. When would you have me do it?
Presently?
Fungoso. O, ay, I pray you, good uncle! [*Aside, as Sogliardo and
Sordido step to one side*] God send me good luck! Lord,

---

446. *mark*] valued at 13s 4d, or two-thirds of a pound (*OED*).

447. *redeem*] purchase (*OED* 7).

447-8. *Plowden . . . Fitzherbert*] eminent   jurists.   Edmund   Plowden
(Middle Temple), 1518-85, wrote the standard reference work, *Les Comen-
taries . . . de dyvers cases esteantes matters en ley, & de les Argumentes sur yceux*
(1571), covering law from Edward VI to Elizabeth I, reprinted and enlarged
in 1578, 1579, and 1599; the cost of used copies varied from 4s to 8s. *Abridgement of dyvers reports* by Sir James Dyer (Middle Temple), 1512-82, Chief
Justice of the Court of Common Pleas, edited and published in 1588, and
subsequently reissued, was a collection of law cases stating material facts,
arguments of counsel, and judge's decision; in 1597, the volume was
appraised at 6d. Sir Robert Brooke (Middle Temple), Chief Justice of the
Court of Common Pleas and Speaker of the House of Commons, compiled
a digest of year-books, or court records: *La Graunde Abridgement*, 1568
(reprinted 1570, 1573, 1576, 1586), is based on Fitzherbert's work, but more
coherent in arrangement and commentary; a complete set in 1599 was
appraised at 23s 4d. Brooke also reported more recent cases, published in
1578, and reprinted 1587 and subsequently; these cost 8d in 1597. Sir
Anthony Fitzherbert (Gray's Inn), 1470-1538, Justice of the Common Pleas,
produced *La Graunde Abridgement*, 1514 (reprinted 1565, 1573, 1577), the
authority for precedents not mentioned in the year-books; it cost 16s in 1597.
He also published in 1534 a manual of procedure, *La Novel Natura Brevium*
(reissued frequently to 1598; it cost 2s in 1599) and a commentary on municipal courts, translated as *The new Book of Justices of the Peace* (often reprinted
to 1594; it cost 12d in 1597), as well as texts on landed interests (R. J. Fehrenbach and E. S. Ledham-Green, eds, *Private Libraries in Renaissance England:
A Collection and Catalogue of Tudor and Early Strart Book-lists* (Binghamton
NY, 1992-3), and *DNB*).

448. *divers*] several, sundry; common in legal phraseology (*OED* 3).

449. *were as good*] might as well.

450. *move*] urge, propose; in legal jargon, solicit an action on someone's
behalf (*OED* 12).

453-4. SD] When Sogliardo rejoins his brother, Carlo may take the opportunity to rejoin Puntarvolo and Fastidius, if he has not already done so; see
402n.

an 't be thy will, prosper it! O Jesu! Now, now, if it take   455
(O Christ!) I am made forever!

Fastidius. [*To Puntarvolo*] Shall I tell you, sir? By this air, I am
the most beholding to that lord of any gentleman living.
He does use me the most honourably and with the greatest respect, more indeed than can be uttered with any   460
opinion of truth.

Puntarvolo. Then have you the Count Gratiato?

Fastidius. As true noble a gentleman too as any breathes. I
am exceedingly endeared to his love. By Jesu (I
protest to you, signor, I speak it not gloriously, nor   465
out of affectation, but—[*Shrugs*]) there's he and the
Count Frugale, Signor Illustre, Signor Luculento, and a
sort of 'em, that, when I am at the court, they do share
me amongst 'em. Happy is he can enjoy me most private.
I do wish myself sometime an ubiquitary for their love,   470
in good faith.

Carlo. [*Aside*] There's ne'er a one of these but might lie a week
on the rack ere they could bring forth his name, and yet

---

455. O Jesu] *Q;* O, my starres *F.*   456. (O Christ)] *Q;* now, *F.*   464. By
Jesu] *Q;* by this hand *F.*   468. the court] *Q;* court *F. So l. 521.*

---

458. *beholding*] indebted to; originates in an error for 'beholden', but
common in Elizabethan usage (*OED*).

that lord] unknown courtier, but part of the namedropping now-
heard conversation between Fastidius and Puntarvolo, mimed during the
Sogliardo / Fungoso exchange just completed. See next note.

462.] Puntarvolo asks if Brisk knows and/or has obtained favour and influence with a certain nobleman.

Gratiato] 'adorned. Also favoured, . . . countenanced, privileged' (Florio);
that is, influential at court.

465. *gloriously*] vaingloriously (Gifford).

467. *Frugale . . . Luculento*] All three names, drawn from Florio, are
critical of courtiers: 'Frugale' means niggardly, crass, as of one who likes to
get something for nothing; 'Illustre' means prestigious, or prominent, with a
suggestion of sensationalist glitter; similarly, 'Luculento', means scintillating,
implying a desire to shine brightly, perhaps without desert.

468. *sort*] group.

469. *can . . . private*] who can get me all to himself (with homoerotic
overtones).

470. *ubiquitary*] one who is or can be everywhere at once (*OED* 1).

472–3. *ne'er . . . name*] Carlo shrewdly guesses that no one of any influence at court knows Brisk. After his visit to court, Macilente reports the same
information to Deliro at 4.1.71ff.

473. *rack*] instrument of torture.

he pours them out as familiarly as if he had seem 'em
stand by the fire i' the presence, or ta'en tobacco with   475
them over the stage i' the lords' room.

Puntarvolo. Then you must of necessity know our court-star
there, that planet of wit, Madonna Saviolina?

Fastidius. O Lord, sir! My mistress!

Puntarvolo. Is she your mistress?   480

Fastidius. Faith, here be some slight favours of hers, sir, that
do speak it, she is; as this scarf, sir, or this ribbon in mine
ear, or so. This feather grew in her sweet fan sometimes,
though now it be my poor fortunes to wear it, as you see,
sir: slight, slight, a foolish toy.   485

Puntarvolo. Well, she is the lady of a most exalted and ingenious spirit.

Fastidius. Did you ever hear any woman speak like her? Or
enriched with a more plentiful discourse?

Carlo. O, villainous! Nothing but sound, sound, a mere echo!   490
She speaks as she goes 'tired, in cobweb lawn—light, thin.
Good enough to catch flies withal.

Puntarvolo. O, manage your affections!

---

482. ribbon] *Q, F (*ribband*)*.

---

475. *stand . . . fire*] that is, stand in a privileged spot, in the warmth.
the presence] the presence chamber, or reception room.

476. *over . . . lords' room*] in one of the partitioned boxes in the gallery
above the stage. Jonson himself is warned in Dekker's *Satiromastix* not 'to
venture on the stage, when your play is ended, and to exchange courtesies,
and compliments with gallants in the Lords' rooms' (*H&S*).

479. *mistress*] in the Petrarchan sense: a woman who dominates and influ-
ences her admirer by her virtuous perfection; in this case, by her wit. The
term implies no carnal intimacy.

481. *favours*] love-tokens.

482. *speak it, she is*] announce that she is; redundant use of 'it', as prepara-
tory object, anticipatory of noun clause or phrase (Partridge, *Syntax*, pp.
21–2).
ribbon] used for belts, hatbands, garters, shoelaces, and hair-ties
(Linthicum, p. 283). Fastidius wears his as an earring.

486. *the lady*] use of 'the' to emphasize unique and outstanding quality
(Partridge, *Syntax*, p. 90).

491. *'tired*] attired.
cobweb lawn] flimsy transparent linen. This derogatory image appears in
Satiromastix I.2.148: Horace/Jonson refers to Fannius/Dekker as 'the slight-
est cobweb-lawn piece of a poet, oh God!'

493.] Restrain your outbursts.

Fastidius. [*To Carlo*] Well, if thou be'st not plagued for this
    blasphemy one day—   495
Puntarvolo. [*To Fastidius*] Come, regard not a jester. It is in
    the power of my purse to make him speak well or ill
    of me.
Fastidius. [*To Puntarvolo*] Sir, I affirm it to you (upon my
    credit and judgement) she has the most harmonious and   500
    musical strain of wit that ever tempted a true ear, and yet
    to see—A rude tongue will profane heaven!
Puntarvolo. I am not ignorant of it, sir.
Fastidius. O, it flows from her like nectar, and she doth give
    it that sweet, quick grace and exornation in the compo-   505
    sure that (by this good heaven) she does observe as pure
    a phrase and use as choice figures in her ordinary con-
    ferences as any be i' the *Arcadia.*
Carlo. Or rather in Greene's works, whence she may steal with
    more security.   510
   [*Sordido and Fungoso speak together before joining the others.*]
Sordido. Well, if ten pound will fetch 'em, you shall have it,
    but I'll part with no more.
Fungoso. I'll try what that will do, if you please.
Sordido. Do so, and, when you have 'em, study hard.
Fungoso. Yes, sir. [*Aside*] An I could study to get forty shillings   515
    more now! Well, I will put myself into the fashion, as far
    as this will go, presently.
Sordido. I wonder it rains not! The almanac says we should
    have store of rain today.

---

502. will] *Q;* would *F*   heaven] *Q;* heauen, if it could *F*   506. (by this
good heaven)] *Italic in Q;* (by this good aire, as I am an honest man, would
I might neuer stirre, sir, but) *F*

---

   505. *exornation*] rhetorical embellishment.
   505–6. *composure*] composition.
   507. *figures*] figures of speech.
   508. Arcadia] Sir Philip Sidney's pastoral romance (1590); Jonson did not
admire it (*Conv. Drum.* 190–3, 611–12), but Fungoso does (3.1.307).
   509. *Greene's works*] short romances, with more popular appeal than the
Arcadia, written in the style of Lyly's *Euphues.* Carlo suggests that a vastly
overpraised poseur like Saviolina more likely resembles the wit of Greene's
Pandosto, rather than a work written by a genuine courtier-wit like Sidney.
   511. *'em*] the law books (444–53).
   515. *study*] figure out how.

Puntarvolo. [*To Fastidius*] Why, sir, tomorrow I will associate   520
    you to the court myself, and from thence to the city about
    a business, a project I have. I will expose it to you, sir.
    Carlo, I am sure, has heard of it.
Carlo. What's that, sir?
Puntarvolo. I do intend this year of jubilee to travel, and   525
    (because I will not altogether go upon expense) I am
    determined to put forth some five thousand pound to be
    paid me five for one upon the return of myself, my wife,
    and my dog from the Turk's court in Constantinople. If
    all or either of us miscarry in the journey, 'tis gone. If we   530

---

525. jubilee to] *Q (Iubile to); Iubile*, comming on, to *F*

520. *associate*] accompany (affected Latinate language).
522. *expose*] expound (another Latinate term).
525. *this year of jubilee*] 1600. The phrase in Jewish history refers to a year
of emancipation and restoration which, according to Leviticus 25, was to be
held every fifty years. Pope Boniface VIII instituted a year of remission as a
Roman Catholic practice in 1300, when plenary indulgence might be earned
by a pilgrimage to Rome or other acts of piety. The jubilee was at first every
hundred years, then shortened to every fifty years by Jonson's day, and subsequently became an irregular occasion.
526. *upon expense*] at my own expense.
527. *put . . . pound*] Gambling on returns from dangerous or unlikely
journeys was a form of insurance; five for one is better than usual odds. See
Chars.19n. The wager indicates the risks of travel, since the expectation is
that the traveller will *not* return. Very few met expenses or made a profit.
Costs were high for ship-passage, horse-rental, carts or carriages, baggage
transport, border tolls and duties, passports, meals, and lodging. For personal safety, a traveller to the east hired a Janizary as a bodyguard to protect
him from robbers, disbanded soldiers, white-slavers, kidnappers, or pirates,
any of whom might torture or murder him for spite or profit. Other risks
included death from disease, with subsequent confiscation of goods by the
state, and either the purchase of new clothes or suffering fines or imprisonment because of the sumptuary laws in various countries. See Bates, *Touring
in 1600*, pp. 327–68.
529. *Constantinople*] Nashe refers to wagers on a journey to Constantinople in *The Terrors of the Night* (1.348). Fynes and Henry Moryson stopped
there during their journey to Jerusalem, 1595–7; Henry lost his three-for-one
investment of £400 when he died in Aleppo (Bates, pp. 4–5). The Inns of
Court may have taken a parochial interest in the east, piqued by Robert Carr
of the Middle Temple, translator of *The Mahumetan or Turkish History* (mentioned in G. B. Harrison, *A Last Elizabethan Journal* (London, 1933), 20
March 1600).

be successful, why, there will be twenty-five thousand
pound to entertain time withal. [*Sordido starts to leave.*]
Nay, go not, neighbour Sordido. Stay tonight and help to
make our society the fuller. Gentlemen, frolic! [*Fastidius
joins Sordido, Sogliardo, and Fungoso.*] Carlo? What? Dull   535
now?

Carlo. I was thinking on your project, sir, an you call it so. Is
this the dog goes with you?

Puntarvolo. This is the dog, sir.

Carlo. He do' not go barefoot, does he?   540

Puntarvolo. Away, you traitor, away!

Carlo. Nay, afore God, I speak simply. He may prick his foot
with a thorn, and be as much as the whole venture is
worth. Besides, for a dog that never travelled before, it's
a huge journey to Constantinople. I'll tell you now, an he   545
were mine, I'd have some present conference with a
physician, what antidotes were good to give him, and
preservatives against poison, for, assure you, if once your
money be out, there'll be divers attempts made against
the life of the poor animal.   550

Puntarvolo. Thou art still dangerous.

Fastidius. Is Signor Deliro's wife your kinswoman?

Sogliardo. Ay, sir, she is my niece, my brother's daughter here,
and my nephew's sister.

Sordido. Do you know her, sir?   555

Fastidius. O God, sir, Signor Deliro, her husband, is my
merchant.

547–8. and preservatives] *Q;* preseruatiues *F.*

531–2. *twenty-five thousand pound*] provided the wagerers pay up; in *Nine
Day's Wonder,* ed. G. B. Harrison (London, 1923), p. 27, Kemp remarks of
his three-for-one gains: 'some that love me, regard my pains and respect their
promise, have sent home the treble worth; some other at first sight have paid
me, if I came to seek them; others I cannot see, nor will they willingly be
found, and these are the greater number'.

541. *traitor*] rascal, rogue.

548. *assure you*] I assure you.

549. *out*] put down for the wager.

551. *still dangerous*] always chary, reluctant to take risks or accede to
another's views (*OED* 1c).

557. *merchant*] usurer; cf. 2.2.299–305. London merchants made money
in trade first, then turned to usury. By law, they received 10 per cent interest, but could extort more. Between 1580 and 1620, all merchants seemed

Fungoso. [*To Sordido*] Ay, I have seen this gentleman there
often.

Fastidius. I cry you mercy, sir. Let me crave your name, pray   560
you.

Fungoso. Fungoso, sir.

Fastidius. Good Signor Fungoso, I shall request to know you
better, sir.

Fungoso. I am her brother, sir.   565

Fastidius. In fair time, sir.

Puntarvolo. Come, gentlemen. I will be your conduct.

Fastidius. [*To Fungoso*] Nay, pray you, sir. We shall meet at
Signor Deliro's often.

Sogliardo. [*Following*] You shall ha' me at the heralds' office,   570
sir, for some week or so, at my first coming up. Come,
Carlo.

Exeunt.

GREX

Mitis. Methinks, Cordatus, he dwelt somewhat too long on
this scene: it hung i' the hand.

---

558. Ay, I] *Q, F (* I, I*)*.

---

to have some money-lending schemes, and were frequently pilloried for it in
Jacobean drama; e.g., Thomas Sutton, reputedly the model for Volpone, had
£45,000 lent out at interest when he died (Stone, p. 534).

566. *In fair time*] a casual greeting, like 'Well met' (Onions); see the
similar greeting, 'In good time', at 3.1.456 and 4.3.118.

567. *I . . . conduct*] I will lead or escort you. He may be addressing
Sordido, the reluctant guest, directly.

568. *Nay, pray you, sir*] As the other characters prepare to exit, Fastidius
gives Fungoso precedence, although Fungoso, out of admiration, has stood
back to let him go first. Sogliardo follows closely (570–2), trying to associate himself with the courtier, but making sure Carlo is at his heels.

570. *ha' me*] find me.
heralds' office] Derby House, home of the College of Heralds, 1555–1666,
in the immediate neighbourhood of St Paul's Cathedral; cf. 2.2.352; 3.1.82
(Nason, p. 90).

571. *coming up*] coming to London.

573. *he*] Asper, the playwright.

574. *hung . . . hand*] The image of dangling or trailing a dead weight suggests that Mitis felt the scene dragged on, suspending the action without
much purpose.

Cordatus. I see not where he could have insisted less, and   575
    t'have made the humours perspicuous enough.

Mitis. True, as the subject lies. But he might have altered the
    shape of argument, and explicated 'em better in single
    scenes.

Cordatus. That had been single indeed. Why? Be they not the   580
    same persons in this as they would have been in those?
    And is it not an object of more state to behold the scene
    full and relieved with variety of speakers to the end than
    to see a vast empty stage and the actors come in, one by
    one, as if they were dropped down with a feather into the   585
    eye of the audience?

Mitis. Nay, you are better traded with these things than I, and
    therefore I'll subscribe to your judgement. Marry, you
    shall give me leave to make objections.

Cordatus. O, what else? It's the special intent of the author   590
    you should do so, for thereby others that are present may
    as well be satisfied, who happily would object the same
    you do.

---

578. of argument] *Q;* of his Argument *F.*   586. audience] *Q;* spectators
F.

---

575. *and*] and at the same time. Cordatus defends the scene as of necessary
length to develop fully the various characters and their 'humours'.

576. *perspicuous*] easily comprehended. Cordatus has conceivably picked
up the term from Carlo (369).

577. *as the subject lies*] as the matter of 'humours' is now being presented.

578. *argument*] plot.

578–9. *single scenes*] *F*, in fact, does subdivide this long scene at 189 and
281.

580. *single*] singular (*OED* 7), sarcastically playing on 'single' in the previous speech.

582. *state*] sound theatrical practice, playing on *state* as a proper or normal
condition in which something might flourish (*OED* 6) and as a key issue or
major question in a debate (*OED* 12), referring to Mitis's use of the term
'argument' (578).

585. *feather*] Feathers were used as eyedroppers, and still are used non-
medically to deposit small precise amounts of liquid, as in oiling fine firearms
or musical instruments.

587. *traded*] conversant (*OED* 2).

591. *others . . . present*] the theatre audience.

592. *happily*] haply, perhaps; with wordplay on pleasurable involvement
in the act of criticism. *Happily* in Elizabethan English signified both *haply*
and *happily*.

Mitis. So, sir. But when appears Macilente again?

> *Enter* MACILENTE, DELIRO, *and* FIDO,
> *with herbs and perfumes.*

Cordatus. Marry, he stays but till our silence give him leave.   595
Here he comes, and with him Signor Deliro, a merchant
at whose house he is come to sojourn. Make your own
observation now. Only transfer your thoughts to the city
with the scene, where suppose they speak.

ACT 2   SCENE 2

Deliro. I'll tell you by and by, sir.
Welcome, good Macilente, to my house
To sojourn even forever, if my best

594.1.] *Q; not in* F

2.2. ACT 2 SCENE 2] SCENA TERTIA. *Q; Act II. Scene IIII.* / DELIRO,
MACILENTE, FIDO, / FALLACE. F

---

599. *scene*] scene change.
2.2.] The scene shifts to Deliro's house in London. Jonson's focus on
marital discord reflects the times; the worst period of marital breakdowns
among the nobility was recorded between 1595 and 1620, when something
like one-third of the older peers were estranged from or actually separated
from their wives. Middle-class marriages are less easy to track: usually private
arbitration, pre-existing marriage settlement provisions, and local courts
resolved matters at a community level, but some suits for separate maintenance brought by wives of merchants and yeomen do appear in Chancery
court records and in the ecclesiastical courts. Such court actions suggest that
neighbours and family did expect proper separation procedures to be followed in law; see Amy Louise Erickson, *Women and Property in Early Modern
England* (London, 1993), 124–8. Stone, pp. 661–2, suggests several reasons
why this generation of women voiced dissatisfaction: (*a*) a response by
women to the Puritan doctrine of greater equality between the sexes; (*b*) the
improved legal postition of women regarding separation and separate own-
ership of property (Doctrine of the Wife's Separate Estate); (*c*) the better
education of this generation of women than ever before. But see Sara
Mendelson and Patricia Crawford, *Women in Early Modern England* (Oxford,
1998), pp. 126–48, for a darker view. Love-matches were still regarded with
suspicion, if not derision, as in this scene.
   1.] The audience is to understand that Deliro is concluding a conversation
on another subject.

In cates and every sort of good entreaty
May move you stay with me.
>   *Deliro turns to his* Boy, *and falls a-strewing of flowers.*
Macilente.   I thank you, sir.   5
[*Aside*] And yet the muffled Fates (had it pleased them)
Might have supplied me from their own full store
Without this word, 'I thank you', to a fool.
I see no reason why that dog called Chance
Should fawn upon this fellow more than me.   10
I am a man, and I have limbs, flesh, blood,
Bones, sinews, and a soul as well as he.
My parts are every way as good as his;
If I said better, why, I did not lie.
Nath'less, his wealth (but nodding on my wants)   15
Must make me bow and cry, 'I thank you, sir'.
Deliro. [*To Fido*] Dispatch. Take heed your mistress see you
>   not.
Fido. I warrant you, sir.   *Exit* FIDO.
Deliro. Nay, gentle friend, be merry. Raise your looks
>   Out of your bosom. I protest, by heaven,   20
>   You are the man most welcome in the world.

---

5. SD] *Q; Deliro censeth. His boye strewes flowres. F in margin.*   18. SD] *Q; not in F. F adds:* I'll steale by her softly.

---

4. *cates*] choice foods.

5. SD turns to his *Boy*] turns to Fido, who holds the herbs and flowers which Deliro is strewing. Green rushes were strewn on bare floors to act as carpets and primitive air fresheners; the flowers are intended to sweeten the air further.

6. *muffled*] concealing the face or figure in the traditional image of inscrutable destiny.

8. *word*] utterance; actor's line, as at 22.

10. *fellow*] term usually used of a social inferior.

14. *did not lie*] would not have lied.

15. *Nath'less*] none the less.
nodding] suggests the complacency behind Deliro's largess.

17. *Dispatch*] Hurry.

19. *gentle*] distinguished (complimentary address to a person of good family).

Macilente. 'I thank you, sir.' [*Aside*] I know my cue, I think.

Enter FIDO *with two censers.*

Fido. Where will you have 'em burn, sir?
Deliro.   Here, good Fido.
     What? She did not see thee?
Fido.   No, sir.
Deliro.   That's well.
     Strew, strew, good Fido, the freshest flowers, so.   25
Macilente. What means this, Signor Deliro?
Deliro. [*To Fido*] Cast in more frankincense. Yet more. Well
     said.
     [*To Macilente*] O Macilente, I have such a wife!
     So passing fair, so passing-fair unkind,
     And of such worth and right to be unkind   30
     (Since no man can be worthy of her kindness)!
Macilente. What, can there not?
Deliro.   No, that is sure as death,
     No man alive! I do not say *is not*,
     But *cannot possibly be*, worth her kindness.
     Nay, that is certain. Let me do her right.   35
     How said I? 'Do her right?' As though I could!

22.1.] *Q; not in F. In margin at ll. 23–4, F adds: With more perfumes and herbes.*
26. Deliro?] *Q;* DELIRO, all this censing? *F.*   29. passing-fair unkind]
*This ed.; passing faire vnkind Q; passing farre vnkind F; passing fair-unkind
Whalley.*   30. And] *Q; But F*   34. *cannot possibly be*] *This ed.; roman in
Q, F*   35. that] *Q; it F*

_____

22. *cue*] (*a*) status or place, a wry comment on social roles, anticipated
by his earlier complaints; (*b*) theatrical cue for the actor to say his line, and
hence for the character Macilente to play the part of the grateful guest.
   22.1. censers] incense-burners. According to the SDs in *F*, Deliro swings
one of the censers to spread the scent in a virtual parody of church practice;
Jonson used a similar effect in the opening scene of *Volp.* when Volpone
adores his gold in a morning prayer ritual. Here, Deliro describes his wife
as the goddess he adores, and decorates his house like an altar.
   27. *said*] done.
   29. *passing fair*] surpassingly beautiful.
   passing-fair] superlatively.
   unkind] (*a*) not affectionate or sexually complaisant in temperament (cf.
Williams, *kind*); (*b*) lacking the gentle and submissive disposition considered
natural in women, who were expected to be chaste, silent, and obedient.

> As though this dull gross tongue of mine could utter
> The rare, the true, the pure, the infinite rights
> That sit (as high as I can look) within her.

Macilente. This is such dotage as was never heard.   40
Deliro. Well, this must needs be granted.
Macilente.   Granted, quoth you?
Deliro. Nay, Macilente, do not so discredit
> The goodness of your judgement to deny it,
> For I do speak the very least of her;
> And I would crave and beg no more of heaven,   45
> For all my fortunes here, but to be able
> To utter first in fit terms what she is,
> And then the true joys I conceive in her.

Macilente. Is 't possible she should deserve so well
> As you pretend?

Deliro.   Ay, and she knows so well   50
> Her own deserts that (when I strive t'enjoy them)
> She weighs the things I do with what she merits;
> And (seeing my worth outweighed so in her graces)
> She is so solemn, so precise, so froward,
> That no observance I can do to her   55
> Can make her kind to me. If she find fault,
> I mend that fault, and then she says I faulted
> That I did mend it. Now, good friend, advise me
> How I may temper this strange spleen in her.

---

40. *dotage*] (*a*) feebleness of mind or understanding; (*b*) infatuation; (*c*) folly.

41. *this*] i.e., what I have said about Fallace.

48. *conceive*] imagine; perhaps punning on Deliro's desire to produce children.

50. *pretend*] (*a*) profess (*OED* 3a); (*b*) assert, apparently without foundation (*OED* 3b); (*c*) contend, as in a legal action (*OED* 2).

51. *when ... them*] with a suggestion of Deliro's attempts to claim his sexual rights as husband. This hint of sexual inadequacy carries over into 'the things I do' at 52, and elsewhere.

54. *solemn*] formal; awe-inspiring.
precise] scrupulous; Puritanical.
froward] hard to please; headstrong.

55. *observance*] respectful and courteous attention; with a hint at sexual pleasuring.

59. *spleen*] The spleen was regarded anatomically as both the seat of melancholy and the seat of mirth or humour.

Macilente. You are too amorous, too obsequious,   60
        And make her too assured she may command you.
        When women doubt most of their husbands' loves,
        They are most loving. Husbands must take heed
        They give no gluts of kindness to their wives,
        But use them like their horses, whom they feed   65
        Not with a mangerful of meat together,
        But half a peck at once, and keep them so
        Still with an appetite to that they give them.
        He that desires to have a loving wife
        Must bridle all the show of that desire;   70
        Be kind, not amorous, nor bewraying kindness
        As if love wrought it, but considerate duty:

---

66. mangerful] *Q (*manger-full*); manger—full *F*

60. *amorous*] fond; lustful; uxorious.

62–74.] Macilente reduces Deliro's idealization of his wife to sexual enslavement, based partly on Deliro's unconsciously (?) punning references to his wife's 'unkindness', or sexual coldness to her husband, who apparently cannot please or arouse her. Although the advice in this passage mouths commonplaces about training wives generally, the chief resonance is sexual.

65. *use . . . horses*] a common analogy, reinforced by both the law and the church; cf. Joan Hartwig, 'Horses and Women in *The Taming of the Shrew*', *HLQ* (1982): 285–94.

66. *meat*] (*a*) fodder; (*b*) hinting also at the sexual organ, as in *Shoemaker's Holiday* 5.2.223–4: 'And I'll promise you meat enough, for simp'ring Susan keeps the larder' (Henke); (*c*) pun on 'meet' = grapple with sexually in copulation; as in *1 Honest Whore* 2.1.160–1 (Henke).

68. *appetite*] sexual desire; cf. *EMI* (*F*) 2.3.14–20.

70. *bridle*] curb, continuing the horse analogy for the training of brides. The husband must control his own desires, if he hopes to dominate his wife.

71–2.] According to this advice, prudence, not passion, is what makes a marriage work. A husband should dominate his wife and perform sexually as is natural and normal for the species and as the marriage contract entitles him, not out of uncontrollable lust or romantic idealizing but out of an awareness of marital responsibility.

71. *bewraying*] revealing, exposing.

72. *considerate*] (*a*) deliberate, prudent (*OED* 2); (*b*) in the law of contracts, pertaining to a thing given or done by the promisee in exchange for the promise. Natural affection, as in a marriage contract, was formerly called 'good consideration', as opposed to 'valuable' or pecuniary consideration (*OED, Consideration* 6).

duty] legal and moral obligation. The husband should show kindness not out of amorous passion but out of judicious commitment to fulfilling the marital bond.

'Offer no love-rites, but let wives still seek them,
For when they come unsought, they seldom like them.'
Deliro. Believe me, Macilente, this is gospel!   75
          O, that a man were his own man so much
          To rule himself thus! I will strive, i' faith,
          To be more strange and careless. Yet I hope
          I have now taken such a perfect course
          To make her kind to me and live contented   80
          That I shall find my kindness well returned
          And have no need to fight with my affections.
          She late hath found much fault with every room
          Within my house. One was too big (she said),
          Another was not furnished to her mind,   85
          And so through all—all which I have altered.
          Then here she hath a place, on my backside,
          Wherein she loves to walk, and that (she said)
          Had some ill smells about it. Now this walk
          Have I (before she knows it) thus perfumed   90
          With herbs and flowers, and laid in divers places—
          As 'twere on altars consecrate to her—
          Perfumèd gloves and delicate chains of amber
          To keep the air in awe of her sweet nostrils.
          This have I done, and this I think will please her.   95
          Behold, she comes.

                    Enter FALLACE.

Fallace.   Here's a sweet stink indeed!
          What, shall I ever be thus crossed and plagued?

86. which] *Q;* which, now, *F*

73-4.] quoted in *England's Parnassus* (1600), p. 200, under the heading of 'Marriage' (*H&S*). Manningham also quotes it from a sermon given by Robert Scott, Junior Dean of Trinity College, Cambridge, in an undated diary entry, *c.* 1601 (p. 41).

78. *strange and careless*] dispassionately distant and emotionally uninvolved.

85. *to her mind*] according to her taste.

87. *backside*] (*a*) back garden; (*b*) quibble on posteriors or rump.

89. *ill smells*] continuing the scatalogical joke about Deliro's 'backside'.

92. *consecrate*] dedicated, sanctified.

93. *Perfumèd gloves*] popular lover's gift, especially at court (*H&S*).

amber] sweet-smelling fossil resin, used for ornaments, especially amulets for attracting lovers (*OED*).

And sick of husband? O, my head doth ache
As it would cleave asunder with these savours!
All my rooms altered, and but one poor walk   100
That I delighted in, and that is made
So fulsome with perfumes that I am feared
(My brain doth sweat so) I have caught the plague.
Deliro. Why, gentle wife, is now thy walk too sweet?
Thou said'st of late it had sour airs about it,   105
And found'st much fault that I did not correct it.
Fallace. Why, an I did find fault, sir?
Deliro.   Nay, dear wife,
I know thou hast said thou hast loved perfumes,
No woman better.
Fallace.   Ay, long since, perhaps,
But now that sense is altered. You would have me,   110
Like to a puddle or a standing pool,
To have no motion nor no spirit within me.
No, I am like a pure and sprightly river
That moves forever, and yet still the same;
Or fire that burns much wood, yet still one flame.   115
Deliro. But yesterday I saw thee at our garden
Smelling on roses and on purple flowers,
And since, I hope, the humour of thy sense
Is nothing changed.
Fallace.   Why, those were growing flowers,
And these within my walk are cut and strewed.   120
Deliro. But yet they have one scent.
Fallace.   Ay, have they so?
In your gross judgement. If you make no difference
Betwixt the scent of growing flowers and cut ones,

---

99. *savours*] smells.
107. *Why, an*] what if.
111. *standing*] stagnant.
113. *sprightly*] quickly flowing.
116. *But*] only.
121. *one*] the same.

You have a sense to taste lamp-oil, i' faith.
And with such judgement have you changed the
    chambers,   125
Leaving no room that I can joy to be in
In all your house. And now, my lord, and all
You smoke me from, as if I were a fox,
And long, belike, to drive me quite away.
Well, walk you there, and I'll walk where I list.   130
                                    [*She flounces away.*]

Deliro. What shall I do? O, I shall never please her!
Macilente. [*Aside*] Out on thee, dotard! What star ruled his
    birth,
That brought him such a star? Blind Fortune still
Bestows her gifts on such as cannot use them.
How long shall I live ere I be so happy   135
To have a wife of this exceeding form?
Deliro. Away with 'em! Would I had broken a joint
When I devised this that should so dislike her!
Away! Bear all away!   FIDO *bears all away.*
Fallace.   Ay, do, for fear
Aught that is there should like her. O, this man!   140
How cunningly he can conceal himself,
As though he loved! Loved? Nay, honoured and adored!
Deliro. Why, my sweetheart!
Fallace.   'Sweetheart'? O, better still!
And asking 'Why?' and 'Wherefore?' and looking
    strangely,

---

137. *Deliro.*] *Q2, F; speech prefix not in Q1.*   139. SD] *Q; in margin of F.*

---

124. *sense . . . lamp-oil*] i.e., insensitivity. Cf. Dent, C43: 'It smells of the candle (lamp, oil)', suggesting too much plodding study to acquire understanding, and too little practical experience.

128. *smoke . . . fox*] method of starting game from coverts; cf. *Lear* 5.1.22–3: 'He that parts us shall bring a brand from heaven, / And fire us hence like foxes'.

132. *star*] astrological influence.

133. *star*] sparkling gem, prize of high quality.
still] continually.

137. *'em*] the flowers, love tokens, etc.

138. *dislike*] displease.

140. *like*] please. Similarly, *liked*, 149 below.
her] Fallace herself.

As if he were as white as innocence.   145
Alas, you're simple, you! You cannot change,
Look pale at pleasure, and then red with wonder.
No, no, not you! I did but cast an amorous eye e'en now
Upon a pair of gloves that somewhat liked me,
And straight he noted it and gave command   150
All should be ta'en away.
Deliro.   Be they my bane then.
What, sirrah Fido!

Enter FIDO.

                    Bring in those gloves again
You took from hence.
Fallace.   'Sbody, sirrah, but do not!
Bring in no gloves to spite me. If you do—
                                        [*Exit* FIDO.]
Deliro. Ay me, most wretched! How am I misconstrued? 155
Macilente. [*Aside*] O, how she tempts my heart-strings with
     her eye
To knit them to her beauties, or to break!
What moved the heavens, that they could not make
Me such a woman, but a man, a beast,
That hath no bliss like to others? Would to God   160
(In wreak of my misfortunes) I were turned

---

148. you!] *This ed.;* you: *Q;* you: 'tis pitty o' your naturalls. *F*   I . . . now]
lineation as in Q; separate line in F   152. SD] *In Q, appears at end of l. 152;
not in F*   154.1.] *This ed.; at end of l. 154 in Q; not in F*   160. God] *Q;*
heauen *F*

---

146. *simple*] i.e., ignorant and uncomplicated, incapable of subtlety or
sophistication.
   151. *Be . . . then*] May they be poison to me, in that case, if I have them
removed.
   153. *'Sbody*] by God's (Christ's) body.
   156–65.] Macilente's most extreme expression of envy: dazzled by her
beauty, he desires not only to possess Fallace, but also to become a beautiful woman himself, instead of a mere man. In his fantasy, he prays for transformation into a naiad or siren whose fatal gaze might magnetically lure the
'iron world' to destruction. See introd., p. 75. The iron age, as the last and
worst era in classical mythology, the age of absolute evil, is like the satirist's
view of the corrupt world of 1599.
   161. *wreak of*] revenge for.
     turned] transformed.

To some fair water-nymph, that, set upon
The deepest whirlpit of the rav'nous seas,
My adamantine eyes might headlong hale
This iron world to me, and drown it all!   165

Enter FUNGOSO *in Brisk's suit.*

Cordatus. Behold, behold: the translated gallant!
Mitis. O, he is welcome.

Fungoso. [*To Deliro and Fallace*] God save you, brother and
sister. [*To Macilente*]—God save you, sir. [*To Fallace*]—I
have commendations for you out i' the country. [*Aside*] I   170
wonder they take no knowledge of my suit. [*Aloud*] Mine
uncle Sogliardo is in town. Sister, methinks you are
melancholy. Why are you so sad? I think you took me for
Master Fastidius Brisk, sister, did you not?
Fallace. Why should I take you for him?   175
Fungoso. Nay, nothing. I was lately in Master Fastidius his
company, and methinks we are very alike.
Deliro. You have a fair suit, brother. God give you joy on 't.
Fungoso. Faith, good enough to ride in, brother. I made it to
ride in.   180
Fallace. O, now I see the cause of his idle demand was his
new suit.
Deliro. [*Aside to Fungoso*] Pray you, good brother, try if you
can change her mood.
Fungoso. [*Aside to Deliro*] I warrant you. Let me alone. I'll put 185
her out of her dumps.—Sister, how like you my suit?

165.1.] *Q; not in F.*   168.] *Q; Act II. Scene V. /* FVNGOSO. *In margin: To the
rest. F.*   168-9. God save . . . God save] *Q;* Saue . . . Saue *F.*   178. God
give] *Q;* 'giue *F.*

---

163. *whirlpit*] whirlpool.
164. *adamantine*] magnetic.
166. *translated*] transformed.
168. *brother*] brother-in-law.
176. *Fastidius his*] Fastidius's.
179. *made it*] ordered it, had it made.
181. *idle demand*] frivolous question (i.e., whether Fallace took her
brother to be Brisk).

Fallace. O, you are a gallant in print now, brother.

Fungoso. Faith, how like you the fashion? It's the last edition,
    I assure you.

Fallace. I cannot but like it to the desert.   190

Fungoso. Troth, sister, I was fain to borrow these spurs. I ha'
    left my gown in gage for 'em. Pray you, lend me an angel.

Fallace. Now beshrew my heart then.

Fungoso. Good truth, I'll pay you again at my next exhibition.
    I had but bare ten pound of my father, and it would not   195
    reach to put me wholly into the fashion.

Fallace. I care not.

Fungoso. I had spurs of mine own before, but they were not
    jinglers. Monsieur Fastidius will be here anon, sister.

Fallace. You jest!   200

Fungoso. Never lend me penny more while you live, then, and
    that I'd be loath to say, in truth.

Fallace. When did you see him?

Fungoso. Yesterday. I came acquainted with him at Sir
    Puntarvolo's. [*Wheedling*] Nay, sweet sister—   205

Macilente. [*Aside*] I fain would know of heaven now why yond
    fool

---

187. *gallant in print*] a perfect gallant (*OED*, *Print* 14b); thoroughly in the
fashion (Dent, M239).

188. *last edition*] latest fashion, a variation on the metaphor of 'in print',
above.

190.] I cannot help admiring it as it deserves. Here, *desert* means 'deserving' (*OED* sb.1, 1).

192. *in gage*] as surety.

angel] gold coin worth about 10*s*.

193.] A refusal: I'll be damned if I will. *Beshrew* means 'curse, invoke evil
upon'.

194. *exhibition*] payment of an allowance. Law students did not live on
'common stipends' as at Oxford or Cambridge, but maintained themselves
privately, either by 'their places', i.e., paid positions in a law practice, or by
'exhibition', i.e., family support; few had independent means (Johansson,
Law, pp. 22–3).

202. *loath*] reluctant.

204. *came*] became.

206–15.] Comparisons between the scholar and the gallant abound in
Elizabethan literature and proverb-lore. Erondell's *French Garden* (1605),
in Byrne, pp. 74–5, is typical: 'Truly 'tis a vice which beareth too much sway
in our time, that one doth respect more the gilding of the body, than the
riches of the mind. So that one may be bravely apparelled, it booteth not;
one (a Latinism) passeth everywhere.'

Should wear a suit of satin? He? That rook?
That painted jay with such a deal of outside?
What is his inside, trow? Ha, ha, ha, ha, ha!   210
Good heaven, give me patience!
A number of these popinjays there are
Whom, if a man confer and but examine
Their inward merit with such men as want—
Lord, lord, what things they are!   215

Fallace. [*Giving money*] Come, when will you pay me again,
now?

Fungoso. O God, sister!

Enter FASTIDIUS BRISK in a new suit.

Macilente. [*Aside*] Here comes another.

Fastidius. Save you, Signor Deliro. How dost thou, sweet lady?   220
Let me kiss thee.

Fungoso. How? A new suit? Ay, me!

Deliro. And how does Master Fastidius Brisk?

Fastidius. Faith, live in court, Signor Deliro, in grace, I thank
God, both of the noble masculine and feminine. I must   225
speak with you in private by and by.

Deliro. When you please, sir.

---

211. patience] *Q;* patience, patience, patience *F.*   218.1.] *Q; not in F.*
220.] *Q; Act II. Scene VI. /* FASTIDIVS BRISKE. *In margin: To the rest. F.*

---

212. *popinjays*] chattering, fine-feathered birds.

213. *confer*] compare (a Latinism).

214. *men as want*] poor men like Macilente who have 'inward merit' but
no money for clothes.

216. SD] Fallace's line suggests that money is changing hands, but since
she does not refer to a specific sum, as she does in 4.1.127, her question here
may simply test a precondition for a loan.

218. *O God, sister!*] a response to one or both of (*a*) the notion of repayment, and (*b*) the entry of Brisk, now dressed in another presumably even
more splendid suit.

219. *another*] that is, another popinjay.

224. *live in court*] I live in court (affectation of insouciance).
in grace] in the good graces.

225. *both . . . feminine*] of the nobility, both male and female; i.e., of both
lords and ladies.

226. *speak . . . private*] i.e., in order to borrow money.

Fallace. Why look you so pale, brother?

Fungoso. 'Slid, all this money is cast away now.

Macilente. Ay, there's a newer edition come forth.   230

Fungoso. 'Tis but my hard fortune. Well, I'll have my suit
    changed. I'll go fetch my tailor presently, but first I'll
    devise a letter to my father.—Ha' you any pen and ink,
    sister?

Fallace. What would you do withal?   235

Fungoso. I would use it. [*Muttering*] 'Slight, an it had come
    but four days sooner, the fashion!   *Exit.*

Fastidius. There was a countess gave me her hand to kiss
    today i' the presence, 'did me more good, by Jesu, than—
    and yesternight sent her coach twice to my lodging to   240
    entreat me accompany her and my sweet mistress, with
    some two or three nameless ladies more—O, I have been
    graced by 'em beyond all aim of affection—this' her
    garter my dagger hangs in—and they do so commend and
    approve my apparel, with my judicious wearing of it, it's   245
    above wonder!

Fallace. Indeed, sir, 'tis a most excellent suit, and you do wear
    it as extraordinary.

Fastidius. Why, I'll tell you now, in good faith, and by this
    chair, which, by the grace of God, I intend presently to   250
    sit in, I had three suits in one year, made three great ladies

---

237. SD] *Q; not in F.*   239. 'did] *Q;* did *F.*   by Jesu] *Q;* by that light *F*
243. this'] *Q;* this's *F.*

236–7. *'Slight . . . fashion*] The degree to which this line (like 222 and
231–3) is an aside is problematic, and perhaps irrelevant for an obsessive
character like Fungoso.

239. *'did*] which did. As a mark of personal style, Brisk drops strategic
words from his sentences, or leaves them otherwise incomplete. Here
he omits the relative pronoun; at 224, he omits the subject, and at 243 the
verb. His conversation is often, as at 238–46, a series of overlapping self-
interruptions.

242. *nameless*] not to be named, for reasons of discretion.

243. *this'*] this is.

244. *garter*] a ribbon worn either around the leg to keep the hose up, or
around the waist as a sash or belt (*OED* 1a, b). Like the scarf, ribbon, and
feather in 2.1.482–3, a popular love-token at court.

249–51. *by this chair . . . sit in*] instance of Fastidius's ability to swear
oaths 'with variety' (Chars.37).

in love with me. I had other three, undid three gentlemen
in imitation, and other three, gat three other gentlemen
widows of three thousand pound a year.

Deliro. Is 't possible?   255

Fastidius. O, believe it, sir. Your good face is the witch, and
your apparel the spells, that bring all the pleasures of the
world into their circle.

Fallace. Ah, the sweet grace of a courtier!

Macilente. [*Aside*] Well, would my father had left me but a   260
'good face' for my portion yet; though I had shared the
unfortunate wit that goes with it, I had not cared. I might
have passed for somewhat i' the world then.

Fastidius. [*Still addressing Deliro*] Why, assure you, signor, rich
apparel has strange virtues. It makes him that hath it   265
without means esteemed for an excellent wit; he that
enjoys it with means puts the world in remembrance of
his means. It helps the deformities of nature and gives
lustre to her beauties; makes continual holiday where it
shines; sets the wits of ladies at work that otherwise would   270
be idle; furnisheth your two-shilling ordinary; takes
possession of your stage at your new play; and enricheth
your oars, as scorning to go with your scull.

Macilente. Pray you, sir, add this: it gives respect to your fools,
makes many thieves, as many strumpets, and no fewer   275
bankrupts.

---

252. *other three, undid*] another three suits which financially ruined.

253–4. *other three, gat . . . year*] another three suits which enabled three
other gentlemen (who imitated the style) to marry widows with an annual
income of £3000.

261. *yet*] even, at the least (intensifying the extreme case: Macilente
apparently received nothing as his share of the family estate, except his wits).

271. *two-shilling ordinary*] a relatively expensive tavern meal. Prices
ranged from sixpence to half a crown (5s), but Dyce's note on Middleton,
The Phoenix 4.4, mentions three-half penny, ten-crown and even five-pound
dinners. Brisk's point is that rich apparel provides the topic of conversation
over meals at fashionable taverns.

271–2. *takes . . . play*] upstages the actors in a new play with a fashion
show.

273. *oars . . . scull*] See Chars.26–8n. The fashionable water-taxi was a
substantial boat with one or more pair of oars; a sculler was a cheap light
craft with only one oar.

Fallace. Out, out, unworthy to speak where he breatheth!

Fastidius. [*To Deliro*] What's he, signor?

Deliro. A friend of mine, sir.

Fastidius. By heaven, I wonder at you citizens, what kind of   280
creatures you are!

Deliro. Why, sir?

Fastidius. That you can consort yourselves with such poor
seam-rent fellows.

Fallace. He says true.   285

Deliro. Sir, I will assure you, however you esteem of him, he's
a man worthy of regard.

Fastidius. Why? What has he in him of such virtue to be
regarded? Ha?

Deliro. Marry, he is a scholar, sir.   290

Fastidius. Nothing else?

Deliro. And he is well travelled.

Fastidius. He should get him clothes. I would cherish those
good parts of travel in him and prefer him to some nobleman of good place.   295

Deliro. Sir, such a benefit should bind me to you forever in
my friend's right, and I doubt not but his desert shall
more than answer my praise.

Fastidius. Why, an he had good clothes, I'd carry him to the
court with me tomorrow.   300

Deliro. He shall not want for those, sir, if gold and the whole
city will furnish him.

Fastidius. You say well, sir. Faith, Signor Deliro, I am come

---

299–300. the court] *Q;* court *F.*

278.] Here and in the ensuing conversation, Macilente is talked about as
a curious object, but does not join in: Brisk's manner is an implicit snub.
The actor playing Macilente may react with anything from a weary sneer to
barely concealed rage.

284. *seam-rent*] ragged, with torn seams in one's garments.

294. *prefer*] recommend.

296–7. *in . . . right*] for my friend's sake.

297. *desert*] deserving.

298. *answer*] balance or justify.

to have you play the alchemist with me and change the
species of my land into that metal you talk of.   305
Deliro. With all my heart, sir. What sum will serve you?
Fastidius. Faith, some three- or fourscore pound.
Deliro. Troth, sir, I have promised to meet a gentleman this
morning in Paul's, but upon my return I'll dispatch you.
Fastidius. I'll accompany you thither.   310
Deliro. As you please, sir, but I go not thither directly.
Fastidius. 'Tis no matter. I have no other designment in hand,
and therefore as good go along.
Deliro. [*Aside*] I were as good have a quartan fever follow me
now, for I shall ne'er be rid of him. [*Calls off-stage.*] Bring   315
me a cloak there, one. [*Aside*] Still, upon his grace at the
court am I sure to be visited. I was a beast to give him
any hope. Well, would I were in that I am out with him
once, and—[*Turns to the others.*] Come, Signor Macilente,
I must confer with you as we go.—Nay, dear wife, I   320
beseech thee, forsake these moods. Look not like winter
thus. Here, take my keys, open my counting-houses,

---

307. fourscore pound] *Q;* foure hundred *F*

---

304. *play the alchemist*] Deliro is to lend Fastidius ready cash, with landed
property as collateral; in alchemical terms, he will turn a base substance
(land) into gold.

305. *species*] (*a*) ingredients compounded in an alchemical preparation
(*OED* 11a); (*b*) outward or visible form of some real thing (*OED* 3); (*c*) kind
of coin or money. Although *OED* 12 lists nothing earlier than 1617 for this
last sense, clearly the money pun is intended here.

309. *Paul's*] St Paul's Cathedral. See Chars.81–2n and 3.2–3n.

dispatch you] settle or execute our business transaction speedily (*OED* 5).

314. *quartan fever*] ague characterized by the occurrence of a paroxysm
every fourth (third, by modern reckoning) day.

316. *one*] someone (Partridge, *Syntax*, p. 73).

upon his grace] with the aid of his favour.

317. *visited*] provided with rich customers.

318. *in . . . out*] (*a*) refers to the cash previously lent to Fastidius, not yet
repaid. Deliro implies that, if he were repaid, he would not lend more; (*b*)
bawdy innuendo on Deliro's desire to satisfy his wife, who rejects her
husband's advances and favours Fastidius's. This unconscious irony in
Deliro's speech may be furthered by flirtatious stage-business between Brisk
and Fallace. Deliro's attempts to arouse or give 'delights' to his wife by giving
her keys (phallic symbols) to his counting (pronounced cunting) houses
(322) only increase the irony. She, however, is already sensually aroused by
Brisk (332–8 and *passim* to 357).

spread all my wealth before thee, choose any object that
delights thee. If thou wilt eat the spirit of gold and drink
dissolved pearl in wine, 'tis for thee.   325
Fallace. So, sir.
Deliro. Nay, my sweet wife—
Fallace. Good Lord! How you are perfumed in your terms
    and all! Pray you, leave us.
Deliro. Come, gentlemen.   330
Fastidius. Adieu, sweet lady.

                                        Exeunt all but Fallace.

Fallace. Ay, ay, let thy words ever sound in mine ears and thy
    graces disperse contentment through all my senses. O,
    how happy is that lady above other ladies that enjoys so
    absolute a gentleman to her servant! A countess give him   335
    her hand to kiss! Ah, foolish countess! He's a man worthy
    (if a woman may speak of a man's worth) to kiss the lips
    of an empress.

                Enter FUNGOSO *with his* Tailor.

Fungoso. What, 's Master Fastidius gone, sister?
Fallace. Ay, brother. [*Aside*] He has a face like a *cherubin*— 340
Fungoso. God's me, what luck's this? I have fetched my tailor
    and all. Which way went he, sister? Can you tell?
Fallace. Not I, in good faith. [*Aside*]—and he has a body like
    an angel—
Fungoso. How long is't since he went?   345
Fallace. Why, but e'en now. Did you not meet him? [*Aside*]—
    and a tongue able to ravish any woman i' the earth!

---

328. perfumed in] *Q;* perfumed! in *F*   331.1.] *Q; not in F*   338.1.] *Q;*
Returnd with / his taylor. F, in margin, ll. 338–9.   339. What, 's] *This ed.;*
What's *Q, F*

324–5. *eat . . . pearl*] thought to have restorative and revitalising powers;
cf. M. P. Tilley, *Elizabethan Proverb Lore* (New York, 1926), p. 242, referring
to the proverb, 'Pearls dissolved in wine are restorative'. The same proverb
recurs in *Alc.* 2.2.75 and *Volp.* 3.6.172. Horace satirizes it as a form of
madness in *Sat.* 2.3.239–46.
    332. *thy*] Fastidius Brisk's.
    333. *graces*] (*a*) elegance of manner; (*b*) physical charms.
    335. *servant*] Petrarchan admirer, but Fallace is also contemplating him
as a carnal lover.
    347. *tongue . . . ravish*] Fallace fantasizes about (*a*) seductive flattery; (*b*)
exciting kisses; (*c*) perhaps cunnilingus (Henke).

Fungoso. O, for God's sake. [*To Tailor*] I'll please you for your
    pains. [*To Fallace*] But e'en now, say you? [*To Tailor*]
    Come, good sir. [*Aside*] 'Slid, I had forgot it, too. [*To* 350
    Fallace] Sister, if anybody ask for mine uncle Sogliardo,
    they shall ha' him at the heralds' office yonder by Paul's.
                                                    Exit with his Tailor.
Fallace. Well, I will not altogether despair. I have heard of a
    citizen's wife has been beloved of a courtier, and why not
    I? Heigh ho! Well, I will into my private chamber, lock 355
    the door to me, and think over all his good parts, one
    after another.   *Exit.*

Mitis. Well, I doubt this last scene will endure some grievous
    torture.
Cordatus. How? You fear 'twill be racked by some hard 360
    construction?
Mitis. Do not you?
Cordatus. No, in good faith. Unless mine eyes could light me
    beyond sense, I see no reason why this should be more
    liable to the rack than the rest. You'll say perhaps the city 365

352.1. *Exit* . . . Tailor.] *Q; not in F.*   357. *Exit.*] *Q; not in F.*

348. *please*] satisfy, pay.
    355–7. *I will* . . . *another*] suggestive of auto-erotic fantasy: *into my private
chamber* implies sexual ingression of some kind; *private chamber* means both
vagina and bedroom (Williams). Similarly, *door* had a bawdy sense of
'vagina'. Henke cites Furnival's recording of a song about Priapus who
'openeth every woman's door', and Greene's warning, in *Groatsworth of Wit*
(1592), about 'doors' of a prostitute 'ever open to entice youth to destruction'. A key and *lock* are symbolic of penis and vagina; cf. the folk-riddle in
Buckley, *Oxford Libel* (1564): 'There is a key of long time known; it cannot
rust, the use is great, yet entereth in where seed is sown; in every lock it
playeth feat' (cited in Williams). Finally, 'his good parts' refers to genitals;
cf. in *EMI* (*Q*) 3.4.192–6, when Bianca admires a man 'of very excellent
good parts', jealous Thorello asks himself, 'Good parts? How should she
know his parts?' (Williams).
    358. *doubt*] fear.
    358–9. *grievous torture*] the rack, as at 360, 365. Words will be twisted and
stretched beyond their original senses, and the playwright charged with the
slanderous presentation of malicious personal satire. Cf. Ind.83.
    363–4. *light* . . . *sense*] enable me to see beyond the physical limits of sight.

will not take it well, that the merchant is made here to
dote so perfectly upon his wife, and she, again, to be so
Fastidiusly affected as she is.

Mitis. You have uttered my thought, sir, indeed.

Cordatus. Why, by that proportion, the court might as well   370
take offence at him we call the courtier, and with much
more pretext, by how much the place transcends and goes
before in dignity and virtue. But can you imagine that
any noble or true spirit in the court whose sinewy and
altogether unaffected graces very worthily express him a   375
courtier will make any exception at the opening of such
an empty trunk as this Brisk is? Or think his own worth
impeached by beholding his motley inside?

Mitis. No, sir, I do not.

Cordatus. No more, assure you, will any grave wise citizen or   380
modest matron take the object of this folly in Deliro and
his wife, but rather apply it as the foil to their own virtues.

---

368. *Fastidiusly*] Q, F (*Fastidiously*).   374. sinewy] Q, F (Sinewie,
sinowie).   387. malicious and] Q; malicious, or F.

367. *perfectly*] entirely.

370. *proportion*] analogy (*OED* 3).

372. *pretext*] excuse, apparently valid claim.

372-3. *by . . . virtue*] by the extent to which the court has superior power
in social, legal, and cultural matters.

374. *sinewy*] lean and lithe; hence, manly.

376. *exception*] complaint; more dangerously in a litigious age, legal objection; cf. Ind.122n.

377. *his own*] the true courtier's.

378. *his motley inside*] referring to Fastidius, the sham courtier. Motley
was worn by fools.

380-96.] As *H&S* point out, Jonson frequently inserted disclaimers of
this kind as defences against legal charges; see *Volp.* Ded.56ff., and *BF*
Ind.137-41. The concern here is also to establish through contrast what the
'sound or safe judgement' consists of: 'the office of a true *critic*, or *censor*, is,
not to throw by a letter anywhere, or damn an innocent syllable, but lay the
words together, and amend them; judge sincerely of the author and his
matter, which is the sign of solid and perfect learning in a man' (*Disc.*
2586-90).

381. *take the object of*] object to.

382. *foil*] a thin leaf of metal placed under a gem to increase its brilliancy
(*OED* sb.1, 5); here, a metaphor for the contrasting folly that sets off the
spectators' virtues.

For that were to affirm that a man writing of Nero should
mean all emperors; or speaking of Machiavel, comprehend all statesmen; or in our Sordido, all farmers; and   385
so of the rest—than which nothing can be uttered
more malicious and absurd. Indeed, there are a sort of
these narrow-eyed decipherers, I confess, that will extort
strange and abstruse meanings out of any subject, be it
never so conspicuous and innocently delivered. But to   390
such—where'er they sit concealed—let them know the
author defies them and their writing-tables, and hopes
no sound or safe judgement will infect itself with their
contagious comments, who, indeed, come here only
to pervert and poison the sense of what they hear, and   395
for nought else.

Mitis. Stay. What new mute is this that walks so suspiciously?

---

383. *that*] taking personal affront at satire.

390. *conspicuous*] obvious.

392. *writing-tables*] tablets of paper (here, for writing down slanders imagined to have been heard in the theatre).

Act 3

ACT 3   SCENE I

Enter CAVALIER SHIFT *with two siquisses in his hand.*

Cordatus. O, marry, this is one for whose better illustration we
must desire you to presuppose the stage the middle aisle
in Paul's, and that [*Pointing to the door on which Shift is
posting his bills*] the west end of it.

Mitis. So, sir. And what follows?   5

ACT 3 SCENE I] *Q (ACTUS TERTIUS, SCENA PRIMA.); beginning at l.21 in F
(Act III. Scene I. / SHIFT, ORANGE, CLOVE.)*

0.1. *CAVALIER*] (*a*) a dashing military man, or, pejoratively, a roistering
swaggering fellow (*OED* 2); (*b*) a pimp (Rubinstein). Stage-pimps frequently
have quasi-military titles, like Barry's echo of Shift in 'Captain Puff' (*Ram
Alley*, 1604) or Jonson's 'Captain Face' (*Alc.*)

siquisses] advertisements, frequently exhibited on posts or doors, request-
ing information, lost articles, employment, etc. Derives from Latin, *si quis* =
'if anyone', the words beginning the notice becoming the name for the bill
itself (Johannson, *Religion*, pp. 92, 94).

2. *presuppose*] imagine in advance or as a necessary preceding condition.

2–3. *middle aisle in Paul's*] The setting for this scene in St Paul's Cathedral is a fashionable strolling-area for courtiers, professionals, tradesmen,
prostitutes, thieves, and rowdies; also called 'Paul's Walk', 'Duke Humphrey's
Walk', '*Insula Paulina*' (312). See Greene, *Cony-catching* pamphlets, and
Dekker, 'Paul's Steeple's Complaint' in *The Dead Term* (1608), or *Gull's Horn-
book* (1609), for the variety of classes and types to be found there. The object
of meetings in Paul's might be business, gossip, fashion, or just smoking,
despite repeated proclamations from Mary I and Elizabeth I against 'any of
her Majesty's subjects who shall walk up and down, or spend the time in the
same, in making any bargain or other profane cause, and make any kind of
disturbance during . . . divine service, . . . [on] pain of imprisonment and
fine'; the only effect of the proclamations was to prevent the aisle from being
used as a thoroughfare for livestock and wagon-loads of produce (Henry
Hart Milman, *Annals of St Paul's Cathedral* (London, n.d.), 284–6). John
Earle, in *Micro-cosmographie* (1628) (Autograph Manuscript, Leeds: Scolar
Press, 1966), 142–3, summed up Paul's Walk as 'the whole world's map,
which you may here discern in its proper'st motion, jostling and turning'.

4. *west end*] where advertisements were posted on the door. Respondents
left messages below the siquis appointing a time and place for meeting.

215

Cordatus. Faith, a whole volume of humour, and worthy the unclasping.

Mitis. As how? What name do you give him [*Indicating Shift*] first?

Cordatus. He hath shift of names, sir. Some call him Apple   10
John, some Signor Whiff. Marry, his main standing name is Cavalier Shift; the rest are but as clean shirts to his natures.

Mitis. And what makes he in Paul's now?

Cordatus. Troth, as you see, for the advancement of a siquis   15
or two, wherein he has so varied himself that, if any one of 'em take, he may hull up and down i' the humorous world a little longer.

Mitis. It seems, then, he bears a very changing sail?

Cordatus. O, as the wind, sir. Here comes more.   20

6–7.] a book metaphor; folio books were frequently fastened with one or more clasps to keep the pages straight and the binding secure when the volumes were not in use.

10. *shift of names*] punning on Cavalier Shift's name.

10–11. *Apple John*] 'Apple-squire', pander or pimp; *apple* refers reductively and facetiously to a woman's virginity (Williams). Originally, *apple-john* meant an apple with long-keeping qualities, and was subsequently applied to a pimp with a reliable supply of whores.

11. *Whiff*] puff of tobacco smoke. Tobacco was thought to have extraordinary medical powers when first introduced into England by Sir Walter Ralegh: 'It cureth any grief, dolor, oppilation, impostume, or obstruction proceeding of cold or wind, especially in the head or breast. The leaves are good against the migraine, cold stomachs, sick kidneys, toothaches, fits of the mother, naughty breath, scaldings or burnings . . . The fume taken in a pipe is good against rheums, catarrhs, hoarseness, ache in the head, stomach, lungs, breast; also in want of meat, drink, sleep, or rest', according to Henry Buttes, *Diet's Dry Dinner* (1599), P4–6.

standing] more or less permanent (as distinguished from aliases).

12–13. *the rest . . . natures*] i.e., he changes his name to suit his various personalities as often as some men change their shirts.

14. *makes*] does.

16. *so varied himself*] signed his bills with a variety of aliases, a fact he would like to keep secret.

17. *take*] elicit a response.

hull] float or drift on the sea, like a ship with sails furled, moving by the action of winds or waves on the hull (Skeat).

19. *bears . . . changing sail*] keeps veering in different directions.

Enter ORANGE.

Shift. [*Aside*] This is rare. I have set up my bills without
discovery.

Orange. What? Signor Whiff? What fortune has brought you
into these west parts?

Shift. Troth, signor, nothing but your rheum. I have been   25
taking an ounce of tobacco hard by here with a gentleman, and I am come to spit private in Paul's. God save
you, sir.

Orange. Adieu, Signor Whiff.   [*Walks aside.*]

Enter CLOVE.

Clove. Master Apple John! You are well met. When shall we   30
sup together, and laugh and be fat with those good
wenches? Ha?

Shift. Faith, sir, I must now leave you, upon a few humours
and occasions; but when you please, sir.   *Exit.*

Clove. Farewell, sweet Apple John.—I wonder there are no   35
more store of gallants here.

GREX

Mitis. What be these two, signor?

Cordatus. Marry, a couple, sir, that are mere strangers to the
whole scope of our play—only come to walk a turn or
two i' this scene of Paul's by chance.   40

20.1.] *Q; not in F.*   27. God save] *Q;* Saue *F.*   29.1.] *Q; not in F.*   34.
SD] *Q; not in F.*

---

21. *rare*] splendid (see 1.2.26n).

22. *discovery*] (*a*) being found out; (*b*) a legal quibble: disclosing documents necessary to maintain a title.

25. *your rheum*] phlegm; *your* is colloquial and indefinite.

27. *spit*] Apparently a common physical reaction in the pipe-smoker was
an increase in phlegm.

31. *laugh and be fat*] proverbial (Dent, L91).

33–4. *humours and occasions*] Shift's language may parody Nym's in *H5.*

35–6. *no more store*] no greater supply or number.

38–9. *strangers . . . play*] As *H&S* remark, 'an extraordinary confession for
a dramatist to make'; see introd., p. 57.

39–40. *a turn or two*] Four turns was the limit for a man of fashion
(Dekker, *Gull's Horn-book*, 2.231).

Orange. [*Joining Clove*] Save you, good Master Clove.
Clove. Sweet Master Orange.   *They walk together.*

GREX

Mitis. How? Clove and Orange?
Cordatus. Ay, and they are well met, for 'tis as dry an Orange
   as ever grew: nothing but salutation, and 'O God, sir!'   45
   and 'It pleases you to say so, sir!'; one that can laugh at
   a jest for company with a most plausible and extemporal
   grace, and some hour after, in private, ask you what it
   was. The other, Monsieur Clove, is a more spiced youth.
   He will sit you a whole afternoon sometimes in a book-   50
   seller's shop reading the Greek, Italian, and Spanish when

---

42. SD] *In Q, after l. 27; not in F.*   45. 'O God, sir!'] *Italic in Q, F.*   46.
'It . . . sir!'] *Italic in Q, F.*

---

44. *well met*] well matched. Cloves were often stuck in oranges; see
Chars.103–4n.

dry] (*a*) in 'humours' physiology, a fundamental quality (opposed to
moist); (*b*) of fruit, withered, without substance; (*c*) of a person, reserved,
uncommunicative, lacking wit.

45. *'O God, sir!'*] a fashionable temporizing reply. Article 10 of the 29 articles of behaviour in the Middle Temple Revels, 1597/8, cautions against
'answerless answers' of this kind (Baker, p. 131).

47–8. *with . . . grace*] in a believable and spontaneous manner, as if he
understood the joke.

49. *spiced*] dainty, delicate, over-particular (*OED* 2); playing on the fact
that a clove is a spice.

50. *sit you*] sit. *You* is the ethical dative, occurring chiefly in vivid colloquial conversation, indicating the speaker's rising intensity and his presumption that the listener has a sympathetic interest in the narrative
(Partridge, *Syntax*, p. 37).

50–1. *bookseller's shop*] *Patient Grissel* 2.1.20–3 depicts a similar moment
in a stationer's shop; and the Page in *2 Return from Parnassus* 1277–90 elab-
orates on his master Amoretto's intellectual pretentions in a bookbinder's
shop: he will 'first look on the title and wrinkle his brow; next make as though
he read the first page and bite the lip; then with his nail score the margin,
as though there were some notable conceit; and lastly, when he thinks he
hath gulled the standers-by sufficiently, throw the book away in a rage, swearing that he could never find books of a true print since he was last in Padua,
enquire after the next mart, and so depart'.

he understands not a word of either. If he had the tongues
to his suits, he were an excellent linguist.

————————————————

Clove. Do you hear this reported for certainty?
Orange. O God, sir!   [*They continue to walk together.*]   55

> *Enter* PUNTARVOLO [*and*] CARLO,
> *two* Servingmen *following, one leading the dog*
> [*and the other holding a cat in a bag*].

Puntarvolo. [*To Servingman with cat*] Sirrah, take my cloak—
[*To servingman with dog*] and you, sir knave, follow me
closer. If thou losest my dog, thou shalt die a dog's death:
I will hang thee.
Carlo. Tut, fear him not. He's a good lean slave. He loves a   60
dog well, I warrant him; I see by his looks, I—mass, he's
somewhat like him. [*Aside to Servingman*] 'Sblood, poison
him, make him away with a crooked pin or somewhat,
man. Thou mayst have more security of thy life. [*To Pun-*
tarvolo] And so, sir, what? You ha' not put out your whole   65
venture yet? Ha' you?

————————————————

55. O God, sir!] *F*; O good sir *Q*.   55.1–3. *Enter . . . dog*] *Q; Act III. Scene*
II. / PVNTARVOLO, CARLO. F.   62. 'Sblood] *Q;* S'lud *F.*

————————————————

52–3. *tongues to his suits*] languages to match his pretences. *H&S* suggest
this refers to popular satire on the international costume of the Elizabethan
fop, as in *MerVen.* 1.2.66–8. It may also refer to the emblem of Rumour, pictured in a suit decorated with several twisting tongues to illustrate the spread
of idle or unfounded report; cf. *2H4* Ind.
58. *die a dog's death*] traditional; cf. Nashe, *The Unfortunate Traveller*
(1594): 'Iohn Leyden . . . died like a dog, he was hanged and the halter paid
for' (2.241).
60. *fear him not*] don't worry about the servant's vigilance.
slave] rascal, servant.
61–2. *he's . . . like him*] the servant and the dog resemble each other.
Carlo's remarks to the servant have a lewd edge; *dog* was an epithet for a
promiscuous homosexual lover (cf. 2.1.188.5n).
63. *with a crooked pin*] not a literal suggestion, but a variant of 'with a
merry pin', meaning in a merry humour, or for a joke (*OED, Pin* 15).
64. *security of thy life*] freedom from the anxiety or care of guarding the
valuable greyhound.
65. *put out*] i.e., found sufficient financial backers for.

Puntarvolo. No, I do want yet some fifteen or sixteen hundred
pounds. But my lady (my wife) is out of her humour: she
does not now go.

Carlo. No? How then?   70

Puntarvolo. Marry, I am now enforced to give it out upon the
return of myself, my dog, and my cat.

Carlo. Your cat? Where is she?

Puntarvolo. My squire has her there in the bag. [*To Servingman with cat*] Sirrah, look to her. [*To Carlo*] How lik'st   75
thou my change, Carlo?

Carlo. O, for the better, sir. Your cat has nine lives, and your
wife ha' but one.

Puntarvolo. Besides, she will never be seasick, which will
save me so much in conserves. When saw you Signor   80
Sogliardo?

Carlo. I came from him but now. He is at the heralds' office
yonder. He requested me to go afore and take up a man

---

67. *want*] lack.

68. *out of her humour*] the first character exploded in the play. The conventional view was that 'Nature herself desires that women should stay at
home': 'Infants, decrepit persons, fools, [and] women' were considered hin-
drances on the road. Only poor or 'fast' women travelled (Howard, pp. 28,
34).

69. *go*] intend to go.

71. *give it out*] offer the wager.

72. *cat*] with a suggestion of 'whore' (Partridge, *Slang*). This substitute
for Lady Puntarvolo suggests the reputation of women who travelled.
Manningham, p. 196, explains the analogy: 'A whore is no worse than a cat,
for she plays with her tail, and a whore does no more.'

74. *squire*] (*a*) knight's attendant; (*b*) apple-squire, or pimp.

76. *my change*] my substituting the cat for my wife.

77. *cat has nine lives*] proverbial (Dent, C154).

79. *never be seasick*] based on the fact that ships commonly sailed with
cats on board; perhaps alluding to the superstitious belief that cats could
raise or influence the course of tempests at sea without being affected themselves. This latter assumption was an issue in the case of the North Berwick
witches who allegedly used a cat to raise a tempest in order to destroy James
VI and his bride as they sailed home from Denmark in 1590; see Margaret
Alice Murray, *The God of the Witches* (London, 1952), p. 154.

80. *so much*] a substantial amount of money (and perhaps time, stores, or
aggravation).

conserves] medications.

83. *take up a man*] hire a servant, who would then wear Sogliardo's livery
advertising his new heraldic colours and badge, thus giving him social
consequence.

or two for him in Paul's, against his cognizance was ready.

Puntarvolo. What? Has he purchased arms then?   85

Carlo. Ay, and rare ones too: of as many colours as e'er you
    saw any fool's coat in your life. I'll go look among yond
    bills an I can fit him with legs to his arms.

Puntarvolo. With legs to his arms! Good! I will go with you,
    sir.   *They go to look upon the bills.*   90

    Enter FASTIDIUS, DELIRO, [*and*] MACILENTE.

Fastidius. Come, let's walk in the *Mediterraneum.* I assure
    you, sir, I am not the least respected among ladies, but
    let that pass. Do you know how to go into the presence,
    sir?

Macilente. Why, on my feet, sir.   95

Fastidius. No, on your head, sir, for 'tis that must bear you
    out, I assure you. As thus, sir: you must first have an espe-
    cial care to wear your hat that it oppress not confusedly

---

90. SD] *Q; They goe to / looke vpon the / bills. F in margin.*   90.1.] *Q; Act III.
Scene III. /* FASTIDIUS, DELIRO, MACILENTE. *F*   91. in the *Mediterraneum*] *Q;* in *Mediterraneo F.*

---

84. *against*] preparing for the time when.

cognizance] badge, or cullisen; device worn by followers of a house, not by
family members (Nason, pp. 58, 91).

85. *arms*] 'A complete coat of arms, or heraldic achievement, consists
regularly of the escutcheon, or shield, with the crest and other accessories
according to the rank of the bearer' (Nason, p. 91).

86. *colours*] the three classes of heraldic tinctures.

87. *fool's coat*] (*a*) foolish coat of arms; (*b*) motley, the parti-coloured suit
worn by court jesters.

88. *an I can*] to see if I can.

legs] witty antithesis to 'arms', based on the conventional 'little legs' of
menservants (see 128).

91. *in the* Mediterraneum] literally, in the middle of land, or between two
bodies of land; also referring to the Sea; another nickname for the middle
aisle in St Paul's. *H&S* cite Dekker: 'pick out such an hour, when the main
shoal of islanders [punning on 'aisle-landers'] are swimming up and down'
(*Gull's Horn-book* 2.230).

92–3. *but let that pass*] trendy expression also mocked in Shakespeare (see,
for example, *LLL* 5.1.96–7, 100, and *MWW* 1.4.13; Shift uses it at 372–3).

93. *presence*] reception room at court.

96–7. *bear you out*] carry the day for you.

98. *that*] so that.

this your predominant, or foretop, because, when you
come at the presence door, you may, with once or twice   100
stroking up your forehead thus, enter with your predominant perfect; that is, standing up stiff.

Macilente. As if one were frighted?

Fastidius. Ay, sir.

Macilente. Which, indeed, a true fear of your mistress should   105
do, rather than gum water, or whites of eggs. Is 't not so,
sir?

Fastidius. An ingenious observation. Give me leave to crave
your name, sir.

Deliro. His name is Macilente, sir.   110

Fastidius. Good Signor Macilente, if this gentleman, Signor
Deliro, furnish you (as he says he will) with clothes, I will
bring you tomorrow by this time into the presence of the
most divine and acute lady of the court. You shall see
sweet silent rhetoric and dumb eloquence speaking in her   115
eye, but, when she speaks herself, such an anatomy of wit,
so sinewized and arterized that 'tis the goodliest model
of pleasure that ever was to behold. O, she strikes the

---

113. of the] *Q;* in *F.*

99. *predominant, or foretop*] modish hair style in which the front lock of
hair was grown long and brushed upward. Cf. *1 Return from Parnassus*
3.1.994ff.: '*Gullio:* I stood stroking up my hair, which became me very
admirably'; later, Ingenioso refers to him contemptuously as 'this foretop',
4.1.1237. Marston, *Scourge of Villainy* 11.119, also describes the mincing
courtier's pause to 'Stroke up his foretop'.

101. *stroking up*] innuendo of sexual caressing (Henke), or copulation
(Williams); cf. 'come . . . enter . . . standing up stiff', 100–2.

102. *standing up stiff*] innuendo of erect penis (Partridge, *Bawdy*).

106. *gum . . . eggs*] used as hair-dressing preparations.

114. *acute*] keen-witted—a new and perhaps euphuistic term (*H&S*).

115–16. *sweet . . . eye*] a parody of Daniel, in *The Complaint of Rosamund*
(1592), stanza 28; Davies mocks it in *Epigrams* 45, *c.* 1599 (*H&S*).

115. *dumb*] mute.

116. *anatomy of wit*] model or embodiment of understanding; echoing the
subtitle of Lyly's *Euphues: The Anatomy of Wit*, but Jonson satirically misap-
plies the reference to Saviolina.

117. *so . . . arterized*] examined in every detail, much as an anatomy
would dissect every sinew and artery.

world into admiration of her—O, O, O!—I cannot express
'em, believe me.   120
Macilente. O, your only admiration is your silence, sir.
                                            [*They walk.*]
Puntarvolo. [*Reading the first bill*] 'Fore God, Carlo, this is
good. Let's read 'em again: 'If there be any lady or gentlewoman of good carriage that is desirous to entertain
(to her private uses) a young, straight, and upright gen-   125
tleman of the age of five- or six-and-twenty, at the most,
who can serve in the nature of a gentleman-usher, and
hath little legs of purpose and a black satin suit of his own
to go before her in—which suit (for the more sweeten-
ing) now lies in lavender—and can hide his face with her   130

---

122. [*Reading... bill*]] *Fb in margin (The first bill); not in Q, Fa.*   123–33.
'If... given.'] *Italic in Q, F.*

119–20. *express 'em*] speak for all her admirers, or describe all her
charms.

121.] Macilente expresses veiled contempt for Fastidius's affectation of
ineffable awe, but his use of 'your' is indefinite, as at 1.2.11, or 25 above. His
words are a variation on Musonius, as quoted by Aulus Gellius, V, 1, cited
in Burton Stevenson, *The Home Book of Proverbs, Maxims and Familiar Phrases*
(New York, 1948), p. 15: '*Admirationem autem quae maxima est non verba
parere, sed silentium*' ('The greatest admiration produces not words but
silence').

123. *read 'em again*] The bawdy suggestiveness of the whole siquis suggests why Puntarvolo wants to read it again; the notice, apparently for a
gentleman-usher (see 127n), seems to deal with prostitution, the writer
offering his services (*a*) as a bully, to protect a whore on her rounds, or (*b*)
as a clandestine lover for a woman willing to hire him.

123–4. *gentlewoman of good carriage*] (*a*) woman of good deportment or
character; (*b*) a whore, or female willing to carry the weight of the male
during sexual intercourse; cf. *R&J* 1.4.93, and *I Honest Whore* 2.1.230–1
(Henke). The euphemism appears frequently in *Gesta Grayorum*.

124–5. *desirous to entertain... private uses... straight... upright*] with
bawdy innuendo of sexual services to be provided by an erect male.

127. *gentleman-usher*] a male attendant on a lady; crudely, understood to
provide potent sexual service himself, or to act as pimp (Williams).

128. *little legs*] used colloquially for a page or usher; as in *Gull's Horn-book*
2.253, suggesting trim nimbleness in running errands, especially as a go-
between or sexual object himself, and perhaps elegance in making bows, to
complete the fashionable look suggested by the black satin suit.

of purpose] for the purpose (of running errands, etc.).

130. *lies in lavender*] (*a*) literally, lies packed away with lavender to sweeten
its scent and preserve it from moths; (*b*) colloquially, is pawned (*OED* 2a,b;
Dent, L96).

fan, if need require, or sit in the cold at the stair foot for
her as well as another gentleman, let her subscribe her
name and place, and diligent respect shall be given.' This
is above measure excellent, ha?

Carlo. [*Pointing to the second bill*] No, this, this! Here's a fine   135
slave.

Puntarvolo. [*Reads.*] 'If this city, or the suburbs of the same,
do afford any young gentleman of the first, second, or
third head, more or less, whose friends are but lately
deceased, and whose lands are but new come to his   140
hands, that (to be as exactly qualified as the best of our
ordinary gallants are) is affected to entertain the most
gentlemanlike use of tobacco: as first, to give it the most
exquisite perfume; then, to know all the delicate sweet
forms for the assumption of it; as also, the rare corollary   145
and practice of the Cuban Ebullition, Euripus, and Whiff,

---

133. This] *Q; begins new line in F; Fb adds speech-heading:* PVNT.   135. SD]
Fb in margin (The second / bill); not in Q, Fa.   137. Puntarvolo.] *Q, Fa; not
in Fb, thereby tacitly assigning the speech to Carlo.*   137–53. 'If . . . ministered.] *Italic in Q, F.*

130–1. *hide . . . fan*] as a sign of discretion, to give the mistress privacy.

132. *subscribe*] write at the bottom of the siquis.

133. *respect*] attention.

134. *above measure*] exceedingly.

135–6. *fine slave*] superb servant, ironically referring to the writer of the
advertisement.

138–9. *first . . . head*] first, second, or third generation gentleman of his
family; an upstart gentleman. Cf. 4.1.12: Fungoso is 'the first head of our
house', the father being a yeoman (*H&S*).

139. *friends*] relatives or guardians.

142. *is affected to entertain*] wants to learn how to make use of.

145. *assumption of it*] taking it into the body (*OED* 4).

corollary] supplement, added feature.

146. *Cuban Ebullition*] a method of inhaling and rapidly exhaling a large
quantity of pipe-smoke. 'Cuban' may refer to a source or kind of tobacco;
'Ebullition', in pathology, is a state of agitation in the blood or 'humours'
due to heat, causing the heart to pump (*OED* 1b); also, the action of gushing
forth (*OED* 3), here referring to billows of smoke.

Euripus] derived from the strait of Euboea, known for its violence and
uncertain currents (*OED*). As a smoking technique, it suggests gulping a
large quantity of smoke and then exhaling it, with some re-inhaling, in erratic
bursts.

Whiff] a technique of inhaling and exhaling tobacco nasally, as in
Marston, *Jack Drum's Entertainment* (B3): 'Just like a whiff of tobacco, no
sooner in at the mouth, but out at the nose'.

which he shall receive or take in here at London, and
evaporate at Uxbridge, or farther, if it please him—if
there be any such generous spirit that is truly enamoured
of these good faculties, may it please him but by a note   150
of his hand to specify the place or ordinary where he uses
to eat and lie, and most sweet attendance with tobacco
and pipes of the best sort shall be ministered. *Stet quaeso,
candide lector.*' Why, this is without parallel, this!

Carlo. Well, I'll mark this fellow for Sogliardo's use presently.   155

Puntarvolo. Or, rather, Sogliardo for his use.

Carlo. Faith, either of 'em will serve. They are both good
properties. I'll design the other a place too, that we may
see him.

Puntarvolo. No better place than the Mitre, that we may be   160
spectators with you, Carlo. Soft, behold who enters here.

153–4. *Stet quaeso, candide lector*] *Upper case in Q, F.*   154. Why . . . this!]
Q; in F, on a separate line, adding the speech-heading PVNT. *(although only Fb
takes the line as a response to Carlo's reading).*

---

147. *receive or take in*] inhale.

148. *evaporate*] exhale (a Latinism).

Uxbridge] a market town sixteen miles from London (Chalfant), a ludicrous distance over which to retain inhaled smoke, as the bill claims.

150. *faculties*] skills (*OED* 8).

151. *uses*] is accustomed.

152. *lie*] lodge.

most sweet attendance] Possibly, as in the previous advertisement, the
wording is erotically suggestive—here, homoerotic. The hint is followed up
in *use*, 155–6.

153–4. *Stet . . . lector*] 'Please let this stand, honest reader'; a request not
to tear the advertisement down. *H&S* cite an anecdote about a wit who, when
houses near St Paul's were slated for demolition, wrote this slogan on his door.

155. *Sogliardo's use*] employment by Sogliardo; hinting at sexual use.

156. *his use*] Shift's purpose, making money out of a credulous social
climber like Sogliardo.

157–8. *good properties*] (*a*) implements or tools for a purpose (Schmidt);
(*b*) stage properties.

158. *design . . . too*] fix a meeting-place with the other writer as well.

160. *Mitre*] Taverns of this name existed in both Cheapside and Bread
Street. The Cheapside Mitre was near the north-east end of Cheapside by
Mercer's Hall. The Bread Street Mitre, near the south end of Bread Street,
drew its patrons from nearby landing places at Queenhithe and Three Cranes.
Jonson could have been referring to either tavern, since both are conveniently
close to one of the city Counters (one on Milk Street, the other in the Poultry),
where 5.3 ends (Chalfant). Article 15 of the 29 articles of behaviour in the
Middle Temple Revels, 1597/8, names 'the Mitre, the Mermaid, or the Kings-
head in old Fish-street' as the only fashionable dining spots (Baker, p. 131).

161. *Soft*] Slow down, or be quiet (*OED* 8).

Enter SOGLIARDO.

Signor Sogliardo! God save you.

Sogliardo. Save you, good Sir Puntarvolo. Your dog's in health,
sir, I see. How now, Carlo?

Carlo. We have ta'en simple pains to choose you out fol-   165
lowers here.

Puntarvolo. Come hither, signor.   *They show him the bills.*

Clove. Monsieur Orange, yond gallants observes us. Prithee,
let's talk fustian a little and gull 'em, make 'em believe
we are great scholars.   170

Orange. O Lord, sir!

Clove. Nay, prithee, let's, by Jesu. You have an excellent habit
in discourse.

Orange. It pleases you to say so, sir.

Clove. By this church, you ha', la! Nay, come, begin.—Aris-   175
totle, in his *Daemonologia*, approves Scaliger for the best

161.1.] *In Q, at end of l. 162; Act III. Scene IIII.* / SOGLIARDO. *In margin: To
them. F.*   162. God save] *Q;* saue *F.*   167. SD] *Q; They shew him / the bills.*
F in margin.   168. observes] *Q1, Q2;* obserue *Q3, F.*   172. by Jesu] *Q;*
beleeue me *F.*

168–70.] Clove and Orange have been strolling together, without overhearing the other men's conversation, since 42. It is understood that each
group of strollers mimes private chat when not delivering lines, and over-
hears only snatches of other conversations in passing.

169. *fustian*] pretentious chatter.

175. *you ha', la!*] emphatic: you have [an excellent habit in discourse],
indeed!

175–200. *Aristotle . . . species*] For the degree to which Clove's monologue parodies Marston, see introd., pp. 33–6. Marstonian echoes are indicated below. This sequence is in the absurd style of Inns of Court
mock-orations, which rely on improbable attributions, anachronisms,
obscenities, pretentious rhetoric, and factual distortions.

176. Daemonologia] not, of course, by Aristotle. Demonology was a
popular sixteenth-century scholarly interest on which several books were
available, notably *Demonologie, in form of a dialogue* (1597) by James VI of
Scotland, later James I of England,

Scaliger] Julius Caesar Scaliger (1484–1558), a classical scholar, who initially made a name for himself through his virulent attack on Erasmus in
Oratio pro M. Tullio Cicerone contra Des. Erasmum Roterdamum (1529); Erasmus
responded with 'Penny-Pinching' (pp. 489–90), satirizing uncritical pedantic
imitation of Ciceronian diction and style. See Vernon Hall, 'Life of Julius
Caesar Scaliger', *Transactions of the American Philosophical Society*, 40.2

navigator in his time; and, in his *Hypercritics*, he reports
him to be *Heautontimorumenos*. You understand the
Greek, sir?

Orange. O God, sir!   180

Macilente. [*Aside*] For society's sake, he does. O, here be a
couple of fine tame parrots.

Clove. Now, sir, whereas the ingenuity of the time and the
soul's *synderisis* are but *embryons* in nature, added to the
paunch of Esquiline and the *intervallum* of the zodiac,   185

(1950): 96–114. Scaliger's later work on poetics was particularly influential
in establishing neoclassical 'laws', such as Jonson objects to in Ind.243–65.

177. *navigator*] Books on travel and exploration were also enjoying a
vogue; the best known of these is Hakluyt, *The Principal Navigations, Voyages,
Traffics and Discoveries of the English Nation* (1598–1600). Scaliger did not
contribute to this popular genre.

Hypercritics] 'Hypercriticus', meaning 'severely and minutely critical', is
the title of book 7 of Scaliger's *Poetics*. The term was applied vituperatively to
the younger Scaliger by R. Titius in 1589 (*OED*), and Jonson's use of it here
reveals that he immersed himself early in his career in Renaissance secondary
sources as well as in the classics. See David MacPherson, 'Some Renaissance
Sources for Jonson's Early Comic Theory', *ELN* 8 (1971): 180–2.

178. Heutontimorumenos] self-abuser; from Terence's play *Heautontimorumenos* (usually translated *The Self-tormenter*), 163 BC, trans. Nicholas Udall,
1533; based on Menander's comedy of the same name, now lost.

181–2.] Macilente could be addressing Deliro (but not Fastidius, who
is too much like Clove and Orange to appreciate the comment); but his
remark is probably intended as a private sneer, perhaps directly addressed
to the audience. None of the other men is listening, as Clove points out at
201.

182. *fine tame parrots*] expensive pets or frivolous toys to amuse women;
cf. Lodge, *A Larum for London* (1599): 'Here is she, that would not have been
seen with a mouth upon her for a thousand pound, that spent as much on
monkeys, dogs, and parrots as would have kept ten soldiers all the year' (Hoy,
3.261; 4.16).

184. synderisis] Burton, *Anatomy of Melancholy* (1.166), defines it as
'the purer part of the conscience', the innate understanding of good and
evil, as distinct from the rationalized application of that understanding to
particular behaviour. Marston refers to it in *Scourge of Villainy* 7.211 and
11.236.

embryons] embryos, rudimentary lives in the uterus.

185. *paunch of Esquiline*] latrine. The expression originated in Spenser's
allegorical description of the human body, *FQ* 2.9, stanza 32; Marston uses
it in *Scourge of Villainy* 7.185 (*H&S*). The Esquiline gate in Imperial Rome
was a common dump for refuse and offal.

intervallum] intervening space or time.

185–6. *zodiac . . . ecliptic line*] *H&S* cite *Histriomastix* (1599): 'In the eclip-

besides the ecliptic line being optic and not mental,
but by the contemplative and theoric part thereof, doth
demonstrate to us the vegetable circumference and the
ventosity of the tropics; and whereas our intellectual or
mincing capriole (according to the *Metaphysics*) as you   190
may read in Plato's *Histriomastix*—You conceive me, sir?
Orange. O Lord, sir!
Clove. Then coming to the pretty animal, as 'Reason long
since is fled to animals', you know, or indeed for the more
modelizing or enamelling, or rather diamondizing of   195

193–4. 'Reason . . . animals'] *Italic in Q, F.*

---

tic line, which parts the Zodiac', in Act I (B2), part of the play Marston did
not revise, according to Small, p. 67.

186. *optic*] visible to the naked eye.

188. *vegetable*] according to the principle of simple life and growth (*OED*
2c).

circumference] used figuratively in Marston, *Scourge of Villainy* 10.78
(*H&S*).

189. *ventosity*] (*a*) flatulence; (*b*) figuratively, bombast. 'Untraced in
Marston, but he is made to disgorge it in the Quarto text of *Poet.*, 5.3.494'
(*H&S*).

190. *mincing capriole*] dainty leap or caper in dancing (*OED* 1). The same
image of the intellect is in Marston's *Scourge of Villainy* 11.13–14 (*H&S*).

Metaphysics] title applied, at least since the first century AD, to the
thirteen books of Aristotle dealing with questions of 'first philosophy' or
ontology.

191. Histriomastix] Marston revised this play, his hand being apparent
from Act 2, from an earlier version that was not, of course, by Plato; see
Small, pp. 67–89. It was probably performed in 1599 as an Inns of Court
play; see Finkelpearl, *Histrio-Mastix*.

193–4. 'Reason . . . animals'] misquotation from *JC*, probably acted at the
Globe in 1599; a play Jonson did not admire because of its misrepresenta-
tion of Roman life. Antony's actual lines are: 'O judgment, thou art fled to
brutish beasts, / And men have lost their reason' (3.2.106–7). An echo of
Jonson's gibe appeared in *The Wisdom of Doctor Dodypoll* (1600), sc.2, where
a madman commits an assault: '*Alp.* Lay hold upon him, help the Doctor
there. / *Alb.* Then reason's fled to animals I see, / And I'll vanish like tobacco
smoke. *Exit*.' See J. Dover Wilson, 'Ben Jonson and *Julius Caesar*', *ShS* 2
(1949): 36–43.

195. *modelizing*] (*a*) shaping or framing (*OED* 1); (*b*) symbolizing (*OED*
2).

enamelling] figuratively, embellishing artistically.

diamondizing] bedecking brilliantly. The coinage is typical of Marston's
style.

your subject, you shall perceive the hypothesis
(whereof the meteors long since had their first conceptions and notions) to be merely pythagori-
cal, and aristocratical; for, look you, sir, there is ever a
kind of concinnity and *species*—Let us return to our   200
former discourse, for they mark us not.

[*They continue to walk.*]

Fastidius. Mass, yonder's the knight Puntarvolo.

Deliro. And my cousin Sogliardo, methinks.

Macilente. Ay, and his familiar that haunts him, the devil with
a shining face.   205

Deliro. Let 'em alone. Observe 'em not.

Sogliardo, Puntarvolo, [and] Carlo walk.

Sogliardo. Nay, I will have him. I am resolute for that. By this
parchment, gentlemen, I have been so toiled among the
harrots yonder, you will not believe. They do speak i' the

---

205. a shining] *Q;* the shining *F.*   206.1.] *Q; Sogliardo, Pun-/taruolo, Carlo,/
walke. F in margin.*

196. hypothesis] amplification or elaboration of a particular statement in
a thesis (*OED* 1a).

galaxia] the Milky Way; here metaphorically, the brilliantly assembled
details of the hypothesis.

198. *pythagorical*] (*a*) pertaining to Pythagoras, the Greek philosopher
and mathematician of Samos, sixth century BC (*b*) associated with the belief
in transmigration of souls; hence, metamorphosed, transformed (*OED*,
Pythagorean 1a, b).

199. *aristocratical*] malapropism for aristotelian? Clove may in fact
mean 'platonic', alluding to ideal form, since the previous terms suggest
abstraction.

200. *concinnity*] (*a*) harmony of parts; (*b*) elegance of literary style.

species] appearance of beauty (Latin).

204–5. *devil . . . face*] (*a*) Lucifer, the shining one (Carlo is called Damnation and Wickedness, 2.1.133, 141); (*b*) flushed, as from a hot-house; cf.
4.3.68–70; (*c*) greasy from eating pork; cf. 5.3.133–5.

207. *him*] the writer of the second siquis. Sogliardo, Puntarvolo, and
Carlo have been assessing the posted bills while Orange and Clove have been
trying to impress other passers-by.

208. *parchment*] sketch, or tricking, of the arms given by the Heralds'
office (Nason, p. 95).

208–9. *toiled . . . harrots*] hard at work trying to understand the heralds'
jargon; Sogliardo speaks with rustic expression and pronunciation (Nason,
p. 92).

209. *yonder*] at the nearby College of Heralds; see 2.1.570n.

strangest language and give a man the hardest terms for   210
his money that ever you knew.

Carlo. But ha' you arms? Ha' you arms?

Sogliardo. I' faith, I thank God I can write myself gentleman
now. Here's my patent [*Showing it to them*]. It cost me
thirty pound, by this breath.   215

Puntarvolo. A very fair coat, well charged and full of armory.

Sogliardo. Nay, it has as much variety of colours in it as you
have seen a coat have. How like you the crest, sir?

Puntarvolo. I understand it not well. What is 't?

---

212. you . . . you] *Q2, F;* you . . . your *Q1.*   213. God] *Q, Fa;* them *Fb.*

213ff.] This passage satirizes the granting of arms to the unworthy, when
'heraldry moved into a baroque phase, a lush profusion of improbable quar-
terings supplanting the simple coats of a less sophisticated and pretentious
age' (Stone, p. 24). Jonson and many of his friends took up heraldry as a
hobby; one, Edmond Bolton, wrote a manual of heraldry for do-it-
yourselfers, printed 1610 (the main text before that was Gerard Legh, *Accidence of Armory* (1576), frequently reprinted); Camden served as a king at
arms in the College of Heralds; and Jonson himself devised impresas for his
masques. See Nason for details. Erasmus had experimented with satirical
insignia for faking noble descent: 'Two milking-pails, if you like, and a
tankard of beer'; or a silver butcher-knife and three golden geese on a field
gules: 'a memorial of blood bravely spilled' (pp. 426–8). Dekker used heraldry in *The Double P. P.* to itemize various kinds of papists, including 'A
Papist Rampant' (2.171–9).

213. *gentleman*] 'man entitled to coat-armour; *arma gerens* in the words
of Lord Chief Justice Coke; any man above the rank of yeoman, including
not only the gentry and the nobility, but even the king himself' (Nason,
p. 92).

214. *patent*] The King of Arms granted patents for arms and crests to
qualified applicants, who paid set fees (Nason, p. 92).

216. *charged*] bearing heraldic devices (Nason, pp. 26, 92).

217. *colours*] tinctures, categorized as 'metals', 'colours', or 'furs' (Nason,
pp. 14–15, 93). 'Two colours are necessary and most highly honourable; . . .
three are very honourable; *four* commendable; *five* excusable; more, dis-
graceful. Yet have I seen a *Coat of Arms* (I mean within the Escutcheon) so
piebald that if both *Metals* and all the *Colours* (*seven* in all) were lost elsewhere, they might have been found therein' (Fuller, *Worthies of England*, cited
in *H&S*, via Small).

218. *crest*] 'heraldic emblem which, in a complete coat of arms, is borne,
upon a wreath or coronet, above the helmet, which, in turn, surmounts the
shield' (Nason, p. 50).

Sogliardo. Marry, sir, it is your boar without a head, rampant.   220
Puntarvolo. A boar without a head. That's very rare.
Carlo. [*To him, aside*] Ay, and rampant too. Troth, I commend
    the herald's wit. He hath deciphered him well: a swine
    without a head, without brain, wit, anything, indeed,
    ramping to gentility.—You can blazon the rest, signor?   225
    Can you not?
Sogliardo. O, ay, I have it in writing here of purpose. It cost
    me two shillings the tricking.
Carlo. Let's hear! Let's hear!
Puntarvolo. It is the most vile, foolish, absurd, palpable, and   230
    ridiculous escutcheon that ever this eye survised.—Save
    you, Monsieur Fastidius.
                    They salute as they meet in the walk.
Carlo. Silence, good knight. [*To Sogliardo*] On, on!

---

220. boar] *Q, Fa* (Bore); *Fb* (Boore).

220. *your*] colloquial and indefinite usage; see 25n.

boar . . . rampant] The wild boar, a common heraldic charge, was usually
blazoned as *passant*, walking, with the head in profile (Nason, p. 93); the
crest on the liveries worn by Sir Francis Bacon's servants was a boar (Aubrey,
p. 26). But a boar *without a head* is satiric (a stupid boor), not heraldic,
as in Webster, *The Duchess of Malfi* 4.2: 'You do give for your crest a woodcock's head, with the brains picked out on't; you are a very ancient gentleman' (Nason, p. 93). If *rampant*, the figure stands upon the hind legs—an
improper heraldic pose for a boar (though acceptable for a horse, unicorn,
or lion), because it contravenes the 'one rule: you shall not set forth any beast
in arms to do anything against his kind [its nature]' (Legh, cited in Nason,
p. 93).

221. *rare*] (*a*) uncommon; (*b*) excellent.

225. *ramping*] (*a*) vulgarly and boldly climbing up, a derisive term; (*b*)
sexual innuendo, usually used of women as wanton and riotous, like 'ramping
Alice' in *BF* 4.5.85 (Henke).

blazon] describe in technical heraldic language, as at 234–7 (Nason,
p. 94).

227. *of purpose*] on purpose; in order to show the design.

228. *tricking*] drawing of a coat of arms in outline with pen and ink,
indicating the tinctures merely by abbreviations (Nason, pp. 19, 94). See
Appendix B for Nason's tricking of Sogliardo's arms.

231. *escutcheon*] shield, the principal element in a complete coat of arms,
around which are marshalled the helm, crest, motto, etc. (Nason, p. 94).

survised] looked over (a Latinism).

Sogliardo. [*Reading*] '*Gyrony* of eight pieces, *azure* and *gules*;
    between three plates, a *chevron* engrailed checky, *or*, *vert*,   235
    and *ermines*; on a chief *argent* between two *ann'lets* sables,
    a boar's head *proper.*'
Carlo. How's that? 'On a chief *argent*'?
Sogliardo. [*Checking*] 'On a chief *argent* . . . a boar's head
    proper . . . between two *ann'lets* sables.'   240
Carlo. 'Slud, it's a hog's cheek and puddings in a pewter field,
    this.
Sogliardo. How like you them, signor?
Puntarvolo. Let the word be *Not without mustard.* Your crest is
    very rare, sir.   245

---

234. Gyrony . . . gules] The *gyrony*, or lower two-thirds of the escutcheon's field, is divided into eight triangles, meeting at the centre, and alternating in tincture, blue and red. The colours provide satiric commentary on Sogilardo's social ambition: blue (*azure*), the heraldic symbol of power, honour, and wisdom, was commonly the colour worn by servants in the sixteenth century; red (*gules*) was usually associated with gallant courtiers, not bumpkins (Nason, pp. 24, 94; Linthicum, p. 41).

235–6. between . . . ermines] The *plates* or 'roundels argent' are circular silver charges, each marking a corner of the lower field; the *chevron* (one of the nine features of a coat of arms) is shaped like an inverted letter V, representing 'the rafter of an house. Howbeit it be a very honourable bearing, yet it is never seen in the coat of a King or Prince because it pertaineth to a mechanical profession' (Peacham, *The Gentleman's Exercise* (1634), cited in Nason, p. 96). Sogliardo's chevron is *engrailed checky*, or divided by curving lines marking small squares of alternating tinctures, like a chess-board, but in three colours: *or*, the heraldic metal gold; *vert*, the heraldic colour green; and *ermines*, heraldic fur, black with white spots. They signify a travesty of gentlemanly quality in Sogliardo's *nouveau-riche* vulgarity: sick or 'humorous' appetites (*OED*, Green 3, 8c–d) and poor judgement (judges and peers wear ermine as a sign of authority).

236–7. chief . . . proper] The *chief*, another standard feature of the coat of arms, consists of the upper third of the field, its tincture the heraldic metal silver (*argent*); in the centre is a boar's head in its natural colours (*proper*), flanked on either side by rings (*ann'lets*) in the heraldic colour black (*sables*) (Nason, p. 98).

244. word] motto, usually placed in a scroll below the shield (Nason, pp. 52, 98).

Not without mustard] *H&S* cite Baskervill's suggestion that the reference is to Nashe's *Pierce Penniless* 1.171. An improvident London gallant, having wasted his resources, goes to sea to recoup his losses by taking Spanish ships. However, he suffers from sea-sickness, scurvy, and unpalatable nourishment, including dinners of salt fish, served without mustard, its usual condiment. He prays to God for deliverance, vowing never to eat salt fish again, but,

Carlo. A frying pan to the crest had had no fellow.

> *Here they shift [companions, strolling back and forth on*
> *the stage. In one direction,] Fastidius mixes with*
> *Puntarvolo; Carlo and Sogliardo; [in the other direction,]*
> *Deliro and Macilente; Clove and Orange: four couple.*

Fastidius. [*To Carlo*] Entreat your poor friend to walk off a
little, signor. I will salute the knight.

Carlo. [*To Sogliardo, drawing him ahead*] Come. Lap 't up, lap
't up.   250

Fastidius. [*To Puntarvolo*] You are right well encountered, sir.
How does your fair dog?

Puntarvolo. In reasonable state, sir. What citizen is that you
were consorted with? A merchant of any worth?

Fastidius. 'Tis Signor Deliro, sir.   255

Puntarvolo. Is it he? [*To Deliro*] Save you, sir.

> [*They*] *salute* [*as they pass in the walk*].

Deliro. Good Sir Puntarvolo.

Macilente. [*Aside*] O, what copy of fool would this place minister to one endued with patience to observe it!

246.1–4.] *This ed.; Here they Shift, Fast. mixes / with Punt. Carl. and Sogli. /*
Deliro and Macilente, Cloue / and Orenge, foure couple. Q (printed over at the
right beside ll. 240–5); Here they shift. / Fastidius mixes / with Puntarvolo / Carlo,
and Sogli-/ardo, Deliro, and / Macilente, Cloue / and Orange, fou / couple. F (in
margin between ll. 239–45).   256.1.] *This ed.; Salute. Q (interlineated at ll.*
254–5), F (in margin).

---

when he lands safely home, he qualifies his oath to: 'Not without mustard,
good Lord, not without mustard'. For the theory that this motto glances at
Shakespeare's heraldic motto, *Non sans droict*, see James P. Bednarz, 'Shakespeare's Purge of Jonson: the Literary Context of *Troilus and Cressida*', *ShS*
21 (1993): 175–212.

    246.] i.e., sarcastically, you couldn't do better than add a frying pan to
the crest of your coat of arms.

    246.4. four couple] four couples. Puntarvolo is still followed by the two
servants with dog and cat, but Jonson does not count this train in his SD.

    247. *your poor friend*] Sogliardo.

    249. *Lap 't up*] apparently a dog joke: (*a*) directed at Sogliardo, follow-
ing up on the command 'Come'? (*b*) a gibe at Fastidius's sycophancy? (*c*) a
cue for Puntarvolo's dog, implying some stage-business?

    254. *consorted with*] keeping company with.

    258–9. *what copy . . . minister*] what an abundance (from the Latin *copia*)
of fools or folly would this cathedral serve or supply (from the Latin *min-
istro*). The word 'minister' resonates particularly in the St Paul's setting, in
which foolish display has become the new religion.

Carlo. [*To Sogliardo*] Nay, look you, sir: now you are a gen-   260
tleman, you must carry a more exalted presence, change
your mood and habit to a more austere form, be exceeding proud, stand upon your gentility, and scorn every
man. Speak nothing humbly. Never discourse of any
nobleman; though you ne'er saw him but riding to the   265
Star Chamber, it's all one. Love no man. Trust no
man. Speak ill of no man to his face, nor well of any
man behind his back. Salute fairly on the front, and wish
'em hanged upon the turn. Spread yourself upon his
bosom publicly, whose heart you would eat in private.   270
These be principles. Think on 'em. I'll come to you again
presently.   *Exit* CARLO.
            Sogliardo mixes with Puntarvolo and Fastidius.
Puntarvolo. [*To Servingman with dog*] Sirrah, keep close; yet
not so close, thy breath will thaw my ruff.

---

272. SD–272.1.] *on one line in Q; not in* F.

---

263. *stand . . . gentility*] assert your right to be a gentleman; be a snob.

264–6. *Never . . . one*] Never converse with anyone below the status of nobleman, even if you've never met, but you have merely seen him going to the Star Chamber on government business—it doesn't matter.

266. *Star Chamber*] highest court, held by the Lord Chancellor, the Privy Council, other lords, barons and judges, dealing primarily with crimes against the state (riot, rebellion, etc.), and secondarily with appeals of decisions in civil or criminal cases tried in other courts (Prothero, pp. 180–3).

268–9. *Salute . . . turn*] Greet any man warmly to his face and speak ill of him behind his back.

269–70. *Spread . . . bosom*] embrace the man.

274. *so . . . breath*] capable of two readings: (*a*) 'so close *that* thy breath', a comparative statement; (*b*) *so* close: thy breath, 'so' acting as a demonstrative, and the rest of the sentence becoming descriptive, almost prescriptive.

breath will thaw] The bad breath of the lower classes, here powerful enough to collapse a starched ruff, was frequently remarked upon; cf. *Old Fortunatus* 2.1.173–6: 'I scorned to crowd among the muddy throng / Of the rank multitude, whose thick'ned breath / Like to condensed fogs do choke that beauty / Which else would dwell in every kingdom's cheek'.

274.1ff.] In *Gull's Horn-book*, ch. 4 (2.234–5), the tailor hides behind a pillar, unseen by the fashion-plates he is observing; perhaps a reconstruction of the staging here. In ch. 1, Dekker describes a tailor as a pander for the seven deadly sins (p. 209). Cf. *Ep.* 88, in which the gallant is reduced to a soulless mannequin.

Enter FUNGOSO *with his* Tailor.

Sogliardo. [*To Fungoso, in passing*] O good cousin, I am a little   275
    busy. How does my niece? I am to walk with a knight
    here.
Fungoso. [*To Tailor*] O, he is here. Look you, sir, that's the
    gentleman.
Tailor. What, he i' the blush-coloured satin?   280
Fungoso. Ay, he, sir. Though his suit blush, he blushes not.
    Look you, that's the suit, sir. I would have mine such a
    suit without difference: such stuff, such a wing, such a
    sleeve, such a skirt, belly and all. Therefore, pray you,
    observe it. Have you a pair of tables?   285
Fastidius. [*To Puntarvolo*] Why, do you see, sir? They say I am
    fantastical. Why, true. I know it, and I pursue my humour
    still in contempt of this censorious age. 'Slight, an a
    man should do nothing but what a sort of stale judge-
    ments about this town will approve in him, he were a   290
    sweet ass. I'd beg him, i' faith. I ne'er knew any more find
    fault with a fashion than they that knew not how to put

274.1.] *In Q, at end of l. 277; Act III. Scene V.* / FVNGOSO, Taylor. *In margin:*
To them. F.

    275. *cousin*] nephew. 'Cousin' was a flexible term, and the fact that
Fungoso does not reply simply accords with his obsessive self-absorption.
Deliro refers to Sogliardo, his wife's uncle, as 'cousin' at 203, meaning a
relative by marriage, but carefully avoids greeting him in this scene.
    278. *he*] Fastidius Brisk.
    280. *blush-coloured*] maiden's blush, a delicate damask-rose, popular for
suits worn by gallants (Linthicum, p. 36).
    283. *without difference*] identical; also in a heraldic sense, referring to the
coat of arms worn by the head of a family (Nason, p. 91). Fungoso's quest
for a 'fool's coat' parallels his uncle's.
    wing] flat tab lined with buckram extending out from the armhole, widest
at the shoulder and narrowing towards the underside, used to disguise the
join of the detachable outer sleeve to the garment (Linthicum, p. 76).
    284. *skirt*] the lower portion of a man's coat.
    285. *pair of tables*] writing tablet.
    289. *sort*] group.
    291. *beg him*] Fastidius is sneering at any man who governs his life by
conventional public opinion. The expression 'beg him for a fool' refers to a
legal process by which one could apply to the court of wards for custody of
a well-to-do but mentally impaired person, and enjoy the profits of the estate.
Gifford cites *Jack Drum's Entertainment*: 'Be my ward, John. Faith I'll give
thee two coats a year, an thou'lt be my *fool*.' This legal process also under-
lies the Fool's quips in *Lear*.

themselves into 't. For mine own part, so I please mine
own appetite, I am careless what the fusty world speaks
of me. Puh!   295

Fungoso. [*To Tailor*] Do you mark how it hangs at the knee
there?

Tailor. I warrant you, sir.

Fungoso. For God's sake, do. Note all. Do you see the collar,
sir?   300

Tailor. Fear nothing. It shall not differ in a stitch, sir.

Fungoso. Pray God it do not! You'll make these linings serve?
And help me to a chapman for the outside, will you?

Tailor. I'll do my best, sir. You'll put it off presently?

Fungoso. Ay. Go with me to my chamber; you shall have it,   305
but make haste of it, for the love of Christ, for I'll sit i'
my old suit or else lie a-bed and read the *Arcadia* till you
have done.   *Exit with* Tailor.

Enter CARLO.

Carlo. [*To Puntarvolo, Fastidius, and Sogliardo*] O, if ever you
were struck with a jest, gallants, now, now! I do usher in   310
the most strange piece of military profession that ever was
discovered in *Insula Paulina.*

Fastidius. Where? Where?

Puntarvolo. What is he for a creature?

Carlo. A pimp, a pimp that I have observed yonder, the rarest   315
superficies of a humour. He comes every morning to
empty his lungs in Paul's here, and offers up some five

302. God] *Q;* heau'n *F.*   306. Christ] *Q;* a customer *F.*   308. SD] *Q; not
in F.*   308.1.] *Q; not in F.*

---

294. *fusty*] stale-smelling, as of wine casks; hence, stuffy, old-fashioned.
Marston uses the phrase twice in *Scourge of Villainy*: at 2.13, and in the final
comment to the reader, 'I take a solemn congee of this fusty world'.

303. *chapman*] merchant.

304. *put it off*] take off the suit you are now wearing.

307. Arcadia] prose pastoral romance by Sir Philip Sidney, here viewed
as indicative of Fungoso's rustic tastes.

312. Insula Paulina] English/Latin pun: Paul's Isle/Aisle.

314.] What kind of creature is he?

316. superficies] face or surface, implying brazenly superficial affectation.
Carlo chooses this word deliberately to twit Puntarvolo for the pedantic
affectation of his sundial analogy at 2.1.207ff.

317. *empty his lungs*] cough and spit (see 25 above).

or six hecatombs of faces and sighs, and away again. Here
he comes. Nay, walk, walk, be not seen to note him, and
we shall have excellent sport.   320

    Enter SHIFT; *walks by and uses action to his rapier.*

Puntarvolo. 'Slid, he vented a sigh e'en now, I thought he
    would have blown up the church.
Carlo. O, you shall have him give a number of those false fires
    ere he depart.
Fastidius. See now! He is expostulating with his rapier. Look,   325
    look!
Carlo. Did you ever in your days observe better passion over
    a hilt?
Puntarvolo. Except it were in the person of a cutler's boy, or
    that the fellow were nothing but vapour, I should think   330
    it impossible.
Carlo. See, again he claps his sword o' the head, as who
    should say, 'Well, go to!'

320.1.] *Q; Act III. Scene VI.* / SHIFT. *In margin: To them. F*

   318. *hecatombs*] literally, counting in hundreds, great public animal sacri-
fices; here, an exaggerated metaphor for 500 or 600 public displays of
sacrificial emotion by Shift.
   320.1. *uses action to*] demonstrates flashy fencing techniques with.
   321. *a sigh*] such a sigh.
   I thought] that I thought.
   323. *false fires*] phony sighs of passion.
   329. *Except*] unless.
   cutler's boy] apprentice to an artisan who makes, sells, or repairs knives, etc.
   329–31.] Puntarvolo's point is that only an apprentice trying to perfect his
skill at working on knives and blades, or some humour-driven fool fascinated
by swordsmanship, could produce such a display.
   330. *vapour*] (*a*) medically, emanation from some humour in the body
(*OED* 3); (*b*) unsubstantial or worthless fellow (*OED* 2c).
   332. *claps . . . head*] Either he slaps the hilt, or in executing a fencing skill
he accidentally strikes himself on the head with his rapier, perhaps by exaggerating a salute with the rapier held upright before the face, or by seeming
to defend his head from attack. According to George Silver, *Paradoxes of
Defence* (1599), 'the hilt as well serveth to defend the head as the hand, and
is a more sure and strong ward than is the blade of the rapier . . . because in
the true carriage of the gardant fight, the hand must lie above the head in
such straightness and narrowness of space that which way soever the agent
shall strike or thrust at the head, face, or body, the removing of two or four
inches [provided by the hilt] shall save all' (p. 52).
   333. *go to!*] expression of impatience or indignation.

Puntarvolo. O, violence! I wonder the blade can contain itself,
    being so provoked.   335

Carlo. [*Declaiming*] *With that, the moody squire thumped his*
    breast,
    And reared his eyen to heaven for revenge.

Sogliardo. Troth, an you be gentlemen, let's make 'em friends,
    and take up the matter between his rapier and he.

Carlo. Nay, if you intend that, you must lay down the matter,   340
    for this rapier, it seems, is in the nature of a hanger-
    on, and the good gentleman would happily be rid of
    him.

Fastidius. By my faith, an 'tis to be suspected, I'll ask him.
             [*He approaches Shift, while Carlo, Puntarvolo, and*
             Sogliardo comment on Shift's reactions from a distance.]

Macilente. [*To Deliro*] O, here's rich stuff! For Christ' sake,
    let us go.   345
    A man would wish himself a senseless pillar
    Rather than view these monstrous prodigies:
    Nil habet infelix paupertas, durius in se,
    Quam quod ridiculos homines facit.   *Exit with* DELIRO.

Fastidius. [*To Shift*] Signor.   350

Shift. At your service.

Fastidius. Will you sell your rapier?

---

338. gentlemen] *Q;* good gentlemen *F.*   339. he] *Q;* him *F.*   344.
Christ'] *Q (*Christ*);* lifes *F.*   349. SD] *Q;* not in *F.*

336–7.] Untraced, though *H&S* found it quoted again in J. C., *The Two
Merry Milke-maids* (1620), 3.1 where the source might be *EMO*.

337. eyen] eyes.

339. take . . . matter] mend the quarrel.

he] grammatically, *F*'s 'him' is correct, but perhaps Jonson was
mocking Sogliardo's attempts at verbal refinement, or simply mocking his
rusticity.

340. lay . . . matter] dispose of the problem.

341–2. hanger-on] (*a*) sword which hung by a loop to the wearer's belt;
(*b*) used disparagingly of a follower or dependant (*OED* 5).

343. him] the rapier, or metaphorical 'hanger-on'.

344.] If you think he'd like to be rid of his rapier, I'll ask him (to sell
it).

346. pillar] probably indicating the stage pillar; another example of self-
conscious staging.

348–9.] 'Poverty, harsh in itself, has no effect so unfortunate as that it
turns men into butts of jokes' (Juvenal, 3.152–3).

Carlo. 'Sblood, he is turned wild upon the question! He looks
    as he had seen a sergeant.

Shift. Sell my rapier! Now God bless me!   355

Puntarvolo. Amen.

Shift. You asked me if I would sell my rapier, sir?

Fastidius. I did indeed.

Shift. Now Lord have mercy upon me!

Puntarvolo. Amen, I say still.   360

Shift. 'Slud, sir, what should you behold in my face, sir, that
    should move you (as they say, sir) to ask me, sir, if I would
    sell my rapier?

Fastidius. Nay, let me pray you, sir, be not moved. I protest I
    would rather have been silent than any way offensive, had   365
    I known your nature.

Shift. [*Protesting loudly*] Sell my rapier? God's lid! Nay, sir, for
    mine own part, as I am a man that has served in causes
    or so, so I am not apt to injure any gentleman in the
    degree of falling foul, but—sell my rapier? I will tell you,   370
    sir, I have served with this foolish rapier where some of
    us dare not appear in haste. I name no man, but let that
    pass. Sell my rapier? Death to my lungs! This rapier, sir,
    has travelled by my side, sir, the best part of France and
    the Low Country. I have seen Flushing, Brill, and the   375

---

355. God] *Q;* fate *F*   367. God's] *Q;* 'ods *F*

---

354. *as . . . sergeant*] as if he were afraid of being arrested. The sergeant
was the sheriff's officer, empowered to enforce sentences, arrest offenders,
and summon people to court; he was known for his zeal in watching outside
St Paul's or taverns frequented by known criminals (Johansson, *Law*, pp.
26–7).

356.] Puntarvolo's ironic support of Shift's prayer reminds us of the St
Paul's setting and the secular interests that draw people there; also at 360.

364. *moved*] distressed, angered; playing on *move*, prompt, at 362.

368–9. *causes or so*] military actions and such.

370. *falling foul*] behaving dishonourably.

371. *foolish*] worthless; said with polite self-deprecation.

373. *Death . . . lungs!*] exclamation of outrage, perhaps to be accompanied by stage business of coughing and spitting.

374. *France*] Religious wars lasted, with intervals, from 1562 to 1594.

375. *the Low Country*] (*a*) the Netherlands, where the war against Spanish
rule, 1566–1609, ended in the liberation of the Northern Provinces. The
English assisted the Dutch in a Protestant pact against Catholic power; (*b*)
colloquially, pudendum (cunt-ry); cf. *Ham.* 3.2.100–5.

375–6. *Flushing . . . Hague*] Flushing and Brill were ceded to the English;

Hague with this rapier, sir, in my Lord of Leicester's time, and, by God's will, he that should offer to disrapier me now, I would—[*Quietly*] Look you, sir: you presume to be a gentleman of good sort, and so likewise your friends here. If you have any disposition to travel, for the sight   380
of service or so—one, two, or all of you—I can lend you letters to divers officers and commanders in the Low Countries that shall, for my cause, do you all the good offices that shall pertain or belong to gentlemen of your—
[*Begging more directly*] Please you to show the bounty of   385
your mind, sir, to impart some ten groats or half a crown to our use, till our ability be of growth to return it, and we shall think ourself—[*Protesting loudly again, as Fastidius turns away and joins the others*] 'Sblood, sell my rapier?

Sogliardo. I pray you, what said he, signor? [*Admiringly*] He's   390
a proper man.

Fastidius. Marry, he tells me, if I please to show the bounty of my mind, to impart some ten groats to his use or so.

---

379. good sort] *Q;* sort *F*

The Hague was the English headquarters. Soldiers who went only to Flushing were held in contempt as idle boasters who saw no action; in *1 Return from Parnassus* 3.1, Ingenioso says of Gullio, who brags of his sword and his patriotism: 'He was never any further than Flushing, and then he came home sick of the scurvies'.

376. *my Lord . . . time*] Robert Dudley, Earl of Leicester (1532–1588), the Queen's favourite (and step-father of a later favorite, Robert Devereux, Earl of Essex), was commander of the English army, 1585–7, defeated by the Spanish in 1586 after an ill-managed campaign; many were killed, including Sir Philip Sidney, wounded at Zutphen. Leicester returned to London, where he remained during the Armada crisis of 1588, after which he mysteriously died (*DNB*).

377. *offer*] attempt.

379. *sort*] breeding or social standing.

380–4. *disposition to travel . . . service . . . good offices*] sexual quibbles, suggesting that Shift can procure sexual favours for gentlemen in quest of adventure.

383. *cause*] sake.

386. *impart*] lend (euphemism).

387. *ability . . . growth*] professional skill earns enough.

391. *proper man*] good-looking fellow.

Puntarvolo. Break his head, and give it him.

Carlo. I thought he had been playing on the Jews' trump, I!   395
                    [*Fastidius returns to Shift.*]

Shift. [*Still protesting*] My rapier? No, sir. My rapier is my
    guard, my defence, my revenue, my honour—[*Aside to
    Fastidius*] If you cannot impart, be secret, I beseech you.
    [*Protesting as before*]—and I will maintain it where there
    is a grain of dust or a drop of water! [*Aside as before*] Hard   400
    is the choice when the valiant must eat their arms or
    clem. [*Protesting as before*] Sell my rapier? No, my dear, I
    will not be divorced from thee yet. I have ever found thee
    true as steel, and—[*Aside, following Fastidius, who rejoins
    the others*] You cannot impart, sir? [*Greets the others.*] God   405
    save you, gentlemen. [*To Fastidius*] Nevertheless, if you
    have a fancy to it, sir . . .

Fastidius. Prithee, away! [*To the others*] Is Signor Deliro
    departed?

Carlo. Ha' you seen a pimp out-face his own wants better?   410

Sogliardo. I commend him that can dissemble them so well.

Puntarvolo. True, and having no better a cloak for it than he
    has, neither.

Fastidius. God's precious, what mischievous luck is this!
    Adieu, gentlemen.   415

Puntarvolo. Whither in such haste, Monsieur Fastidius?

Fastidius. [*Leaving*] After my merchant, Signor Deliro, sir.

405–6. God save] *Q;* Saue *F.*   411. them] *Q;* 'em *F.*   412–13. for it than
he has] *Q1;* than he has for it *Q2;* for it, then he has *F.*

394.] Advice to Fastidius: strike Shift violently (for his impudence), but
give him the money. To *break* a head is to draw blood, break the skin.

395. *playing . . . trump*] anti-semitic remark, meaning 'scheming to
acquire money', punning on the Jews' harp, a twanging instrument held
between the teeth. Its sound might be described as intrusive and importunate, like Shift's voice.

401. *eat their arms*] sell their weapons to have money for food.

402. *clem*] starve.

my dear] addressing the rapier as a soldier's most cherished and valuable
possession.

410. *out-face*] brazen out.

414. *God's precious*] by God's (Christ's) precious body (an oath).

Carlo. [*To the others*] O, hinder him not. He may hap lose his
tide: a good flounder, i' faith.

Exit [FASTIDIUS].

Orange. Hark you, Signor Whiff: a word with you.   420

Orange and Clove call Shift aside.

Carlo. How? Signor Whiff?

Orange. [*To Shift*] What was the difference between that
young gallant that's gone and you, sir?

Shift. No difference. He would ha' given me five pound for
my rapier, and I refused it. That's all.   425

Clove. O, was it no otherwise? We thought you had been upon
some terms.

Shift. No other than you saw, sir.

Clove. Adieu, Good Master Apple John.

Exeunt ORANGE *and* CLOVE.

Carlo. How? Whiff, and Apple John too? 'Heart, what'll   430
you say if this be the *appendix* or label to both yond
indentures?

Puntarvolo. It may be.

Carlo. [*Declaiming*] Resolve us of it, Janus, thou that lookst

---

419.1.] *Q; not in F.*   420.1.] *Q, F (Oren. & Cloue / call Shift aside.) in
margin at ll. 420–1.*   423. young] *Q; not in F.*   426. was it] *Q;* was't *F.*
429.1.] *Q; not in F.*   430. Apple John] *Q (Apple Ioan), F (APPLE-IOHN).*

418–19. *lose his tide*] miss his opportunity to 'fish' for money, because
Deliro (the tide) has gone out.

419. *flounder*] (*a*) struggler in the mire of debt, the flounder being a
bottom feeder; (*b*) gaping fish, the flounder being large-mouthed; Carlo's
metaphor suggests the probable stage-business of Fastidius's gaping facial
expression at 414.

422. *difference*] dispute.

422–3. *that . . . gallant*] Fastidius.

426–7. *been . . . terms*] had words, argued.

430. *'Heart*] by God's heart (an oath).

431. *appendix*] i.e. the name that should be attached.

432. *indentures*] i.e. the posted bills in which Shift has offered his services.
Literally, service contracts (for apprentices or bondsmen) that had been
signed and then cut in half with a serrated edge, so that when brought
together again at any time, the edges tallied, proving that they were the original documents. Carlo has figured out that Shift is the author of both posted
notices.

434. *Janus*] the two-faced Roman god; see 1.2.204n. But Carlo may here
be thinking of the four-faced Janus mentioned as a symbol of circumspec-
tion in Martial's *Epigrams* 8.2.3, 5 (Loeb), and others cited in Wheeler, pp.
121–2.

every way; or thou, Hercules, that hast travelled all   435
    countries.

Puntarvolo. Nay, Carlo, spend not time in invocations now.
    'Tis late.

Carlo. [*To Shift*] Signor, here's a gentleman [*Indicating
    Sogliardo*] desirous of your name, sir.   440

Shift. Sir, my name is Cavalier Shift. I am known sufficiently
    in this walk, sir.

Carlo. Shift? I heard your name varied e'en now, as I take it.

Shift. True, sir. It pleases the world, as I am her excellent
    tobacconist, to give me the style of Signor Whiff. As I am   445
    a poor esquire about the town here, they call me Master
    Apple John. Variety of good names does well, sir.

Carlo. Ay, and good parts to make those good names, out of
    which I imagine yond bills to be yours.

Shift. Sir, if I should deny the scriptures, I were worthy to be   450
    banished the middle aisle forever.

Carlo. I take your word, sir. This gentleman has subscribed to
    'em, and is most desirous to become your pupil. Marry,
    you must use expedition.—Signor Insulso Sogliardo, this
    is the professor.   455

Sogliardo. [*Nods as Shift doffs his hat.*] In good time, sir. Nay,
    good sir, house your head. Do you profess these sleights
    in tobacco?

---

450. scriptures] *Q;* manuscripts *F.*   457. these] *Q, Fa;* those *Fb.*

---

435. *Hercules*] 'Jupiter, upon the arrival of Claudius among the Gods, dis-
patches Hercules who had travelled all countries, to know who he was'
(Seneca, *De morte Claudii,* cited in Whalley).

440. *desirous of*] wanting to know.

443. *varied*] altered; i.e. given instead as Whiff and Apple John.

448. *parts to make*] qualities to be associated with.

450. *scriptures*] writings; punning on holy writ and 'bills' of excommuni-
cation, by which he might be 'banished' from the church.

454. *expedition*] haste; in military terms, setting forth with warlike
intentions.

455. *professor*] i.e. Shift; one who professes or claims a skill. So too *profess,*
457, 459.

456. *In good time*] like 'Well met', a conventional greeting.

457. *house your head*] put on your hat; imitating Puntarvolo's magnanimity at 2.1.300–1.

457–8. *sleights in tobacco*] sophisticated tricks of smoking, as in the
advertisement.

Shift. I do more than profess, sir, and, if you please to be a
practitioner, I will undertake in one fortnight to bring you   460
that you shall take it plausibly in any ordinary, theatre, or
the Tilt Yard, if need be: the most popular assembly that
is.

Puntarvolo. But you cannot bring him to the whiff so soon?

Shift. Yes, as soon, sir. He shall receive the first, second,   465
and third whiff, if it please him, and, upon the receipt,
take his horse, drink his three cups of Canary, and expose
one at Hounslow, a second at Staines, and a third at
Bagshot.

Carlo. Bow-wow!   470

Sogliardo. You will not serve me, sir, will you? I'll give you
more than countenance.

---

459. I do] *Q;* I, do *F*   460. practitioner] *Q2, F;* practioner *Q1.*   462.
be: the] *Q;* be, i' the *F*

460–1. *bring you that*] train you so effectively that.

462. *Tilt Yard*] sports-field at the northwest end of Whitehall Palace, the
royal residence in Westminster; site of the Accession Day Tilts and other
large-scale public entertainments.

465. *receive*] inhale; similarly, *receipt*, 466.

467. *take*] mount.

Canary] sweet wine from the Canary Islands (see Ind.328).

expose] exhale, used here to imply a deliberate demonstration of prowess.

468. *Hounslow*] Middlesex village about thirteen miles west of London,
noted for its taverns and for the highwaymen on its adjoining heath (Chalfant).

Staines] Surrey village on the north bank of the Thames, nineteen miles
west of London; a favourite destination for excursions from London
(Chalfant), where couples 'Rode all to Staines for no cause serious, / But
for their mirth, and for their lechery' (Sir John Davies, cited in Hoy, 3.24).

469. *Bagshot*] Surrey coaching town, thirty miles southwest of London;
'no brief jaunt, considering the circumstances' (Chalfant, p. 103). See the
advertised boast at 147–8.

470. *Bow-wow!*] a bark evidently meant to deride Shift's boast; cf. Nashe,
Lenten Stuff: 'bow-wow, quoth Bagshaw' (3.212), and *Misogonus* 4.1.57
(McKerrow, 4.410). The proverb, 'Bow-wows is no wedding' (Dent, B572),
seems to mean that noisy protests are no guarantee of truth, an implication
that suits this context. In addition, Puntarvolo's greyhound may have had
some stage business, perhaps cued by 'Hounslow', to which this comment
doubles as a response.

471. *serve*] surface meaning: work for hire as a servant (as opposed to gentlemanly service in the military). Unconscious *double entendre*: (*a*) procure
for, as in Shift's earlier offer at 380–4, made privately to Fastidius. Publicly,
Shift must 'scorn to serve'; (*b*) copulate with.

472. *countenance*] surface meaning: what is necessary for maintenance
(Gifford). Unconscious *double entendre*: pronounced 'cunt'nance', a bawdy

Shift. Pardon me, sir, I do scorn to serve any man.

Carlo. Who? He serve? 'Sblood, he keeps high men and low
    men, he. He has a fair living at Fulham.   475

Shift. But in the nature of a fellow, I'll be your follower, if you
    please.

Sogliardo. Sir, you shall stay and dine with me, and, if we can
    agree, we'll not part in haste. I am very bountiful to men
    of quality. Where shall we go, signor?   480

Puntarvolo. Your Mitre is your best house.

Shift. I can make this dog take as many whiffs as I list, and
    he shall retain or effume them at my pleasure.

Puntarvolo. [*In huffy farewell*] By your patience. [*To serving-
    men*] Follow me, fellows.   485

Sogliardo. Sir Puntarvolo!

Puntarvolo. Pardon me. My dog shall not eat in his company
    for a million.   *Exit* PUNTARVOLO *with his* Followers.

Carlo. Nay, be not you amazed, Signor Whiff, whate'er that
    stiff-necked gentleman says.   490

---

483. effume] efume *Q1, F*; refume *Q2*.   486. Sir Puntarvolo] *Q;* Sir,
PVNTARVOLO *F.*   488. SD] *Q; not in F.*

---

quibble (Henke). Sogliardo's offer of 'more than countenance' suggests (*a*)
a generous salary; (*b*) more money than he would otherwise pay for Shift's
procuring a woman for him; or (*c*) more than Shift could make as a pimp
from the services of whores.

474–5. *high men and low men*] The literal implication is that Shift keeps
his own servants, or perhaps his own gang of thieves, but the phrase in gambling means loaded dice, also called 'high and low fullams'. Whalley suggests
that the dice were named topographically for Fulham, six miles south-west
of the City, either because the town was notorious for gamesters or because
the dice were made there. H&S trace the word to 'fullan', in *Dice-Play*
(*c.* 1550), probably meaning 'full one'. According to Judges, the dice were
wrongly numbered on one face; usually 5 was substituted for 2 in a 'high
man', and 2 for 5 in a 'low man'.

476. *fellow*] companion, rather than servant.

480. *quality*] skill; good birth.

481. *Your . . . your*] indeterminate and colloquial usage, as at 25 and 220
above.

483. *effume*] puff out smoke (an affected coinage).

484. *By your patience*] i.e., excuse me. Puntarvolo is offended at the suggestion that his valuable dog might be taught to smoke.

490. *stiff-necked*] referring to Puntarvolo's characteristic rigidity of
posture.

Sogliardo. No, for you do not know the humour of the dog as
we do. Where shall we dine, Carlo? I would fain go to one
of these ordinaries, now I am a gentleman.

Carlo. So you may. Were you never at none yet?

Sogliardo. No, faith, but they say there resorts your most   495
choice gallants.

Carlo. True, and the fashion is, when any stranger comes in
amongst 'em, they all stand up and stare at him as he
were some unknown beast brought out of Africa, but
that'll be helped with a good adventurous face. You must   500
be impudent enough, sit down, and use no respect. When
anything's propounded above your capacity, smile at it,
make two or three faces, and 'tis excellent: they'll think
you have travelled. Though you argue a whole day in
silence thus, and discourse in nothing but laughter, 'twill   505
pass. Only now and then give fire, discharge a good full
oath, and offer a great wager. 'Twill be admirable.

Sogliardo. I warrant you, I am resolute. [*To Shift*] Come, good
signor, there's a poor French crown for your ordinary.

[*He gives money.*]

---

494. none] *Q;* any *F.*

---

491. *humour of the dog*] Puntarvolo's extreme devotion to his dog. Jonson
may have based this 'humour' on Sir John Harington and his dog Bungey,
although Small discounts this suggestion (pp. 47–9). Equally, Jonson may
have had in mind popular stories told of another dog-lover, Dr Bullen; Manningham, p. 210, records a story also alluded to in *TwN* 5.1.1–6. 'Mr. Francis
Curle told me how one Dr. Bullen [Boleyn], the Q[ueen's] kinsman, had a
dog which he doted on, so much that the Q[ueen], understanding of it,
requested he would grant her one desire, and he should have whatsoever he
would ask. She demanded his dog; he gave it, and "Now, Madam," q[uoth]
he, "you promised to give me my desire." "I will," q[uoth] she. "Then I pray
you give me my dog again."'

497ff.] based on Erasmus, 'Inns', pp. 147–52. *H&S* cite a similar passage
in Chapman, *May-Day* (1601/2). Dekker varies the theme in ch. 5, 'How a
young Gallant should behave himself in an Ordinary', *Gull's Horn-book*
2.238.

499–500. *but . . . face*] but that hostility can be overcome with a bold
manner.

501. *use no respect*] don't be deferential or polite.

502. *propounded . . . capacity*] contended or proposed beyond your
understanding.

Shift. It comes well, for I had not so much as the least   510
portcullis of coin before.

Exeunt.

Mitis. I travail with another objection, signor, which I fear will
be enforced against the author ere I can be delivered
of it.

Cordatus. What's that, sir?   515

Mitis. That the argument of his comedy might have been of
some other nature, as of a duke to be in love with a countess, and that countess to be in love with the duke's son,
and the son to love the lady's waiting-maid: some such
cross-wooing, with a clown to their servingman, better   520
than to be thus near and familiarly allied to the time.

Cordatus. You say well, but I would fain hear one of these
autumn-judgements define once *Quid sit comedia?* If he
cannot, let him content himself with Cicero's definition
(till he have strength to propose to himself a better), who   525

511.1.] *Q; not in F.*

511. *portcullis*] 'a popular name for the silver halfpenny of Queen
Elizabeth (the smallest silver coin issued by her), which bore on the obverse
a portcullis and a mint-mark' (*OED* 3a).

512. *travail*] am in labour. The childbirth trope is completed by the
reference to being *delivered*. Mitis fears that his own uneasy perception of
the Paul's Walk scene as particular satire will be more quickly voiced by
someone with political standing in the audience. A charge of particular satire,
seen as sedition, might mean arrest and imprisonment, which Jonson had
already experienced for his share in writing *The Isle of Gulls* (1597), and
would experience again for *Eastward Ho!* (1605).

516–21.] defines Jonson's satirical attitude to romantic comedy as written
by Greene and Shakespeare through the 1590s; cf. prologue to *EMI* (*F*).

521. *thus . . . time*] so closely and particularly (even impertinently) linked
to current life.

523. *autumn-judgements*] elderly critics; waning or diminished minds.

Quid sit comedia?] What is comedy, or what might (or should) comedy
be? The present subjunctive, *sit*, little used in English, invited in Latin a hypothetical or theoretical response. Cordatus's reply is from Minturno's *De Poeta*
(1559), book 4, on comedy; Jonson borrowed a marginal gloss '*Quid sit
Comoedia*' (p. 280) and the Ciceronian catchphrase, translated literally part
of the adjacent text, and paraphrased another part. See Henry L. Snuggs,
'The Source of Jonson's Definition of Comedy', *MLN* 65 (1950): 543–4.

would have a comedy to be *imitatio vitae, speculum con-*
suetudinis, imago veritatis: a thing throughout pleasant
and ridiculous, and accommodated to the correction of
manners. If the maker have failed in any particle of this,
they may worthily tax him, but if not, why, be you (that   530
are for them) silent, as I will be for him; and give way to
the actors.

ACT 3   SCENE 2

Enter SORDIDO *with a halter about his neck*
[*and carrying a ladder*].

Sordido. Nay, God's precious, if the weather and the season

3.2.] SCENA SECUNDA. *Q; Act III. Scene VII.* / SORDIDO, HINE. *F*   0.1.
Enter... neck] *Q; in margin of F:* With a halter / about his necke.

526–7. imitatio... veritatis] an imitation of life, a mirror of social intercourse, a representation of truth. Attributed to Cicero by Donatus, and subsequently echoed by various Renaissance critics, including Sidney.
527. *pleasant*] jocular, roughly equivalent to 'ridiculous' (*OED* 4); *iucun-*
dam in Minturno.
528. *ridiculous*] (*a*) laughable, amusing; (*b*) causing laughter at a figure by
rendering him satirically as the sum of his own incongruities. Cf. 348–9n.
529. *manners*] social behaviour.
maker] poet.
530. *worthily tax*] justifiably criticize.
531. *for them*] on their side, sharing their opinion.
for him] on his side.
3.2.] Sordido's attempted suicide is in line with several recorded cases of
grain speculators who saw the bottom fall out of their markets; see *H&S*,
9.455–7. Small, p. 54, cites the thirteenth-century *Exempla of Jacques de Vitry*
(London Folklore Society, 1890), p. 164: 'I heard of a certain man who
amassed a lot of grain and waited for many years so that he could sell it profitably. However God gave seven good seasons, as a result of which the wretch,
frustrated of his hope, at last for sorrow hanged himself above his own grain'
(my translation of the original Latin). The apocryphal element appears in
the recurrent detail of the complaint over the cut rope, which Bang traced
to Castiglione's *The Courtier* (1516), first translated into English by Hoby in
1561 (*Englische Studien* 26.2, pp. 330–2). The figure of a man with a halter
around his neck is a traditional emblem of suicidal despair, appearing in
morality plays such as *Magnificence* (*c.* 1516), where the halter is rejected in
favour of the knife, and in poetry as late as *FQ* 1.9. For staging details
on theatre hangings, which relied on ropes attached to a body harness supporting the actor, see John H. Astington, 'Gallows Scenes on the Elizabethan
Stage', *ThN* 37 (1983): 3–9; and introd. p. 56.

be so respectless that beggars shall live as well as their
betters; and that my hunger and thirst for riches shall not
make them hunger and thirst with poverty; that my sleeps
shall be broken and their hearts not broken; that my   5
coffers shall be full and yet care, theirs empty and yet
merry; 'tis time that a cross should bear flesh and blood,
since flesh and blood cannot bear this cross.

GREX

Mitis. What, will he hang himself?
Cordatus. Faith, ay. It seems his prognostication has not kept   10
 touch with him, and that makes him despair.
Mitis. Beshrew me, he will be out of his humour then indeed!

Sordido. Tut, these star-monger knaves! Who would trust 'em?
 One says 'dark and rainy' when 'tis clear as crystal.
 Another says 'tempestuous blasts and storms', and 'twas   15
 as calm as a milk bowl. Here be sweet rascals for a man
 to credit his whole fortunes with. You sky-staring coxcombs, you! You fat brains, out upon you! You are good
 for nothing but to sweat night-caps and make rug-gowns

---

 2. *respectless*] indifferent to or disregarding social distinctions.
 6. *yet care*] I shall still worry (an elliptical structure).
 6–7. *yet merry*] they shall still be merry (elliptical).
 7. *cross*] gibbet; probably metaphorical, since the scene does not require
an official place of execution. Chambers (3.107) suggests that a wayside cross
was thrust up from the trap; however, a cross strong enough to bear the
actor's weight would more likely be thrust through one of the stage doors,
or even be 'discovered' below the gallery. Possibly the standard property tree
might have been used for this purpose.
 8. *bear this cross*] tolerate this reversal of fortune.
 10–11. *kept touch*] kept faith (*H&S*).
 12. *Beshrew me*] i.e., damn me (oath).
 13. *star-monger knaves*] prognosticating charlatans, i.e., almanac-writers.
 17. *credit . . . with*] trust . . . to.
 18. *fat*] sweaty.
 out upon you!] a curse upon you.
 19. *to sweat night-caps*] to make your night-caps sweaty (cf. 'fat brains',
above). Not simply donned as sleeping gear, night-caps were worn in the
study by scholars and lawyers, who might sweat into them simply by pro-
longed thinking.
 rug-gowns] robes made of coarse woollen cloth with a hairy nap on one
side, usually worn by scholars (Hoy, 1.219).

dear. You learned men, and have not a legion of devils *à*   20
votre service, à votre service? By heaven, I think I shall die
a better scholar than they. But soft—How now, sirrah?

Enter a Hind *with a letter.*

Hind. Here's a letter come from your son, sir.
Sordido. From my son, sir? What would my son, sir? Some
good news, no doubt.   [*He reads*] *the letter.*   25
'Sweet and dear father,
Desiring you first to send me your blessing, which is more
worth to me than gold or silver, I desire you likewise to
be advertised that this Shrovetide (contrary to custom)
we use always to have revels, which is, indeed, dancing,   30
and makes an excellent show, in truth, especially if we
gentlemen be well attired, which our seniors note and

22.1.] *Q; not in F.*   25. SD] *Q, Fa; in margin of Fb.*

20. *dear*] expensive (because the forecasters are inaccurately predicting cold weather, thus driving up the price of warm clothing).

legion of devils] a common assumption about 'learned men' as interested in forbidden knowledge such as necromancy and alchemy; best represented by Doctor Faustus's bargain with the devil. In Sordido's sarcastic reference, forecasters cannot be considered very learned if they fail to conjure up reliably informative devils.

20–1. *à votre service*] at your service.

22.1. *Hind*] servant.

24–5.] heavily sarcastic.

27. *your blessing*] a conventional piety. According to *Dialogues from Hollyband* (c. 1566), in Byrne, p. 3, sons regularly greeted their parents each morning with 'father, give me your blessing, if it please you'.

29. *advertised*] informed.

Shrovetide] Shrove Sunday, Monday, and Tuesday preceding Lent.

contrary to custom] Although revels were usually held from Christmas to Candlemas, they sometimes lasted until Shrove Tuesday, as did the *Gesta Grayorum* of 1594/5. Nevertheless, Gifford correctly notes that 'Fungoso imposes on his father'.

30. *use*] make it a practice.

revels . . . dancing] 'Dancing . . . formed part of the established corporate life of the Inns from before 1471 until at least 1733' (Brissenden, pp. 6–7). In Solemn Revels, older members of an Inn performed the stately measures of a formal dance like a pavan; the younger men conducted Post Revels, which included more vigorous dancing as well as stage-plays and various witty 'law-sports' (Finkelpearl, *Temple*, pp. 32–44).

32. *well attired*] One of the rules for a reveller was 'Item, That he have the wit to mislike the fashion of his clothes before he pawn them; and that he

think the better of our fathers, the better we are maintained, and that they shall know if they come up and have
anything to do in the law. Therefore, good father, these   35
are (for your own sake as well as mine) to re-desire you
that you let me not want that which is fit for the setting
up of our name in the honourable volume of gentility,
that I may say to our calumniators with Tully: *Ego sum
ortus domus meae, tu occasus tuae.* And thus (not doubting   40
of your fatherly benevolence) I humbly ask you blessing,
and pray God to bless you.

> Yours, if his own . . .'

How's this? 'Yours, if his own'? Is he not my son, except
he be his own son? Belike this is some new kind of sub-   45
scription the gallants use. [*To the Hind*] Well, wherefore
dost thou stay, knave? Away, go!

> *Exit* Hind.

Here's a letter indeed! Revels? And benevolence? Is this
a weather to send benevolence? Or is this a season to revel
in? 'Slid, the devil and all takes part to vex me, I think.   50
This letter would never have come now else, now, now,

47.1.] *Q; not in* F.

---

be always furnished with reasons for the convenience of every fashion'
(Finkelpearl, *Temple*, p. 58).

seniors] barristers and benchers of the Inns of Court.

34–5. *that they . . . law*] our fathers will learn of the seniors' good opinion
if our fathers come up to London to pursue a legal matter. Fungoso implies
that free legal services or influence in court may be the reward of fathers
who support their sons generously.

35. *these*] these lines in the letter.

37. *want*] lack.

39. *Tully*] Cicero.

39–40. *Ego . . . tuae*] 'I am the rising star of my house, you the falling
star of yours.' Derived from Plutarch, who does not mention Cicero
(*H&S*).

41. *benevolence*] generosity.

43. *Yours, if his own*] a subscription usually not found in letters to a parent,
where duty, respect, or obedience should figure as key concepts (*H&S*).
Angel Day, in *The English Secretary; or Method of Writing of Epistles and Letters*
(1599), gives several subscriptions popular at the time, including the apt
'Your honour's most faithful and obedient son' and the silly 'Yours as you
like to have me' and 'Yours or not his own' (pp. 15–16).

44. *except*] unless.

45. *Belike*] perchance, probably.

45–6. *subscription*] complimentary close to a letter, before the signature.

50. *takes part*] conspire.

when the sun shines and the air thus clear. Soul, if this
hold, we shall shortly have an excellent crop of corn
spring out of the highways. The streets and the houses of
the town will be hid with the rankness of the fruits that   55
grow there in spite of good husbandry. Go to! I'll prevent
the sight of it. [*He climbs the ladder and attaches the halter.*]
I have this remedy, heaven! Stay. I'll try the pain thus a
little. [*He pulls upward on the halter.*] O, nothing, nothing.
Well now! Shall my son gain a benevolence by my death?   60
Or anybody be the better for my gold, or so forth? No.
Alive I kept it from 'em, and dead my ghost shall walk
about it and preserve it. My son and daughter shall starve
ere they touch it. I have hid it as deep as hell from the
sight of heaven, and to it I go now.   *Falls off.*   65

Enter Rustici, *five or six, one after another.*

First Rustic. Ay me, what pitiful sight is this? Help! Help!
Help!

---

62. dead] *This ed.;* (dead) *Q, F*   65. SD] *Q; in margin of F*   65.1.] *Q;
Act III. Scene VIII.* / RVSTICI. *In margin: To him. F.*

---

52. *Soul*] by my soul (mild oath).

52–6. *if . . . husbandry*] if the good weather continues, we will have a
virtual plague of fertility, with crops bursting out of the highways, and
burying houses and streets in town, to spite the thrifty practices of farmers
who expect to make vast profits from hoarded harvests. Good husbandry, in
this context, is not a farmer's satisfaction at a fruitful yield but a miser's
gloating over inflated prices during periods of dearth. Cf. the Porter's story
of 'a farmer, that hanged himself on th'expectation of plenty' (*Mac.* 2.3.4–5),
as Sordido plans to do.

58. *try the pain*] Stone, p. 277, records a story of the Earl of Oxford, who
asked his men whether they thought hanging a painful death: ' "Marry," quod
one of his, "that shall your Lordship presently know, seeing the experience." '
He then took off his garters, made a halter, tied it round his own neck, was
hoisted up on the back of another man, and then let fall until he 'waxed very
black in the face, strangling and labouring for life'. On being cut down, he told
the Earl that he would not endure such pain for all the world. Not content with
this experiment, however, another of the Earl's men insisted on carrying out a
further test, with the same result.

59. *nothing*] Having tested the pain of hanging by yanking upwards to
tighten the rope around his neck, Sordido decides the pain of death by
hanging would be negligible.

60. *benevolence*] generous inheritance. Cf. 41, 49: Sordido is irked by his
son's vocabulary and assumptions.

65.1. *Rustici*] rustics, country folk.

Second Rustic. How now, what's the matter?

First Rustic. O, here's a man has hanged himself! Help to get
 him again!   [*He seems to cut the rope as others,*   70
                                 one by one, enter to assist.]

Second Rustic. Hanged himself? 'Slid, carry him afore a
 justice. 'Tis chance-medley, on my word!

Third Rustic. How now, what's here to do?

Fourth Rustic. How comes this?

Second Rustic. One has executed himself contrary to the order   75
 of law and, by my consent, he shall answer 't.

Fifth Rustic. Would he were in case to answer it!

First Rustic. Stand by. He recovers! Give him breath.

Sordido. O!

Fifth Rustic. [*To First Rustic*] Mass, 'twas well you went the   80
 footway, neighbour.

First Rustic. Ay, an I had not cut the halter—

Sordido. How? Cut the halter? Ay me, I am undone, I am
 undone!

Second Rustic. Marry, if you had not been undone, you had   85
 been hanged, I can tell you.

---

72. on] *Q;* o' *F.*   75. the order] *Q;* order *F.*

---

69. *get*] revive.

70.1–2.] The First Rustic probably stands on the ladder, apparently
cutting the body down, but actually detaching the ropes from the harness.
In order for him to do so, the others, beginning with the Second Rustic,
must lift up the body to keep the weight off the ropes. The continuing noisy
entry of several rustics, who assist in some way during Sordido's detachment
and lowering to the ground, distracts attention from, or obscures the trick
involved in, what looks like a rope-cutting.

72. *chance-medley*] The Second Rustic misuses the legal term, which could
hardly be applied to deliberate suicide, also a criminal offence. It refers to
manslaughter, or 'the casual killing of a man, not altogether without the killer's
fault, though without an evil intent; homicide by misadventure' (*OED*). In
diary entries for August 1598 Henslowe recorded payments to Dekker and
others for 'A book called *Chance-Medley, or Worse Afeared than Hurt*'.

77. *in case*] in a condition.

80–1. *the footway*] by the footpath, not the main road.

82, 83. *cut the halter*] Manningham records a version of this story in April
1603, without reference to Jonson: 'A covetous fellow had hanged himself,
and was angry with him that cut the rope to save his life. A covetous man
will rather lose his life then his goods' (p. 220).

83. *undone*] ruined financially.

85. *undone*] released from the noose.

Sordido. You threadbare, horsebread-eating rascals, if you
    would needs have been meddling, could you not have
    untied it, but you must cut it? And in the midst too? Ay me!
First Rustic. Out on me, 'tis the caterpillar Sordido! How   90
    cursed are the poor, that the viper was blessed with this
    good fortune!
            [The other Rustics turn on the First Rustic.]
Second Rustic. Nay, how accursed art thou, that art cause to
    the curse of the poor!
Third Rustic. Ay, and to save so wretched a caitiff!   95
Fourth Rustic. Cursed be thy fingers that loosed him!
Second Rustic. Some desperate fury possess thee, that thou
    mayst hang thyself too!
Fifth Rustic. Never mayst thou be saved, that saved so
    damned a monster!   100
Sordido. *[Aside]* What curses breathe these men! How have my
    deeds
    Made my looks differ from another man's,
    That they should thus detest and loathe my life?
    Out on my wretched humour! It is that
    Makes me thus monstrous in true human eyes.   105
    [To the Rustics] Pardon me, gentle friends. I'll make fair
    'mends

---

87. *horsebread-eating*] 'Horse-corn' meant beans and grains used as
fodder (peas, oats, lentils), but eaten by the poor in times of dearth when
wheat and rye were too expensive.

90. *caterpillar*] parasite or bloodsucker; in *Old Fortunatus* 3.1.417: 'They
are as all horses are, caterpillars to the commonwealth, they are ever munch-
ing' (Hoy, 1.122). As used in *R2* 2.3.165, it implies a loafer getting fat on the
work of others.

95. *caitiff*] villain (*OED* 3).

101.] The switch into blank verse emphasizes the miracle of the conversion by heightening the language. The same rhetorical switch occurs earlier
when Sordido suddenly waxes poetic at 1.3.54, thanking his 'blessed angel'
for the miracle of bad weather.

106–21.] During the corn scarcity of 1596, the Queen and council sent a
request to the Archbishop of Canterbury to order preachers to 'admonish
the farmers and owners of corn of this dishonest and unchristian kind of
seeking gain by oppressions of their poor neighbours, and recommend to the
richer sort keeping of hospitality for relief of the poor and avoiding of excess

For my foul errors past, and twenty-fold
Restore to all men what with wrong I robbed them.
My barns and garners shall stand open still
To all the poor that come, and my best grain   110
Be made alms-bread to feed half-famished mouths.
Though hitherto amongst you I have lived
Like an unsavoury muckhill to myself,
Yet now my gathered heaps, being spread abroad,
Shall turn to better and more fruitful uses.   115
Bless then this man [*Indicating First Rustic*]. Curse him
     no more for saving
My life and soul together. O, how deeply
The bitter curses of the poor do pierce!
I am by wonder changed. Come in with me
And witness my repentance. Now I prove   120
No life is blessed that is not graced with love.   *Exit.*
Second Rustic. O, miracle! See when a man has grace!
Third Rustic. Had 't not been pity so good a man should have
     been cast away?

---

121. SD] *Q; not in F.*

. . . and convert that which they spend superfluously that way to the relief of the poorer sort' (de Bruyn, p. 56). Manningham records fragments of several sermons on covetousness six years later, at least half of those years affected by dearths and corn-hoarding: 'Covetousness, the root of all wickedness, maketh men desire to be great rather than good, and this desire causes them to suck even the life from one another' (p. 94); 'Take heed of covetousness, for though a man have abundance, his life standeth not in riches' (p. 197); 'The use of riches is to serve our own necessity, God's glory, to do good to the poor, to lend to the needy, to reward the virtuous, to make friend of, etc. Yet the gift cannot merit, for if I give all that I have, yet if I want charity, etc.' (p. 198).

   109. *still*] continually.
   111. *alms-bread*] food distributed as charity to the poor.
   113. *unsavoury muckhill*] stinking manure-heap, used for fertilizer; a proverbial image for hoarded wealth, as in Dent, M1071: 'Money, like dung, does no good till it is spread'. The image is literal in *CisA* 4.9.20: 'The old proverb's true, I see: gold is but muck. [*He removes the dung, and shows him the gold.*]'
   114 *abroad*] outside of my house.
   119. *by wonder*] by a miracle.
   124. *cast away*] damned (as a suicide).

Second Rustic. Well, I'll get our clerk to put his conversion in   125
the chronicle.

Fourth Rustic. Do, for I warrant him he's a virtuous man.

Second Rustic. O God, how he wept, if you marked it! Did you
see how the tears trilled?

Fifth Rustic. Yes, believe me, like Master Vicar's bowls upon   130
the green, for all the world.

Third or Fourth Rustic. [*To First Rustic*] O neighbour, God's
blessing o'your heart, neighbour! 'Twas a good grateful
deed.

Exeunt [*with the ladder*].

GREX

Cordatus. How now, Mitis? What's that you consider so   135
seriously?

Mitis. Troth, that which doth essentially please me: the
warping condition of this green and soggy multitude.

---

126. chronicle] *Q; Acts, and Monuments F.*   127. virtuous man] *Q; Martyr
F.*   128. *Second Rustic*] *Rust. Q, F1.*   133. blessing o'your] *F;* blessing
your *Q.*   134.1. *Exeunt*] *Q;* not in *F.*

---

126. *chronicle*] perhaps church records; possibly a record of contemporary
events like Edward Hall's *Chronicle*, Raphael Holinshed's *Chronicles of
England, Scotland, and Ireland*, or John Stow's *Annals, or General Chronicle of
England. F* changes the reference to John Foxe's *Acts and Monuments* (1563,
reissued for the fifth time in 1596, and a sixth in 1610) also called *The Book
of Martyrs*, as suggested by *F*'s changing 'virtuous man' to '*Martyr*' at 127.
Its popularity is a tribute to Foxe's style, vigorous and vivid in depicting the
persecutions of Protestant martyrs, and coarsely ribald in belabouring his
opponents; but Foxe, like Jonson's rustics, was also frequently inaccurate.
See *DNB*.

129. *trilled*] (*a*) flowed in a steady stream (*OED* v², *arch.*); (*b*) in dialect,
rolled or bowled (*OED* v¹ 1b). The latter usage explains the next line's reference to the vicar's lawn-bowling.

133. *grateful*] pleasing, welcome.

138. *soggy*] waterlogged; perhaps an indication that the Rustics have been
weeping in sympathy with Sordido's tears; perhaps similar to Donne's
'spungy hydroptique Dutch' in *Elegies*, 'On his Mistris', 16.42, meaning
'boggy' or 'sopping'. The reference to 'warping condition' and 'green' suggests a damp and decaying moisture; Skeat records 'soggy' as meaning 'heavy
(like damp and green hay)', citing the *English Dialect Dictionary* for various
provincial uses. *OED* does not record 'soggy' before 1722, and suggests that
Jonson's use is a misprint for 'foggy', meaning (*a*) fat, gross; as in Nashe, *A
Choice of Valentines* (3.405): 'Therewith out stepped a foggy three-chinned
dame, / That us'd to take young wenches for to tame' (McKerrow, 4.481);

But, in good faith, signor, your author hath largely out-
stripped my expectation in this scene, I will liberally   140
confess it. For when I saw Sordido so desperately
intended, I thought I had had a hand of him then.

Cordatus. What? You supposed he should have hung himself
indeed?

Mitis. I did, and had framed my objection to it ready, which   145
may yet be very fitly urged, and with some necessity:
for, though his purposed violence lost th'effect and
extended not to death, yet the intent and horror of the
object was more than the nature of a comedy will in any
sort allow.   150

Cordatus. Ay? What think you of Plautus, in his comedy called
Cistellaria, there where he brings in Alcestimarchus with
a drawn sword ready to kill himself and, as he is e'en
fixing his breast upon it, to be restrained from his
resolved outrage by Silenium and the Bawd? Is not his   155
authority of power to give our scene approbation?

Mitis. Sir, I have this your only evasion left me to say: I think
it be so indeed—your memory is happier than mine. But
I wonder what engine he will use to bring the rest out of
their humours?   160

Cordatus. That will appear anon. Never preoccupy your imagination withal. Let your mind keep company with the
scene still, which now removes itself from the country

---

150. allow] *Q;* admit *F.*   157–8. I think . . . mine.] *Italic in Q, F.*

---

or (*b*) bemuddled, confused (*OED* 4b), as in *Pilgrimage to Parnassus* 5.536–7:
'Rude foggy squires / That know not to esteem of wit or art'. The final possibility is that the word was 'sappy', or sapping: to sap is 'to dig or delve, or
grub the ground' (Florio, *Zappare*). The idea of 'warping' may simply be
related to 'green', as in green wood which warps if used for building.

   141–2. *desperately intended*] bent on a desperate act.
   142. *had a hand of him*] got rid of him (*OED, Rid* 43b).
   145. *framed*] fashioned, constructed.
   146. *fitly*] aptly, appropriately (with regard to the laws of comedy).
   necessity] appropriateness, urgency.
   152. Cistellaria] *The Casket,* adapted from Menander.
   156. *of power*] sufficiently powerful.
   157. *this your only*] this single. The indefinite *your* suggests sarcasm.
   158. *happier*] more felicitous. Mitis perhaps facetiously acknowledges
defeat because he cannot recall another specific classical reference to outdo
Cordatus's.
   159. *engine*] device.

to the court. Here comes Macilente and Signor Brisk,
freshly suited. Lose not yourself, for now the *epitasis*, or   165
busy part of our subject, is in action.

ACT 3   SCENE 3

Enter MACILENTE [*and*] BRISK [*in new suits*],
[*and*] CINEDO *with tobacco*.

Fastidius. Well now, Signor Macilente, you are not only
welcome to the court, but also to my mistress's
withdrawing-chamber.—Boy, get me some tobacco.
[*Cinedo stands aside preparing a pipe. To Macilente*] I'll but
go in and show I am here, and come to you presently,   5
sir.   *Exit.*
Macilente. [*Aside*] What's that he said? By heaven, I marked
     him not.
My thoughts and I were of another world.
I was admiring mine own outside here,
To think what privilege and palm it bears   10
Here in the court. Be a man ne'er so vile
In wit, in judgement, manners, or what else,
If he can purchase but a silken cover,

---

166. action] *Q; act F.*

ACT 3 SCENE 3] SCENA TERTIA *Q; Act III. Scene IX. F.*   0.1–2] *Q;* MACI-
LENTE, BRISKE, CINEDO, / SAVIOLINA. *F.*   2. mistress's] *This ed.;* mistresse *Q;* mistris *F.*   6. SD] *Q; not in F.*

---

165. *freshly suited*] wearing new clothes.
Lose not yourself] i.e., don't distract yourself with side-issues, or non-
issues.
     epitasis] The Renaissance view of plot, based on Roman comedy and later
commentators like Donatus, demanded a tripartite division into protasis,
epitasis, and catastrophe; see Mary C. Williams, *Unity in Jonson's Early Comedies* (Salzburg, 1972), pp. 22–8. Jonson divides the play almost in half, the
protasis parading the humours, and the epitasis setting up complications in
which the characters are put out of their humours; the catastrophe, by
Jonson's own label, is narrowly limited to the final scene (5.4 in this edition).
     3. *withdrawing-chamber*] drawing-room.
     9. *outside*] personal appearance, now fashionably attired.
     10. *palm*] emblem of excellence or supreme honour, like that carried by
a victor in ancient Rome (*OED* 3).

He shall not only pass, but pass regarded;
Whereas, let him be poor and meanly clad,   15
Though ne'er so richly parted, you shall have
A fellow that knows nothing but his beef,
Or how to rinse his clammy guts in beer,
Will take him by the shoulders or the throat
And kick him down the stairs. Such is the state   20
Of virtue in bad clothes—ha, ha, ha, ha!—
That raiment should be in such high request!
How long should I be ere I should put off
To my lord chancellor's tomb, or the sheriff's posts?
By heaven, I think, a thousand thousand year.   25
His gravity, his wisdom, and his faith
To my dread sovereign—graces that survive him—
These I could well endure to reverence,
But not his tomb, no more than I'll commend
The chapel organ for the gilt without,   30

---

24. To my] *Q;* To the *F.*   sheriff's] *Q, F (Shriues).*   29. I'll] *Q (I'le);*
I'ld *F.*

14.] He will be not only socially accepted but also admired.

16. *richly parted*] talented and intelligent; see Chars.7.

17. *that . . . beef*] i.e. ignorant and uncouth; a contemptible attribute, as in 'beef-witted' or 'beef-brained', thick-headed or stupid; 'beaf-eater', well-fed menial (*OED, Beef* 5).

18. *rinse . . . guts*] imbibe copiously.

23. *be*] live, wait.

put off] doff my hat. Dekker similarly satirizes the new protocol of the fashionable: 'Suck this humour up especially. Put off to none, unless his hatband be of a newer fashion than yours, and three degrees quainter' (*Gull's Horn-book* 2.234).

24. *my lord chancellor's tomb*] the massive tomb of Sir Christopher Hatton in St Paul's choir, one of the sights of London (*H&S*).

sheriff's posts] posts set up before the doors of a sheriff's or a mayor's house, for hanging up (posting) proclamations (*H&S*). To doff one's cap to a mere sign (as opposed to a person) of authority suggests meaningless and ludicrously punctilious ceremony.

26–8]. I could easily spend time showing respect to Hatton's gravity, wisdom, and faith to the Queen, since these are admirable qualities that outlive his mortal being.

30. *the gilt without*] the gold-leaf decoration on its cabinet.

Or this bass viol [*Indicating an instrument hanging on wall*]
for the varnished face.

Enter FASTIDIUS.

Fastidius. In faith, I have made you stay somewhat long, sir,
but—[*To Cinedo*] Is my tobacco ready, boy?

Cinedo. Ay, sir.

Fastidius. Give me. [*To Macilente*] My mistress is upon   35
coming. You shall see her presently, sir. ([*Puffs*] *tobacco.*)
You'll say you never accosted a more piercing wit. [*To
Cinedo*] This tobacco is not dried, boy, or else the pipe's
defective. [*To Macilente*] O, your wits of Italy are nothing
comparable to her! Her brain's a very quiver of jests, and   40
she does dart them abroad with that sweet loose and judi-
cial aim that you would—Here she comes, sir.

31.1.] *Q; not in F.*   32. In faith] *Q; I feare* F.   36. SD] *This ed.; Tab.* Q,
F.   42. that you] *Q, Fb; not in Fa.*

31. *bass viol*] viola da gamba, a small cello held between the legs while
being played; hence, associated with bawdy innuendo. Viols frequently signify
sexual play in drama, as in *2 Return from Parnassus* 3.2.1243–4: 'Her viol *da
gamba* is her best content, / For twixt her legs she holds her instrument'. The
viol was popular among amateur and professional musicians in 1599, when
Anthony Holborne published *Pavans, galliards, almains, and other short airs for
viols, etc 5 pts.* Manningham (p. 32) lists several devices and mottos taken
from escutcheons in the gallery at Whitehall; among them, 'A viol well
strung; the word, *Adhibe dextram*' ('Treat it right'), punning on skill and
fidelity. Macilente thus sets the scene by mentioning the prop, and by suggesting the emblematic meaning of that prop, handled unskilfully by Fastidius, and rejected as a pledge of fidelity and as a sexual invitation by
Saviolina, who comments stringently on his bad playing and on his inadequacy as a lover.

varnished face] wood finish on the instrument.

35. *Give me*] idiomatic omission of pronoun 'it', probably owing to lack
of emphasis; Carlo gives the same order to his boy at Ind.324 (Partridge,
Syntax, p. 39).

35–6. *upon coming*] about to come in.

36. ([*Puffs*] *tobacco.*)] Jonson's SD, '(*Tab.*)', an abbreviation of '*tabacco*',
now seems less vivid than *Puff* which Marston used in *Jack Drum's Entertainment*, imitating Jonson: M. Puffe punctuates his sentences with '(*Puff*)',
as in 'Sir, I enroll you in the legend of my (*Puff*) intimates' (B4v). Marston
is clearly reproducing what he saw on stage in *EMO*.

41. *loose*] discharge [of an arrow] (*OED* 1). A noun, not another adjec-
tive, in the archery metaphor.

Enter SAVIOLINA.

Macilente. [*Aside*] 'Twas time. His invention had been bogged
   else.

Saviolina. [*Calling off-stage*] Give me my fan there.   45
                                        And goes in again.

Macilente. How now, Monsieur Brisk?

Fastidius. A kind of affectionate reverence strikes me with a
   cold shivering, methinks.

Macilente. [*Aside*] I like such tempers well as stand before
   their mistresses with fear and trembling and before their   50
   Maker like impudent mountains.

Fastidius. By Jesu, I'd spend twenty pound my vaulting horse
   stood here now, she might see me do but one trick!

Macilente. Why, does she love activity?

Cinedo. Or, if you had but your long stockings on, to be   55
   dancing a galliard as she comes by.

42.1.] *This ed.; Enter Saviolina, and goes in againe. Q; She is seene and / goes
in againe. In margin of F*   45.1. *And . . . again*] *In Q, appears at end of l.
42.1. See collation note above.*   52. By Jesu] *Q;* By this hand *F*

43–4. *had . . . else*] had bogged down otherwise.

47. *affectionate*] passionate.

52. *vaulting horse*] wooden horse used for gymnastic exercise. Like the references to dancing and the viol, evidence of educational residence abroad to
acquire 'the qualities of ornation'; namely, weapon-handling, music,
drawing, poetry, dancing, vaulting, running, and 'dexterity', as well as languages, the art of government, and various sciences, including architecture
(Stone, p. 694, citing Thomas Palmer, 1606). Vaulting was popular as a
courtship display; cf. *CR* 2.1.63–6; *NI* 1.3.73–4; and Webster, *The White
Devil* 2.2.37ff. On the other hand, a 'vaulting-house' was a brothel, an
innuendo not lost on Macilente.

53. *she might*] that she might.

trick] (*a*) feat of dexterity; (*b*) one of the elaborate steps in the
galliard; hence Cinedo's quip at 55–6 about the galliard (see Brissenden,
p. 116).

54. *activity*] innuendo of copulation, as in 'do the act', or 'do the deed'
(Partridge, *Bawdy*).

56. *galliard*] lively dance demanding agility, and giving male dancers
opportunities for virtuoso solo performance; steps include the 'cinquepace',
five rapid steps danced to the six beats of the music, with a pause on the
fifth beat; the 'fleuret', rapid crossing and uncrossing of the feet; the 'ruade',
kicking the foot backwards; and the 'caper', high leap in which the dancer
makes two revolutions in the air before landing (Brissenden, pp. 56–7,
113–14).

Fastidius. Ay, either. O, these stirring humours make ladies
mad with desire! She comes. My good genius embolden
me! [*To Cinedo*] Boy, the pipe, quickly.

Macilente. [*Aside*] What? Will he give her music?   60

Enter SAVIOLINA.

Fastidius. A second good morrow to my fair mistress.

Saviolina. Fair servant, I'll thank you a day hence, when the
date of your salutation comes forth.

Fastidius. [*To Macilente*] How like you that answer? Is 't not
admirable?   65

Macilente. I were a simple courtier, sir, if I could not admire
trifles, sir.

[*Fastidius*] *talks, and takes tobacco between* [*phrases*].

Fastidius. Troth, sweet lady, I shall—(*Tobacco.*)—be prepared
to give you thanks for those thanks, and—(*Tobacco*)—
study more officious and obsequious regards—   70
(*Tobacco*)—to your fair beauties. (*Tobacco*)—Mend the
pipe, boy.

Macilente. [*Aside*] I ne'er knew tobacco taken as a *parenthesis*
before.

Fastidius. 'Fore God, sweet lady, believe it, I do honour the   75
meanest rush in this chamber for your love.

60.1.] *In Q, at end of l. 58; not in F.*   67.1.] *He talkes, and / takes tabacco /
betweene. In margin of F; not in Q.*   69. SD] *This ed.; Tab. Q, F. Also at 70,
100, 103, 106, 107, 108, 111, 115, 118, 123, 128, and 129.*

---

57. *stirring*] (*a*) sexually exciting (Partridge, *Bawdy*); (*b*) physically active,
with innuendo of copulation (Henke). Brisk's sexual allusions do not necessarily communicate real desire; he merely makes 'a good jest' (108) to show
off his wit.

58. *genius*] personal guardian spirit, protecting him and giving him valour.

60. *music*] punning on tobacco-pipe and the musical instrument; see 121n
below.

62. *a day hence*] tomorrow. Saviolina's quip depends on 'morrow' being
understood literally as 'next day' (*OED* 2), although the archaic meaning is
'morning' (*OED* 1).

66. *simple*] simpleminded.

67. *trifles*] foolish or trivial jests, nonsensical jokes (*OED* 1).

76. *meanest*] lowliest.

rush] Rushes, cylindrical grasslike needs, were used as floor-
coverings, before carpets became common. Brisk declares that he adores any
wisp of rush on the floor simply because she has touched it with her foot.

for your love] for love of you (Partridge, *Syntax*, p. 44).

Saviolina. Ay, you need not tell me that, sir. I do think you
  do prize a rush before my love.

Macilente. [*Aside*] Is this the wonder of nations?

Fastidius. O, by Jesu, pardon me, I said 'for your love', by   80
  this light; but it is the accustomed sharpness of your
  ingenuity, sweet mistress, to—Mass, your viol's new
  strung, methinks.   *Takes down the viol.*

Macilente. [*Aside*] 'Ingenuity'? I see his ignorance will not
  suffer him to slander her, which he had done most   85
  notably if he had said 'wit' for 'ingenuity', as he meant it.

Fastidius. By the soul of music, lady—(*Hum, hum*)

Saviolina. Would we might hear it once.

Fastidius. —I do more adore and admire your—(*Hum,
  hum*)—predominant perfections than—(*Hum, hum*)—   90
  ever I shall have power and faculty to express. (*Hum*)

Saviolina. Upon the viol da gamba, you mean?

Fastidius. It's miserably out of tune, by this hand.

Saviolina. Nay, rather by the fingers.

Macilente. [*Aside*] It makes good harmony with her wit.   95

Fastidius. [*Handing her the viol.*] Sweet lady, tune it. [*To
  Cinedo*] Boy, some tobacco.

Macilente. [*Aside*] Tobacco again? He does court his mistress
  with very exceeding good changes.

Fastidius. Signor Macilente, you take none, sir? (*Tobacco*)   100

---

80. by Jesu] *Q;* by this ayre *F.*   83. SD] *Q; He takes downe / the violl, and /
playes betweene. In margin of F.*   92. da gamba] *Q, F (de Gambo).*

77–8.] Saviolina's quip is to reinterpret Fastidius's 'for' (76) as 'fore' or
'before', hence reversing his meaning.

82. *ingenuity*] Brisk means 'sharpness of wit'.

84–6.] Macilente does not define 'ingenuity' as 'wit' or 'ingeniousness',
which he sees Saviolina lacks. He quibbles on 'ingenuousness', the condition of being born to a high social station (*OED* 1). In this period, 'ingenuity' served as the abstract noun for either 'ingenious' or 'ingenuous' (*OED*).

87. Hum, hum] an attempt to mimic the resonance of the bow on the
viola da gamba's strings; or perhaps the sound of Fastidius's humming as he
tries to tune the instrument.

94.] Saviolina quibbles with the conventional oath *by this hand*: one tunes
with the fingers, not the hand.

95.] The out-of-tune viola da gamba is a perfect match for her wit.

99. *changes*] modulations in his conduct; a musical quibble.

Macilente. No. Unless I had a mistress, signor, it were a great
    indecorum for me to take tobacco.

Fastidius. How like you her wit? (*Tobacco*)

Macilente. Her *ingenuity* is excellent, sir.

Fastidius. [*Watching Saviolina tune the viol*] You see the subject   105
    of her sweet fingers there? (*Tobacco*) O, she tickles it so,
    that—(*Tobacco*)—she makes it laugh most divinely.
    (*Tobacco.*) I'll tell you a good jest now, and yourself shall
    say it's a good one: I have wished myself to be that instru-
    ment, I think, a thousand times, and not so few, by   110
    heavens! (*Tobacco*)

Macilente. Not unlike, sir. But how? To be cased up and hung
    by the wall?

Fastidius. O, no, sir, to be in use, I assure you, as your judi-
    cious eye may testify. (*Tobacco*)   115

Saviolina. [*Offering him the viol*] Here, servant, if you will
    play, come.

Fastidius. Instantly, sweet lady. (*Tobacco*) In good faith, here's
    most divine tobacco.

Saviolina. [*Recoiling from the smoke*] Nay, I cannot stay to   120
    dance after your pipe.

---

111. heavens] *Q;* heauen *F.*

105–10.] 'The point of this "good jest" is that it was a stale lover's conceit'
(*H&S*), already satirized by Marston in *Scourge of Villainy* 8.118–37. It may
also echo Shakespeare's Sonnet 128, 'How oft when thou, my music, music
play'st', which describes 'sweet fingers', a tickling touch, and a desire to trade
places with the instrument. See Thomas H. McNeal, '*Every Man Out of His
Humour* and Shakespeare's *Sonnets*', *N&Q* 197 (1952): 376.

110. *not so few*] even more than a thousand.

112. *cased up*] (*a*) hung on the wall in a case; (*b*) innuendo of sexual pen-
etration (Hoy, 2.115): the male sexual 'instrument' in the female 'case'. Legal
jokes relying on the term *case* appear frequently, as in *Gesta Grayorum* (1594),
p. 39, enjoining revellers to perform 'all requisite and manly service, be it
night-service, or otherwise, as the case requireth, to all ladies' (Williams).

114. *in use*] active, continuing the pun on musical and sexual
performance.

121. *dance . . . pipe*] Pipe jokes were very common; cf. Asinius Bubo's
remark, prior to reading Horace's poem in *Satiromastix*: 'Here's the best leaf
in *England*, but on, on, I'll but tune this pipe' (1.2.43–4). Most pipe jokes,
especially when dance accompanies the music reference, include the innuendo of copulation: 'Dance after my Pipe' is an alternative title of the ballad
generally known as 'The Shaking of the Sheets', referring to bedding, or 'The
Dance of Death', punning on orgasm (Henke), as in the opening lines of

Fastidius. Good! Nay, dear lady, stay! By this sweet smoke, I
 think your wit be all fire. (*Tobacco*)
Macilente. [*Aside*] And he's the salamander that lives by it.
Saviolina. Is your tobacco perfumed, sir, that you swear by 125
 the sweet smoke?
Fastidius. Still more excellent! Before God and these bright
 heavens, I think—(*Tobacco*)—you are made of ingenuity,
 (*Tobacco*) I!
Macilente. [*Aside*] True, as your discourse is. O, abominable! 130
Fastidius. Will your ladyship take any?
Saviolina. O, peace, I pray you. I love not the breath of a
 woodcock's head.
Fastidius. Meaning my head, lady?
Saviolina. Not altogether so, sir. But (as it were fatal to their 135
 follies that think to grace themselves with taking tobacco
 when they want better entertainment) you see your pipe
 bears the true form of a woodcock's head.
Fastidius. O, admirable simile!
Saviolina. 'Tis best leaving of you in admiration, sir. *Exit.* 140

---

124. that lives by] *Q;* belongs to *F.* 125. sir] *Q;* seruant *F.* 127–8.
Before God . . . heavens] *parenthetical in Q;* (before heauen, and these
bright lights) *F.* 140. SD] *Q; not in F.*

Heywood's *Woman Killed with Kindness*: 'Francis. Some music there! None
lead the bride a dance? / Charles. Yes, would she dance *The Shaking of the
Sheets*; / But that's the dance her husband means to lead her.'
 122. *Good! . . . stay!*] This phrase is capable of at least three readings: (*a*)
'Good' is a compliment on Saviolina's pipe joke; she hears it as an insult
('Good, you cannot stay'), but he restrains her from leaving and offers a
clearer compliment. (*b*) She accepts the compliment. He pauses, saying 'Nay
. . . stay', because he wants time to invent a witty response worthy to follow
her pipe-joke. He then delivers his next line. (*c*) She rises to leave, and Fastidius fumbles for the appropriate epithet to make his admiration for her
clear: 'Good—nay! *dear* lady, stay!'
 124. *salamander*] lizard purportedly able to live in flames and to put out
fire (Browne, 3.14).
 132–3. *breath . . . head*] a quibble on the pipe-smoker's bad breath; for
Bellafront in *1 Honest Whore* 2.1.83, tobacco 'makes your breath stink, like
the piss of a fox'. The woodcock, a bird easily caught, was a type of the fool;
also a popular carving on pipe-bowls.
 135–8. *But . . . head*] The woodcock's head carved on the pipe-bowl is a
true symbol of those foolish enough to smoke when they have nothing better
to do. Ironically, such fools think they look sophisticated and accomplished,
but they really create the opposite effect.

Macilente. Are these the admired lady-wits that, having so
good a plainsong, can run no better division upon it?
'Sheart, all her jests are of the stamp March was fifteen
years ago. Is this the comet, Monsieur Fastidius, that your
gallants wonder at so?   145

Fastidius. Heart of a gentleman, to neglect me afore presence
thus! Sweet sir, I beseech you, be silent in my disgrace.
By Jesu, I never was in so vile a humour in my life! And
her wit was at the flood too. Report it not for a million,
good sir. Let me be so far endeared to your love.   150

Exeunt.

GREX

Mitis. What follows next, Signor Cordatus? This gallant's
humour is almost spent, methinks. It ebbs apace, with
contrary breath of his mistress.

Cordatus. O, but it will flow again for all this, till there come
a general drought of humour among all our actors, and   155

---

148. Jesu] *Q;* the *Muses F.*   never was] *Q;* was never *F.*   150.1.] *Q; not
in F.*

---

142. *plainsong . . . run . . . division*] In early music, the plainsong is the
theme, and the division is a variation on it, either by dividing the slow notes
of the theme into rapid passages or by harmonizing with the theme to form
a descant, or by some combination of the two. Macilente's complaint is that
women like Saviolina lack inventiveness on the standard theme of courtship.

143. *stamp*] fashion or kind (*OED* 13e).

March] The play takes place in March around Shrovetide, just before
Lent; see Fungoso's letter, 3.2.29. Macilente emphasizes the very ordinary,
out-of-date ('fifteen years ago'), predictable quality of Saviolina's so-called
witticisms by using a proverbial description (Tilley, M640: 'as sure as March
in Lent').

144. *comet*] blazing star that stands out even in a heaven full of stars. The
trope was common in love-poetry; e.g. see Puntarvolo's poem to '*heavenly
pulchritude*' at 2.1.305–10.

146. *Heart . . . gentleman*] mild oath.

afore presence] in front of company, before a guest.

147. *be silent in*] do not tell anyone about.

149. *for a million*] on any account.

152. *spent*] exhausted.

152–4. *ebbs . . . flow*] tidal images, picking up on Saviolina's 'flood' of wit
(149).

then I fear not but his will fall as low as any. See who presents himself here?

> [*Indicating Fungoso, who is about to enter.*]

Mitis. What, i' the old case?

Cordatus. I' faith, which makes it the more pitiful. You understand where the scene is?   160

------

156. *fear not but*] do not doubt but that.

158. *old case*] same predicament (of needing money to keep up with the
latest fashions); possibly, same clothing as before.

160. *where . . . is*] at Deliro's house. This line, under the performance conditions of continuous staging at the Globe, would coincide with Fallace's
entrance in 4.1.

Act 4

ACT 4   SCENE 1

Enter FUNGOSO, FALLACE *following him.*

Fallace. Why are you so melancholy, brother?

Fungoso. I am not melancholy, I thank you, sister.

Fallace. Why are you not merry then? There are but two of
us in all the world, and if we should not be comforts to
one another, God help us!   5

Fungoso. Faith, I cannot tell, sister, but if a man had any true
melancholy in him it would make him melancholy to see
his yeomanly father cut his neighbours' throats to make
his son a gentleman, and yet, when he has cut 'em, he
will see his son's throat cut too ere he make him a true   10
gentleman indeed before death cut his own throat. I must
be the first head of our house, and yet he will not give
me the head till I be made so. Is any man termed a
gentleman that is not always i' the fashion? I would know
but that.   15

Fallace. If you be melancholy for that, brother, I think I have
as much cause to be melancholy as one, for I'll be sworn
I live as little in the fashion as any woman in London. By
the bible of heaven (beast that I am to say it), I have not
one friend i' the world besides my husband. When saw   20
you Master Fastidius Brisk, brother?

ACT 4 SCENE 1] *Q (ACTUS QUARTUS, SCENA PRIMA), F (ACT IIII.
SCENE I.).*   0.1.] *Q;* FALLACE. FUNGOSO. *F.*   4–5. to one] *Q;* one to *F.*
18–19. By the bible of heaven] *Q;* By the faith of a Gentlewoman *F.*
19. have] *Q;* ha' *F.*

---

12. *first head*] first generation gentleman; cf. 3.1.138–9.

12–13. *give me the head*] let me do what I want, give me my indepen-
dence.

14. *i' the fashion*] fashionably dressed.

17. *as one*] as anyone (Partridge, *Syntax*, p. 74).

20. *friend*] (*a*) lover; cf. *Alc.* 3.2.33–7; (*b*) patron. Fallace may be unin-
tentionally punning on the aphorism in Lyly, *Euphues* (Croll and Clemons),
p. 461: 'I know that a friend in the court is better than a penny in the purse'

268

Fungoso. But a while since, sister, I think—I know not well,
in truth. By God's lid, I could fight with all my heart,
methinks.
Fallace. Nay, good brother, be not resolute.   25
Fungoso. [*Brooding, oblivious of Fallace*] I sent him a letter, and
he writes me no answer neither.
Fallace. [*Rhapsodizing, oblivious of Fungoso*] O sweet Fastidius
Brisk! O fine courtier! Thou art he mak'st me sigh and
say, 'How blessed is that woman that hath a courtier   30
to her husband! And how miserable a dame she is that
hath neither husband nor friend in the court!' O sweet
Fastidius! O fine courtier! How comely he bows him in
his courtesy! How full he hits a woman betwixt the lips
when he kisses! How upright he sits at the table! How   35
daintily he carves! How sweetly he talks and tells news
of this lord and of that lady! How cleanly he wipes his
spoon at every spoonful of any white meat he eats, and
what a neat case of pick-tooths he carries about him still!
O sweet Fastidius! O fine courtier!   40

---

23. By God's lid] *Q;* By this hand *F.*   32. in the] *Q, Fa;* i' the *Fb.*   34.
courtesy] *Q, Fa;* court'sie *Fb.*   betwixt] *Q, Fa;* betweene *Fb.*

(cited in M. P. Tilley, *Elizabethan Proverb Lore* (New York, 1926)). Fallace
quotes from *Euphues* at 5.3.512–14.

25. *resolute*] physically violent, eager to brawl.

26ff.] All semblance of communication between brother and sister stops;
cf. *Disc.* 215–18, and 'Non-sequiturs' in Erasmus, pp. 422–4, a duologue in
which one speaks of a wedding and the other of a rough voyage at sea, neither
listening to the other.

26. *him*] Sordido (see 3.2.26–43).

33. *bows him*] makes a bow.

38. *white meat*] food made of milk, eggs, curds, and cheese, perhaps mixed
with bread or flour (McKerrow, 4.393; Skeat). Other descriptions may be
found in Henry Buttes, *Diet's Dry Dinner* (1599), ch. 5.

39. *neat*] (*a*) elegantly made (*OED* 7); (*b*) cleverly contrived (*OED* 8c).
case of pick-tooths] a courtly affectation. Cf. setting the table in Dekker, *If
This Be Not a Good Play, the Devil Is in It* 1.3.7–10: 'So: the Lord Prior's
napkin here, there the Subprior's: his knife and case of pick-tooths thus: as
for the convent, let them lick their fingers instead of wiping, and suck their
teeth instead of picking'. A toothpick case may have a retractable pick that
slides into its own gold or enamelled sheath, or have a sickle-shaped pick
made of gold or silver, fixed on an intricately carved or jewelled handle, as
displayed in the Jewellery Room, Victoria and Albert Museum.

still] always.

Enter DELIRO *with* Musicians.

Deliro. See, yonder she is, gentlemen. Now, as ever you'll bear
the name of musicians, touch your instruments sweetly.
She has a delicate ear, I tell you. Play not a false note, I
beseech you.

Musicians. Fear not, Signor Deliro.   45

Deliro. O, begin, begin—some spritely thing. [*Aside*] Lord,
how my imagination labours with the success of it. [*To
Musicians as they play*]—Well said, good, i' faith! [*Aside*]
Heaven grant it please her. I'll not be seen, for then she'll
be sure to dislike it.   [*He conceals himself.*]   50

Fallace. [*Hearing the music*] Hey da, this is excellent! I'll lay
my life this is my husband's dotage. [*She spies Deliro.*] I
thought so. [*To him*] Nay, never play peek-a-boo with me.
I know you do nothing but study how to anger me, sir.

Deliro. Anger thee, sweet wife? Why, didst thou not send for 55
musicians to supper last night thyself?

Fallace. 'To supper', sir! Now, come up—'to supper', I
beseech you! As though there were no difference between
supper time, when folks should be merry, and this time,
when they would be melancholy! I would never take upon   60

40.1.] *Q; Act IIII. Scene II. /* DELIRO, Musicians, MACILENTE, /
FVNGOSO. *F.*   53. peek-a-boo] *Q, F1* (peeke-boe)*;* boo-peep *F2.*
57. Now come up—'to supper'] *This ed.;* now come up to supper *Q, F.*

43. *delicate ear*] sensitive faculty of discriminating sound, especially in
appreciating music (*OED, Ear* 5); hence the warning against 'a false note'.

51. *lay*] bet.

53. *peek-a-boo*] called 'bo-peep' in *F2* and *Lear* 1.4.173. The game seems
to have been not a nursery amusement but a form of hide-and-seek: cf.
Satiromastix 1.257: 'Our unhandsome-faced poet does play at bo-peeps with
your Grace, and cries "all-hid" as boys do' (cited in the Arden *Lear*, ed.
Kenneth Muir). It is also associated with an anxious husband in *MWW*:
Master Ford is described as a 'peaking cornuto' (3.5.66), a comment on the
horns of a cuckold and on the game of hide-and-seek he plays with his wife.

57–8. *'To supper'... beseech you!*] The mimicry suggests Fallace's contempt for Deliro's understanding. 'Now, come up' has the sense of the
modern 'Now, come off it'. Cf. Nell's show of temper in Beaumont's *The
Knight of the Burning Pestle* (Revels), 3.533: 'Marry, come up, sir saucebox!'
H&S see 'come up to supper' as an ironic invitation, citing *John Heywood's
Works* (1562), 2.1 (F2); and Chapman, *The Blind Beggar of Alexandria* (1598),
5.59 (D2).

me to take a wife, if I had no more judgement to please
her.

Deliro. Be pleased, sweet wife, and they shall ha' done. And
would to Christ my life were done, if I can never please
thee!   65

Exeunt Musicians.

Enter MACILENTE.

Macilente. God save you, lady. Where is Master Deliro?

Deliro. Here, Master Macilente. You're welcome from the
court, sir. No doubt you have been graced exceedingly of
Master Brisk's mistress and the rest of the ladies for his
sake?   70

Macilente. Alas, the poor fantastic, he's scarce known
To any lady there, and those that know him
Know him the simplest man of all they know;
Deride and play upon his amorous humours,
Though he but apishly doth imitate   75
The gallant'st courtiers: kissing ladies' pumps,
Holding the cloth for them, praising their wits,
And servilely observing everyone,
May do them pleasure; fearful to be seen
With any man (though he be ne'er so worthy)   80

---

64. Christ] *Q;* fate *F.*   65.1–2.] *Q; not in F.*   66. God save you] *Q;* Saue
you *F.*   67. You're] *Q (*you'r*);* you are *F.*   67–8. the court] *Q, Fa;* court
Fb.

---

71. *fantastic*] one who indulges in fanciful ideas or wild notions (*OED*
B1).

73. *simplest*] most foolish; least sophisticated; most insignificant.

74. *amorous humours*] attempts to represent himself as a lover.

76. *kissing ladies' pumps*] kissing ladies' shoes or slippers: an extravagance
of the kind mocked in the Inns of Court 'Rules' for revellers: 'If any man
kissing his hand superstitiously hath taken his mistress's dog by the tail,
swearing her breath hath perfumed the same; he is to be punished for the
first part as an idolater, and for the second as a blasphemer . . . If any man
kiss the seat of his mistress's saddle, or the stool whereon she hath sitten, he
shall be taken as a vain worshipper of idols' (Finkelpearl, *Temple*, p. 57).

77. *Holding . . . them*] holding aside a wall-hanging over a doorway,
equivalent to modern gentlemen opening a door for ladies. Cf. *CR* 5.4.40–1,
of a courtier: 'This holds up the arras', and Marston, *What You Will* 4.1:
'a fine courtier . . . supports the tapestry, when I pass into the presence'
(cited in *H&S*).

79. *May*] who may.

272   EVERY MAN OUT OF HIS HUMOUR   [ACT 4

That's not in grace with some that are the greatest.
Thus courtiers do, and these he counterfeits,
But sets not such a sightly carriage
Upon their vanities as they themselves,
And therefore they despise him, for indeed   85
He's like a zany to a tumbler,
That tries tricks after him to make men laugh.

Fallace. [*Aside*] Here's an unthankful spiteful wretch! The
good gentleman vouchsafed to make him his companion
(because my husband put him into a few rags) and now   90
see how the unrude rascal backbites him.

Deliro. Is he no more graced amongst 'em then, say you?

Macilente. Faith, like a pawn at chess. Fills up a room,
that's all.

Fallace. [*Aside*] O monster of men! Can the earth bear such   95
an envious caitiff?

Deliro. Well, I repent me I e'er credited him so much, but,
now I see what he is, and that his masking visor is off, I'll

---

86. a zany] *Q, Fa (*a *Zani); the *Zani *Fb.*

83–4.] But cannot carry off their vain mannerisms as attractively as the
courtiers do themselves.

86. *zany*] derived from the clown-servant (*zanni*) in the Commédia
dell'arte; a comic attendant on a more skilled performer, who imitates his
master's acts in a ludicrously awkward way (*OED*), as indicated in 'apishly
doth imitate', 75. Cf. Lodge, *Wit's Misery* (1596), in *The Complete Works of
Thomas Lodge* (New York, 1963), 4.88: 'This is an only fellow for making
faces, showing lascivious gestures, singing like the great organ pipe in Paul's,
counterfeiting any deformity you can devise'. Dekker comments that 'your
knights are apes to the lords, . . . your Inn-a-court-man is zany to the knights,
and (marry, very scurvily) comes likewise limping after' (*The Gull's
Horn-book* 2.251).

89. *good gentleman*] Fastidius Brisk.

vouchsafed] condescended graciously (a courtly affectation of language).
Cf. 2.1.387–8.

90. *put . . . rags*] purchased him a new outfit.

91. *unrude*] dreadful, unmannerly; a variant of 'unride', severe, causing
suffering, but probably associated with 'rude' (*OED*).

93. *pawn*] least significant, most expendible piece on the chessboard.

96. *envious caitiff*] malicious, despicable wretch (*OED* 3).

98. *masking visor*] mask or vizard covering the face; more figuratively,
outward appearance or show, hiding a person's true condition. This spelling
(*Q* and *F*) seems tautological; the term may be 'masquing visor', the disguise or costume one might wear at court when participating in a revels
during a masque.

forbear him no longer. All his lands are mortgaged to me,
and forfeited. Besides, I have bonds of his in my hand for   100
the receipt of now twenty pound, now thirty, now twenty-
five. Still, as he has had a fan but wagged at him, he would
be in a new suit. Well, I'll salute him by a sergeant the
next time I see him, i' faith. I'll suit him!

Macilente. Why, you may soon see him, sir, for he is to   105
meet Signor Puntarvolo at a notary's by the Exchange
presently, where he means to take up upon return.

Fallace. [*To Macilente*] Now out upon thee, Judas! Canst thou
not be content to backbite thy friend, but thou must
betray him? Wilt thou seek the undoing of any man? And   110
of such a man, too? [*To Deliro*] And will you, sir, get your
living by the counsel of traitors?

Deliro. Dear wife, have patience.

Fallace. [*In a rage*] The house will fall! The ground will open
and swallow us! I'll not bide here for all the gold and   115
silver in heaven.   *Exit.*

---

101. twenty] *Q (*xx*); fifty *F.*   thirty] *Q (*xxx*); a hundred *F.*   101–2.
twenty-five] *Q (*xxv*); two hundred *F.*   116. SD] *Q; not in *F.*

101–2. *twenty . . . thirty . . . twenty-five*] The discrepancy in sums from *Q*
to *F* (see collation) may suggest the jump in the cost of living between 1600
and 1616.

102. *as he . . . at him*] since a few women have fluttered their fans in his
direction, raising his hopes.

103. *salute . . . sergeant*] have him arrested for debt.

104. *I'll suit him!*] punning on law suit and suit of clothes. The Inns of
Court students might expect that the appropriate action against Fastidius
would be 'fresh suit', an appeal made immediately upon discovery of a loss
and leading to restitution of the injured party's goods (Rastell).

106. *notary's*] A *notary* was a secretary or scrivener, publicly authorized
to draw up or attest contracts, to write a protest concerning non-payment
of bills of exchange, and to discharge other formal duties; he also received
money to place out at interest, and supplied those who wanted to raise
money on security (*OED*). This latter business venture, sustained by bro-
kerage fees, began as a sideline prior to 1600, and became really lucrative
after James's accession (Stone, pp. 536–7).

the Exchange] the Royal Exchange, a shopping area on Cornhill built in
1566 'near unto the Cathedral Church of Saint Paul, and is to this day commonly called the old 'Change' (Stow, 1.54). The New Exchange was built in
the Strand in 1609.

107. *take up upon return*] formalize the travel wager by having it written
up as a contract.

Deliro. [*In a panic*] O good Macilente, let's follow and appease
  her, or the peace of my life is at an end.   *Exit.*
Macilente. Now pease, and not peace, feed that life whose
  head hangs so heavily over a woman's manger!   120

                              Exit [*following* DELIRO].

      Enter FALLACE *running at another door, and claps it to.*

Fallace. [*To Fungoso*] Help me, brother. [*To Deliro, within*]
  God's body, an you come here, I'll do myself a mischief!
Deliro. (*Within*) Nay, hear me, sweet wife. Unless thou wilt
  have me go, I will not go.
Fallace. Tut, you shall ne'er ha' that vantage of me, to say you   125
  are undone by me. I'll not bid you stay, I! [*To Fungoso,
  giving money*] Brother, sweet brother, here's four angels
  I'll give you toward your suit. For the love of Jesu, and
  as ever you came of Christian creature, make haste to
  the waterside (you know where Master Fastidius uses to   130
  land) and give him warning of my husband's intent, and

---

118. SD] *Q; not in F.*   120.1. SD] *Q; not in F.*   120.2.] *Q; not in F. In margin
of F beside ll. 122–3: Deliro follow's / his wife.*   122. God's body] *Q;* 'ods body
F.   123. SD] *In Q appears at end of l. 124, not parenthetically; not in F.*   128.
Jesu] *Q;* gentry *F.*   131. intent] *Q, Fa;* malitious intent *Fb.*

117, 118. *appease, peace*] Deliro echoes the need to placate his wife with
his desire for household harmony in this desperate pun.
  119.] Macilente puns on 'appease', suggesting with irritation that Deliro
is an ass to be fed with *pease*, horse-corn or fodder, rather than soothed with
peace and quiet in his household.
  120. *woman's manger*] mysogynist metaphor reducing the woman to a
supply of fodder for men's sexual appetite. Cf. Emilia on men in
Oth. 3.4.101–2: 'They eat us hungerly, and when they are full, / They belch
us'.
  120.2] The Globe, like the Swan and the Fortune, had at least two entry-
doors from the tiring-house to the stage, although some of the private
theatres, like the Blackfriars, may have had three; see Gurr, pp. 131–4.
  123–4. *Unless . . . not go*] i.e., without your consent, I will not leave the
house to have Brisk arrested.
  125. *vantage*] advantage or superiority in a contest.
  127. *angels*] gold coins worth about 10 shillings each, stamped with the
Archangel Michael standing upon and piercing a dragon (*OED* 6). See
5.3.508.
  129. *came . . . creature*] were born a Christian.
  130–1. *where . . . land*] which stairs Brisk usually lands at, when he travels
by boat.

tell him of that lean rascal's treachery. O Jesu, how my
flesh rises at him! Nay, sweet brother, make haste. You
may say I would have writ to him, but that the necessity
of the time would not suffer it—[*Aside*] he cannot choose   135
but take it extraordinarily from me—[*To Fungoso*] and
commend me to him, good brother. Say I sent you.

                                                            Exit.

Fungoso. Let me see: these four angels, and then forty shillings
more I can borrow on my gown in Fetter Lane. Well, I
will go presently, say on my suit, pay as much money as   140
I have, and swear myself into credit with my tailor for the
rest.   *Exit.*

                    ACT 4   SCENE 2

        Enter DELIRO *with* MACILENTE, *speaking as they pass
                        over the stage.*

Deliro. O, on my soul, you wrong her, Macilente.
        Though she be froward, yet I know she is honest.
Macilente. Well, then have I no judgement. Would any woman
        but one that were wild in her affections have broke out
        into that immodest and violent passion against her   5
        husband? Or is 't possible—

132. Jesu] *Q;* heauens *F.*   135. suffer it] *Q;* permit *F.*   137.1. *Exit.*] *Q;
not in F.*   142. SD] *Q; not in F.*

ACT 4 SCENE 2] Q *(SCENA SECUNDA.); no scene-change in F.*   0.1–2.] *Q;
in margin of F: Deliro and Ma-/cilente, passe o-/uer the stage.*

___

132. *that lean rascal's*] Macilente's.
133. *flesh*] gorge.
136. *take . . . me*] see this as an extrordinary sign of favour on my part.
139. *gown*] his professional gown, as a fledgling lawyer (Linthicum,
pp. 183–4).
Fetter Lane] running south from Holborn, near the Inns of Court, a street
associated with pawnbrokers. Cf. *Ram Alley* 3.1: 'Take thou these books, go
to the broker's in Fetter Lane, lay them in pawn for a velvet jerkin and a
double ruff' (Chalfant).
140. *say on*] assay on, try on.
141. *swear . . . credit*] obtain credit on my personal oath.
2. *froward*] unruly.
honest] chaste.
4. *wild*] licentious, giving way to sexual passion (*OED* 7b), as well as reck-
less, unruly (*OED* 6b).

Deliro. If you love me, forbear. All the arguments i' the world
shall never wrest my heart to believe it.

Exeunt.

GREX

Cordatus. How like you the deciphering of his dotage?
Mitis. O, strangely, and of the other's envy too, that labours   10
so seriously to set debate betwixt a man and his wife.
Stay, here comes the knight adventurer.
Cordatus. Ay, and his scrivener with him.

ACT 4   SCENE 3

Enter PUNTARVOLO [*and*] Notary, *with* Servingmen
[*in charge of the dog and cat, as before*].

Puntarvolo. I wonder Monsieur Fastidius comes not! But,
notary, if thou please to draw the indentures the while, I
will give thee the theory.
Notary. With all my heart, sir, and I'll fall in hand with 'em
presently.   5

[*As Puntarvolo gives his instructions,
the Notary writes them down.*]

Puntarvolo. Well then, first: the sum is to be understood.

8.1.] *Q; not in F.*

ACT 4 SCENE 3] *Q* (SCENA TERTIA), *F (Act IIII. Scene III.).*   0.1–2.] *This
ed.; Enter Puntarvolo, Notarie, with Serving-men. Q;* PVNTARVOLO, NOTARIE,
CARLO, / SERVANTS. *F*   3. the theory] *Q (the Theorie); thy instructions
F.*

---

9. *deciphering*] depiction.
10. *envy*] malice.
13. *scrivener*] notary; see 4.1.106n. The scrivener draws up the contract
for the travel wager, and presumably arranges all the money matters.
2. *indentures*] sealed agreement or contract between two or more parties
with mutual convenants, in two or more copies, the edges of which were serrated correspondingly for identification and security (*OED* 2). See 3.1.432.
3. *theory*] systematic statement of rules or principles to be followed (*OED*
3).
4–5. *fall . . . presently*] write them down immediately. This scribal stage-
business is continuous from 6 to 55.
6. *the sum . . . understood*] the amount of the wager is to be clearly stated.

Notary. Good, sir.

Puntarvolo. Next: our several appellations and character of
my dog and cat must be known. [*To Servingman*] Show
him the cat, sirrah.   10

Notary. So, sir.

Puntarvolo. Then: that the intended point is the Turk's court
in Constantinople; the time limited for our return, a year;
and that, if either of us miscarry, the whole venture is
lost—These are general, conceiv'st thou?—or if either of   15
us turn Turk.

Notary. Ay, sir.

Puntarvolo. Now, for particulars: that I may make my travels
by sea or land, to my best liking; and that, hiring a coach
for myself, it shall be lawful for my dog and cat to ride   20
with me in the said coach.

Notary. Very good, sir.

Puntarvolo. That I may choose to give my dog or cat fish, for
fear of bones, or any other nutriment that (by the judge-

---

12. point] *Italic in* Q; bound F   Turk's] Q, F *(Turkes)*.   20. dog and
cat] Q; dog, or cat, or both F

8. *appellations*] names.
character] description.
12. *point*] destination.
13. *the time . . . year*] Not over-long for the journey at that time. Thomas
Dallam, the royal master organ-builder, left for Constantinople in 1599 with
an elaborate organ, the Queen's gift to the Sultan, and returned in 1600,
travelling mostly overland. Fynes Moryson and his brother Henry left for
Jerusalem, by way of Constantinople, 29 November 1595, and Fynes
returned 10 July 1597, Henry having died in Aleppo (Bates, pp. 4–5).
14. *miscarry*] fail to return on schedule.
16. *turn Turk*] (*a*) become a Muslim; (*b*) become a traitor (*OED* 3b).
These possibilities were not uncommon at a time when Turkey, at its peak
of power, offered opportunities of advancement to men of ability. Many of
the Grand Turk's eminent subjects were renegade foreigners; e.g., the English
consul at Cairo turned Turk in 1601, retaining possession of considerable
English merchandise left in his care (Bates, p. 55). (*c*) A third possibility, not
intended by Puntarvolo: engage in buggery with beautiful youths; or more
simply, yield to lust; innuendo suited to the erotic suggestiveness of *dog* and
cat in the context of *travel* = sexual labour (Williams). The idea of the cat or
dog turning Turk is deliciously absurd.
23. *choose*] choose whether or not. Although *choose* implies no negative
meaning on its own, according to *OED*, Puntarvolo would be acting against
his own interests if he chose to give his animals dangerous food.

ment of the most authentical physicians where I travel)   25
shall be thought dangerous.

Notary. Well, sir.

Puntarvolo. That, after receipt of his money, he shall, neither
in his own person nor any other, either by direct or
indirect means, as magic, witchcraft, or other such exotic   30
arts, attempt, practise, or complot anything to the
prejudice of me, my dog, or my cat. Neither shall I use
the help of any such sorceries or enchantments as unctions to make our skins impenetrable, or to travel invisible by virtue of a powder or a ring, or to hang any   35
three-forked charm about my dog's neck, secretly con-

---

25. *authentical*] authoritative as to opinion, as well as duly authorized to
practise medicine (archaic term).

28. *he*] Brisk, who is holding the wagered amount during the contracted
period, but must pay back five to one if he loses the bet.

30. *magic*] a facet of Puntarvolo's quixotic fascination with chivalry. Up
to 1550, participants in ordeals by battle had to swear an oath that they used
no magic, and submit to a stripped search for incantations written on the
body or for the *alettoria*, a stone rendering invincibility if held in the mouth;
see Bryson, pp. 41–2.

31. *complot*] conspire (*OED* v).

33–4. *unctions . . . impenetrable*] like the one given to Jason by Medea.

35. *powder or a ring*] The powder is fernseed: 'Before the mode of repro-
duction of ferns was understood, they were popularly supposed to produce
an invisible seed, which was capable of communicating its invisibility to any
person who possessed it' (*OED*). The ring of King Gyges of Lydia made him
invisible when he turned the gem inwards towards the palm of his hand
(Cicero, *De Officiis* 3.19.78); Angelica's ring, in Boiardo's *Orlando Inamorato*
and Ariosto's *Orlando Furioso*, has the same effect when put into the bearer's
mouth (*H&S*).

36. *three-forked charm*] (*a*) in folk-magic, a herb or twig over which a
magic spell would be chanted. Bryson (p. 42) mentions that knights wore
necklaces with pendants containing peony, wormwood, St-John's-wort, or
pellitory of Spain, this last particularly effective for counteracting other
charms; (*b*) in the learned tradition of occult philosophers and astrologers
such as Dr John Dee or Cornelius Agrippa von Nettesheim (Whalley cites
the story of the magic emblems in his dog's collar), the charm might be one
of several esoteric signs. The most likely talismanic symbol is the T-shaped
St Anthony's cross, which St Francis used as his signature, and which was
adapted for heraldic use; it is also called the Tau cross, related to the
Egyptian ansated cross, or *ankhu*, an ancient symbol of life, or the Tunc cross,
representing the Edenic tree, and often confused with the 'Hammer of Thor',
a Scandinavian sign representing the wrath of God felling his enemies. The
Y-shaped cross, called the *furca*, was a medieval symbol of the Trinity (if

veyed into his collar—understand you?—but that all be
performed sincerely, without fraud or imposture.

Notary. So, sir.

Puntarvolo. That, for testimony of the performance, myself   40
am to bring thence a Turk's *mustachio*; my dog, a hare's
lip; and my cat, the train or tail of a rat.

Notary. 'Tis done, sir.

Puntarvolo. 'Tis said, sir, not done, sir. But forward: that upon
my return and landing on the Tower Wharf with the afore-   45
said testimony, I am to receive five for one, according to
the proportion of the sums put forth.

Notary. Well, sir.

Puntarvolo. Provided that if, before our departure or setting
forth, either myself or these be visited with sickness or   50
any other casual event, so that the whole course of the
adventure be hindered thereby, that then he is to return,
and I am to receive, the prenominated proportion upon
fair and equal terms.

Notary. Very good, sir. Is this all?   55

Puntarvolo. It is all, sir. And dispatch them, good notary.

Notary. As fast as possible, sir.   *Exit.*

Enter CARLO.

Puntarvolo. O Carlo, welcome! Saw you Monsieur Brisk?

41–2. hare's lip] *Q; Graecian* hares lip *F*   42. rat] *Q; Thracian* rat *F*
57.1.] *Q; not in F*

---

inverted, of salvation descending from heaven), and also a Pythagorean
emblem of the course of life. See Rudolph Koch, *The Book of Signs*, trans.
Vyvyan Holland (New York, 1955), pp. 5, 7, 14, 16.

40. *testimony of the performance*] proof that the wagered deed was performed. To validate the three-for-one wager on his journey, Fynes Moryson,
in *Itinerary* (1617), I.235, mentions a certificate given him at the Latin
Monastery in Jerusalem as proof of his visit (cited in *H&S*).

43. *'Tis done*] That point is written down. Puntarvolo quibbles in his reply
(44): 'I haven't completed the trip yet'.

45. *Tower Wharf*] located on the river frontage where the Tower guns were
mounted (Chalfant).

49–54.] This provision insures Puntarvolo against accident prior to his
departure, in which event all bets are to be returned without penalty.

50. *these*] the dog and cat.

51. *casual*] unexpected.

56. *dispatch them*] copy out the articles of the agreement in due legal form
immediately.

Carlo. Not I. Did he appoint you to meet here?

Puntarvolo. Ay, and I muse he should be so tardy. He is to   60
take an hundred pounds of me in venture, if he maintain
his promise.

Carlo. Is his hour past?

Puntarvolo. Not yet, but it comes on apace.

Carlo. Tut, be not jealous of him. He will sooner break all the   65
ten commandments than his hour. Upon my life, in such
a case, trust him.

Puntarvolo. Methinks, Carlo, you look very smooth, ha?

Carlo. Why, I come but now from a hot-house. I must needs
look smooth.   70

Puntarvolo. From a hot-house?

Carlo. Ay, do you make a wonder on 't? Why, it's your only
physic. Let a man sweat once a week in a hot-house, and
be well rubbed and frotted with a good plump juicy
wench, and sweet linen, he shall ne'er ha' the pox.   75

Puntarvolo. What? The French pox?

Carlo. The French pox—our pox! 'Sblood, we have 'em in as
good form as they, man, what?

---

60. *muse*] wonder that.

64. *comes on apace*] approaches quickly.

65. *jealous*] mistrustful.

68, 70. *smooth*] (*a*) clean-shaven, glowing (as at 3.1.204–5, where Carlo is
'the devil with a shining face'); (*b*) glib, plausible; cf. Greene, *A Notable Discovery of Cosenage* 10.16: 'The cony-catchers, apparelled like honest civil
gentlemen, or good fellows, with a smooth face, as if butter would not melt
in their mouths' (Hoy, 2.255); (*c*) implication of licentiousness; cf. *John*,
2.1.573: 'That smooth-faced gentleman, tickling Commodity ... This bawd,
this broker'.

69, 71. *hot-house*] bath-house (see 2.1.25 and note).

73. *physic*] medical cure that purges the system.

74. *frotted*] (*a*) massaged (*H&S*); (*b*) stroked or caressed (*OED*); (*c*)
rubbed sexually (Williams, *Fricatrice*).

75. *sweet linen*] Burton, 2.236, also recommends good hygiene as a pre-
ventive: 'neatly dressed, washed, and combed, according to his ability at least,
in clean sweet linen ... for nothing sooner dejects a man than want, squalor,
and nastiness, foul or old clothes out of fashion'.

pox] any disease with eruptive pustules on the skin, from chicken-pox to
plague.

76. *French pox*] syphilis. But as Carlo points out in his next line,
any nation may suffer from sexually transmitted disease, including the
English.

Puntarvolo. Let me perish but thou art a villain! Was your
    new-created gallant there with you? Sogliardo?   80
Carlo. O, porpoise—hang him, no. He's a lieger at Horn's
    Ordinary yonder. His villainous Ganymede and he ha'
    been droning a tobacco pipe there ever sin' yesterday
    noon.
Puntarvolo. Who? Signor Tripartite, that would give my dog   85
    the whiff?
Carlo. Ay, he. They have hired a chamber and all private
    to practise in for the making of the *Petun*, the *Receipt*

79. villain] *Q;* salt one *F.*   88. *Petun*] *Q, F (Patoun).*

---

79. *Let . . . villain*] I'll be damned if you're not an utter scoundrel
(exclaiming at Carlo's cynicism).
   81. *porpoise*] (*a*) swinish fellow, from the Latin, *porcus piscus*, hog-fish or
sea-swine (see 'snout', 93 below); (*b*) social anomaly: the porpoise is a
mammal that lives like a fish, though it keeps leaping out of the sea, and
hence is 'neither flesh nor fish' (*OED*, citing Greene, *Never Too Late*), comparable to Sogliardo's attempt to leap class lines, instead of remaining in one
identifiable element; (*c*) dreadful hanger-on. Sailors identified porpoises as
a bad omen at sea: 'they say they're half fish, half flesh; a plague on them,
they ne'er come but I look to be washed!' (*Per.* 2.1.25–6).
   lieger] resident; cited in *OED, ledger* 7b, as the first use of the word in this
sense.
   81–2. *Horn's Ordinary*] the Horn on the Hoop, a tavern popular with
lawyers on Fleet Street near the Temple. Mentioned prominently in various
local and literary records, the tavern was as famous as the Mitre or the
Mermaid for its food and drink (Chalfant).
   82. *Ganymede*] Shift. In Greek myth, a mortal boy of extraordinary
beauty brought to Olympus to serve Zeus (*Iliad* 20.232–5); the implication
that he was Zeus's catamite derives from Lucian, *Dialogues of the Gods*
(Oxford), 4 and 20, and Ovid, *Metamorphoses* (Loeb), 10.160–1 (Wheeler,
p. 102).
   83. *droning . . . pipe*] quibble on the 'drone' or brass pipe of a bagpipe
(*H&S*). See 3.3.121 and note for a similar pipe joke.
   85. *Tripartite*] Shift, because he has three names.
   85–6. *that . . . whiff*] who wanted to teach my dog how to smoke. Cf.
3.1.482–8.
   88. *Petun*] a native South American name for tobacco; cf. John Taylor the
Water Poet, *Works* (1630), N1: 'whereas . . . the herb (alias weed) ycleped
tobacco, (alias trinidado, alias petun, alias nicotinin) a long time hath been
in continual use and motion' (*OED*). Dekker refers to 'petoones' in *The Welsh
Ambassador* 5.3.101.
   88–9. Receipt Reciprocal] Gifford suggests, citing Dekker, that it refers
to the *ring*, passing the pipe from one smoker to another. Alternatively, it
may be a form of 'French inhaling', inhaling smoke through the nose and
mouth simultaneously.

Reciprocal, and a number of other mysteries not yet extant.
I brought some dozen or twenty gallants this morning to   90
view 'em (as you'd do a piece of perspective) in at a keyhole, and there we might see Sogliardo sit in a chair,
holding his snout up like a sow under an apple tree, while
th'other opened his nostrils with a poking-stick to give the
smoke a more free delivery. They had spit some three- or   95
fourscore ounces between 'em afore we came away.

Puntarvolo. How? Spit three- or fourscore ounces?

Carlo. Ay, and preserved it in porringers, as a barber does his
blood when he pricks a vein.

Puntarvolo. Out, pagan! How dost thou prick the vein of thy   100
friend!

Carlo. Friend? Is there any such foolish thing i' the world?
Ha? 'Slid, I ne'er relished it yet.

Puntarvolo. Thy humour is the more dangerous.

99. pricks] *Q;* opens *F.*   100. prick] *Q;* open *F.*

89. *extant*] seen in public (*OED* 3) or known to exist.

91. *perspective*] In perspective art, the only 'true' perspective on the painting is through a peep-hole fixed to the frame; from all other angles, the viewer
sees only a distorted image, as in the *Anamorphosis of Edward VI* by William
Scrots, 1546 (National Portrait Gallery, London).

94. *poking-stick*] laundress's tool. The pleats of a laundered ruff were
folded, while still wet with starch, and left to dry over small steel rods or
poking-sticks (Linthicum, p. 160). The poking-sticks were apparently heated
first. Cf. *Blurt, Master Constable* 3.3.104–5: 'Next, your ruff must stand in
print; and for that purpose get poking-sticks with fair and long handles, lest
they scorch your lily sweating hands' (Hoy, 2.27).

95. *spit*] The sheer volume of phlegm mentioned here (60–80 oz) testifies
hyperbolically to their commitment to the art of smoking; see 3.1.25–7 and
27n.

98. *porringers*] soup bowls.

barber] then also a surgeon and dentist; the Company of Barber-Surgeons,
incorporated in 1462, became the Company of Barbers and Surgeons under
Henry VIII, and in the eighteenth century was divided into two distinct
corporations (*OED*).

99. *pricks a vein*] in order to 'bleed' his patient (medical term). Puntarvolo's repetition at 100 quibbles on injurious attack; so too Macilente, 'stabbing similes', 227.

100. *pagan*] infidel, faithless fellow (imprecation). Puntarvolo is shocked
at the ease with which Carlo attacks Sogliardo behind his back.

104. *dangerous*] seeing or fearing dangers, as well as causing them; see
2.1.551.

Carlo. No, not a whit, signor. Tut, a man must keep time in   105
    all. I can oil my tongue when I meet him next, and look
    with a good slick forehead. 'Twill take away all soil of sus-
    picion, and that's enough. What Lynceus can see my
    heart? Pish, the title of a friend, it's a vain idle thing, only
    venerable among fools. You shall not have one that has   110
    any opinion of wit affect it.

Enter DELIRO *and* MACILENTE.

Deliro. Save you, good Sir Puntarvolo.
Puntarvolo. Signor Deliro! Welcome.
Deliro. Pray you, sir, did you see Master Fastidius Brisk? I
    heard he was to meet your worship here.   115
Puntarvolo. You heard no figment, sir. I do expect him every
    minute my watch strikes.
Deliro. In good time, sir.   *[He walks aside with Macilente.]*
Carlo. *[Indicating Deliro]* There's a fellow now, looks like one
    of the patricians of Sparta. Marry, his wit's after ten i'   120
    the hundred. A good bloodhound, a close-mouthed dog,

III.I.] *Q; Act IIII. Scene IIII.* / DELIRO, MACILENTE. *In margin: To them. F*
116–17. every . . . strikes] *Q;* at euery pulse of my watch *F*

    105–6. *keep . . . all*] suit his behaviour to all occasions.

    106. *oil my tongue*] speak flatteringly.

    107. *slick*] (*a*) sleek (*H&S*); (*b*) hypocritically smooth, as at 68, 70 above.
soil] moral stain.

    108. *Lynceus*] an Argonaut reputed for his keen sight. Cf. 'Fain would I
meet the Lynceus now, that eagle's eye' in *BF* 2.1.4.

    110. *venerable*] respected.

    110–11. *You . . . affect it*] You won't see any discerning person entering
into friendship.

    116. *figment*] invented statement (*OED* 2a).

    117. *my watch strikes*] Some pocket-watches were designed to strike the
hours. Travellers were warned to carry a pocket sundial, or 'if a watch, not
a striker, for that warns the wicked you have cash' (Bates, p. 37).

    118.] a polite expression of thanks and farewell.

    119–20. *like . . . Sparta*] The comparison suggests that Deliro looks (*a*)
severe or stern; and (*b*) like a Spartan bloodhound, a conceit that continues
in 121–2.

    120–1. *ten i' the hundred*] the legal rate of interest. See Bacon, 'Of Usury',
in *Essays* (London, 1900), 41.104. Carlo implies that Deliro is a tenacious
collector of debts owed to him.

    121. *close-mouthed*] silent in following a scent. A good dog does not bay
unless the game is in sight or its location is otherwise clear.

he follows the scent well. Marry, he's at a fault now,
methinks.

Puntarvolo. I should wonder at that creature is free from the
danger of thy tongue.   125

Carlo. O, I cannot abide these limbs of satin, or rather Satan,
indeed, that'll walk like the children of darkness all day
in a melancholy shop, with their pockets full of blanks,
ready to swallow up as many poor unthrifts as come
within the Verge.   130

Puntarvolo. So, and what hast thou for him [*Indicating
Macilente*] that is with him now?

Carlo. O, damn me, immortality! I'll not meddle with him,
the pure element of fire, all spirit, extraction!

Puntarvolo. How, Carlo? What is he, man?   135

Carlo. A scholar, Macilente. Do you not know him? A lank
raw-boned anatomy, he walks up and down like a charged
musket. No man dares encounter him. That's his rest
there.

---

122. *he's at a fault*] he has lost the scent (*OED* 8). A hunting term.

124–5.] I would be surprised if anyone could escape your criticisms.

126. *limbs of satin*] Respectable tradesmen wore satin doublets; cf. *EH*
1.1.114 (*H&S*). The pun on 'Satan' was a common one, as in *Satiromastix*
1.2.337. The limbs of Satan are the devils that do his bidding.

127. *children of darkness*] imps or demons.

128. *melancholy shop*] A poorly lit shop allowed a dishonest tradesman to
cheat his customers with shoddy goods. This practice is dramatised in Middleton's *Michaelmas Term* (1607), at 2.3.109–11 (*H&S*).

blanks] documents (bonds or mortgages) with spaces left blank, to be
filled with specifics at the request of a borrower (*OED* 6).

129. *unthrifts*] spendthrifts or prodigals (*OED* 3).

130. *the Verge*] a Westminster area extending from Charing Cross down
Whitehall to the river and including Hyde Park, St James's Park, and Green
Park, within which people were safe from arrest for debt or other crimes
(Sugden).

133. *immortality*] the answer to Puntarvolo's question about what Carlo
has in store for Macilente. Carlo swears ('damn me') to give Macilente a life
eternally free from Carlo's taunts.

134. *fire*] one of the four elements, beyond which nothing can be reduced
or destroyed.

extraction] applying heat to obtain the constituent elements of any substance (*OED* 3), an alchemical process.

136. *lank*] lean, shrunken.

137. *anatomy*] skeleton.

138. *rest*] Carlo expands on his simile of Macilente as a loaded musket to
describe Deliro as his support, punning on (*a*) support for a musket, con-

Puntarvolo. His rest? Why, has he a forked head?   140
Carlo. Pardon me, that's to be suspended. You are too quick,
    too apprehensive.
        [*They walk aside, as Deliro and Macilente return.*]
Deliro. Troth, now I think on 't, I'll defer it till some other
    time.
Macilente. God's precious, not by any means, signor. You shall   145
    not lose this opportunity. He will be here presently now.
Deliro. Yes, faith, Macilente, 'tis best, for look you, sir, I shall
    so exceedingly offend my wife in 't, that—
Macilente. Your wife? Now for shame, lose these thoughts,
    and become the master of your own spirits. Should I, if   150
    I had a wife, suffer myself to be thus passionately carried
    to and fro with the stream of her humour? And neglect
    my deepest affairs to serve her affections? 'Sblood, I
    would geld myself first!
Deliro. O, but, signor, had you such a wife as mine is, you   155
    would—
Macilente. Such a wife? Now God hate me, sir, if ever I dis-
    cerned any wonder in your wife yet, with all the specula-
    tion I have. I have seen some that ha' been thought fairer

---

153. 'Sblood] *Q;* S'light *F*   157. God hate me] *Q;* hate me *F*

---

sisting of a wooden pole with an iron spike at the bottom to fix it in the
ground, and a semicircular piece of iron at the top ('forked head', 140) to
rest the musket on; the soldier carried it 'suspended' (141) by strings fastened over the shoulder (Hoy, 3.50); (*b*) financial support of Macilente as
house-guest and companion.

140.] Aside from offering support (*rest*) for a musket, a *forked head* also
suggests cuckoldry.

141. *Pardon . . . suspended*] Still punning on a musket-support (138n), but
now Carlo wants to 'suspend' or discontinue the joke.

141–2. *You . . . apprehensive*] You catch on to my jokes too quickly and go
beyond me in wit.

143. *it*] having Brisk arrested for debt. See 4.1.97–107.

150. *master . . . spirits*] (*a*) self-determined, in control of the animating
forces of your life; (*b*) master of your sex-life, in a ribald pun on ejaculation
(Henke), as in Sonnet 129: 'Th'expense of spirit in a waste of shame / Is lust
in action'. Macliente's contempt for Deliro's 'dotage', which he interprets as
a purely sexual monomania, is clear in his comment that he would rather
'geld' (154) himself than be so enslaved by a woman.

153. *affairs*] affairs of business.

158–9. *speculation*] power of sight.

than she, in my time; and I ha' seen those ha' not been
altogether so tall, esteemed proper women; and I have   160
seen less noses grow upon sweeter faces that have done
very well too, in my judgement. But, in good faith, signor,
for all this, the gentlewoman is a good, pretty, proud,
hard-favoured thing, marry, not so peerlessly to be doted   165
upon, I must confess. Nay, be not angry.

Deliro. Well, sir, however you please to forget yourself, I have
not deserved to be thus played upon, but henceforth, pray
you, forbear my house, for I can but faintly endure the
savour of his breath at my table that shall thus jade me   170
for my courtesies.

Macilente. Nay then, signor, let me tell you, your wife is no
proper woman, by Jesu, and I suspect her honesty, that's
more, which you may likewise suspect—if you please. Do
you see? I'll urge you to nothing against your appetite,   175
but if you please, you may suspect it.

Deliro. Good sir.   *Exit.*

Macilente. 'Good sir'? Now horn upon horn pursue thee,
thou blind egregious dotard!

160. proper] *Q;* properer *F*   173. woman, by Jesu] woman by *Iesu Q;*
woman, and, by my life *F*   177. Good sir] *Q;* Good, sir *F*   SD] *Q; not
in F*

---

159. *ha' not*] who have not.
160. *tall*] perhaps a joke about the height of the boy-actor playing Fallace,
who may have been taller than most women.
   proper] handsome; punning on decorous or well-behaved, certainly the
meaning intended at 173.
165. *hard-favoured*] unpleasant, unsympathetic.
167. *forget yourself*] i.e., behave inexcusably.
170. *jade*] befool or jape at (*OED* 3).
171. *for*] in return for.
173. *honesty*] chastity.
177. *Good sir*] Here and in Macilente's mimicry in the next line, either
the *Q* or *F* reading (see collation) is plausible. *Q*'s line is a vocative (quali-
fier and substantive), implying a formally polite bow and farewell. Macilente's reply balances the first vocative against a second: 'thou blind
egregious dotard!' In *F*, 'Good' is the response to Macilente's sneer that
Deliro may suspect his wife if he chooses, and represents Deliro's awareness
that the choice exists, whether or not Macilente gives him permission to avail
himself of it. It is a dismissal, not a concession.
178. *horn . . . thee*] may you be cuckolded time and time again. The usual
image of the cuckold's horns is here multiplied and rendered aggressive by
Macilente's anger.

Carlo. [*Aside to Puntarvolo*] O, you shall hear him speak like   180
    envy.—Signor Macilente! You saw Monsieur Brisk lately?
    I heard you were with him at the court.
Macilente. Ay, Buffone, I was with him.
Carlo. And how is he respected there? (I know you'll deal
    ingeniously with us.) Is he made of amongst the sweeter   185
    sort of gallants?
Macilente. Faith, ay, his civet and his casting-glass
    Have helped him to a place amongst the rest,
    And there his seniors give him good slight looks
    After their garb, smile, and salute in French   190
    With some new compliment.
Carlo.   What, is this all?
Macilente. Why, say that they should show the frothy fool
    Such grace as they pretend comes from the heart,
    He had a mighty windfall, out of doubt.   195
    Why, all their graces are not to do grace
    To virtue or desert, but to ride both
    With their gilt spurs quite breathless from themselves.

---

182. the court] *Q;* court *F*   185. ingeniously] *Q;* ingenuously *F*

180–1. *shall . . . envy*] shall hear Macilente speak maliciously.

184–5. *(I know . . . us.)*] The parentheses suggest the snicker-and-nudge familiarity of jeerers who have contempt for the outsider (here, Brisk). The questions before and after the parentheses act as 'straight lines' eliciting Macilente's vitriolic response. *Ingeniously* means 'honestly'.

185. *made of*] made much of; treated with courtesy and affection (*OED* 21).

187. *civet*] perfume, often derived from the flux or excrement of a civet cat, and frequently derided as a decadent luxury. See 2.1.109–12 and notes; and *AYL* 3.2.64–7.

casting-glass] small bottle for sprinkling perfume; cf. Marston, *Antonio and Mellida* 3.2.24–5 (*H&S*).

189. *slight*] (*a*) effete, performed with little exertion (*OED* 5f); (*b*) slighting, disdainful (*OED* 6).

190. *After their garb*] according to their habit; cf. 2.1.97.

193–5.] If they were to grace Brisk with a show of friendship, it would be a huge benefit to him, no doubt.

193. *frothy*] frivolous, trifling; cf. *Meas.*, 'FROTH, *a foolish Gentleman*', *Dramatis Personae*.

196–8.] These courtiers do not acknowledge goodness or merit, but drive both away with their silly affectations (for which their gilt spurs are a symbol).

'Tis now esteemed precisianism in wit
And a disease in nature to be kind   200
Toward desert, to love or seek good names.
Who feeds with a good name? Who thrives with loving?
Who can provide feast for his own desires
With serving others? Ha, ha, ha!
'Tis folly by our wisest worldlings proved,   205
If not to gain by love, to be beloved.

Carlo. [*To Puntarvolo*] How like you him? Is 't not a good
spiteful slave? Ha?

Puntarvolo. Shrewd, shrewd.

Carlo. Damn me, I could eat his flesh now. Divine sweet   210
villain!

Macilente. Nay, prithee, leave.—[*Drawing Carlo aside*] What's
he there?

Carlo. [*Aside to Macilente*] Who? This i' the starched beard?
'Tis the dull stiff knight Puntarvolo, man. He's to travel   215

199–201.] 'Nowadays, trendy people regard the reward of true merit and
good reputation as pedantically puritanical [*precisianism in wit*]'. Macilente's
analogy is based on a major intellectual controversy of the 1590s. Puritans
(Calvinists) opposed the Act of Uniformity of 1559 (forcing all clergy to
follow the Prayer Book instead of the Bible alone) and wanted to reform the
Anglican church so that it accorded with the Genevan standard. This conflict exploded in the anonymous Martin Marprelate tracts, biting satires
fiercely attacking pro-Anglican prelates, and advocating certain doctrinal and
ethical outlooks rooted in individual consideration and merit. The open hostilities ceased with the banning of printed satires in 1599 and the accession
in 1603 of James I, who demanded that dissenting clergy should either subscribe to the Act of Uniformity or exile themselves to Amsterdam, where
they eventually formed the nucleus of the Mayflower pilgrims, 1620; the
English remnant expanded into the Roundheads of 1642, the victorious side
in the English Civil War (Johansson, *Religion*, pp. 33–50).

202–4.] ironic rhetorical questions: who can get ahead by means of altru-
istic practices?

205–6.] It is a foolish waste of time to be loved unless you can exploit
your admirers for some advantage to yourself.

212. *leave*] stop embarrassing me with fulsome praise.

214. *starched*] bristly, short-cropped. Gifford and *H&S* cite John Taylor,
Superbiae Flagellum, on beards: 'Some seem as they were starched stiff and
fine, / Like to the bristles of some angry swine'.

215. *stiff*] (*a*) old-fashioned, pompous, like Morose in *SW*: 'that stiff piece
of formality'; (*b*) physically inflexible; as at 2.1.273–6.

now presently. He has a good knotty wit. Marry, he
carries little on 't out of the land with him.

> [*They continue to talk aside.*]

Macilente. How then?

Carlo. He puts it forth in venture, as he does his money, upon
the return of a dog and cat.   220

Macilente. Is this he?

Carlo. Ay, this is he. A good tough gentleman: he looks like a
chine of brawn at Shrovetide, out of date and ready to
take his leave; or a dry pool of ling upon Easter Eve, that
has furnished the table all Lent, as he has done the city   225
this last vacation.

Macilente. Come, you'll never leave your stabbing similes. I
shall ha' you aiming at me with 'em by and by, but—

Carlo. O, renounce me then. Pure, honest, good devil, I love
thee above the love of women. I could e'en melt in admi-   230

---

217. on 't] *Q;* o 't *F.*

---

216. *knotty*] (*a*) full of complicated or puzzling thoughts (*OED* 2); (*b*)
implying 'knotty-pated', blockheaded (*OED* 5); (*c*) possibly punning on
'naughty'.

217. *carries . . . him*] hasn't much intelligence to take with him on his trip.

219. *it*] Puntarvolo's wit, which he is risking along with his money in the
foolish venture.

223. *chine of brawn*] sirloin roast of boar.

at Shrovetide] at the last meat meal before Lent, the forty weekdays
between Ash Wednesday and Easter Eve, observed as a time of fasting (i.e.,
no meat) and penitence.

223-4. *out . . . leave*] old and ready to be thrown out.

224. *dry pool of ling*] store of dried or salted cod; what was left over at the
end of Lent.

225. *furnished the table*] been served at (Lenten) meals.

227. *stabbing*] backbiting.

228. *ha' you*] catch you.

229.] parody of Puritan speech. The 'pure' (enlightened) and virtuous
Macilente must 'renounce' the vicious Carlo.

230. *above . . . women*] above my love for women; ambiguous *of* with
objective genitive (Partridge, *Syntax*, pp. 15–16).

ration of thee now. God's so', look here, man: Sir Dagonet
and his squire.

Enter SOGLIARDO *and* SHIFT.

Sogliardo. Save you, my dear *gallantos*. [*To Shift*] Nay, come,
approach, good cavalier. [*To Puntarvolo*] Prithee, sweet
knight, know this gentleman. He's one that it pleases me   235
to use as my good friend and companion, and therefore
do him good offices. [*To Carlo and Macilente*] I beseech
you, good gentles, know him.

Puntarvolo. Sir, for Signor Sogliardo's sake, let it suffice I
know you.   240

Sogliardo. Why, by Jesu, I thank you, knight, and it shall
suffice. Hark you, Sir Puntarvolo, you'd little think it: he's
as resolute a piece of flesh as any 's in the world.

Puntarvolo. Indeed, sir?

Sogliardo. Upon my gentility, sir.—Carlo, a word with you. Do   245
you see that same fellow there?

Carlo. What? Cavalier Shift?

Sogliardo. O, you know him. Cry you mercy. Before God,
I think him the tallest man living within the walls of
Europe.   250

232.1.] *Q; Act IIII. Scene v.* / SOGLIARDO, SHIFT. *In margin: To them. F.*
238. know him.] *Q;* know him, know him all ouer. *F.*   241. by Jesu] *Q; (as
I am true gentleman) F.*   243. any's] *Q;* any is *F.*   248. God] *Q;* me *F.*

---

231. *God's so*] mild oath, 'by God's soul', but also hinting at 'catso',
sometimes represented as 'codso', based on the Italian *cazzo*, a term for male
genitalia (see 2.1.30).

Sir Dagonet] the king's fool in *Morte d'Arthur*, here referring to Sogliardo.
The same joke appears in Beaumont's *Knight of the Burning Pestle* 4.49, referring to the context in which the name might have been popularized: the
archery exhibit known as Arthur's Show at Mile-End Green (now Stepney
Green), where London citizens portrayed knights of the Round Table. Cf.
Shallow's reminiscences in *2H4* 3.2.274–6: 'I remember at Mile-End Green,
when I lay at Clement's Inn [one of the Inns of Chancery associated with
the Inns of Court]—I was then Sir Dagonet in Arthur's show'.

233. gallantos] gallants; inept Italian approximating two words in Florio:
galante, describing one who is 'gallant, handsome, . . . gracious'; and *galano*,
one who is 'gay in clothes, brave in apparel'.

243. *resolute . . . flesh*] brave a man.

245. *Upon my gentility*] on my word as a gentleman.

248. *Cry you mercy*] I beg your pardon.

249. *tallest*] most valiant, warlike. Cf. *EMI* (*Q*) 4.3.8–12: 'a tall man is
never his own man till he be angry . . . What's a tall man unless he fight?'

Carlo. 'The walls of Europe!' Take heed what you say, signor.
Europe's a huge thing within the walls.

Sogliardo. Tut, an 'twere as huge again, I'd justify what I
speak. 'Slid, he swaggered e'en now in a place where we
were: I never saw a man do it more resolute.   255

Carlo. Nay, indeed, swaggering is a good argument of resolution. [*To Macilente*] Do you hear this, signor?

Macilente. Ay, to my grief. [*Aside*] O, that such muddy flags,
For every drunken flourish, should achieve
The name of manhood, whilst true perfect valour   260
(Hating to show itself) goes by despised!
'Sblood, I do know now, in a fair just cause,
I dare do more than he, a thousand times.
Why should not they take knowledge of this? Ha?
And give my worth allowance before his?   265
Because I cannot swagger. Now the pox
Light on your Pict Hatch prowess!

Sogliardo. Why, I tell you, sir, he has been the only bid-stand
that ever was, kept Newmarket, Salisbury Plain, Hockley

262. 'Sblood] *Q;* Heart *F.*   269. ever was] *Q;* euer *F.*

---

253. *as huge again*] twice as huge.

256–7. *resolution*] Carlo's sarcasm depends on the several meanings of this
term: (*a*) positively, 'determination, firmness of temper', 'valour', or 'self-
confidence' (*OED* 13, 15); but (*b*) negatively, 'dissolution' or 'decay' (*OED*
1, 3), whether mental, moral, or physical (e.g., the purulence associated with
sexually transmitted disease); perhaps simply verbal, applied to the colloquial use of 'resolute' to mean 'tough'. If resolution means 'valour' here, then
'swaggering' reduces it to a caricature, as Macilente's next speech points out.
If resolution means 'decay', then the swagger of a bully or pimp is the perfect
physical correlative of diminished times.

258. *muddy flags*] referring to rogues like Shift, while punning on (*a*)
soiled battle-standards and (*b*) coarse meadow grasses or pieces of turf.

259. *flourish*] flourishing, or waving, the sword in the air.

260. *name of manhood*] reputation for manly valour.

264. *they*] the people whose opinion counts for something.

267. *Pict Hatch*] a tavern/brothel; see Chars.82.

268. *bid-stand*] highwayman, who bids his victims to stand and deliver
(Grose).

269. *Newmarket, Salisbury Plain*] Newmarket Heath, fifty-six miles north-
east of London, and Salisbury Plain, seventy miles south-west of London,
were isolated stretches of ground crossed by major thoroughfares and thus
frequented by highwaymen (Sugden); both locations are mentioned as
recourses for dismissed servants in J. M., *A Health to the Gentlemanly Profession of Servingmen* (1598), 13v (*H&S*).

i' the Hole, Gadshill: all the high places of any request.   270
He has had his mares and his geldings, he, ha' been worth
forty, threescore, a hundred pound a horse, would ha'
sprung you over hedge and ditch like your greyhound.
He has done five hundred robberies in his time, more or
less, I assure you.   275

Puntarvolo. What? And 'scaped?

Sogliardo. 'Scaped, i' faith, ay! He has broken the jail when he
has been in irons and irons; and been out, and in again;
and out, and in—forty times, and not so few, he!

Macilente. [*Aside*] A fit trumpet to proclaim such a person.   280

Carlo. But can this be possible?

Shift. Why, 'tis nothing, sir, when a man gives his affections
to it.

Sogliardo. Good Pylades, discourse a robbery or two, to satisfy
these gentlemen of thy worth.   285

Shift. Pardon me, my dear Orestes. Causes have their
quiddits, and 'tis ill jesting with bell-ropes.

269–70. *Hockley i' the Hole*] a Bedfordshire village situated in a valley on
the main road to London, notorious for robberies (Chalfant).

270. *Gadshill*] on the London road, twenty miles south-east of London,
also notorious for highway robbery; cf. *1H4* 1.2, 4. See *H&S* for other references.

high] chief, principal, main (*OED* 7).

of any request] that anyone asks about, especially of a vogue or fashion.

271. *ha'*] which have.

273. *you, your*] indefinite and colloquial usage.

278. *irons and irons*] fettered with many iron chains. The repetition acts
as a naive intensifier, representing Shift as the Houdini of his age.

280.] Macilente describes Sogliardo as a herald or trumpeter who plays
loudly in order to attract attention to forthcoming announcements or introductions.

282. *affections*] emotional commitment.

284, 286. *Pylades, Orestes*] classical exemplars of male friendship. They
were represented in the 'Masque of Amity', *Gesta Grayorum* (p. 35).

284. *discourse*] describe.

286. *Causes*] (*a*) in law, cases pleaded for one side in suits; court actions
(*OED* 7, 8); (*b*) motives for action (*OED* 3) here, the robberies, dignified as
though they were affairs of honour; cf. *H5* 5.1.3–4: 'There is occasions and
causes why and wherefore in all things'; (*c*) agents of misfortune (*OED* 2).

287. *quiddits*] quiddities, captious subtleties or quibbles in an argument
(*OED*).

'tis ill . . . bell-ropes] gallows humour: Shift facetiously suggests his reluctance to incriminate himself before witnesses. The wording plays on proverbs
like 'It is ill jesting with edged tools', and thieves' cant: a hanged thief, or a

Carlo. How? Pylades and Orestes?

Sogliardo. Ay, he is my Pylades, and I am his Orestes. How
  like you the conceit?   290

Carlo. O, it's an old stale interlude device. No, I'll give you
  names myself. Look you, he shall be your Judas, and you
  shall be his Elder Tree, to hang on.

Macilente. Nay, rather let him be Captain Pod, and this his
  Motion, for he does nothing but show him.   295

Carlo. Excellent! Or thus: you shall be Holden, and he your
  Camel.

Shift. You do not mean to ride, gentlemen?

---

thief that deserves hanging, is a 'gallows-clapper', so called from the swing-
ing of the body to and fro like the clapper of a bell; hence, 'bell-ropes'
(Stevenson, *The Home Book of Proverbs, Maxims and Familiar Phrases* (New
York, 1948), p. 930).

290. *conceit*] comparison.

291. *old . . . device*] old-fashioned entertainment; perhaps a glance at
Pykering's *Horestes* (1567); or the more recent 'Masque of Amity' in the *Gesta
Grayorum*. As a scoffer at friendship (cf. 100–11), Carlo mocks the bonds
of affection as melodramatic and insincere. Cf. Goneril's comment, 'An
interlude!', *Lr* 5.3.90, when she is accused of breaking all bonds of natural
affection.

292–3. *Judas . . . Elder Tree*] According to medieval tradition, Judas
hanged himself from an elder tree, although Gerrard, in his *Herbal* (1597,
p. 1240), says of the *Arbor Iudae*: 'It may be called in English Judas tree,
whereon Judas did hang himself, and not upon the Elder tree, as it is said'
(*H&S*). Carlo's facetious jest places Shift as a traitorous rogue hanging on
Sogliardo for profit.

294–5. *Captain Pod . . . Motion*] Sogliardo is to be Captain Pod, a popular
puppet-show entertainer, and Shift his puppet. Cf. Dekker and Wilkins's *Jests
to Make you Merry* (1607), p. 32: 'he thought like *Banks* his horse, or the
baboons, or Captain *Pold* with his motion, she would have shown him some
strange and monstrous sight' (cited in *H&S* with other references). Leather-
head, the puppet-master in *BF*, claims to have been Pod's apprentice (5.1.7).

296–7. *Holden . . . Camel*] Sogliardo is to be Holden, an animal-trainer,
and Shift his camel. Holden may have tried to teach his camel to dance, as
in the proverb mentioned in Topsell, *History of Four-footed Beasts*, p. 96: 'The
wantonness thereof appeareth by the proverb of a dancing camel, when one
taketh upon him more than his skill will serve to discharge' (cited in Tilley,
C30).

298. *ride*] quibbling on 'camel': (*a*) harass (*OED* 17b); (*b*) mount
sexually (Partridge, *Bawdy*). Shift's question is typical of the vulgarity he
injects into all his conversations; hence the jokes on 'countenance' that
follow.

Puntarvolo. Faith, let me end it for you, gallants. You shall be
    his Countenance, and he your Resolution.   300
Sogliardo. Troth, that's pretty. How say you, cavalier? Shall it
    be so?
Carlo. Ay, ay, most voices.
Shift. Faith, I am eas'ly yielding to any good impressions.
Sogliardo. Then give hands, good Resolution.   305
Carlo. Mass, he cannot say 'good Countenance' now,
    properly, to him again.
Puntarvolo. Yes, by an irony.
Macilente. O sir, the countenance of Resolution should, as he
    is, be altogether grim and unpleasant.   310

Enter BRISK.

Fastidius. Good hours make music with your mirth, gentle-
    men, and keep time to your humours.—How now, Carlo?

309–10. should, as he is, be altogether] *F;* should, as he's altogether *Q.*
310.1.] *Q; Act IIII. Scene VI. /* FASTIDIVS BRISKE. *In margin: To Them. F.*

---

300. *Countenance*] Sogliardo, who will give Shift an allowance for maintenance (see 3.1.472) and thus seem to *countenance,* condone or endorse, his
criminal behaviour. For a similar affectation in nicknaming, see 'Protection',
NI 3.1.186.
    Resolution] valour, swagger; colloquially, the attribute of a bravo, street
bully, or pimp. See 256–7n.
    303. *most voices*] the majority wins.
    307. *properly*] (*a*) appropriately, but playing on 'handsomely'. Sogliardo
has already been represented as an ugly swine: he does not have a *good counte-*
nance, or attractive face, although he can pay *good countenance,* or a handsome
allowance; (*b*) alternatively, Carlo may mean that Sogliardo cannot now call
Shift a *good countenance,* because, as a proper name, it belongs to Sogliardo.
    309–10.] *F*'s reading makes better grammatical sense than *Q*'s without sub-
stantially altering the meaning; *Q*'s line may be the result of a printer's error.
So far, the joke has been that Sogliardo is ugly and consequently can be
addressed as *good Countenance* only ironically. The irony is double-barrelled,
because *countenance,* pronounced *cunt'nance,* implies pimping as well as
patronage and appearance. Macilente's use of the word *countenance* seems
to ring changes on all meanings, and not to be simply a reference to the new
nickname: the *countenance* (face in general, or Sogliardo's endorsement of
Shift's services in particular) put on *resolution* (Shift, or what he
represents—swaggering bravado, moral laxness) should be suitably repellent,
and consequently no irony attaches to the phrase *good countenance.* Sogliardo's
ugly features (*countenance*) illustrate Shift's character (*resolution*) perfectly.
    311–12. *Good . . . humours*] May the times harmonize with your mirth and
mark the beat of your desires.

Puntarvolo. Monsieur Brisk! Many a long look have I
    extended for you, sir.

Fastidius. Good faith, I must crave pardon. I was invited this   315
    morning, ere I was out of my bed, by a bevy of ladies to
    a banquet, whence it was almost one of Hercules' labours
    for me to come away, but that the respect of my promise
    did so prevail with me. I know they'll take it very ill,
    especially one that gave me this bracelet of her hair but   320
    over night, and this pearl another gave me from her fore-
    head. Marry, she—What? Are the writings ready?

Puntarvolo. I will send my man to know. [*To Servingman
    leading the dog*] Sirrah, go you to the notary's and learn
    if he be ready. Leave the dog, sir.   325

                                        Exit Servingman.

Fastidius. [*Greeting the others*] And how does my rare qualified
    friend, Sogliardo?—O Signor Macilente! By these eyes,
    I saw you not. I had saluted you sooner else, on my
    troth. [*Aside to Macilente*] I hope, sir, I may presume upon
    you that you will not divulge my late check or disgrace,   330
    indeed, sir.

Macilente. You may, sir.

Carlo. [*Aside*] 'Sheart, he knows some notorious jest by this
    gull, that he hath him so obsequious.

Sogliardo. Monsieur Fastidius, do you see this fellow there?   335
    [*Gesturing to Shift*] Does he not look like a clown? Would
    you think there's anything in him?

325.1.] *Q; not in F.*   328. on] *Q; o' F.*   337. there's] *Q, Fa;* there were *Fb.*

---

317. *banquet*] snack or refreshment, also called a *running banquet*; usually
a course of sweetmeats, fruit, and wine (*OED* 2, 3).

Hercules' labours] The twelve labours of Hercules were legendary for their
difficulty.

320. *bracelet of her hair*] love-token. Cf. in Donne, 'The Relic' 6: 'A
bracelet of bright hair about the bone', found in the grave, signifies 'a loving
couple'.

320–1. *but over night*] just last night.

321–2. *pearl . . . forehead*] pearl dangling from the hairline, a style affected
by Elizabeth I, as in the engraving by Crispin van de Passe the Elder
(National Portrait Gallery).

326. *rare qualified*] highly distinguished.

330. *my late check*] my recent discomfiture. See 3.3.120–50.

334. *he hath . . . obsequious*] Macilente has rendered Fastidius so
obsequious (abjectly deferential).

336. *clown*] simple peasant; uncouth, ill-bred man (*OED* 1, 2).

Fastidius. Anything in him? Beshrew me, ay. The fellow hath
a good ingenious face.

Sogliardo. By this element, he is an ingenious tall man as ever   340
swaggered about London. He and I call Countenance
and Resolution, but his name is Cavalier Shift.

Puntarvolo. [*To Shift*] Cavalier, you knew Signor Clog, that
was hanged for the robbery at Harrow on the Hill?

Sogliardo. [*Interrupting*] Knew him, sir! Why, 'twas he gave all   345
the directions for the action.

Puntarvolo. How? [*To Shift*] Was 't your project, sir?

Shift. [*To Sogliardo*] Pardon me, Countenance, you do me
some wrong to make that public which I imparted to you
in private.   350

Sogliardo. God's will, here are none but friends, Resolution.

Shift. That's all one. Things of consequence must have their
respects: where, how, and to whom. [*To Puntarvolo*] Yes,
sir, he showed himself a true clog in the coherence of that
affair, sir; for, if he had managed matters as they were   355
corroborated to him, it had been better for him by a forty
or fifty score of pounds, sir, and he himself might ha'
lived, in despite of fate, to have fed on woodcocks with

339. an ingenious] *Q;* as ingenious a *F.*   344. on] *Q;* o' *F.*   347. Was 't]
Q, Fa; was it *Fb.*   349. that] *Q, Fa;* occasions *Fb.*

---

339. *ingenious*] (*a*) clever, enterprising; (*b*) noble, frank.

340. *By this element*] a mild oath imitating Brisk's style.

tall] bold, brave.

341. *call*] call each other.

343. *Clog*] (*a*) heavy block of wood attached to the leg or neck of a
prisoner to prevent his escape (*OED* 2); (*b*) hindrance to any action, with
a glance at 'blockhead' (*OED* 3); (*c*) shoe with a thick wooden sole worn
by rustics (*OED* 6).

344. *Harrow on the Hill*] then a Middlesex village, twelve miles north-west
of London; an excellent rendezvous for highwaymen because it occupies the
highest ground in Middlesex with views from the summit embracing several
counties (Chalfant).

352–3. *must . . . respects*] must follow certain proprieties.

354. *he . . . true clog*] Clog, a type of the inept thief, lived up to his name
by hampering his own performance in the plot and getting himself arrested
(and hanged) for the crime as a result.

coherence] progress, smooth operation depending on sticking together.

356. *corroborated to*] confirmed with, as of formal legal acts (*OED* 4), but
here used of illegal actions.

358. *fed on woodcocks*] (*a*) eaten a good meal at an ordinary; i.e., celebrated
the success of the caper; (*b*) preyed on dupes who assemble at ordinaries
(Gifford).

the rest. But it was his heavy fortunes to sink, poor Clog,
and therefore talk no more of him.   360

Puntarvolo. Why, had he more agents then?

Sogliardo. O God, sir! Ay, there were some present there that
were the Nine Worthies to him, i' faith.

Shift. Ay, sir, I can satisfy you at more convenient conference. But, for mine own part, I have now reconciled   365
myself to other courses, and profess a living out of my
other qualities.

Sogliardo. [*To the others*] Nay, he has left all now, I assure you,
and is able to live like a gentleman by his quality. By this
dog, he has the most rare gift in tobacco that ever you   370
knew.

Carlo. [*To Macilente*] 'Sheart, he keeps more ado with this
monster than ever Banks did with his horse, or the fellow
with the elephant.

---

359. fortunes] *Q;* fortune *F.*   361. agents] *Q;* aiders *F.*

---

361. *agents*] confederates.

363. *the Nine Worthies*] a celebrated group of three biblical heroes (Joshua,
David, Judah Maccabeus), three classical heroes (Hector, Alexander, Julius
Caesar), and three medieval heroes (Arthur, Charlemagne, Sir Guy of
Warwick), all of whom represent the best that man can be. General disagreement or misinformation about the members of this group, or perhaps simply
the interests of comedy, caused discrepancies: Shakespeare includes Hercules
and Pompey in *LLL* 5.2, and Nashe adds Solomon and Gideon in *The Unfortunate Traveller* (2.253). Sogliardo's point is that very worthy men took part.

to] compared to.

366. *profess*] earn, maintain.

367. *qualities*] skills.

368. *he . . . all*] Shift has stopped being a criminal.

369. *quality*] skill (as a specialist in tobacco).

369–70. *By this dog*] an oath imitating Brisk's style.

373. *Banks*] the horse-trainer who owned Morocco, a bay gelding famous
for its repertoire of odd tricks. According to Sir Kenelm Digby, *Of Bodies and
Of Man's Soul*, p. 393 (cited in Whalley), it could dance, add up a throw of dice,
play cards, tell the number of pence in a silver coin, bow at the mention of Elizabeth, or James of Scotland, and 'bite and strike at you' for naming the King of
Spain. Tarlton's *Jests* notes that the horse was exhibited a the Cross Keys in
Grace Street in 1588, and the preface to the tract *Maroccus Extaticus, or Banks'
Bay Horse in a Trance* (1595), places it that year as shown at Bel-Savage near
Ludgate. Dekker mentions Banks's horse in several pamphlets, and alludes to
a story of a horse 'walking a'th' top of Paul's', reputedly Morocco, in *Satiromastix* 1.2.128 (Hoy, 1.213, 221). Jonson refers in *Ep.* 133.156–9 to the rumour
that both Banks, 'our PYTHAGORAS', and his 'learned horse' were 'burned for
one witch' in Rome, thus ending an illustrious career.

373–4. *the fellow . . . elephant*] another performer in London in the mid-

Macilente. [*To Carlo*] He will hang out his picture shortly in   375
a cloth, you shall see.

Sogliardo. O, he does manage a quarrel the best that ever you
saw for terms and circumstances.

Fastidius. Good faith, signor, now you speak of a quarrel, I'll
acquaint you with a difference that happened between a   380
gallant and myself. Sir Puntarvolo, you know him if I
should name him: Signor Luculento.

Puntarvolo. Luculento! What inauspicious chance interposed
itself betwixt your two loves?

Fastidius. Faith, sir, the same that sundered Agamemnon and   385

1590s. Gifford quotes Donne, *Satires* 1.79–82, and *H&S* cite Davies, *Epigrams* 30. Browne, 'Of the Elephant' 3.1, mentions that errors in describing
the anatomy of elephants could have been corrected by 'experience, whereof
not many years past, we have had advantage in England, by an elephant
shown in many parts thereof'. This elephant may merely have been exhibited, but alternatively may have performed spelling tricks like Banks's horse.
Browne goes on to mention stories of elephants able to write sentences and
even to speak. Jonson notes similarly in *Disc.* 322–6: 'That an elephant . . .
came hither ambassador from the great Mogul (who could both write and
read) and was every day allowed twelve cast of bread, twenty quarts of
Canary sack; besides nuts and almonds the citizens' wives sent him'.

375–6. *picture . . . cloth*] advertisement; cf. 2.1.431.

377–8.] Shift knows all the duelling formalities and techniques, as
illustrated, for example, in *Vincentio Saviolo, His Practice* (1595), translated
from the Italian treatise of 1588.

382. *Luculento*] first mentioned at 2.1.467.

384. *your two loves*] the friendship of you two.

385ff.] Fleay noted the similarity between this duel and the one reported
in *Patient Grissel* 3.2.19–61, performed early in 1600 (cited in *H&S*, 9.468).
Both *H&S* (9.369) and Chambers (3.292) think the scene was based on an
actual courtiers' duel in which only the clothing was damaged, although
Dekker and Chettle may merely have copied Jonson. The abortive duel is in
the *miles gloriosus* tradition, which Jonson had explored earlier with Bobadilla
in *EMI* (*Q*) 3.4 and 4.2. But in *EMO* Shift is the braggart soldier, not Fastidius, who only 'duels' to stay in fashion.

Brisk's duel is appropriate for a 'Frenchified' courtier. Although duelling in
Italy was defunct by the end of the sixteenth century, in France it had reached
its acme: Henri III (1574–89) favoured celebrated duelists, Henri IV
(1589–1610) commuted the punishment of seven thousand duellists, and
during their reigns one-third of the French nobles were killed in duels (Bryson,
pp. 118–19, 131). The Inns of Court attitude towards formalized European
duelling appears in the *Gesta Grayorum*, p. 38: 'Item, no Knight of this Order
shall, in point of honour, resort to any grammar-rules out of the books *De
Dullo*, or such like, but shall, out of his own brave mind, and natural courage,
deliver himself from scorns, as to his own discretion shall seem convenient'.

great Thetis' son, but let the cause escape, sir. He sent
me a challenge (mixed with some few braves) which I
restored and, in fine, we met. Now, indeed, sir (I must
tell you), he did offer at first very desperately but without
judgement, for look you, sir: [*Adopting a fencing stance*] I   390
cast myself into this figure. Now he comes violently on,
and withal advancing his rapier to strike. I thought to
have took his arm—for he had left his whole body to my
election, and I was sure he could not recover his guard.
Sir, I missed my purpose in his arm, rashed his doublet   395
sleeve, ran him close by the left cheek and through his
hair. He again lights me here—I had a gold cable hatband
then new come up (which I wore about a murrey French
hat I had)—cuts my hatband (and yet it was massy,

---

394. for . . . guard] *Parenthetical in Q, F.*   397. here—I had a] *This ed.;*
Here, I had a *Q;* here (I had on, a *F*   398. (which] *Q;* which *F*

385–6. *the same . . . son*] In the *Iliad*, Agamemnon and Achilles quarrel over
a woman. After Agamemnon returns his mistress to Troy in exchange for
Greek prisoners, he takes Achilles' mistress as a relacement. Achilles,
offended, sulks in his tent and refuses to fight. Jonson uses this frame of
reference to set off the mock-heroic duel between Fastidius and Luculento. A
duel over a love affair was not usually considered honourable (Bryson, p. 71).

386. *let . . . escape*] never mind the cause.

387. *braves*] dares, threats, or boasts; some display of defiance. In a proper
duel of honour, the challenge was supposed to be brief, modest, and uncon-
ditional; an abusive tone showed ill-breeding and was not acceptable
(Bryson, p. 7).

388. *restored*] responded to.

in fine] in the end; in short.

389. *offer*] fence, fight.

392–3. *to . . . arm*] to have hit or pinked him on the arm.

393–4. *to my election*] as an open target for me to score a hit wherever I
chose to strike.

394. *recover his guard*] regain the 'guard' position in fencing, the traditional oblique posture that protects vital areas.

395. *rashed*] slashed.

397. *again*] in return.

lights me] strikes a blow upon me (*OED* 10a).

gold cable hatband] thick twists of gold rope; cf. Ind.109.

398. *new come up*] in the latest fashion.

murrey] mulberry or dull purplish-red; in colour-symbolism, 'steadfast-
ness in love' (Linthicum, pp. 39–40).

398–9. *French hat*] broad-brimmed hat, probably made of velvet. A velvet
hat with a gold band and gold feather cost 40s in 1576 (Linthicum, pp.
219–21); Emulo, in *Patient Grissel*, claims costs of £9 to £10 in 1600.

goldsmith's work), cuts my brims, which by good fortune   400
(being thick embroidered with gold twist and spangles)
disappointed the force of the blow. Nevertheless, it grazed
on my shoulder, takes me away six purls of an Italian cut-
work band I wore, cost me three pounds in the Exchange
but three days before.   405

Puntarvolo. This was a strange encounter.

Fastidius. Nay, you shall hear, sir. With this, we both fell out
and breathed. Now, upon the second sign of his assault,
I betook me to the former manner of my defence. He, on
the other side, abandoned his body to the same danger   410
as before, and follows me still with blows. But I (being
loath to take the deadly advantage that lay before me of
his left side) made a kind of *stramazoun*, ran him up to
the hilts, through the doublet, through the shirt, and yet
missed the skin. He, making a reverse blow, falls upon   415
my embossed girdle (I had thrown off the hangers a little

---

404. wore, cost] *Q;* wore (cost *F.*   405. before.] *Q;* before.) *F.*   408.
upon . . . assault] *Parenthetical in Q, F.*   409–10. on . . . side] *Parenthetical
in Q, F.*   415. making . . . blow] *Parenthetical in Q, F.*

---

400. *cuts my brims*] bawdy quibble: (*a*) sheers off the brims of the hat; (*b*)
disables sexually (castrates?). Cf. *OED, Brim* v., 'Of swine, to be in heat, to
rut, to copulate'; and *Westward Ho!* 4.2.243–5: 'he doted on my wife, / He
would have wrought on her and played on me, / but to pare of these brims,
I cut off her'.

403. *purls*] minutely looped and scalloped edging on the collar, made of
silk, silver, or gold needlework, and sold by the weight; up to four angels a
pound for silk (Linthicum, pp. 141–2).

403–4. *Italian . . . band*] lace-like linen collar made by cutting away the
material in squares and filling the spaces with geometric designs of needlework. Purls were a usual part of cut-work (Linthicum, p. 139).

404. *the Exchange*] the Royal Exchange, a shopping area (see 4.1.106n).

408. *breathed*] rested.

413. stramazoun] descending blow, as opposed to a *stoccata*, or thrust; a
fencing term derived from the Italian *stramazzare*, to slay or murder. The
stramazoun might, therefore, be called a murdering blow (Nares). Brisk's use
of the term is either ignorant or pretentious.

414. *hilts*] Jonson usually uses the plural with singular meaning (Partridge, *Accidence*, p. 25), but see 3.1.328.

415. *a reverse blow*] a *reverso*, a backhand stroke.

416. *embossed girdle*] fitted belt, fastened in front, used by men to support
the hanger for the sword; usually made of embossed leather for daily wear
(Linthicum, p. 265).

hangers] fringed loops appended to the girdle for hanging the dagger or

before), strikes off a skirt of a thick laced satin doublet I
had (lined with some four taffetas), cuts off two panes
embroidered with pearl, rents through the drawings-out
of tissue, enters the linings, and skips the flesh.   420

Carlo. [*To Macilente*] I wonder he speaks not of his wrought
shirt.

Fastidius. Here, in the opinion of mutual damage, we paused.
But (ere I proceed) I must tell you, signor, that in this
last encounter, not having leisure to put off my silver   425
spurs, one of the rowels catched hold of the ruffle of my
boot, and (being Spanish leather and subject to tear)
overthrows me, rends me two pair of silk stockings (that

---

423. in . . . damage] *Parenthetical in Q, F.*   424-5. in . . . encounter] *Parenthetical in Q, F.*

---

small-sword (Gifford). Wrought or embroidered hangers were often gifts
from ladies to their favourites (Linthicum, p. 265).

418. *panes*] French breeches were made of strips or pleats of fabric which
parted slightly to show a rich lining, and were often embroidered with a goldsmith's work (Linthicum, p. 205).

419-20. *rents . . . tissue*] rips though the rich cloth often including gold or
silver threads (*tissue*) which has been partly drawn through the decorative
slits in the jacket's fabric.

421-2. *wrought shirt*] long-sleeved, high-necked shirt made of linen or
silk, either cut-worked to resemble lace, or ornamented with embroidered
fruits, flowers, historical tableaux, etc. on the band, front, and cuffs
(Linthicum, p. 213). Carlo mentions the shirt as the one major item of clothing not yet injured in the duel. See 433.

423. *in . . . damage*] in view of the hurts we had given each other.

426-7. *ruffle of my boot*] The fashion was for high wide boots, made of
soft leather, folded over and hanging loosely to expose the lace or fringe
inside; cf. 1.2.62-3n.

428. *overthrows me*] If a duelist falls accidentally, his opponent is not
obliged to permit him to rise, although killing him in that position would be
considered infamous. The fall is thought to be an intervention of God, ending
the duel, and the opponent is then the victor (Bryson, p. 59). Brisk's opponent does not grasp his advantage. Brisk falls a victim to his own fashion
sense by duelling in unsuitable clothes that serve as a virtual booby-trap.

silk stockings] favoured by gallants because 'they showed off the comeli-
ness of the wearer's leg much better than did the woollen ones' (Linthicum,
p. 261). Cf. *Gull's Horn-book*, of the gallant in Paul's Walk: 'He therefore that
would strive to fashion his legs to his silk stockings, and his proud gait to
his broad garters, let him whiff down these observations; for, if he once get
to walk by the book . . . Paul's may be proud of him, . . . whilst all the Inns
of Court rejoice to behold his most handsome calf' (2.230).

I put on, being somewhat a raw morning: a peach colour
and another) and strikes me some half-inch deep into the   430
side of the calf. He, seeing the blood come, presently
takes horse and away. I (having bound up my wound with
a piece of my wrought shirt)—

Carlo. [*To Macilente*] O, comes it there?

Fastidius.—rid after him, and, lighting at the court gate both   435
together, embraced and marched hand in hand up into
the presence.

Macilente. [*To Carlo*] Well, by this we can guess what apparel
the gentleman wore.

Puntarvolo. 'Fore God, it was a designment begun with much   440
resolution, maintained with as much prowess, and ended
with more humanity.

---

431. seeing . . . come] *Parenthetical in Q, F.*   434. there?] *Q;* in there? *F.*
435-6. lighting . . . together] *Parenthetical in Q, F.*   437. presence.] *Q;*
presence: was not this businesse well carried? *F.*   438. Well, by] *Q;* Well?
yes, and by *F.*   440. God] *Q;* valour *F.*

---

429. *peach colour*] according to courtly colour-symbolism, the colour of
love; a deep pink (Linthicum, pp. 25-6, 40). The implication is that Brisk's
stockings brand him as licentious and possibly vulgar; cf. Prince Hal's comic
dismay at Poins, *2H4* 2.2.13-19.

431-2. *seeing . . . away*] A duel is usually fought to the agreed finish,
which may be either first blood, capture, surrender, recanting, or fleeing the
field. The last is most shameful, because flight proves the fugitive's cause was
unjust, and the opponent may follow and kill him. If he flees to court,
as Luculento does, he has the right of sanctuary (Bryson, pp. 62-7). The
complication here is that the first blood is accidental, not inflicted by the
opponent, and therefore problematic, like the fall itself, as an indicator of
Luculento's victory. However, since Brisk does not formally surrender before
Luculento flees the field, Luculento has violated the rules and thus forfeits
victory. The reason for fleeing was probably fear of arrest for manslaughter,
which Jonson himself had experienced in 1598 (see introd., p. 30).

435. *lighting*] alighting, dismounting.

436. *embraced*] At the end of a duel, if the loser did his best, the winner
should become his friend; if the loser behaved improperly, the winner should
refuse to associate with him further (Bryson, p. 81). Brisk's forgiveness of an
unworthy opponent can be excused only on the basis of Brisk's own unwor-
thiness as a victor; in this duel, both men are losers.

440-2.] Whereas Carlo and Macilente have been snickering at the
sartorial focus of Brisk's duel, Puntarvolo has apparently been approving of
its chivalric style.

440. *designment*] undertaking.

His Servingman *enters.*

How now, what says he?

Servingman. The notary says he is ready, sir. He stays but
your worship's pleasure.   445

Puntarvolo. [*To Brisk*] Come, we will go to him, Monsieur.
[*To the others*] Gentlemen, shall we entreat you to be
witnesses?

Sogliardo. You shall entreat me, sir.—Come, Resolution.

Shift. I follow you, good Countenance.   450

Carlo. [*To Macilente*] Come, signor, come, come.

Macilente. [*Aside*]   O, that there should be fortune
To clothe these men, so naked in desert,
And that the just storm of a wretched life
Beats 'em not ragged for their wretched souls,   455
And since as fruitless, even as black, as coals!

Exeunt.

GREX

Mitis. Why, but, signor, how comes it that Fungoso appeared
not with his sister's intelligence to Brisk?

Cordatus. Marry, long of the evil angels that she gave him,
who have, indeed, tempted the good simple youth to   460
follow the tail of the fashion and neglect the imposition

442.1.] *In Q appears after l. 443; not in F.*   443. he] *Q;* the Notarie *F.*
444. The notary] *Q;* He *F.*   456.1.] *Q1; Exit. Q2; not in F.*

---

443. *he*] the notary.

452–6.] What a sad state of affairs, that such utterly undeserving men
should have the fortune to wear fine clothes and pose as gentlemen, and that
there is no just storm of fortune to beat them into ragged poverty as
punishment for their spiritual wretchedness!

456. *since as ... even as*] not only ... but also.

458. *intelligence*] information, warning that Deliro is threatening to arrest
Brisk for debt.

459. *long of*] because of.

evil angels] (*a*) money given to Fungoso at 4.1.126–42; (*b*) demons.
A common pun.

461. *imposition*] (*a*) request, charge (*OED* 5b); (*b*) laying on of hands
in a religious ceremony such as blessing or confirmation (*OED* 1b),
but quibbling on the *evil angels* that *tempted* him away from the righteous
path.

of his friends. Behold, here he comes, very worshipfully
attended and with good variety.

ACT 4   SCENE 4

Enter FUNGOSO *with* Tailor, Shoemaker,
and Haberdasher.

Fungoso. Gramercy, good shoemaker. I'll put to strings
myself.

Exit Shoemaker.

[*To Haberdasher*] Now, sir, let me see. What must you have
for this hat?

Haberdasher. Here's the bill, sir.   5

Fungoso. How does 't become me? Well?

Tailor. Excellent, sir, as ever you had any hat in your life.

Haberdasher. Nay, faith, sir, the hat's as good as any man i'
this town can serve you, and will maintain fashion as
long. Ne'er trust me for a groat else.   10

Fungoso. Does it apply well to my suit?

Tailor. Exceeding well, sir.

Fungoso. How lik'st thou my suit, haberdasher?

Haberdasher. By my troth, sir, 'tis very rarely well made. I
never saw a suit sit better, I can tell on.   15

Tailor. Nay, we have no art to please our friends, we!

ACT 4 SCENE 4] *Q* (SCENA QUARTA.*); ACT IIII. SCENE VII. F*   0.1–2.]
Q; FVNGOSO, TAYLOR, SHOO-MAKER,/ HABERDASHER. *F*   2.1. SD] *Q; not
in F   After l. 7.] F adds new line:* FVNG. Nay, you'll say so, all.   8. Nay,
faith] *Q;* In faith, *F*

---

462. *he*] Fungoso.

worshipfully] (*a*) with followers who praise clothes and expense as worthy
objects of worship; and (*b*) attended by flatterers addressing Fungoso as 'your
worship' to indicate that he is now a person of note. Cordatus continues the
quibble on temptation into sin.

1–2. *I'll . . . myself*] I'll obtain my own shoelaces.

3. *must you have*] do I owe you.

9. *serve you*] make for you.

11. *apply well to*] go well with, complement.

15. *sit*] fit.
I can tell on] that I can recall.

16. *we . . . friends*] (ironically, with seeming modesty) we don't know how
to please our customers. Oh, no, not we!

Fungoso. [*Giving money*] Here, haberdasher, tell this same.

Haberdasher. Good faith, sir, it makes you have an excellent
    body.

Fungoso. Nay, believe me, I think I have as good a body in   20
    clothes as another.

Tailor. You lack points to bring your apparel together.

Fungoso. I'll have points anon. [*To Haberdasher, still counting
    money*] How now? Is 't right?

Haberdasher. Faith, sir, 'tis too little, but upon farther hopes.   25
    Good morrow to you, sir.

Fungoso. Farewell, good haberdasher.

                                   Exit Haberdasher.

Well now, Master Snip, let me see your bill.

GREX

Mitis. Methinks he discharges his followers too thick.

Cordatus. O, therein he saucily imitates some great man. I   30
    warrant you, though he turns off them, he keeps this
    tailor, in place of a page, to follow him still.

Fungoso. This bill is very reasonable, in faith. Hark you,
    Master Snip. Troth, sir, I am not altogether so well fur-
    nished at this present as I could wish I were, but if you'll   35

22. together] *Q;* together, sir. *F.*   25. hopes.] *Q;* hopes—*F.*   27.1.] *In Q
appears after l. 26; not in F.*

17. *tell*] count.

21. *as another*] as anyone else (Partridge, *Syntax*, p. 74).

22. *points*] thongs or ties with metal tags, used in combination with eyelets
to attach hose to doublet ('trussing'); they were also used to fasten the sleeve
to the doublet, or the codpiece to the hose (Linthicum, p. 282).

25. *upon farther hopes*] I have hopes of being paid more later. Fungoso has
paid only part of the bill, and now requires credit.

28. *Snip*] nickname, frequently derisive, for a tailor; *H&S* trace the origin
to the jingle: 'Snip-snap quoth the tailor's sheers. / Alas, poor louse, beware
thy ears.'

29. *discharges*] pays and sends away.

too thick] in too close or too rapid a succession (*OED, Thick* adv., 3).

30. *therein . . . great man*] (*a*) Fungoso is aping the extravagance (and the
inability to pay bills) of some powerful figure at court; (*b*) Asper, the playwright, is deliberately satirizing some particular figure of note, whom some
members of the audience may recognize.

34–5. *furnished*] provided with money.

do me the favour to take part in hand, you shall have all
I have, by Jesu—

Tailor. Sir—

Fungoso.—and but give me credit for the rest till the beginning of the next term—   40

Tailor. O Lord, sir—

Fungoso.—'fore God and by this light, I'll pay you to the
utmost, and acknowledge myself very deeply engaged to
you, by this hand.

Tailor. Why, how much have you there, sir?   45

Fungoso. Marry, I have here four angels and fifteen shillings
of white money. It's all I have, as 'hope to be saved!

Tailor. You will not fail me at the next term with the rest?

Fungoso. No. An I do, pray God I be hanged! Let me never
breathe again upon this mortal stage, as the philosopher   50
calls it. By this air, and as I am a gentleman, I'll hold!

GREX

Cordatus. [*Wryly*] He were an iron-hearted fellow, in my
judgement, that would not credit him upon these monstrous oaths.

Tailor. Well, sir, I'll not stick with any gentleman for a trifle. 55
You know what 'tis remains?

Fungoso. Ay, sir, and I give you thanks, in good faith. [*As Tailor
is leaving*] O God, how happy am I made in this good
fortune! Well, now I'll go seek out Monsieur Brisk. God's

---

37. by Jesu] *Q;* by this hand *F*   44. by this hand] *Q;* by the courtesie *F*
47. 'hope] *Q, Fa;* I hope *Fb.*   saved] *Q;* blest *F*   53–4. these mon-
strous] *Q;* this volley of *F*   58. God] *Q;* fate *F*   59. God's] *Q;* 'Ods *F*

---

36. *take part in hand*] accept a partial payment of ready cash.
43. *engaged*] (*a*) obliged; (*b*) indebted to.
47. *white money*] silver change.
50. *the philosopher*] either Democritus, as *H&S* suggest, or Pythagoras, as
suggested in Dent, w882, citing R. Edwards, *Damon and Pithias* (1571).
51. *hold*] keep my word.
53. *credit him*] (*a*) believe him; (*b*) extend him credit for his purchases.
55. *stick*] be unreasonable.

so', I have forgot ribbon for my shoes, and points! 'Slid,   60
what luck's this? How shall I do? [*Calling him back*]
Master Snip! Pray let me reduct some two or three
shillings for points and ribbon. By Jesu, I have utterly dis-
furnished myself in the default of memory. Pray, le' me
be beholding to you. It shall come home i' the bill, believe   65
me.

Tailor. Faith, sir, I can hardly depart with money, but I'll take
up and send you some by my boy presently. What
coloured ribbon would you have?

Fungoso. What you shall think meet, i' your judgement, sir, to   70
my suit.

Tailor. Well, I'll send you some presently.

Fungoso. And points too, sir?

Tailor. And points too, sir.

Fungoso. Good lord, how shall I study to deserve this kind-   75
ness of you, sir? Pray let your youth make haste, for I
should have done a business an hour since, that I doubt
I shall come too late.

Exit Tailor.

Now, in good truth, I am exceeding proud of my suit!

Exit.

GREX

Cordatus. Do you observe the plunges that this poor gallant   80
is put to, signor, to purchase the fashion?

---

63. By Jesu] *Q;* as I am an honest man *F.*   67. money] *Q;* ready money
F.   78.1.] *In Q appears after l. 74; not in F.*   79. truth] *Q;* faith *F.*   79.1.]
Q; not in F.

---

62. *reduct*] draw back, call back (Latin).
64. *in . . . memory*] because of my defective memory. A *default* in law is a
failure to perform some requirement or obligation (*OED* 3).
65. *beholding*] beholden, indebted.
come . . . bill] be included when I pay the whole bill.
67. *depart . . . money*] part with the cash.
67–8. *take . . . some*] select from my stock and send you some ribbon and
points (instead of cash).
70–1.] Whatever you think, with your experience, will match my outfit.
75. *study*] endeavour.
76. *youth*] boy, servant. See 68 above.
77. *doubt*] fear.
80. *plunges*] depths.

Mitis. Ay, and to be still a fashion behind with the world, that's the sport.

Cordatus. Stay. O, here they come from *sealed and delivered.*

ACT 4   SCENE 5

Enter PUNTARVOLO, FASTIDIUS BRISK, [*and*] Servingmen *with the dog* [*and cat*].

Puntarvolo. Well, now my whole venture is forth, I will resolve to depart shortly.

Fastidius. Faith, Sir Puntarvolo, go to the court and take leave of the ladies first.

Puntarvolo. I care not if it be this afternoon's labour. Where   5
is Carlo?

Fastidius. Here he comes.

Enter CARLO, SOGLIARDO, SHIFT, *and* MACILENTE.

Carlo. Faith, gallants, I am persuading this gentleman [*Indicating Sogliardo*] to turn courtier. He is a man of fair revenue, and his estate will bear the charge well. Besides,   10
for his other gifts of the mind, or so, why, they are as nature lent him 'em: pure, simple, without any artificial drug or mixture of these two threadbare beggarly qualities, learning and knowlege, and therefore the more accommodate and genuine. Now, for the life itself—   15

ACT 4 SCENE 5] *Q (SCENA QUINTA.); Act IIII. Scene VIII. F* 0.1–2.] *Q;* PVNTARVOLO, FASTIDIVS BRISKE, SER-/VANTS, CARLO, SOGLIARDO, MA-/CILENTE, SHIFT,/ FVNGOSO. *In margin: To them. F* 7.1.] *Q; not in F.*

82–3.] The joke is that all of Fungoso's stratagems and expenditures still leave him wearing yesterday's fashions.

84. *they . . . delivered*] Puntarvolo and Brisk come from signing the contract and having it officially notarized by the scrivener.

1. *my . . . forth*] that my entire trip to Constantinople is covered by wagers.

5. *I care . . . labour*] I don't mind spending the afternoon that way.

10. *charge*] expense.

11–12. *gifts . . . 'em*] Sogliardo is completely uneducated: by implication, a natural fool. The apparently flattering description of his unspoiled nature is ironic.

15. *accommodate*] suitable.
life] life of a courtier.

Fastidius. O, the most celestial, and full of wonder and delight
that can be imagined, signor, beyond all thought and
apprehension of pleasure! A man lives there in that divine
rapture that he will think himself i' the third heaven for
the time, and lose all sense of mortality whatsoever, when   20
he shall behold such glorious (and almost immortal)
beauties, hear such angelical and harmonious voices, discourse with such flowing and ambrosian spirits, whose
wit's as sudden as lightning and humorous as nectar. O,
it makes a man all quintessence and flame, and lifts him   25
up in a moment to the very crystal crown o' the sky,
where (hovering in the strength of his imagination) he
shall behold all the delights of the Hesperides, the *Insulae
Fortunatae*, Adonis' Gardens, Tempe, or what else, con-
fined within the amplest verge of poesy, to be mere   30

---

19. third] *Q*; ninth *F.*   24. wit's as] *This ed.;* wits as *Q;* wits are as *F.*
29. Adonis'] *Q, F (Adonis).*

---

18. *apprehension*] understanding.
    there] at court.
    19. *third heaven*] 'The Jews spoke of the heaven of the clouds as the first,
that of the stars as the second, and of God's abode as the third'; de Vocht
cites 2 Cor. 12.2, 'referring to Saint Paul's experience' (p. 85). *H&S* use *F*'s
reading, based on W. Alley, *The Poor Man's Library* (1571), 2.59, which refers
to ten heavens, the ninth being '*coelem aqueum, vel crystallynum*' in Ptolemy,
or the crystal-clear heaven, which *H&S* take as the reference in 26 to 'the
very crystal crown o' the sky'.
    23. *ambrosian*] divine (*OED* 1), intellectually 'flowing' like the drink of the
gods (see *OED, Ambrosia* 2); usually *ambrosia* is considered the food and
nectar the drink of the gods.
    24. *humorous*] moist (*OED* 1); honeyed.
    25. *quintessence*] the 'fifth' essence of ancient and medieval philosophy,
thought to be the substance from which heavenly bodies were composed; a
perfect manifestation of the 'soul' of life, latent in all things, and sought by
alchemists as the basic ingredient of the philosopher's stone.
    flame] fire, the most upward-moving of the four elements.
    28. *Hesperides*] the mythical garden of the golden apples in the Isles of
the West (see 2.1.390), also called *Insulae Fortunatae*, the Fortunate Isles (see
Ind.268).
    29. *Adonis' Gardens*] The Greek phrase originally referred to potted
plants grown for the festival of Adonis (*H&S*), but was misunderstood
by Elizabethans as a synonym for an earthly paradise, as in *FQ* 3.6.42–
50.
    Tempe] a beautiful vale in Thessaly celebrated by classical pastoral
poets.

umbrae and imperfect figures conferred with the most
essential felicity of your court.

Macilente. [*To Carlo*] Well, this *encomion* was not extemporal;
it came too perfectly off.

Carlo. [*Ostensibly to Sogliardo*] Besides, sir, you shall never   35
need to go to a hot-house. You shall sweat there with
courting your mistress, or losing your money at primero,
as well as in all the stoves in Flanders. Marry, this, sir:
you must ever be sure to carry a good strong perfume
about you, that your mistress' dog may smell you out   40
amongst the rest. And, in making love to her, never fear
to be out, for you may have a pipe of tobacco, or a bass
viol shall hang o' the wall of purpose, will put you in
presently. The tricks your Resolution has taught you in
tobacco (the Whiff and those sleights) will stand you   45
in very good ornament there.

Fastidius. Ay, to some, perhaps. But, an he should come

38. Flanders] *Q; Sweden F.*

---

31. umbrae . . . *figures*] shadows; superficial and misleading likenesses.
conferred] compared.

33-4.] This comment may not be an aside, like Carlo's remarks (at 8-15
and subsequently) which Sogliardo is too naive to appreciate as jibes.

33. encomion] encomium, a set speech of high-flown praise or flattery
(*OED*).

34. *too . . . off*] sounding too much as though memorized and rehearsed
(as opposed to *extemporal* or ad-lib speech).

36-7. *sweat there . . . mistress*] Carlo compares the effort of flirting with a
lady at court to the sweating treatment for syphilis, available in hot-houses.

37. *primero*] card game. See notes at Chars.12 and 1.2.50.

38. *stoves in Flanders*] Elizabethans were vague in their geographical
references; 'Flanders' might imply all the Netherlands, and even Germany
(Sugden). In German (and Swedish, as in *F*) inns, the room with several
sleeping-benches was called the 'stove', because the stove was the most
important piece of furniture in it; to retain the heat, the windows were never
opened, and all the travellers, whatever their sex or class, lay as near the stove
as possible (Bates, p. 242); cf. Erasmus, 'Inns', pp. 147-55, in which he
describes these public stove-rooms as overheated and uncongenial, especially
in stormy weather when the close quarters were rendered even more uncom-
fortable by the wet outer clothing hung to dry.

41. *making love to*] courting.

42. *to be out*] (*a*) at a loss for words; theatre term for forgetting lines (see
Ind.292); (*b*) sexual rejection or dysfunction.

43. *will put you in*] (*a*) that will prompt you; help you recall lines after
being 'out'; (*b*) that will gain entry for you sexually.

45. *sleights*] tricks.

to my mistress with tobacco—this gentleman knows
[*Indicating Macilente*]—she'd reply upon him, i' faith. O,
by this bright sun, she has the most acute, ready, and   50
facetious wit that—tut, there's no spirit able to stand her.
[*To Macilente*] You can report it, signor. You have seen her.

Puntarvolo. Then he can report no less out of his judgement,
    I assure him.

Macilente. Troth, I like her well enough, but she's too self-   55
    conceited, methinks.

Fastidius. Ay, indeed, she's a little too self-conceited. An
    'twere not for that humour, she were the most-to-
    be-admired lady in the world.

Puntarvolo. Indeed, it is a humour that takes from her other   60
    excellencies.

Macilente. Why, it may easily be made to forsake her, in my
    thought.

Fastidius. Easily, sir? Then are all impossibilities easy.

Macilente. You conclude too quick upon me, signor. What will   65
    you say if I make it so perspicuously appear now that
    yourself shall confess nothing more possible?

Fastidius. Marry, I will say I will both applaud you and admire
    you for it.

Puntarvolo. And I will second him.   70

Macilente. Why, I'll show you, gentlemen.—Carlo, come
    hither.   *Macilente, Carlo, Puntarvolo, and Brisk whisper.*

Sogliardo. Good faith, I have a great humour to the court.
    What thinks my Resolution? Shall I adventure?

58–9. most-to-be-admired] *F; no hyphens in Q.*   68. applaud you] *Q;*
applaud *F.*   70. him.] *Q;* him, in the admiration. *F.*   72. SD] *Q; They*
whisper. In margin of F.

---

49. *reply upon*] (*a*) respond sharply by word or gesture; used of returning
gun fire; (*b*) send away or repudiate (*OED* 5b); (*c*) in law, answer a defen-
dant's plea, as the third step in common pleadings (*OED* 3).

51. *facetious*] polished and urbane (*OED* 1).

53. *out of*] based on.

60. *takes*] detracts.

62. *it . . . her*] she can easily be taught to forgo self-conceit.

66. *perspicuously*] clearly, evidently.

67. *yourself*] you yourself; absolute use as emphatic subject. The omission
of the personal pronoun subject was very popular in the sixteenth and seventeenth centuries (Partridge, *Syntax*, pp. 41–2); so too 111, 'Myself'.

73. *humour to*] fancy to go to; see text and notes at Ind.86–112, 212.

Shift. Troth, Countenance, as you please. The place is a place   75
    of good reputation and capacity.

Sogliardo. O, my tricks in tobacco (as Carlo says) will show
    excellent there.

Shift. Why, you may go with these gentlemen now and see
    fashions, and after, as you shall see correspondence.   80

Sogliardo. You say true. You will go with me, Resolution?

Shift. I will meet you, Countenance, about three or four of
    clock, but to say to go with you, I cannot, for (as I am
    Apple John) I am to go before the cockatrice you saw this
    morning, and therefore, pray, present me excused, good   85
    Countenance.

Sogliardo. Farewell, good Resolution, but fail not to meet.

Shift. As I live.   *Exit* SHIFT.
                                            They break silence.

Puntarvolo. Admirably excellent!

Macilente. If you can but persuade Sogliardo to the court,   90
    there's all now.

Carlo. O, let me alone. That's my task.
                            [*Carlo takes Sogliardo aside.*]

Fastidius. Now, by Jesu, Macilente, it's above measure excel-
    lent! 'Twill be the only courtly exploit that ever proved
    courtier ingenious.   95

Puntarvolo. Upon my soul, it puts the lady quite out of her
    humour, and we shall laugh with judgement.

Carlo. [*Returning*] Come, the gentleman was of himself
    resolved to go with you afore I moved it.

Macilente. Why then, gallants, you two and Carlo go afore to   100

88. SD] *Q; not in F.*   88.1.] *Q; not in F.*   93. by Jesu] *Q;* by wit *F.*
94. courtly exploit] *Q;* court-exploit *F.*

---

76. *capacity*] force of mind, mental ability, talent.
80. *see correspondence*] see fit, or find agreeable.
84. *cockatrice*] whore; see 1.2.224.
85. *present me excused*] make my excuses.
88.1. They] Macilente, Carlo, Puntarvolo, and Brisk have been whispering during 73–88.
91. *there's all now*] that's the main thing.
92. *let me alone*] leave it to me.
97. *judgement*] critical discernment; i.e., the satisfaction of having been
right.
98. *of himself*] independently by himself.
99. *moved*] urged.

prepare the jest. Sogliardo and I will come some while
after you.

Carlo. Pardon me, I am not for the court.

Puntarvolo. That's true. Carlo comes not at the court indeed.
Well, you shall leave it to the faculty of Monsieur Brisk   105
and myself. Upon our lives, we will manage it happily.
Carlo shall bespeak supper at the Mitre against we come
back, where we will meet and dimple our cheeks with
laughter at the success.

Carlo. Ay, but will you all promise to come?   110

Puntarvolo. Myself shall *mansuete* it for them. He that fails, let
his reputation lie under the lash of thy tongue.

Carlo. God's so', look who comes here.

Enter FUNGOSO [*in his new outfit*].

---

103. the court] *Q*, *Fb*; court *Fa*.   104. the court] *Q*; court *F.*
111. *mansuete*] *This ed.*; *manfrede Q*, *Fa*; vndertake *Fb.*   113.1. Enter
FUNGOSO] *Q*; *not in F.*   *in his new outfit*] *This ed.*; *not in Q, F.*

---

105. *faculty*] capability in general; aptitude for any special action (*OED* 1).
106. *happily*] successfully; with enjoyment.
107. *bespeak*] order.
against] in anticipation of.
111. mansuete *it for them*] conduct them personally; literally, accustom
them to the hand; tame them, render them docile or gentle. Puntarvolo's
guarantee also implies his superior status: 'I'll bring them along tamely, like
well-trained animals.' The redundant 'it' is idiomatic, a syntactical device to
emphasize a whole implied situation, as in 'He lords it over us'; the construction is frequent in nonce-formations of verbs from nouns or adjectives,
used transitively to give the verb its force, and translates as 'behaving in the
characteristic manner of' (Partridge, *Syntax*, p. 36). For similar construc-
tions, see 5.2.58: 'What, and shall we see him clown it?'
My reconstruction of *Q*'s *manfrede*, generally agreed to be either a printer's
error or a lost allusion, is partly confirmed by my examination of a page of
Jonson's autograph manuscript of *MQ* (British Library, Royal MS 18 A.14,
F3). Jonson habitually used a modified secretary hand, writing v for u, except
in initial position, and making little clear distinction of letters in words
formed from several minims; hence, the ease with which one might confuse
u with r, for example. He also used the long s, easily confused with p or f.
He used the secretary e inconsistently in the median position; such an e followed closely by t might be mistaken for d, and in any case he was not always
careful to close his d. The Latinate *mansuete* was in use in various contexts;
cf. Browne, 3.23, describing the unicorn as 'a tame and mansuete animal';
for other citations see *OED*. For a fuller argument see Ostovich, '"Manfrede"?: Reconstruction of a Misprint in Jonson's *Every Man Out of His
Humour* (1600)', *N&Q* 36.3 (September 1989): 320–1.

Sogliardo. What, nephew!

Fungoso. Uncle, God save you. Did you see a gentleman, one   115
   Monsieur Brisk? He goes in such a suit as I do.

Sogliardo. Here is the gentleman, nephew, but not in such a
   suit.

Fungoso. Another suit!   *He swoons.*

Sogliardo. How now, nephew?   120

Fastidius. [*To Fungoso*] Would you speak to me, sir?

Carlo. Ay, when he has recovered himself, poor poll.

Puntarvolo. Some *rosa-solis*!

Macilente. [*To Fungoso, who is reviving*] How now, signor?

Fungoso. I am not well, sir.   125

Macilente. Why, this it is, to dog the fashion.

Carlo. Nay, come, gentlemen. Remember your affairs. His
   disease is nothing but the flux of apparel.

Puntarvolo. [*To Servingmen*] Sirs, return to the lodging. Keep
   the cat safe. I'll be the dog's guardian myself.   130
                              Exit Servingmen [*and cat*].

Sogliardo. Nephew, will you go to the court with us? These
   gentlemen and I are for the court. Nay, be not so
   melancholy.

Fungoso. By God's lid, I think no man in Christendom has
   that rascally fortune that I have.   135

Macilente. Faith, your suit is well enough, signor.

Fungoso. Nay, not for that, I protest, but I had an errand to
   Monsieur Fastidius, and I have forgot it.

130.1.] *Q; not in F.*   131. the court] *Q; court F. So too at ll. 132.*

---

122. *poor poll*] i.e., parrot, because of his unintelligent copying or mimicry
of others. Cf. Sir Politic Would-Be in *Volp.*, also called Pol, for similar reasons.

123. rosa-solis] literally, rose of the sun; a cordial originally made from,
or flavoured with, the juice of the sundew plant; later, brandy or other spirits
were added (*OED*). Cf. *Patient Grissel* 4.2.203, where it is used to revive the
shocked Grissel; or Dekker's *News from Gravesend* (1604), 1.78–9: 'drink off
this draught of *Rosa solis* to fetch life into them again, after their so often
swooning' (Hoy, 1.170).

126. *to dog*] to follow pertinaciously.

127. *Remember your affairs*] Remember the plot under way against Saviolina, and don't get distracted by Fungoso's humour.

128. *flux*] in the context of *disease*: (*a*) discharge (of humours, etc.) (*OED*
2); (*b*) abnormally copious flow, usually of blood, excrement, etc. from the
bowels or other organs, associated with dysentery (*OED* 1), but here applied
to fashion. *Flux* may also refer to any state of constant fluctuation, such as
Fungoso's perpetual clothes-envy.

Macilente. Why, go along to the court with us and remember
    it.—Come. Gentlemen, you three take one boat, and   140
    Sogliardo and I will take another. We shall be there
    instantly.
Fastidius. Content. [*To Fungoso*] Good sir, vouchsafe us your
    pleasance.
Puntarvolo. Farewell, Carlo. Remember.   145
Carlo. I warrant you. Would I had one of Kemp's shoes to
    throw after you!
Puntarvolo. Good fortune will close the eyes of our jest, fear
    not, and we shall frolic.

Exeunt.

GREX

Mitis. This Macilente, signor, begins to be more sociable on   150
    a sudden, methinks, than he was before. There's some
    portent in 't, I believe.

149.1.] *Q; not in F.*

143–4. *vouchsafe . . . pleasance*] grant us the pleasure of your company.

145. *Remember*] Cf. 127. Puntarvolo echoes Carlo as a sign of their
complicity in the plot against Saviolina.

146–7. *one . . . you*] Carlo combines a theatrical reference with the tradition of throwing an old shoe after someone for good luck, a custom still
observed at weddings; cf. *2 Return from Parnassus* 1.4.433, and Dent, S372.
One comic routine for which Kemp (an original shareholder at the Globe)
was noted apparently involved farcically large slippers. Wilhelm Creizenach,
The English Drama in the Age of Shakespeare (1916; trans./rpt New York, 1967)
mentions an English clown, Sackville, at the Frankfort Fair in 1597, wearing
'shoon, neither of which pincheth him a whit', i.e., imitating Kemp's large
shoes. Chambers (3.362) adds that, when the Chamberlain's Men moved
into the Globe, Kemp may have been playing at the Curtain in the comedy
described by Thomas Platter 'in which a servant took off his shoe and threw
it at his master, . . . a bit of common-form stage clownery'. On the other
hand, Gifford suggests that Kemp himself might have played Carlo at the
Globe, 'though his name does not appear among the performers'. The most
likely explanation is that Jonson inserted a pre-publication reference to
Kemp's *Nine Days' Wonder*, recounting the morris dance to Norwich in 1600,
and entered just two weeks before *EMO* in the Stationers' Register. As Bruce
Boehrer points out, this quip ironically mocks Puntarvolo for his money-
making travel plan to Constantinople, as well as for this much less impressive 'voyage' to Whitehall. See 'The Case of Will Kemp's Shoes', *BJJ* 7
(2000):271–95, esp. 280–3.

148–9.] Good luck will prevent anyone from seeing through our prank,
don't worry, and we'll have fun.

Cordatus. O, he's a fellow of a strange nature. Now does he,
in this calm of his humour, plot and store up a world of
malicious thoughts in his brain till he is so full with 'em   155
that you shall see the very torrent of his envy break forth
and, against the course of all their affections, oppose itself
so violently that you will almost have wonder to think
how 'tis possible the current of their dispositions shall
receive so quick and strong an alteration.   160

Mitis. Ay, marry, sir, this is that on which my expectation has
dwelt all this while. For I must tell you, signor, though I
was loath to interrupt the scene, yet I made it a question
in mine own private discourse how he should properly
call it *Every Man Out of His Humour*, when I saw all his   165
actors so strongly pursue and continue their humours.

Cordatus. Why, therein his art appears most full of lustre and
approacheth nearest the life, especially when, in the flame
and height of their humours, they are laid flat. It fills the
eye better, and with more contentment. How tedious a   170
sight were it to behold a proud, exalted tree lopped and
cut down by degrees when it might be felled in a moment!
And to set the axe to it before it came to that pride and
fullness were as not to have it grow.

Mitis. Well, I shall long till I see this fall you talk of.   175

Cordatus. To help your longing, signor, let your imagination

156–7. forth and,] *Q;* forth like a land-floud: and, *F.*

154–9. *calm . . . torrent . . . course . . . current*] Jonson retrieves this image
of the torrent and violent alteration at the beginning of 5.4, especially 12–19.
Dowgate Torrent was a channel of floodwater running to the watergate at
the bottom of Dowgate Hill; according to Stow, p. 34, 'after a strong shower
of rain', the water ran to the Thames 'with such a violent swiftness, as no
man could rescue or stay' anyone who fell in, and by the time the unfortunate reached the watergate, he would be 'drowned, and stark dead'
(Chalfant). Cf. Asper's definition of true humour, Ind.86–107.

157. *their affections*] the passionate emotions aroused by his malicious
thoughts.

164. *discourse*] process of reasoning or understanding (*OED* 2).

168. *nearest the life*] with verisimilitude.

171. *exalted*] lofty, great.

172. *in a moment*] all at once; with one blow.

173–4. *And . . . grow*] And to proceed to the catastrophe immediately,
before all the various humours are at their proud height, would be to frustrate the whole design of comedy.

be swifter than a pair of oars, and, by this, suppose
Puntarvolo, Brisk, Fungoso, and the dog arrived at the
court gate, and going up to the great chamber. Macilente
and Sogliardo, we'll leave them on the water till possibil-   180
ity and natural means may land 'em. Here come the gallants. Now, prepare your expectation.

179. *great chamber*] great hall.

Act 5

ACT 5   SCENE I

Enter PUNTARVOLO, FASTIDIUS BRISK,
FUNGOSO, *and the dog.*

Puntarvolo. Come, lordings. [*To Fungoso*] Signor, you are sufficiently instructed?

Fastidius. Who? I, sir?

Puntarvolo. [*Indicating Fungoso*] No, this gentleman. But stay:
I take thought how to bestow my dog. He is no compe-   5
tent attendant for the presence.

Fastidius. Mass, that's true indeed, knight. You must not carry
him into the presence.

Puntarvolo. I know it, and I, like a dull beast, forgot to bring
one of my cormorants to attend me.   10

Fastidius. Why, you're best leave him at the porter's lodge.

Puntarvolo. Not so. His worth is too well known amongst
them to be forthcoming.

Fastidius. 'Slight, how'll you do then?

Puntarvolo. I must leave him with one that is ignorant of his   15
quality, if I will have him to be safe. And see: here comes

ACT 5 SCENE I] *Q, F* (ACTUS QUINTUS, SCENA PRIMA; *Act V. Scene I).*
0.1–2.] *Q;* PVNTARVOLO, FASTIDIVS BRISKE, FVN-/GOSO, GROOME,
MACILENTE, / SOGLIARDO. *F.*   1. lordings] *Q;* gentles *F.*   11. you're]
Q, Fa; you were *Fb.*

---

1. *lordings*] sirs, or gentlemen; frequent as a plural form of address (*OED*
1), though distinctly old-fashioned in Jonson's day.

2. *instructed*] coached to participate in the plot to present Sogliardo to
Saviolina.

10. *cormorants*] gluttons (Schmidt), an abusive term frequently used of
servants, who, their employers claimed, cost more in food than their services
were worth. Cf. Shylock's complaint that Launcelot was 'a huge feeder',
MerVen. 2.5.45. Literally, large and voracious seabirds.

13. *forthcoming*] in safe custody, ready to be produced when required
(*OED* 1).

one that will carry coals; *ergo*, will hold my dog.

Enter a Groom *with a basket.*

Honest friend, may I commit the tuition of this dog to
    thy prudent care?

Groom. You may if you please, sir.   20

Puntarvolo. Pray thee, let me find thee here at my return. It
    shall not be long till I will ease thee of thy employment
    and please thee. [*To the others*] Forth, gentles!

Fastidius. Why, but will you leave him with so slight
    command, and infuse no more charge upon the fellow?   25

Puntarvolo. Charge? No, there were no policy in that. That
    were to let him know the value of the gem he holds, and
    so to tempt frail nature against her disposition. [*To
    Groom*] No, pray thee, let thy honesty be sweet and short.

Groom. Yes, sir.   30

Puntarvolo. [*To the others*] But hark you, gallants, and chiefly
    Monsieur Brisk. When we come in eyeshot of this lady,
    let not other matters carry us from our project, but, if we
    can, single her forth to some place.

Fastidius. I warrant you.   35

17.1.] *In Q appears after l. 19; not in F.*   29. sweet and short] *Q;* sweet, as
it shall be short *F.*

---

   17. *carry coals*] The task of the meanest drudges in great houses was to
transport charcoal; hence, (*a*) do any dirty work; (*b*) endure any insult. The
Groom is not necessarily carrying coals on stage, as *H&S* suggest; he is
merely identified as a servant of the lowest status.
   ergo] therefore (Latin).
   hold my dog] a degrading job: see 39–47, and Carlo's dig at Puntarvolo as
'a yeoman fewterer', 2.1.378. 'To give one the dog to hold' proverbially meant
to serve one a nasty trick (J. Ray, *A Compleat Collection of English Proverbs*,
London, 1768).
   17.1. *Groom*] manservant, not limited in the seventeenth century to a
stable-hand.
   18. *Honest*] good, trustworthy.
   tuition] safe-keeping, protection, or custody (*OED* 1).
   23. *please thee*] i.e., give you a tip.
   gentles] gentlemen.
   25. *infuse*] impart (a Latinism).
   charge] (*a*) responsibility for a burden or trouble undertaken; (*b*) admo-
nition; in law, an official instruction (*OED* 15).
   26. *policy*] prudent strategy, expedient procedure (*OED* 4).
   28. *against her disposition*] against a natural inclination to be honest.

320   EVERY MAN OUT OF HIS HUMOUR   [ACT 5

Puntarvolo. And be not too sudden, but let the device induce
    itself with good circumstance. On!
Fungoso. Is this the way? Good truth, here be fine hangings.

              Exeunt PUNTARVOLO, BRISK, [*and*] FUNGOSO.

Groom. 'Honesty'? 'Sweet and short'? Marry, it shall, sir,
    doubt you not; for, even at this instant, if one would give   40
    me twenty pounds, I would not deliver him: there's for
    the 'sweet'. But now, if any man come offer me but
    twopence, he shall have him: there's for the 'short' now.
    'Sblood, what a mad, humorous gentleman is this, to
    leave his dog with me! I could run away with him now,   45
    an he were worth anything. Well, I pray God send him
    quickly again.

              Enter MACILENTE *and* SOGLIARDO.

Macilente. Come on, signor. Now prepare to court this all-
    witted lady most naturally and like yourself.
Sogliardo. Faith, an you say the word, I'll begin to her in   50
    tobacco.
Macilente. O, fie on 't, no. You shall begin with 'How does
    my sweet lady?' or 'Why are you so melancholy,
    madam?'—though she be very merry, it's all one. Be sure
    to kiss your hand often enough. Pray for her health, and   55

38.1.] *Q; not in F.*   44. 'Sblood] *Q;* Slid *F.*   47.1.] *Q; not in F.*

36–7. *induce . . . circumstance*] seem plausible, arise naturally out of the
situation.
38. *hangings*] tapestries. Fungoso is impressed by the decor.
39–47.] The groom's remarks are based on the before-and-after picture
he sets up with 'even at this instant . . . But now': 'Up to now I would not
have given the dog to anyone but Puntarvolo, even if others had offered me
twenty pounds. But now (since Puntarvolo has been so patronizing) anyone
else can have the dog for twopence'. The groom is angry but not seriously
intending to betray this unwanted trust; therefore, he hopes the dog's owner
will return quickly so that he won't be tempted to act on this just-vented
petulance.
41. *deliver him*] hand the dog over.
46–7. *send . . . again*] send Puntarvolo back again quickly (with the
promised tip).
49. *naturally . . . yourself*] (*a*) informally, without artifice; (*b*) just like the
natural-born fool that you are. The advice is 'Be yourself'; the joke depends
on Sogliardo's not realizing that being himself (a rustic boor) is no advantage with a court lady. The whole of 5.2 depends on his smug complacency
at being himself.

tell her how 'more than most fair' she is. Screw your face
at one side thus [*Demonstrating*] and protest—let her fleer
and look askance, and hide her teeth with her fan when
she laughs a fit—to bring her into more matter: that's
nothing. You must talk forward (though it be without   60
sense, so it be without blushing); 'tis most courtlike and
well.
Sogliardo. But shall I not use tobacco at all?
Macilente. O, by no means! 'Twill but make your breath suspected and that you use it only to confound the rankness   65
of that.
Sogliardo. Nay, I'll be advised, sir, by my friends.
Macilente. God's my life, see where Sir Puntar's dog is!
Groom. I would the gentleman would return for his follower
here. I'll leave him to his fortunes else.   70
Macilente. [*Aside*] 'Sheart, 'twere the only jest in the world to

---

56–60. *Screw . . . nothing*] Macilente is attempting to say two sentences at
once; consequently, the one interupts the other. One sentence is an instruction: 'Screw your face at one side, thus, and protest [i.e., vow your devo-
tion], to bring her into more matter [to prompt her to further replies]'. The
other is a warning of anticipated behaviour: 'Let her fleer [scoff, sneer] and
look askance, and hide her teeth with her fan when she laughs a fit'. The
final comment, 'That's nothing', may cap either sentence, or both: that is,
Sogliardo's facial expressions and oaths are nothing, mere social tricks that
require neither worry nor thoughtful preparation; and the lady's reactions
are nothing that should put him off as a courtier; they are not to be inter-
preted as critical or mocking.
    56–7. *Screw . . . side*] Macilente describes the courtly affectation termed
'the oblique leer, or the Janus' in *CR* 5.4.233; 'Janus . . . look a-squint', in
Westward Ho! 5.1.260–1. See 1.2.204 and 3.1.434 for other Janus references
in which facial expression may also play a part.
    59. *laughs a fit*] (a) affects a musical laugh: *fit* meaning 'melody' was
current in the sixteenth and seventeenth centuries (*OED, Fit* sb.1, 2); (b)
laughs on a capricious impulse or humour (*OED, Fit* sb.², 4e); (c) bursts out
laughing (*OED* 4f): unseemly behaviour in one striving for courtly
elegance.
    60. *forward*] (a) continuously, without hesitation; (b) eagerly; (c) in a pejo-
rative sense, boldly and pertly.
    65–6. *confound . . . that*] cover up your bad breath.
    67.] I want to be guided by my friends' opinions.
    69. *his follower*] his dog.
    70. *him*] the dog.
    71. *only*] best.

poison him now. Ha! By God's will, I'll do it, if I could
but get him of the fellow.—Signor Sogliardo, walk aside,
and think upon some device to entertain the lady with.

Sogliardo. So I do, sir.   *Sogliardo walks off, meditating.*   75

Macilente. [*To Groom*] How now, mine honest friend? Whose
   dog-keeper art thou?

Groom. Dog-keeper, sir? I hope I scorn that, i' faith.

Macilente. Why? Dost thou not keep a dog?

Groom. Sir, now I do—(*Throws off the dog.*)—and now I do   80
   not. I think this be sweet and short. Make me his dog-
   keeper?   *Exit.*

Macilente. This is excellent above expectation. [*To the dog*]
   Nay, stay, sir. You'd be travelling, but I'll give you a dram
   shall shorten your voyage: here. [*He poisons the dog.*] So,   85
   sir, I'll be bold to take my leave of you. Now to the Turk's
   court in the devil's name, for you shall never go on God's
   name.   *Kicks him out.*
   Sogliardo! Come.

Sogliardo. I ha' 't, i' faith, will sting it.   90

Macilente. Take heed you lose it not, signor, ere you come
   there. Preserve it.

                                              Exeunt.

---

75. SD] *Q; not in F.*   80. SD] *Throwes off the Dogge, & Exit. Q, not parenthetical, on a separate line after l. 83; Hee throwes / off the dogge. In margin of F.*
82. SD] *Q (see previous note); not in F.*   88. SD] *In Q appears in square brackets; not in F.*

71–2. *to poison him*] The suggestion would not have shocked Jonson's
audience unduly. Customarily in times of plague, all dogs found in the streets
were killed for fear of infection, and dog-killers received a bounty. But the
licence to kill excluded dogs held on a leash (McKerrow, 4.164). Here, the
dog is the 'carrier' for Puntarvolo's 'plague' of humour.

73. *of the fellow*] away from the groom.

77. *dog-keeper*] with a suggestion of pimp, especially for homosexuals.
Rainolds, *The Overthrow of Stage-Plays* (1599), blames theatres and trans-
vestism on stage for inciting homosexual affairs: 'he who condemneth the
female whore and male, and detesting specially the male by terming him a
dog . . . might well control likewise the means and occasions whereby men
are transformed into dogs' (Williams).

87. *on*] in.

90.] I have a witty device that will cover up any social breach (*sting*, in Mid-
lands dialect, meant 'repair the thatch', using the pointed tool called a *sting*; cf.
OED v.2). The clumsy rusticity of the claim puts the wittiness in some doubt.

91. *it*] Sogliardo's witty device.

GREX

Cordatus. How like you this first exploit of his?

Mitis. O, a piece of true envy! But I expect the issue of the
other device.   95

Cordatus. Here they come, will make it appear.

ACT 5   SCENE 2

Enter PUNTARVOLO, SAVIOLINA, FASTIDIUS BRISK,
[*and*] FUNGOSO.

Saviolina. Why, I thought, Sir Puntarvolo, you had been gone
your voyage.

92.1.] *Q; not in* F.

ACT 5 SCENE 2] *Q,* F *(SCENA SECUNDA; Act V. Scene II).*   0.1–2.] *Q;*
SAVIOLINA, PVNTARVOLO, FASTIDIVS / BRISKE, FVNGOSO, / MACILENTE,
SOGLIARDO. *In margin: To them.* F.

94. *envy*] malice.
94–5. *expect . . . device*] am looking forward to the outcome of the other
plot against Sogliardo and Saviolina.
96. *will*] who will.
5.2.] The practical joke on Saviolina derives from Castiglione's *The
Courtier*, trans. Hoby (1561), Y3v–Y4, a 'merry prank' that 'was wrought unto
a couple of great ladies' concerning a handsome cowherd from Bergamo
who, when dressed in fine clothes, seemed to be a gentleman, provided he
kept his mouth shut: 'And so when those two ladies were informed that there
was arrived . . . a very witty man, a musician, a dancer and the best courtier
in all Spain, they longed very much to speak with him, and sent inconti-
nently for him, and after they had received him honorably, they caused him
to sit down, and began to entertain him with a very great respect in the presence of all men, and few there were present that knew him not to be a Bergomask cowherd. Therefore seeing those ladies entertain him with such respect,
and honour him so much, they fell all in a-laughing, the more because the
silly fellow spake still his native language, the mere Bergamask tongue. But
the gentlemen that devised this prank had first told those ladies that among
other things he was a great dissembler and spake all tongues excellently well,
and especially the country speech of Lombardy, so that they thought he
feigned, and many times they beheld the one the other with certain marvel-
lings, and said: What a wonderful matter is this, how he counterfeiteth this
tongue! In conclusion this communication lasted so long that every man's
sides ached for laughing, and he could not choose himself but utter so many
tokens of his nobleness of birth, that at length those ladies (but with much
ado) believed he was the man that he was indeed' (*H&S*, citing Bang).

Puntarvolo. Dear and most amiable lady, your divine beauties
do bind me to those offices that I cannot depart when I
would.   5
Saviolina. 'Tis most courtlike spoken, sir. But how might we
do to have a sight of your dog and cat?
Fastidius. His dog's in the court, lady.
Saviolina. And not your cat? How dare you trust her behind
you, sir?   10
Puntarvolo. Troth, madam, she hath sore eyes, and she doth
keep her chamber. Marry, I have left her under sufficient
guard. There are two of my hinds to attend her.
Saviolina. I'll give you some water for her eyes. When do you
go, sir?   15
Puntarvolo. Certes, sweet lady, I know not.
Fastidius. He doth stay the rather, madam, to present your
acute judgement with so courtly and well-parted a
gentleman as yet your ladyship hath never seen.
Saviolina. What's he, gentle Monsieur Brisk? Not that   20
gentleman?   [*Indicating Fungoso*]
Fastidius. No, lady, this is a kinsman of Justice Silence.
Puntarvolo. Pray, sir, give me leave to report him. He's a
gentleman, lady, of that rare and admirable faculty as, I

---

8. dog's] *Q;* dogge is *F.*   13. hinds] *Q;* followers *F.*   22. of] *Q;* to *F.*

3. *amiable*] worthy of being loved; cf. 2.1.265.
4. *offices*] courtly services, attentions.
8. *court*] courtyard.
9. *behind*] left behind.
14. *I'll . . . eyes*] One of the attributes of the female courtier was skill
at medicines. This is parodied more fully in Lady Politic Would-Be,
Volp. 3.4.
16. *Certes*] certainly, assuredly (archaic, from Old French).
22. *kinsman of Justice Silence*] i.e., provincial lawyer. Justice Shallow, in
2H4, is Justice Silence's cousin (3.2.3–4), both former law-students of rustic
origins who became inept country justices. Fungoso is akin to them in status-
seeking. Dekker, in *Satiromastix* 2.2.135, similarly refers to 'these true heirs
of Master Justice Shallow'. Cf. *Disc.* 716–18, concerning shallow minds: 'You
may sound these wits, and find the depth of them, with your middle finger.
They are *cream-bowl*, or but puddle deep.'
23. *report him*] describe Sogliardo, the so-called courtly gentleman.

protest, I know not his like in Europe. He is exceedingly   25
valiant, an excellent scholar, and so exactly travelled that
he is able in discourse to deliver you a model of any
prince's court in the world; speaks the languages with
that purity of phrase and facility of accent that it breeds
astonishment; his wit, the most exuberant and—above   30
wonder!—pleasant of all that ever entered the concave of
this ear.

Fastidius. 'Tis most true, lady. Marry, he is no such excellent
proper man.

Puntarvolo. His travels have changed his complexion, madam.   35

Saviolina. O Sir Puntarvolo, you must think every man was
not born to have my servant Brisk's feature.

Puntarvolo. But that which transcends all, lady: he doth so
peerlessly imitate any manner of person for gesture,
action, passion, or whatever—   40

Fastidius. Ay, especially a rustic or a clown, madam, that it is
not possible for the sharpest-sighted wit in the world to
discern any sparks of the gentleman in him when he
does it.

Saviolina. O Monsieur Brisk, be not so tyrannous to confine   45
all wits within the compass of your own. Not find the
'sparks' of a gentleman in him, if he be a gentleman?

Fungoso. No, in truth, sweet lady, I believe you cannot.

---

44. does it] *Q, Fb;* does *Fa.*

---

26. *so exactly*] with such careful attention to detail (*OED* 2).

33-4. *no . . . man*] not a conventionally handsome man. Sogliardo has
been described as 'an essential clown' (Chars.74) and as not having a 'good
countenance' (4.3.307n).

35. *complexion*] the combination of the four humours of the body in a
certain proportion; hence, the physical constitution (*OED* 1, 2). Also,
Sogliardo's appearance; see previous note.

36-7. *every . . . born*] that not every man was born.

37. *feature*] bodily form, implying exquisite or well-made elegance. The
singular was used commonly until the late seventeenth century with the same
meaning as the plural used now; in the restrictive sense of 'lineaments of the
face', the singular was used as late as 1887 in Trollope (Partridge, *Accidence*,
p. 23).

45-6. *be . . . own*] don't presume to judge others' wit by your own.

Saviolina. Do you believe so? Why, I can find sparks of a
gentleman in you, sir.   50
Puntarvolo. Ay, he is a gentleman, madam, and a reveller.
Fungoso. Indeed, I think I have seen your ladyship at our
revels.
Saviolina. Like enough, sir. But would I might see this
wonder you talk of. May one have a sight of him for any   55
reasonable sum?
Puntarvolo. Yes, madam. He will arrive presently.
Saviolina. What, and shall we see him clown it?
Fastidius. I' faith, sweet lady, that you shall. See, here he
comes.   60

Enter MACILENTE *with* SOGLIARDO.

Puntarvolo. This is he. Pray observe him, lady.
Saviolina. Beshrew me, he clowns it properly indeed.
Puntarvolo. Nay, mark his courtship.
Sogliardo. How does my sweet lady? [*He takes her hand.*] Hot
and moist? Beautiful and lusty? Ha?   65
Saviolina. Beautiful, an it please you, sir, but not lusty.
Sogliardo. Oho, lady, it pleases you to say so, in truth! And

60.1.] *Q; not in F.*

---

51. *reveller*] law-student. Beaumont, in his burlesque 'Grammar Lecture'
at the Inner Temple, *c.* 1601, defined three classes of students: young students, equivalent to naive freshmen; revellers, the sophisticated, upper-class
dilettantes; and plodders, the serious students who intended to make law
their careers. Cf. Mark Eccles, 'Francis Beaumont's *Grammar Lecture*', *RES*
16 (1940): 402–14. To be called a reveller implied desirable social status. See
notes at Chars.67 and 3.2.30–5.
53. *revels*] Inns of Court festivities, to which members of the royal court
would be invited.
58. *shall . . . clown it?*] shall we watch him play the clown?; idiomatic construction frequent with nonce-formations of verbs from nouns. The neutral
'it' was supplied as object to give the borrowed verb its force, there being no
suffix to distinguish it from the noun; cf. 'fast it', *EMI* (*F*) 5.5.52; 'wanton
it', *SW* 5.1.28 (Partridge, *Syntax*, p. 36).
64–5. *Hot and moist?*] the dominant humours for lechery, supposed to be
indicated by the palm; cf. *Oth.* 3.4.35ff.: 'Hot, hot, and moist, this hand of
yours requires / A sequester from liberty . . . / For here's a young and sweating devil here, / That commonly rebels'.
65. *lusty*] (*a*) beautiful, pleasant (*OED* 2); (*b*) full of sexual desire (*OED*
4). Saviolina denies the second implication at 66.
67. *it . . . so*] Cf. one of Orange's catch-phrases, 3.1.46, 174.

how does my sweet lady? In health? *Bona roba, quaeso que novelles? Que novelles?* Sweet creature.

Saviolina. O, excellent! Why, gallants, is this he that cannot   70
be deciphered? They were very blear-witted, i' faith, that
could not discern the gentleman in him.

Puntarvolo. But do you? In earnest, lady?

Saviolina. Do I, sir? Why, if you had any true court-
judgement, in the carriage of his eye and that inward   75
power that forms his countenance you might perceive his
counterfeiting as clear as the noonday. Alas! Nay, if you
would have tried my wit indeed, you should never have
told me he was a gentleman, but presented him for a true
clown indeed, and then have seen if I could have deci-   80
phered him.

Fastidius. 'Fore God, her ladyship says true, knight. But does
he not affect the clown most naturally, mistress?

Puntarvolo. O, she cannot but affirm that, out of the bounty
of her judgement.   85

Saviolina. Nay, out of doubt he does well, for a gentleman, to
imitate, but I warrant you he becomes his natural carriage of the gentleman much better than his clownery.

Fastidius. 'Tis strange, in truth, her ladyship should see so far
into him.   90

Puntarvolo. Ay, is 't not?

Saviolina. Faith, as easily as may be! Not decipher him, quoth
you?

Fungoso. Good sadness, I wonder at it.

Macilente. Why, has she deciphered him, gentlemen?   95

---

77. Alas! Nay] *This ed.;* Alas; Nay *Q;* Alas—Nay *F.*

---

68. Bona roba] from Italian, *buona roba,* 'good stuff', slang for a wench,
but commodifying her as if pricing the material of her dress (Florio).

68–9. quaeso que novelles?] 'I ask what news?' (fractured Italian). The
question 'What news?' frequently opened jigs or satiric skits on current
events, especially as part of Inns of Court revels or mock-rules like the *Prince
D'Amour* (Baskervill, *Jig,* pp. 59–63).

71. *blear-witted*] dim-witted.

78. *tried*] tested.

83. *naturally*] (*a*) realistically, as though born to it; (*b*) like a 'natural' or
half-wit.

87–8. *carriage*] bodily deportment, mien.

94. *Good sadness*] in sober truth.

Puntarvolo. O, most miraculously and beyond admiration!

Macilente. Is 't possible?

Fastidius. She hath given most infallible signs of the gentleman in him, that's certain.

Saviolina. Why, gentlemen, let me laugh at you a little. Was   100
this your device, to try my judgement in a gentleman?

Macilente. Nay, lady, do not scorn us, though you have this
gift of perspicacy above others. What if he should be no
gentleman now, but a clown indeed, lady? Would not your
ladyship be out of your humour?   105

Fastidius. O, but she knows it is not so.

Saviolina. What if he were not a man, ye may as well say! Nay,
if your worships could gull me so indeed, you were wiser
than you are taken for.

Macilente. In good faith, lady, he is a very perfect clown, both   110
by father and mother. That I'll assure you.

Saviolina. O sir, you are very pleasurable.

Macilente. Nay, do but look on his hand, and that shall resolve
you. Look you, lady, what a palm here is.

> [*He shows her Sogliardo's hand.*]

Sogliardo. Tut, that was with holding the plough.   115

Macilente. The plough! Did you discern any such thing in
him, madam?

Fastidius. Faith, no, she saw the gentleman as bright as at
noonday, she. She deciphered him at first.

---

98. given] *Q;* gather'd *F.*   113. *his hand*] *Q;* this hand *F.*

---

98. *given*] given statement or proof of; uttered before witnesses; discerned
and imparted knowledge of (*OED* 23, 25, 29). *F*'s 'gather'd' suggests, rather,
that she has simply drawn certain inferences, which may or may not be
correct and which she may alter if she so chooses. *Q*'s wording implies that
she will not, or cannot, revise her opinion now. Either word traps the lady.

103. *perspicacy*] clear-sightedness, discernment.

108. *gull*] deceive, trick. Cf. 1.2.5n.

112. *pleasurable*] jocular, mirthful.

113–14. *resolve you*] resolve the matter for you.

119. *at first*] from the first, at once. Usage of the article varies; cf.
1.2.102–3, 'you must keep your men gallant at the first', where modern
English might be disposed to drop the article, because *at first* suggests a contrast to action taken later. The same problem recurs in official titles, like
'justice of peace', 1.2.19–20, where modern usage retains the article (Partridge, *Syntax*, p. 97).

Macilente. Troth, I am sorry your ladyship's sight should be   120
    so suddenly struck.

Saviolina. O, you're goodly beagles!   [*She starts to leave.*]

Fastidius. What, is she gone?

Sogliardo. Nay, stay, sweet lady! *Que novelles? Que novelles?*

Saviolina. Out, you fool, you!   *Exit* SAVIOLINA.   125

Fungoso. She's out of her humour, i' faith.

Fastidius. Nay, let's follow it while 'tis hot, gentlemen.

Puntarvolo. Come! On mine honour, we'll make her blush in
    the presence. My spleen is great with laughter.

Macilente. [*Aside*] Your laughter will be a child of a feeble life,   130
    I believe, sir. [*To Fungoso*] Come, signor, your looks are
    too dejected, methinks. Why mix you not mirth with the
    rest?

Fungoso. By God's will, this suit frets me at the soul. I'll have
    it altered tomorrow sure.   135

Exeunt.

Enter SHIFT.

Shift. I am come to the court to meet with my Countenance,
    Sogliardo. Poor men must be glad of such countenance,
    when they can get no better. Well, need may insult upon
    a man, but it shall never make him despair of conse-
    quence. The world will say 'tis base. Tush, base! 'Tis base   140

---

125. SD] *Q; not in F.*   128. we'll] *Q; wee shall F.*   135.1.] *Q; not in F.*
135.2.] *Q; Act V. Scene III. /* SHIFT, / FASTIDIVS, PVNTARVOLO,
SOGLIARDO,/ FVNGOSO, MACILENTE. *In margin: To them. F.*

---

122. *beagles*] term of abuse, based on the idea of hunting down game in
packs. Cf. *Sej.* 2.410–13: '*Sabinus.* How is it, that these beagles haunt the
house / Of Agrippina? *Arruntius.* O, they hunt, they hunt. / There is some
game here lodged, which they must rouse, / To make the great-ones sport.'
See also Dekker, *Gull's Horn-book* 2.251: 'be thou a beagle to them all, and
never lin snuffing, till you have scented them'.

124. *Que novelles?*] What news?

129. *spleen*] regarded as the seat of laughter or mirth *c.* 1600, although
usually considered the *locus* of melancholy and ill-humour (*OED*).

130. *a child . . . life*] short-lived.

135.1.] *Exeunt* might normally signal a new scene, but the reappearance
of Puntarvolo and the others at 142.1–2 indicates that Shift enters here at
135.2 to fill up a brief interval while the rest have followed after Saviolina.

138. *need*] poverty.
insult upon] triumph jeeringly over; wound, humiliate.

139–40. *despair of consequence*] give up dreams of status and position.

to live under the earth, not base to live above it, by any
means.

Enter PUNTARVOLO, FASTIDIUS, SOGLIARDO,
FUNGOSO, [and] MACILENTE.

Fastidius. The poor lady is most miserably out of her humour,
i' faith.

Puntarvolo. There was never so witty a jest broken at the Tilt,   145
of all the court wits christened.

Macilente. [*Aside*] O, this applause taints it foully.

Sogliardo. I think I did my part in courting. [*Seeing Shift*] O
Resolution!

Puntarvolo. [*Looking around for the Groom*] Ay me, my dog!   150

Macilente. Where is he?

Fastidius. [*To Fungoso*] God's precious, go seek the fellow,
good signor!

Sends away FUNGOSO.

Puntarvolo. Here, here I left him.

Macilente. Why, none was here when we came in now but   155
Cavalier Shift. Inquire of him.

Fastidius. [*To Shift*] Did you see Sir Puntarvolo's dog here,
cavalier, since you came?

Shift. His dog, sir? He may look his dog, sir. I see none of his
dog, sir.   160

142.1–2.] *Q; not in F.*   153.1–2.] *Q; not in F.*   159. see] *Q;* saw *F.*

140–1. *'Tis . . . it*] It's base to be dead and buried, not base to find a way
of living. The sentiment puns on *base* as physically low (underground) and
morally low.

145. *the Tilt*] the Tilt Yard, the sports field near Whitehall Palace where
courtiers could 'exercise themselves in jousting, tourn[ey]ing, and fighting
at barriers' (Stow, 2.101). See 3.1.462.

146. *christened*] i.e., who were ever born.

147.] O, all this self-congratulation by courtiers spoils or discredits the
joke against courtly affectations. *Taints* means 'breaks (a lance) in tilting'
(*OED* 5b); Macilente continues the tilting metaphor ('so witty a jest broken')
begun by Puntarvolo in the previous speech.

148–50. *O Resolution! . . . dog!*] The simultaneous recognitions have an
apparently fortuitous appositeness in their equation of followers.

159–60.] A truculent reply, based on the insult implied in holding dogs
(cf. 5.1.17n) and on Shift's reputation as a 'tall man', which he tacitly
defends.

159. *look*] look for.

Macilente. Upon my life, he hath stolen your dog, sir, and
 been hired to it by some that have ventured with you. You
 may guess by his peremptory answers.

Puntarvolo. Not unlike, for he hath been a notorious thief
 by his own confession. [*To Shift*] Sirrah, where's my   165
 dog?

Shift. Charge me with your dog, sir? I ha' none of your dog,
 sir.

Puntarvolo. Villain, thou liest!

 > [*Puntarvolo and Shift threaten each other.*]

Shift. Lie, sir? 'Sblood, you're but a man, sir!   170

Puntarvolo. Rogue and thief, restore him!

Sogliardo. Take heed, Sir Puntarvolo, what you do. He'll bear
 no coals, I can tell you—of my word!

Macilente. [*Aside*] This is rare.

Sogliardo. [*To Puntarvolo*] It's mar'l he stabs you not. By this   175
 light, he hath stabbed forty for forty times less matter, I
 can tell you, of my knowledge.

Puntarvolo. [*To Shift*] I will make thee stoop, thou abject!

Sogliardo. Make him stoop, sir!—Gentlemen, pacify him, or
 he'll be killed!   180

Macilente. Is he so tall a man?

Sogliardo. Tall a man? If you love his life, stand betwixt 'em.
 Make him stoop!

Puntarvolo. My dog, villain, or I will hang thee! Thou hast
 confessed robberies and other felonious acts to this   185
 gentleman, thy Countenance—

---

165. where's] *Q;* where is *F.*   173. of] *Q;* o' *F.*

---

161. *he*] Shift.

165. *Sirrah*] insulting address, as to a menial.

169–70. *thou liest! / Lie, sir?*] To give one the lie (*mentita*) is a provocation
to a duel, inviting the challenge (Bryson, p. 111). See 5.3.86–91.

170. *you're . . . man*] i.e., you are merely a man, and I could kill you for
that insult.

172–3. *bear no coals*] accept no insult.

173. *of*] on.

175. *It's mar'l*] It's a marvel that (colloquial).

178. *stoop*] (*a*) thieves' cant for 'yield', 'confess' (Judges); (*b*) said of a dog
putting its nose to the ground to find a scent (*OED* 1e); (*c*) bow or humble
oneself to a superior power (*OED* 2, 7).

180. *he'll be killed*] Puntarvolo will be killed.

Sogliardo. I'll bear no witness.

Puntarvolo. —and, without my dog, I will hang thee for
   them.   *Shift kneels.*

Sogliardo. What? Kneel to thine enemy?   190

Shift. Pardon me, good sir. God is my judge, I never did
   robbery in all my life.

> *Enter* FUNGOSO.

Fungoso. O Sir Puntarvolo, your dog lies giving up the ghost
   in the Woodyard.

Macilente. [*Aside*] 'Sblood, is he not dead yet?   195

Puntarvolo. O my dog, born to disastrous fortune! Pray you,
   conduct me, sir.

> *Exit* PUNTARVOLO, *with* FUNGOSO.

Sogliardo. How? Did you never do any robbery in your life?

Macilente. [*Aside*] O, this is good. [*To Sogliardo*] So he swore,
   sir.   200

Sogliardo. Ay, I heard him. And did you swear true, sir?

Shift. Ay, as God shall have part of my soul, sir, I ne'er robbed
   any man, I; never stood by the highwayside, sir, but
   only said so because I would get myself a name and be
   counted a tall man.   205

---

189. SD] *Q; in margin of F.*   191. judge] *Q;* witness *F.*   192.1.] *Q; in
margin of F: Fungoso return'd.*   195. 'Sblood] *Q;* Heart *F.*   197.1.] *Q; not
in F.*   201. Ay, I] *Q, F (*I, I*).*   202. as God shall have part of my soul,
sir] *Parenthetical in Q; (*as I hope to be forgiuen, sir*) F*   203. man, I;] *This
ed.;* man I; *Q;* man, I *F.*

---

194. *Woodyard*] the area for chopping and storing wood, adjacent to the
Whitehall kitchen and out-buildings (bake-houses, brewery, charcoal house,
etc.), at the north of the palace along the Thames.

196. *O . . . fortune!*] Besides its parody of inflated Arcadian language, this
line suggests all the proverbial effects of association with the dog-star, under
which influence, presumably, the dog was born: e.g., souring wine, rendering dogs mad, causing fish and seaweed to rise to the surface of the ocean.
Cf. Pliny, *Natural History* 2.40; 9.25; 14.22; 18.68. In general, the dog-star
meant fatally bad luck, as in Erasmus, *Parabolae*, p. 1289: '*canicula pestilens
est omnibus sidus*' ('the dog-star is unhealthy for all') (cited in McKerrow,
4.21).

202. *part of*] interest in, concern for, possession of (*OED* 7).

202–3. *I ne'er . . . I; never*] The emphatically repeated pronoun construction is common in Jonson; cf. 1.2.129–30; 4.3.271; 4.4.16. The emphatic *never*
after the semicolon indicates that it begins a new syntactical unit.

Sogliardo. Now out, base *viliaco*! Thou, my Resolution? I, thy
 Countenance?—By this light, gentlemen, he hath confessed to me the most inexorable company of robberies,
 and damned himself that he did 'em. You never heard
 the like!—Out, scoundrel, out! Follow me no more, I   210
 command thee! Out of my sight! Go! Hence! Speak not!
 I will not hear thee. Away, *camouccio*!
                                   [*Exit* SHIFT.]
Macilente. [*Aside*] O, how I do feed upon this now, and fat
 myself! Here were a couple unexpectedly dishumoured!
 Well, by this time, I hope Sir Puntarvolo and his dog are   215
 both out of humour to travel. [*To the others*] Nay, gentlemen, why do you not seek out the knight and comfort
 him? Our supper at the Mitre must of necessity hold
 tonight, if you love your reputations.
Fastidius. 'Fore God, I am so melancholy for his dog's disas-   220
 ter, but I'll go.
Sogliardo. Faith, and I may go too, but I know I shall be so
 melancholy.
Macilente. Tush, melancholy? You must forget that now, and
 remember you lie at the mercy of a fury: Carlo will rack   225
 your sinews asunder and rail you to dust if you come not.
                                   Exeunt.

212.1.] *Schelling; not in Q, F.*   226.1.] *Q; not in F.*

206. viliaco] common term of abuse, from the Italian '*vigliacco*': 'a rascal,
a villain, a base, vile, abject scurvy fellow, a scoundrel' (Florio). Cf. *Satiromastix* 1.1.72; and Chapman, *Sir Giles Goosecap* 3.1.154.
   208. *inexorable*] unforgivable.
   company] collection (*OED* 36).
   212. camouccio] From the Italian *camoscio*: 'a kind of stuff worn in Italy'
(Florio), but used as a slang term of contempt. Cf. Middleton, *Blurt, Master
Constable* 1.2.82–3: 'Whosoever says you have a black eye, is a *camooch*'. *H&S*
suggest that the word is 'a back-formation from "camooch"—an unhappy
attempt to quote what Jonson conjectured to be the native Italian form'.
Given that the speaker is a posturing ignoramus, it more likely continues the
fractured Italian used earlier.
   213–14. *fat myself*] proverbial; cf. 'laugh and be fat', 3.1.31.
   218. *Mitre*] the Mitre Tavern. See 3.1.160n.
   hold] be held, take place.
   225. *fury*] one of the three avenging goddesses sent from Tartarus to
avenge wrong and punish crime.
   226. rail . . . dust] pulverize you with his vituperative scolding. *Rail* means
'scold'.

Mitis. O, then their fear of Carlo, belike, makes them hold
their meeting.
Cordatus. Ay. Here he comes. Conceive him but to be entered
the Mitre, and 'tis enough.   230

ACT 5   SCENE 3

[*A table and chairs are brought on.*] *Enter* CARLO.

Carlo. Holla! Where be these shot-sharks?
Drawer. [*Calling from off-stage*] By and by.

Enter Drawer.

You're welcome, good Master Buffone.
Carlo. Where's George? Call me George hither quickly.
Drawer. What wine please you have, sir? I'll draw you that's   5
neat, Master Buffone.
Carlo. Away, neophyte! Do as I bid. Bring my dear George to
me.
[*Exit* Drawer.]
Mass, here he comes.

ACT 5 SCENE 3] *Q, F* (SCENA TERTIA; *Act V. Scene IIII*).   0.1. *Enter*
CARLO] *Q;* CARLO, DRAWER, GEORGE. *F*   2.1.] *In Q appears at end of l.*
1; not in F.   7. bid] *Q;* bid thee *F*

227. *belike*] in all likelihood, probably.
229. *Conceive him but*] only imagine him.
1. *shot-sharks*] a mild epithet for tavern waiters, the rascals (*sharks*; see
Chars.8on) who bring the tavern-bill (*shot*).
2.] The drawer's line borrows a laugh from *1H4* 2.4, recalling the practical joke Prince Hal plays on Francis, the drawer.
4. *George*] Perhaps a real name, as *H&S* suggest; '*George* the drawer at
the Mitre' is mentioned in *Westward Ho!* 4.1.62, but probably refers inter-
textually to this scene in *EMO*. George is here represented as the more
experienced drawer.
5–6. *that's neat*] drink that is not diluted with water.
7. *neophyte*] apprentice; newcomer or upstart. Although Jonson uses the
word, perhaps in mockery of the fad for inflated language, it was not in
general use until the nineteenth century; cf. *CR* 3.1.3 and 4.55; *Poet.* 1.2.123.

Enter GEORGE.

George. Welcome, good Master Carlo.   10
Carlo. What, 's supper ready?
George. Ay, sir, almost. Will you have the cloth laid, Master
    Carlo?
Carlo. O, what else? Are none of the gallants come yet?
George. None yet, sir.   15
Carlo. Stay, take me with you, George. Let me have a good
    fat loin of pork laid to the fire presently.
George. It shall, sir.
Carlo. And withal—hear you?—draw me the biggest shaft you
    have out of the butt you wot of. Away! You know my   20
    meaning, George. Quick!
George. Done, sir.   *Exit.*
Carlo. 'Sblood, I never hungered so much for thing in my life
    as I do to know our gallants' success at the court. Now
    is that lean bald-rib, Macilente, that salt villain, plotting   25
    some mischievous device, and lies a-soaking in their
    frothy humours like a dry crust, till he has drunk 'em all

---

9.1.] *In Q appears at end of l. 9; not in F.*   11. What, 's] *This ed.;* What's *Q;*
What! is *F.*   22. SD] *Q; not in F.*   23. 'Sblood] *Q; not in F.*   24. the
court] *Q;* court *F.*

---

16. *take me with you*] not so fast, I have more orders to give you.
17. *presently*] at once.
19–20. *draw . . . butt*] fill me up the biggest flagon from the wine cask.
20. *you wot of*] that you know about—you know which one I mean.
24. *success*] result, termination of something, whether favourable or not
(*OED*).
25. *bald-rib*] man so thin that his ribs show. See Chars.6n and 5.3.136–8n.
salt] witty, clever; stinging (rubbing salt in the wound).
26–8. *and lies . . . all up*] and immerses himself in the pleasure of absorb-
ing and obliterating their humours. An alehouse simile: Carlo compares the
gallants' flighty affections to foaming ale, and Macilente to the dry bread or
toast which was floated in mugs of ale as a bar-snack. The alehouse meal of
cakes and ale was the traditional English sustenance of all classes (Elizabeth
herself ate it for breakfast), easily prepared and cheap; the stale leftovers
could be given away with the drink or distributed as alms. See Frederick W.
Hackwood, *Inns, Ales, and Drinking Customs of Old England* (London, 1909),
pp. 88–91, and Peter Clark, *The English Alehouse: A Social History, 1200–1830*
(London, 1983), p. 132.

up. Could the kex but hold up's eyes at other men's happiness in any reasonable proportion, 'slid, the slave were
to be loved next heaven, above honour, wealth, rich fare,   30
apparel, wenches—all the delights of the belly and the
groin whatever.

Enter GEORGE.

George. Here, Master Carlo. [*He sets down wine and two cups.*]
Carlo. Is 't right, boy?
George. Ay, sir, I assure you 'tis right.   35
Carlo. Well said, my dear George. Depart. Come, my small
gimlet, you in the false scabbard, away!

Puts forth [GEORGE] *the* Drawer *and shuts the door.*
So. Now to you, Sir Burgomaster: let's taste of your
bounty.

---

28. kex] *Q;* pummise *F.*   up's] *Q;* vp his *F.*   32.1.] *In Q1 appears at end of*
l. 32; not in Q2 or F.   37.1.] *In Q appears beside indented ll. 38–9; in margin of F.*

---

28. *kex*] dry or hollow stem of a plant; hence, a dried-up sapless person
(*OED* 4). The dry-nurse in Jonson's *E.Blackfriars* is called 'Mistress Kecks'
(*H&S*). Similarly, in Middleton's *A Chaste Maid in Cheapside*, the infertile
husband and wife of one subplot are Lord and Lady Kix. Here Carlo refers
to Macilente's cadaverous appearance (*that lean bald-rib*), and to his condition
of being so shrivelled with envy that he cannot tolerate another's happiness.
    hold up's eyes] look directly and objectively, without squinting in envy.
    29–30. *the slave . . . heaven*] Macilente as a social critic would be someone
to appreciate highly, were he not so malicious.
    31–2. *the belly and the groin*] (*a*) gluttony and lust. Cf. *Disc.* 53–5, describ-
ing hypocrites: 'Only they set the sign of the cross over their outer doors,
and sacrifice to their gut and their groin in their inner closets'. See also *Ep.*
117, 'On Groin', and 118, 'On Gut'. Hence by extension, (*b*) appetites and
passions in general. Cf. *Disc.* 1394–404: 'O! if a man could restrain the fury
of his gullet, and groin, and think how many fires, how many kitchens, cooks,
pastures, and ploughed lands; what orchards, stews, ponds, and parks, coops,
and garners he could spare: what velvets, tissues, embroideries, laces he
could lack; and then how short, and uncertain his life is; he were in a better
way to happiness, than to live the emperor of these delights; and be the dic-
tator of fashions! But we make ourselves slaves to our pleasures; and we serve
Fame, and Ambition, which is an equal slavery'. So too *SN* 3.4.45–6.
    37. *gimlet*] small boring-tool used to draw liquor from barrels; similarly,
in *BF* 2.2.48, Ursula calls her drawer a 'false faucet'.
    you . . . scabbard] you unconvincing facsimile of a grown man. A *scabbard*
is a sheath for a sword or dagger.
    38. *Sir Burgomaster*] facetiously addressing the huge flagon of wine. *H&S*
conjecture that it refers to a big-bellied jug with a bearded figure in front,
in the style of the Dutch Bellarmines.

Mitis. What, will he deal upon such quantities of wine alone?   40
Cordatus. You shall perceive that, sir.

He drinks.

Carlo. Ay, marry, here's purity. O George, I could bite off thy
nose for this now! Sweet rogue, he has drawn nectar, the
very soul of the grape. I'll wash my temples with some
on 't presently, and drink some half-a-score draughts.   45
'Twill heat the brain, kindle my imagination. I shall talk
nothing but crackers and firework tonight. So, sir. Please
you to be here, sir, and I here. So.

*He sets the two cups asunder, and first drinks
with the one, and pledges with the other.*

Cordatus. This is worth the observation, signor.

Carlo. *1 Cup.* Now, sir, here's to you, and I present you with   50
so much of my love.
    2 Cup. I take it kindly from you, sir, (*Drinks*) and will

---

41. shall] *Q;* will *F.*   41.1.] *In Q appears at end of l. 41; not in F.*   42. thy]
Q; his *F.*   48.1–2.] *Q; in margin of F.*   50. *1 Cup.*] *This ed., passim;* 1 Cup.
Q, F, but subsequently only the numeral.   52. *2 Cup.*] *This ed., passim;* 2 Cup.

---

40. *upon*] with.
42–3. *bite . . . nose*] an endearment; cf. 4.3.210.
47. *crackers*] firecrackers.
    firework] used in both the singular and plural in the sense of pyrotechnic
display. Jonson uses both forms; cf. *SN* Ind.53: 'these carry no fireworks to
fright you' (Partridge, *Accidence*, pp. 23–4).
    48.1–2ff.] *H&S* cite Fynes Moryson, *Itinerary* (1617), 3.2, ch. 4, p. 99,
who notes that, in the Netherlands, 'Some wanting companions to drink lay
down their hat or cloak for a companion, so playing themselves both parts,
of drinking to and pledging, till they have no more sense or use of reason
than the cloak or hat hath'. Whalley cites the parallel to Dryden, *The Wild
Gallant*, in which the actor plays backgammon, throwing the dice out of alter-
nate dice-boxes, then quarrelling, and finally 'overturning the tables, and
throwing the men about the floor'.

return you the like proportion, but withal, sir, remem-
bering the merry night we had at the countess's—you
know where, sir.   55
1 Cup. By Jesu, you do put me in mind now of a very necessary office, which I will propose in your pledge, sir: the
health of that honourable countess and the sweet lady
that sat by her, sir.
2 Cup. I do vail to it with reverence. (*Drinks*) And now,   60
signor, with these ladies, I'll be bold to mix the health of
your divine mistress.
1 Cup. Do you know her, sir?
2 Cup. O lord, sir, ay, and in the respectful memory and
mention of her I could wish this wine were the most pre-   65
cious drug in the world.
1 Cup. Good faith, sir, you do honour me in 't exceedingly.   (*Drinks.*)

GREX

Mitis. Whom should he personate in this, signor?
Cordatus. Faith, I know not, sir. Observe, observe him.   70

2 Cup. If it were the basest filth or mud that runs in the
channel, I am bound to pledge it, by God, sir. (*Drinks.*)

Q, F, but subsequently only the numeral.   SD] *Q; not in F.*   56. Jesu] *Q;*
heauen *F.*   do put] *Q;* put *F.*   60–8.] *F prints each cup as separate speech*
on new line; Q prints as one paragraph. So ll. 71–9, 82–94.   60. SD] *Q; not in*
F.   And] *F;* 2. And *Q.*   68. SD] *Q; not in F.*   72. by God] *Q;* respec-
tiuely *F.*   SD] *Q; not in F.*

60. *vail*] bow.
61. *mix*] Wine was often mixed with water.
69–70.] Another disclaimer of personal satire. Carlo mimics the courtly
style of speech: the name-dropping, hints of amorous favours, and exaggera-
tions resemble Fastidius's conversation. Cordatus's evasion has been taken
as confirmation of satire on a particular man. According to Jasper Mayne in
Jonsonus Viribus (1638), Jonson wrote the scene as revenge on a man he had
quarrelled with: 'That thou didst quarrel first, and then in spite / Did 'gainst
a person of such vices write; / That 'twas revenge, not truth; that on thy stage
/ CARLO was not presented, but thy rage'.
71–2. *the channel*] the gutter which carried sewage to the Thames. Cf.
4.5.154–9 and 5.4.12–13.

And now, sir, here is again a replenished bowl, sir, which
I will reciprocally return upon you to the health of the
Count Frugale.   75
1 Cup. The Count Frugale's health, sir? I'll pledge it on
my knees, by Jesu!
2 Cup. Will you, sir? I'll drink it on my knees then, by the
Lord.   (*Drinks.*)

GREX

Mitis. Why, this is strange.   80
Cordatus. Ha' you heard a better drunken dialogue?

---

2 Cup Nay, do me right, sir.
1 Cup. So I do, in good faith.
2 Cup. Good faith, you do not. Mine was fuller.
1 Cup. Why, by Jesu, it was not.   85

---

73. again] *Q; not in F.*   bowl, sir] *Q;* bowl, *F.*   74. return] *Q;* turn *F.*
77. by Jesu] *Q;* by this light *F*   78. knees] *Q;* knee *F.*   79. Lord] *Q;*
light *F.*   SD] *Q; not in F.*   85. by Jesu] *Q;* beleeue me *F.*

---

73. *replenished bowl*] Carlo keeps filling up the cups after drinking from
them.
76–7. *pledge . . . knees*] a courtly affectation, especially in toasting a mistress. Cf. Chapman, *All Fools* (Regents), 5.2.55–8: '*Dariotto.* Well, ladies, here
is to your honour'd healths. *Fortunio.* What, Dariotto, without hat or knee?
Dariotto. Well said, Fortunio. Oh, y'are a rare courtier! Your knee, good
signor, I beseech your knee.'
78. *drink . . . knees*] not simply a *reductio ad absurdum.* Cf. *A Yorkshire
Tragedy* (1608), in *Disputed Plays of William Shakespeare,* ed. William Kozlenko
(New York, 1974), 1.1, p. 120: 'The bravest humor! 'twould do a man
good to be drunk in it: they call it knighting in London, when they drink
upon their knees'; and *1 Return from Parnassus* 3.1: 'it pleased me to bestow
love, this pleasing fire, upon Lady Lesbia: many a health have I drunk to
her upon my native knees, eating that happy glass in honour of my
mistress!'
82. *do me right*] a common expression in pledging healths: 'By the rules
of drinking, a man was to pledge the other in the same quantity of liquor,
which he drank to him' (Whalley).

2 Cup. By Jesu, it was, and you do lie.

1 Cup. Lie, sir?

2 Cup. Ay, sir.

1 Cup. 'Swounds, you rascal!

2 Cup. O, come, stab if you have a mind to it.   90

1 Cup. Stab? Dost thou think I dare not?

(In his own person). Nay, I beseech you, gentlemen, what means this? Nay, look, for shame, respect your reputations.   *Overturns wine, pot, cups, and all.*

Enter MACILENTE.

Macilente. Why, how now, Carlo? What humour's this?   95

Carlo. O my good Mischief, art thou come? Where are the rest? Where are the rest?

Macilente. Faith, three of our ordnance are burst.

Carlo. Burst? How comes that?

Macilente. Faith, overcharged, overcharged.   100

Carlo. But did not the train hold?

Macilente. O, yes, and the poor lady is irrecoverably blown up.

Carlo. Why, but which of the munitions is miscarried? Ha?

Macilente. *Imprimis*, Sir Puntarvolo. Next, the Countenance and Resolution.   105

---

86. By Jesu] *Q;* Beleeue me *F.*   89. 'Swounds, you rascal!] *Q;* S'wounds! *F.*   92. *(In his own person)*] *Q, in square brackets;* CARL. *F.*   94. SD.] *Q; in margin of F: Speakes in his owne person, and ouerturnes wine, pot, cups, and all.* 94.1.] *Q; Act V. Scene V. /* MACILENTE, CARLO, GEORGE. *F.*

---

86. *lie*] Cf. 5.2.169–70n. In his copy of Clement Edmondes's *Observations upon Caesar's Commentaries* (1609?), Jonson marked a passage on the folly of duelling which focuses on the *mentita*: 'But that which is yet worst of all, is that custom hath now made it so familiar, that every trifle seemeth sufficient to call the matter to a private combat; the word *lie* is of as great consequence, as any stab or villainy whatsoever' (*H&S*, 9.326, commenting on *NI* 4.4.166). For its effect in Kastril's quarrelling lessons and practice, see *Alc.* 4.2–3.

98. *three . . . burst*] three of our big guns have exploded. This reference to cannonry begins a series of war-machine images in which the men involved in the trick are compared to weapons which end up backfiring, and Saviolina is compared to a target under siege.

100. *overcharged*] loaded with excessive explosives.

101. *train*] (*a*) artillery and other apparatus for battle or siege, including transport and men following in the rear (*OED* 9b); (*b*) retinue of followers, here consisting of Puntarvolo and the rest.

103. *munitions*] weapons.

miscarried] (*a*) perished, self-destructed (*OED* 1); (*b*) failed (*OED* 3, 4).

104. Imprimis] in the first place.

Carlo. How? How, for the love of God?

Macilente. Troth, the Resolution is proved recreant; the Countenance hath changed his copy; and the passionate knight is shedding funeral tears over his departed dog.

Carlo. What, 's his dog dead? 110

Macilente. Poisoned, 'tis thought. Marry, how, or by whom, that's left for some cunning woman here o' the Bankside to resolve. For my part, I know nothing more than that we are like to have an exceeding melancholy supper of it.

Carlo. 'Slight, and I had purposed to be extraordinarily 115 merry. I had drunk off a good preparative of old sack here. But will they come, will they come?

Macilente. They will assuredly come. Marry, Carlo, as thou lov'st me, run over 'em all freely tonight, and especially the knight. Spare no sulphurous jest that may come out 120 of that sweaty forge of thine, but ply 'em with all manner of shot: minion, saker, culverin, or anything what thou wilt.

---

106. God] *Q;* wit *F*   110. What, 's] *This ed.;* What's *Q, F*

---

107. *recreant*] cowardly.

107-8. *the Countenance . . . copy*] Sogliardo has (*a*) altered his behaviour; (*b*) changed his role-model, i.e., Shift; and possibly (*c*) rejected the fake. Jonson may be playing on the expression 'copy of one's countenance', meaning a pretence or sham, as in *Westward Ho!*: 'I shall love a Puritan's face the worse, whilst I live, for that copy of thy countenance' (cited in Partridge, *Slang*).

112. *cunning . . . Bankside*] one of the quacks and fortune-tellers who flourished in the suburb of Southwark on the south bank of the Thames, known for its theatres (the Globe, the Rose, the Hope, and the Swan) and brothels (the Bordello, or Stews). Heywood, in *The Wise Woman of Hogsden* 2.1, refers to 'Mother Phillips of the Bankside, for the weakness of the back' and 'Mistress Mary on the Bankside . . . for 'recting a figure'.

116. *preparative*] (*a*) medicinal draught taken before a meal (*OED* 1b); (*b*) military signal as an order to make ready (*OED* 4); in this sense, it signals a resurgence of the war-machine imagery at 120-5 and later at 169-70.

119. *run . . . all*] i.e., be unsparing of them with your satirical attacks.

122. *shot*] projectiles to be discharged by a big gun, such as a *minion*, a kind of small cannon or gun, capable of discharging a shot of four pounds; a *saker*, an old form of cannon smaller than a demi-culverin, formerly employed in sieges and on ships, and capable of discharging a shot of about five pounds; and a *culverin*, a large cannon, very long in proportion to its bore, capable of discharging a shot of 17-20 pounds. The demi-culverin discharged 9 or 10 pounds.

what] whatsoever.

Carlo. I warrant thee, my dear case of petronels, so I stand
     not in dread of thee, but that thou'lt second me.   125
Macilente. Why, my good German tapster, I will.
Carlo. [*Calling*] What, George! *Lomtero, lomtero!* (*Etc.*)
                              [*While singing, he*] *danceth.*

                    [Enter GEORGE.]

George. Did you call, Master Carlo?
Carlo. More nectar, George. *Lomtero!* (*Etc.*)
George. Your meat's ready, sir, an your company were come.   130
Carlo. Is the loin o' pork enough?
George. Ay, sir, it is enough.   [*Exit.*]
Macilente. Pork? 'Sheart, what dost thou with such a greasy

---

127. (*Etc.*)] *Not parenthetical in Q, F; so too at l. 129.*   127.1. [*While singing,
he*] *danceth*] *This ed.; danceth Q; He danceth. F*   131. o'] *This ed.; a Q; of
F*   133. 'Sheart] *Q; Heart F*

---

124. *warrant*] assure.
case of petronels] pair of large pistols, here metaphorically representing
weapons of satire.
124–5. *so . . . thee*] provided that I need not fear your deserting me.
125. *second me*] back me up, support me in satirical duels.
126. *German tapster*] one who drinks as heavily as a Dutchman. Like
'tippler', 'tapster' referred either to the barman or to the drinker. Elizabethans made no distinction between the Dutch and the Germans, especially in their proverbial capacity for drink; cf. William Parkes, *The Curtain-
drawer of the World* (1612) (Grosart, 1876), 26: 'There's Tom the Tapster
peereless for renown, / That drank three hundred drunken Dutchmen
down'.
127. *Lomtero*] The tune is untraced, but this refrain is echoed as a song
of victory in *Jack Drum's Entertainment*, D2, when Mammon believes his rival
in love, Pasquil, is dead: '*Mammon sings, Lantara, etc. Pasquil riseth and striketh
him*'.
131. *enough*] cooked sufficiently (*OED* B 1c).
133–68. *Pork? . . . swine else.*] In the discourse on pork, Carlo argues that
pork is the best food because it is most like man's flesh; specifically, that if
one eats what is closest to one's own nature, one derives nourishment more
quickly, and becomes stronger. This comment is both moral and physical.
Carlo's Circean similes and Macilente's earlier description of him as one
'That bites at all, but eats on those that feed him' (1.2.235) suggest that pork-
eating, virtually a kind of cannibalism, is an analogue of wanton appetite in
a world of moral anarchy. Although Galen, like Carlo, affirmed the nutri-
tional value of pork, Thomas Cogan, in *The Haven of Health* (London, 1584),

dish? I think thou dost varnish thy face with the fat on
't, it looks so like a glue-pot.   135
Carlo. True, my rawboned rogue, and if thou wouldst farce
thy lean ribs with it too, they would not, like ragged laths,
rub out so many doublets as they do. But thou know'st
not a good dish, thou. O, it's the only nourishing meat in
the world! No marvel though that saucy stubborn gen-   140
eration, the Jews, were forbidden it, for what would they
ha' done, well pampered with fat pork, that durst murmur
at their Maker out of garlic and onions? 'Sblood, fed with

---

143. 'Sblood] *Q;* S'light *F*

p. 118, argued, like Macilente, that 'young pigs . . . are not very wholesome,
by reason of their overmuch moisture, and they breed in our bodies much
superflouous humours' (cited in Rhodes, *Elizabethan Grotesque* (London,
1980), p. 185). Henry Buttes, *Diet's Dry Dinner* (1599), agrees, but notes that
pork is so tasty that 'our appetite captivates our reason in this matter' (16r).
So too Burton, 1.218: 'Pork, of all meats, is . . . altogether unfit for such as
. . . are anyways unsound of body or mind: too moist, full of humours, and
therefore *noxia delicatis*, saith Savonarola'. For the anti-semitic context see
Ostovich, 'Two Jonsonian Neologisms', *Cahiers Élisabéthains* 38 (October
1990): 65–7.

133. *greasy*] (*a*) oily; (*b*) filthy, obscene (Partridge, *Bawdy*). Cf. in *BF*
2.5.175–6, Winwife remarks of Ursula's bawdy diatribes: 'Let's away. Her language grows greasier than her pigs.'

136. *farce*] stuff, flesh out.

137. *laths*] slats of thin wood serving as frame for plaster walls and ceil-
ings, and much resembling ribs.

138. *rub out*] wear out, fray.

140. *saucy*] (*a*) insolent, scornful; (*b*) having a dainty or fastidious palate
(*OED* 3).

stubborn] for refusing to convert to Christianity.

142–3. *murmur at*] complain to, grumble at.

143. *garlic and onions*] a common anti-semitic association: 'The Jews, anx-
iously observing the prohibited eating of blood, keep their flesh covered with
onions and garlic till it putrify and contract as bad a smell as that of rot-
tenness from those strong sauces, and so by continual use thereof emit a
loathsome savour, as Mr. Fulham experimented in Italy at a Jewish meeting,
with the hazard of life till he removed into the fresh air' (Wren, cited by
Robin Robbins, ed., in Browne, 2.922).

143–5. *'Sblood . . . gigantomachized*] By Christ's blood, if the Jews had
eaten pork, the vile, beggarly, bulging-eyed complainers would have rebelled
more powerfully against God. (See following notes.)

it, the whoreson, strummel-patched, goggle-eyed grumbledories would ha' gigantomachized.   145

[*Enter* GEORGE *with wine.*]

Well said, my sweet George! Fill, fill!

[GEORGE *fills the cups, and exit.*]

GREX

Mitis. This savours too much of profanation.

---

144. strummell-patched] *H&S, after Gifford*; strummel patcht *Q*; strum-
mell, patcht *F.*

---

144. *strummel–patched*] an ambiguous term, not found elsewhere. *Strummel* is thieves' cant for straw; *patched* is depreciatory, suggesting something
made up in a hasty, clumsy, or otherwise imperfect fashion; botched. Conceivably the epithet is a variation on 'a man of straw' or 'Jack Straw', a person
of no consideration (cf. Nashe, *Have With You to Saffron Walden* 3.109); Jack
Straw was the 'anti-king' of the Lincoln's Inn Revels (*Black Books* 1.189–90).
Straw is associated with scolds and complainers, on whom 'a wisp, or small
twist, of straw or hay, was often applied as a mark of opprobrium' (Nares).
Possibly Jonson's coinage is a variant of 'patch-panel', an abusive appella-
tion for one who is shabby or wears worn-out clothes (according to
Creizenach, *The English Drama in the Age of Shakespeare* (New York, 1967),
p. 110, 'traffic in old clothes' was a common occupation among Jews); consequently, a person of little value (Hoy, 1.248).
    goggle-eyed] assumed to be a racial trait (Burton, 1.211).
144–5. *grumbledories*] another Jonson coinage with an obscure etymology,
perhaps constructed by analogy to 'drumbledory', bumblebee (*H&S*). A
'grumboll' is a peevish, discontented person, a confirmed grumbler; Dekker
used the term in *Satiromastix* 4.3.262, and as the name of one of the devils
in *If This Be Not a Good Play, the Devil Is in It* (1611), 1.1.81. Jonson may
have been punning on 'grummel', now spelled 'gromwell' (*OED*), a seed used
generally for an equivalent to a usurer's gain; in T. Wilson's *Discourse upon
Usury* (1572), the usurer is called 'Grummelgainer, the wrong merchant or
evil occupier' (McKerrow, 4.388). This possibility not only evokes the usual
prejudice equating Jews and money-lenders, but also suggests itself by asso-
ciative rhyme with 'strummel'.
    145. *gigantomachized*] re-enacted the battle of the giants; another coinage,
invented on the Rabelaisian principle of compounding Greek or Latin words
with italianate '-ize' endings. For an analysis of this kind of neologism see
Rhodes, *The Elizabethan Grotesque*, pp. 24–6. *H&S* suggest it means 'the Jews
would have fought like the Giants against the Gods; passed from murmur-
ing to open rebellion'.
    146. *Well said*] Well done. See Ind.324.

Cordatus. O, servetur ad imum, qualis ab incepto processerit, et
    sibi constet. The necessity of his vein compels a toleration;
    for bar this, and dash him out of humour before his time.   150

Carlo. 'Tis an axiom in natural philosophy: what comes
    nearest the nature of that it feeds converts quicker to
    nourishment and doth sooner essentiate. Now, nothing
    in flesh and entrails assimulates or resembles man more
    than a hog or swine.   (*Drinks.*)   155
Macilente. True, and he, to requite their courtesy, oftentimes
    doffeth off his own nature and puts on theirs, as when he
    becomes as churlish as a hog, or as drunk as a sow. But
    to your conclusion.
Carlo. (*Drinks.*) Marry, I say, nothing resembling man more   160
    than a swine, it follows nothing can be more nourishing;
    for indeed (but that it abhors from our nice nature) if we
    fed one upon another, we should shoot up a great deal
    faster, and thrive much better. I refer me to your Long
    Lane cannibals, or such like. But since 'tis so contrary,   165
    pork, pork is your only feed.

155. SD] *Q; not in F.*   157. doffeth off] *Q;* d'offeth *F.*   160. SD] *In Q
appears at end of l. 159, thus mistakenly giving the SD to Macilente; not in F.*
164–5. Long Lane] *Q;* vsurous *F.*   165. 'tis] *Q;* it is *F.*

148–9. *O, servetur . . . constet*] 'O, he is preserved at the end in the same
condition as he had appeared from the beginning and has consistently maintained'; from Horace, *Ars Poetica* 126–7.
    149–50. *The necessity . . . time*] We have to be tolerant of his compulsive
humour of (drunken blasphemy) because, if we don't allow it, we'll put him
out of his humour too early, before the time for the best dramatic effect
occurs in the play.
    153. *essentiate*] become converted into bodily substance (*OED* 2, citing
this line as its first instance).
    154. *assimulates*] simulates, counterfeits.
    156. *he*] man.
    158. *as drunk as a sow*] proverbial (Dent, S1042). The SD and comment at
153–5, repeated at 160–1, act as asterisks, emphasizing the relation of men
to swine, and the fact that Carlo is intoxicated, if not incapacitated.
    162. *abhors from*] a Latinism: shrinks from, disagrees with.
    nice] squeamish, fastidious.
    164–5. *Long Lane cannibals*] old-clothes dealers and pawnbrokers, gener-
ally reputed to be rapacious, operating on the thoroughfare running from
Smithfield to Aldersgate Street (Chalfant). *F*'s wording, 'usurous cannibals',
emphasizes the money-lending in which any tradesman, including Deliro,
might profitably engage.

Macilente. I take it your devil be of the same diet; he would
ne'er ha' desired to been incorporated into swine else. O,
here comes the melancholy mess. Upon 'em, Carlo!
Charge, charge!   170

Enter PUNTARVOLO, FASTIDIUS, SOGLIARDO,
[*and*] FUNGOSO.

Carlo. 'Fore God, Sir Puntarvolo, I am sorry for your heaviness. Body o' me, a shrewd mischance! Why, had you no
unicorn's horn nor bezoar's stone about you? Ha?
Puntarvolo. Sir, I would request you be silent.
Macilente. [*Aside to Carlo*] Nay, to him again.   175

170.1–2.] *Q; not in F.*   173. unicorn's] *Italic in Qb, F; Vnicorne Qa.*   174.]
*Q; Act V. Scene VI. / PVNTARVOLO, CARLO, MACILENTE, / FAST. BRISKE,
SOGLIARDO, / FVNGOSO. F*

---

167. *your devil*] the devil (ethical dative).
168. *to been incorporated*] to have been incorporated; an elliptical perfect
infinitive (Partridge, *Accidence*, p. 248). So too *SW* 4.7.2: 'O see! here hath
like to been murder since you went!'. The reference is to devils entering into
swine; see Mark 5.11–16.
169. *mess*] dinner-party.
169–70. *Upon . . . charge!*] Macilente urges Carlo to exert all his satirical
skills in attacking this group, as though in a military charge. See above at 120ff.
171–2. *heaviness*] grief.
172. *Body o' me*] euphemistic oath for 'by the body of Christ'.
shrewd mischance] galling misfortune (i.e., the death of the dog).
173. *unicorn's horn*] believed in the sixteenth century to be a remedy
against poison, although Browne, 3.23, calls it 'an insufferable delusion' con-
cocted of fossils or teeth of sea-animals: 'none of the ancients ascribed any
medicinal or antidotal virtue unto the unicorn's horn'. Nevertheless, Browne
is reluctant to abandon the notion of cure altogether, suggesting that the
horn may have been known by another name in former days, and only half-
heartedly admitting that the animal itself may not have existed.
bezoar's stone] another supposed antidote, derived from stomachs ·or
intestines of ruminant animals. Not a stone, Browne explains, but the 'stony
seed of some *Lithospermum* or greater Gromwell; or the *Lobus Echinatus* of
Clusius, called also the Bezoar Nut; for being broken, it discovereth a kernel of
a leguminous smell and taste, bitter like a Lupin, and will swell and sprout if set
in the ground, and therefore more serviceable for issues than dangerous and
virulent diseases'. *H&S* cite sources suggesting that the stone was a coales-
cence recovered from certain animals and fraudulently used as a cure. Burton
refers to it both as a stone 'found in the belly of a little beast in the East Indies,
brought into Europe by Hollanders and our countrymen merchants' (2.219),
and as a spice, classed with saffron, cinnamon, and myrrh (2.259).

Carlo. [*To Puntarvolo*] Take comfort, good knight. If your cat
ha' recovered her cataract, fear nothing. Your dog's mischance may be holpen.

Fastidius. Say how, sweet Carlo, for, so God mend me, the
poor knight's moans draw me into fellowship of his mis-   180
fortunes.—But be not discouraged, good Sir Puntarvolo.
I am content your adventure shall be performed upon
your cat.

Macilente. [*Aside*] I believe you, musk-cod, I believe you;
for rather than thou wouldst make present repayment,   185
thou wouldst take it upon his own bare return from
Calais.

Carlo. [*Overhearing, aside to Macilente*] Nay, God's life, he'd
be content (so he were well rid out of his company) to
pay him five for one at his next meeting him in Paul's.   190
[*To Puntarvolo*] But for your dog, Sir Puntar, if he be not

---

177. cataract] *Q;* catarrhe *F*   188. God's] *Q;* 'ds *F.*

177. *cataract*] Cf. 'sore eyes', 5.2.11. *F*'s change to 'catarrhe' is probably
not a reference to the common cold, which would imply discharges from the
nose, but rather to any 'humid flux', as in *Volp.* 2.2.94 (Revels), meaning an
excess of the watery humour, phlegm, changing the balance of the four
humours in the body, according to the theories of Hippocrates and Galen.
In either word, the joke depends on the first syllable, 'cat-'.

178. *be holpen*] be of use (*OED* 2b).

182–3. *your adventure . . . cat*] that your wager depend on your successful
journey with your cat, leaving the dog out of it.

184. *musk-cod*] literally, a small bag or purse used for perfumes; figuratively, a perfumed fop like Fastidius. See *Ep.* 19, 'On Sir Cod the perfumed',
and *Satiromastix* 2.2.24 (*H&S*). For a common variant see 2.1.109,
'musk-cat'.

186–7. *bare . . . Calais*] a spiteful comment on Brisk's constant need for
ready money. Puntarvolo has deposited with Brisk a sum of £100 as part of
the five-for-one wager; rather than return the money now, Brisk (in Macilente's opinion) would prefer to revise the bet to cover any trip, no matter
how tame and nearby, even *bare* or unaccompanied by dog, cat, or wife. *Bare*
also means 'mere'.

189. *(so he . . . company)*] if he could get away with it; if he could avoid
having to witness Puntarvolo's grief.

191. *Puntar*] The nickname mocks the knight as a gambler ('punter'); see
Char.12ff. and notes. Disrespectful address is allowable in licensed fools
(e.g., Lear's fool calls the king 'nuncle'), but Carlo is only an unofficial jester.

outright dead, there is a friend of mine, a quacksalver,
shall put life in him again, that's certain.

Fungoso. O no, that comes too late.

Macilente. [*To Puntarvolo*] God's precious, knight, will you   195
suffer this?

Puntarvolo. [*Calling*] Drawer! Get me a candle and hard wax
presently.

Sogliardo. [*Also calling*] Ay, and bring up supper—[*To the
others*] for I am so melancholy.   200

Carlo. Ah, signor, where's your Resolution?

Sogliardo. Resolution! Hang him, rascal! O Carlo, if you love
me, do not mention him.

Carlo. Why, how so? How so?

Sogliardo. O, the arrant'st crocodile that ever Christian was   205
acquainted with! By Jesu, I shall think the worse of
tobacco while I live for his sake. I did think him to be as
tall a man—

Macilente. [*Aside to Carlo*] Nay, Buffone, the knight, the
knight!   210

Carlo. [*To the others, baiting Puntarvolo*] 'Sblood, he looks like
an image carved out of box, full of knots. His face is for
all the world like a Dutch purse with the mouth down-
ward; his beard's the tassels. And he walks (let me see)
as melancholy as one o' the Master's side in the   215
Counter.—Do you hear, Sir Puntar?

---

206. Jesu] *Q;* my gentrie *F.*   211. 'Sblood] *Q;* S'lud *F.*   214. beard's]
Q; beard *F.*

---

192. *quacksalver*] a charlatan or fraud who claims to know medical or
miraculous remedies.

195–6.] Macilente deliberately encourages Puntarvolo to retaliate against
Carlo for deriding the loss of the dog.

200. *so melancholy*] cf. 5.2.223.

209–10.] Macilente redirects Carlo away from Sogliardo to continue his
attacks on Puntarvolo.

211. *he*] Puntarvolo.

212. *box*] a wood similar to pine.

full of knots] see 'knotty', 4.3.216.

213. *Dutch purse*] bag with its mouth gathered up by a string ending in
two tassels (Sugden, p. 164). The pursing of Puntarvolo's lips, caused by his
growing anger, has given his face a tightly drawn look.

215–16. *the Master's . . . Counter*] the best ward in the prison, located
in the same part of the house as the warden's apartments. The Knights'
ward was probably on the same side of the building, but on the upper
storey, and was therefore not so expensive. Cf. *Westward Ho!* 3.2.77–81:

Puntarvolo. Sir, I do entreat you no more, but enjoin you to
   silence, as you affect your peace.
Carlo. Nay, but, dear knight, understand (here are none but
   friends and such as wish you well) I would ha' you do   220
   this now: flay me your dog presently—but, in any case,
   keep the head—and stuff his skin well with straw, as you
   see these dead monsters at Bartholomew Fair—
Puntarvolo. I shall be sudden, I tell you.
Carlo. —or, if you like not that, sir, get me somewhat a less   225
   dog and clap into the skin. Here's a slave about the town
   here, a Jew, one Yohan, or a fellow that makes periwigs,
   will glue it on artificially; it shall ne'er be discerned.
   Besides, 'twill be so much the warmer for the hound to
   travel in, you know.   230
Macilente. Sir Puntarvolo, 'sdeath, can you be so patient?
Carlo. Or thus, sir: you may have (as you come through

---

220. you] *Q;* ye *F.*   227. periwigs] *Q;* purrukes *F.*   231. 'sdeath] *Q;*
'death *F.*

'*Monopoly.* Which is the dearest ward in prison, Sergeant: the Knights'
ward? / *Ambush.* No sir, the Master's side. / *Monopoly.* Well, the knight is
above the master, though his table be worse furnished: I'll go thither.'
The Twopenny ward accommodated those who could pay something
towards better board and room in order to avoid staying in the Hole, the
worst part of the prison: a large windowless room with wooden shelves
instead of beds and food generally unfit for human consumption (Johansson, *Law*, pp. 34–6).
   218. *affect your peace*] wish to stay out of a fight.
   221. *flay me*] skin. The colloquial *me* is the ethical dative, as at 3.1.50 and
elsewhere.
   223. *dead monsters*] preserved curiosities and freaks, like the five-legged
bull mentioned in *Alc.* 5.1.7–9 and *BF* 3.6.6–7.
   Bartholomew Fair] the annual event, including markets for cloth, cattle,
and the hiring of servants, held in West Smithfield between 1120 and 1855,
opening on St Bartholomew's day, 24 August, and lasting from three days
to a week.
   225. *get . . . less*] acquire a somewhat smaller.
   226. *clap . . . skin*] put the smaller dog into your dog's skin. An idiomatic
omission of 'it', probably owing to lack of emphasis (Partridge, *Syntax*, p. 39).
   227. *a Jew, one Yohan*] a topical allusion, perhaps to some Bankside
alehouse-keeper. In his long note on 'Yaughan', *Ham.* 5.1.60, Harold Jenkins,
pp. 547–8, cites Brinsley Nicholson's conjecture linking Yohan, Yaughan, and
the 'deaf John' of *Alc.* 1.1.85. *H&S* note that 'Jew' often meant Dutchman
or Fleming, and that the name Johan was popular among Low Germans,
but not among Jews.
   228. *will*] who will.

Germany) a familiar, for little or nothing, shall turn itself
into the shape of your dog, or anything—what you will—
for certain hours. [*Puntarvolo threatens.*] God's my life,   235
knight, what do you mean? You'll offer no violence, will
you? [*Puntarvolo draws his rapier and beats Carlo with the
hilt.*] Hold, hold!
Puntarvolo. 'Sblood, you slave! You bandog, you!
Carlo. As you love God, stay the enraged knight, gentlemen!   240

[*The* Drawer *enters with candles and wax.*]

Puntarvolo. By my knighthood, he that stirs in his rescue
dies.—Drawer, be gone!

[*Exit* Drawer.]
Carlo. Murder, murder, murder!
Puntarvolo. Ay, are you howling, you wolf?—Gentlemen, as
you tender your lives, suffer no man to enter till my revenge   245
be perfect.—Sirrah Buffone, lie down. Make no exclama-

---

235. God's] *Q;* 'ods *F.*   237–8. SD] *This ed.; in margin of F: The knight /
beates him; not in Q.*   239. 'Sblood] *Q;* S'death *F.*   240. God] *Q;* wit *F.*

---

233. *a familiar*] an attendant demon or spirit, usually taking the shape of
an animal, commonly a dog: Margaret Alice Murray, *The God of the Witches*
(London, 1952), pp. 81–7, cites Elizabeth Style of Somerset, who divined by
a black dog; Alse Gooderidge in Derbyshire, who used a parti-coloured dog;
and John Walsh, the Dorset witch, who divined by a brindled dog; Agnes
Sampson, executed 1590, divined by a large black dog called Elva.
   shall] that shall.
   237–8. SD] In dealing with an unworthy opponent, a knight need not be
meticulous as to choice of weapons. In *Orlando Furioso*, Mandricardo fights
with his lance, then with fragments of broken lance used as clubs, and then
with fists. In Alamanni's *Gyrone*, Danaino, fighting to restore a lady's stolen
greyhound, stuns his opponent, removes the latter's helmet, and beats him
with the hilt of his sword until the thief surrenders the dog (Bryson,
pp. 194–5).
   239. *bandog*] ferocious mastiff, as described at 1.2.234–5; often kept
chained as a watchdog. See 2.1.382n.
   240. *stay*] restrain.
   241. *stirs . . . rescue*] moves in an attempt to help Carlo.
   242. *Drawer, be gone!*] Puntarvolo ejects the drawer either for attempting
to help Carlo, a good customer, or simply because the knight wants no
unsupportive witness to his revenge. The other gentlemen are tacitly complying with Puntarvolo.
   245. *tender*] value.
   246. *perfect*] complete.

tions, but down! Down, you cur, or I will make thy blood
flow on my rapier hilts!   [*Carlo is forced down.*]

Carlo. Sweet knight, hold in thy fury and, 'fore God, I'll
honour thee more than the Turk does Mahomet.   250

Puntarvolo. Down, I say! [*He hears knocking at the door.*] Who's
there?

Constable. (*Within*) Here's the constable. Open the doors.

Carlo. [*Pleading*] Good Macilente!

Puntarvolo. Open no door! If the *Adelantado* of Spain were   255
here, he should not enter. On! Help me with the light,
gentlemen. [*He melts wax in the candle flame.*] You knock
in vain, sir officer!   [*Knocking continues.*]

Carlo. [*To Macilente*] Et tu, Brute.

Puntarvolo. Sirrah, close your lips, or I will drop it in thine   260
eyes, by heaven!

Carlo. O! O!   *They seal up his lips.*

249. God] *Q;* heauen *F.*   256. On] *Q;* One *F.*   262. SD] *Q; in margin of*
F: He seales vp his / lips.

---

255. Adelantado] Spanish title of the governor of a province.

259.] The person addressed here is uncertain. Carlo has already pleaded
for Macilente's assistance at 254. If he receives no tacit reply and sees Macilente join Puntarvolo at the call for help with the light (256), as Gifford suggests, then the line is an apt reproach. If Macilente gestures refusal at 254,
then Carlo might address Sogliardo, particularly if he anglicized the pronunciation of *Brute*. The line is a burlesque of Shakespeare's in *JC* (1599),
3.1.77; cf. Dover Wilson, 'Ben Jonson and *Julius Caesar*', *ShS* 2 (1949):37.

262. SD] Aubrey, p. 264, recounts an anecdote told of Sir Walter Ralegh:
'In his youthful time, was one Charles Chester, that often kept company with
his acquaintance; he was a bold impertinent fellow, and they could never be
at quiet because of him; a perpetual talker, and made a noise like a drum in
a room. So one time at a tavern Sir Walter Ralegh beats him and seals up
his mouth (i.e., his upper and nether beard) with hard wax. From him, Ben
Jonson takes his Carlo Buffono [*sic*] (i.e. "jester") in *Every Man Out of his
Humour.*' (See Chars.22n for other references.) Collier, repeating this story,
claims that the same man appears in *Pierce Penniless* 1.190ff., 'which Nashe
disguises by laying the scene near Chester, and by calling the hero a friar'
(McKerrow, 4.117).

Physical attack following satirical abuse was a pattern familiar to the Inns
of Court audience. The Middle Temple had a particular recent history of
going too far, losing control, and ending with violence. On 9 February 1598,
in the week following his resignation as Prince D'Amour in the revels,
Richard Martin was attacked and beaten severely by Sir John Davies, who
had been a frequent butt of jokes during the festivities; the scandalous reper-
cussions for Davies lasted for a number of years (Finkelpearl, *Temple*, pp.
54–5).

Constable. (*Within*) Open the door, or I will break it open!
Macilente. Nay, good constable, have patience a little. You
shall come in presently. We have almost done.   265
Puntarvolo. So. Now, are you out of your humour, sir?—Shift,
gentlemen.

> *They all draw, and exeunt.*
> [*Carlo remains; Fungoso hides under the table.*]

Enter Constable *with* Officers, *and stay* BRISK.

Constable. Lay hold upon this gallant, and pursue the rest.

> [*Exeunt some* Officers.]

Fastidius. Lay hold on me, sir! For what?
Constable. Marry, for your riot here, sir, with the rest of your   270
companions.
Fastidius. My riot! God's my judge, take heed what you do!
Carlo, did I offer any violence?

267.1. *exeunt*] *Q; disperse. In margin of* F.   267.2.] *Q; Act V. Scene VII.* /
CONSTABLE, OFFICERS, DRAWERS. *In margin: To them.* F.   272. God's my
judge] *Q;* master Constable F.

---

266. *Shift*] move quickly, make your escape.

267.1. *exeunt*] technically inaccurate, since Carlo remains in view,
Fungoso dives under the table, and Brisk is captured before he can complete an exit. F's choice, *disperse*, does not convey the sense of everyone dis-
appearing from view, except for Brisk. And even Brisk might actually exit
through the stage-door before being hauled back on stage by an officer.

267.2–285.1.] The staging seems to require a Keystone Kops effect of
great numbers of officers and rapid, generally ineffectual movement. For the
policing practice of arresting gallants as they leave taverns or ordinaries, see
Westward Ho! 3.2 and *Northward Ho!* 1.2; also, *Gull's Horn-book*, where the
gallant is advised to arrive at an ordinary 'in a coach, for that will both hide
you from the baselisk-eyes of your creditors and out-run a whole kennel of
bitter-mouthed sergeants' (2.326).

270. *riot*] usually applied to a tavern brawl; 'where three (at the least) or
more do some unlawful act: as to beat a man, enter upon the possession
of another, or such like' (Rastell). But William Lambard, *Eirenarcha; or of
The Office of the Justices of Peace* (1579, enl. 1599), pp. 181–2, distinguishes
between 'sudden affray', such as a spontaneous brawl, and *riot*, which not
only assumes violence perpetrated by a group but also includes the 'manner
and circumstance of the doing'; that is, the purpose of the gathering (which
may have begun as a lawful assembly) and the intention behind the violent
act.

273. *Carlo . . . violence?*] The comedy of Brisk's question depends on
Carlo's obvious inability to answer, as the Constable points out in the next
line.

Constable. O sir, you see he is not in case to answer you, and
   that makes you so peremptory.   275
Fastidius. Peremptory? 'Slife, I appeal to the drawers if I did
   him any hard measure!

     Enter GEORGE [*with the other* Drawer].

George. They are all gone. There's none of them will be laid
   any hold on.
Constable. [*To Fastidius*] Well, sir, you are like to answer till the   280
   rest can be found out.
Fastidius. 'Sblood, I appeal to George here!
Constable. Tut, George was not here.—Away with him to the
   Counter, sirs. [*To Carlo*] Come, sir, you were best get
   yourself dressed somewhere.   285
     Exeunt [Officers *with* BRISK *and* CARLO].
          Manent two Drawers.
George. Good Lord, that Master Carlo could not take heed,
   and knowing what a gentleman the knight is if he be
   angry!
Drawer. A pox on 'em! They have left all the meat on our
   hands. Would they were choked with it for me!   290

---

275. peremptory] *Q1, Q2, F1* (paramptorie*); peramptorie *Q3*; peremptorie
F2.   276. Peremptory] *Q, F* (Peremptorie).   277.1.] *Q; not in F*.
282. 'Sblood] *Q;* Slid *F*   appeal] *Q;* appeare *F*   285.1. *Exeunt*] *Q; not
in F*   285.2.] *Q; not in F*

---

275. *peremptory*] contradictory. Possibly the spelling in *Q1, Q2*, and *F1*
(see collation notes) is an attempt to convey a vulgarism; *H&S* point out
Constable Haggis's 'parantory' in *BF* 4.1.70, justified by the Stage-keeper's
comment (Ind.44–5) on 'mistaking words, as the fashion is, in the *stage*-
practice'. Although this line of humour is not developed in *EMO*, and the
Constable is not presented as a Dogberry, the audience's expectation of
broad farce in the playing of constable-scenes should not be discounted. The
constable may be using the term in its legal sense: arbitrarily dismissive of
another opinion or request, as in one-sided but binding objections or writs
(*OED* 1).
  280. *like to answer*] being held responsible.
  284–5. *get . . . dressed*] have your injuries medically treated.
  285.2. Manent] they remain onstage.
  289. *meat*] food.
  290. *for me*] as far as I'm concerned.

Enter MACILENTE.

Macilente. What, are they gone, sirs?

George. O, here's Master Macilente.

Macilente. Sirrah George, do you see that concealment there? That napkin under the table?

George. [*Seeing Fungoso under the table*] God's so', Signor   295
Fungoso!

Macilente. He's a good pawn for the reckoning. Be sure you keep him here and let him not go away till I come again, though he offer to discharge all. I'll return presently.   [*Exit.*]   300

George. [*To the other Drawer*] Sirrah, we have a pawn for the reckoning.

Drawer. What? Of Macilente?

George. No. Look under the table.

Fungoso. I hope all be quiet now. If I can get but forth of this   305
street, I care not.   *Looks out under the table.*
Masters, I pray you, tell me: is the constable gone?

George. What? Master Fungoso?

Fungoso. Was 't not a good device, the same of me, sirs?

George. Yes, faith. Ha' you been here all this while?   310

Fungoso. O God, ay. Good sirs, look an the coast be clear. I'd fain be going.

George. All's clear but the reckoning, and that you must clear and pay before you go, I assure you.

Fungoso. I pay? 'Slight, I ate not a bit since I came into the   315
house yet.

290.1.] *Q; in margin of F: Macilente comes backe.*   297. He's a] *Q;* Hei's *F.*
306. SD] *Q; in margin of F.*   309. the] *Q;* this *F.*

---

297. *pawn . . . reckoning*] pledge guaranteeing that the bill will be paid.

299. *though . . . all*] even if Fungoso offers to pay the entire bill (as a way of escaping).

305. *get . . . of*] only get away from.

309. *device*] trick (of hiding under the table).

of me] usually equivalent to the possessive 'my', but also connotes causation. Although the phrase recurs in popular speech, it may hint at the bucolic, betraying Fungoso's country origins. The constuction is sportive, emphasizing his premature elation, and thereby setting him up for a fall (Partridge, *Syntax*, p. 51).

Drawer. Why, you may when you please, sir. 'Tis all ready
   below that was bespoken.

Fungoso. Bespoken? Not by me, I hope!

George. By you, sir? I know not that, but 'twas for you and   320
   your company, I am sure.

Fungoso. My company? I was an invited guest, so I was.

Drawer. Faith, we have nothing to do with that, sir. They're
   all gone but you, and we must be answered. That's the
   short and the long on 't.   325

Fungoso. Nay, if you will grow to extremities, my masters,
   then would this pot, cup, and all were in my belly, if I
   have a cross about me.

George. What, and have such apparel? Do not say so, signor.
   That mightily discredits your clothes.   330

Fungoso. By Jesu, the tailor had all my money this morning,
   and yet I must be fain to alter my suit too. Good sirs, let

---

331. By Jesu, the] *Q;* As I am an honest man, my *F*

317–18. *'Tis . . . bespoken*] The food that was ordered is all prepared below
(i.e., in the kitchen, usually located in the cellar). For this idiomatic construction, used for emphasis in the seventeenth century, see Partridge,
Syntax, pp. 32–3.

320–1.] bizarrely legalistic defeat of a law-student by an apprentice.
Usually confrontations between apprentices and law-students were more
violent, as in the traditional street battles between Inns of Court gangs who
attacked parading apprentices on Shrove Tuesday. For the Shrovetide setting
of *EMO* see introd., pp. 31ff.

324. *answered*] paid.

326. *extremities*] quibbling on (*a*) exaggerated views based on extreme
ends of a scale instead of the mean (*OED* 3), referring to George's last words,
'the short and the long on't'; and (*b*) conditions of extreme need (*OED* 7),
here referring to financial embarrassment.

327. *would . . . belly*] A colloquial way of retorting to an insult, the phrase
is a jeering offer to eat his words if he is lying.

328. *a cross*] i.e., any money at all; a quibble on the crosses with which
many small coins (the silver penny and half penny, for example) were
stamped. Cf. *Westward Ho!* 3.2.60 (Hoy, 2.209).

329. *apparel*] a legal in-joke, again from the one-upping apprentice. Aside
from the usual sense of the word as clothing, 'apparels' in Inns of Court
jargon means 'debts': either a debit balance or an undischarged debt to a
particular Inn, usually for catering. See R. J. Schoeck, 'Inns of Court Nomenclature', *N&Q* (1953): 3. Hence Fungoso's later reference to 'purse or
apparel' at 434, and his request for 'a capon's leg' at 445, once his debts are
paid.

me go: 'tis Friday night, and, in good truth, I have no
stomach in the world to eat anything.

Drawer. That's no matter, so you pay, sir.   335

Fungoso. Pay? God's light, with what conscience can you ask
me to pay that I never drank for?

George. Yes, sir, I did see you drink once.

Fungoso. By this cup (which is silver) but you did not. You do
me infinite wrong. I looked in the pot once, indeed, but   340
I did not drink.

Drawer. Well, sir, if you can satisfy my master, it shall be all
one to us.   *One calls George within.*
[*Calling back*] By and by!

                                        Exeunt.

<hr>

GREX

Cordatus. Lose not yourself now, signor.   345

<hr>

Enter MACILENTE *and* DELIRO.

Macilente. Tut, sir, you did bear too hard a conceit of me in
that, but I will now make my love to you most transparent, in spite of any dust of suspicion that may be raised
to dim it; and henceforth, since I see it is so against your
humour, I will never labour to persuade you.   350

342. my] *Q;* our *F.*   343. SD] *Q; not in F.*   344.1.] *Q; not in F.*   345.1.]
Q; Act V. Scene VIII./ MACILENTE, DELIRO, FALLACE. *F.*   349. dim] *Q;*
cloud *F.*

<hr>

333. *Friday night*] a fast night; cf. Cob's outburst against 'villainous
Fridays' in *EMI* (*Q*) 3.1.131–6. Fast days, when fish was eaten instead of
meat, were a political-economic convenience, not just a religions custom,
and were not strictly observed. Fungoso pleads both a fast night and lack of
appetite ('no stomach') to avoid eating and thus paying for the meal. But
see 445.

340–1. *I looked . . . drink*] a law-student's quibble, prompted by the
drawers' stolid disbelief.

345.] Get a hold of yourself. This warning also prepares us for the increasingly rapid pace in the rest of the act as the scene changes to Deliro's house,
back to the Mitre (429.1–2), and then to the Counter (478.1), and finally,
in 5.4, to court, before returning to the playhouse frame of the Induction.

346. *conceit*] personal opinion (*OED* 4).

346–7. *in that*] in our earlier quarrel. See next note.

Deliro. Why, I thank you, signior. But what's that you tell me
   may concern my peace so much?

Macilente. Faith, sir, 'tis thus. Your wife's brother, Signor
   Fungoso, being at supper tonight at a tavern with a
   sort of gallants, there happened some division amongst   355
   'em, and he is left in pawn for the reckoning. Now, if
   ever you look that time shall present you with a happy
   occasion to do your wife some gracious and acceptable
   service, take hold of this opportunity, and presently
   go and redeem him; for, being her brother, and his   360
   credit so amply engaged as now it is, when she shall
   hear (as he cannot himself but he must out of extremity
   report it) that you came and offered yourself so
   kindly and with that respect of his reputation, 'slud, the
   benefit cannot but make her dote and grow mad of your   365
   affections.

Deliro. Now, by heaven, Macilente, I acknowledge myself
   exceedingly indebted to you by this kind tender of your
   love, and I am sorry to remember that I was ever so rude
   to neglect a friend of your worth. [*Calling off-stage*] Bring   370
   me shoes and a cloak there! [*To Macilente*] I was going to
   bed if you had not come. What tavern is it?

Macilente. The Mitre, sir.

Deliro. O. [*Calling*] Why, Fido, my shoes! [*To Macilente*] Good
   faith, it cannot but please her exceedingly.   375

   Enter FALLACE [*and* FIDO *with shoes and cloak*].

Fallace. [*To Deliro*] Come, I mar'l what piece of nightwork you

---

364. 'slud] *Q;* Why *F.*   370. worth] *Q;* importance *F.*   375.1. *Enter*
FALLACE] *Q; not in F.*

---

350. *persuade you*] persuade you that your wife is inconstant; see
4.3.172–6.
   355. *sort*] group.
   division] disagreement, dissension (*OED* 4).
   360. *redeem him*] pay his tavern bill.
   362. *he cannot himself*] he himself cannot behave otherwise.
   extremity] condition of extreme urgency, need, or embarrassment (see
326).
   365–6. *grow . . . affections*] parallels 'dote': fall madly in love with you for
you feelings of goodwill.
   368. *tender*] offer.

have in hand now, that you call for your cloak and your
shoes. What, is this your pander?

Deliro. O sweet wife, speak lower. I would not he should hear
thee for a world—   380

Fallace. Hang him, rascal! I cannot abide him for his treachery, with his wild quick-set beard there. Whither go you
now with him?

Deliro. No whither with him, dear wife. I go alone to a place
from whence I will return instantly. [*Aside to Macilente*]   385
Good Macilente, acquaint not her with it by any
means; it may come so much the more accepted.
Frame some other answer. [*To Fallace*] I'll come back
immediately.   *Exit* DELIRO [*and* FIDO].

Fallace. [*Calling after him*] Nay, an I be not worthy to know   390
whither you go, stay till I take knowledge of your coming
back.

Macilente. Hear you, Mistress Deliro.

Fallace. So, sir, and what say you?

Macilente. Faith, lady, my intents will not deserve this slight   395
respect, when you shall know 'em.

Fallace. Your intents? Why, what may your intents be, for
God's sake?

Macilente. Troth, the time allows no circumstance, lady.
Therefore know this was but a device to remove your   400
husband hence and bestow him securely, whilst
(with more conveniency) I might report to you a
misfortune that hath happened to Monsieur Brisk.
Nay, comfort, sweet lady. This night, being at supper, a
sort of young gallants committed a riot, for the which he   405
only is apprehended and carried to the Counter, where,
if your husband and other creditors should but have
knowledge of him, the poor gentleman were undone
forever.

389. *Exit* DELIRO] *Q; not in* F.

382. *wild . . . beard*] Whalley and *H&S* quote from Taylor's description of
beards in *Superbiae Flagellum* (1621), c7v: 'And some (to set their love's desire
on edge) / Are cut and pruned like to a quickset hedge'.
388. *Frame*] invent.
399. *circumstance*] beating about the bush; circumlocution.

Fallace. Ay me, that he were!   410
Macilente. Now, therefore, if you can think upon any present
      means for his delivery, do not forslow it. A bribe to the
      officer that committed him will do it.
Fallace. O God, sir, he shall not want for a bribe. Pray you,
      will you commend me to him, and say I'll visit him   415
      presently?
Macilente. No, lady, I shall do you better service in protract-
      ing your husband's return, that you may go with more
      safety.
Fallace. Good truth, so you may. Farewell, good sir.   420
                                    Exit [MACILENTE].
      Lord, how a woman may be mistaken in a man! I would
      have sworn upon all the testaments in the world he
      had not loved Master Brisk. [*Calling*] Bring me my
      keys there, maid.—Alas, good gentleman, if all I have i'
      this earthly world will pleasure him, it shall be at his   425
      service.   *Exit.*

Mitis. How Macilente sweats i' this business, if you mark him!
Cordatus. Ay, you shall see the true picture of spite anon. Here
      comes the pawn and his redeemer.

              Enter DELIRO, [*and*] FUNGOSO, [*with* GEORGE, *the*]
                        Drawer, *following them.*

Deliro. Come, brother, be not discouraged for this, man,   430
      what?
Fungoso. No, truly, I am not discouraged, but I protest to you,
      brother, I have done imitating any more gallants either in

---

420.1. *Exit*] *Q; not in F.*   426. SD] *Q; not in F.*   429.1–2.] *Q, with bracketed words supplied by this ed.; Act V. Scene IX. /* DELIRO, FVNGOSO, DRAWERS,
/ MACILENTE. *F.*   432. *Fungoso.*] *F* (FVNG.); *Drawer. Q.*

  410.] How terrible if that should happen to him!
  412. *forslow*] delay.
  413. *him*] Brisk.
  424–5. *gentleman . . . him . . . his*] referring obsessively to Brisk.

purse or apparel, but as shall become a gentleman for
good carriage or so.   435

Deliro. You say well. [*To George*] This is all i' the bill here? Is
't not?

George. Ay, sir.

Deliro. [*Giving money*] There's your money: tell it. [*To
Fungoso*] And, brother, I am glad I met with so good occa-   440
sion to show my love to you.

Fungoso. I will study to deserve it, in good truth, and I live.

Deliro. [*To George*] What, is 't right?

Geroge. Ay, sir, and I thank you.

Fungoso. Let me have a capon's leg saved, now the reckoning   445
is paid.

George. You shall, sir.   *Exit.*

Enter MACILENTE.

Macilente. Where is Signor Deliro?

Deliro. Here, Macilente.

Macilente. [*Drawing him aside*] Hark you, sir, ha' you dis-   450
patched this same?

Deliro. Ay, marry, have I.

Macilente. Well then, I can tell you news: Brisk is i' the
Counter.

Deliro. I' the Counter?   455

Macilente. 'Tis true, sir, committed for the stir here tonight.
Now would I have you send your brother home afore,
with the report of this your kindness done him to his

---

447. SD] *Q; not in F.*   447.1.] *Q; not in F.*

434. *purse or apparel*] (*a*) spending or clothing; (*b*) credit or debt, especially for food and drink (Inns of Court jargon). See 329n.

435. *carriage*] appearances, manners.

439. *tell*] count.

445. *capon's leg*] Aside from his comic admission of hunger and his readi-
ness to eat provided someone else pays the bill, Fungoso's choice of food
indicates that he is now 'out of his humour' and intends to remain so: capon
'procureth an equal temperature of all the humours', according to Buttes,
Diet's Dry Dinner (1599), K3r.

457. *brother*] brother-in-law.

sister, which will so pleasingly possess her, and out of his
mouth too, that i' the meantime you may clap your action   460
on Brisk, and your wife, being in so happy a mood,
cannot entertain it ill by any means.

Deliro. 'Tis very true. She cannot indeed, I think.

Macilente. Think? Why, 'tis past thought! You shall never meet
the like opportunity, I assure you.   465

Deliro. I will do it. [*They join Fungoso.*] Brother, pray you, go
home afore—this gentleman and I have some private
business—and tell my sweet wife I'll come presently.

Macilente. [*To Fungoso*] And, signor, acquaint your sister how
liberally and out of his bounty your brother has used   470
you—do you see?—made you a man of good reckoning;
redeemed that you never were possessed of, credit; gave
you as gentlemanlike terms as might be; found no fault
with your coming behind the fashion; nor nothing.

Fungoso. Nay, I am out of those humours now.   475

Macilente. Well, if you be out, keep your distance, and be not
made a shot-clog no more. [*To Deliro*] Come, signor, let's
make haste.

                              Exeunt.

                    Enter BRISK *and* FALLACE.

Fallace. O Master Fastidius, what pity is 't to see so sweet a
man as you are in so sour a place!   *And kisses him.*   480

---

464. Why, 'tis] *This ed.;* why'ts *Q;* why, 'tis *F*   473. no] *Q;* any *F*
478.1–2.] *Q; Act V. Scene X. /* FALLACE, FASTIDIVS BRISKE. *F*   480. SD]
Q; not in F.

---

460. *clap your action*] slap your law-suit.

467. *afore*] i.e., before us.

471. *made . . . reckoning*] established you as a man of good credit, a man
who pays his bills.

472. *that*] that which.

473. *gentlemanlike terms*] courteous terms of repayment, as between gentlemen; in this case amounting to a refusal of repayment on the grounds of
family affection (see 440–1).

474. *coming . . . fashion*] trying to keep up with the latest fashions.

477. *a shot-clog*] a dupe; one who is tolerated because he pays the shot,
or reckoning, for the rest; otherwise a mere clog upon the company (Nares,
Skeat).

Cordatus. As upon her lips, does she mean?

Mitis. O, this is to be imagined the Counter, belike?

Fastidius. Troth, fair lady, 'tis first the pleasure of the fates,
and next of the constable, to have it so, but I am patient
and, indeed, comforted the more in your kind visitation.   485

Fallace. Nay, you shall be comforted in me more than this, if
you please, sir. I sent you word by my brother, sir, that
my husband laid to 'rest you this morning. I know not
whether you received it or no?

Fastidius. No, believe it, sweet creature. Your brother gave me   490
no such intelligence.

Fallace. O, the Lord!

Fastidius. But has your husband any such purpose?

Fallace. O God, Master Brisk, yes, and therefore be presently
discharged, for if he come with his actions upon you—   495
Lord deliver you!—you are in for one-half a score year!
He kept a poor man in Ludgate once twelve year for
sixteen shillings. Where's your keeper? For God's
love, call him! Let him take a bribe and dispatch you.

485. visitation] *Q;* visit *F.*   494. God, Master] *Q;* sweet master *F.*
498-9. God's love] *Q;* loues sake *F.*

481.] a facetious remark, prompting Mitis's articulation of the change in
location.

485. *visitation*] pompous diction, probably court usage for a friendly
social call. Cf. *Journal of the Earl of Nottingham* (1605), p. 50: 'Sunday,
Monday, and Tuesday were . . . spent only in visitation and matters of compliment with one or other' (cited in *OED* 5). The term usually connotes an
official inspection, or a visit to the distressed as an act of charity (*OED* 1,
3); the latter may apply to Brisk.

486. *comforted in me*] comforted by my visit; with an inadvertent erotic
suggestion of sexual entry. Fallace is in a panic trying to hurry Brisk out of
jail; Brisk misreads her 'passion' (502) as seductive, and kisses her (515).

488. *laid to 'rest*] lay in wait to arrest.

494-8.] Prisoners could not be released until their debts were settled or
their creditors forgave them; potentially, their imprisonment was permanent
(Johansson, *Law*, p. 34).

496. *one-half a score year*] ten years. Measurements of time, value, or distance were generally indicated in the singular after numerals (Partridge,
Accidence, p. 14). But see 3.3.143-4: 'March was fifteen years ago'.

Lord, how my heart trembles! Here are no spies, are   500
there?

Fastidius. No, sweet mistress. Why are you in this passion?

Fallace. O Christ, Master Fastidius, if you knew how I took
up my husband today, when he said he would arrest you;
and how I railed at him that persuaded him to 't, the   505
scholar there (who, on my conscience, loves you now);
and what care I took to send you intelligence by my
brother; and how I gave him four sovereigns for his pains;
and now how I came running out hither without man or
boy with me, so soon as I heard on 't; you'd say I were   510
in a passion indeed. Your keeper, for God's sake! O
Master Brisk, as 'tis in *Euphues*: 'Hard is the choice when
one is compelled either by silence to die with grief or by
speaking to live with shame.'

Fastidius. Fair lady, I conceive you, and may this kiss assure   515
you that, where adversity hath (as it were) contracted,
prosperity shall not—God's light, your husband!

Fallace. O me!

       Enter DELIRO [*and*] MACILENTE.

Deliro. Ay! Is 't thus?

---

503. Christ, Master] *Q*; Lord, Master *F*   513. either by] *Q*, *Fb*; by *Fa*.
517. God's light] *Q*; gods me *F*   518.1.] *Q*; *Act V. Scene XI.* / DELIRO,
MACILENTE, FALLACE, / FASTIDIVS BRISKE. *F*

503-4. *took up*] rebuked, opposed.
505. *at him*] at Macilente.
508. *four sovereigns*] gold coins virtually interchangeable with angel-nobles, worth about 10 shillings each. Fallace gave 'four angels' at 4.1.127, just the 40 shillings Fungoso needed for his wardrobe.
512. *as 'tis in* Euphues] Cf. Lyly, *Euphues and his England* (1580), ed. Bond, 2.123, but the original has 'writing' instead of 'speaking'. The line was frequently quoted; see *H&S*, 9.480.
515. *kiss*] It is not clear whether this kiss is actually given, although the attempt is certainly in progress until interrupted at 517.
516-17. *where ... not*] although misfortune has brought us together, good fortune will not [separate us afterwards]. Brisk seems to be promising a courtly lover's eternal devotion, but is interrupted by the lady's husband.

Macilente. Why, how now, Signor Deliro? Has the wolf seen   520
    you? Ha? Hath Gorgon's head made marble on you?
Deliro. Some planet strike me dead!
Macilente. Why, look you, sir, I told you you might have sus-
    pected this long afore, had you pleased, and ha' saved this
    labour of admiration now, and passion, and such extrem-   525
    ities as this frail lump of flesh is subject unto. Nay, why
    do you not dote now, signor? Methinks you should say it
    were some enchantment, *deceptio visus*, or so, ha? If you
    could persuade yourself it were a dream now, 'twere
    excellent. Faith, try what you can do, signor. It may be   530
    your imagination will be brought to it in time. There's
    nothing impossible.
Fallace. Sweet husband?
Deliro. Out, lascivious strumpet!   *Exit* DELIRO.
Macilente. What? Did you see how ill that stale vein became   535
    him afore, of 'sweet wife' and 'dear heart'? And are you
    fallen just into the same now, with 'sweet husband'?
    Away! Follow him! Go! Keep state, what? Remember you
    are a woman: turn impudent. Gi' him not the head,
    though you gi' him the horns. Away! And yet methinks   540

---

534. SD] *Q; not in F.*

520–1. *Has . . . you?*] Cf. Browne, 3.8: 'That a wolf, first seeing a man,
begets a dumbness in him'. Gifford cites Virgil's *Eclogues* 9.53–4, as evidence
of the ancient belief that if a wolf saw a man before the man saw the wolf,
the man would lose his power of speech; *H&S* cite Pliny, *Natural History*
8.22.
    521. *Gorgon's head*] According to the Greek myth, the gorgon Medusa
had serpents instead of hair on her head; the sight was so loathsome and ter-
rifying that it turned her enemies to stone. Perseus killed Medusa, and presented her head to the goddess Athene, who used it as a final weapon on the
battlefield (cf. Apollodorus 2 and Pindar, *Pythian* 10.46.8, cited in Wheeler,
pp. 104–5, 108).
    on] of.
    522.] an outcry against an awful destiny; cf. 2.1.309n.
    524. *and ha' saved*] and that you might have saved.
    527. *dote*] i.e., make excuses for Fallace's behaviour.
    528. deceptio visus] deception of sight, illusion.
    538. *Keep state*] Hold on to your dignity (*OED* 19).
    539–40. *Gi' . . . horns*] Do not allow him to have his head (his freedom,
used of horses freed from the bridle), even though you have given him horns

you should take your leave of *enfant-perdu* here, your
forlorn hope.

Exit FALLACE.

How now, Monsieur Brisk? What? Friday at night? And
in affliction too? And yet your *pulpamenta*, your delicate
morsels? I perceive the affection of ladies and gentle-   545
women pursues you wheresoever you go, monsieur.

Fastidius. Now, in good faith, and as I am gentle, there
could not have come a thing i' this world to have distracted me more than the wrinkled fortunes of this poor
dame.   550

---

541. *enfant-perdu*] *This ed.; Infans-perdus Q; Enfans-perdus F.*   542.1.] *Q;
not in F.*   550. dame] *Q; spinster F.*

(by cuckolding him). See *OED, Head,* 6, 26, and 57. The ironic advice is that
she should not admit she is wrong, or cede control of the marriage to her
husband.

541. *you . . . your*] said to the departing Fallace.

541–2. *enfant–perdu . . . forlorn hope*] equivalent military terms denoting
a sentinel placed in an extremely perilous and desperate battle position,
where he will probably not survive. The epithet, appropriately French
with English translation (mocking Brisk's humour), applies financially,
as one 'past hope of recovery' (Blount's *Glossographia* (1656), cited in
OED, Perdu 2a). Cf. Dekker, *Work for Armourers* (Grosart, 4.120): 'These
younger brothers were appointed to stand *Infans perdus* (or the *Forlorn
hope*) because though they had little to lose but their lives; yet they should
win honour, nay perhaps knighthood, which in these days are better than
lands'.

543–4. *Friday . . . too?*] Macilente pretends that Brisk is undergoing a
spiritual conversion: Friday is a fast-day (Brisk also missed supper at the
Mitre) and he has just been humiliated by arrest, incarceration, and exposure as a would-be adulterer by his new mistress's husband—the man he
hoped to borrow money from. In mock-religious terms, Brisk is piously
fasting and sorrowing, as Macilente remarks sarcastically, but he has not yet
attained a state of true penitence.

544. pulpamenta] 'delicate dish of meat finely seasoned' (Cooper, *The-
saurus Linguae Romanae & Britannicae* (1578), cited in *H&S*). But the
delicate morsel Brisk has been nibbling is Fallace; Jonson is following
Persius, the satirical poet of AD 34–62, who used the expression *pulpa sceler-
ata* ('stolen flesh') figuratively to refer to the flesh as a sign of sensuality
(cited in *Cassell's New Latin Dictionary,* 1968).

547. *Now . . . gentle*] Compare these fashionable oaths to the simpler responses at 557 and 562; the latter are more direct 'prayers' to go with his
fasting and sorrow.

549. *wrinkled*] spoiled, imperfect.

550. *dame*] The term was used of any lady of position, especially poeti-

366 EVERY MAN OUT OF HIS HUMOUR [ACT 5

Macilente. O yes, sir, I can tell you a thing will distract you
much better, believe it. Signor Deliro has entered three
actions against you, three actions, monsieur: marry, one
of them (I'll put you in comfort) is but three thousand
mark, and the other two, some five thousand pound 555
together—trifles, trifles.

Fastidius. O God, I am undone!

Macilente. Nay, not altogether so, sir. The knight must have
his hundred pound repaid. That'll help, too. And then
sixscore pound for a diamond: you know where. These 560
be things will weigh, monsieur, they will weigh.

Fastidius. O Jesu!

Macilente. What, do you sigh? This it is to kiss the hand of a
countess, to have her coach sent for you, to hang poniards
in ladies' garters, to wear bracelets of their hair, and, for 565
every one of these great favours, to give some slight jewel
of five hundred crowns or so. Why, 'tis nothing! Now,
monsieur, you see the plague that treads o' the heels of
your foppery. Well, go your ways in. Remove yourself to
the twopenny ward quickly to save charges, and there set 570

---

555. mark] *Q; not in F.*   555–6. pound together] *Q;* a peece *F.*   557. O
God] *Q;* O *F.*   562. O Jesu!] *Q;* O, heauen! *F.*

---

cally; otherwise: (*a*) a woman in rank next below a lady; the wife of a citizen
(*OED* 7b); (*b*) generally, the mistress of a household. Cf. Bilson, *The Per-
petual Government of Christ's Church* (1593), p. 58: 'Every poor woman that
hath either maid or apprentice is called Dame: and yet Dame is as much as
Domina and used to Ladies of greatest account, as Dame Isabel and Madam'
(*OED* 2).

554–5. *three thousand mark, five thousand pound*] A mark was worth
two-thirds of a pound. The total of £7000 was a large but not unusual
debt for a gentleman trying to keep up appearances at court. Tradesmen
offered easy credit despite the risk of loss, partly because they needed
the court patronage to survive, and, once given, the credit was hard to
stop; and partly because they discovered opportunities for exceeding
the legal rate of interest (10 per cent) by persuading the debtor to buy
goods on credit in order to sell them at a lower price for cash (Stone, pp.
513–16).

558. *The knight*] Puntarvolo.

560. *diamond*] This barbed comment reminds Brisk of his earlier boasts
of giving and receiving expensive gifts, as at 4.3.315–22.

568. *treads . . . of*] follows hard upon.

570. *the twopenny ward*] Cf. 215–16n. Brisk is probably in the knights'

up your rest to spend Sir Puntar's hundred pound for
him. Away, good pomander, go!

Exit BRISK.

ACT 5   SCENE 4

[*The* Actor *portraying the* Queen *passes over the stage.*]

*The very wonder of her presence strikes Macilente to the
earth, dumb and astonished; from whence, rising and
recovering heart, his passion thus utters itself.*

Macilente. Blessèd, divine, unblemished, sacred, pure,
Glorious, immortal, and indeed immense—
O, that I had a world of attributes

572.1.] *Q; not in F.*

[ACT 5 SCENE 4]] *The original catastrophe, printed as an appendix with the
apology in Q; Q's revised catastrophe concludes 5.3; F's catastrophe concludes 5.11.*
0.2–4.] *See 'Apology for the Original Catastrophe', ll. 30–3, in Appendix A:1.*

ward, which cost a groat a night for a private room, plus a groat for every
pair of sheets. The twopenny ward cost only twopence a night for a private
bed; one penny if it were shared (Hoy, 3.41–2).

570–1. *set . . . rest*] venture your final stake; risk what funds you have left
on one play. Cf. Gascoigne, *Supposes* (1566), 3.2. In primero, the stakes to
be kept in reserve are agreed upon at the beginning of the game; if a player
is forced to gamble his reserved stake and wins, then the game continues; if
he loses, the game is terminated (*OED, rest* sb.2, 6b). But Brisk has no money
left, as Macilente's taunt reminds him: his only ready cash at this point is
the bet with Puntarvolo, and that will have to be returned, according to the
terms of the agreement signed earlier; see 4.3.60–2.

572. *pomander*] scent container; cf. 2.1.110.

0.1.] See Appendix A: I, 'Apology', in which Jonson explains that the
original ending was not well received because the Queen was portrayed on
the stage by an actor. She may have been 'discovered' by drawing curtains
over the discover-space, or revealed 'above' in state, perhaps in the lords'
room, but Jonson gave no SD for her exit. Passing over the stage is not unusual
(see 4.2.0.1–2) and is certainly convenient. At the court performance,
however, the actual queen probably 'played the part' from her position in
state in the audience. See Appendix I:3, AT COURT.

0.4. *passion*] (*a*) feeling by which the mind is powerfully affected or
moved; a vehement, commanding, overpowering emotion, in art often in
reaction to a personified force (*OED* 6); (*b*) condition of being acted upon
by an external agency; an effect or impression produced by action from
without (*OED* 5).

To lend or add to this high majesty!   5
Never till now did object greet mine eyes
With any light content, but in her graces
All my malicious powers have lost their stings.
Envy is fled my soul at sight of her,
And she hath chased all black thoughts from my bosom,
Like as the sun doth darkness from the world.   10
My stream of humour is run out of me,
And as our city's torrent, bent t'infect
The hallowed bowels of the silver Thames,
Is checked by strength and clearness of the river
Till it hath spent itself e'en at the shore,   15
So in the ample and unmeasured flood
Of her perfections are my passions drowned,
And I have now a spirit as sweet and clear
As the most rarefied and subtle air;
With which, and with a heart as pure as fire   20
(Yet humble as the earth), do I implore,   *He kneels.*

5–40.] *Reprinted separately in F, with titles:* Which, in the presentation before
Queene E. was thus varyed, / BY MACILENTE. *F1;* The Epilogue at the
presentation before Queen ELIZABETH. *F2.*   21. SD] *Q; not in F.*

---

7. *light content*] enlightening pleasure, illuminating happiness. Macilente
is experiencing a kind of epiphany, a spiritual and intellectual revelation.
  10. *Like as*] just as.
  11.] Appropriately, Macilente's is the final instance in the play-within-the-
frame of a character thrust 'out of his humour'.
  12. *our city's torrent*] Dowgate Torrent. In the image of the torrent, 11–19,
Macilente's malice and jealousy of people with superior, if undeserved,
advantages is compared to sewage or human excrement flushed through
Dowgate Torrent (see 4.5.154–9n) into the Thames—representing the dignity
and virtue of the Queen—which, because of its greater strength and clean-
ness, immediately dissipates and purifies the puny 'stream of humour' before
it can infect the 'hallowed bowels' of the river. For the implications of this
sensationalistic image so close to the Queen see John Gordon Sweeney III,
Jonson and the Psychology of Public Theater (Princeton, 1985), p. 27.
  21. SD] the conventional prelude to prayer. 'A practice of offering up a
prayer for the lord's well-being at the end of a performance was probably of
ancient derivation, although whether it survived in the public theatres may
perhaps be doubted' (Chambers, 1.311). Specific praise and prayer for Queen
Elizabeth emerged early in her reign; Bale's *King Johan* (1538–60), ends with
speeches by Civil Order, Nobility, and Clergy lauding her superior virtue
and strength, 'Which may be a light to other princes all / For the godly ways
whom she doth daily move / To her liege people, through God's word special'
(2672–4). Similarly, Discipline, Piety, and Exercitation pray for Queen,

O heaven, that she whose figure hath effected
This change in me may never suffer change
In her admired and happy government!
May still this island be called Fortunate   25
And rugged Treason tremble at the sound,
When Fame shall speak it with an emphasis.
Let foreign Policy be dull as lead,
And pale Invasion come with half a heart
When he but looks upon her blessèd soil;   30
The throat of War be stopped within her land;
And turtle-footed Peace dance fairy rings
About her court; where never may there come

---

22. figure] *Q;* prescence *F.*   23. never suffer] *Q;* suffer most late *F.*

Lords, Council, Church, and Commons at the end of Wager's *The Longer
Thou Livest* (1559); so too Fulwell's *Like Will to Like* (1568), 1231–42, and the
last two lines of R. B.'s *Apius and Virginia* (1575). The practice of 'kneeling
after the play' is mocked in Middleton's *A Mad World, My Masters* (1608)
(Regents), 5.2.178–82 (cited in *H&S*). Shakespeare apparently liked the traditional prayer to powerful patrons, although he transferred the sense to
include the whole audience; see the epilogues to *MND* and *Temp.* Jonson
reserved future compliments to royalty for his masques.

22–40.] The personifications are conventional emblems of the Queen's
power. Cf. *Speeches to the Queen at Bisham* (1592) in John Nichols, *The Progresses and Public Processions of Queen Elizabeth* (London, 1823), 3.134–5: 'One
hand she stretcheth to France, to weaken Rebels; the other to Flanders, to
strengthen Religion; her heart to both countries, her virtues to all. This is
she at whom Envy hath shot all her arrows, and now for anger broke her
bow; on whom God hath laid all his blessings, and we for joy clap our hands.
Heedless Treason goeth headless; and close Treachery restless: Danger
looketh pale to behold her Majesty; and Tyranny blusheth to hear of her
mercy . . . We, upon our knees, will entreat her to come into the valley, that
our houses may be blessed with her presence, whose hearts are filled with
quietness by her government.'

27. *emphasis*] vigour or intensity of expression.

28. *foreign Policy*] the strategies undertaken by foreign governments; not
the attitudes of the English Foreign Office.

32. *turtle-footed*] *H&S* suggest 'slowfooted' but the reference is more
likely to mean 'dancing like a lover', or 'moving to the rhythms of a love-
song'. The turtle-dove is the symbol of love and constancy, like the 'turtle-
billing lovers' of *EMI* (*F*) 1.5.68, and the Song of Solomon 2.12: 'The time
of singing is come, / And the voice of the turtle is heard in our land'. Ford
and Dekker, in *The Sun's Darling* 5.1, imitate Jonson in describing the cathartic effect of love on malice: 'and turtle-footed Peace / Dance like a fairy
through his realms, while all / That envy him shall like swift comets fall'.

Suspect or Danger, but all Trust and Safety.
Let Flattery be dumb and Envy blind   35
In her dread presence; Death himself admire her,
And may her virtues make him to forget
The use of his inevitable hand.
Fly from her, Age! Sleep, Time, before her throne!
Our strongest wall falls down when she is gone.   40

> *Here the trumpets sound a flourish, in which time*
> *Macilente converts himself to them that*
> *supply the place of Grex, and speaks.*

GREX

Macilente. How now, sirs? How like you it? Has 't not been
    tedious?
Cordatus. Nay, we ha' done censuring now.
Mitis. Yes, faith.
Macilente. How so?   45
Cordatus. Marry, because we'll imitate your actors and be out
    of our humours. Besides, here are those round about you
    [*Indicating audience*] of more ability in censure than we,
    whose judgements can give it a more satisfying allowance.
    We'll refer you to them.   50
Macilente. Ay, is 't e'en so? [*To Audience*] Well, gentlemen, I
    should have gone in and returned to you as I was, Asper,

40.1–3.] *Q; not in F.*

34. *Suspect*] suspicion.
40.1. sound a flourish] play a fanfare as the final sounding (cf. Ind.0.1
and 283.1) concluding the play; here signalling the return to the frame-play.
40.2. converts himself] (*a*) turns and, clearly no longer as acting in the
play-proper, joins the Grex; see Appendix A:II, 1, THE QUARTO, 13. (*b*) transforms himself into Asper either by removing Macilente's beard (cf. 5.3.382),
or some minor undoing of his costume or make-up, or simply by discarding
Macilente's stage voice and idiosyncrasies and retrieving Asper's (compare
Marston, *The Malcontent* 1.4.43.1: 'Bilioso *entering*, Malevole *shifteth his*
speech'). This dropping of the stage character and returning to mere actor
status has become, since Brecht, a modern trick to dispel illusion. Shakespeare plays the same trick in the epilogue of *AYL*, with 'Rosalind's' remark,
'If I were a woman', reminding the audience that a boy actor is speaking,
not the heroine.
43. *censuring*] giving critical commentary.
46–7. *be . . . humours*] abandon the critical 'humours' we adopted earlier.
49. *can . . . allowance*] can express their approval of the play more amply.

at the first. But (by reason the shift would have been
somewhat long, and we are loath to draw your patience
any farther) we'll entreat you to imagine it. And now—   55
that you may see I will be out of humour for company—
I stand wholly to your kind approbation, and, indeed, am
nothing so peremptory as I was in the beginning. Marry,
I will not do as Plautus in his *Amphitryo* for all this:
Summi Iovis causa, plaudite; beg a plaudit for God's sake.   60
But, if you, out of the bounty of your good liking, will
bestow it, why, you may, in time, make lean Macilente as
fat as Sir John Falstaff.

Exeunt.

NON EGO VENTOSAE PLEBIS SUFFRAGIA VENOR.

55. any farther] *Q* (any farder); farder *F*.   63.1.] *Q; not in F.*   63.2. NON
. . . VENOR.] *Q; not in F.*

53. *shift*] costume-change.
55. *imagine it*] perhaps another dig at the Chorus of *H5* with his repeated
requests to 'let us . . . / On your imaginary forces work' (Prol.17–18) and
other injunctions to 'Suppose' or 'but think' or 'Work, work your thoughts'
to imagine actions too difficult to stage (Chorus 3.3, 13, 25).
56. *for company*] along with everyone else, joining in to keep the others
company.
60. *Summi . . . plaudite*] 'For great Jove's sake, applaud', the last line of
Plautus's *Amphitryon*. Dekker imitated the line in the address to the reader
in *The Wonderful Year* (1603): 'Besides, if that which he presents upon the stage
of the world be good, why should he basely cry out (with that old poetical
mad-cap in his *Amphitrio*) *Iouis summi causa clare plaudite*, beg a plaudit for
God-sake' (*H&S*).
plaudit] round of applause, or any noisy expression of approval, such as
shouts or whistles; cf. Dekker, *The Belman of London* (1608) (Grosart,
3.90–1): 'all the bench-whistlers from one end to the other, gave a ringing
plaudit to the epilogue of his speech, in sign of approbation'.
63. *Falstaff*] another allusion to *1 and 2H4*; cf. *EMO* 5.2.22, referring to
Justice Silence.
63.2. *NON . . . VENOR*] from Horace *Epistles* 1.19.37: 'I do not chase after
approval from the fickle masses'. The sentiment, as well as the feel of direct
address to the reader, is Aristophanic; cf. the parabasis of *The Acharnians*
(trans. Douglass Parker, Ann Arbor, 1961), pp. 57–8, speaking of the poet's
objective: 'His integrity remains absolute. He will not knuckle, truckle, /
hoax, or coax his way into favor. He will not adulterate / the pure matter of
his plays with soft soap, bunkum, / or grease, / simply to win a prize. His
aim is not your applause, / or votes, / but your EDIFICATION: / ONWARD
AND UPWARD WITH HIS ART!'

Appendix A

THE APOLOGY AND VARIANT ENDINGS

The apology, followed by the original catastrophe, was appended to the quartos, in which a revised conclusion ended the play. The conclusion was revised again for the first folio, which appended the quarto revision and part of the original catastrophe, but eliminated the apology.

I

[APOLOGY FOR THE ORIGINAL CATASTROPHE]

It had another *catastrophe*, or conclusion, at the first playing, which (*dia to ten basilissan prosopopoesthai*) many seemed not

---

This apology is only in Q; not in F.   2. *dia . . . prosopopoesthai*] *Upper-case Roman letters in Q3; Greek letters in Q1, Q2.*

0.1. CATASTROPHE] the change or revolution that produces the conclusion or final event in a drama (*OED* 1).

2. dia . . . prosopopoesthai] because of the Queen's having been portrayed on stage by an actor. The degree of impersonation is not clear, although the concept of the Queen's effect on Macilente is flattering, and not unlike the idea of Spenser's Gloriana (or Jonson's Cynthia in *CR*) in projecting a virtue that uplifts and transforms those around her. The verb *prosopopoesthai* refers literally to the putting on of the mask worn by classical actors; this suggests a remote and formal embodiment of queenliness, rather than an imitation of Elizabeth's personal mannerisms. Certainly in rhetoric, *prosopopoeia* only applies to a person in whom some quality of abstraction is embodied (*OED* 2b). It is hard to know, at this remove, whether the objections to the scene were political or literary, but Jonson's apology speaks merely to dramatic concerns. However, in post-Reformation England, where Latin was seen as popish, and Greek was viewed by puritans both as a heathen heresy and as a sign of aggressively maintained class difference though divergence of educational opportunities (see Jack Cade's diatribes in *2H6*, for example), Jonson's disclaimer may project more than a touch of contempt for those who disagree with him. For a fuller defence of Jonson's representation of the Queen see H. Ostovich, '"So Sudden and Strange a Cure": A Rudimentary Masque in *Every Man Out of his Humour*', *ELR* 22.3 (November 1992): 315–32.

to relish it, and therefore 'twas since altered. Yet, that a right-
eyed and solid reader may perceive it was not so great a part
of the heaven awry as they would make it, we request him but 5
to look down upon these following reasons:

1. There hath been precedent of the like presentation in
divers plays, and is yearly in our city pageants or shows of
triumph.

2. It is to be conceived that Macilente, being so strongly 10
possessed with envy (as the poet here makes him), it must be
no slight or common object that should effect so sudden and

2–3. *many . . . relish it*] The reason does not seem to be antagonism to
the dramatic principle involved (see 8n and 8–9n below), but may indicate
either disapproval of the elaborate compliment given to an aged queen whose
popularity was waning, or suspicion of the sincerity of such a compliment
in the context of a comical satire.

3–4. *right-eyed*] clear-sighted.

4. *solid*] of sound scholarship and sober judgement in matters of learning or speculation (*OED* 12, citing this example).

4–5. *part . . . awry*] error in the nature of things; mistake in the course of
the universe.

6. *look . . . upon*] read and consider.

7–8. *in divers plays*] Some occasional pieces, like Sidney's *Lady of May*
(1578) and Peele's *The Arraignment of Paris* (1581?), depended on the Queen's
presence to resolve the conflicts in the plot. Presumably, when Peele's play
was subsequently performed at the first Blackfriars playhouse, an actor took
the Queen's part. Similarly, in Marston's revision of *Histriomastix* (1598), Act
6, an actor presumably plays Astraea, identified both in the marginal gloss
and by Peace herself as 'Q. Eliza'. Cf. Finkelpearl, *Histrio-Mastix*, and Anne
Barton, *Ben Jonson, Dramatist* (Cambridge, 1984), pp. 67–8.

8–9. *city . . . triumph*] Like occasional pieces, pageants usually depended
on the actual presence of the Queen, not a substitute. However, in the
progress through the city on 14 January 1559, the day before Elizabeth's coro-
nation, the Queen saw three complimentary representations of herself, performed by boy actors. Often such representations invoked a mythical parallel,
as in Peele's *Descensus Astraeae* (1591), in *The Life and Works of George Peele*,
ed. Prouty (New Haven, 1952), pp. 214–19, in which Astraea appears as 'Our
fair Eliza, or Zabeta fair', sitting at the top of the pageant 'Shadowing the
person of a peerless Queen' (l. 75). Similar representations of the Queen
appeared in pageants at which Elizabeth herself was not present. During
Leicester's progress through the Low Countries in 1586, several cities,
including Haarlem, Amsterdam, and Utrecht, offered royal tableaux specifically showing the Queen emblematically purging the state of envy and
tyranny (David M. Bergeron, *English Civic Pageantry, 1558–1642* (London,
1971), pp. 51–5). For details see Ostovich, '"So Sudden and Strange a
Cure"', pp. 325–6, and introd. pp. 36–7.

strange a cure upon him as the putting him clean *out of his humour.*

3. If his imagination had discoursed the whole world over   15
for an object, it could not have met with a more proper,
eminent, or worthy figure than that of her Majesty's; which
his election (though boldly, yet respectively) used to a moral
and mysterious end.

4. His greediness to catch at any occasion that might   20
express his affection to his sovereign may worthily plead for
him.

5. There was nothing (in his examined opinion) that could
more near or truly exemplify the power and strength of
her invaluable virtues than the working of so perfect a miracle   25
on so opposed a spirit, who not only persisted in his humour,
but was now come to the court with a purposed resolution
(his soul, as it were, new dressed in envy) to malign at anything that should front him, when suddenly (against expectation and all steel of his malice) the very wonder of her   30
presence strikes him to the earth, dumb and astonished; from
whence, rising and recovering heart, his passion thus utters
itself.

26. not] *Q1b*; no: *Q1a*.

---

15. *discoursed*] travelled (*OED* 1).
18. *election*] exercise of deliberate choice or preference (*OED* 2).
respectively] respectfully.
19. *mysterious*] godly, religious (*OED* 1c).
20. *greediness*] eagerness.
26. *opposed*] inimical. Cf. Reginald Scot, *The Discovery of Witchcraft* (1584), 13.30 (1886), p. 277: 'Lay a wager with your confederate (who must seem simple, or obstinately opposed against you)' (*OED* 3).
27–33. *now . . . itself*] A similar shock of powerlessness in face of a great good affects the malcontents in Peele's *Descensus Astraeae*, 108–13: '*1 Malcontent*: What meaneth this, I strive and cannot strike, / She is preserved by miracle belike: / If so then, wherefore threaten we in vain / That Queen, whose cause the gracious heavens maintain? / *2 Malcontent*. No marvel then although we faint and quail / For mighty is the truth and will prevail.'
27. *purposed*] intended.
29. *front*] meet face to face, confront; especially, face in defiance or hostility. Cf. Spenser, *A View of the Present State of Ireland* (1596) (Globe, 1633), 600–1: 'He dare now to front princes' (cited in *OED* 3).
30. *all steel*] rapier wit; firm determination.
32. *passion*] Cf. 5.4.0.4n.

II

THE REVISED CATASTROPHES

I. THE QUARTO

After 5.3.573.1.
[*Macilente.*] Why, here's a change! Now is my soul at peace.
　　I am as empty of all envy now
　　As they of merit to be envied at.
　　My humour, like a flame, no longer lasts
　　Than it hath stuff to feed it, and their virtue,   5
　　Being now raked up in embers of their folly,
　　Affords no ampler subject to my spirit.
　　I am so far from malicing their states
　　That I begin to pity 'em. It grieves me
　　To think they have a being. I could wish   10
　　They might turn wise upon it, and be saved now,
　　So heaven were pleased. But let them vanish, vapours.
　　And now with Asper's tongue (though not his shape),

---

1. The Quarto   3. of] *Q*; *not in F.*   5. virtue] *Q*; Follie *F.*   6. embers
of their folly] *Q*; their repentant ashes *F.*   7. spirit] *Q*; spleene *F.*
13–44.] *Q*; *not in F.*

---

3. *they*] those whom Macilente has been dis-humouring.
5. *stuff*] fuel.
5–6. *their virtue . . . folly*] their good qualities, now banked or protected
by the burnt residue of their foolish humours. The image is of a hearth, in
which the ashes are raked over the coals of the fire to keep it from being
utterly extinguished. The implication is that 'virtue' can be rekindled from
the ashes of 'folly' after a period of inactivity.
8. *malicing*] regarding with malice or envy; seeking or desiring to injure.
10. *being*] position or standing in the world.
11. *turn . . . it*] learn from their experience.
12. *So*] provided.
vapours] (*a*) insubstantial or worthless visions; cf. *Tp.* 4.1.167–70, where
Prospero similarly dismisses the 'baseless fabric of this vision' that he has
conjured up: 'These our actors, / As I foretold you, were all spirits and / Are
melted into air, into thin air'. (*b*) In older medical use, vapours were exha-
lations developed within the organs of the body, and supposed to have an
injurious effect upon the health; cf. Sir Thomas Elyot, *The Castle of Health*
(1541), p. 53: 'Of humours some are more gross and cold, some are subtle
and hot, and are called vapours' (*OED* 3).
13.] Asper has not taken the time to change his costume; he still looks like
Macilente, but speaks like Asper, the playwright. Cf. 5.4.40.2 and 51.5.

Kind patrons of our sports (you that can judge,
And with discerning thoughts measure the pace   15
Of our strange muse in this her maze of humour,
You whose true notions do confine the forms
And nature of sweet poesy), to you
I tender solemn and most duteous thanks
For your stretched patience and attentive grace.   20
We know (and we are pleased to know so much)
The cates that you have tasted were not seasoned
For every vulgar palate, but prepared
To banquet pure and apprehensive ears.
Let then their voices speak for our desert.   25
Be their applause the trumpet to proclaim
Defiance to rebelling ignorance
And the green spirits of some tainted few
That (spite of pity) betray themselves

29. pity] *Q*; pietie *conj. W.W. Greg.*

16. *maze of humour*] Cf. *PR* 261–2: 'all actions of mankind / Are but a labyrinth, or maze'.

20. *stretched*] strained to capacity.

22. *cates*] delicacies. Jonson frequently used the image of the cook as setting standards of taste: see *SN* 3.2.168–80, where Lickfinger, the cook, proposes to send cooks to America to reform cannibals with 'plain cooking'; *NT* has a dialogue between the Cook and the Poet (illustrated by a huge pot of characters on stage to 'present the meats'), in which the Poet accepts, not without irony, the role of cook instead of reformer-critic; *GM* offers a comical cannibal's menu in song, in which the delicacies described are humorous or satiric characters and types; in *PR*, Comus the Belly-god is seen as the challenge to the ideal of art and poetry, and the Bowl-bearer sums up the dilemma of taste by condemning the audience as incorrigible: 'But when the belly is not edified by it, it is not well: for where did you ever read, or hear, that the belly had any ears? . . . Beware of dealing with the belly, the belly will not be talked to, especially when he is full' (48–58). See Don K. Hedrick, 'Cooking for the Anthropophagi: Jonson and His Audience', *SEL* 17 (1977): 242–4.

24. *apprehensive*] understanding; cf. Ind.199–201, where Asper defines his ideal audience as 'Attentive auditors' who 'come to feed their understanding parts'.

25. *their voices*] the voices of discerning viewers.
desert] meritoriousness.

26–32.] The discriminating members of the audience will, by applauding, defy (and so defeat) the ignorant detractors who are too immature to keep their foolish opinions to themselves.

28. *green*] not ripe, unseasoned; cf. 3.2.139 and n.

To scorn and laughter; and, like guilty children,   30
Publish their infancy before their time
By their own fond exception. Such as these,
We pawn 'em to your censure, till time, wit,
Or observation set some stronger seal
Of judgement on their judgements, and entreat   35
The happier spirits in this fair-filled Globe
(So many as have sweet minds in their breasts,
And are too wise to think themselves are taxed
In any general figure, or too virtuous
To need that wisdom's imputation)   40
That with their bounteous hands they would confirm
This as their pleasure's patent, which, so signed,
Our lean and spent endeavours shall renew
Their beauties with the spring to smile on you.

FINIS.

2. THE FOLIO

The folio retains lines 1–12 of the quarto's revised catastophe,
and concludes the play with lines from the original catastrophe, 5.4.41–63.1:

[*Macilente.*] Why, here's a change! Now is my soul at peace.
    I am as empty of all envy now
    As they of merit to be envied at.
    My humour, like a flame, no longer lasts

---

31. infancy] *Q*; infamie *conj. P. Simpson.*

31–2. *Publish . . . exception*] expose their childishness too soon through
their own foolish disparagements. Jonson objects here to audiences who blurt
out opinions too early in a play, since they can have only an inadequate
understanding of how a scene or character is being developed; a discerning
audience waits before judging.
    33. *We . . . censure*] We place them in the keeping of your superior critical
power. The analogy is to wards being placed, until they come of age, with
guardians.
    38–9. *taxed . . . figure*] personally criticized in any general satiric repre-
sentation. Cf. Ind.139–45 and 191–3.
    41–2. *with . . . patent*] indicate by applauding that they accept this play as
entertainment that fulfils a contract between playwright and audience.
    43–4.] Jonson seems to promise more plays to please his discerning
audience.

Than it hath stuff to feed it, and their virtue,   5
Being now raked up in embers of their folly,
Affords no ampler subject to my spirit.
I am so far from malicing their states
That I begin to pity 'em. It grieves me
To think they have a being. I could wish   10
They might turn wise upon it, and be saved now,
So heaven were pleased. But let them vanish, vapours.
Gentlemen, how like you it? Has 't not been tedious?

GREX

Cordatus. Nay, we ha' done censuring now.
Mitis. Yes, faith.   15
Macilente. How so?
Cordatus. Marry, because we'll imitate your actors and be out
     of our humours. Besides, here are those round about you
     [*Indicates audience*] of more ability in censure than we,
     whose judgements can give it a more satisfying allowance.   20
     We'll refer you to them.
Macilente. Ay, is 't e'en so?—[*To audience*] Well, gentlemen, I
     should have gone in and returned to you as I was, Asper,
     at the first; but (by reason the shift would have been
     somewhat long, and we are loath to draw your patience   25
     farther) we'll entreat you to imagine it. And now—that
     you may see I will be out of humour for company—I
     stand wholly to your kind approbation, and, indeed, am
     nothing so peremptory as I was in the beginning. Marry,
     I will not do as Plautus, in his *Amphitryo*, for all this: 30
     Summi Iovis causa, plaudite; beg a plaudit for God's sake.
     But if you (out of the bounty of your good liking) will
     bestow it, why, you may (in time) make lean Macilente
     as fat as Sir John Falstaff.

THE END.

3. AT COURT

According to the folio, in the presentation before Queen
Elizabeth during the Christmas season of 1599, part of the

13.] *F, a metrical line; in Q, 5.4.41–2, prose.*

original catastrophe (5.4) was retained in a slightly altered form:

> Which, in the presentation before
> *Queen E[lizabeth] was thus varied,*
> By Macilente.

This revised catastrophe comprises lines 5–40 ('Never till now did object greet mine eyes / . . . / Our strongest wall falls down when she is gone'), but there is no indication of a return to the Grex. If this were the performed version, it is surprising that Jonson should not have mentioned that fact in his defence of the original catastrophe in the first quarto, published shortly afterward. Possibly this version represents the performance at King James's court in 1605.

Appendix B

The arms of Sogliardo and the tricking of the arms of Sogliardo are taken from Arthur Huntington Nason, *Heralds and Heraldry in Ben Jonson's Plays, Masques, and Entertainments* (New York, 1907), pp. 95 and 97.

The arms of Sogliardo: '*Gyrony* of eight pieces, *azure* and *gules*; between three plates, a *chevron* engrailed checky, *or*, *vert*, and *ermines*; on a chief *argent*, between two *ann'lets* sables, a boar's head *proper*.' (3.1.234–7).
Crest: a 'boar without a head, rampant' (3.1.220).

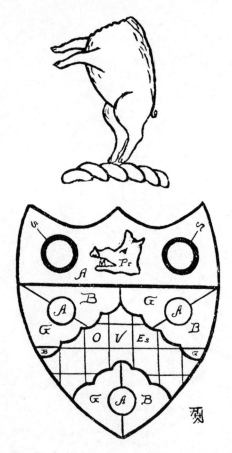

Tricking of the arms of Sogliardo. A = Argent (silver); G = Gules
(red); B = Azure Blue; O = Or (gold); V = Vert (green); Es = Ermines
(white with black spots); S = Sable (black); Pr = Proper (i.e., a colour
appropriate to a boar).

Appendix C

To the Noblest Nurseries
of Humanity and Liberty
in the Kingdom:
The Inns of Court

I understand you, gentlemen, not your houses; and a worthy
succession of you, to all time, as being born the judges of these
studies. When I wrote this poem, I had friendship with diverse
in your societies who, as they were great names in learning,
so they were no less examples of living. Of them, and then   5
(that I say no more), it was not despised. Now that the printer,

---

0.1. *Nurseries*] nurturers; metaphor for the gentlemen of the Inns of
Court, not for the institution itself. Collectively they provide nourishment
for 'Humanity and Liberty'. See Finkelpearl, p. 79.

0.2. *Humanity*] interest in humanist concerns, or the humanities; i.e.,
classical forms, concentration on the comic.

Liberty] Finkelpearl (*Temple*, pp. 79–80) suggests that the prime meaning
here is 'the spirit which appears during the revels, when "the Lord of Liberty
reigns" [l. 9] and "liberty plucks justice by the nose" (*Meas.*, 1.3.29)'. The
term suggests a combination of 'revelry, rebellion, uninhibited satire, relaxed
playfulness, libertine wantonness, licensed fooling, and political freedom'.

1. *you . . . not your houses*] emphasis on *you*: I understand the taste and character of you law-students, not the content of your studies at the Inns of Court.

1–3. *a worthy . . . studies*] I hope that succeeding generations of lawyers
will continue your tradition of merit, perpetually producing worthy judges
of law (and literature; see next note).

2. *judges*] a light Inns of Court conceit: distinguished lawyers often became
benchers or judges, although Jonson uses the word in the sense of literary
critics or intelligently appreciative audiences, like the Grex in the play.

3. *poem*] Jonson habitually referred to his plays and masques as poems in
the classical sense; cf. *Disc.* 2346–73.

3–4. *friendship . . . societies*] Jonson's acquaintance with literary men in
several of the law societies, or Inns, included Donne (Lincoln's Inn),
Campion and Guilpin (Gray's Inn), Beaumont (Inner Temple), Davies,
Harington, Hoskyns, and Marston (Middle Temple).

6. *(that . . . more)*] of which I shall speak no further; a modest disclaimer
as prelude to the understatement that completes the sentence.

by a doubled charge, thinks it worthy a longer life than commonly the air of such things doth promise, I am careful to put
it a servant to their pleasures who are the inheritors of the first
favour born it. Yet I command it lie not in the way of your   10
more noble and useful studies to the public. For so I shall
suffer for it. But, when the gown and cap is off and the Lord
of Liberty reigns, then to take it in your hands perhaps may
make some bencher, tincted with humanity, read and not
repent him.   15

By your true honourer,
Ben Jonson

16. true] *Fb*; *not in Fa.*

---

7. *by a doubled charge*] by twice undertaking the responsibility of publishing; perhaps a reference to the fact that both Smethwick and Stansby
authorized the folio edition of the play, or simply reminding the readers that
this is the second edition of *EMO* (see the textual history in the introd.).
But the phrase may merely convey emphasis; in Marston's *What You Will*,
Induction, 101–4, Philomuse mentions only a single promise 'to the author
to give a kind of inductive speech to his comedy', but defends his word by
claiming: 'Tut, I have vowed it; I am double charged', the implication being
that he has sworn an oath to the author and to God.

a longer life] Plays were considered *ephemera*, and had always been
published in quarto, as befits casual 'pocketbook' reading, not intended
to remain on anyone's bookshelves.

8–10. *I am ... born it*] elaborate compliment to the Inns of Court, for
whom the play was originally written in 1599, and to whom he rededicates
the play in 1616. The lawyers of 1616 inherit the pleasures and status enjoyed
by those lawyers back in 1600 who favoured and supported Jonson's original *Q* publication.

12. *suffer*] be blamed (for distracting you from your legal studies).

when ... off] when studies are laid aside, especially at the end of a law-
term. Lawyers still wear cap and gown in the upper courts.

12–13. *the Lord ... reigns*] i.e., when lawyers are at leisure, or attending
revels. 'He alludes to the custom of creating at Christmas (the Saturnalia of
the ancients) in the palace, the inns of court, and houses of the nobility, a
lord of misrule, whose office it was to lead and regulate the revels presented
at this season of festivity' (Gifford). By extension, any time dedicated to
entertainment.

14. *bencher*] one of the senior members elected by each Inn of Court to
govern its affairs and call members to the bar (*OED*).

tincted] imbued. In alchemy, a material object may be *tincted* by a
spiritual quality or character infused into it. In this instance, the bencher is
spiritually enriched by his studies in the humanities.

15. *repent him*] regret the spending of his time.

Appendix D

CASTING ANALYSIS

As the following chart, speculative though it is, illustrates, Jonson is efficient and considerate in his management of actors. He introduces new characters gradually, so that each actor can make his role distinctive for the audience before another new character appears. The casting of parts is balanced, giving all the actors approximately the same number of scenes, although the number of lines varies. Most of the actors appear in seven to nine of the play's eighteen scenes, and often the bit-players have at least one line to speak (see the Rustics of 3.3, for example).

The notable exceptions are the first three actors. Actors 2 and 3 are on stage for all eighteen scenes, but their roles after the induction are not onerous, and, even supposing that they engage in mute stage-business at various points in the play, they have considerable stage time in which they do not attract audience attention. Actor 1 is on stage for fifteen scenes, but he, like the Grex, also spends considerable time observing from the sidelines. On the other hand, Actor 4 (Carlo), with only seven scenes, is 'on' during all his stage time: his speeches are flamboyant and unusually lengthy, and even when he speaks aside, he exerts himself to attract dramatic and extra-dramatic attention. But the real restriction on Carlo's doubling is his greasy make-up, giving him the glistening appearance of the 'devil with a shining face' (3.1.204–5), the frequenter of hot-houses and eater of pork.

There is little opportunity for Actors 2 to 9 to double. However, any actor from 5 to 11, or Boy B or C, might play the Prologue. Traditionally, the Prologue wore a large black cloak that hid whatever costume he might be dressed in. I have arbitrarily assigned the part to Actor 11 because his later role as Groom seems to repeat the Prologue's trick of taking an arrogant social superior at his word. If the audience recognizes the doubled role in 5.1, or if the actor plays the part deliberately to force that recognition, then the doubling adds a spice to an already comic scene.

Doubling assignments, by theatrical convention, follow a rather obvious logic. The actor must have time to change his costume

385

(twenty-five lines, at a loose estimate; more if make-up is involved), and there should be a strong contrast between roles to inhibit audience recognition. Of course, these rules do not apply to Asper, who makes no secret of his role as a 'humorist' in the play proper. But the rest of the doubling possibilities in the play would usually follow the conventions, unless there were a suggestive or comic reason for not doing so. If Sordido and Shift are doubled, as I speculate in the chart, the contrasts are very pronounced between the ageing surly miser, dressed as a farmer and probably speaking in the traditional west-country accent of the stage rustic, and the brash urban con-artist in worn-out soldier's garb. Manner, tone, and costume all militate against any easy recognition of the actor behind the roles. The costume changes are simple, and in any case there is only one quick change between 3.1 and 2. The same holds true for Actors 11, 12, and 13: props, as well as manner, tone, and costume, serve to differentiate small tradesmen with their tools from rustics with appropriate implements, petty fops with pomanders, police officers

CASTING ANALYSIS

Actors	Ind	1.1	1.2	1.3	2.1	2.2	3.1	3.2	3.3
1	Asper	Mac	x	x		x	x		x
2	Cord	x	x	x	x	x	x	x	x
3	Mitis	x	x	x	x	x	x	x	x
4	Carlo		x		x		x		
5			Sogli		x		x	6 Rus	
6					Brisk	x	x		x
7					Punt		x	4 Rus	
8					Fung	x	x		
9						Deliro	x	5 Rus	
10				Sord	x		Shift	Sord	
11	Pro			Hind			Tailor	1 Rus	
12	(ST)				Hunt		Orang	2 Rus	
13	(ST)						Clove	3 Rus	
A	Boy				WG	Fido			Saviol
B					Lady P	Fallace	S/Dog		
C					Cinedo		S/Cat		Cinedo

ST = Sounding Trumpet
X = Continues in the same role
S/ = Servant with
WG = Waiting-Gentlewoman
Rus = Rustic

with truncheons, the huntsman with his horn, and musicians with their instruments.

The boys may have required more dress-time to play women's roles, but the likelihood is that only Actor C, in his final appearance as the Queen, would require much cosmetic elaboration. The effectiveness of Actor A as Saviolina and B as Fallace probably depends more on fashionable dress and headgear than on make-up.

The casting suggested here assigns the forty-four roles to the minimum number of players needed to present the play: thirteen men and three boys. If *EMO* were taken on tour, the smaller touring company could play the piece without difficulty. However, I would guess that the full London company at the Globe was approximately equivalent to the numbers Henslowe recorded from time to time in his diary: eighteen men and between six and twelve boys. In that case, such careful doubling might not be required, and supernumaries could be used to fill out crowd scenes, such as the Paul's Walk scene or the tavern scenes.

	4.1	4.2	4.3	4.4	4.5	5.1	5.2	5.3	5.4
Mac	x	x		x	x	x	x	x	x
Cord	x	x	x	x	x	x	x	x	x
Mitis	x	x	x	x	x	x	x	x	x
			Carlo		x			x	
			Sogli		x	x	x	x	
			Brisk		x	x	x	x	
			Punt		x	x	x	x	
Fung				x	x	x	x	x	
Deliro	x	x						x /5 Off	
			Shift		x		x	3 Off	
			Notary	Tailor		Groom		1 Off	
Mus				Shoe				Const	(ST)
Mus				Haber				2 Off	(ST)
							Saviol	Geo/Fi	
Fallace			S/Dog		S/Dog			Fal/4 Off	
			S/Cat		S/Cat			Dra/6 Off	Queen

Off = Officer
Mus = Musician
Fal = Fallace
Dra = Drawer
Const = Constable

Index

An asterix (*) before an entry indicates that the note contains information about meaning, usage or date which supplements *OED*. 'App. A' refers to Appendix A.